DATE DUE

PRINTED IN U.S.A.

SOMETHING ABOUT THE AUTHOR

ISSN 0276-816X

something ABOUT THE AUTHOR

**Facts and Pictures about Authors
and Illustrators of Books for Young People**

EDITED BY
ANNE COMMIRE

VOLUME 49

GALE RESEARCH COMPANY
BOOK TOWER
DETROIT, MICHIGAN
48226

Editor: Anne Commire

Associate Editors: Agnes Garrett, Helga P. McCue

Senior Assistant Editor: Dianne H. Anderson

Assistant Editors: Elisa Ann Ferraro, Eunice L. Petrini, Linda Shedd

Sketchwriters: Marguerite Feitlowitz, Rachel Koenig

Researcher: Catherine Ruello

Editorial Assistants: Kathleen Betsko, Catherine Coray, Joanne J. Ferraro, Nigel French

Permissions Assistant: Susan Pfanner

In cooperation with the Young People's Literature staff

Editor: Joyce Nakamura

Senior Assistant Editor: Heidi Ellerman

External Production Manager: Mary Beth Trimper

External Production Assistants: Linda Davis, Patty Farley

Internal Production Associate: Louise Gagné

Internal Senior Production Assistant: Sandy Rock

Layout Artist: Elizabeth Lewis Patryjak

Art Director: Arthur Chartow

Special acknowledgment is due to the members of the *Contemporary Authors* staff
who assisted in the preparation of this volume.

Chairman: Frederick G. Ruffner

President: J. Kevin Reger

Publisher: Dedria Bryfonski

Associate Editorial Director: Ellen T. Crowley

Director, Biography Division: Christine Nasso

Senior Editor, Something about the Author: Adele Sarkissian

Library of Congress Catalog Card Number 72-27107

ISBN 0-8103-2259-5
ISSN 0276-816X
Computerized photocomposition by
Typographics, Incorporated
Kansas City, Missouri
Printed in the United States

Contents

Introduction 9

Illustrations Index 227

Acknowledgments 15

Author Index 245

A

Alexander, Lloyd (Chudley) 1924- 21

Anderson, Leone Castell 1923-
Brief Entry..................................35

Andrews, Jan 1942-
Brief Entry..................................35

Angelou, Maya 1928- 35

B

Ballard, Lowell Clyne 1904-1986
Obituary Notice 49

Ballard, Mignon Franklin 1934-
Brief Entry..................................49

Barker, Cicely Mary 1895-1973 49

Barrett, William E(dmund) 1900-1986
Obituary Notice 52

Bellville, Cheryl Walsh 1944-
Brief Entry..................................53

Blauer, Ettagale 1940- 53

Bond, Felicia 1954- 54

Bonham, Frank 1914- 57

Born, Adolf 1930- 62

Britton, Kate
see Stegeman, Janet Allais 182

C

Cartlidge, Michelle 1950- 64

Christopher, Louise
see Hale, Arlene 122

Cleaver, Hylton (Reginald) 1891-1961 66

Coatsworth, Elizabeth 1893-1986
Obituary Notice 68

Cole, Joanna 1944- 68

Coleman, William L(eRoy) 1938- 74

Conrad, Pam(ela) 1947-
Brief Entry.................................75

Cooke, Ann
see Cole, Joanna 68

Craig, Helen 1934- 75

Crunden, Reginald
see Cleaver, Hylton (Reginald).............66

D

Dean, Karen Strickler 1923- 77

Duff, Annis (James) 1904(?)-1986
Obituary Notice 79

E

Edens, Cooper 1945- 79

Edwards, Linda Strauss 1948- 86

Egielski, Richard 1952- 90

Everett, Gail
see Hale, Arlene 122

F

Fleisher, Robbin 1951-1977
Brief Entry.................................96

Ford, Brian J(ohn) 1939- 96

French, Michael 1944- 99

Friedman, Ina R(osen) 1926- 101

Furniss, Tim 1948- 101

G

Galdone, Paul 1914-1986
Obituary Notice 103

5

Gard, (Sanford) Wayne 1899-1986
    Obituary Notice 103

Gardner, Hugh 1910-1986
    Obituary Notice 103

Gasperini, Jim 1952-
    Brief Entry.............................103

Gevirtz, Eliezer 1950- 103

Gilmore, Mary (Jean Cameron) 1865-1962 105

Goodman, Deborah Lerme 1956-
    Brief Entry.............................110

Gould, Chester 1900-1985 110

Gregory, Diana (Jean) 1933- 118

Grummer, Arnold E(dward) 1923- 120

H

Hague, (Susan) Kathleen 1949- 121

Hale, Arlene 1924-1982....................122

Hind, Dolores (Ellen) 1931-
    Brief Entry.............................123

Hoffman, Edwin D. 123

Hoopes, Lyn L(ittlefield) 1953- 123

Hughes, Ted 1930- 125

I

Ipcar, Dahlov (Zorach) 1917- 135

J

Jefferds, Vincent H(arris) 1916-
    Brief Entry.............................146

K

Kent, David
    see Lambert, David (Compton) 153

Kirkland, Will
    see Hale, Arlene 122

Korman, Gordon 1963- 146

Kouhi, Elizabeth 1917-
    Brief Entry.............................151

Krahn, Fernando 1935- 151

L

Lambert, David (Compton) 1932-
    Brief Entry.............................153

Lampert, Emily 1951-
    Brief Entry.............................153

Lauré, Ettagale
    see Blauer, Ettagale 53

Laux, Dorothy 1920- 154

Laviolette, Emily A. 1923(?)-1975
    Brief Entry.............................154

Le Tord, Bijou 1945- 154

Levinson, Riki
    Brief Entry.............................156

Levoy, Myron.....................157

Lewis, Francine
    see Wells, Helen 201

M

Mace, Varian 1938- 158

Mays, Lucinda L(a Bella) 1924- 160

McCaffrey, Mary
    see Szudek, Agnes S(usan) P(hilomena) 184

McInerney, Judith W(hitelock) 1945- 162

Mearian, Judy Frank 1936- 163

Melady, John 1938-
    Brief Entry.............................164

Mertz, Barbara (Gross) 1927- 164

Michaels, Barbara
    see Mertz, Barbara (Gross) 164

Michel, Anna 1943- 166

Moldon, Peter L(eonard) 1937- 167

Moore, Patrick (Alfred) 1923- 168

N

Nerlove, Miriam 1959-
    Brief Entry.............................172

Ness, Evaline (Michelow) 1911-1986
    Obituary Notice 172

Nestor, William P(rodromos) 1947- 172

Noble, Iris 1922-1986
    Obituary Notice 173

O

O'Connell, Margaret F(orster) 1935-1977 173

P

Panowski, Eileen Thompson 1920- 174

Peters, Elizabeth
   see Mertz, Barbara (Gross) 164

Pierce, Tamora 1954-
   Brief Entry...........................174

Piowaty, Kim Kennelly 1957- 175

Q

Quigg, Jane (Hulda) (?)-1986
   Obituary Notice 175

R

Ransom, Candice F. 1952-
   Brief Entry...........................175

Roop, Constance Betzer 1951-
   Brief Entry...........................176

Roop, Peter 1951-
   Brief Entry...........................176

Ross, David 1896-1975 176

Roth, Harold
   Brief Entry...........................176

Rubinstein, Robert E(dward) 1943- 177

Rushmore, Robert (William) 1926-1986
   Obituary Notice 178

S

Satchwell, John
   Brief Entry...........................178

Scholz, Jackson (Volney) 1897-1986
   Obituary Notice 178

Schur, Maxine 1948-
   Brief Entry...........................178

Shachtman, Tom 1942- 179

Shefts, Joelle
   Brief Entry...........................180

Stasiak, Krystyna 181

Stegeman, Janet Allais 1923-
   Brief Entry...........................182

Stevens, Kathleen 1936- 182

Szudek, Agnes S(usan) P(hilomena)
   Brief Entry...........................184

T

Tate, Mary Anne
   see Hale, Arlene 122

Thompson, Eileen
   see Panowski, Eileen Thompson 174

Thompson, Hilary 1943-
   Brief Entry...........................184

Treadgold, Mary 1910- 185

U

Underhill, Liz 1936-
   Brief Entry...........................186

Unwin, Nora S. 1907-1982
   Obituary Notice 186

Uris, Leon (Marcus) 1924- 186

W

Walsh, Ellen Stoll 1942- 200

Wells, Helen 1910-1986..................201

Wheeler, Cindy 1955- 204

Wilkin, Eloise (Burns) 1904- 206

Williams, Lynn
   see Hale, Arlene 122

Y

Yaffe, Alan
   see Yorinks, Arthur 211

Yorinks, Arthur 1953- 211

Z

Zallinger, Peter Franz 1943- 217

Zelinsky, Paul O. 1953- 218

Zemach, Kaethe 1958- 224

Introduction

As the only ongoing reference series that deals with the lives and works of authors and illustrators of children's books, *Something about the Author (SATA)* is a unique source of information. The *SATA* series includes not only well-known authors and illustrators whose books are most widely read, but also those less prominent people whose works are just coming to be recognized. *SATA* is often the only readily available information source for less well-known writers or artists. You'll find *SATA* informative and entertaining whether you are:

—a student in junior high school (or perhaps one to two grades higher or lower) who needs information for a book report or some other assignment for an English class;

—a children's librarian who is searching for the answer to yet another question from a young reader or collecting background material to use for a story hour;

—an English teacher who is drawing up an assignment for your students or gathering information for a book talk;

—a student in a college of education or library science who is studying children's literature and reference sources in the field;

—a parent who is looking for a new way to interest your child in reading something more than the school curriculum prescribes;

—an adult who enjoys children's literature for its own sake, knowing that a good children's book has no age limits.

Scope

In *SATA* you will find detailed information about authors and illustrators who span the full time range of children's literature, from early figures like John Newbery and L. Frank Baum to contemporary figures like Judy Blume and Richard Peck. Authors in the series represent primarily English-speaking countries, particularly the United States, Canada, and the United Kingdom. Also included, however, are authors from around the world whose works are available in English translation, for example: from France, Jean and Laurent De Brunhoff; from Italy, Emanuele Luzzati; from the Netherlands, Jaap ter Haar; from Germany, James Krüss; from Norway, Babbis Friis-Baastad; from Japan, Toshiko Kanzawa; from the Soviet Union, Kornei Chukovsky; from Switzerland, Alois Carigiet, to name only a few. Also appearing in *SATA* are Newbery medalists from Hendrik Van Loon (1922) to Sid Fleischman (1987). The writings represented in *SATA* include those created intentionally for children and young adults as well as those written for a general audience and known to interest younger readers. These writings cover the spectrum from picture books, humor, folk and fairy tales, animal stories, mystery and adventure, science fiction and fantasy, historical fiction, poetry and nonsense verse, to drama, biography, and nonfiction.

Information Features

In *SATA* you will find full-length entries that are being presented in the series for the first time. This volume, for example, marks the first full-length appearance of Felicia Bond, Hylton Cleaver, Joanna Cole, Cooper Edens, Patrick Moore, Mary Treadgold, Leon Uris, Eloise Wilkin, and Paul O. Zelinsky.

Brief Entries, first introduced in Volume 27, are another regular feature of *SATA*. Brief Entries present essentially the same types of information found in a full entry but do so in a capsule form and without illustration. These entries are intended to give you useful and timely information while the more time-consuming process of compiling a full-length biography is in progress. In this volume you'll find Brief Entries for Jan Andrews, Pam Conrad, Vincent H. Jefferds, Elizabeth Kouhi, Tamora Pierce, Maxine Schur, Janet Allais Stegeman, Agnes S. P. Szudek, and Hilary Thompson, among others.

Obituaries have been included in *SATA* since Volume 20. An Obituary is intended not only as a death notice but also as a concise view of a person's life and work. Obituaries may appear for persons who have entries in earlier *SATA* volumes, as well as for people who have not yet appeared in the series. In this volume Obituaries mark the recent deaths of Elizabeth Coatsworth, Paul Galdone, Evaline Ness, Nora S. Unwin, and others.

Revised Entries

Since Volume 25, each *SATA* volume also includes newly revised and updated entries for a selection of *SATA* listees (usually four to six) who remain of interest to today's readers and who have been active enough to require extensive revision of their earlier biographies. For example, when Beverly Cleary first appeared in *SATA* Volume 2, she was the author of twenty-one books for children and young adults and the recipient of numerous awards. By the time her updated sketch appeared in Volume 43 (a span of fifteen years), this creator of the indefatigable Ramona Quimby and other memorable characters had produced a dozen new titles and garnered nearly fifty additional awards, including the 1984 Newbery Medal.

The entry for a given biographee may be revised as often as there is substantial new information to provide. In this volume, look for revised entries on Lloyd Alexander, Frank Bonham, Richard Egielski, and Arthur Yorinks.

Illustrations

While the textual information in *SATA* is its primary reason for existing, photographs and illustrations not only enliven the text but are an integral part of the information that *SATA* provides. Illustrations and text are wedded in such a special way in children's literature that artists and their works naturally occupy a prominent place among *SATA*'s listees. The illustrators that you'll find in the series include such past masters of children's book illustration as Randolph Caldecott, Kate Greenaway, Walter Crane, Arthur Rackham, and Ernest L. Shepard, as well as such noted contemporary artists as Maurice Sendak, Edward Gorey, Tomie de Paola, and Margot Zemach. There are Caldecott medalists from Dorothy Lathrop (the first recipient in 1938) to Richard Egielski (the latest winner in 1987); cartoonists like Charles Schulz, ("Peanuts"), Walt Kelly ("Pogo"), Hank Ketcham ("Dennis the Menace"), and Georges Rémi ("Tintin"); photographers like Jill Krementz, Tana Hoban, Bruce McMillan, and Bruce Curtis; and filmmakers like Walt Disney, Alfred Hitchcock, and Steven Spielberg.

In more than a dozen years of recording the metamorphosis of children's literature from the printed page to other media, *SATA* has become something of a repository of photographs that are unique in themselves and exist nowhere else as a group, particularly many of the classics of motion picture and stage history and photographs that have been specially loaned to us from private collections.

Indexes

Each *SATA* volume provides a cumulative index in two parts: first, the Illustrations Index, arranged by the name of the illustrator, gives the number of the volume and page where the illustrator's work appears in the current volume as well as all preceding volumes in the series; second, the Author Index gives the number of the volume in which a person's biographical sketch, Brief Entry, or Obituary appears in the current volume as well as all preceding volumes in the series. These indexes also include references to authors and illustrators who appear in *Yesterday's Authors of Books for Children*. Beginning with Volume 36, the *SATA* Author Index provides cross-references to authors who are included in *Children's Literature Review*.

Starting with Volume 42, you will also find cross-references to authors who are included in the *Something about the Author Autobiography Series*. This companion series to *SATA* is described in detail below.

What a *SATA* Entry Provides

Whether you're already familiar with the *SATA* series or just getting acquainted, you will want to be aware of the kind of information that an entry provides. In every *SATA* entry the editors attempt to give as complete a picture of the person's life and work as possible. In some cases that full range of information may simply be unavailable, or a biographee may choose not to reveal complete personal details. The information that the editors attempt to provide in every entry is arranged in the following categories:

1. The "head" of the entry gives

   —the most complete form of the name,
   —any part of the name not commonly used, included in parentheses,
   —birth and death dates, if known; a (?) indicates a discrepancy in published sources,
   —pseudonyms or name variants under which the person has had books published or is publicly known, in parentheses in the second line.

2. "Personal" section gives

   —date and place of birth and death,
   —parents' names and occupations,
   —name of spouse, date of marriage, and names of children,
   —educational institutions attended, degrees received, and dates,
   —religious and political affiliations,
   —agent's name and address,
   —home and/or office address.

3. "Career" section gives

   —name of employer, position, and dates for each career post,
   —military service,
   —memberships,
   —awards and honors.

4. "Writings" section gives

   —title, first publisher and date of publication, and illustration information for each book written; revised editions and other significant editions for books with particularly long publishing histories; genre, when known.

5. "Adaptations" section gives

   —title, major performers, producer, and date of all known reworkings of an author's material in another medium, like movies, filmstrips, television, recordings, plays, etc.

6. "Sidelights" section gives

   —commentary on the life or work of the biographee either directly from the person (and often written specifically for the *SATA* entry), or gathered from biographies, diaries, letters, interviews, or other published sources.

7. "For More Information See" section gives

   —books, feature articles, films, plays, and reviews in which the biographee's life or work has been treated.

How a *SATA* Entry Is Compiled

A *SATA* entry progresses through a series of steps. If the biographee is living, the *SATA* editors try to secure information directly from him or her through a questionnaire. From the information that the biographee supplies, the editors prepare an entry, filling in any essential missing details with research. The author or illustrator is then sent a copy of the entry to check for accuracy and completeness.

If the biographee is deceased or cannot be reached by questionnaire, the *SATA* editors examine a wide variety of published sources to gather information for an entry. Biographical sources are searched with the aid of Gale's *Biography and Genealogy Master Index*. Bibliographic sources like the *National Union Catalog*, the *Cumulative Book Index*, *American Book Publishing Record*, and the *British Museum*

Catalogue are consulted, as are book reviews, feature articles, published interviews, and material sometimes obtained from the biographee's family, publishers, agent, or other associates.

For each entry presented in *SATA*, the editors also attempt to locate a photograph of the biographee as well as representative illustrations from his or her books. After surveying the available books which the biographee has written and/or illustrated, and then making a selection of appropriate photographs and illustrations, the editors request permission of the current copyright holders to reprint the material. In the case of older books for which the copyright may have passed through several hands, even locating the current copyright holder is often a long and involved process.

We invite you to examine the entire *SATA* series, starting with this volume. Described below are some of the people in Volume 49 that you may find particularly interesting.

Highlights of This Volume

LLOYD ALEXANDER......announced at age fifteen his intention to become a poet, "writing long into the night and studying verse forms to the scandalous neglect of my homework." Because his grades were "too wretched" for a scholarship and his parents were unable to afford college tuition, he worked in a bank as a mail boy after high school graduation, writing his stories and poetry during his spare time. For adventure and a chance for "real deeds and derring-do" he joined the army during World War II. In Paris, he fell in love with both the city and a young Parisian student, his future bride. When they returned stateside, Alexander continued to support himself with odd jobs, finding precious time to write during the evening and early morning hours. It was not until seventeen years after he began writing that he found his literary niche in fantasy for children with his creation of a mythical world in the "Prydain Chronicles," five books inspired by the Arthurian legends. The fifth book, *The High King,* won the 1969 Newbery Medal. "Fantasy . . . tells us that we're considerably more than we think we are. After all, how can we be less than our dreams?"

FRANK BONHAM......author of adventure stories for young people. Bonham was raised in California ". . . before smog and freeways." Describing himself as a "hard-core unemployable," he has managed to support himself as a free-lance writer for the past five decades. After twenty years of writing mysteries, television scripts, and westerns, he discovered that ". . . the real satisfaction was in writing adventure books for young people." In an effort to impart realism and fact in his stories, Bonham relies heavily on research—"in the field, not only in books." Research among juvenile gangs in the Los Angeles area led to *Durango Street* and other books about minority groups, including *Mystery of the Fat Cat* and *The Nitty Gritty.* "Young people today . . . not only grow taller . . . , they are taller inside, their minds keener and more skeptical."

JOANNA COLE......author of fiction and science books for children. In grade school, Cole discovered that she liked writing reports and stories and that her favorite subject was science. Those early experiences were "much more influential than my later education. Maybe that's why as an adult I ended up writing books for children." Her first science book, *Cockroaches,* was followed by stories about "animal birth with the photographer Jerome Wexler, and from those books grew the idea for a series on animals' bodies." Many of her science books have been recognized as outstanding by the Children's Book Council and the National Science Teachers Association. In recent years, she has added fiction for children and books on parenting to her long list of publications. "I consistently try to do things in my writing and in my life that are all but impossible."

COOPER EDENS......grew up on Lake Washington in Washington state, spending "hours alone . . . daydreaming." Labeled the "art guy" in junior high school, Edens was encouraged by his teachers and parents to develop his talent. His paintings helped support him while he attended the University of Washington. Edens wrote his first book, *The Starcleaner Reunion,* around a series of his paintings, although his later books have been written more conventionally—text first, then illustrations. Merging the real world with the dream world, he uses a recurring symbol in his books of "a heart/star [that] embodies both the infinite and the individual." Since 1979, he has produced ten books of images and poems.

RICHARD EGIELSKI......1987 winner of the prestigious Caldecott Medal for his illustrations in *Hey, Al* by Arthur Yorinks. Raised in New York City, Egielski attended the High School of Art and Design, Pratt

Institute, and Parsons School of Design. At Parsons, he was critically influenced by the renowned author and illustrator Maurice Sendak, who taught a course in picture books. Sendak later introduced Egielski to children's author Arthur Yorinks, thus initiating a successful collaboration between them. Since their first effort, *Sid and Sol,* was published in 1977, they have produced three additional award-winning children's books. "I love to interpret good writing. I only illustrate texts I truly believe in, and never go against them."

CHESTER GOULD......creator of the "Dick Tracy" comic strip, grew up in Oklahoma where his father owned a weekly newspaper. "[My father's business] got me into the frame of mind to become a cartoonist," Gould wrote. At the age of seven, he had his first attempts at cartooning pasted on the window of the newspaper office of the *Pawnee Courier Dispatch.* Later, as a young man, he moved to Chicago determined to break into the "big-time cartoon world." It took another ten years, however, before he would join the elite group of newspaper cartoonists with his "Dick Tracy" comic strip. Proud of his forty-six-year involvement in American cartooning, Gould believed that "the American comic strip . . . has sold more newspapers . . . than any other feature in American journalism."

ARTHUR YORINKS......New York-born writer, playwright, and teacher, was "always involved in some form of the arts." He credits his early musical interests to his classical piano teacher, and artistic interests to his mother who spent hours painting and drawing with him. In junior high school, he was already collaborating on comic books with an illustrator friend. At the age of sixteen, he mustered up enough courage to show his stories to Maurice Sendak, who later teamed Yorinks' writing with Egielski's illustrations. Subsequently, the Yorinks-Egielski team has produced four successful, award-winning picture books for children. About their collaborations, Yorinks says: "I tend to discover what I had in mind . . . after I've seen Richard's illustrations."

These are only a few of the authors and illustrators that you'll find in this volume. We hope you find all the entries in *SATA* both interesting and useful.

Something about the Author Autobiography Series

You can complement the information in *SATA* with the *Something about the Author Autobiography Series (SAAS),* which provides autobiographical essays written by important current authors and illustrators of books for children and young adults. In every volume of *SAAS* you will find about twenty specially commissioned autobiographies, each accompanied by a selection of personal photographs supplied by the authors. The wide range of contemporary writers and artists who describe their lives and interests in the *Autobiography Series* includes Joan Aiken, Betsy Byars, Leonard Everett Fisher, Milton Meltzer, Maia Wojciechowska, and Jane Yolen, among others. Though the information presented in the autobiographies is as varied and unique as the authors, you can learn about the people and events that influenced these writers' early lives, how they began their careers, what problems they faced in becoming established in their professions, what prompted them to write or illustrate particular books, what they now find most challenging or rewarding in their lives, and what advice they may have for young people interested in following in their footsteps, among many other subjects.

Autobiographies included in the *SATA Autobiography Series* can be located through both the *SATA* cumulative index and the *SAAS* cumulative index, which lists not only the authors' names but also the subjects mentioned in their essays, such as titles of works and geographical and personal names.

The *SATA Autobiography Series* gives you the opportunity to view "close up" some of the fascinating people who are included in the *SATA* parent series. The combined *SATA* series makes available to you an unequaled range of comprehensive and in-depth information about the authors and illustrators of young people's literature.

Please write and tell us if we can make *SATA* even more helpful to you.

Acknowledgments

Grateful acknowledgment is made to the following publishers, authors, and artists
for their kind permission to reproduce copyrighted material.

AMERICAN LIBRARY ASSOCIATION. Sidelight excerpts from an article "A Personal Note by Lloyd Alexander on Charles Dickens" by Lloyd Alexander, November, 1968 in *Top of the News*. Copyright © 1968 by American Library Association. Reprinted by permission of American Library Association.

ANGUS & ROBERTSON LTD. Sidelight excerpts from *Old Days, Old Ways: A Book of Recollections* by Mary Gilmore. Reprinted by permission of Angus & Robertson Ltd.

ATHENEUM PUBLISHERS. Illustration by Rick Schreiter from *How The Whale Became and Other Stories* by Ted Hughes. Copyright © 1963 by Ted Hughes./ Jacket illustration by Michael Garland from *The Candle and the Mirror* by Lucinda Mays. Text copyright © 1982 by Lucinda Mays. Jacket illustration copyright © 1982 by Michael Garland. Both reprinted by permission of Atheneum Publishers.

AVON BOOKS. Cover photograph by Doyle Gray from *Stay on Your Toes, Maggie Adams!* by Karen Strickler Dean. Text copyright © 1986 by Karen Strickler Dean. Cover photograph copyright © 1985 by Doyle Gray. Reprinted by permission of Avon Books.

BANTAM BOOKS, INC. Cover photograph by Pat Hill from *Two's a Crowd* by Diana Gregory. Copyright © 1985 by Diana Gregory and Cloverdale Press, Inc./ Photographs by Jill Uris from *Ireland, a Terrible Beauty: The Story of Ireland Today* by Jill and Leon Uris. Both reprinted by permission of Bantam Books, Inc.

BLACKIE & SON LTD. Illustrations by Cicely Mary Barker from *A Flower Fairy Alphabet* by Cicely Mary Barker. Copyright © 1985 by The Estate of Cicely Mary Barker./ Illustrations by Cicely Mary Barker from *Flower Fairies of the Garden* by Cicely Mary Barker. Copyright © 1985 by The Estate of Cicely Mary Barker./ Illustration by Cicely Mary Barker from *Flower Fairies of the Seasons* by Cicely Mary Barker. Copyright © 1981 by Blackie & Son Ltd./ Illustration by Cicely Mary Barker from *Flower Fairies of the Wayside* by Cicely Mary Barker. Copyright © 1985 by The Estate of Cicely Mary Barker. All reprinted by permission of Blackie & Son Ltd.

BERKLEY PUBLISHING GROUP. Cover illustration from *Ammie, Come Home* by Barbara Michaels. Copyright © 1968 by Barbara Michaels. Reprinted by permission of Berkley Publishing Group.

CENTURY HUTCHINSON LTD. Sidelight excerpts from *Sporting Rhapsody* by Hylton Cleaver. Reprinted by permission of Century Hutchinson Ltd.

CHELSEA HOUSE PUBLISHERS. Illustration by Chester Gould from *The Celebrated Cases of Dick Tracy, 1931-1951* by Chester Gould. Edited by Herb Galewitz. Copyright © 1980 by Chelsea House Publishers./ Sidelight excerpts from an article "Interview with Chester Gould" in *The Celebrated Cases of Dick Tracy, 1931-1951* by Chester Gould. Edited by Herb Galewitz. Copyright © 1970 by Chelsea House, Inc./ Illustration by Chester Gould from "The First Appearance of Junior, September 8, 1932-October 12, 1932" in *Dick Tracy, the Thirties: Tommy Guns and Hard Times* by Chester Gould. Copyright © 1978 by Chelsea House Publishers./ Sidelight excerpts from *Dick Tracy, the Thirties: Tommy Guns and Hard Times* by Chester Gould. Copyright © 1978 by Chelsea House Publishers. All reprinted by permission of Chelsea House Publishers.

CHILDREN'S PRESS. Illustration from *Learning about Ghosts* by Sylvia R. Tester. Illustrated by Krystyna Stasiak. Copyright © 1981 by Regensteiner Publishing Enterprises, Inc. Reprinted by permission of Children's Press.

THOMAS Y. CROWELL, INC. Sidelight excerpts from *My Love Affair with Music* by Lloyd Alexander./ Illustration by Felicia Bond from *Poinsettia and Her Family* by Felicia Bond. Copyright © 1981 by Felicia Bond./ Illustration by Felicia Bond from *Mary Betty Lizzie McNutt's Birthday* by Felicia Bond. Copyright © 1983 by Felicia Bond./ Jacket illustration by

Arthur Shilstone from *Speedway Contender* by Frank Bonham. Copyright © 1964 by Frank Bonham./ Illustration by Margot Zemach from *Molly, McCullough, and Tom the Rogue* by Kathleen Stevens. Text copyright © 1982 by Kathleen Stevens. Illustrations copyright © 1983 by Margot Zemach. All reprinted by permission of Thomas Y. Crowell, Inc.

DELL PUBLISHING CO., INC. Illustration by Bill Sokol from *Time Cat* by Lloyd Alexander. Text copyright © 1963 by Lloyd Alexander. Illustrations copyright © 1963 by William Sokol./ Illustration by Alvin Smith from *Mystery of the Fat Cat* by Frank Bonham. Copyright © 1968 by Frank Bonham./ Cover illustration from *Viva Chicano* by Frank Bonham. Copyright © 1970 by Frank Bonham. All reprinted by permission of Dell Publishing Co., Inc.

DIAL BOOKS FOR YOUNG READERS. Jacket illustration by Diane De Groat from *Two Ways about It* by Judy Frank Mearian. Copyright © 1979 by Judy Frank Mearian. Reprinted by permission of Dial Books for Young Readers.

DODD, MEAD & CO. Illustration by Paul O. Zelinsky from *Hansel and Gretel*, retold by Rika Lesser. Text copyright © 1984 by Rika Lesser. Illustrations copyright © 1984 by Paul O. Zelinsky. Reprinted by permission of Dodd, Mead & Co.

DOUBLEDAY & CO., INC. Illustration by Dahlov Ipcar from *Hard Scrabble Harvest* by Dahlov Ipcar. Copyright © 1976 by Dahlov Ipcar./ Jacket illustration by Dahlov Ipcar from *The Marvelous Merry-Go-Round* by Dahlov Ipcar./ Jacket illustration by Dahlov Ipcar from *Lost and Found: A Hidden Animal Book* by Dahlov Ipcar. Copyright © 1981 by Dahlov Ipcar./ Jacket illustration by Dahlov Ipcar from *Horses of Long Ago* by Dahlov Ipcar. Copyright © 1965 by Dahlov Ipcar./ Illustration by Judith Gwyn Brown from "Disobedience" by A. A. Milne in *A New Treasury of Children's Poetry: Old Favorites and New Discoveries*. Selected by Joanna Cole. Copyright © 1984 by Joanna Cole. All reprinted by permission of Doubleday & Co., Inc.

E. P. DUTTON, INC. Illustration by Laszlo Kubinyi from "The Painter's Cat" in *The Town Cats and Other Tales* by Lloyd Alexander. Text copyright © 1977 by Lloyd Alexander. Illustrations copyright © 1977 by Laszlo Kubinyi./ Jacket illustration by Charles Mikolaycak from *Westmark* by Lloyd Alexander. Copyright © 1981 by Lloyd Alexander./ Illustration by Laszlo Kubinyi from *The Wizard in the Tree* by Lloyd Alexander. Text copyright © 1975 by Lloyd Alexander. Illustrations copyright © 1975 by Laszlo Kubinyi./ Illustration by Tom Feelings from *Now Sheba Sings the Song* by Maya Angelou. Text copyright © 1987 by Maya Angelou. Illustrations copyright © 1987 by Tom Feelings./ Jacket illustration by Symeon Shimin from *Durango Street* by Frank Bonham. Copyright © 1965 by Frank Bonham./ Illustration by Bari Weissman from *Golly Gump Swallowed a Fly* by Joanna Cole. Text copyright © 1981 by Joanna Cole. Illustrations copyright © 1981 by Bari Weissman./ Jacket illustration by Paul O. Zelinsky from *Rumpelstiltskin*, retold by Paul O. Zelinsky. All reprinted by permission of E. P. Dutton, Inc.

FABER & FABER LTD. Sidelight excerpts from *Poetry in the Making* by Ted Hughes./ Illustration by Peter L. Moldon from *Your Book of Ballet* by Peter L. Moldon. Copyright © 1974, 1980 by Peter L. Moldon. Both reprinted by permission of Faber & Faber Ltd.

FARRAR, STRAUS & GIROUX, INC. Photograph by Jason Lauré from *South Africa: Coming of Age under Apartheid* by Jason Lauré and Ettagale Lauré. Text copyright © 1980 by Jason Lauré and Ettagale Lauré. Photographs copyright © 1977, 1978, 1979, 1980 by Jason Lauré./ Illustrations by Richard Egielski from *It Happened in Pinsk* by Arthur Yorinks. Text copyright © 1983 by Arthur Yorinks. Illustrations copyright © 1983 by Richard Egielski./ Illustrations by Richard Egielski from *Sid and Sol* by Arthur Yorinks. Text copyright © 1977 by Arthur Yorinks. Illustrations copyright © 1977 by Richard Egielski./ Illustrations by Richard Egielski from *Hey, Al* by Arthur Yorinks. Text copyright © 1986 by Arthur Yorinks. Illustrations copyright © 1986 by Richard Egielski./ Illustration by Richard Egielski from *Louis the Fish* by Arthur Yorinks. Text copyright © 1980 by Arthur Yorinks. Illustrations copyright © 1980 by Richard Egielski./ Illustration by Margot Zemach from *The Princess and Froggie* by Harve and Kaethe Zemach. Copyright © 1975 by Farrar, Straus & Giroux, Inc. All reprinted by permission of Farrar, Straus & Giroux, Inc.

PHILIPP FELDHEIM, INC. Illustration by Chanan Mazal from *The Mystery of the Missing Pushke* by Eliezer Gevirtz. Copyright © 1982 by Eliezer Gevirtz. Reprinted by permission of Philipp Feldheim, Inc.

FOUR WINDS PRESS. Illustration by Bijou Le Tord from *Nice and Cozy* by Bijou Le Tord. Copyright © 1980 by Bijou Le Tord. Reprinted by permission of Four Winds Press.

GANNETT BOOKS. Illustration by Dahlov Ipcar from *A Flood of Creatures* by Dahlov Ipcar. Copyright © 1985 by Dahlov Ipcar./ Illustration by Dahlov Ipcar from *Bug City* by

Dahlov Ipcar. Copyright © 1975 by Dahlov Ipcar. Both reprinted by permission of Gannett Books.

THE GREEN TIGER PRESS. Illustration by Cooper Edens from *If You're Afraid of the Dark, Remember the Night Rainbow* by Cooper Edens. Copyright © 1979 by Cooper Edens./ Illustrations from *Inevitable Papers* by Cooper Edens. Copyright © 1982 by Cooper Edens./ Illustration by Cooper Edens from *Caretakers of Wonder* by Cooper Edens. Copyright © 1980 by Cooper Edens./ Illustration by Cooper Edens from *With Secret Friends* by Cooper Edens. Copyright © 1981 by Cooper Edens./ Illustration by Cooper Edens from *The Starcleaner Reunion* by Cooper Edens. Copyright © 1979 by Cooper Edens. All reprinted by permission of The Green Tiger Press.

GROSSET & DUNLAP, INC. Jacket illustration by Ralph Crosby Smith from *Cherry Ames, Student Nurse* by Helen Wells. Copyright 1943 by Grosset & Dunlap, Inc./ Frontispiece illustration from *Cherry Ames, Chief Nurse* by Helen Wells. Copyright 1944 by Grosset & Dunlap, Inc./ Frontispiece illustration from *Cherry Ames, Visiting Nurse* by Helen Wells. Copyright 1947 by Grosset & Dunlap, Inc./ Jacket illustration from *Cherry Ames, Department Store Nurse* by Helen Wells. Copyright © 1956 by Grosset & Dunlap, Inc. All reprinted by permission of Grosset & Dunlap, Inc.

HARPER & ROW, PUBLISHERS, INC. Illustration by Richard Egielski from *Lower! Higher! You're A Liar!* by Miriam Chaikin. Text copyright © 1984 by Miriam Chaikin. Text copyright © 1984 by Miriam Chaikin. Illustrations copyright © 1984 by Richard Egielski./ Photograph by Jaap Stolp from *Single Lens: The Story of the Simple Microscope* by Brian J. Ford./ Illustration by Arieh Zeldich from *Nana* by Lyn Littlefield Hoopes. Text copyright ©1981 by Lyn Littlefield Hoopes. Illustrations copyright ©1981 by Arieh Zeldich./ Jacket illustration by Leonard Baskin from *Crow: From the Life and Songs of the Crow* by Ted Hughes. Copyright © 1971 by Ted Hughes./ Jacket illustration by Leonard Baskin from *Gaudete* by Ted Hughes. Copyright © 1977 by Ted Hughes./ Illustration by Leonard Baskin from "Second Glance at a Jaguar" in *Selected Poems, 1957-1967* by Ted Hughes. Text copyright © 1972 by Ted Hughes. Illustrations copyright © 1973 by Harper & Row, Publishers, Inc./ Illustration by Gabriel Lisowski from *The Witch of Fourth Street and Other Stories* by Myron Levoy. Text copyright © 1972 by Myron Levoy. Illustrations copyright © 1972 by Gabriel Lisowski. All reprinted by permission of Harper & Row, Publishers, Inc.

HAMISH HAMILTON LTD. Illustration by Paul O. Zelinsky from *Ralph S. Mouse* by Beverly Cleary. Copyright © 1982 by Beverly Cleary. Reprinted by permission of Hamish Hamilton Ltd.

HOLIDAY HOUSE, INC. Illustration by Leslie Morrill from *Judge Benjamin: Superdog* by Judith Whitlock McInerney. Text copyright © 1982 by Judith Whitlock McInerney. Illustrations copyright © 1982 by Leslie Morrill. Reprinted by permission of Holiday House, Inc.

HOLT, RINEHART & WINSTON GENERAL BOOK. Illustration by Margot Zemach from "The True Enchanter" in *The Foundling and Other Tales of Prydain* by Lloyd Alexander. Text copyright © 1973 by Lloyd Alexander. Illustrations copyright © 1973 by Margot Zemach./ Jacket illustration by Evaline Ness from *The Black Cauldron* by Lloyd Alexander. Copyright © 1965 by Lloyd Alexander./ Jacket illustration by Evaline Ness from *The book of Three* by Lloyd Alexander. Copyright © 1964 by Lloyd Alexander./ Jacket illustration by Evaline Ness from *The High King* by Lloyd Alexander. Text copyright © 1968 by Lloyd Alexander./ Illustration by Lester Abrams from *The Four Donkeys* by Lloyd Alexander. Text copyright © 1972 by Lloyd Alexander. Illustrations copyright © 1972 by Lester Abrams./ Illustration by Michael Hague from *Numbears: A Counting Book* by Kathleen Hague. Text copyright © 1986 by Kathleen Hague. Illustrations copyright © 1986 by Michael Hague. All reprinted by permission of Holt, Rinehart & Winston General Book.

THE HORN BOOK, INC. Sidelight excerpts from an article "The Flat-Heeled Muse" by Lloyd Alexander in *Horn Book Reflections on Children's Books and Reading,* edited by Elinor Whitney Field. Copyright © 1969 by The Horn Book, Inc./ Sidelight excerpts from an article "Newbery Award Acceptance Speech" by Lloyd Alexander, August, 1969 in *Horn Book*./ Sidelight excerpts from an article "The World of Rufus Henry" by Frank Bonham, February, 1966 in *Horn Book*./ Sidelight excerpts from an article "Making Pictures on the Farm" by Dahlov Ipcar in *The Illustrator's Notebook,* edited by Lee Kingman. Copyright © 1978 by The Horn Book, Inc./ Sidelight excerpts from an article "Interview with Paul O. Zelinsky" by Sylvia and Kenneth Marantz, May-June, 1986 in *Horn Book.* All reprinted by permission of The Horn Book, Inc.

HOUGHTON MIFFLIN CO. Illustration by Fernando Krahn from *Amanda and the Mysterious Carpet* by Fernando Krahn. Copyright © 1985 by Fernando Krahn. Reprinted by permission of Houghton Mifflin Co.

ALFRED A. KNOPF, INC. Illustration by Helen Craig from *Susie and Alfred in the Knight, the Princess and the Dragon* by Helen Craig. Copyright © 1985 by Helen Craig./ Illustration by Dahlov Ipcar from *The Cat Came Back,* adapted by Dahlov Ipcar. Copyright © 1971 by Dahlov Ipcar./ Photograph from *The Story of Nim: The Chimp Who Learned Language* by Anna Michel. Text copyright © 1980 by Anna Michel. Photographs copyright © 1979, 1980 by Herbert S. Terrace./ Illustration by Paul O. Zelinsky from *Three Romances: Love Stories from Camelot Retold* by Winifred Rosen. All reprinted by permission of Alfred A. Knopf, Inc.

J. B. LIPPINCOTT CO. Illustration by Cindy Wheeler from *A Good Day, A Good Night* by Cindy Wheeler. Copyright © 1980 by Cindy Wheeler. Reprinted by permission of J. B. Lippincott Co.

LITTLE, BROWN & CO. Jacket illustration by Ben Stahl from *The Other Side of the World* by Arlene Hale. Copyright © 1976 by Arlene Hale. Reprinted by permission of Little, Brown & Co.

MACMILLAN PUBLISHING CO. Photograph by Chuck Saaf from *Parade!* by Tom Shachtman. Copyright © 1985 by Tom Shachtman. Copyright © 1985 by Chuck Saaf. Reprinted by permission of Macmillan Publishing Co.

JULIA MacRAE BOOKS. Illustration by Paul O. Zelinsky from *Dear Mr. Henshaw* by Beverly Cleary. Copyright © 1983 by Beverly Cleary. Reprinted by permission of Julia MacRae Books.

McGRAW-HILL, INC. Jacket illustration by Leonard Leone from *Topaz* by Leon Uris. Copyright © 1967 by Leon Uris. Reprinted by permission of McGraw-Hill, Inc.

MELBOURNE UNIVERSITY PRESS. Sidelight excerpts and photographs from *Letters of Mary Gilmore,* selected and edited by W. H. Wilde and T. Inglis Moore. Copyright © 1962 by The Public Trustee and the State of New South Wales. Copyright © 1980 by William H. Wilde and Pacita Alexander. All reprinted by permission of Melbourne University Press.

WILLIAM MORROW & CO., INC. Jacket illustration by Donald Carrick from *Doctor Change* by Joanna Cole./ Photographs by Jerome Wexler from *A Chick Hatches* by Joanna Cole. Text copyright © 1976 by Joanna Cole. Photographs copyright © 1976 by Jerome Wexler./ Illustration by Paul O. Zelinsky from *Dear Mr. Henshaw* by Beverly Cleary. Copyright © 1983 by Beverly Cleary./ Illustration by Paul O. Zelinsky from *Ralph S. Mouse* by Beverly Cleary. Copyright © 1982 by Beverly Cleary. All reprinted by permission of William Morrow & Co., Inc.

ODEON. Illustration by Adolf Born from the Czechoslovakian translation of Daniel Defoe's *Robinson Crusoe.* Reprinted by permission of Odeon.

PANTHEON BOOKS, INC. Illustration by Linda Strauss Edwards from *The Downtown Day* by Linda Strauss Edwards. Copyright © 1983 by Linda Strauss Edwards. Reprinted by permission of Pantheon Books, Inc.

THE PUTNAM PUBLISHING GROUP. Jacket illustration by Bob Travers from *Soldier Boy* by Michael French. Copyright © 1985 by Michael French. Reprinted by permission of The Putnam Publishing Group.

RANDOM HOUSE, INC. Jacket illustration by Janet Halverson and Sidelight excerpts from *Singin' and Swingin' and Gettin' Merry Like Christmas* by Maya Angelou. Copyright © 1976 by Maya Angelou./ Jacket illustrations by Janet Halverson and Sidelight excerpts from *All God's Children Need Traveling Shoes* by Maya Angelou. Copyright © 1986 by Random House, Inc./ Sidelight excerpts from *I Know Why the Caged Bird Sings* by Maya Angelou. Copyright © 1969 by Maya Angelou./ Jacket illustration by Janet Halverson and Sidelight excerpts from *The Heart of a Woman* by Maya Angelou. Copyright © 1981 by Maya Angelou./ Jacket illustration by Janet Halverson from *Gather Together in My Name* by Maya Angelou. Copyright © 1974 by Maya Angelou./ Illustration by Tom Stimpson from *The Space Shuttle Action Book* (a pop-up book) by Patrick Moore. Paper engineering by Vic Duppa-Whyte. Copyright © 1983 by Aurum Press Ltd. First American edition copyright © 1983 by Random House, Inc./ Illustration by Eloise Wilkin from "Spring Rain" by Marchette Chute in *Poems to Read to the Very Young,* selected by Josette Frank. Copyright © 1982 by Random House, Inc./ Illustration by Eloise Wilkin from *Baby's Christmas* by Eloise Wilkin. Copyright © 1980 by Random House, Inc. All reprinted by permission of Random House, Inc.

SCHOLASTIC, INC. Cover illustration by Ruth Sanderson from *The Rascals from Haskell's Gym* by Frank Bonham. Copyright © 1977 by Frank Bonham./ Illustration by Dirk Zimmer from *Bony-Legs* by Joanna Cole. Text copyright © 1983 by Joanna Cole. Illustrations copyright © 1983 by Dirk Zimmer./ Cover photograph from *A Time to Dance* by Karen Strickler Dean./ Cover illustration by Tom Newsom from *This Can't Be Happening at Macdonald Hall!* by Gordon Korman. Text copyright © 1978 by Gordon Korman. Illustrations copyright © 1978 by Scholastic Books, Inc./ Cover illustration from *No Coins, Please* by Gordon Korman. Copyright © 1984 by Gordon Korman./ Jacket illustration by Bruce Emmett from *Son of Interflux* by Gordon Korman. Copyright © 1986 by Gordon Korman Enterprises, Inc. Jacket illustration copyright © 1986 by Bruce Emmett./ Jacket illustration by Bruce Emmett from *Don't Care High* by Gordon Korman. Copyright © 1985 by Gordon Korman. Jacket illustration copyright © 1985 by Bruce Emmett. All reprinted by permission of Scholastic, Inc.

TROUBADOUR PRESS, INC. Illustration by Varian Mace from *Fairy Tales Color and Story Album* by Ann Moen. Reprinted by permission of Troubadour Press, Inc.

THE VIKING PRESS. Illustration by Michelle Cartlidge from *Teddy's Birthday Party: A Cutout Model Book* by Michelle Cartlidge. Copyright © 1985 by Michelle Cartlidge./ Illustration by Leonard Baskin from "The Loon" in *Under the North Star* by Ted Hughes. Text copyright © 1981 by Ted Hughes. Illustrations copyright © 1981 by Leonard Baskin./ Illustration by Alan E. Cober from *The Tiger's Bones and Other Plays for Children* by Ted Hughes. Copyright © 1974 by The Viking Press, Inc./ Illustration by Leonard Baskin from "The Interrogator" in *Cave Birds: An Alchemical Cave Drama* by Ted Hughes. Text copyright © 1978 by Ted Hughes. Illustrations copyright © 1978 by Leonard Baskin./ Jacket painting by Charles Mikolaycak from *A Dark Horn Blowing* by Dahlov Ipcar. Copyright © 1978 by Dahlov Ipcar. All reprinted by permission of The Viking Press.

FRANKLIN WATTS, INC. Cover illustration by Andrew Farmer from *Space* by Tim Furniss. Copyright © 1985 by Aladdin Books Ltd. Reprinted by permission of Franklin Watts, Inc.

WESTERN PUBLISHING CO., INC. Illustration by Eloise Wilkin from *My Goodnight Book* by Eloise Wilkin. Copyright © 1981 by Western Publishing Co., Inc. Reprinted by permission of Western Publishing Co., Inc.

Sidelight excerpts from an article "Two Worlds in Balance" by Dahlov Ipcar in *Bookmark*. Reprinted by permission of *Bookmark*./ Sidelight excerpts from *More Books by More People* by Lee Bennett Hopkins. Copyright © 1974 by Lee Bennett Hopkins. Reprinted by permission of Curtis Brown Ltd./ Sidelight excerpts from an article "An Interview with Gordon Korman" by Chris Ferns in *Canadian Children's Literature*, number 38. Reprinted by permission of *Canadian Children's Literature*./ Sidelight excerpts from an article "Dick Tracy" by Chester Gould, March, 1973 in *Cartoonist Profile*. Reprinted by permission of *Cartoonist Profile*./ Sidelight excerpts from an article "The American Comic Strip Has Sold More Newspapers Than Any Other Feature in American Journalism" by Chester Gould, March, 1973 in *Cartoonist Profile*. Reprinted by permission of *Cartoonist Profile*.

Comic strip featuring Gravel Gertie in the year of her initial appearance. Copyright 1944 by *Chicago Tribune*. Reprinted by permission of *Chicago Tribune*./ Illustration from the comic strip "Dick Tracy" by Chester Gould. Copyright 1949 by *Chicago Tribune*. Reprinted by permission of *Chicago Tribune*./ Sidelight excerpts from an article "Myth and Education" by Ted Hughes in *Children's Literature in Education*. Copyright by Ted Hughes. Reprinted by permission of *Children's Literature in Education*./ Sidelight excerpts from an article "Ted Hughes," March 23, 1965 in *The Guardian*. Reprinted by permission of *The Guardian*./ Sidelight excerpts from an article "Ted Hughes' Crow," July 30, 1970 in *The Listener*. Reprinted by permission of *The Listener*./ Sidelight excerpts from an article "Ted Hughes," February, 1962 in *The London Magazine*. Reprinted by permission of *The London Magazine*./ Gould's first daily strip of "Dick Tracy," October 12, 1931. Copyright 1931 by News Syndicate Co., Inc. Reprinted by permission of News Syndicate Co., Inc./ Theater still from the New York stage production of "The Blacks" with Maya Angelou. Reprinted by permission of Martha Swope.

Appreciation also to the Performing Arts Research Center of the New York Public Library at Lincoln Center for permission to reprint the theater still from the musical "Ari."

PHOTOGRAPH CREDITS

Lloyd Alexander: Alexander Limont; Maya Angelou: Susan Mullally Weil; Frank Bonham: Keith Bonham Photography; Adolf Born: Vlasta Gronska; Helen Craig: Geoff Shields; Michael French: Jane Hull; Chester Gould: Michael Lawton, Cirama; Diana Gregory: Claudia O'Keefe;

Kathleen Hague: Meghan M. Hague; Arlene Hale: National Studio (Burlington, Iowa); Ted Hughes: Layle Silbert; Dahlov Ipcar: Adolf Ipcar; Bijou Le Tord: Roxanne Lowit; Barbara Mertz: Joan Bingham; William P. Nestor: Flo Nestor; Margaret F. O'Connell: Haidi Kuhn; Robert E. Rubinstein: Brian Lanker; Tom Shachtman: Fabio Mucchi; Leon Uris (with wife, Jill): Norm Clasen; Helen Wells: Bill Stone Photography; Cindy Wheeler: Patrick Lee; Arthur Yorinks (with Richard Egielski): Copyright © 1986 by Todd Weinstein.

SOMETHING ABOUT THE AUTHOR

ALEXANDER, Lloyd (Chudley) 1924-

PERSONAL: Born January 30, 1924, in Philadelphia, Pa.; son of Alan Audley (a stockbroker and importer) and Edna (a homemaker; maiden name, Chudley) Alexander; married Janine Denni, January 8, 1946; children: Madeleine. *Education:* Attended West Chester State Teachers College, 1942, Lafayette College, 1943, and Sorbonne, University of Paris, 1946. *Home:* 1005 Drexel Ave., Drexel Hill, Pa. 19026. *Agent:* Brandt & Brandt, 1501 Broadway, New York, N.Y. 10036.

CAREER: Author of children's books; free-lance writer and translator, 1946—. Has worked as a layout artist, cartoonist, advertising copywriter and magazine editor. Author-in-residence, Temple University, 1970-74. Member, Library Committee, *World Book Encyclopedia*, Chicago, Ill., 1973-74. *Military service:* U.S. Army, Intelligence, 1942-46; became staff sergeant. *Member:* Authors Guild, P.E.N., International Board on Books for Young People (U.S. section), Amnesty International, Children's Reading Round Table, Carpenter Lane Chamber Music Society (member of board of directors, 1973—). *Cricket* magazine (advisory board member, 1975—).

AWARDS, HONORS: Isaac Siegel Memorial Juvenile Award from the Jewish Book Council, 1959, for *Border Hawk: August Bondi;* Newbery Honor Book from the American Library Association, 1966, for *The Black Cauldron; Taran Wanderer* was selected one of *School Library Journal*'s Best Books of the Year, 1967; *The Truthful Harp* was selected one of American Institute of Graphic Arts Children's Books, 1967-68; *The High King* was chosen one of Child Study Association of America's Children's Books of the Year, 1968, *The King's Fountain*, 1971, *The Cat Who Wished to Be a Man*, 1973, *The Foundling and Other Tales of Prydain*, 1974, *The Wizard in the Tree*, 1975, *The Kestrel*, 1982, and *The Black Cauldron* and *Time Cat*, 1985; Newbery Medal from the American Library Association, 1969, for *The High King;* National Book

LLOYD ALEXANDER

Award finalist in children's literature, 1969, for *The High King,* and 1979, for *The First Two Lives of Lukas-Kasha.*

The Marvelous Misadventures of Sebastian was selected one of Library of Congress' Best Books of the Year, 1970, and received the National Book Award in children's literature, 1971; *The King's Fountain* was chosen one of *School Library Journal*'s Best Books for Spring, 1971; Drexel Award from the Graduate School of Library Science of Drexel University, 1972, and from the Pennsylvania School Libraries Association, 1976, for an outstanding contribution to literature for children; *Boston Globe-Horn Book* honor for text, 1973, for *The Cat Who Wished to Be a Man; The Foundling and Other Tales of Prydain* was chosen one of *New York Times* Outstanding Books of the Year, 1973; nominated for the Laura Ingalls Wilder Award, 1975; CRABbery Award from Oxon Hill Branch of Prince George's County Library (Md.), 1979, The Silver Pencil Award, 1981, and Austrian Children's Book Award, 1984, all for *The First Two Lives of Lukas-Kasha.*

American Book Award finalist for fiction (paperback), 1980, for *The High King,* and 1982, for *The Wizard in the Tree;*

Flowers blossomed at each motion of his fingers. ■ (From "The True Enchanter" in *The Foundling and Other Tales of Prydain* by Lloyd Alexander. Illustrated by Margot Zemach.)

Westmark was chosen one of American Library Association's Best Books for Young Adults, 1981, one of *School Library Journal*'s Best Books for Young Adults, 1982, and one of *School Library Journal*'s Best of the Best Books, 1970-1983, and received the American Book Award for children's hardcover fiction, 1982; Parents' Choice Award for literature from the Parents' Choice Foundation, 1982, for *The Kestrel,* 1984, for *The Beggar Queen,* and 1986, for *The Illyrian Adventure; The Kestrel* was selected one of American Library Association's Best Books for Young Adults, 1982, and *The Beggar Queen,* 1984; Golden Cat Award from Sjöstrands Förlag (Swedish publisher), 1984, for excellence in children's literature; Regina Medal from the Catholic Library Association, 1986.

WRITINGS—Juvenile, except as noted: *And Let the Credit Go* (adult novel), Crowell, 1955; *My Five Tigers* (adult), Crowell, 1956; *Janine Is French* (adult), Crowell, 1958; *Border Hawk: August Bondi* (illustrated by Bernard Krigstein), Farrar, Straus, 1959; *My Love Affair with Music* (adult; illustrated by Vasiliu), Crowell, 1960; *The Flagship Hope: Aaron Lopez* (illustrated by B. Krigstein), Farrar, Straus, 1960; (with Louis J. Camuti) *Park Avenue Vet* (adult), Holt, 1962; *Time Cat: The Remarkable Journeys of Jason and Gareth* (illustrated by Bill Sokol), Holt, 1963 (published in England as *Nine Lives,* Cassell, 1963); *Fifty Years in the Doghouse* (adult), Putnam, 1963 (published in England as *Send for Ryan!,* W. H. Allen, 1965); *The Book of Three* (ALA Notable Book; *Horn Book* honor list; teacher's guide available), Holt, 1964; *The Black Cauldron* (ALA Notable Book; *Horn Book* honor list; teacher's guide available), Holt, 1965; *Coll and His White Pig* (illustrated by Evaline Ness), Holt, 1965; *The Castle of Llyr* (ALA Notable Book; *Horn Book* honor list; teacher's guide available), Holt, 1966; *Taran Wanderer* (ALA Notable Book; *Horn Book* honor list; teacher's guide available), Holt, 1967; *The Truthful Harp* (illustrated by E. Ness), Holt, 1967; *The High King* (ALA Notable Book; *Horn Book* honor list; teacher's guide available), Holt, 1968.

The Marvelous Misadventures of Sebastian (ALA Notable Book; *Horn Book* honor list), Dutton, 1970; *The King's Fountain* (illustrated by Ezra Jack Keats), Dutton, 1971; *The Four Donkeys* (ALA Notable Book; Junior Literary Guild selection; illustrated by Lester Abrams), Holt, 1972; *The Foundling and Other Tales of Prydain* (ALA Notable Book; illustrated by Margot Zemach), Holt, 1973; *The Cat Who Wished to Be a Man* (ALA Notable Book), Dutton, 1973; *The Wizard in the Tree* (Junior Literary Guild selection; illustrated by Laszlo Kubinyi), Dutton, 1975; *The Town Cats and Other Tales* (illustrated by L. Kubinyi), Dutton, 1977; *The First Two Lives of Lukas-Kasha* (Junior Literary Guild selection), Dutton, 1978; *Westmark* (ALA Notable Book; *Horn Book* honor list; Junior Literary Guild selection), Dutton, 1981; *The Kestrel* (*Horn Book* honor list), Dutton, 1982; *The Beggar Queen,* Dutton, 1984; *The Illyrian Adventure,* Dutton, 1986; *The El Dorado Adventure,* Dutton, 1987.

Translator from the French; published by New Directions, except as indicated: Jean-Paul Sartre, *The Wall and Other Stories,* 1948, published as *Intimacy and Other Stories,* Peter Nevill, 1949, New Directions, 1952; J. Sartre, *Nausea,* 1949 (published in England as *The Diary of Antoine Roquentin,* Lehmann, 1949); Paul Eluard, *Selected Writings,* 1951, published as *Uninterrupted Poetry: Selected Writings,* 1975; Paul Vialar, *The Sea Rose,* Spearman, 1951.

Author of afterword of E. Nesbit's *Five Children and It.* Work included in New Directions anthologies. Contributor to *Cricket's Choice,* Open Court, 1974. Member of editorial board,

Cricket magazine, 1975—. Contributor to *Contemporary Poetry* and of articles to periodicals, including *School Library Journal, Harper's Bazaar, Horn Book.*

ADAPTATIONS: ''The High King'' (filmstrip with cassette), Miller-Brody, 1979; ''The Black Cauldron'' (animated feature film), Walt Disney Productions, 1985; ''The King's Fountain'' (cassette), Holt (Canada), 1986.

SIDELIGHTS: **January 30, 1924.** Born and raised in Philadelphia, Pennsylvania. ''Family life as a child was unextraordinary. My childhood was certainly no more miserable than anyone else's, although at the time, I thought it was. I learned to read quite young and have been an avid reader ever since, even though my parents and relatives were not great readers. I was more or less left to my own devices and interests, which, after all, may not be such a bad idea. My relatives were as Dickensian an assortment of people as anyone could imagine, and that might have been an advantage, too.'' [Lee Bennett Hopkins, *More Books by More People*, Citation, 1974.[1]]

When he was seven, a Christmas present in the form of a toy xylophone prompted a passion for music. ''My first true instrument was our piano, a black giant named Bellak. It could be played manually, in the usual way, but its mechanical aspect was what fascinated me. Sliding open a panel revealed a long metal fixture with square holes, something like an elongated mouth organ, a wooden cylinder with a hook set in the middle, and mysterious sprockets and chains—a secret shrine where the music roll fitted; on either side, when the panels were opened as wide as they could yawn, a vista of the piano's dark and dusty guts. Below, a trap door opened with a swish and a snap when someone operated a lever, and two flat, rubber-covered treadles, smelling like a pair of galoshes, swung down to the floor.

''Attached to these galoshes were bellows that squeaked and gasped. Before I had grown enough to sit on the piano bench and reach the pedals with my feet, I lay on my stomach on the floor and pumped them by hand. . . . From end to end of the keyboard just above my head, the keys clicked in their sockets; the felt hammers attacked the strings faster than my eye could follow, until the piano's whole thorax heaved and writhed with motion. On one side, the notes of the treble cut my eardrum like splinters of glass; on the other, the bass chords plunged into my head and stayed there, even after I had stopped pumping, where they finally sank and drowned.

''No one in my family played the piano well, or frequently, and for the most part the Bellak's business was to act like a piece of furniture.

''Music lessons out of the question, . . . my best teacher was the old Bellak itself. The Bellak had resources I never suspected and I tried to make use of them.'' [Lloyd Alexander, *My Love Affair with Music*, Crowell, 1960.[2]]

Alexander's mother managed to find a piano teacher, Miss Porter, who agreed to give lessons at a reduced rate. ''Privately, in my own mind, E above the good old familiar middle C had a pale orange sound—a slightly raised voice, a person on his way somewhere; D was a dullard, F bland and easy, and G a little stricter; A lay tantalizingly beyond my little finger; B stretched and reached still farther—as my own hand had to stretch—until, suddenly, the octave smiled and became complete.''[2]

The music lessons lasted until Miss Porter's retirement. ''As it was, Miss Porter's retirement had not only ended my inter-

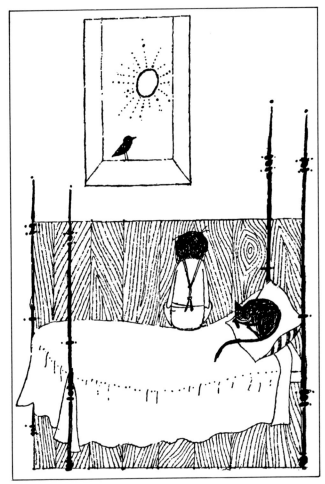

Jason sat in his room on the end of his bed, with his chin in his hands, and wished the past five minutes had never happened. ■ (From *Time Cat* by Lloyd Alexander. Illustrated by Bill Sokol.)

est, but had somehow wiped out the enthusiasm that had drawn me in the first place. As time passed, it grew harder to remember when music had been important to me. That I had once taken a pencil and marked out the position of a chord on the piano seemed childish and faintly embarrassing. Music, as far as I was concerned, was a waste of time and I had other concerns. I spent most of my days calculating how, without actually starving to death, I could save enough from my lunch money to ask a girl for a date. The rest of my efforts went into developing the nerve to ask the girl once I had saved the money.

''In any case, I wanted no more of music; it pained me to listen to it. Yet I could not escape entirely; music lay in wait for me and constantly assailed me wherever I went or whatever I did.''[2]

1939. At the age of fifteen Alexander announced to his family his intentions to become a poet. ''Poetry, my father warned, was no practical career; I would do well to forget it. My mother came to my rescue. At her urging, my father agreed I might have a try, on condition that I also find some sort of useful work. For my part, I had no idea how to find any sort of work—or, in fact, how to go about being a poet. For more than a year I had been writing long into the night and studying verse forms to the scandalous neglect of my homework. My

"**I confess to a certain artistic license.**" ▪ (From "The Painter's Cat" in *The Town Cats and Other Tales* by Lloyd Alexander. Illustrated by Laszlo Kubinyi.)

parents could not afford to send me to college and my grades were too wretched for a scholarship.''[1]

Besides writing, Alexander read books, especially Greek and Celtic mythology. ''. . . Since my family traditionally distrusted public libraries—like banks, government buildings, and other official-type structures best left alone—I scavenged our home collection, a wondrous compost of the wildest conglomeration of gems and junk; Shakespeare and Warwick Deeping; Melville and Marie Corelli; something called *The Little Leather Library;* plus a few blurry volumes in imitation morocco, given as inducements by a local newspaper trying to raise the number as well as the cultural level of its subscribers. What came to hand one day was a badly scuffed red buckram school reader.

''Whose it had been I still do not know. My sister disclaimed ownership. It could have been discarded by a lodger (we sometimes took them in those days). It might have belonged to a late aunt, a retired schoolteacher who had retreated to my grandmother's house in West Philadelphia among many other relatives or near-relatives, indigent or plain luckless, who lived there at no time or another. Be that as it may, I opened the book and discovered Nicholas Nickleby.

''We never know ahead of time what books will affect us, and in what ways. Dickens was one of many authors who helped me grow up (and are still helping). For a long while he was both refuge and encouragement. If he helped me escape from my daily life, . . . he also sent me back somehow better able to face up to it.'' [Lloyd Alexander, ''A Personal Note by Lloyd Alexander on Charles Dickens,'' *Top of the News,* November, 1968.[3]]

1940. After graduating from high school, Alexander took a job as a mail boy in a bank. ''My high-school graduation came as a relief and a shock. I had never been fond of school and was glad to be rid of it; on the other hand, I had no place else to go. Most of my friends were getting ready for college, but my parents were in no position to send me; my application for a scholarship had, justifiably, been turned down because of mediocre grades.

''Instead of homework, I preferred writing stories. In addition to poor marks, I collected rejection slips. My goal was to become an author and it appeared that I would reach it only if I inserted the qualifying word 'unpublished.'

''For the first time, I regretted not having taken music more seriously. Had I done so, I thought, I might at least have been able to get a scholarship based on musicianship rather than intelligence. Then, if worse came to worst, I could always teach piano.

''In any case, I was forced to admit that I could choose only the more disagreeable alternative and look for a job. My writing would have to be confined to spare time; other trivia, music included must go.

''To my mind, the only thing worse than looking for a job was actually finding one. However, the job I did find required no previous experience, no great intelligence, and no special skill, thereby suiting my qualifications exactly. I became a messenger boy in a bank.

''My time for writing was limited to evenings and week ends. Once again, I saw no room for music—certainly not among tellers' wickets and canceled checks.

''Working offered one small compensation: a salary. To be sure after deducting my share of expenses at home, plus cloth-ing, razor blades, shoe polish and all the other details required to make a presentable bank employee, I ended up with little more than what I had received as allowance at school. Still, I considered myself a man and a wage earner and felt free to use the remains of my money as I saw fit. . . .''[2]

Alexander also attended a local college, hoping to learn more about writing. Instead, he found that the courses were more elementary than what he needed, so he quit at the end of the term.

1943. ''Adventure, I decided, was the best way to learn writing. The United States had already entered World War II and I joined the Army, convinced that here was a chance for real deeds of derring-do.

''They shipped me not into the thick of some bold fray, but to Texas, where I became in discouraging succession an artilleryman, a cymbal player in the band, a harmonium player in the post chapel, and a first aid man. Finally I was assigned to a military intelligence training center in Maryland.

''There my hopes for adventure brightened. In my barracks I met former Foreign Legionnaires, Spanish Civil War veterans, refugees, writers, painters, scholars, Cherokee Indians, and a genuine Count. Rumors flew that we would be parachuted into France to work with the Resistance.

''This, to my intense relief, did not happen. Adventurous in imagination, a real parachute jump would have scared me out

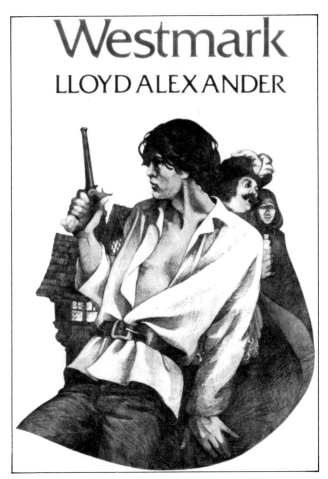

He had lived all his life in Dorning, but the town had suddenly changed. ■ (Jacket illustration by Charles Mikolaycak from *Westmark* by Lloyd Alexander.)

of my wits. Instead, we sailed to England and in late autumn, we were ordered to Wales to be outfitted for combat.

"Wales was an enchanted world. The Welsh language fascinated me, as did English spoken with a Welsh lilt, more song than speech. How much was imagination, how much reality. I hesitate now to guess; but it seemed I recognized faces from all the hero tales of my childhood. My sense of Wales was of a land far more ancient than England, wilder and rougher hewn. The Companions of Arthur might have galloped from the mountains with no surprise to me. Wales, to my eyes, appeared still a realm of bards and heroes; even the coal-tips towered like dark fortresses. Not until years afterwards did I realize I had been given, without my knowing, a glimpse of another enchanted kingdom.

"Armed to the teeth with typewriters and submachine guns, we went to France and I went to the Seventh Army in Alsace-Lorraine as a translator-interpreter. When the war ended, I was attached to a counter-intelligence unit in Paris."

1945. "In post-war Paris, I found, the people had barely enough food and clothing. But, to make up for this, there was a whole world of music in the streets. Along the boulevards I heard the sound of accordions, hurdy-gurdies, one-man bands, *chanteurs de rue*. In the *bals musette*, short-skirted women and men wearing caps danced to the rhythms of *la java* and the music flooded out over the cobblestones.

"I fell in love with the city at first sight and sound. So naturally, when the army announced that soldiers would be allowed to receive discharges there and attend the university, I

applied at once. Some weeks later, a civilian in Paris, I moved into the student dormitories at the Foundation des Etats-Unis. Then by accident, one rainy summer afternoon, I met a beautiful, vivacious Parisienne named Janine. For me, at least, it was love at first sight; I intended to marry her."[2]

1946-1953. Married Janine Denni and with her small daughter, Madeleine, returned to the United States. "I wanted to be home, feeling if I were to do anything at all I would have to be closer to my own roots, to where I had been born and raised. Aside from that, I was homesick. Janine, Madeleine, and I went back to Philadelphia, where I turned out a novel, which the publishers unhesitatingly turned down, then wrote two more, which did every bit as well as the first.

"My writing time was limited to evening and early mornings; for luckily, I had found a job—or jobs, since they included, in succession, working as a cartoonist, advertising writer, layout artist for a painter, and associate editor for an industrial magazine.

"I had been writing grimly for seven years, in a stubborn kind of hopeless hopefulness, ready to admit I was no writer at all and would have been better off had I stayed a bank messenger all my life. Looking back on those days, what seemed a catastrophe now struck me as deeply funny. I was able to laugh at it; and at myself. And enjoy it. I wrote a novel about it, as my fourth and last attempt. The novel was published.

"One thing I had learned during those seven years was to write about things I knew and loved. Our cats delighted me. So did music; I had acquired a battered Welsh harp whose strings had

What a morning it had been! ■ (From *The Four Donkeys* by Lloyd Alexander. Illustrated by Lester Abrams.)

the habit of breaking unexpectedly; and had tried to learn the violin, piano, and guitar. I relished Janine's war with the English language and her bafflement at the peculiar customs of Americans. All this found its way into books and was published. I was writing out of my own life and experience. But nearly ten more years passed before I learned a writer could know and love a fantasy world as much as his real one."

1963. Made his first venture into fantasy with the publication of *Time Cat*. It was the story of a boy and a cat who were able to visit nine different eras in history. Alexander's editor, Ann Durrell, also a cat lover, encouraged him to write this fantasy. Alexander had been writing for seventeen years before he began writing for children. "The muse in charge of fantasy wears good, sensible shoes. . . . She does not carry a soothing lyre for inspiration, but is more likely to shake you roughly awake at four in the morning and rattle a sheaf of subtle, sneaky questions under your nose. And you had better answer them. The Muse will stand for no nonsense (that is, nonsense). Her geometries are no more Euclidean than Einstein's, but they are equally rigorous.

"I was aware of the problems and disciplines of fantasy, but in a left-handed sort of way; because there is a difference between knowing and doing. Until I met the Muse in Charge of Fantasy personally, I had no hint of what a virago she could be.

"Our first encounter was relatively cordial and came in the course of working on a book called *Time Cat*. I suspect I learn more from writing books than readers very likely learn from reading them, and I realize now that *Time Cat* is an example of a fantasy perhaps more realistic than otherwise. Basically, only one fantastic premise moved the story: that Gareth, a black cat, could take the young boy Jason into nine historical periods. The premise included some built-in and plausible hedges. Boy and cat could talk together during their journeys—but only when no one else was around to overhear them; after their return home they could no longer speak to each other, at least not in words. They enjoyed no supernatural protection or privilege; what happened to them, happened—indeed, if Gareth met with a fatal accident, Jason would be forever marooned in the past. They weren't allowed to interfere with or change the course of history, or do anything contrary to laws of the physical world and their personal capacities. Jason was a boy and Gareth was a cat.

"Within those boundaries, the problem became one of straightforward historical research, with some investigation into how cats were regarded in various eras. Ichigo, the boy emperor in the Japanese adventure, really existed. His wanting to dress kittens in kimonos was valid; there was an extravagant preciousness in the Japanese court of that epoch, and historical records state that such things happened. In other adventures, only slight accommodations made it acceptable for Jason and Gareth to be where they were, doing what they were doing.

"The creation of a fantasy that starts from the ground up is something else again. Melancholy men, they say, are the most incisive humorists; by the same token, writers of fantasy must be, within their own frame of work, hardheaded realists. What appears gossamer is, underneath, solid as prestressed concrete. What seems so free in fantasy is often inventiveness of detail rather than complicated substructure. Elaboration—not improvisation.

"And the closer a self-contained imaginary world draws to a recognizably real one . . . the more likely its pleasant meadows are to conceal unsuspected deadfalls and man-traps. The writer is wise if he explores it thoroughly and eliminates them. . . .

"I began discovering the importance of consistency as a result of some of the research for *Time Cat*, originally planned to include an adventure in ancient Wales. Surely everyone cherishes a secret, private world from the days of childhood. Mine was Camelot, and Arthur's Round Table, Malory, and the *Mabinogion*. The Welsh research brought it all back to me. Feeling like a man who has by accident stumbled into an enchanted cavern lost since boyhood, both terrified and awestruck, I realized I would have to explore further. Perhaps I had been waiting to do so all these years, and some kind of moment had come. In any case, I replaced the Welsh episode with an Irish one and later turned all my attention not to the beautiful land of Wales I knew in reality, but an older, darker one." [Lloyd Alexander, "The Flat-Heeled Muse," *Horn Book Reflections on Children's Books and Reading*, edited by Elinor Whitney Field, Horn Book, 1969.⁴]

1964. Began the "Prydain" Chronicles with the publication of *The Book of Three*. The series comprised five books and was inspired by the Arthurian legends and the *Mabinogion*, a collection of Welsh myths and legends. "I didn't have any idea in the world I was going to write five books. It's a funny thing, but I thought at the beginning that I was going to do something quite easy. I had become very fond of mythology, and I was fascinated by the *Mabinogion* . . . . It's a very difficult book: there are so many things mixed up in it—courtly romance combined with Stone Age mythology, a mixture which can never be sorted out. Unlike the Irish and Scandinavian mythologies, which are pretty much of a piece, I don't think the Welsh mythology has been lucky. As far as I knew, with the possible exception of Gwyn Jones, nobody had tried to make much sense out of the *Mabinogion*. That's what I wanted to do; and I thought it would be a pleasant and simple thing to do. All I needed to do was retell the magnificent mythology, and being bone lazy this appealed to me. I tried this at first, but strange things happened to me. I found I had been kidding myself: I didn't want simply to retell anybody's mythology. What I really wanted to do was invent my own, or at least use my own in some way. So originally I did not foresee a work of that length involving that amount of time. I thought at the very most it might be three books. I began on that basis, not quite knowing where I was going. But the more I worked on *The Book of Three* the more I realized the personal importance it was taking on. As regards the *Mabinogion*, I found that what I liked I could use, but I no longer felt obliged to do a scholarly work. It was a tremendously liberating decision. I found myself, to my amazement, tapping into various areas of my personality that I never even knew existed. So the work that began as external became internal.

"I still had no idea how things were going to work out. I realized pretty early on that I was accumulating debts that had to be paid; that there were situations, objects and characters that had to be accounted for. I knew that there would be a day of reckoning when I would have to pull together all the promises I had made and all the hints I had dropped. Interestingly enough, the same way Taran changed and grew in unforeseen ways, the same happened to me. I had to engage ideas and attitudes and really examine my own feelings and beliefs in ways I had never done before. I didn't do this in my adult books—not that I hadn't wanted to, but it never became an issue somehow. All of a sudden I found myself immersed in a work that was becoming larger and larger and more and more personal." [Justin Wintle and Emma Fisher, editors, "Lloyd Alexander," *The Pied Pipers: Interviews with the Influential Creators of Children's Literature*, Paddington Press, 1974.⁵]

The company had gone less than a quarter mile when large raindrops pattered into the dust of the lane. ■ (From *The Wizard in the Tree* by Lloyd Alexander. Illustrated by Laszlo Kubinyi.)

From his first book in the ''Prydain'' series to his fifth and last one, Alexander wrote a quarter of a million words in six years. ''After I finished *The Castle of Lyr* I thought I was nearing the end when a funny thing happened. I was walking down a street in Philadelphia past a construction site; when I went home that evening I saw in the papers that a gigantic steel girder had fallen down on the pavement where I had passed. I thought to myself, what a disaster to end my life before finishing the *Prydain Chronicles*. It scared me. Seriously. So I got down to it and wrote the last volume, *The High King*. I sent it to my editor, who made one small criticism: she said that I needed another book to precede it. Evidently, without realizing it, I had implied certain things in *The High King*—characters and situations—which had never existed in the previous books, and which needed some kind of introduction. This rather took me by surprise. I had to put aside the semi-finished manuscript I'd just done and spend another year or so writing *Taran Wanderer,* the book which bridges *The Castle of Llyr* and *The High King*. I realized that my editor was right, that *Taran Wanderer* was an essential step I hadn't seen.

''Using the device of an imaginary world allowed me in some strange way to go to the central issues. In other words I used the imaginary kingdom not as a sentimentalized fairyland, but as an opening wedge to express what I hoped would be some very hard truths. I never saw fairy tales as an escape or a cop out. I think Tolkien would have borne me out on this. I don't think he or anybody else working in the high fantasy medium would see it as an escape from reality. On the contrary, speaking for myself, it is the way to understand reality. In the *Chronicles* there are questions about the nature and use of power, of self-aggrandizement at the expense of others, of kindness and of other humane qualities. If you set up a conflict between good and evil, how can you define the two camps? I suppose one rule of thumb is that the evil thing dehumanizes people, that evil has an absorption with death rather than an absorption with life. In the *Prydain Chronicles* the Lord of Death lives in a kind of static, unchanging world.

''I am amazed and delighted by how many adults read the *Prydain Chronicles*. I don't think adults stop growing, or at least they shouldn't. If you stop growing you're dead. At any rate, I've never tried to pull any punches with the kids. There are a great number of hard situations in those books, and I've tried to go at them head-on. For example, the scene in *The Black Cauldron* where Taran must trade his magical brooch,

(From the animated filmstrip "The High King." Produced by Random House/Miller Brody Productions, 1979.)

which is the greatest thing that has ever happened to him, for a cauldron that is going to be destroyed: it's a terrible decision. The feeling tone is most anguishing, at least from my point of view. And I'm sure that every adult and every child has gone through that in one way or another. It's one of the deeper levels of the emotions that we share in common, whatever our age or nationality."[5]

1969. Awarded the Newbery Medal from the American Library Association for *The High King*. "After Isabella Jinnette told me the Committee's decision—and assured me it was true, and there was no danger of their changing their minds—I lapsed into a state of bedazzlement, bewilderment, and general incoherency. On top of being insufferably pleased with myself. Luckily, whenever we start feeling too insufferably pleased with ourselves, something always brings us down to earth again. In this instance, I was playing first violin in our Sunday-afternoon-rank-amateur-chamber-music society. At a glorious moment, when the first violin has a solo passage, a sublime, superb melody that soars up from the ensemble—I botched it. We collapsed in total musical disaster. The cellist put down his bow, looked at me, and shook his head.

"'No doubt about it,' he said, 'the Newbery Medal's a wonderful thing for you. But it doesn't do anything for Johann Sebastian Bach.'

"I went home in disgrace, chewing over that idea. By the time I had digested it, I was able to face up to a sobering thought:

Writing books or playing Bach, I still have a lot to learn and a long way to go.

"Coming to the last page of *The High King* was a sad moment for me, a feeling more akin to loss than liberation; as if something one had loved deeply for a long time had suddenly gone away. Yet, it was a loss with more than equal gain. Throughout the writing of the book, and even from the first of the five books of Prydain, I believe I had a glimpse of what it felt like to create something; of how it felt, if only for a moment, truly to be a writer. Now, perhaps, I can start being one. Certainly no work has given me greater joy in the doing; and writing for children has been the happiest discovery of all.

"I have to smile, remembering myself as a very much younger man. Then, had the oracular pig, Hen Wen, foretold I would write for young people, I wouldn't have believed her. I was still looking for a way to say . . . whatever it was, if anything, I had to say. I was unsure of both form and content: a double discouraging combination for me—and very likely more so for my wife. . . . The aggravations and exasperations generated by the literary temperament must be appalling, but she did put up with them. She still does. And will. I hope.

"Although it didn't feel that way at the time, those years were a blessing—heavily disguised. Or, say, the kind of gift the enchantresses Orddu, Orwen, and Orgoch bestow on the unwitting recipient. Perhaps we have to serve an apprenticeship to life before we can serve one to art. We can't begin doing our best for children until we ourselves begin growing up.

Melyngar's hoofs clicked over the stones. Taran, snuffling and shivering, looked toward the waiting hills. ■ (Jacket illustration by Evaline Ness from *The Book of Three* by Lloyd Alexander.)

"At heart, the issues raised in a work of fantasy are those we face in real life. In whatever guise—our own daily nightmares of war, intolerance, inhumanity; or the struggles of an Assistant Pig-Keeper against the Lord of Death—the problems are agonizingly familiar. And an openness to compassion, love, and mercy is as essential to us here and now as it is to any inhabitant of an imaginary kingdom." [Lloyd Alexander, "Newbery Award Acceptance Speech," *Horn Book,* August, 1969.⁶]

1971. Received the National Book Award for *The Marvelous Misadventures of Sebastian.* Speaking about the book, Alexander commented: "In one sense it is my homage to Mozart. It's a Mozartian book in background and atmosphere, and there are some little secret Mozart references that a Mozart fan is going to pick up. Essentially it is a very personal book indeed. . . . I've tried to play the violin. Even though I've failed, it has meant I've been able to hear music in ways that I never heard before in all my life. It was the most insightful thing that happened to me. And I make a direct analogy between that and writing for children. For years I wrote for adults. I was perfectly happy with it, having a certain modest success, and that's how I thought I would continue. But what happened to me when I began writing for children was the same thing in literary terms as had happened to me in musical terms in trying to play the violin: I discovered things about writing and the creative process that I never knew were there.

"Essentially this is what *Sebastian* is all about. He begins, as you know, as a fairly competent fiddler and a fairly light-hearted young man. He has facility, but he has never scratched below the surface. In the course of the story he comes into possession of a fiddle that allows him to play and hear music as he has never done before. It changes his life. The fiddle, of course, is a mixed blessing because it also drains his life away the more he understands his magnificent discovery. Without being pretentious about it, I suppose *Sebastian* attempts to say something about what it feels like to be an artist. The Gallimaufry Theatricus involves the idea of art as illusion—the interchange between reality and illusion runs through the book. As far as I can remember, in nearly every chapter there's a flip in which what seemed make-believe or illusory turns out to be real, and vice versa. The concept of the theater becomes an analogue for the concept of art in general. Quicksilver, the proprietor of the theater, says this: that his theater provides people with a balloon they can go up in, in the belief they are going to the moon, at least for a moment. And to an extent that's real in a way."⁵

Alexander explained his work habits: ". . . I start work at the crack of dawn, but if things go badly at the typewriter, I may sneak back to bed. Janine claims I'm snoozing. I claim I'm thinking horizontally.

"Or, I'll go into the backyard and feed peanuts to the squirrels. Or have philosophical conversations with our four cats. Or play the fiddle; usually Mozart, the composer I love best. Or draw pictures. Or read books.

"I've learned that you needn't go any distance at all for story ideas. . . . For example, I live near Philadelphia, in Drexel Hill. Well, actually there's no hill in Drexel Hill, unless you count a bump in the road across from the barber shop. There's a street named Riverview—bone dry, not a river in sight. But,

(Jacket illustration by Evaline Ness from *The Black Cauldron* by Lloyd Alexander.)

if I want, I can turn that bump into Mt. Everest, that invisible river into the raging Mississippi, my cats into tigers, my backyard into Sherwood Forest. The real excitement is creating something that didn't exist before. And writing for young people—that's the best adventure of all.'' [Lloyd Alexander, ''Meet Your Author,'' *Cricket,* December, 1976.[7]]

1982-1984. *The Westmark Trilogy* published. ''It would be convenient if the inspiration for every book came directly from a specific incident in the writer's life. More often than not, the connection probably isn't so direct or immediate; not one-to-one, but slantwise. This is by way of saying there was no extraordinary event to set me thinking about one project more than another. My life was no more bedeviled than anyone's. The world was in its usual condition. I recall nothing that made me especially receptive to the moods and materials that became part of *Westmark*. The issues and questions that were to underlie the story had been nagging at me long before.

''Early in December 1979, I finished a rough draft and sent it along with much trepidation to Ann Durell, my editor. I simply did not know how to describe the work. A fantasy? Sort of. Historical novel? Not really. I held my breath, apprehensive and anxious. Ann saved me from self-inflicted asphyxiation by telephoning soon after she received the manuscript. Her enthusiasm was the best Christmas present I could have hoped for.

''Ann wanted to confer in detail, at length, and promptly. Where? The winter had been particularly severe. I was afraid of getting caught in a blizzard between Drexel Hill and New York. Ann was equally unthrilled about a journey to the snowbound suburbs.

''Ann proposed a compromise. We could meet at the Free Library of Philadelphia. Carolyn Field, Director of Children's Services, gave us the use of her office. We jokingly assured her that she was contributing to an historic occasion. (We did not neglect to remind Carolyn of our prophecy when, in 1982, *Westmark* received the American Book Award in Children's Literature.)

''Ann and I worked in Carolyn's office for most of a morning and afternoon. The main thing involved the tonality of the story. We agreed on an important principle: not to pull punches, not to soften or avoid harsh situations.

''Since Ann was being so gratifyingly agreeable, I ventured to reveal a dark secret: I was thinking of writing a second volume; perhaps others after that. I did not know whether Ann would swallow hard, ponder a while, then kindly advise me to let well enough alone. Ann did not hesitate for a second. 'Do it,' she said.'' [*The Advocate,* fall, 1984.[8]]

The second volume, *The Kestrel,* appeared in 1983. The trilogy was completed in 1984 with the publication of *The Beggar Queen.*

1985. *The Black Cauldron*, the second book in the ''Prydain'' series, was adapted into an animated film by Walt Disney Pictures. It took twelve years to complete at a cost of over $25 million. ''Fantasy in its own way tells us that we're considerably more than we think we are; and in this sense fantasy also tells the truth. Despite capabilities and potential, such a capacity for humanity—if we can only get at it—that indeed someday we can write our own happy endings.

(Jacket illustration by Evaline Ness from *The High King* by Lloyd Alexander.)

(From the animated movie "The Black Cauldron," based on Lloyd Alexander's "Prydain" series. Copyright © 1985 by Walt Disney Productions.)

Dallben (left) and his young assistant, Taran, prepare to witness a startling vision brought forth by their oracular pig, Hen Wen. ■ (From the animated movie "The Black Cauldron." Copyright © 1985 by Walt Disney Productions.)

"This may be no more than wishful thinking. But a wish is certainly a good way to start. There's no law in the fantasy world or in the real world that says some wishes can't come true. If fantasy is a kind of hopeful dream, it's nevertheless one that we made up ourselves.

"And, after all, how can we be less than our own dreams?" [Lloyd Alexander, "Truth about Fantasy," *Top of the News,* January, 1968.⁹]

1986. "Writing the 'Westmark' trilogy had been difficult and in many ways an anguishing work. Though changed, manipulated, and dramatized, a lot of the material came from my own wartime experiences. I found myself dredging up emotions and situations I would have preferred to forget. It wasn't an attempt to exorcise my own demons. That didn't happen, nor did I want it to. I want to keep those demons. I call them: my conscience.

"In any event, I needed something to heal my spirits. I wanted to lighten up and laugh a little bit. Even serious writers are allowed to be playful.

"What emerged was *The Illyrian Adventure,* in every way different from anything I'd written before. It was intended as an entertainment—for its author as much as anyone—with a gloriously fearless heroine, legendary heroes, inscrutable mysteries, and fiendish villains. What surprised me shouldn't have surprised me at all. In what was meant as sheer amusement, below the surface I realized that my own concerns and questions were still there, even though set in different terms.

"After her adventures in Illyria, I supposed that Miss Vesper Holly would settle into proper Philadelphia tranquility. But I have grown too fond of Vesper and her somewhat bumbling chronicler, dear old Brinnie, to let them sit idle. They have given me great pleasure and allowed me to have affectionate fun with the mode of the old-fashioned melodrama-thriller. This does not imply a lack of substance. The situations which the intrepid pair confront are, in different guise, very familiar to us. Even so, their adventures are offered not with solemnity but with a measure of lightheartedness. Playfulness is a much-needed part of literary ecology, refreshing to both writer and reader."

HOBBIES AND OTHER INTERESTS: Music, particularly violin, piano, and guitar, animals, especially cats, drawing, and printmaking.

FOR MORE INFORMATION SEE: Philadelphia Sunday Bulletin, March 22, 1959; *Horn Book,* April, 1965, August, 1968, August, 1969, February, 1970, August, 1971, October, 1971, December, 1971, August, 1974, October, 1982, August, 1983, May/June, 1985; *Library Journal,* December, 15, 1966, May 15, 1969, April 15, 1971; *Top of the News,* January, 1968, November, 1968; *Publishers Weekly,* February 17, 1969; *Saturday Review,* March 22, 1969, April 22, 1972; *New York Times Book Review,* May 4, 1969, November 4, 1973; Lloyd Alexander, "The Flat-Heeled Muse," *Horn Book Reflections on Children's Books and Reading,* edited by Elinor Whitney Field, Horn Book, 1969; Eleanor Cameron, *The Green and Burning Tree,* Atlantic-Little, Brown, 1969.

Wilson Library Bulletin, October, 1970, June, 1974; *Writer,* May, 1971; Martha E. Ward and Dorothy A. Marquardt, *Authors of Books for Young People,* 2nd edition, Scarecrow, 1971; Jacqueline S. Weiss, "Profiles in Literature," Temple

A rare cartoon by Lloyd Alexander, who confesses "secret yearnings to be an artist."

University, 1972; Doris de Montreville and Donna Hill, editors, *Third Book of Junior Authors,* H. W. Wilson, 1972; Dee Stuart, "An Exclusive Interview with Newbery Award-Winning Author: Lloyd Alexander," *Writer's Digest,* April, 1973; Virginia Haviland, *Children and Literature,* Scott, Foresman, 1973; *Cricket,* January, 1974, December, 1976, September, 1983; Lee Bennett Hopkins, *More Books by More People,* Citation, 1974; Virginia Haviland, *Children and Literature: Views and Reviews,* Lothrop, 1974.

Lee Kingman, editor, *Newbery and Caldecott Medal Books: 1966-1975,* Horn Book, 1975; "Meet the Newbery Author: Lloyd Alexander" (filmstrip with record or cassette), Miller-Brody, 1975; Justin Wintle and Emma Fisher, *The Pied Pipers,* Paddington Press, 1975; Myra Cohn Livingston, *A Tribute to Lloyd Alexander,* Drexel Institute, 1976; *Children's Literature Review,* Gale, Volume 1, 1976, Volume 5, 1983; *Language Arts,* April, 1978, April, 1984; D. L. Kirkpatrick, editor, *Twentieth-Century Children's Writers,* St. Martin's, 1978, new edition, 1983; *New York Times,* March 19, 1979; *Los Angeles Times,* March 22, 1979; Betsy Hearne and Marilyn Kaye, editors, *Celebrating Children's Books: Essays on Children's Literature in Honor of Zena Sutherland,* Lothrop, 1981; Jim Roginski, compiler, *Newbery and Caldecott Medalists and Honor Book Winners,* Libraries Unlimited, 1983; M. J. Greenlaw, "Profile: Lloyd Alexander," *Language Arts,* April, 1984; *Advocate,* fall, 1984; Lois R. Kuznets, "'High Fantasy' in America: A Study of Lloyd Alexander, Ursula LeGuin, and Susan Cooper," *The Lion and the Unicorn,* Volume 9, 1985.

ANDERSON, Leone Castell 1923-

BRIEF ENTRY: Born August 12, 1923, in Los Angeles, Calif. Taught by her three older sisters, Anderson was reading long before she attended school and began writing stories at the age of eight. To help out her financially-stressed family during the end of the Depression, she held a variety of jobs after graduating from high school in 1939, including those in hymn book publishing, educational movie review magazine publishing, electrical meter manufacturing, and advertising. Following her marriage in 1946, Anderson was a free-lance writer until 1969 when she reentered the work force as a staff member of the young people's department at Elmhurst Public Library in Illinois. Five years later, she moved to the country where she took up residence in a 100-year-old schoolhouse renovated by her architect husband, J. Eric Anderson. Feeling somewhat isolated, in 1979 Anderson opened her own paperback bookstore, Lee's Booklover's Shop, in Stockton, Illinois. With the store open only in the afternoons, Anderson devotes her mornings to writing. Thus far, she has produced more than a half dozen children's books, including *It's O.K. to Cry* (Child's World, 1979), *The Wonderful Shrinking Shirt* (Whitman Publishing, 1983), and *The Good-By Day* (Golden Press, 1984). A student of piano and voice, Anderson attributes the rhythm and melodic line in her books to her "feel for music." Her performances in community theaters help her to "visualize and 'hear' the scenes of my books."

Anderson has contributed to the *Burlington Northern Railroad Commuter News, Elmhurst Press,* and *Stockton Herald News,* as well as to numerous children's magazines and other adult publications. A speaker at schools, she is a member and Midwest representative of the Society of Children's Book Writers, and a member of the Children's Reading Round Table and the Authors Guild. *Home:* 13115 East Chelsea Rd., Stockton, Ill. 61085.

ANDREWS, Jan 1942-

BRIEF ENTRY: Born June 6, 1942, in England. A free-lance writer and editor, Andrews now resides in Ontario, Canada—a move she considers responsible for the reason she writes at all: "There is something about the way of the land—its vastness and strength, the space of it—that speaks to me very deeply." Andrews claims she writes for children because she can't help it. "I have a passionate interest in adult life but still the children's stories are the ones that grow in my head. . . . I think about children a great deal and about how, when it comes to raising them, we really ought to be doing a better job." Andrews has written *Fresh Fish . . . and Chips* (Women's Educational Press, 1973); a bilingual text, *Ella, an Elephant: Ella, un éléphant* (Tundra Books, 1976); and *Very Last First Time* (Atheneum, 1986), a story of the ancient Eskimo custom of collecting mussels on the ocean floor.

Andrews edited *The Dancing Sun* (Press Porcepic, 1981), an anthology of children's literature from various Canadian ethnic traditions selected by young readers. The anthology contains Elizabeth Kaufman's award-winning "Grandfather's Special Magic" and R. Guttormsson's "The Rescue of the Prince." According to *Canadian Children's Literature,* the poetry in the collection "briefly, succinctly and wonderfully . . . is able to suggest the variety of cultures which enrich the Canadian experience." Andrews has contributed stories to *Cricket, Canadian Children's Annual,* and language arts publications in Canada and the United States. Besides writing, she organizes activities such as workshops on children's literature, readings, exhibitions, and panel discussions. She developed on oral history/story-telling program, "Out of the Everywhere," for Expo 86. *Home and office:* 444 Athlone Ave., Ottawa, Ontario, Canada K1Z 5M7.

ANGELOU, Maya 1928-

PERSONAL: Surname pronounced *An*-ge lō; given name, Marguerite Annie Johnson; born April 4, 1928, in St. Louis, Mo.; daughter of Bailey (a naval dietician) and Vivian (Baxter) Johnson; married Tosh Angelos, 1950 (divorced); married Paul Du Feu, December, 1973 (divorced, 1981); children: Guy. *Education:* Attended public schools in Arkansas and California; studied music privately, dance with Martha Graham, Pearl Primus, and Ann Halprin, and drama with Frank Silvera and Gene Frankel. *Residence:* Sonoma, Calif. *Office:* c/o Random House, 201 East 50th St., New York, N.Y. 10017. *Agent:* Gerard W. Purcell Associates Ltd., 964 Second Ave., New York, N.Y. 10022.

CAREER: Author, poet, playwright, professional stage and screen performer and singer. Appeared in "Porgy and Bess" on twenty-two nation tour sponsored by the U.S. Department of State, 1954-55; appeared in Off-Broadway plays, "Calypso Heatwave," 1957, and "The Blacks," 1960; with Godfrey Cambridge wrote, produced, and performed in "Cabaret for Freedom," Off-Broadway, 1960; appeared in "Mother Courage" at University of Ghana, 1964, and in "Medea" in Hollywood, 1966; made Broadway debut in "Look Away," 1973, directed film, "All Day Long," 1974; directed her play, "And Still I Rise," in California, 1976. *Arab Observer* (English-language newsweekly), Cairo, Egypt, associate editor, 1961-62; University of Ghana, Institute of African Studies, Legon-Accra, Ghana, assistant administrator of School of Music and Drama, 1963-66; free-lance writer for *Ghanaian Times* and Ghanaian Broadcasting Corp., 1963-65; *African Review,* Ac-

MAYA ANGELOU

cra, Ghana, feature editor, 1964-66. Lecturer, University of California, Los Angeles, 1966; writer-in-residence, University of Kansas, 1970; distinguished visiting professor, Wake Forest University, 1974, Wichita State University, 1974, California State University, Sacramento, 1974. Northern coordinator, Southern Christian Leadership Conference, 1959-60; appointed member of American Revolution Bicentennial Council by President Ford, 1975-76; television narrator, interviewer, and host for Afro-American specials and theater series, 1972—.

MEMBER: American Film Institute (member of board of trustees, 1975—), Directors Guild of America, Actors' Equity Association, American Federation of Television and Radio Artists, Women's Prison Association (member of advisory board). *Awards, honors:* Nominated for National Book Award, 1970, for *I Know Why the Caged Bird Sings;* Pulitzer Prize nomination, 1972, for *Just Give Me a Cool Drink of Water 'fore I Diiie;* Tony Award nomination, 1973, for performance in "Look Away"; named Woman of the Year in Communications by *Ladies' Home Journal,* 1976; appointed first Reynolds Professor of American Studies at Wake Forest University, 1981; Matrix Award in the field of books from Women in Communication, Inc., 1983. Yale University fellowship, 1970; Rockefeller Foundation scholar in Italy, 1975; honorary degrees from Smith College, 1975, Mills College, 1975, Lawrence University, 1976.

WRITINGS—Books; all published by Random House, except as noted: *I Know Why the Caged Bird Sings* (autobiography), 1970; *Just Give Me a Cool Drink of Water 'fore I Diiie* (poetry), 1971; *Gather Together in My Name* (autobiography),

1974; *Oh Pray My Wings Are Gonna Fit Me Well* (poetry), 1975; *Singin' and Swingin' and Gettin' Merry Like Christmas* (autobiography), 1976; *And Still I Rise* (poetry), 1978; *The Heart of a Woman* (autobiography), 1981; *Shaker, Why Don't You Sing?* (poetry), 1983; *All God's Children Need Traveling Shoes* (autobiography), 1986; *Poems: Maya Angelou,* four books, Bantam, 1986; *Now Sheba Sings the Song* (illustrated by Tom Feelings), Dutton, 1987.

Plays: (With Godfrey Cambridge) "Cabaret for Freedom" (musical revue), first produced in New York at Village Gate Theatre, 1960; "The Least of These" (two-act drama), first produced in Los Angeles, 1966; (adaptor) Sophocles, "Ajax" (two-act drama), first produced in Los Angeles at Mark Taper Forum, 1974; "And Still I Rise" (one-act musical), first produced in Oakland, Calif., at Ensemble Theatre, 1976. Also author of two-act drama, "The Clawing Within," 1966, and of two-act musical, "Adjoa Amissah," 1967.

Screenplays: "Georgia, Georgia," Independent-Cinerama, 1972; "All Day Long," American Film Institute, 1974.

Television: "Blacks, Blues, Black" (ten one-hour programs), National Educational Television (NET-TV), 1968; "Assignment America" (six one-half-hour programs), 1975; "The Legacy" and "The Inheritors" (two Afro-American specials), 1976; "Sister, Sister," NBC-TV, 1982.

Recordings: "Miss Calypso" (songs), Liberty Records, 1957; "The Poetry of Maya Angelou," GWP Records, 1969; "An Evening with Maya Angelou," Pacific Tape Library, 1975; "Women in Business," University of Wisconsin, 1981.

Composer of songs, including two songs for movie, "For Love of Ivy," and composer of musical scores for both her screenplays. Contributor of articles, short stories, and poems to periodicals, including *Harper's, Ebony, Mademoiselle, Redbook, Ladies' Home Journal,* and *Black Scholar.*

ADAPTATIONS: "I Know Why the Caged Bird Sings" (cassette; filmstrip with cassette; teacher's guide), Center for Literary Review, 1978, (television movie), CBS-TV, 1979.

WORK IN PROGRESS: A sixth book about her life; another volume of poetry.

SIDELIGHTS: **April 4, 1928.** Born in St. Louis, Missouri to Bailey and Vivian (Baxter) Johnson.

1931. Sent by her divorced parents to live with her grandmother in Stamps, Arkansas. "When I was three and [my brother] Bailey four, we had arrived in the musty little town, wearing tags on our wrists which instructed—'To Whom It May Concern'—that we were Marguerite and Bailey Johnson Jr., from Long Beach, California, en route to Stamps, Arkansas, c/o Mrs. Annie Henderson.

"Our parents had decided to put an end to their calamitous marriage, and Father shipped us home to his mother. A porter had been charged with our welfare—he got off the train the next day in Arizona—and our tickets were pinned to my brother's inside coat pocket.

"I don't remember much of the trip, but after we reached the segregated southern part of the journey, things must have looked up. Negro passengers, who always traveled with loaded lunch boxes, felt sorry for 'the poor little motherless darlings' and plied us with cold fried chicken and potato salad.

Mother told her secrets to me
When I rode
Low in the pocket
Between her hips.

■ (From *Now Sheba Sings the Song* by Maya Angelou. Illustrated by Tom Feelings.)

(Jacket illustration by Janet Halverson from *The Heart of a Woman* by Maya Angelou.)

"The town reacted to us as its inhabitants had reacted to all things new before our coming. It regarded us a while without curiosity but with caution, and after we were seen to be harmless (and children) it closed in around us, as a real mother embraces a stranger's child. Warmly, but not too familiarly.

"We lived with our grandmother and uncle in the rear of the Store (it was always spoken of with a capital *s*), which she had owned some twenty-five years.

"Early in the century, Momma (we soon stopped calling her Grandmother) sold lunches to the sawmen in the lumberyard (east Stamps) and the seedmen at the cotton gin (west Stamps). Her crisp meat pies and cool lemonade, when joined to her miraculous ability to be in two places at the same time, assured her business success. From being a mobile lunch counter, she set up a stand between the two points of fiscal interest and supplied the workers' needs for a few years. Then she had the Store built in the heart of the Negro area. Over the years it became the lay center of activities in town. . . ." [Maya Angelou, *I Know Why the Caged Bird Sings*, Random House, 1969.[1]]

Angelou learned from her paternal grandmother "grace under pressure." She also taught her that through hard work, courage, and a strong determination to succeed, a black person could control his own destiny, even in the bigoted south of the Depression era. "'Thou shall not be dirty' and 'Thou shall not be impudent' were the two commandments of Grandmother Henderson upon which hung our total salvation.

"Each night in the bitterest winter we were forced to wash faces, arms, necks, legs and feet before going to bed. She used to add, with a smirk that unprofane people can't control when venturing into profanity, 'and wash as far as possible, than wash possible.'

"We would go to the well and wash in the ice-cold, clear water, grease our legs with the equally cold stiff Vaseline, then tiptoe into the house. We wiped the dust from our toes and settled down for schoolwork, cornbread, clabbered milk, prayers and bed, always in that order. Momma was famous for pulling the quilts off after we had fallen asleep to examine our feet. If they weren't clean enough for her, she took the switch (she kept one behind the bedroom door for emergencies) and woke up the offender with a few aptly placed burning reminders.

"Stamps, Arkansas, was Chitlin' Switch, Georgia; Hang 'em High, Alabama; Don't Let the Sun Set on You Here, Nigger, Mississippi; or any other name just as descriptive. People in Stamps used to say that the whites in our town were so prejudiced that a Negro couldn't buy vanilla ice cream. Except on July Fourth. Other days he had to be satisfied with chocolate.

"During these years in Stamps, I met and fell in love with William Shakespeare. He was my first white love. Although

(Jacket illustration by Janet Halverson from *Gather Together in My Name* by Maya Angelou.)

(From the television movie "I Know Why the Caged Bird Sings," starring Esther Rolle and Constance Good. Presented on CBS-TV, April 28, 1979.)

I enjoyed and respected Kipling, Poe, Butler, Thackeray and Henley, I saved my young and loyal passion for Paul Lawrence Dunbar, Langston Hughes, James Weldon Johnson and W.E.B. Du Bois' 'Litany at Atlanta.' But it was Shakespeare who said, 'When in disgrace with fortune and men's eyes.' It was a state with which I felt myself most familiar. I pacified myself about his whiteness by saying that after all he had been dead so long it couldn't matter to anyone any more."[1]

1936. Sent to St. Louis, where she and her brother lived for a year with their mother. "To describe my mother would be to write about a hurricane in its perfect power. Or the climbing, falling colors of a rainbow. . . . It is remarkable how much truth there is in the two expressions: 'struck dumb' and 'love at first sight.' My mother's beauty literally assailed me. Her red lips (Momma said it was a sin to wear lipstick) split to show even white teeth and her fresh-butter color looked see-through clean. Her smile widened her mouth beyond her cheeks beyond her ears and seemingly through the walls to the street outside. I was struck dumb. I knew immediately why she had sent me away. She was too beautiful to have children. I had never seen a woman as pretty as she who was called 'Mother.' Bailey on his part fell instantly and forever in love. I saw his eyes shining like hers; he had forgotten the loneliness and the nights when we had cried together because we were 'unwanted children.' He had never left her warm side or shared the icy wind of solitude with me. She was his Mother Dear and I resigned myself to his condition. They were more alike than she and I, or even he and I. They both had physical beauty and personality, so I figured it figured.

"I had decided that St. Louis was a foreign country. I would never get used to the scurrying sounds of flushing toilets, or the packaged foods, or doorbells or the noise of cars and trains and buses that crashed through the walls or slipped under the doors. In my mind I only stayed in St. Louis for a few weeks. As quickly as I understood that I had not reached my home, I sneaked away to Robin Hood's forest and the caves of Alley Oop where all reality was unreal and even that changed every day. I carried the same shield that I had used in Stamps: 'I didn't come to stay.'"[1]

When she was eight years old, Angelou was raped by her mother's boyfriend, who was found "dropped . . . [or] kicked to death" shortly afterward by her uncles. She felt responsible for his murder, and decided "to stop talking."[1] And so she did—for five years she was silent.

Shortly after the murder, Angelou and her brother were returned to their grandmother in Arkansas. "The barrenness of Stamps was exactly what I wanted, without will or consciousness. After St. Louis, with its noise and activity, its trucks and buses, and loud family gatherings, I welcomed the obscure lanes and lonely bungalows set back deep in dirt yards.

''The resignation of its inhabitants encouraged me to relax. They showed me a contentment based on the belief that nothing more was coming to them, although a great deal more was due. Their decision to be satisfied with life's inequities was a lesson for me. Entering Stamps, I had the feeling that I was stepping over the border lines of the map and would fall, without fear, right off the end of the world. Nothing more could happen, for in Stamps nothing happened.

''Into this cocoon I crept.

''For an indeterminate time, nothing was demanded of me or of Bailey. We were, after all, Mrs. Henderson's California grandchildren, and had been away on a glamourous trip way up North to the fabulous St. Louis. . . .''[1]

Slowly she regained her confidence, pride and speech. She was befriended by an educated black woman, Mrs. Flowers, who ''Made me proud to be a Negro, just by being herself.''[1]

1940. Graduated at the top of her eighth grade class. At her grandmother's request, Angelou and her brother were sent to San Francisco, California to live. ''Knowing Momma, I knew that I never knew Momma. Her African-bush secretiveness and suspiciousness had been compounded by slavery and confirmed by centuries of promises made and promises broken.

We have a saying among Black Americans which describes Momma's caution, 'If you ask a Negro where he's been, he'll tell you where he's going.' To understand this important information, it is necessary to know who uses this tactic and on whom it works. If an unaware person is told a part of the truth (it is imperative that the answer embody truth), he is satisfied that his query has been answered. If an aware person (one who himself uses the stratagem) is given an answer which is truthful but bears only slightly if at all on the question, he knows that the information he seeks is of a private nature and will not be handed to him willingly. Thus direct denial, lying and the revelation of personal affairs are avoided.

''Momma told us one day that she was taking us to California. She explained that we were growing up, that we needed to be with our parents, that Uncle Willie was, after all, crippled, that she was getting old. All true, and yet none of those truths satisfied our need for The Truth. . . .

''I was as unprepared to meet my mother as a sinner is reluctant to meet his Maker. And all too soon she stood before me, smaller than memory would have her but more glorious than any recall. She wore a light-tan suede suit, shoes to match and a mannish hat with a feather in the band, and she patted my face with gloved hands. Except for the lipsticked mouth, white teeth and shining black eyes, she might have just emerged from a dip in a beige bath. My picture of Mother and Momma embracing on the train platform has been darkly retained through the coating of the then embarrassment and the now maturity.

(From the stage production "Look Away," starring Geraldine Page and Maya Angelou. Opened at Playhouse Theatre, January 7, 1973.)

Maya Angelou. (Photograph by Jill Krementz.)

Mother was a blithe chick nuzzling around the large, solid dark hen. The sounds they made had a rich inner harmony. Momma's deep, slow voice lay under mother's rapid peeps and chirps like stones under rushing water.

"The younger woman kissed and laughed and rushed about collecting our coats and getting our luggage carted off. She easily took care of the details that would have demanded half of a country person's day. I was struck again by the wonder of her, and for the length of my trance, the greedy uneasinesses were held at bay.

"We moved into an apartment, and I slept on a sofa that miraculously transformed itself at night into a large comfortable bed. Mother stayed in Los Angeles long enough to get us settled, then she returned to San Francisco to arrange living accommodations for her abruptly enlarged family."[1]

After a six months stay in Los Angeles, Angelou's grandmother ("Momma") returned to Stamps, Arkansas and Angelou and her brother moved to San Francisco to live with their mother.

1941-1945. Attended George Washington High School in San Francisco and took dance and drama lessons at the California Labor School. "In the early months of World War II, San Francisco's Fillmore district, or the Western Addition, experienced a visible revolution. On the surface it appeared to be totally peaceful and almost a refutation of the term 'revolution.'

"In San Francisco, for the first time, I perceived myself as part of something. Not that I identified with the newcomers, nor with the rare Black descendants of native San Franciscans, nor with the whites or even the Asians, but rather with the times and the city. . . . The undertone of fear that San Francisco would be bombed which was abetted by weekly air raid warnings, and civil defense drills in school, heightened my sense of belonging. Hadn't I, always, but ever and ever, thought that life was just one great risk for the living?

"George Washington High School was the first real school I attended. My entire stay there might have been time lost if it hadn't been for the unique personality of a brilliant teacher. Miss Kirwin was that rare educator who was in love with information. I will always believe that her love of teaching came not so much from her liking for students but from her desire to make sure that some of the things she knew would find repositories so that they could be shared again.

"I never knew why I was given a scholarship to California Labor School. It was a college for adults, and many years later

I found that it was on the House Un-American Activities list of subversive organizations. At fourteen I accepted a scholarship and got one for the next year as well. In the evening classes I took drama and dance, along with white and Black grownups. I had chosen drama simply because I liked Hamlet's soliloquy beginning, 'To be, or not to be.' I had never seen a play and did not connect movies with the theater. In fact, the only times I had heard the soliloquy had been when I had melodramatically recited to myself. In front of a mirror.

"The allegiances I owed at this time in my life would have made very strange bedfellows: Momma with her solemn determination, Mrs. Flowers and her books, Bailey with his love, my mother and her gaiety, Miss Kirwin and her information, my evening classes of drama and dance.

"Our house was a fourteen-room typical San Franciscan post-Earthquake affair. We had a succession of roomers, bringing and taking their different accents, and personalities and foods. . . ."[1]

While still in high school, Angelou obtained a job as the first black woman streetcar conductor in San Francisco.

1945. Angelou, an unmarried teenager, gave birth to a baby boy. "My son was born when I was sixteen, and determined

(Jacket illustration by Janet Halverson from *All God's Children Need Traveling Shoes* by Maya Angelou.)

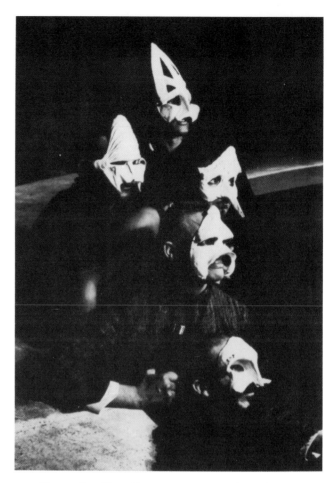

(From the New York stage production of "The Blacks" with Maya Angelou [third row, right]. Opened at the St. Marks Playhouse, May 4, 1961.)

to raise him, I had worked as a shake dancer in night clubs, fry cook in hamburger joints, diner cook in a Creole restaurant and once had a job in a mechanic's shop, taking the paint off cars with my hands." [Maya Angelou, *Singin' and Swingin' and Gettin' Merry Like Christmas*, Random House, 1976.[2]]

By the time she was eighteen, she had "managed in a few tense years to become a snob at all levels, racial, cultural and intellectual. I was a madam and thought myself morally superior to the whores. I was a waitress and believed myself cleverer than the customers I served. I was a lonely unmarried mother and held myself to be freer than the married women I met." [Lynn Z. Bloom, "Maya Angelou," *Dictionary of Literary Biography*, Gale, 1985.[3]]

1950. Married Tosh Angelos, an ex-sailor and white. "Tosh grew up in a Greek community, where even Italians were considered foreign. His contact with Blacks had been restricted to the Negro sailors on his base and the music of the bebop originators.

"I would never forget the slavery tales, or my Southern past, where all whites, including the poor and ignorant, had the right to speak rudely to and even physically abuse any Negro they met. I knew the ugliness of white prejudice. Obviously there was no common ground on which Tosh and I might meet.

"Tosh and I were married in the Courthouse on a clear Monday morning. To show her displeasure, Mother moved her fourteen rooms of furniture to Los Angeles three days before the ceremony.

"During the first year of marriage I was so enchanted with security and living with a person whose color or lack of it could startle me on an early-morning waking, and I was so busy keeping a spotless house, teaching myself to cook and serve gourmet meals and managing a happy, rambunctious growing boy that I had little time to notice public reactions to us. Awareness gradually grew in my mind that people stared, nudged each other and frowned when we three walked in the parks or went to the movies. The distaste on their faces called me back to a history of discrimination and murders of every type. Tosh, I told myself, was Greek, not white American; therefore I needn't feel I had betrayed my race by marrying one of the enemy, nor could white Americans believe that I had so forgiven them the past that I was ready to love a member of their tribe. . . . I stared back hard at whites in the streets trying to scrape the look of effrontery off their cruel faces. But I dropped my eyes when we met Negroes. I couldn't explain to all of them that my husband had not been a part of our degradation. I fought against the guilt which was slipping into my closed life as insidiously as gas escaping into a sealed room."[2] The ill-fated marriage ended after a few years.

Early 1950s. Studied dance in New York City and appeared as a singer in San Francisco's "Purple Onion" cabaret.

1954-1955. Toured twenty-two countries as a member of the cast of "Porgy and Bess." In Rome and Tel Aviv Angelou managed to teach modern dance as well. "I made an arrangement with a dance teacher to give classes in modern ballet and African movement for three weeks in exchange for lessons in Middle Eastern dance.

"We boarded a plane for Morocco where we would give a concert and continue to Spain. I was downcast at leaving Tel Aviv. I had felt an emotional attachment to Egypt and made an intellectual identification with Israel. The Jews were reclaiming a land which had surrendered its substance to the relentless sun centuries before. They brought to my mind grammar school stories of pioneer families and wagon trains. The dislodged Palestinians in the desert were as remote in my thoughts as the native Americans whose lives had been stifled by the whites' trek across the plains of America.

"In Barcelona we were tired. Too many planes, hotel rooms and restaurant meals were exacting a toll on the company's spirits. But the Spaniards had no way of telling the extent of exhaustion the singers experienced. Years of training sustained the quality of performance, and an affection which bordered on kinship reduced the exhibition of ill humor which lay just under everyone's skin.

"We went to Lausanne, Switzerland, performed and left, associating the white and icily beautiful town only with one more stop to be checked off our list. Our interests narrowed into petty little concerns and the cities and countries were beginning to melt together."[2]

Angelou, during one of her many interviews. (Photograph copyright © by Mary Ellen Mark, Archive Pictures, Inc.)

(Jacket illustration by Janet Halverson from *Singin' and Swingin' and Gettin' Merry Like Christmas* by Maya Angelou.)

Left the tour in Italy to return to her son who missed her so much that he suffered from a skin rash and depression. "Before my eyes a physical and mental metamorphosis began as gradually and inexorably as a seasonal change. At first the myriad bumps dried and no fresh ones erupted. His skin slowly regained its smoothness and color. Then I noticed that he no longer rushed panting to my room to assure himself that I was still there. And when I left the house to shop we both took the parting normally, with a casual 'See you in a minute.' His shoulders began to ride high again and he had opinions about everything from the planning of meals to what he wanted to be called.

"'Mother, I've changed my name.'

"I'm certain that I didn't look up. 'Good. What is it today?'

"In the space of one month, he had told . . . the family to call him Rock, Robin, Rex and Les.

"'My name is Guy.'

"'That's nice. Guy is a nice name.'

"'I mean it, Mother.'

"'Good, dear. It's quite a nice name.'

"When I called to him later in the day, he refused to answer. I stood in the doorway of his room watching him spraddled on the bed.

"'Clyde, I called you. Didn't you hear me?'

"He had always been rambunctious, but never outright sassy.

"'I heard you calling Clyde, Mother, but my name is Guy. Did you want me?'

"He gave me a mischievous grin.

"One day I asked him quietly why he didn't like Clyde. He said it sounded mushy. I told him about the Clyde River in Scotland, but its strength and soberness didn't impress him.

"'It's an O.K. name for a river, but my name is Guy.' He looked straight into my eyes. 'Please tell your friends that I never want to be called Clyde again. And, Mother, don't you do it either.' He remembered 'Please.'

"Whenever anyone in the family called him Clyde, he would sigh like a teacher trying to educate a group of stubborn kindergarten students and would say wearily, 'My name is Guy.'

"It took him only one month to train us. He became Guy and we could hardly remember ever calling him anything else."[2]

Late 1950s. ". . . I worked months singing in West Coast and Hawaiian night clubs and saved my money. I took my young son, Guy, and joined the beatnik brigade. To my mother's dismay, and Guy's great pleasure, we moved across the Golden Gate Bridge and into a houseboat commune in Sausalito where I went barefoot, wore jeans, and both of us wore rough-dried clothes. Although I took Guy to a San Francisco barber, I allowed my own hair to grow into a wide unstraightened hedge, which made me look, at a distance like a tall brown tree whose branches had been clipped. My commune mates, an icthyologist, a musician, a wife, and an inventor, were white, and had they been political, (which they were not), would have occupied a place between the far left and revolution.

"Strangely, the houseboat offered me respite from racial tensions, and gave my son an opportunity to be around whites who did not think of him as too exotic to need correction, nor so common as to be ignored.

"In less than a year, I began to yearn for privacy, wall-to-wall carpets and manicures. Guy was becoming rambunctious and young-animal wild. He was taking fewer baths than I thought healthy, and because my friends treated him like a young adult, he was forgetting his place in the scheme of our mother-son relationship.

"I had to move on. I could go back to singing and make enough money to support myself and my son.

"I had to trust life, since I was young enough to believe that life loved the person who dare to live it.

"I packed our bags, said goodbye and got on the road." [Maya Angelou, *The Heart of a Woman*, Random House, 1981.[4]]

1958. ". . . I had written and recorded six songs for Liberty Records, but I didn't seriously think of writing until John [Killens; social activist and author] gave me his critique. After that I thought of little else. John was the first published black author I had really talked with. (I'd met James Baldwin in

Maya Angelou goes over her script "Sister, Sister" with Diahann Carroll. In June, 1982, the teleplay, concerning three sisters in a black middle-class family, aired on NBC-TV. The movie had been sitting on the network shelf for nearly three years, until feminists generated a campaign of protest.

Paris in the early fifties, but I didn't really know him.) John said, 'Most of your work needs polishing. In fact, most of everybody's work could stand rewriting. But you have undeniable talent.' He added, 'You ought to come to New York. You need to be in the Harlem Writers Guild.' The invitation was oblique but definitely alluring.''[4]

Inspired by Killens, Angelou moved to Brooklyn to learn the writing craft. Through weekly meetings of the Harlem Writers Guild she studied and accepted the constructive criticism offered by the group.

1960. Starred in Genet's ''The Blacks'' at St. Mark's Playhouse, and, with Godfrey Cambridge, produced, directed, wrote and starred in ''Cabaret for Freedom'' at New York's Village Gate. ''Time, opportunity and devotion were in joint. Black actors, bent under the burden of unemployment and a dreary image of cinematic and stage Uncle Tom characterizations, had the chance to refute the reflection and at the same time, work toward the end of discrimination.

''After 'Cabaret for Freedom,' they would all be employed by suddenly aware and respectful producers. After Martin Luther King won freedom for us all, they would be paid honorable salaries and would gain the media coverage that their talents deserved.

''It was the awakening summer of 1960 and the entire country was in labor. Something wonderful was about to be born, and we were all going to be good parents to the welcome child. Its name was Freedom.

''Then, too soon, summer and the revue closed. The performers went back to the elevator-operating or waiting-on-tables jobs they had interrupted. A few returned to unemployment or welfare lines. No one was hired as a leading actor in a major dramatic company nor as a supporting actor in a small ensemble, or even as a chorus member in an Off-Off-Broadway show. Godfrey was still driving his beat-up cab, Hugh continued to work split shifts in his family's liquor stores, and I was broke again. I had learned how to work office machines, and how to hold a group of fractious talented people together, but a whole summer was gone; I was out of work and Guy needed school clothes.''[4]

1961. Left New York with South African freedom fighter Vusumzi Make. In Cairo, Egypt, Angelou worked as an associate editor for an English language weekly newspaper. ''I stayed at the *Arab Observer* for over a year and gradually my ignorance receded. I learned from Abdul Hassan how to write an opinionated article with such subtlety that the reader would think the opinion his own. Eric Nemes, the layout artist, showed me that where an article was placed on a page, its typeface, even the color of ink, were as important as the best-written copy. David DuBois demonstrated how to select a story and persevere until the last shred of data was in my hands. Vus supplied me with particulars on the politically fluid, newly independent African states. I received a raise from Dr. Nagati, the respect of my fellow workers and a few compliments from strangers.

''Guy graduated from high school and then took a knapsack and joined Egyptian friends for a trek in the Sahara. . . . More women were hired in my office and some found my presence incongruous and unacceptable. I spoke halting Arabic, smoked cigarettes openly, was not a Muslim, and was an American on top of that. On the day when President Kennedy and Khrushchev had their confrontation over the independence of Cuba, in the hours when the next world war hung like an unpaid debt over our heads, no one spoke to me. The male employees ignored me; as if by a time warp we were all returned to my first day at the *Arab Observer*. The women were openly hostile. Papers which they needed to bring to my desk were handed over by the coffee server or the copy boy. Actions by people thousands of miles away, men who didn't know I was alive and whose sympathy I would never expect, influenced my peace, and rendered me odious. Kennedy was an American, and so was I. I didn't have the language to explain that being a black American was qualitatively different from being An American. I worried like everyone else, but made myself scarce in the office.''[4]

1962. Left Egypt for Africa. ''The breezes of the West African night were intimate and shy, licking the hair, sweeping through cotton dresses with unseemly intimacy, then disappearing into the utter blackness. Daylight was equally insistent, but much more bold and thoughtless. It dazzled, muddling the sight. It forced through my closed eyelids, bringing me up and out of a borrowed bed and into brand new streets.

''After living nearly two years in Cairo, I had brought my son Guy to enter the University of Ghana in Accra. I planned staying for two weeks with a friend of a colleague, settling Guy into his dormitory, then continuing to Liberia to a job with the Department of Information.

''Guy was seventeen and quick. I was thirty-three and determined. We were Black Americans in West Africa, where for the first time in our lives the color of our skin was accepted as correct and normal.

''Guy had finished high school in Egypt, his Arabic was good and his health excellent. He assured me that he would quickly learn a Ghanaian language and he certainly could look after himself. . . . Another adventure. The future was plump with promise.

''For two days Guy and I laughed. We looked at the Ghanaian streets and laughed. We listened to the melodious languages and laughed. We looked at each other and laughed out loud.

''On the third day, Guy, on a pleasure outing, was injured in an automobile accident. One arm and one leg were fractured and his neck was broken.

''July and August of 1962 stretched out like fat men yawning after a sumptuous dinner. They had every right to gloat, for they had eaten me up. Gobbled me down. Consumed my spirit, not in a wild rush, but slowly, with the obscene patience of certain victors. I became a shadow walking in the white hot streets, and a dark spectre in the hospital.

''There was no solace in knowing that the doctors and nurses hovering around Guy were African, nor in the company of the Black American expatriates who, hearing your misfortune, came to share some of the slow hours. Racial loyalties and cultural attachments had become meaningless.

''Trying utterly, I could not match Guy's stoicism. He lay calm, week after week, in a prison of plaster from which only his face and one leg and arm were visible. His assurances that he would heal and be better than new drove me into a faithless silence. Had I been less timid, I would have cursed God. Had I come from a different background, I would have gone further and denied His very existence. Having neither the courage nor the historical precedent, I raged inside myself like a blinded bull in a metal stall.

''Admittedly, Guy lived with the knowledge that an unexpected and very hard sneeze could force the fractured vertebrae

Historian and long-time friend, Nell Painter (right), interviews Maya Angelou for the television special, "And Still I Rise: Maya Angelou." Based on Angelou's book, it was filmed on the grounds of her home in Winston Salem, North Carolina. Produced by the University of North Carolina Center for Public Television, it was broadcast on PBS-TV, February 3, 1985.

against his spinal cord, and he would be paralyzed or die immediately, but he had only an infatuation with life. He hadn't lived long enough to fall in love with this brutally delicious experience. He could lightly waft away to another place, if there really was another place, where his youthful innocence would assure him a crown, wings, a harp, ambrosia, free milk and an absence of nostalgic yearning. . . . My wretchedness reminded me that, on the other hand, I would be rudderless.

"I had lived with family until my son was born in my sixteenth year. When he was two months old and perched on my left hip, we left my mother's house and together, save for one year when I was touring, we had been each other's home and center for seventeen years. He could die if he wanted to and go off to wherever dead folks go, but I, I would be left without a home." [Maya Angelou, *All God's Children Need Traveling Shoes,* Random House, 1986.⁵]

Guy recovered from his injuries, entered the University of Ghana, and Angelou found a job as an assistant administrator

of the School of Music and Drama at the University. "I worked wherever I was needed. [One of the professor's] wrote *Kple, Music of the Gods,* a book on the liturgy of the Ewe, and despite my scanty knowledge of typewriters, I was asked to type the manuscript, and did so. Reports on students' development, their absences and illnesses were kept in my files. Sometimes I handled theatre reservations or sold tickets at the box office in town. When Ireland's Abbey Theatre director Byrd Lynch, came to teach at Legon, she chose to present Bertolt Brecht's *Mother Courage* in full production, and I was chosen to play the title role.

"My son was growing into manhood on the university campus, under my eye, but not my thumb. Ana Livia and Julian, Efua and her children, my housemates and our lusty friends provided recreation enough. At last life was getting itself in joint.

"It was agreed in the house that as far as work was concerned, I was the most fortunate. As administrative assistant at the

University of Ghana, I had direct contact with African students, faculty, administrators and small traders. While the job was a blessing, the pay was not bounteous.

"I received no housing, tuition, or dislocation allowances. On the first day of every month, when the small manilla envelopes of cash were delivered to the offices, I would open mine with a confusion of sensations. Seventy-five pounds. Around two hundred dollars. In San Francisco, my mother spent that much on two pairs of shoes. Then I would think, seventy-five pounds, what luck! Many Ghanaians at the university would take home half that amount with gratitude. My feelings slid like mercury. Seventy-five pounds. Sheer discrimination. The old British philosopher's packet was crammed with four times that, and all I ever saw him do was sit in the Lecturers' Lounge ordering Guinness stout and dribbling on about Locke and Lord Acton and the British Commonwealth.

"I would count out the paper money, loving the Black president's picture. Thirty pounds for rent; thirty for my son's tuition, being paid on the installment plan; ten for beer, cigarettes, food. Another five for the houseman who my friends and I paid fifteen pounds per month to clean the bungalow."⁵

During the three years that Angelou lived in Ghana, she worked as a free-lance writer and as a feature editor for *African Review* as well as an assistant administrator at the University.

1966. Returned to Los Angeles and lectured at the University of California in Los Angeles. "Many years earlier I, or rather someone very like me and certainly related to me, had been taken from Africa by force. This second leave-taking would not be so onerous, for now I knew my people had never completely left Africa. We had sung it in our blues, shouted it in our gospel and danced the continent in our breakdowns. As we carried it to Philadelphia, Boston and Birmingham we had changed its color, modified its rhythms, yet it was Africa which rode in the bulges of our high calves, shook in our protruding behinds and crackled in our wide open laughter.

"I could nearly hear the old ones chuckling."⁵

1970. First book, an autobiography, *I Know Why the Caged Bird Sings* was nominated for the National Book Award. Since that time, she has written four additional autobiographies that cover the period from 1928 into the mid-1960s.

Besides writing, books, plays, and poetry, Angelou has also been a television narrator, interviewer, and host for Afro-American specials and theater series. She wrote and produced a ten-part television series on African traditions in American life; was author and executive producer of the five-part miniseries for CBS-TV, "Three Way Choice;" and received the Golden Eagle Award for her PBS documentary "Afro-American in the Arts."

1973-1981. Married to Paul Du Feu.

1975. Received the *Ladies' Home Journal* "Woman of the Year Award" in Communications. Appointed member of the American Bicentennial Council by President Ford.

December, 1981. Appointed the first Reynolds Professor of American Studies at Wake Forest University, a life-time appointment.

1983. Angelou, who speaks six languages, received the Matrix Award in the field of books from Women in Communications, Inc. "The fact that the adult American Negro female emerges

a formidable character is often met with amazement, distaste and even belligerence. It is seldom accepted as an inevitable outcome of the struggle won by survivors and deserves respect if not enthusiastic acceptance.'"¹

1986. Fifth book in her series of autobiographical works, *All God's Children Need Traveling Shoes,* which describes her four-year stay in Ghana, drew praise from reviewers. With just a high school education, Angelou has been an author, a poet, journalist, historian, educator, producer, songwriter, playwright, and is presently a college instructor and lecturer. "I believe all things are possible for a human being, and I don't think there's anything in the world I can't do. Of course, I can't be five foot four because I'm six feet tall. I can't be a man because I'm a woman. The physical gifts are given to me, just like having two arms is a gift. In my creative source, wherever that is, I don't see why I can't sculpt. Why shouldn't I? Human beings sculpt. I'm a human being. I refuse to indulge any man-made differences between myself and another human being. I will not do it. I'm not going to live very long. If I live another fifty years, it's not very long. So I should indulge somebody else's prejudice at their whim and not for my own convenience! Never happen! Not me!

"All my work, my life, everything is about survival. All my work is meant to say, 'You may encounter many defeats, but you must not be defeated.' In fact, the encountering may be the very experience which creates the vitality and the power to endure." ["Maya Angelou," *Black Women Writers at Work,* edited by Claudia Tate, Continuum, 1983.⁶]

Angelou speaks English, French, Spanish, Italian, Arabic, and Fanti.

FOR MORE INFORMATION SEE: New York Times, February 25, 1970, March 24, 1972; *Newsweek,* March 2, 1970; *Harvard Educational Review,* November, 1970; Maya Angelou, *I Know Why the Caged Bird Sings,* Random House, 1970; *New York Post,* November 5, 1971; *Harper's Bazaar,* November, 1972; Sheila Weller, "Work in Progress: Maya Angelou," *Intellectual Digest,* June, 1973; Sidonie Ann Smith, "The Song of a Caged Bird: Maya Angelou's Quest for Self-Acceptance," *Southern Humanities Review,* fall, 1973; *Times Literary Supplement,* February 17, 1974, June 14, 1985, January 24, 1986; *Viva,* March, 1974; *New York Times Book Review,* June 16, 1974; *New Republic,* July 6, 1974; *Village Voice,* July 11, 1974, October 28, 1981; M. Angelou, *Gather Together in My Name,* Random House, 1974; *Writers Digest,* January, 1975; *Black World,* July, 1975; *Ladies' Home Journal,* May, 1976; *Poetry,* August, 1976; M. Angelou, *Singin' and Swingin' and Gettin' Merry Like Christmas,* Random House, 1976; *Ms.,* January, 1977; *Parnassus: Poetry in Review,* fall-winter, 1979.

Washington Post Book World, October 4, 1981, June 26, 1983, May 11, 1986; *Washington Post,* October 13, 1981; *Chicago Tribune,* November 1, 1981; M. Angelou, *The Heart of a Woman,* Random House, 1981; *Black Scholar,* summer, 1982; *Los Angeles Times,* May 29, 1983; "Maya Angelou," *Black Women Writers at Work,* edited by Claudia Tate, Continuum, 1983; *Observer,* April 1, 1984; *Chicago Tribune Book World,* March 23, 1986; *Time,* March 31, 1986; *Los Angeles Times Book Review,* April 13, 1986; *Detroit Free Press,* May 9, 1986; M. Angelou, *All God's Children Need Traveling Shoes,* Random House, 1986.

His studies were pursued but never effectually overtaken.

—H.G. Wells

BALLARD, Lowell Clyne   1904-1986

OBITUARY NOTICE—See sketch in *SATA* Volume 12: Born December 29, 1904, in Bisbee, Ariz.; died September 20, 1986; buried in Greenwood Memorial Park, San Diego, Calif. Educator, administrator, game maker, and author. Ballard worked for thirty years as a principal of various elementary schools in southern California. With Frank L. Beals, he wrote children's books such as *Real Adventure with the Discoverers of America, Real Adventure with the Pilgrim Settlers, Real Adventure with American Plainsmen, Real Adventure with American Patriots,* and *Spanish Adventure Trails.* He also contributed poems to periodicals and created the game American Heroes.

FOR MORE INFORMATION SEE: Contemporary Authors, Permanent Series, Volume 1, Gale, 1975. Obituaries: *Tribune* (San Diego), September 23, 1986.

BALLARD, Mignon Franklin   1934-

BRIEF ENTRY: Born October 29, 1934, in Calhoun, Ga. A former newspaper editor and third-grade teacher, Ballard works in the Artists in Education program in South Carolina schools. She attributes her love for words to her parents, both story-tellers who encouraged Ballard to use her imagination. Besides two books for middle-graders, she has contributed short stories to periodicals such as *American Girl, Instructor, Child Life,* and *Woman's World.* Both of her published books, *Aunt Matilda's Ghost* (Aurora, 1978) and *Raven Rock* (Dodd, 1986), are mysteries, and another is near completion. According to Ballard, "Having been born close to Halloween and raised across the street from a funeral home might have something to do with my love of ghost stories and mysteries." Of *Aunt Matilda's Ghost,* for which Ballard received an Excellence in Writing Award in Children's Literature from Winthrop College in 1978, *Booklist* observed, ". . . There is enough ghost-liness to attract middle-grade sleuths, and the mystery is attention-holding." In this story a ghost, a lost diary, a kidnapped dog, and a trip to a cemetery help Peggy and her friends clear the name of an ancestor and find his lost invention. *Raven Rock* relates the mystery of Henrietta Meredith's search for a mother who abandoned her in infancy, a decades-old crime, and a murderer known as The Chuckler. *Publishers Weekly* noted that this novel "tells its tale credibly." A member of Mystery Writers of America, Ballard was a Girl Scout leader for eight years and worked as chairman and publicity chairman of the Fort Mill Community Playhouse. *Residence:* Fort Mill, S.C.

BARKER, Cicely Mary   1895-1973

PERSONAL: Born June 28, 1895, in Waddon, Croydon, Surrey, England; died February 16, 1973, in Worthing, Sussex, England; daughter of Walter and Mary Eleanor Oswald Barker. *Education:* Attended Croydon School of Art.

CAREER: Free-lance artist, author and illustrator of books for children. Best known for her "Flower Fairies" series, Barker executed commissions of paintings for St. Georges Church, Waddon, Norbury Methodist Church, and St. Andrew's Church, Croydon, and stained glass for St. Edmund's Church, West Croydon. Work was exhibited at Royal Institute of Painters in Water-Colours, Society of Women Artists, Society of Graphic Art, Pastel Society, and Bologna International Children's Book Fair, 1985, and elsewhere. *Member:* Croydon Arts Society (vice-president, 1961-72).

WRITINGS—All for children; all self-illustrated; all originally published by Blackie & Son, except as noted: *Flower Fairies of the Spring* (verse), 1923, Macmillan, 1927, reissued, Peter Bedrick, 1985; *Flower Fairies of the Summer* (verse), 1925, Macmillan, 1927, reissued, Peter Bedrick, 1985; *Flower Fairies of the Autumn, with the Nuts and Berries They Bring* (verse), 1926, Macmillan, 1927, reissued, Peter Bedrick, 1985; *The Book of Flower Fairies* (verse), 1927; (editor) *Old Rhymes for All Times,* 1928, Dodge, 1932; (editor) *Rhymes New and Old,* 1933, Artists and Writers Guild (Poughkeepsie, N.Y.), 1935, published as *A Little Book of Rhymes New and Old,* Blackie & Son, 1937; *A Flower Fairy Alphabet,* 1934, Peter Bedrick, 1985; (editor) *A Little Book of Old Rhymes,* 1936, Hippocrene, 1977; *The Lord of the Rushie River* (fiction), 1938, Hippocrene, 1977; *Fairies of the Trees* (verse), 1940, published as *Flower Fairies of the Trees,* 1961, Peter Bedrick, 1985; *When Spring Came in at the Window* (one-act play; music by Olive Linnell), 1942; *Flower Fairies of the Garden* (verse), 1944, Peter Bedrick, 1984; *Groundsel and Necklaces* (fiction), 1946, published as *The Fairy's Gift,* Hippocrene, 1977; *Flower Fairies of the Wayside* (verse), 1948, Peter Bedrick, 1985.

Lively Stories (readers), five volumes, St. Martin's (New York), 1954-55; *Flower Fairy Picture Book* (selection of verse), 1955; *Lively Numbers* (readers), three volumes, St. Martin's, 1960-62; *Lovely Words* (readers), two volumes, St. Martin's, 1961-62; *The Sand, the Sea, and the Sun* (textbook), Gibson, 1970; (editor) *The Rhyming Rainbow: Poems,* Hippocrene, 1977; *An A.B.C. of Flower Fairies,* 1978, Hippocrene, 1980; *Flower Fairies Miniature Library* (contains "Blossom Flower Fairies," "Berry Flower Fairies," "Spring Flower Fairies," and "Summer Flower Fairies"), four volumes, Philomel, 1981 (published in England as *Flower Fairies: Poems and Pictures,* four volumes, Blackie & Son, 1981); *Flower Fairies of the*

Cicely Mary Barker, at eight years.

(From *Flower Fairies of the Seasons* by Cicely Mary Barker. Illustrated by the author.)

(From *Flower Fairies of the Wayside* by Cicely Mary Barker. Illustrated by the author.)

(From *A Flower Fairy Alphabet* by Cicely Mary Barker. Illustrated by the author.)

(From *A Flower Fairy Alphabet* by Cicely Mary Barker. Illustrated by the author.)

(From *Flower Fairies of the Garden* by Cicely Mary Barker. Illustrated by the author.)

Seasons (selection of verse), Hippocrene, 1981, Harper, 1984; *Flower Fairies of the Woodland* (fold-out book), Peter Bedrick, 1984; *Flower Fairies of the Winter*, Peter Bedrick, 1985. Also author of play, "When Spring Came in at the Window."

Illustrator: (With Beatrice A. Waldram) *The "Guardian Angel" Series of Birthday Cards*, S.P.C.K., 1923; *Beautiful Bible Pictures* (cards), Blackie & Son, 1932; *The Little Picture Hymn Book*, Blackie & Son, 1933; Dorothy O. Barker, *He Leadeth Me: A Book of Bible Stories*, Blackie & Son, 1936; *The Flower Fairies Address Book*, Hippocrene, 1980; *The Flower Fairies Birthday Book*, Hippocrene, 1980; *Seasons of Flower Fairies* (frieze), Hippocrene, 1982; *The Flower Fairies Gardening Year*, Blackie & Son, 1983. Also illustrator of *Laugh and Learn* by Jennett Humphreys and *The Children's Book of Hymns*.

SIDELIGHTS: The Barkers of Sussex were wood carvers for over four hundred years. Cicely Mary Barker's father was no exception. He lovingly carved the pulpit he donated to St. Edmund's Church in Croydon in 1909, a mission church much beloved by the family. Artistry was inborn and natural to young Barker. Born in Waddon, Croydon on June 28, 1895 into a professional middle-class environment, Barker was a delicate child, suffering with epilepsy. It was because of her fragile condition that she was educated at home, her parents and governesses serving in the role of tutors. She engaged in many hours of drawing and painting during that time of informal education. Her formal education took form in a correspondence course in drawing and in evening classes at the Croyden School of Art.

In 1911, at the age of sixteen, Barker won second prize in a poster competition run by the Croydon Art Society. Shortly thereafter, she was elected to life membership in the Society, becoming their youngest member. She remained their longest serving member until her death, ultimately becoming their vice-president from 1961-1972.

Her work became commercially recognized when at the age of fifteen her set of painted post cards were taken up by Raphael Tuck. Other paintings soon followed and were sold by various publishers. Always her paintings were of children at work and at play. To her great joy she discovered after the war years that her epilepsy had disappeared, never to return.

In 1924 she built her studio in 23 The Waldrons, where her sister Dorothy established a kindergarten school. "My sister ran a kindergarten and I used to borrow her students for models. For many years I had an atmosphere of children about me—I never forgot it," she told a *Croydon Advertiser* reporter. Many of her celebrated "Fairies" were chosen from Dorothy's students. Here for the next forty years Barker cultivated her skills. She was twenty-nine years old when the first of her "Flower Fairies" was published. They gave new dimension to children's books, the potential of which was first recognized by publisher Blackie who published Barker's books and spread interest throughout the world.

Uncompetitive and unpretentious in spirit, Barker remained completely devoted to her art, her family, her religion and her quiet life among a select group of friends. Nevertheless, she was very giving to those less fortunate, the deprived young—Girl Guides, Girls Diocesan Association, and every Christmas painted a picture for the Girls Friendly Society.

For St. Edmund's Church in Pitlake where her father had played the organ and carved the pulpit, Barker designed her only window in memory of her sister. During her lifetime she wrote and illustrated numerous books, painted portraits and church murals.

Barker maintained that her greatest influence was the medieval attraction of the Pre-Raphaelites and their fascination with the simplicity, romance and pageantry of the Middle Ages. "I am very much interested in the Pre-Raphaelites. I have been, all my life, and I've tried to see as much of their work as I possibly can. . . . I am to some extent influenced by them—not in any technical sense, but in the choice of subject-matter and the feeling and atmosphere they could achieve. I very much like, for example, the early paintings of Millais and, though he is later, the wonderful things of Burne-Jones." [Sturt-Penrose, "Under Pre-Raphaelite Influence," *Croydon Advertiser*, March 1, 1964.[1]]

It was her habit to carry pencil and sketchbook on holiday and rapidly sketch any interesting child for future use. Flowers were a subject she studied with a botanist's keen eye. She had gleaned from many sources her information about them.

After Dorothy died in 1954, Barker assumed the household duties and the care of her elderly mother, who died at the age of ninety-one. Barker missed the companionship of her mother and became very lonely. She was sixty-five by then and planning another book. Her accessibility to town became very difficult and so she sold 23 The Waldrons and moved to Duppas Avenue. 1967 saw yet another move nearer to the center of the village into a small chalet with adequate room for an upstairs studio. Failing health and eyesight, however, took their toll and meant that she had to put away her brushes and depend on others for her care. She died at Worthy Hospital in Croydon, England on February 16, 1973 at the age of seventy-seven. Her death coincided with the fiftieth anniversary of her internationally famous "Flower Fairies" books. "I have always tried to paint instinctively in a way that comes naturally to me, without any real thought or attention to artistic theories."[1]

FOR MORE INFORMATION SEE: Croydon Times (England), October, 10, 1958; *Croydon Advertiser*, February 10, 1961, January 3, 1964, January 17, 1964, March 1, 1964, September 13, 1985; D. L. Kirkpatrick, editor, *Twentieth-Century Children's Writers*, 2nd edition, St. Martin's, 1983. Obituaries: *Times* (London), February 21, 1973; *Croydon Chronicle* (England), March 2, 1973.

BARRETT, William E(dmund) 1900-1986

OBITUARY NOTICE: Born November 16, 1900, in New York, N.Y.; died following a heart attack, September 14, 1986, in Denver, Colo.; buried in Mount Olivet Cemetery, Denver, Colo. Advertising executive and author. Barrett was an advertising executive for Westinghouse before becoming a prolific author of inspirational works. Among his most popular were the novels *The Left Hand of God*, concerning an overseas American who disguises himself as a priest, and *The Lilies of the Field*, which tells of a black American who helps German nuns build a chapel. Both of these works, of interest to young adults, were adapted into motion pictures. Among Barrett's other writings are *The Glory Tent*, a sequel to *The Lilies of the Field*, and *The Fools of Time*, a science fiction novel. He also wrote *Shepherd of Mankind*, a biography of Pope Paul VI, and *Lady of the Lotus*, a fictionalized biography of the wife of Buddha, and published more than two hundred short stories.

FOR MORE INFORMATION SEE: Catholic Authors: Contemporary Biographical Sketches, Volume II, St. Mary's Abbey, 1952; *Contemporary Authors*, Volumes 5-8, revised, Gale, 1969; *Who's Who in the World*, 4th edition, Marquis, 1978. Obituaries: *Rocky Mountain News*, September 16, 1986; *Detroit Free Press*, September 17, 1986; *Detroit News*, September 17, 1986; *Los Angeles Times*, September 17, 1986; *New York Times*, September 17, 1986; *Facts on File*, September 19, 1986; *Publishers Weekly*, October 17, 1986; *AB Bookman's Weekly*, October 27, 1986.

BELLVILLE, Cheryl Walsh   1944-

BRIEF ENTRY: Born August 27, 1944, in Deming, N.M. An author/photographer, Bellville has taught photography and art in Minneapolis, Minnesota, and has headed her own company, Cheryl Walsh Bellville Photography, since 1968. She also worked as a staff writer and editorial photographer for the newspaper *Hundred Flowers* from 1970 to 1971. Her photographs have been exhibited in Minnesota. Bellville's books are filled with her own photographs. According to *School Library Journal*, "The numerous color and black-and-white photographs are outstanding" in *Farming Today Yesterday's Way* (Carolrhoda, 1984), in which the author explores a dairy farm in Wisconsin where draft horses provide the power for the farm machinery. Similarly, Bellville depicts spring round-up on a South Dakota cattle ranch in *Round-Up* (Carolrhoda, 1982) and rodeo events such as bronc riding, calf roping, and bull riding in *Rodeo* (Carolrhoda, 1985). "I try to provide a bridge between the technical urban present and the fragile, traditional stewardship of the ecosystem," said Bellville. She and her husband Rod, a musician, writer, and photographer, have written *Large Animal Veterinarians* (Carolrhoda, 1983), *Stockyards* (Carolrhoda, 1983), and *All Things Bright and Beautiful* (Winston Press, 1983). *Office:* Cheryl Walsh Bellville Photography, 2823 Eighth St. S., Minneapolis, Minn. 55454.

FOR MORE INFORMATION SEE: Contemporary Authors, Volume 109, Gale, 1983; *International Authors and Writers Who's Who*, 10th edition, International Biographical Centre, 1986.

BLAUER, Ettagale   1940-
(Ettagale Lauré)

PERSONAL: Born June 8, 1940, in New York, N.Y.; daughter of Samuel and Minnie (Cantor) Blauer; married Jason Lauré (a photojournalist) May 5, 1974 (divorced January 16, 1984). *Education:* Hunter College (now Herbert H. Lehman College of the City University of New York), B.A., 1961. *Home:* New York, N.Y.

CAREER: Worked as a public relations writer for Chemstrand, Seligman & Lantz, Walter Dorwin Teague Associates, Clairol Inc., and Monsanto Co., 1961-71; Chilton Co., New York

(From *South Africa: Coming of Age under Apartheid* by Jason Lauré and Ettagale Lauré. Photograph by Jason Lauré.)

ETTAGALE BLAUER

City, writer, 1971-83; *Jeweler's Circular Keystone,* New York, N.Y., editor, 1972-83; *Lauré Communications,* writer, 1983—. *Awards, honors:* National Book Award finalist, 1975, and selected a Notable Book in the Field of Social Studies by the joint committee of the National Council of Social Studies and the Children's Book Council, 1975, both for *Joi Bangla! The Children of Bangladesh;* Jesse Neal Editorial Achievement Award from American Business Press, 1977, for stories on women and discrimination, and 1979, for a series on gold; *Joi Bangla! The Children of Bangladesh* and *Jovem Portugal: After the Revolution* were both chosen one of New York Public Library's Books for the Teen Age, 1980, 1981, and 1982, and *South Africa: Coming of Age under Apartheid,* 1981, and 1982.

WRITINGS—All with Jason Lauré; all published by Farrar, Straus, except where indicated: *Joi Bangla! The Children of Bangladesh* (young adult; illustrated with photographs by J. Lauré), 1974; *Jovem Portugal: After the Revolution* (young adult; illustrated with photographs by J. Lauré), 1977; *South Africa: Coming of Age under Apartheid* (young adult; ALA Notable Book), 1980; *Zimbabwe,* Regensteiner, 1987. Contributor to magazines, including *Signature, Junior Scholastic, Ornament, The World and I* and *Savvy.*

SIDELIGHTS: "As a writer of non-fiction, I consider it both my task and my pleasure to learn about foreign subjects and people and bring the information to my readers who cannot make those same journeys except through my writing."

In 1978 Blauer worked and traveled throughout southern Africa for one year, focusing on research for a South Africa book, including border to border coverage of Namibia, trips to Zimbabwe prior to independence; extensive field work on gold and diamond mining including many trips into the mines; also trips to Botswana and Lesotho for diamond mining.

FOR MORE INFORMATION SEE: Los Angeles Times Book Review, August 3, 1980; *Chicago Times Book World,* November 9, 1980.

BOND, Felicia   1954-

PERSONAL: Born July 18, 1954, in Yokohama, Japan; daughter of Oliver James (a retired civil engineer) and Mary Elizabeth (a high school English teacher; maiden name, Stengel) Bond. *Education:* University of Texas, Austin, B.F.A., 1976. *Residence:* New York, N.Y.

CAREER: Spring Branch Science Center, Houston, Tex., botanical illustrator, 1971-78; puppeteer in Austin, Tex., wrote and adapted texts, designed and made puppets and performed for the public library, 1979-80; Reader's Digest Books, New York, N.Y., designer's assistant, 1980-81; Margaret K. McElderry Books, New York, N.Y., art director, 1981-83; free-lance designer and illustrator, 1983—. Substitute grade school art teacher and taught painting to adults in continuing education, Houston, 1980. *Awards, honors: Poinsettia and Her Family* and *If You Give a Mouse a Cookie* were both chosen one of Child Study Association of America's Children's Books of the Year, 1985.

WRITINGS—All self-illustrated; all published by Crowell: *Poinsettia and Her Family,* 1981; *Mary Betty Lizzie McNutt's Birthday,* 1983; *Four Valentines in a Rainstorm,* 1983; *The Halloween Performance,* 1983; *Christmas in the Chicken Coop,* 1983; *Poinsettia and the Firefighters,* 1984; *Wake up, Vladimir,* Crowell, 1987.

Illustrator: Roma Gans, *When Birds Change Their Feathers,* Crowell, 1980; Franklyn M. Branley, *The Sky Is Full of Stars,* Crowell, 1981; Joseph Slate, *How Little Porcupine Played Christmas,* Crowell, 1982; Maria Polushkin, *Mama's Secret,* Four Winds, 1984; Laura Joffe Numeroff, *If You Give a Mouse a Cookie* (Junior Literary Guild selection), Harper, 1985; Stephen P. Kramer, *Getting Oxygen: What Do You Do If You're Cell Twenty-Two?,* Crowell, 1986; S. P. Kramer, *How to Think Like a Scientist: Answering Questions by the Scientific Method,* Crowell, 1987.

ADAPTATIONS—Filmstrips with cassettes, except as noted: "Four Valentines in a Rainstorm," Listening Library, 1984;

FELICIA BOND

She dreamed about the dancing circus horse. ■ (From *Poinsettia and Her Family* by Felicia Bond. Illustrated by the author.)

"The Halloween Performance," Listening Library, 1984; "Mary Betty Lizzie McNutt's Birthday," Listening Library, 1984; "Christmas in the Chicken Coop," Listening Library, 1984; "Poinsettia and Her Family," Reading Rainbow, PBS-TV, 1984; "Poinsettia and the Firefighters" (cassette), Random House, 1986; "If You Give a Mouse a Cookie" (cassette), Random House, 1986.

WORK IN PROGRESS: Three self-illustrated books; illustrating a reissue of *Big Red Barn;* illustrating *The Right Number of Elephants.*

SIDELIGHTS: "I was five years old when I decided to be an artist. I was standing in the doorway of my bedroom in the late afternoon. The room was dark, except for a brilliant, but soft, beam of sunlight filtering through the window. At the base of the window was a red leather window seat, and it glowed a rich, dark color. I was moved somehow, and decided I had to capture that feeling of poignancy and time passing. Art seemed to me to be the best way to do this. My feelings about light and what it represents have not changed to this day.

"When I was six, I was asked to draw the class mural. I was always shy and nervous in school, but somehow let it be known early on that I was an artist. Because I was doing the mural, I was able to skip the exercises the class was engaged in. Instead of being excited, I was nervous at being singled out. The teacher told me to take off my shoes and begin drawing on the large butcher paper unrolled on the floor in front of me. This was all she said. She didn't explain that I would then be able to walk on the clean white paper without smudging it, and draw freely. I was shocked and horrified at her suggestion and burst into tears. The only time I took off my shoes was at home when getting into my pajamas or play clothes. And if I took off my shoes, I reasoned, next I would be taking off *all* my clothes. Right there in the classroom! I certainly didn't

No elaborate preparations were made. ■ (From *Mary Betty Lizzie McNutt's Birthday* by Felicia Bond. Illustrated by the author.)

tell the teacher this, but she managed to reassure me, and once my shoes *were* off, I was surprised at how much sense it made. I enjoyed drawing the mural uninhibited.

"This was the beginning of my awareness that artists have an opportunity to be different. They don't always have to do the same old boring things that other people do. Coming from a family of seven children, when my parents encouraged me and praised me for my art, I found it was a way to stand out and (at that age) to get attention. As I grew older, I developed an intellectual appreciation for art, but it is primarily the early impressions that motivate and inspire me.

"It's fortunate those early impressions and desires of an artist were so strong, since working as one in the 'grown-up' world has proven to be a sometimes frustrating one. To write and draw for children is not taken seriously by some, and the financial rewards, even with successful books, are usually not staggering. The isolation that I find to be necessary is often a struggle for me. Yet, when I look at my past books, I remember a strong sense of freedom mixed with the hard work, and when I look ahead to future books, I feel happy.

"I studied painting in college. After graduating I moved briefly to Edmonton, Alberta, Canada, and without having my painting supplies or a studio to work with or in, I became interested in illustrating some books of fairy and folk tales that my mother had given me. The illustrations were by Dulac, Neilson, and Rackham, etc. I had always loved books as a child—everything from picture books like *Good Night Moon* and *The Velveteen Rabbit* to novels by Elizabeth Enright and Madeleine L'Engle. I also loved Errol LeCain's work, the *Babar* and *Madeline* books, and Golden Books like *The Saggy Baggy Elephant, Little Black Sambo,* and *The Pokey Little Puppy.* So at age twenty-two in Canada, I decided to put together a portfolio of 'children's illustrations.' I do not remember at what point I decided I was going to do children's books, I think it might actually have been *before* I went to Canada, but it wasn't fully articulated until then. Canada was a transition from painting to illustrating. I had always intended to move back to New York since 1967, when I was thirteen and my family moved from Bronxville, New York to Houston, Texas, and six months after college and Canada, I did. For a year or so I worked at various jobs for income and compiled a portfolio. A few weeks after I had moved to New York City, I had a contract with T. Y. Crowell for a 'Let's Read and Find Out' science book, based on the work I already had in my portfolio, and my botanical illustrations done from 1971-78. I illustrated this book, continued work on my portfolio, and pieced together enough other work to stay in New York.

"My portfolio grew. I did my first couple of books slowly, and I started writing. My work always had a narrative sense; I had very little in my portfolio that illustrated someone else's texts. I found it more interesting to invent stories of my own although they were more vignettes than well-crafted stories. I did not, however, think of myself as a writer. But my editor encouraged me, and in 1980 I wrote *Poinsettia and Her Family.* I couldn't believe how hard it was to see the book through to completion. My entire life came to a halt as I executed it. Nor could I believe how good I felt when it was finished. When it did reasonably well, I had more confidence from my publisher and in myself. I really was hooked—there was no turning back.

"Some of my ideas spring forth full-grown, others sometimes gestate for years. I write down things in my sketchbook which now has more words in it than drawings. I try to stay 'free-form' about my ideas so they don't become stiff or mechanical. The process is a personal one and not the same for any two people. It is open and flexible but by no means casual.

"The artist whose work influenced me early on is Charles Schulz. His work is precise, alive, and very specific in it's movements and expressions of the character's bodies and faces. I devoured all his books from first grade on, as did all of my six brothers and sisters. In sixth grade I 'wrote' a class play adapted from a selection of his cartoons. There are several contemporary painters and illustrators whose work I respect, but I have to credit Schulz as one very specific and powerful influence. I also try to incorporate in my own work what I love and respond to in Jean de Brunhoff's Babar books, and Ludwig Bemelman's Madeline books. Both exude warmth and humor in their writing and drawing, and their work is fresh and immediate while still being very thoughtfully executed.

"Time and space and a certain reserve keep me from elaborating in any depth another very strong influence in my work—that of the German Expressionist painters of the late nineteenth century—Nolde, Kirchner, Ensor, Munch and others. A very complex movement politically and emotionally, I respond to some of their ideas about nature, children, birth, death, and purity or transcendence. I often think a painting would be a better way for me to express these ideas, but I find it a challenge to incorporate them in, or use them as seeds for, my books."

BONHAM, Frank 1914-

PERSONAL: Born February 25, 1914, in Los Angeles, Calif.; son of Alfred B. (manager of a brewery) and Cecil (a poet, maiden name, Thompson) Bonham; married Gloria Bailey (a schoolteacher), November 26, 1938; children: David, Bruce, Keith. *Education:* Attended Glendale Junior College (now Glendale College), 1932-34; attended University of California at Los Angeles, 1935. *Politics:* Independent. *Home:* Skull Valley, Ariz.

CAREER: Writer. *Military service:* U.S. Army, 1942-43. *Member:* Writers Guild of America, West; CRASH, Inc. (Community Resources and Self-Help; member of board of directors); Physical Fitness Council; San Diego YMCA. *Awards, honors:* Edgar Allan Poe Award runner-up from Mystery Writers of America special award 1964, for *Honor Bound,* 1967, for *The Mystery of the Red Tide,* and 1969, for *Mystery of the Fat Cat;* Recognition of Merit Award, George G. Stone Center for Children's Books, 1967, for *Durango Street;* Woodward Park School Annual Book Award, 1971, for *Viva Chicano;* Southern California Council on Literature for Children and Young People Award for a "notable body of work," 1980.

WRITINGS—For young people; published by Dutton except as indicated: *Burma Rifles: A Story of Merrill's Marauders,* Crowell, 1960; *War Beneath the Sea,* Crowell, 1962; *Deepwater Challenge,* Crowell, 1963; *The Loud, Resounding Sea,* Crowell, 1963; *Honor Bound,* Crowell, 1963; *Speedway Contender,* Crowell, 1964; *Durango Street* (ALA Notable Book), 1965; *Mystery of the Red Tide* (illustrated by Brinton Turkle), 1966; *Mystery in Little Tokyo* (illustrated by Kazue Mizumura), 1966; *The Ghost Front,* 1968; *Mystery of the Fat Cat* (illustrated by Alvin Smith), 1968; *The Nitty Gritty* (illustrated by A. Smith), 1968; *The Vagabundos,* 1969; *Viva Chicano,* 1970; *Cool Cat,* 1971; *Chief,* 1971; *The Friends of the Loony Lake Monster,* 1972; *Hey, Big Spender!,* 1972; *A Dream of Ghosts,* 1973; *The Golden Bees of Tulami,* 1974; *The Missing Persons League,* 1975; *The Rascals from Haskell's Gym,* 1976;

FRANK BONHAM

Devilhorn, 1978; *The Forever Formula,* 1979; *Gimme an H, Gimme an E, Gimme an L, Gimme a P* (illustrated by David Mostyn), Scribner, 1980; *Premonitions,* Holt, 1984.

Other: *Lost Stage Valley,* Simon & Schuster, 1948; *Bold Passage,* Simon & Schuster, 1950; *Snaketrack,* Simon & Schuster, 1952; *Blood on the Land,* Ballantine, 1952; *Outcast of Crooked River,* Hodder & Stoughton, 1953; *Night Raid,* Ballantine, 1954; *The Feud at Spanish Ford,* Ballantine, 1954; *Border Guns,* Muller, 1956; *Last Stage West,* Dell, 1957; *Tough Country,* Dell, 1958; *Hardrock,* Ballantine, 1958; *One for Sleep,* Gold Medal, 1960; *The Sound of Gunfire,* World Distributors (London), 1960; *The Skin Game,* Gold Medal, 1961; *Trago . . . ,* Dell, 1962; *Defiance Mountain,* World Distributors (London), 1962, Popular Library, 1964; *By Her Own Hand,* Monarch, 1963; *Cast a Long Shadow,* Monarch, 1964; *Rawhide Guns,* Popular Library, 1964; *Logan's Choice,* Fawcett, 1964; *Break for the Border,* Berkley Publishing, 1980; *Fort Hogan,* Berkley Publishing, 1980.

Author of television scripts for "Wells Fargo," "Restless Gun," "Shotgun Slade," and "Death Valley Days" series. Contributor of over five hundred short stories, novels, and novelettes to magazines, including *Saturday Evening Post* serials, short stories to *McCall's, American,* and to mystery and western magazines. Stories and selections from youth novels included in many anthologies.

ADAPTATIONS: "Durango Street" (filmstrip with cassette, book, and teacher's guide), Current Affairs and Mark Twain Media, also available from Listening Library.

She felt her body working for her, everything compact. . . . ■ (Cover illustration by Ruth Sanderson from *The Rascals from Haskell's Gym* by Frank Bonham.)

WORK IN PROGRESS: Street of the Crying Woman, a young adult novel; *To Find the Queen*, an adult mystery.

SIDELIGHTS: "I was born on **February 25, 1914,** in Los Angeles, California, and I was raised there before smog and freeways. My father was born [in California] also, and his mother before him in 1853. We moved around a little, trying to find a place where an asthmatic child—me—could breathe.

"My family life as a child was unremarkable, although my grandfather was a gold camp judge, and both he and my mother were poets. I started writing for pleasure when I was about fourteen. I think I wrote out my dissatisfactions—just as a canary sings out of loneliness." [Lee Bennett Hopkins, *More Books by More People*, Citation, 1974.[1]]

1934. Decided on a writing career at the age of twenty with the ambitious goal of writing a short story a day. "Asthma was one of the big realities of my childhood. It never quite killed me, but it ended my college career, and I moved to a mountain cabin where I started writing. Indirectly I owe a lot to ill health. It kept me from becoming a third-rate newspa-

perman and forced me into a profession I love and for which I am suited. And because I had to take care of myself, I am now in good shape. I run two miles a day."[1]

In the span of two years, Bonham wrote 107 stories, of which he sold ten.

1938. Married Gloria Bailey, a teacher. Three sons, David, Bruce, and Keith were born to the marriage. Two of their children are handicapped. "I am sure that my boys have shaped much of my feeling for the underdog. I have learned much from them. I think we learn a lot more from unhappiness than from happiness, but there are limits to what human beings can absorb in this way. The gods should use more judgement in the matter! But I do know that if everything had gone swimmingly well, I would be a lousy, shallow writer. My oldest son is married, and I have three delightful, little granddaughters [and one grandson]."[1] Son Bruce died in 1984.

1942-1943. Served in the United States Army during World War II.

Calling himself a "hard-core unemployable," Bonham managed to support himself as a free-lance writer. He described

Below him, the buildings of the Project were neatly fitted together in the form of T's, E's, and H's. . . . ■ (Cover illustration from *Viva Chicano* by Frank Bonham.)

Rufus stared down the street, his eyes glazed with disgust and apprehension. ■ (Jacket illustration by Symeon Shimin from *Durango Street* by Frank Bonham.)

himself as, "a shy, self-effacing little man who lives a sort of Walter Mitty existence. I get most of my kicks inside my skull. Yet aware that there is some fun going on out there, I force myself into activities such as skin diving, working out at the Y every night, working as a volunteer at a parolee house in San Diego, researching subjects for stories—dolphins, tuna boats, juvenile delinquency, racial problems, and police work. The necessity to do field research has brought me much pleasure—and a little wisdom.

". . . I have never held a job. Sometimes I think one should start in some other occupation and then become a writer, if only to value and appreciate one's freedom in the profession. Everyone envies me my freedom, except around bill-paying time. There is no floor or ceiling on a free-lancer's finances."[1]

1960. "My first young people's book [*Burma Rifles: A Story of Merrill's Marauders*] was a novel about the Japanese-Americans who fought with Merrill's Marauders as I-and-R men and interpreters. This book necessitated some minor information about navigation, and for that I went to a neighbor who had been a submarine skipper. The submariner got me excited about doing a submarine book, and I wrote one. The submarine book generated an interest in dolphins, and I . . . wrote my dolphin book, *The Loud, Resounding Sea.*" [Frank Bonham, "Hanging in There," *The Writer*, September, 1974.[2]]

Bonham's first children's book resulted in more and more books for young people until he finally turned his attention solely to them. "I had been writing twenty years when I discovered children's books. I was astonished and delighted to learn that almost any subject was a good one for children's stories, and after backing into the field, continued to write mysteries, television scripts, and westerns, I decided the real satisfaction was in writing adventure books for young people."[1]

1965. "The publication of *Durango Street* resulted in correspondence from librarians and teachers working with minority youth, telling me of the need for similar books—those dealing with the problems of ghetto life. I have since done much research into these matters, with the assistance of parole and probation officers, police officers, social workers, and private individuals. A great need still exists for stories pertinent to the lives of black youth and other minorities.

"Although *Durango Street* was written with a general audience in mind, I soon learned that it was of special interest to this neglected black audience. Since 1965 I have written two other books for minority youngsters, *Mystery of the Fat Cat* and *The Nitty Gritty.*

"Delinquency is a field of special interest to me, as it is closely related to ghetto and *barrio* problems. I attend meetings at a San Diego parolee house where a dozen young men and boys on parole from Youth Authority prisons live and attempt to aid one another in finding acceptable ways of handling their problems. Most of my material is drawn from life. My story characters are real people transmuted by merging with other characters, and by sheer imagination."

Research among juvenile gangs in the Los Angeles area led to the story of Rufus Henry, a black boy on parole trying to stay out of trouble. "For a year I roamed the gang districts with agency workers and police officers. I met the sad, tough kids behind bizarre dress and arrogant behavior. Talking with their parents, their parole officers, and their sponsors, I became impressed with the tremendous challenge in rehabilitating a gang boy or girl. If rehabilitation means 'to restore to a former capacity,' then it is impossible. You cannot restore a capacity one has never possessed, and these young people never had a capacity for anything but hard luck and defeat. But with sufficient patience and skill, ideas of ambition, justice, and hope can be implanted.

"My investigations were rich with surprises, but the greatest of all came from friends with whom I discussed this disaster-haunted world of juvenile gangs. A great many adults, I learned, scoff at the suggestion that there is a level of society where you can drown in bad luck and sordidness despite your greatest efforts to crawl out on the bank. Such people seem to suffer from an almost superstitious belief in something called strength of character. As they describe it to me, this quality appears to be a sort of fidget stone you rub to combat evil spirits like heredity and environment. It will either keep you from being born poor, black, or sickly, or bestow on you the strength to rise above those handicaps. While I certainly believe in strength of character, I have noticed that it works best in combination with good luck.

The Oak Street boys. ■ (From *Mystery of the Fat Cat* by Frank Bonham. Illustrated by Alvin Smith.)

"This apparent lack of empathy among so many who should know better perturbed me. . . . So long as people keep believing that some virtue in themselves has shielded them from disaster, they will not support any move to assist those in trouble.

"While observing the problems, I had been vacillating between writing an adult fact book or a book for young readers. I finally decided that the book should be addressed to youngsters, for older minds too often have already set hard within their forms. Children's minds, on the contrary, are as sensitive as sea anemones. Drop an idea in them, and they enfold and consume it, or else reject it. But at least they taste it.

"I decided, too, upon a novel rather than a fact book for the expression of the ancient but apparently still daring idea I wanted to suggest: '*There, but for the grace of God, go I.*'

"The actual writing of *Durango Street* was arduous, and I lost my hold on the story many times. Rufus Henry, the story's protagonist, became in my mind more real than any character I have ever created, and whenever I faltered, I experienced a feeling of guilt for letting him down. Yet each time I went back, like Scott Fitzgerald, 'to where I had left the truth,' he was right there, smiling and smacking his fist against his palm, and saying, 'Okay, man, you got it now? Let's get moving!'" [Frank Bonham, "The World of Rufus Henry," *Horn Book*, February, 1966.[3]]

Other books about minority groups followed *Durango Street*. Of his work habits, Bonham reported: "I studied composition in school and took journalism, but I don't think one can study writing as such. It's a matter of discovering one has a liking and a talent for working with words and developing it by hard work. A woman once asked Robert Frost when he decided to become a poet. He replied, 'When did you decide to become a beautiful woman?' It just happens, but you can help the process a little.

"I run my business the way a businessman runs his—going to work at 8:30 a.m., quitting at 4:30 p.m. But it's not that simple. Magic either happens or doesn't happen. There are traps in writing for young people, and one of these is the temptation to preach. I hope that I do not suffer from this disease in its severest form; I feel sure that I do not, since there are few things of which I myself feel certain and not many topics on which I could care to write a sermon."[1]

1980. Awarded the Southern California Council on Literature for Children and Young People prize for a "notable body of work." Remarked Bonham: "Young people today are concerned about far more things than was my generation. They not only grow taller today, they are taller inside, their minds keener and more skeptical. Yet they are not adults, and the same child who lists *Cyrano de Bergerac* as her favorite play, and thinks *The Odyssey* simply groovy, may still be reading Nancy Drew.

"How do you write for such a creature as this?

"The question perplexes me every time I start a new story. Is the protagonist's problem a young child's, or an adolescent's? Is it universal enough to interest many readers, or only a few? Is it already old hat? Is my protagonist recognizable as a modern youth? Or is he so terribly modern that no one will recognize him two years from now?

"Sometimes lately I have wondered whether Man is not in the process of proving himself one of those experimental models Nature occasionally shelves among layers of fossilized ferns.

(Detail of a jacket illustration by Arthur Shilston from *Speedway Contender* by Frank Bonham.)

"With me, however, and I think with many writers, an experience is never complete until I have told someone about it. I am not a raconteur, merely a blurter. Yet this urge to blurt seems somehow to underly my need and desire to write. Asked which he had found harder to learn, to write or to live, Somerset Maugham replied: 'Let me say that I have never enjoyed living and I have always enjoyed writing.'

". . . I believe that most people do the bulk of their reading in their teens; that, just as they often overfeed their bodies once they achieve marriage, so they seem to starve their minds at the same time. It is important therefore to have an adequate range of literary staples for the young who are still in their prime reading years. Yet the minority child is offered too little that he will recognize as relevant to his world, his special problems, himself.

"The fact that many of these youngsters are poor readers does not mean that one should engage in baby-talk in writing for them. I make little conscious effort to simplify my vocabulary. Nor do I scamp my work, for 'disadvantaged' does not mean 'dumb.' As Daniel Fader writes in *Hooked on Books*, 'Semi-literate readers do not need semiliterate books. . . . The child . . . is immeasurably better off with books that are too difficult for him than books that are too easy.'"

Writers that Bonham admires include: "Conrad, Simenon, Ruth Rendell, Ngaio Marsh, Nicholas Freeling, a number of British mystery writers, a few American mystery writers. Maupassant and Flaubert, and a great many lesser writers I read in between classical experiences."

When not writing, Bonham enjoys exercising and running because "I know it keeps my mind more alive."[1] He collects shells and first editions and enjoys yard work and agriculture.

When asked to give advice to would-be-authors, Bonham responded: "I would advise an aspiring writer to find a subject that interests him/her and research it in depth, in the field, not only in books. Their interest in the story they are planning will be quickened, they will find characters with which to populate the story, dialogue, up-to-date factual material. I would suggest reading Conrad and Flannery O'Connor in order to learn how detail brings a scene to life. I myself have to take notes and transfer them to file cards in order to impress them on my memory. I would keep in mind Matthew Arnold's line, 'Tasks in hours of insight will'd. Can be through hours of gloom fulfill'd.' Writing is not easy for me."

1986. "I have been at work on a mystery novel *To Find the Queen* for two years, and expect to finish it soon.

"I am much less introverted and self-centered than I was when I wrote most of the earlier autobiographical things—thank heaven. A late bloomer, I feel as though I have at last joined the world of people."

Bonham's works are included in the Kerlan Collection at the University of Minnesota.

HOBBIES AND OTHER INTERESTS: Classical music, exercise, running, collecting first editions, horseback riding, "mountain hiking," and woodworking.

FOR MORE INFORMATION SEE: Horn Book, February, 1966; *Library Journal,* September 15, 1966, July, 1970; *New York Times Book Review,* April 14, 1968, August 25, 1968, August 8, 1971, November 10, 1974, January 9, 1977, December 30, 1979; *Book World,* May 5, 1968, October 6, 1968; *Commonweal,* May 24, 1968; *Young Readers' Review,* September, 1968, November, 1968, October, 1969; *Children's Book World,* November 3, 1968; *Saturday Review,* August 16, 1969, November 13, 1971; Martha E. Ward and Dorothy A. Marquardt, *Authors of Books for Young People,* 2nd edition, Scarecrow, 1971; Doris de Montreville and Donna Hill, *Third Book of Junior Authors.* H. W. Wilson, 1972; Lee Bennett Hopkins, *More Books by More People,* Citation Press, 1974; *The Writer,* September, 1974; *Elementary English,* September, 1974; D. L. Kirkpatrick, *Twentieth-Century Children's Writers,* St. Martin's Press, 1978; *Contemporary Literary Criticism,* Volume XII, Gale, 1980.

BORN, Adolf   1930-

PERSONAL: Born June 12, 1930, in Ceske, Velenice, Czechoslovakia; son of Antonin (a railway employee) and Marie (a homemaker; maiden name, Dudova) Born; married Emilie Kayáková (a homemaker), August, 25, 1961; children: Erika. *Education:* Attended Academy of Fine Arts, Prague, 1955. *Religion:* Catholic. *Home and studio:* 14000 Prague 4, M. Cibulkové 9, Czechoslovakia. *Agent:* Dilia, Divadelni a Literarni Agentura, Praha 2, Vysehradska 28, Czechoslovakia.

CAREER: Free-lance illustrator, 1955—. Works on animated films and graphics. *Exhibitions:* Has had over 190 exhibitions in Europe and overseas, including Prague, Czechoslovakia, 1959, 1962, 1965, 1971, 1975, 1977, 1978, and 1985; Lucerne, Switzerland, 1981, 1985; Bremen, West Germany, Gabrovo, Bulgaria, Brno, Czechoslovakia, and Baden-Baden, Germany, all 1981; Konstanz, West Germany, Nuremberg, West Germany, and Vienna, Austria, all 1982; Berlin, Germany, 1983; Hameln, West Germany, 1986.

AWARDS, HONORS: Gold medal from the International Exposition of Illustrations, Leipzig, Germany, 1964, for Bertolt Brecht's *Mother Courage,* and 1976, for Daniel Defoe's *Robinson Crusoe;* prize from the Museum of Modern Art, Skopje, Yugoslavia, 1970, for a collection of cartoons; Cena Nakladatelství Albatros Prize for outstanding book of the Year, 1971, in illustration, for *Míta sám na svete* (title means "Mitya Alone in the World"), 1972, in graphic design, for *Oli, tvuj kamarád z Islandu* (title means "Oli, Your Friend from Iceland"), *Míta sám na svete,* and *Zatoulané písmenko* (title means "The Lost Letter"), and 1974, in illustration, for *Jak jel Vítek do Prahy* (title means "How Little Vitek Went to Prague") and *Vítek je zase doma* (title means "Vitek Is Home Again"); Cartoonist of the Year, Montreal, 1974; *Svete div se* (title means "World, Be Astonished") was chosen one of the "Most Beautiful Books of the Year" in Czechoslovakia, 1974; first prize for animated film, Melbourne, Australia, 1976; Prémie Ceského Literarního Fondu from Czech Literature Foundation, 1978, for *Aprílová skola* (title means "The April School"); Golden Aesop, Bulgaria, 1979, for humour in the graphic arts (lithographs); Golden Apple from Bienále of Illustrations Bratislava, 1979, for *Akadémia pána Machul'ku* (title means "The Academy of Mr. Klecks"); first prize for animated film, "Minderwertigkeits Komplex," Ottawa, Canada and Bilbao, Spain, 1982; International Board on Books for Young People high commendation for illustrations for children, 1986.

WRITINGS—Self-illustrated: *Die Liebe Liebe* (title means, "Loving Love"), Heye Verlag, 1979; *Bilderbuch der Reisekunst* (title means, "Picturebook of the Art of Traveling"), Gerstenberg Verlag, 1985; *Born's Tierreich* (title means, "Born's Animal Kingdom"), Gerstenberg Verlag, 1986.

ADOLF BORN

(From the Czechoslovakian translation of Daniel Defoe's *Robinson Crusoe*. Illustrated by Adolf Born.)

Illustrator: Milos Macourek, *Curious Tales,* translated by Marie Burg, Oxford University Press, 1980.

Also illustrator of over 150 books in Czechoslovakia, including Vera Adlová, *Mirka to ví nejlíp* (title means "Mirka Knows Best"), SNDK (Czechoslovakia), 1964; Jens Sigsgaars, *Míta sám na svete* (title means "Mitya Alone in the World"), Albatros (Czechoslovakia), 1971; Oldrich Syrovátka, *Zatoulané písmenko* (title means "The Lost Letter"), Albatros, 1972; Helena Kadecková, *Oli, tvuj kamarád z Islandu* (title means "Oli, Your Friend from Iceland"), Albatros, 1972; Bohumil Ríha, *Jak jel Vítek do Prahy* (title means "How Little Vitek Went to Prague"), Albatros, 1973; B. Ríha, *Vítek je zase doma* (title means "Vitek Is Home Again"), Albatros, 1974; Milos Macourek, *Svete div se* (title means "World, Be Astonished"), Albatros, 1974; Jan Brzechwa, *Akadémia pána Machul'ku* (title means "The Academy of Mr. Klecks"), Mladé letá (Bratislava), 1978; Jiri Zácek, *Aprílová skola* (title means "The April School"), Albatros, 1978.

WORK IN PROGRESS: Illustrations for Edgar Allan Poe's stories, Arthur Conan Doyle's Sherlock Holmes stories, and Milos Macourek's modern fairytales; "Zofka" (title means "Sophie"), a cartoon film in seven parts about a clever monkey from a zoo.

SIDELIGHTS: Born grew up in Prague where he attended local schools and the Academy of Fine Arts. He began painting and illustrating when he was about seventeen years old. Upon completion of his education he became a free-lance artist specializing in illustration and graphics, and two years later held his first exhibition in Prague. In 1962 he began collaborating on animated films.

A great love for books since childhood, Born remembers *Robinson Crusoe* as one of his favorites, which he has since illustrated twice and adapted into a puppet film.

He has done about fifty animated films, the latest a four-part cartoon film for children about two children and a dog entitled "Mach and Sebestová." He has traveled in Europe, the United States, Canada, India and other places.

"I like to illustrate books with a fine, intellectual humour."

HOBBIES AND OTHER INTERESTS: Travelling, a hat and cap collection.

CARTLIDGE, Michelle 1950-

PERSONAL: Born October 13, 1950, in London, England; daughter of Haydn Derrick (director of transportation) and Barbara (director of a gallery; maiden name, Feistmann) Cartlidge; married Richard Cook (an artist), June 25, 1982; children: Theo. *Education:* Attended Hornsey College of Art, 1967-68, and Royal College of Art, 1968-70. *Agent:* Laura Cecil, 17 Alwyne Villas, London N1 2HG England.

CAREER: Artist, 1970—; writer and illustrator of books for children. *Member:* Society of Authors. *Awards, honors:* Mother Goose Award from Books for Your Children Booksellers, 1979, for *Pippin and Pod.*

WRITINGS—Self-illustrated children's books: *Pippin and Pod,* Pantheon, 1978; *The Bears' Bazaar* (craft book), Lothrop, 1979; *A Mouse's Diary,* Lothrop, 1981; *Mousework,* Heine-

MICHELLE CARTLIDGE

mann, 1982; *Teddy Trucks,* Heinemann, 1981, Lothrop, 1982; *Little Boxes* (cut-out book), Heinemann, 1983; *Dressing Teddy* (cut-out book), Heinemann, 1983, Penguin, 1986; *Munch and Mixer's Puppet Show,* Prentice-Hall, 1983; *Baby Mouse,* Heinemann, 1984, Penguin, 1986; *Teddy's Holiday,* Heinemann, 1984; *Mouse's Christmas Tree,* Penguin, 1985; *Teddy's Birthday Party,* Penguin, 1985; *Little Shops,* Heinemann, 1985; *Bears Room No Peeping,* Methuen, 1985; *Teddy's Dinner,* Simon & Schuster, 1986; *Teddy's Garden,* Simon & Schuster, 1986; *Teddy's House,* Simon & Schuster, 1986; *Teddy's Toys,* Simon & Schuster, 1986; *Teddy's Christmas,* Simon & Schuster, 1986; *A House for Lily Mouse,* Methuen, 1987; *Playground Bunnies,* Walker Books, 1987; *Seaside Bunnies,* Walker Books, 1987; *Toy Shop Bunnies,* Walker Books, 1987; *Birthday Bunnies,* Walker Books, 1987.

SIDELIGHTS: "I am a self-taught illustrator. I left school at fourteen to be apprenticed to a pottery studio in London. At sixteen, I enrolled in a pottery course at Hornsey School of Art and a year later, I moved to the Royal College of Art.

"When I was twenty, I gave up pottery to draw. I felt that the work I was doing was becoming so fragile that I was the only person who could touch it with safety. I tried to transfer my love of detail to my drawing.

"To support myself, I did odd jobs, waitressing and washing up, but had the opportunity to show publisher and illustrator, Jan Pienkowski, a selection of cards I'd produced for my family and friends. This resulted in a commission to design a series of cards for Gallery Five.

"My first picture book *Pippin and Pod* was published by Heinemann in 1979 and I was fortunate enough to win the Mother Goose Award, a prize presented yearly to 'the most exciting newcomer to children's book illustration.' My next picture books were well-received too. Although I like to tell stories about mice and bears, my books are based on real life. For example, the school in *The Bears' Bazaar* was based on the primary school I attended as a child.

"When planning a book, I like to decide on a location, do lots of sketches, and develop the story from them. The amount of detail I include appeals to children, and Theo, my small son, takes a lively and useful interest in my work. I find him a most useful critic.

"I do my best to create a world that a child will recognize, the kind of book he or she can step into to mingle with the characters portrayed. As well as picture books, I have designed a series of cut-out books so that children who have enjoyed reading about my characters can meet them again in active play."

HOBBIES AND OTHER INTERESTS: Travel abroad.

back of Teddy's stand

Teddy's stand

(From *Teddy's Birthday Party: A Cut Out Model Book* by Michelle Cartlidge. Illustrated by the author.)

CLEAVER, Hylton Reginald   1891-1961
(Reginald Crunden)

PERSONAL: Born in 1891, in London, England; died September 9, 1961, in London, England.

CAREER: Author of books for boys, playwright, and journalist. *Evening Standard*, London, England, sports writer, 1937-60. *Military service:* Served in the British Army during World War I.

WRITINGS: The Tempting Thought, Mills & Boon, 1917; *Brother o' Mine: A School Story*, Oxford University Press, 1920; *The Sporting Spirit, and Other Stories*, G. Newnes, 1920; *The Harley First XI*, Oxford University Press, 1920; *Roscoe Makes Good: A Story of Harley*, Oxford University Press, 1921; *Captains of Harley: A School Story*, Oxford University Press, 1921; *On with the Motley*, Mills & Boon, 1922; *The Old Order: A Public School Story*, Oxford University Press, 1922; *The Harley First XV*, Oxford University Press, 1922; *Second Innings: A School Story*, Oxford University Press, 1924; *One Man's Job*, Collins, 1926; *Rugger! The Greatest Game*, Christophers, 1927; *The Greyminster Mystery*, Collins, 1927; *The Short Term at Greyminster*, Collins, 1928; *Fox-Bound: A Novel*, Hutchinson, 1928; *Captains of Greyminster*, Collins, 1929.

A House Divided, Collins, 1930; *The Term of Thrills*, F. Warne, 1931; *The Secret Service of Greyminster*, Collins, 1932; *The New Boy at Greyminster*, Collins, 1932; *Captains of Duke's*, F. Warne, 1933; *Buttle Butts In: A Story of Duke's*, F. Warne, 1933; *The Ghost of Greyminster*, Collins, 1933; *The Forbidden Study*, Collins, 1934, reissued, Childrens Press, 1955; *Boxing for Schools: How to Learn It and How to Teach It*, Methuen, 1934; *The Phantom Pen: A Story of Duke's School*,

Short shook a clenched fist in Kenneth's face. ■ (From "Something for the School," one of Hylton Cleaver's stories, illustrated by H. M. Brock and published in *Captain Magazine*.)

F. Warne, 1934; *They Were Not Amused*, Methuen, 1934; *The Haunted Holiday*, F. Warne, 1934; *The Happy Company*, [Dublin], 1934; *The Test Case*, Collins, 1934; *Gay Charade*, Methuen, 1934.

The Hidden Captain, F. Warne, 1935; *The Further Adventures of the Happy Company*, [Dublin], 1935; *The School That Couldn't Sleep*, F. Warne, 1936; *Double Room*, Methuen, 1936; *The Pilot Perfect*, F. Warne, 1937; *Leave It to Craddock*, F. Warne, 1937; *Sport Problems: One Hundred and Fifty Intricate Sports Questions and Authoritative Rulings*, F. Warne, 1937; *The Blaze at Baron's Royal*, F. Warne, 1938; *The Forgotten Term*, F. Warne, 1939; *The Knight of the Knuckles*, F. Warne, 1940; *Dawnay Leaves School*, F. Warne, 1947; *The Deputy Detective*, Bruce Publishing, 1947; *St. Benedict's Goes Back*, F. Warne, 1948; *Dead Man's Tale: A Detective Story*, F. Warne, 1949; *No Rest for Rusty*, F. Warne, 1949.

Lawson for Lord's, F. Warne, 1950; *Lucky Break*, F. Warne, 1950; *Captain of Two Schools*, F. Warne, 1950; *Sporting Rhapsody* (autobiography), Hutchinson, 1951; *Danger at the Ringside*, Hutchinson, 1952; *Dusty Ribbon*, F. Warne, 1952; *The Vengeance of Jeremy*, F. Warne, 1953; *Nizefela Makes a Name* (autobiography of Wilf White as told by Hylton Cleaver), Museum Press, 1955; *They've Won Their Spurs*, R. Hale, 1956; *A History of Rowing*, H. Jenkins, 1959, reissued, 1967; *Their Greatest Ride*, R. Hale, 1959; *Before I Forget* (autobiography), R. Hale, 1961.

Author of several produced stage plays. Contributor of serials, sometimes under pseudonym Reginald Crunden, to boys periodicals, including *Boy's Own Paper*, *Chums*, and *Captain*.

Hylton Cleaver during World War II.

SIDELIGHTS: English writer and journalist, Cleaver, was born in 1891 in London, England. Throughout his writing career he was known as an author of books for boys and a sports reporter for the *Evening Standard*, a London newspaper. "In the beginning, few men can have had less expectation of sporting rhapsody than I. At school I was not allowed to play games because of acute asthma. I was short-sighted, weedy, and with such bad circulation that at my preparatory school my nose earned me the nickname 'Raspberry Tip.' At St. Paul's I became 'Paint-Brush' because my hair hung over my forehead in one limp lock. In particular I had the worst stutter imaginable; not just an impediment in speech which held up for a while the give and take of conversation; I was practically dumb. Masters gave up oral questions in form; I was not required to do more than nod to my name at roll-call. . . .

"When you stutter as badly as this you use all manner of devices to avoid starting a sentence with a hard consonant— but nothing can escape having to state your name when asked, and Cleaver was always beyond me. All I got out was a succession of k's. People would try to help by saying for me the words they thought I was trying to say for myself, and they were always wrong. This only annoys a stutterer, who redoubles his efforts to proclaim his real thoughts and so sinks more deeply into trouble, which is more embarrassing than ever to his friends. It is a curious fact that stutterers are never so abashed at their own inarticulation as are those to whom they are trying to speak. And, agonizing as asthma is, it is never quite so distressing to suffer as to watch and hear. Basically, asthma is comparable with a horse that roars as it runs. And in my early efforts to run I would make just such a noise, causing others to wonder why I caused myself such unnecessary suffering.

"Being denied most games in school-days, I formed the opinion that the cure was perhaps not coddling but counter-attack. So in my last term at St. Paul's I did begin to play rugby— unknown to my people—though I was so short-sighted that I scored my first try on the twenty-five-yard line instead of the proper place. After I had left school I decided to develop this policy, so I next took up boxing, and had a course of private lessons from Jerry Driscoll in the school gym; feeling better rather than worse, I next tried rowing, because these seemed to me the toughest sports of the lot. And it may encourage others who experience an equally disheartening beginning to know that, although I was never very good, I did eventually play rugby for Middlesex; I did row in the Grand Challenge Cup at Henley, besides going to Yugo-Slavia to coach their eight; and I was vice-captain of Belsize Boxing Club for eight years.

"At my prep school at Putney I was told to report for choir practice, but after I had rendered a few bars the music master made his one and only comment. 'You had better stand among the basses, Cleaver, where you'll do least harm.' On my mother's side they were all musical, and on my father's all were artistic. I could not draw or sing. I took the middle path and became the only writer on the family tree.

"At the time of the First World War I was still stuttering, but sport was beginning to overcome the asthma, so I presented myself as a potential recruit to the Sportsman's battalion of the Royal Fusiliers. We bought our own uniforms in the Strand, drilled at the Hotel Cecil, and an interesting lot the others were. In my platoon were Charlie McGahey, the Essex and England cricketer; Harry Packer, Welsh Rugby selector; and Patsy Cokeley, a professional middle-weight boxer from Limehouse. We all became great friends. In France, in fact, Patsy and I used to start boxing whenever we came out of the line simply for relaxation. Many who were sick of fighting by that time thought us quite incomprehensible.

"Well, having been told by all concerned that I was mad to go into the army at all, and that in any case I should have to remain a private because I could never stand out in front and give an order, I went overseas and stayed with the Sportsman's Battalion until nearly all the friends with whom I had joined had been killed, sent home unfit, or commissioned. By this time I was a Mills bomb specialist and was induced to take stripes chiefly to lead raids. Everyone was very helpful and promised that if I got out in front and made whatever sounds I cared to, they would carry out the order I would obviously have in mind.

"Fortunately I was not by this time so bad in speech as I had been. Physical training, open air, and tough living had built me up, relieving me largely of asthma, and so making articulation more a matter of timing and confidence than of physical imperfection. I took my chance and got away with it so successfully that I was even persuaded to go for a commission, which I did, and which I received.

"I began writing during the First World War when one was generally either bored or frightened, and wanted to take one's mind off the immediate present. I could not then typewrite, and in any case had no typewriter, so everything was written in longhand, and laboriously, either on my knees and in the trenches, or on some makeshift table in a barn. I would then write it out all over again, with corrections, and send it home. Because my school-days had not been very full, but were still a lively memory, I started on school stories. I suppose my instinct then was to write about the good times I would liked to have had.

"In peace-time I developed the art of the short story, and a glance at the bookstalls today shows how completely public taste and the supply of magazines have changed. There is nothing remotely like those collections of short stories which sold so well as *Pearsons Magazine*, *The London*, *The Royal*, *The Twenty Story*, *Cassells*, *The Novel*, and, indeed, *The Strand*. . . .

"I published seven novels and had three plays produced, but I had already such close contacts with sportsmen that I began to discover a market also for diary paragraphs and articles in weekly journals. As time went on it struck me that free-lance writing was all very well so long as one kept health and strength, but that in the event of illness there was nobody who would care how one existed or feel any responsibility as an employer. For that reason I joined the staff of a newspaper, and except for the period of the Second World War have stayed with that newspaper ever since." [Hylton Cleaver, *Sporting Rhapsody*, Hutchinson's Library of Sports and Pastimes, 1951.[1]]

Cleaver retired from the London newspaper a year before his death in London in 1961. His many books included two autobiographies, nonfiction books on boxing, rugby, and rowing, several plays and fiction books for boys.

FOR MORE INFORMATION SEE: Brian Doyle, editor, *Who's Who of Children's Literature*, Schocken Books, 1968; W. O. G. Lofts and D. J. Adley, *The Men behind Boys' Fiction*, H. Baker, 1970.

A wise son maketh a glad father: but a foolish son is the heaviness of his mother.

—Proverbs 10:1

COATSWORTH, Elizabeth 1893-1986

OBITUARY NOTICE—See sketch in *SATA* volume 2: Born May 31, 1893, in Buffalo, N.Y.; died August 31 (one source cites September 2), 1986, in Nobleboro, Me.; buried in Hall Cemetery, Nobleboro, Me. Poet and author of prose works for children and adults. Coatsworth became known for her children's books, which include the Newbery Medal-winning *Cat Who Went to Heaven*. A world traveller, she was an authority on the Orient while still in her twenties; her first book, *Fox Footprints*, was a volume of poetry employing oriental themes. Throughout her career verse continued to play a part, appearing in prose works such as *Cat Who Went to Heaven* and *Away Goes Sally*. Rural New England life was another element of Coatsworth's books, serving as the setting for the critically praised *Country Neighborhood* and *Maine Ways*, among others. Coatsworth's writings also include the novels *Here I Stay* and *The Trunk* as well as *A Personal Geography: Almost an Autobiography*.

FOR MORE INFORMATION SEE: Children's Literature Review, Volume 2, Gale, 1976; *Contemporary Authors, New Revision Series*, Volume 4, Gale, 1981; *Dictionary of Literary Biography*, Volume 22: *American Writers for Children, 1900-1960*, Gale, 1983; *The Oxford Companion to Children's Literature*, Oxford University Press, 1984. Obituaries: *Portland Press Herald*, September 2, 1986; *New York Times*, September 3, 1986; *Facts on File*, September 5, 1986; *Publishers Weekly*, September 19, 1986.

JOANNA COLE

COLE, Joanna 1944-
(Ann Cooke)

PERSONAL: Born August 11, 1944, in Newark, N.J.; daughter of Mario and Elizabeth (Reid) Basilea; married Philip A. Cole (a psychotherapist), October 8, 1965; children: Rachel Elizabeth. *Education:* Attended University of Massachusetts at Amherst and Indiana University—Bloomington; City College of New York (now City College of the City University of New York), B.A., 1967. *Home:* New York, N.Y. *Office:* 171 West 79th St., New York, N.Y. 10024.

CAREER: New York City Board of Education, New York City, elementary school librarian, 1967-68; *Newsweek*, New York City, letters correspondent, 1968-71; Scholastic, Inc., New York City, associate editor of See-Saw Book Club, 1971-73; Doubleday & Co., Garden City, N.Y., senior editor of books for young readers, 1973-80; full-time writer, 1980—. *Member:* Authors Guild, Society of Children's Book Writers, American Association for the Advancement of Science.

AWARDS, HONORS: All of Cole's science books have been named Outstanding Science Trade Books for Children by the joint committee of the National Science Teachers Association and the Children's Book Council; *Cockroaches* was selected one of Child Study Association of America's Children's Books of the Year, 1971, *Giraffes at Home* and *Twins: The Story of Multiple Births*, 1972, *My Puppy Is Born* and *Plants in Winter*, 1973, *Dinosaur Story*, 1974, *A Calf Is Born*, 1975, and *Large as Life: Daytime Animals, Large as Life: Nighttime Animals*, and *The New Baby at Your House*, 1985; *School Library Journal* selected *Fleas* for its Best Books of the Year list, 1973, *A Horse's Body* and *A Snake's Body*, 1981, *Bony-Legs* and *Cars and How They Go*, 1983; *A Chick Hatches* was selected for the Children's Book Showcase of the Children's Book Council, 1977; New York Academy of Sciences Children's Science honor book, 1981, and Children's Choice of the joint committee of the International Reading Association and the Children's Book Council, 1982, both for *A Snake's Body*; Golden Kite Honor Book Award, and selected as a Notable Children's Book by the Association for Library Service to Children, both 1984, for *How You Were Born*.

WRITINGS—Juvenile fiction: *Cousin Matilda and the Foolish Wolf*, A. Whitman, 1970; *The Secret Box*, Morrow, 1971; *Fun on Wheels* (illustrated by Whitney Darrow), Morrow, 1976; *The Clown-Arounds* (illustrated by Jerry Smath), Parents Magazine Press, 1981; (editor and author of introduction) *Best-Loved Folktales of the World* (illustrated by Jill K. Schwarz), Doubleday, 1982; *The Clown-Arounds Have a Party* (illustrated by J. Smath), Parents Magazine Press, 1982; *Golly Gump Swallowed a Fly* (illustrated by Bari Weissman), Parents Magazine Press, 1982; *Get Well, Clown-Arounds!* (illustrated by J. Smath), Parents Magazine Press, 1982; *The Clown-Arounds Go on Vacation* (illustrated by J. Smath), Parents Magazine Press, 1983; *Aren't You Forgetting Something, Fiona?* (illustrated by Ned Delaney), Parents Magazine Press, 1983; *Bony-Legs* (ALA Notable Book; illustrated by Dirk Zimmer), Four Winds, 1983; *Sweet Dreams, Clown-Arounds* (illustrated by J. Smath), Parents Magazine Press, 1985; *Monster Manners* (illustrated by Jared Lee), Scholastic, 1986; *This Is the Place for Me* (illustrated by William Van Horn), Scholastic, 1986; *Doctor Change* (illustrated by Donald Carrick), Morrow, 1986; *Monster Movie* (illustrated by J. Lee), Scholastic, 1987; *Norma Jean, Jumping Bean* (illustrated by Lynn Munsinger), Random House, 1987.

Juvenile nonfiction; all published by Morrow, except where indicated: *Cockroaches* (illustrated by Jean Zallinger), 1971;

(From "Disobedience" by A. A. Milne in *A New Treasury of Children's Poetry: Old Favorites and New Discoveries*, selected by Joanna Cole. Illustrated by Judith Gwyn Brown.)

DOCTOR CHANGE

Written by JOANNA COLE   *Illustrated by* DONALD CARRICK

WILLIAM MORROW & COMPANY

(Jacket illustration by Donald Carrick from *Doctor Change* by Joanna Cole.)

(under pseudonym Ann Cooke) *Giraffes at Home* (illustrated by Robert Quackenbush), Crowell, 1972; (with Madeleine Edmondson) *Twins: The Story of Multiple Births* (illustrated by Salvatore Raciti), 1972; *Plants in Winter* (illustrated by Kazue Mizumura), Crowell, 1973; *My Puppy Is Born* (illustrated with photographs by Jerome Wexler; Children's Book Club choice), 1973; *Fleas* (illustrated by Elsie Wrigley), 1973; *Dinosaur Story* (illustrated by Mort Kunstler), 1974; *A Calf Is Born* (illustrated with photographs by J. Wexler), 1975; *A Chick Hatches* (ALA Notable Book; illustrated with photographs by J. Wexler), 1976; *Saber-Toothed Tiger and Other Ice-Age Mammals* (illustrated by Lydia Rosier), 1977; *A Fish Hatches* (illustrated with photographs by J. Wexler), 1978; (with J. Wexler) *Find the Hidden Insect,* 1979.

A Frog's Body (ALA Notable Book; illustrated with photographs by J. Wexler), 1980; *A Horse's Body* (ALA Notable Book; illustrated with photographs by J. Wexler), 1981; *A Snake's Body* (ALA Notable Book; *Horn Book* honor list; illustrated with photographs by J. Wexler), 1981; *A Cat's Body* (*Horn Book* honor list; Junior Literary Guild selection; illustrated with photographs by J. Wexler), 1982; *A Bird's Body* (Junior Literary Guild selection; illustrated with photographs by J. Wexler), 1982; *Cars and How They Go* (ALA Notable Book; illustrated by Gail Gibbons), Crowell, 1983; *How You*

Were Born (ALA Notable Book), 1984; *An Insect's Body* (illustrated with photographs by J. Wexler and Raymond A. Mendez), 1984.

The New Baby at Your House (illustrated with photographs by Hella Hammid), 1985; *Cuts, Breaks, Bruises, and Burns: How Your Body Heals* (illustrated by True Kelly), Crowell, 1985; *Large as Life: Daytime Animals* (illustrated by Kenneth Lilly), Knopf, 1985; *Large as Life: Nighttime Animals* (illustrated by K. Lilly), Knopf, 1985; *A Dog's Body* (illustrated with photographs by Jim and Ann Monteith), 1985; *Hungry, Hungry Sharks* (illustrated by Patricia Wynne), Random House, 1986; *The Magic School Bus at the Waterworks* (illustrated by Bruce Degen), Scholastic, 1986; *The Human Body: How We Evolved* (illustrated by Walter Gaffney-Kessell), 1987; *Evolution* (illustrated by Aliki), Crowell, 1987.

Other: *The Parents TM Book of Toilet Teaching,* Ballantine, 1983; (editor) *A New Treasury of Children's Poetry: Old Favorites and New Discoveries* (illustrated by Judith Gwyn Brown), Doubleday, 1983; (editor with Stephanie Calmenson) *The Laugh Book* (illustrated by Marylin Hafner; juvenile; anthology), Doubleday, 1986. Contributor of articles to *Parents.*

ADAPTATIONS: ''Bony-Legs'' (cassette), Random House, 1985.

The cat gave Sasha a silver mirror. ■ (From *Bony-Legs* by Joanna Cole. Illustrated by Dirk Zimmer.)

WORK IN PROGRESS: The Magic School Bus inside the Earth to be illustrated by Bruce Degen and published by Scholastic; *The Read-Aloud Treasury for Young Children,* co-edited with Stephanie Calmenson, to be illustrated by Ann Schweninger and published by Doubleday; *A Gift from Saint Francis: The First Crèche,* to be illustrated by Michele Lemieux and published by Morrow; *Asking about Sex and Growing Up* for Morrow; *Animal Sleepyheads One to Ten* to be illustrated by Jenni Bassett and published by Scholastic.

SIDELIGHTS: Born August 11, 1944 in Newark, New Jersey. ''I discovered in the fifth grade what I liked to do: write reports and stories, make them interesting and/or funny and draw pictures to go along with the words. Except for the pictures, I still do that. I remember grade school very clearly when I sat

at my desk, happily interested in whatever subject I was writing about. Science was my favorite. Our teacher, Miss Bair, would assign us to read a science trade book every week. And each week, she would choose one student to do an experiment and report on it to the class. I would have done an experiment every week if she had let me. Grade school was very important to me, much more influential than my later education. Maybe that's why as an adult I ended up writing books for children.

''My first job was as a library-teacher in a Brooklyn elementary school for one year. Toward the end of that year, 1968, my father told me about an article he had read in the *Wall Street Journal* about, of all things, cockroaches. It got me thinking about all those science books I'd read as a kid (insects had been a special interest of mine), and it occurred to me that

Just at that moment, Golly yawned.... ∎ (From *Golly Gump Swallowed a Fly* by Joanna Cole. Illustrated by Bari Weissman.)

In about six months, this baby chick will be a full-grown chicken. ■ (From *A Chick Hatches* by Joanna Cole. Photograph by Jerome Wexler.)

there wasn't one about cockroaches. I wrote a letter to a publisher proposing the idea. An editor wrote back saying she would be interested in seeing what I would do with the subject. For months, I spent every spare moment working on the book. I read just about everything written in English about roaches. I was really quite an expert by the time I mailed in the manuscript.

"Now imagine how I felt when I got the manuscript back with a letter from another editor at the publisher saying, 'We are so sorry but . . .' It seems the house was already doing a book on roaches. I was devastated, but immediately sent the manuscript to William Morrow, where Connie Epstein accepted it and became my first editor. Her guidance was invaluable to me as I developed as a science writer.

"I began doing books about animal birth with the photographer Jerome Wexler and from those books grew the idea for my series on animals' bodies, which are really studies of adaptation and morphology, that is, the form and structure of a living animal as they relate to the animal's way of life.

"While I was working on _A Snake's Body,_ I called the American Museum of Natural History to ask some questions. I live a block away from the Museum, and one of their experts offered to come to my apartment to talk. He and I were sitting in the living room talking about snakes, and Taffy, my Yorkshire terrier was sleeping at our feet. Yorkies are very feisty and unpredictable, and Taffy is kind of a nut. Suddenly, the expert said, 'I thought maybe you'd like to see this,' and pulled a snake skin from his briefcase. In an instant, Taffy leaped up, grabbed the skin right out of his hands and ran off with it. I was mortified, but we never saw that snake skin again."

Cole does not illustrate her books, but her works are consistently praised for their marriage of text to art work. "I often make a dummy as I write. I want to be sure that there isn't too much text on a given page and the words will be reflected in the pictures. When I do _The Magic School Bus_ books, which combine science and humor, I write the text and the word balloons for the pictures at the same time and paste them into a dummy as I go. Even though I get very involved in the pictures, I don't want to interfere with the artist's imagination."

In addition to children's books, Cole writes parenting books and articles for _Parents_ magazine. _How You Were Born_ grew out of both her children's books on animal birth and her adult writing for parents. "Kids are curious about what happens during childbirth. They are always saying, 'Tell me about when I was born.' Sure, they're interested in the facts, but underneath is a desire to be told that they were cherished from the very beginning. In _How You Were Born,_ I wanted to convey scientific information, but my main concern was with children's emotions. It was easy to write that book because I simply imagined that I was talking to the reader the way I talk to my own child. I'm using this same method now as I write a book about sexuality for seven- to ten-year-olds."

In recent years, Cole has added many works of fiction to her long list of nonfiction. Two of these stories were inspired by an anthology of two hundred tales she put together in 1980, _Best-Loved Folktales of the World. Bony-Legs_ is an easy-reader based on a Russian Baba Yaga tale, and _Doctor Change_ is a variation on the sorcerer's apprentice theme. "I like to write about interesting bad guys. I like the villains to be really mean and strong, much stronger than the hero or heroine. But their brute power makes the villains obtuse. When I read _Doctor

Change to kids, there's a scene in which the doctor says to the boy, Tom, 'A stupid boy like you can't get away from me!' I ask the kids if they think Tom is really stupid or not. They have already noticed many ways in which Tom is clever, but Doctor Change has not. He is the one who is stupid, for underestimating Tom.

"In so many folktales, the hero wins, not because he is strong, but because he is able to reach out to others for help, something the greedy, selfish villain cannot do. The hero can also change and develop, and so he can accomplish things at the end of the story that seemed impossible at the beginning. The same thing happens with children as they grow, and that is why children love folktales so much. It is also a main theme of my life; I consistently try to do things in my writing and in my life that are all but impossible. On one level, I am pleased with my work; on another level, dissatisfied. My response to this situation is simply to keep trying and keep doing; that's the only way to grow."

FOR MORE INFORMATION SEE: Horn Book, October, 1980, February, 1982; Sally Holmes Holtze, editor, _Fifth Book of Junior Authors and Illustrators,_ H. W. Wilson, 1983; _Washington Post Book World,_ September 8, 1984.

COLEMAN, William L(eRoy)   1938-

PERSONAL: Born September 25, 1938, in Barkhill, Md.; son of Marion Oscar (a government employee) and Novella (Fringer) Coleman; married Patricia Ann Marshall, August 25, 1962; children: Mary Elizabeth, James Marshall, June Christine. _Education:_ Washington Bible College, B.A., 1962; Grace Theological Seminary, M.Div., 1965. _Politics:_ "Mobile." _Home:_ 1115 9th St., Aurora, Neb. 68818. _Office:_ Professional Building, Aurora, Neb. 68818.

CAREER: Ordained Baptist minister, 1966; pastor of Baptist church in St. Clair Shores, Mich., 1965-70, Mennonite Church in Sterling, Kan., 1970-73, and Evangelical Free Church in Aurora, Neb., 1973-75; writer, 1975—. _Awards, honors:_ Gold Medallion Book Award, children's book category, from Evangelical Christian Publishers Association, 1981, for _The Who, What, When, Where Book about the Bible._

WRITINGS—Juvenile, except as noted; published by Bethany House, except as noted: _Lord, Sometimes I Need Help_ (adult), Hawthorn, 1976; _Counting Stars,_ Bethany Fellowship, 1976; _Those Pharisees_ (adult), Hawthorn, 1977; _My Magnificent Machine,_ 1978; _Understanding Suicide_ (adult), Cook, 1979; _On Your Mark,_ 1979; _Listen to the Animals,_ 1979.

More about My Magnificent Machine, 1980; _Engaged_ (young adult), Tyndale, 1980; _Far Out Facts about the Bible,_ Cook, 1980; _Letters from Dad_ (young adult), Broadman, 1980; _Today I Feel Like a Warm Fuzzy_ (illustrated by Koechel and Peterson), 1980; _The Who, What, When, Where Book about the Bible_ (illustrated by Dwight Walles), Cook, 1980; _Chesapeake Charlie and the Bank Robbers,_ 1980; _The Good Night Book,_ 1980; _My Hospital Book_ (illustrated by D. Walles), 1981; _Singing Penguins and Puffed-up Toads,_ 1981; _Chesapeake Charlie and Blackbeard's Treasure,_ 1981; _Chesapeake Charlie and the Stolen Diamonds,_ 1981; _Jesus, My Forever Friend_ (illustrated by Wayne Hanna), Cook, 1981; _The Sleep Tight Book,_ 1982; _Today I Feel Loved!,_ 1982; _Peter,_ Harvest House, 1982; _The Pharisee's Guide to Total Holiness_ (adult), 1982; _The Great Date Wait and Other Hazards_ (young adult), 1982; _Getting Ready for My First Day of School,_ 1983; _Today

WILLIAM L. COLEMAN

I Feel Shy, 1983; *What Children Need to Know When Parents Get Divorced*, 1983; *Courageous Christians* (illustrated by W. Hanna), Cook, 1983; *Chesapeake Charlie and the Haunted Ship*, 1983; *Making TV Work for Your Family*, 1983; *Today's Handbook of Bible Times and Customs*, 1984; *You Can Be Creative* (adult), Harvest House, 1984; *How, Why, When, Where*, Chariot Books, Books I and II, 1984, Books III and IV, 1985; *Earning Your Wings* (young adult), 1984; *Getting Ready for Our New Baby*, 1984; *Bernie Smithwick and the Super Red Ball*, Cook, 1984; *The Who, What, When, Where Bible Busy Book*, Cook, 1984; *Bernie Smithwick and the Purple Shoestring*, Cook, 1984.

Animals That Show and Tell, 1985; *The Newlywed Book*, 1985; *The Warm Hug Book*, 1985; *Before You Tuck Me In*, 1986; *Bouncing Back: Finding Acceptance in the Face of Rejection* (adult), Harvest House, 1986; *The Friendship Factory*, 1986; *It's Been a Good Year: The Anniversary Book* (adult), 1986; *A Measured Pace* (adult), 1986; *Knit Together* (adult), 1987; *Friends Forever* (young adult), 1987.

"Life Builders" series; all with Charles Colson; all published by Cook, 1986: *Being Good Isn't Easy; Guess Who's at My Party; Trouble in the School Yard; Watch Out for Becky.*

Also author of *The Palestine Herald* (illustrated by Paul Turnbaugh), four volumes published by Cook. Contributor of about ninety articles to Evangelical periodicals.

SIDELIGHTS: "I enjoy writing for two reasons, . . . for the fun of it . . . to help people by making the Christian faith easy to understand."

CONRAD, Pam(ela)   1947-

BRIEF ENTRY: Born June 18, 1947, in New York. Author of several books for elementary-grade readers, Conrad began writing at the age of seven during a bout with chicken pox. Her much-praised second book, *Prairie Songs* (Harper, 1985) received the International Reading Association Award, Western Writers of America Spur Award, and the Boston Globe-Horn Book Honor Book Award, among others. In this story, young Louisa, raised in a sod house on the Nebraska prairie, tells of the harshness, isolation, and beauty of the prairie at the turn of the century. "Conrad artfully deals with all the harsh facts in this fast-paced novel which leaves readers with a real feeling for the difficulties of pioneer life," according to *School Library Journal. Horn Book* noted that "the feeling for and love of the land and the emotional relationships between characters are magnificently created." Strong and clear writing, according to *Publishers Weekly*, draws one into *Holding Me Here* (Harper, 1986), in which fourteen-year-old Robin, daughter of divorced parents, tries to reunite a battered wife with her family. In the process, she realizes her own pain at her parents' separation. "A sad, powerful story of loves gone awry," observed *Booklist*. Conrad has also written *I Don't Live Here!* (Dutton, 1984) and *What I Did for Roman* (Harper, 1987). *Home:* 165 Morris Ave., Rockville Centre, N.Y. 11570.

FOR MORE INFORMATION SEE: Grand Island Daily Independent, December 19, 1985.

CRAIG, Helen   1934-

PERSONAL: Born August 30, 1934, in London, England; daughter of Edward (a writer and designer for theater and

HELEN CRAIG

films) and Helen (Godfrey) Craig; children: Ben Norland. *Education:* Attended King Alfred's School, London, England. *Home:* Vine Cottage, Harroell, Long Crendon, Aylesbury, Buckinghamshire HP18 9AQ, England.

CAREER: Gee & Watson (commercial photographers), London, England, apprentice, 1950-56; owner and operator of photographic studio in Hampstead, London, 1956-63; sculptor and artist in southern Spain, 1964-66; free-lance potter and photographer in London, 1967-69; illustrator of children's books, 1969—; Garland Compton (advertising agency), London, photographer, 1969-72; free-lance photographer, potter, and Chinese wallpaper restorer, 1972-74; OXFAM, Oxford, England, photographer, 1975-77. *Awards, honors: Animal Castle* was chosen one of Child Study Association of America's Children's Books of the Year, 1972; Award from Society of Illustrators (United States), 1977, for *The Mouse House ABC* foldout concertina; Kentucky Blue Grass Award from Northern Kentucky University, 1985, for *Angelina Ballerina.*

WRITINGS—"The Mouse House" series; foldout concertina books; all published by Random House: *The Mouse House ABC,* 1978; *. . . 123,* 1980; *. . . Months of the Year,* 1981; *. . . Days of the Week,* 1982.

Juvenile; self-illustrated: *A Number of Mice,* Aurum Press, 1978; *The Mouse Birthday and Address Book,* Aurum Press, 1982; *Susie and Alfred in the Knight, the Princess and the Dragon,* Random House, 1985; *Susie and Alfred in the Night of the Paper Bag Monsters,* Random House, 1985; *Susie and Alfred in a Welcome for Annie,* Knopf, 1986; *Susie and Alfred in a Busy Day in Town,* Knopf, 1986.

Illustrator: Robert Nye, *Wishing Gold,* Macmillan (England), 1970; Tanith Lee, *Animal Castle,* Farrar, Straus, 1972; T. Lee, *Princess Hynchatti and Some Other Surprises,* Macmillan, 1972; Katharine Holabird, *The Little Mouse Learning House: ABC,* Simon & Schuster, 1983; K. Holabird, *The Little Mouse Learning House: 123,* Simon & Schuster, 1983; K. Holabird, *Angelina Ballerina,* C. N. Potter, 1983; K. Holabird, *Angelina and the Princess,* C. N. Potter, 1984; K. Holabird, *Angelina at the Fair,* C. N. Potter, 1985; K. Holabird, *Angelina's Christmas,* C. N. Potter, 1985; Margaret Mahy, *JAM: A True Story,* Atlantic Monthly Press, 1985; Sarah Hayes, *This Is the Bear,* Harper, 1986; Judy Corbalis, *The Wrestling Princess and Other Stories,* Deutsch, 1986; K. Holabird, *Angelina on Stage,* C. N. Potter, 1986; K. Holabird, *Angelina's Birthday Address Book,* C. N. Potter, 1986.

Also illustrator of one story in *Stories for a Prince,* a compilation of stories written by children, Hamish Hamilton, 1983.

Contributor to *The Children's Book* (Save the Children—Famine in Africa Appeal), Walker, 1985.

WORK IN PROGRESS: Illustrating two more of Katharine Holabird's "Angelina" books; illustrating Nigel Gray's *The One and Only Robin Hood* and Blake Morrison's *The Yellow House,* both for Walker Books.

SIDELIGHTS: "It had always been my ambition that one day I would be a creative artist of some sort but I have only begun to achieve this quite late in life. Many of my family were and are artists. My grandfather was Edward Gordon Craig, well known for his revolutionary ideas and designs for the theater. He was also a brilliant wood engraver. His son (my father)

On the way home Susie wondered if Alfred loved her enough to save her from a dragon. ■ (From *Susie and Alfred in the Knight, the Princess and the Dragon* by Helen Craig. Illustrated by the author.)

and my brother are both excellent artists, too, and I felt rather overwhelmed by this wealth of talent around me.

"I bought Maurice Sendak's book, *Where the Wild Things Are,* for my small son, and that really gave me my direction. As a child I had been strongly impressed by the books I looked at and read, and I can still recall those feelings and try to remember them when I am working.

"I enjoy my work enormously and consider myself extremely lucky to be able to work at something I love and at the same time earn my living. But it is not always easy—many times it is a great struggle to produce one's best work.

"When I illustrate a book, I will first of all read through the story a number of times to really get the feel of it. Then, once I know how many pages will be in the final book, I go through the story marking out the passages where I feel a picture will compliment or extend the story in some way. Then I will make tiny images of each whole page putting in both the picture and the area for the words. This is very important for me as the area filled by the words should balance well with the picture so that the whole page presents an interesting composition. I like to get the feeling of the complete book before I start work and seeing it in miniature can be most helpful.

"Next I make a full-sized dummy of the book, putting in the words as near to the size of the final type as possible and this time working out the drawings more clearly, to show to the publisher, art director, writer, etc. Now I will start the final pictures. I may make two or three more roughs of each picture in order to get everything right before I transfer the final rough onto some thick water colour paper, using a very light pencil. I work in the basic design with a very fine pen and ink, then I will work into this with water colour. After this, I will go back and work up some of the pen lines to get more contrast. This can go on for a long time, alternating with colour line until I am satisfied. This is only one method. I have been experimenting with opaque colours such as gouache and I am hoping to experiment with other techniques later on.

"When I can afford it, I collect children's books and illustrated adult books, contemporary ones as well as those from the past. I work on illustrations and also try to find time for etching and ceramic sculpture."

DEAN, Karen Strickler 1923-

PERSONAL: Born November 24, 1923, in Los Angeles, Calif.; daughter of R. V. (a commercial artist and watercolor painter) and Laura (a teacher; maiden name, Ness) Strickler; married Ervin S. Dean, Jr. (an engineer), June 16, 1947; children: Pamela, Nathan C., Lucie Signa, Thomas S. *Education:* University of California, Los Angeles, B.A., 1946; San Jose State University, elementary teaching credential, 1973, specialist teaching credential, 1976, M.A., 1979. *Residence:* Palo Alto, Calif.

CAREER: Highland-Park News Herald, Los Angeles, Calif., reporter and society editor, 1943-45; Cutter Laboratories, Berkeley, Calif., advertising and publicity copywriter, 1946-47; University of California Press, Berkeley, publicity book jacket copywriter, 1947-49; Palo Alto Unified Schools, Palo Alto, Calif., instructional aide at Wilbur Middle School, 1974-76, volunteer creative writing teacher at Crescent Park Elementary School, 1975; Whisman School District, Mountain

KAREN STRICKLER DEAN

View, Calif., home teacher, 1974-77; Morland School District, San Jose, Calif., teacher of learning-disabled children, 1976-77; New Haven Unified School District, Union City, Calif., teacher of learning-disabled children at Alvarado Middle School, 1977-82, teacher of creative writing and school newspaper sponsor, 1979-81; writer, 1982—. *Member:* Society of Children's Book Writers, California Writers, Writers Connection, National Alliance for the Mentally Ill, Pi Lambda Theta. *Awards, honors:* Winner of numerous prizes in local writing competitions, including Christmas short-story contest in *Peninsula Living,* 1973, for "How Silently, How Silently."

WRITINGS: (Contributor) *Sullivan Reading Comprehension,* Books 5-20, Behavioral Research Labs, 1973; (contributor) Joanne Robinson Mitchell and Anne Libby Pyle, editors, *Prisms,* Heath, 1975; (contributor) *Independent Reading Skills Laboratory,* Educational Progress, 1976.

Young-adult novels: *Maggie Adams, Dancer,* Avon, 1980; *Mariana,* Avon, 1981; *Between Dances: Maggie Adams' Eighteenth Summer,* Avon, 1982; *A Time to Dance,* Scholastic, 1985; *Stay on Your Toes, Maggie Adams!,* 1986.

Contributor of stories to religious magazines.

WORK IN PROGRESS: Research for an adult historical novel; a young-adult novel; *The Voyage of Merely Miranda,* a children's novel for ages nine to twelve; untitled middle-grade novel about Cammy Smith, a minor character in *Stay on Your Toes, Maggie Adams!*

SIDELIGHTS: "I began writing when I was nine or ten years old. Perhaps I did so because of the influence of my mother.

Although from working-class Norwegian emigrants, she read voluminously all during her childhood and at eighteen escaped from what she considered the narrowness of Tuolumne City, California, to study English literature at the University of California at Berkeley. She thrived on Shelley and Keats and graduated in 1919. She tried to write herself, but said that what she wrote sounded like the kind of writing she detested. I think that she didn't give herself enough of a chance. It's a long hard process to learn the craft of writing, at least for us non-geniuses.

"The first fiction I remember writing was a romance set in the seventeenth century. The hero married the heroine, they had twins, and lived happily ever after. I remember my mother telling me to write what I knew and what I felt; not what I thought I should write. I guess the seventeenth-century romance was very contrived.

"My interest in ballet began when I was about twelve, in ninth grade, and I decided to write a story about a dancer who broke her leg on the night of her big chance. At home I continued to write all during junior and senior high—always fiction. At school I became feature editor of the junior high newspaper, *The Genius*, and later of the senior high paper called *The Franklin Press*. I also remember writing a play at that time called 'Murder in the Press Office.' The characters were the students working on the newspaper. The murdered student was Patrick Jerome Hillings who later became a Congressman from Richard Nixon's old district in Los Angeles. The plot involved

Five important events took place on my nineteenth birthday. ■ (Cover photograph from *Stay on Your Toes, Maggie Adams!* by Karen Strickler Dean.)

finding who murdered Hillings by exploring how each of the other characters felt about him.

"After graduating from UCLA, I worked for a year writing publicity and putting out the house organ for Cutter Laboratories in Berkeley. The following year, after time out to get married, I went to work for the University of California Press in Berkeley where I wrote advertising copy, publicity releases, copy for dust jackets, articles about books and authors which I placed in various periodicals including *The Library Journal* and did layout and copy for leaflets and catalogues.

"While working at the Press I studied fiction writing with novelist Margaret Shedd who was teaching through UC Extension. During the two years I attended her classes I wrote an adult novel and had my first child. The adult novel, entitled *Today, Tomorrow, and Then,* received three very generous rejection letters from editors. I then stopped sending it out because my second child, Nathan, was born.

"After Nathan's arrival I continued to write short stories at home. Then twenty-one months after Nathan came Lucie. So I had three children under six, two in diapers. I remember how frantic I used to get, wanting to write and—unlike some clever, contemporary young women writers—seldom having the time or energy to do so. I often took creative writing classes at local high schools and snatched time while the children were napping to write the assignments as well as more short stories.

"Five years after Lucie (we were living in Palo Alto by this time) Tom was born and my writing became even more sporatic. Maybe I would write four or five hours a week, always adult literary short stories which were always rejected. My children used to rush in from the mail box with the rejected manuscript, 'Look, Mama, another rejection slip today!'

"When I turned forty, I gave myself twenty years to become a published writer of fiction. I still didn't write regularly, however, but turned out short stories based on my trips to Mexico in the middle sixties and on my experiences as a wife and mother. When the rejection slips continued to pour in, I decided I should try to do something more financially rewarding and went back to college. I drifted into education courses, not knowing what I wanted to do (except write, of course!) and went along from semester to semester completing without joy or much enthusiasm the requirements for an elementary credential and then, when I couldn't find a job in an elementary classroom (in the middle seventies), went on to acquire a learning handicapped specialist credential and a master's degree in learning disabilities.

"Along with the education courses and the classes for a Spanish minor, I studied fiction writing with novelist Barnaby Conrad. Working with him really sharpened my writing skills. I wrote many short stories and a novel about a Mexican American boy who settled in the Bay area after traveling with his crop-picking family. I later stopped working on the novel, however, after completing fifteen chapters because Jean Feiwel, then my editor at Avon, said that although she was impressed with the vitality of the characters and descriptions, I, being a white middle-aged woman, was not the proper author for the book. She told me the same thing again when several years later I wanted to write *A Time to Dance* from the viewpoint of Summer Jones, the young black character in that novel which Scholastic brought out in 1985. I had to introduce a white character to tell the story.

"Shortly before I took my first full-time teaching job, as a learning disabilities specialist, I wrote six chapters of a young adult novel which became *Maggie Adams, Dancer*. It was based on a short story I had written several years previously but could not sell. The final chapter of Maggie is basically that short story.

"During my first hectic year of teaching, the novel sat on my desk, then during the summer vacation I heard that Avon was looking for a good, realistic ballet story. I set to work to finish the novel, which I did in four months and sent it to Avon. The editors accepted it in April, 1978—one of the biggest thrills of my life—and published it two years later in April, 1980.

"The character Mariana in my second novel developed in my mind while commuting across the southern end of San Francisco Bay over the old Dumbarton Bridge to Union City where I was teaching children with learning disabilities. After writing and rewriting it while teaching full time, I sent it to an agent, who turned it down. She didn't think Adam or his love affair with Mariana was plausible. I then sent the novel straight to Avon and received a postcard from Jean Feiwel, saying, 'I love Mariana!' She bought it, giving me a contract not only for *Mariana* but for a sequel to *Maggie Adams, Dancer*. I had mentioned another Maggie book in the cover letter I sent with *Mariana*. The sequel became *Between Dances*, the second in the Maggie Adams series.''

(Cover photograph from *A Time to Dance* by Karen Strickler Dean.)

HOBBIES AND OTHER INTERESTS: Reading, Mexican-American culture, skiing, swimming, ballet.

FOR MORE INFORMATION SEE: Joette Dignan Weir, ''Her Byline also Seen in Grade Books,'' *Argus*, June 8, 1980; Angelika von der Assen, ''An Inside Look at the World of a Dancer,'' *Peninsula Times Tribune*, July 11, 1980; *Los Angeles Times*, July 13, 1980; *Palo Alto Weekly*, December 4, 1980.

DUFF, Annis (James) 1904(?)-1986

OBITUARY NOTICE: Born about 1904, in Toronto, Ontario, Canada; died August 10, 1986, in Randallstown, Md. Book editor and author. Duff worked in the Toronto library system before turning to bookselling as head of the children's book department for Robert Simpson Company in Toronto. She later joined Viking Press as children's book editor, serving eighteen years before retiring in 1968. Notable among the publications she edited is the winner of the 1963 Caldecott Medal, *Snowy Day*, by Ezra Jack Keats. In addition, Duff wrote the books *''Bequest of Wings'': A Family's Pleasures with Books*, *''Longer Flight'': A Family Grows Up with Books*, and, with Gladys L. Adshead, *Inheritance of Poetry*, an anthology for young adults. She also contributed a number of articles to *Horn Book*.

FOR MORE INFORMATION SEE: Muriel Fuller, ''Annis Duff of the Viking Press,'' *Publishers Weekly*, February 15, 1960. Obituaries: *Publishers Weekly*, October 24, 1986.

EDENS, Cooper 1945-

PERSONAL: Born Gary Drager on September 25, 1945, in Washington D.C.; son of Otto (an electrical engineer) and Garnet (Cooper) Drager; married Louise Arnold, March 3, 1979; children: David, Emily. *Education:* University of Washington, B.A., 1970. *Politics:* ''Universalist.'' *Religion:* ''Universalist.'' *Home:* 4204 NE 11th Ave. #15, Seattle, Wash. 98105. *Agent:* c/o Green Tiger Press, 1061 India St., San Diego, Calif. 92101.

CAREER: Author and illustrator, 1978—. Participant in programs of the Children's Museum of the Museum of Seattle, Wash. *Exhibitions:* Foster-White Gallery, Seattle, Wash, 1970—. *Awards, honors:* Children's Critic Award from the Bologna International Children's Book Fair, 1980, for *The Starcleaners Reunion;* American nominee for the Golden Apple Award from the Czechoslovakian government (Prague), 1983, for *Caretakers of Wonder*.

WRITINGS—All published by Green Tiger Press: *If You're Afraid of the Dark, Remember the Night Rainbow* (self-illustrated), 1978, 2nd edition, 1984; *The Starcleaner Reunion* (self-illustrated), 1979; *With Secret Friends* (self-illustrated), 1981; *Caretakers of Wonder* (self-illustrated), 1981; *Emily and the Shadow Shop* (illustrated by Patrick Dowers), 1982; *Inevitable Papers* (self-illustrated), 1982; *A Phenomenal Alphabet Book* (illustrated by Joyce Eide), 1982; *Nineteen Hats, Ten Teacups, an Empty Birdcage and the Art of Longing* (self-illustrated), 1986; (with others) *Paradise of Ads* (self-illustrated), 1987; *Now Is the Moon's Eyebrow* (self-illustrated), 1987.

Illustrator: Felix Meroux, *The Prince of the Rabbits*, Green Tiger Press, 1984.

Photograph of Cooper Edens by Rex Rystedt. (For _Pacific Northwest Magazine,_ December, 1985.)

WORK IN PROGRESS: Adapting *The Starcleaner Reunion* into a musical, to be entitled *Starcleaners over Broadway.* ''I have written the lyrics and the music and now I'm looking for a choreographer. I think it will be a better play than book because it seems more suited to the stage. I'm hoping to open it in Seattle, but my aim is to take it to Broadway.''

SIDELIGHTS: Edens grew up in Washington State on Lake Washington. ''A huge highway separated me from prospective playmates who might otherwise have come to visit. Consequently, I spent many hours alone by the lake, daydreaming. I would imagine the island in the lake to be a pirate ship, or another world altogether. It seems to me that many artists are, or were in childhood, enchanted by bodies of water—the sea, a lake, a creek or a pond. This was certainly true for me. I had a rowboat which I repainted again and again; first it was a giraffe, then a zebra, then. . . .

''I tended to miss quite a bit of school. I don't remember whether this was for some legitimate reason, or simply because I didn't want to go. My earliest 'textbooks' were coloring books which I would color in peculiar ways, changing the words as I went along. I cut up and reorganized comic strips from the newspaper, superimposing, say, Felix the Cat into the alien world of another comic strip character.

''On very hot days I would invite friends to watch me draw on the walls of my tent, listening to nonsensical recitations of my own stories. I guess my storytelling actually began in those strange tent proceedings. I also wrote songs. My art work began by coloring over other people's drawings. My uncle campaigned for mayor and when he lost the election, I inherited all of his posters. I colored them, and then began to design my own, inspired by such television shows as 'Hopalong Cas-

Even the invisible still vanishes. ■ (From *Inevitable Papers* by Cooper Edens. Illustrated by the author.)

sidy.' In fourth grade when my attendance in school became more regular, I was put in charge of the bulletin board, changing it for each holiday and season. It could be said in relation to my work today that I am *still* doing the bulletin board!

''My confidence grew out of these coloring book and bulletin board escapades. I considered myself master of color. In junior high school, I was regarded the 'art guy,' who was always hanging out in the 'art room.' Philosophically I hold that everyone comes into the world with something great to share. The first authority figure we encounter, be it parent or teacher, encourages or stifles the gift. Our early creativity is fragile, and can be easily crushed. As luck had it, I was encouraged in school.

''My parents did not particularly encourage my drawing but did not discourage it either. When a son starts drawing instead of building erector sets, fathers tend to get fearful. My father's greatest attribute was his tolerance of my interest in drawing. I suspect deep inside he was something of a poet. My mother's brother was an architect, so perhaps he felt my drawing would lead into a respectable field in which to earn a living.''

Attended University of Washington during the Vietnam War. ''I didn't agree with the war, and as the years went on, I became a professional full-time student to avoid the draft, taking degrees in liberal arts, literature, architecture, and painting. Those years sealed my fate. There were certain facts in my life—a highway separating me from playmates, the draft which I avoided by staying in college as long as I did—which clearly helped me to become an artist. If it weren't for these circumstances, I might have become an architect. Art was something I rested back on, and mine was a peaceful path.

''I have always supported myself with my paintings. In the beginning I sold them for fifteen dollars. Pretty soon I raised the price to thirty, and felt guilty. In my fraternity, the fraternity mothers would buy them. Then hairdressers began to buy them, and then galleries. It moved fast. Once I was able to command thirty dollars for them, I made a comparison of my earning to that of busboy in a restaurant. It wasn't too hard to figure out that I had it easier. I acquired a strange wealth, not money, but clientele—I had a list of people who wanted paintings and when I needed money I painted.

''When I began to exhibit my work, I noticed that some of the characters in my paintings tended to recur. One day I

(From *Inevitable Papers* by Cooper Edens. Illustrated by the author.)

randomly laid the paintings on the floor and began to lace the images together with titles. I wrote a story around the paintings, which became *The Starcleaner Reunion*. So my first book was about tying images together with words. Since then, however, I write the story first and then illustrate it.

''My original Starcleaners, as I was to discover, were oversized for standard publishing practice. I put these giant cardboard figures in a suitcase—the combined weight of which was over two hundred pounds—and carried them to New York in the middle of the summer, sweating profusely as I made the rounds of New York publishers. I had visions of publishers occupying grand rooms, where all of an illustrator's art work was hung on white, spotlighted gallery walls. In fact, the of-

fices of these prominent people were often smaller than my suitcase! I often set up my gigantic Starcleaners on top of someone's bologna sandwich. Everyone responded favorably to my work, but felt that it was too expensive to reproduce. This was in 1978, before four-color printing was feasible for large publishers.

''Several editors suggested that I contact Green Tiger Press, which had a reputation for being eccentric. I went to Green Tiger, and they were willing to invest in my work, although they published my second book, *If You're Afraid of the Dark Remember the Night Rainbow*, first. *Night Rainbow* was a song I had many times attempted to have recorded. I submitted the song as a text and Green Tiger okayed it, but they didn't

If you find your socks don't match . . . stand in a flowerbed. ■ (From *If You're Afraid of the Dark, Remember the Night Rainbow* by Cooper Edens. Illustrated by the author.)

know that I could draw. They had already submitted the book to several well-known illustrators, but liked my work and decided to accept my illustrations. Green Tiger put up the money to make four-color separation and we came out with a soft-cover first edition which was very unusual because there weren't many soft-covered children's books. An advantage is that they can be easily mailed as gifts and are, therefore, sold in gift shops. *Night Rainbow* was often the only book sold in such shops. These outside markets helped get 200,000 copies of the book sold because it never had to compete with other children's books.

"Later that year, Green Tiger published *The Starcleaner Reunion*. I had designed the book with the standard dimension of a late nineteenth century lap book, a size created so that two children could sit and hold a book together. Because it was such an odd size, librarians had trouble placing it on their shelves. Such books don't stack well, so we eventually made it smaller.

"With *The Starcleaner Reunion* I couldn't draw mouths. As a result, all the men sport mustaches. This inability got me into other kinds of trouble. I've been asked why there aren't any women in *Starcleaner*. It isn't because I think women can't clean stars, it's simply because women don't have mustaches! Now that I've learned how to paint mouths, I'd like to update it and add many women."

The ones who will load up the night and bring it back to storage. ■ (From *Caretakers of Wonder* by Cooper Edens. Illustrated by the author.)

And what do you remember of your own full moonlight? ■ (From *With Secret Friends* by
Cooper Edens. Illustrated by the author.)

"I think about writing in terms of meter, and I have noticed that when *Night Rainbow* is read out loud it sings. I don't rhyme intentionally, but I consider my books melodic. I hear melodies as I write. I suppose one could say my meter, my phonetic or in-line rhyming has its origins in the melodies of Buddy Holly and the Beatles.''

Edens' general philosophical approach to children's literature is a departure of traditional precepts. "*Alice in Wonderland, Peter Pan, The Wizard of Oz* and Sendak's *Where the Wild Things Are* are the classic big four stories in my opinion, and they all work in a similar way. Essentially these stories transport us to the world of dreams from which we must return. In essence these books are saying, 'You must be home for dinner.' They present a dualistic vision: there is a dream world, and there is a real world to which you must return. I'm trying to break the dualism of the classic tale. My stories embrace the philosophy that these two worlds exist simultaneously— the real world is a dream and the dream world is real. Because of this, there are no classic quests in my books. I don't have people going away to the dream world and returning to reality. In *Caretakers of Wonder,* for example, the characters are real people doing such surreal things as balancing rainbows or mending clouds. My characters are in a real world doing dream things or in a dream doing real things. It isn't a voyage through a door to some strange and secret place. After all, the only real secret is that when you're awake you're in a dream and when you are asleep you're in reality.

"*Starcleaner Reunion* presents an alternate version of the Creation Story. The book does not suggest that the Bible is wrong, nor does it suggest that Buddha is wrong. It says that everyone is capable of making up their own version of the way the world came to be. No one really knows the mystery. The fact that no one knows makes it beautiful, because it ultimately allows everyone to know. If there were but one answer, the world would be very dull. I want everyone to feel that he's 'in on it.'

"People have sent me their own versions of my books. Children in Colombia who were learning English for the first time sent me their response to *Night Rainbow*. 'What if the tomato doesn't ripen? Get a new universe. . . .' were some of their solutions. Many schools use *Caretakers of Wonder* to teach children about ecology. This feels good because it means I'm not sending a completed work into the world, but a catalyst. I want my readers to have the necessary room for a *creative* response to my work.''

Stars and hearts are recurring images in Edens' books. "When I read Carl Jung I realized how very few symbols there are in the world, and how strong the symbols *star* and *heart* really are. They're symbolically odd because a heart doesn't really look like the organ, and a star doesn't look like an astronomical star. I wondered one day, 'What if stars and hearts were really the same thing?' and that is what *The Starcleaner Reunion* is about.''

. . . *Night Rainbow* includes an illustration of a human heart, rather than the traditional heart shape. "I'm lucky I'm with Green Tiger. Most publishers would not have accepted that illustration because they are afraid of anatomical illustrations. In a forthcoming book, I have a drawing of a rib cage which contains the entire universe!

"The symbol of a heart/star embodies both the infinite and the individual. I'm trying to break up dualities and scale; I believe that's the function of art. It's about getting more room to breathe. It's about fighting stagnation. It isn't the verb, it's the loving. It's not what you love it's *that* you love. It's not the art, it's that you're painting. I believe in the verb, and that's why I make books.''

"I'm very organized in terms of keeping myself steeped in imagery which I find inspiring. I have files full of images from poetry. If I see a line I like in, for example, a W. S. Merwin poem, I file it under 'angel' or 'flowers.' I also have a file of aphorisms. A favorite pastime is something I call the 'adjective game.' I write down one hundred of my favorite words, like 'eraser,' and 'night.' I put half the words in one hat and half in another then draw a word from each hat. It's

(From *The Starcleaner Reunion* by Cooper Edens. Illustrated by the author.)

a method of coming up with weird word combinations, like 'chalk angel.'''

Edens' poetic text, *Inevitable Papers* is illustrated with his collage work. "The images in the work were objects juxtaposed on the floor of my house and photographed with a camera set up on the ceiling. *Inevitable Papers* is a study in juxtaposition and whimsy, a book of poetry rather than a children's book. Some people have called it a 'Zen epilogue,' but I think it is just another book about blind evolution. In truth, it is about me playing."

As part of his creative process, Edens quite literally makes a coloring book as he did when he was a child. "I draw the whole book in black and white and then start coloring it in. I do my color work with pastel, gouache and color pencil. Sometimes I glue things—butterflies and so forth—to the illustration. If the flowers are going well, I might do all the flowers in the book—some days I do skies, and sometimes I devote a whole day to hands, because they make me nervous.

"I don't use models, but sometimes my friends end up in books. A number of them are in *Starcleaner Reunion*, but it wasn't conscious, it just happened. I use encyclopedias for detail and color reference when necessary. I also trace images or xerox them which helps me to look at things in new ways. Sometimes a tree looks real, and sometimes it looks like a child's drawing of a tree. I like to shift between making images that are incredibly primitive and absolutely authentic."

"It takes me two to three months to finish a book, but it is a very organic process, by which I mean I don't worry about deadlines or schedules and yet, I'm always right on time. I now have about twenty books written and another ten which only need color added. Green Tiger is committed to publishing at least one book a year and in the future, I may try to work with other publishers as well.

Poet W. S. Merwin and painter Henri Matisse are Edens' heroes. "A rather strange combination, but I respond to them from both my sense of words and my sense of visuals. Their work has given me confidence and kinship. Matisse's cutouts—a series of pieces he did when he was very ill and could no longer paint—was inspiring. He resorted to scissors, as did I in *Inevitable Papers*. I often wonder what would have become of me had I not run across Merwin's poems and the paintings of Matisse—perhaps I would still be drawing Hopalong Cassidy!

"I like to work on many things at once from enchanted, childish projects to new wave rock 'n' roll. Working this way is stalagmitic: I do a bit of everything and pretty soon something has formed on the floor of the cave. I keep a list of priorities which I work on every day. Part of the day I work on projects which may never crystallize. I like the juxtaposition of working on something I'm very good at and at something which I'm not. Working on things I haven't mastered helps me to maintain a certain freshness.

"For example, I've recently outlined movies I would like to make. Whether I'm good at it or not doesn't really matter to me. What's important is that I don't feel comfortable with it; that everyday I come out feeling that I've taken a chance. If I were to spend an entire week on children's books, I would feel my life was too predictable. David Bowie, Fred Astaire and the Beatles were always able to change their course, and I respect that. It is an earmark of tremendous talent to continue innovating and to explore other paths."

Edens lives in Seattle with his wife and her children. "I have come to appreciate Seattle more and more. I love the lakes and the incredible weather which, like London's, is dark, poetic, ethereal. Seattle has become very international and feels a bit like San Francisco in it's heyday. Now that I've been to every city in Europe, I can say that I truly prefer Seattle, with the possible exception of Florence, Italy.

"I married my wife while her children were very young, so I've had the experience of parenting. When they were little, they believed that I drew each book individually! They had no concept of printing, so when I would go to the basement and bring up books, they were certain I'd been up all night making them."

Living with them are all the toys from Edens' childhood. "It's incredible, but everything I had as a child is in my house; all my toys are on display—a museum of my childhood. I have photographs of myself with toys from thirty-eight years ago. It's eerie, but it gives me a sense of continuity in my life. As with dreams and reality, I see no separation between adulthood and childhood. Life and childhood are not separate planets; I'm in the same world as I was when I was a child. The attributes of childhood were lovely enough to keep for an entire life."

Edens offers the following encouragement to young artists: "The hardest step is to admit that you want to do it. But the second you start, something will come back to you—call it God or nature or mystery. I'm a witness to the fact that if you participate you will be joined by some other energy or spirit or friend; then, you're instantly a team, a couplement, and once this happens, everything is easy. When people submit their books to me I always say, 'The one thing that separates you from most people is that you *want* to do it; the minute you want to do it, you're a very select person.' There aren't that many people who consistently work at something, who consistently show up.

"Another lesson is that at first, perhaps only one of ten paintings you make will be good. But one will always be better than the other nine. So you throw away nine and the next day, maybe two of ten will work. Pretty soon half of what you make will be good. You learn that sometimes things come out instantly and sometimes they have to be fixed.

"There is craft involved in any art. You'll have to know the brushes and paints eventually. But there are great victories before you learn the right brush. You can make a lot of spills and still find a reason to show up again. After all, you're with friends. As a philosopher once said, 'The planet exists because life needs it.' It isn't the earth that makes life possible, it's life that makes the earth what it is. That's the way it is with art. It exists because you want it to."

—*Based on an interview by Rachel Koenig*

EDWARDS, Linda Strauss 1948-

PERSONAL: Born June 16, 1948, in White Plains, N.Y.; daughter of Arthur S. (a physician) and Joy (a homemaker; maiden name, Worth) Strauss; married Richard M. Edwards (a physician's assistant), September 12, 1970; children: Aaron Richard, Blythe Ellen. *Education:* Syracuse University, School of Visual Art, B.F.A., 1970. *Home and office:* R.D.2, Box 218A, Lowville, N.Y. 13367.

CAREER: Jefferson-Lewis Board of Cooperative Educational Services, Glenfield, N.Y., graphic artist 1973-74; Individualized Instruction, Inc., Oklahoma City, Okla., artist, 1974-75; South Oklahoma City Junior College, Oklahoma City, instructor, 1975-76; children's book illustrator and writer, 1978—. Member of Lowville Free Library Friends of the Library, 1982 and Board of Trustees, 1983-85; panel member, Regional Decentralization Program, New York State Council of the Arts, 1979-81 and 1984-86.

WRITINGS—Self-illustrated: *The Downtown Day,* Pantheon, 1983.

Illustrator: Marguerita Rudolph, *The Sneaky Machine,* McGraw, 1974; Barbara Williams, *So What If I'm a Sore Loser?,* Harcourt, 1981; Denise G. Orenstein, *When the Wind Blows Hard,* Addison-Wesley, 1982; Jill Ross Klevin, *The Turtle Street Trading Co.,* Delacorte, 1982; J. R. Klevin, *Turtles Together Forever!,* Delacorte, 1982; Jamie Gilson, *Thirteen Ways to Sink a Sub,* Lothrop, 1982; J. R. Klevin, *Meet the Youngest Tycoons in the World!,* Delacorte, 1982; Betty Bates, *Call Me Friday the Thirteenth,* Holiday House, 1983; J. Gilson, *4B Goes Wild,* Lothrop, 1983; Alice Schertle, *Goodnight Hattie, My Dearie, My Dove,* Lothrop, 1985; B. Bates, *Thatcher Payne-in-the-Neck,* Holiday House, 1985; A. Schertle, *Gus Wanders Off,* Lothrop, 1987.

WORK IN PROGRESS: Writing and illustrating *A Game without Words,* a serious story for children.

SIDELIGHTS: ''I guess I have always wanted to be a picture book artist and writer. At least after I found out that being a cowboy or ballet dancer were not in my future. As a kid I really liked drawing and making up stories, so this is a natural outgrowth of those interests.

''I had a happy childhood growing up in what is now described as an 'extended family.' In addition to my parents and brother and sister there were two elderly aunts, a grandfather on and off, and a live-in uncle. Our house was a loving, noisy, busy environment. My book, *The Downtown Day,* is about my two great aunts and myself as a child. The events in the story are fabricated but given their personalities and my normal child self, it could easily have been true. I have recently completed another story about these three characters in which Linda misbehaves. How she and the aunts deal with her naughtiness and anger is the central theme of this book. I read it to my son and daughter and it was quite well received by them. Too bad Aaron isn't my publisher.

''My family, especially my mother, was very encouraging and supportive. My family now is just as supportive. My husband is a perceptive critic and knows just how to cheer me up when the rejection letters come in the mail. But usually I feel very lucky to get paid to do the work I love to do.

''As an illustrator I hope kids will look at my pictures and want to be part of that storybook world. I aim for realism as an artist because I feel that children prefer pictures to be representational so that they can imagine themselves as the hero or heroine of the story. I can also remember feeling patronized by illustrators who drew in a childlike manner. I felt insulted because I wanted to draw the world as it appeared to me. . . . I'm still trying. . . .

LINDA STRAUSS EDWARDS

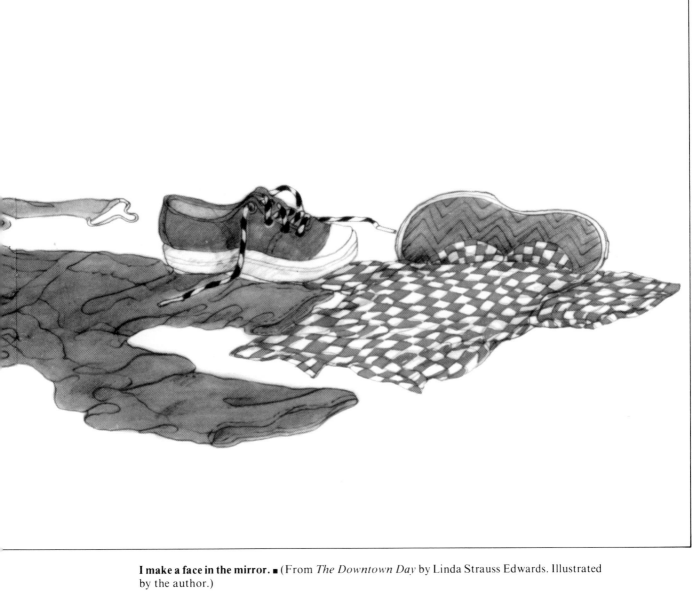

I make a face in the mirror. ■ (From *The Downtown Day* by Linda Strauss Edwards. Illustrated by the author.)

''In writing books for kids I remember my own childhood and the thoughts and feelings I had at that time, to give the stories veracity. As the mother of young children I am also constantly reminded of the priorities and interests and daydreams of little kids. My children help me a lot in my work.

''This job is a great excuse for never growing up. I get to re-experience everything through the new and wondering eyes of a child as a necessary part of it. From this perspective I can forsee easily enjoying the next thirty-seven years of my life as much as the last thirty-seven.''

HOBBIES AND OTHER INTERESTS: Photography, junk stores, window shopping, Sunday crossword, loud music and novels.

EGIELSKI, Richard 1952-

PERSONAL: Born July 16, 1952, in New York, N. Y.; son of Joseph Frank (a police lieutenant) and Caroline (an executive secretary; maiden name, Rzepny). *Education:* Studied at Pratt Institute, 1970-71; Parsons School of Design, graduate, 1974. *Home:* 7 West 14th St., New York, N.Y. 10011.

CAREER: Illustrator, 1973. *Exhibitions:* ''Illustrators 16,'' Society of Illustrators, New York, N.Y., 1974; ''Illustrators 18,'' Society of Illustrators, 1976. *Awards, honors: The Por-*

celain Pagoda was included in the American Institute of Graphic Arts Book Show, 1976; *The Letter, the Witch and the Ring* was selected one of Child Study Association of America's Children's Books of the Year, 1976; *Louis the Fish* was selected one of *School Library Journal*'s Best Books, 1980; Plaque from the Biennale of Illustrations Bratislava, 1985, for *It Happened in Pinsk;* Caldecott Medal from the American Library Association, 1987, for *Hey, Al.*

ILLUSTRATOR: Moonguitars (reader), Houghton, 1974; F. N. Monjo, *The Porcelain Pagoda,* Viking, 1976; John Bellairs, *The Letter, the Witch and the Ring,* Dial, 1976; Arthur Yorinks, *Sid and Sol,* Farrar, Straus, 1977; Miriam Chaikin, *I Should Worry, I Should Care,* Harper, 1979.

A. Yorinks, *Louis the Fish,* Farrar, Straus, 1980; M. Chaikin, *Finders Weepers,* Harper, 1980; Isabel L. Cusack, *Mr. Wheatfield's Loft,* Holt, 1981; M. Chaikin, *Getting Even,* Harper, 1982; Jim Aylesworth, *Mary's Mirror,* Holt, 1982; A. Yorinks, *It Happened in Pinsk,* Farrar, Straus, 1983; M. Chaikin, *Lower! Higher! You're a Liar!,* Harper, 1984; Gelett Burgess, *The Little Father,* Farrar, Straus, 1984; Richard Kennedy, *Amy's Eyes,* Harper, 1985; A. Yorinks, *Hey, Al,* Farrar, Straus, 1986.

ADAPTATIONS: ''Louis the Fish,'' Reading Rainbow, PBS-TV, 1983.

WORK IN PROGRESS: A picture book for Farrar, Straus.

RICHARD EGIELSKI

She held her small *Shabbos* valise in one hand . . . . ■ (From *Lower! Higher! You're a Liar!* by
Miriam Chaikin. Illustrated by Richard Egielski.)

(From *It Happened in Pinsk* by Arthur Yorinks. Illustrated by Richard Egielski.)

SIDELIGHTS: Born July 16, 1952, in New York City. ''As a kid I loved to ride the subways. I often spent entire Saturdays in the trains going uptown, downtown, crosstown, from borough to borough. In those days, the trains were luxurious with their wicker seats and windows you could really see out of. For me, the subway was a netherworld. Just a few stops would bring you into a neighborhood totally different from the one you started out at.

''They called me 'the artist in the family,' but it seemed that there was one in every family. It didn't necessarily mean that you were good at drawing, just that you enjoyed doing it.

He was bigger than the tallest building. ■ (From *Sid and Sol* by Arthur Yorinks. Illustrated by Richard Egielski.)

Cartoons were my first influence, and most of my work had a definite cartoon-like quality. It's interesting to look back on it, because historically picture books gave rise to cartoons, and in my case, where cartoons gave rise to picture books, the cycle is completed. Venus Paradise coloring sets were all the rage then. I had them, of course, but usually turned the paper over and did my own picture rather than color in theirs.

"I wasn't aware of picture books until I was old enough to consider them 'baby books.' Needless to say, by then I wanted nothing to do with them. I had a Golden Book Encyclopedia and a few other things, but books were not an important part of my childhood. I read more Catechisms than anything else.

"Until ninth grade I attended parochial school, which felt like a concentration camp. I remember being frightened almost all of the time. All those things you hear about: nuns throwing erasers at students; rapping kids' knuckles with rulers, is all true. When I complained, my mother agreed, 'Yes, that's the way it was when I went to school.' Not that she was unsympathetic. There was a resigned attitude that school, by its very nature, was a trial by fire. When it came time for high school, I felt I had to make a break. My parents were opposed to my going to a regular public high school, but agreed to the possibility of a specialized school. In my research I came across the High School of Art and Design. They required a portfolio and an entrance exam. I had no idea if I could qualify, but feverishly put together a portfolio, took the test, and to my infinite relief, was accepted. Public high school was a new world for me. Students were *encouraged* to participate in class discussions. Even if you weren't sure you had the right answer, you could raise your hand and speak. Being in an atmosphere where self-expression was emphasized was like breathing good, clean air for the first time in my life. Until that point I had never considered making art a career. After a few months at Art and Design, however, I wanted to be an artist and nothing but.

"Art and Design was essentially a commercial art school, although we did have painting and life drawing classes. My first exposure to art in any formal sense was through commercial art. At the end of four years, I'd resolved to become a painter because I'd discovered such artists as Rembrandt and Goya, whose work made a deep impression on me. They are the most illustrative and most narrative of painters.

"After graduation I went to Pratt. However, the painting program was so heavily oriented toward Abstract Expressionism that I felt like a dinosaur doing representational work. Since I'd studied commercial art and was still attracted to narrative artists like N. C. Wyeth, I figured that illustration was probably my field. I was, afterall, from a middle-class background and reared with the idea that you had to earn a living through your work. Setting up as a painter was too radical for me. Illustration seemed possible, but painting too fantastic, too much like a dream.

"I transferred to Parsons, planning to become a commercial illustrator. One semester I decided to take a course in picture books taught by Maurice Sendak. I hadn't given much thought to picture books as an outlet for my work, but found that I took to it naturally. I had always enjoyed doing sequentials, something I'm sure comes from my love of movies. Maurice Sendak was the most important teacher I ever had. In my opinion, a teacher can't really do that much for you technically. That's something you have to do for yourself by working and practicing every day. An important teacher is one who exposes you to something new, and points out a direction you otherwise might have missed. In introducing me to the art of

picture books, Maurice Sendak became a crucial influence. The quality of his work is a continuing inspiration.

"After graduating from Parsons, I took my portfolio to publishers, but was told by nearly everyone that my work was either too 'sophisticated' or too 'wacky' for children's books. No one, they said, was writing stories that would go with my kind of art. Over and over people suggested that I write my own stories—something I have no desire to do, because I know that I'm not a writer. This was all terribly discouraging. Eventually, I managed to illustrate a few books in spite of what I had been told, but most of my time was spent doing illustrations for magazines.

"And then, things changed, thanks again to Maurice. He suggested me to writer Arthur Yorinks whose first book had languished for over a year *after* having been accepted for want of an illustrator. We talked, he looked at my portfolio, I looked at some of his stories, and we decided to try to do a book together. This turned out to be *Sid and Sol,* which came out in 1977.

"I haven't come across many writers who really know how to do picture books. Too often, I think, they don't want the pictures to dominate and so they put in a lot of description, hoping, I guess, that the illustrator will be forced to do exactly as they dictate. This is one of the many things that sets Arthur's texts apart: there are no descriptions, just wonderful stories, unforgettable characters and vivid atmospheres rendered in the texture and rhythm of the language. His stories, like my illustrations, are very personal and idiosyncratic.

"Arthur and I have evolved a basic working method which, while subject to change due to revisions, stays pretty much intact from book to book. We always start from the story. Arthur will bring me one, or several from which I select one. By the time he has shown it to me, the story is just about final. He tends to draw his inspiration from classic writers— Gogol, Kafka, and so on. *Louis the Fish,* for example, was suggested by Kafka's *The Metamorphosis,* in which a man turns into an insect. I read not only Arthur's piece, but Kafka's as well. I remembered when I first studied *The Metamorphosis* in high school. The teacher divided the story into discrete, but connected, sections. I hadn't thought about that in years and am certain that in some way it affected my illustrations."

The first process for Egielski when illustrating one of Yorinks' stories is to "break the story into thirty-two-page units. I am very concerned with particular images and the flow between those images. I also determine the size of the book at this point. Each story gives me hints about the size and shape the illustrations should assume physically. My first sketches appear, to the inexperienced eye, as little more than scribbles. On one page of a five- by eight-inch notebook, I have representations of each page of the book. The first time I showed these pencil sketches to Arthur, he thought I was insane—they looked like hieroglyphics. But for me, each little squiggle represents an image. Together, they represent the pacing and the rhythm of the entire book. After a couple books together, he learned to 'read' my initial thumbnails. At this point, I may have questions about the story, which he clears up. We might also talk about revisions in the story.

"My storyboard is done in pencil and colored pencil—mediums I can erase. I also work relatively small-scale so I can get down to the bare bones of the picture without getting lost in detail. If I did my storyboards full size, I would spend far too much time on them. At the storyboard stage, I'm mostly

(From *Hey, Al* by Arthur Yorinks. Illustrated by Richard Egielski.)

interested in stringing the images together smoothly and getting down a real nice rhythm. Sometimes I can go through the entire book without hitting a rough spot. Other times, I have problems I can't resolve without talking to Arthur. It's very hard for me to skip over part of the story and try to get to the end. In a picture book, every image is connected to all the others, so I have to solve my problems as they arise.

''Once we have taken story and storyboard as far as we can, we submit the package to our publisher. We may well be showing the fourth draft of the story and the third storyboard. It's easier for our editor to visualize the book with the text and pictures, and better for us because we have a firm grip on what we're doing. Of course this is highly unorthodox with regard to standard publishing practice which generally keeps the artist and writer as far from each other as possible.

''The longest part of our collaborative process is the finishes. I do these full sized in watercolor. I achieve a good sharp line when I need it, as well as a range of opacities and tones. Watercolor is also a very clean medium. Some books go very

smoothly, like *Louis the Fish*. Others, like *It Happened in Pinsk* or our new book, *Hey, Al* are a little bumpier. An interesting thing happened with *Hey, Al*, I was having terrible problems with the illustrations. As it turned out, the snags in the pictures were revealing places where the text needed to be revised. As soon as Arthur did a little fixing, my problems cleared up.

''I love to interpret good writing. A good illustrator is never a slave to a text. The text rarely tells him what to do, but, rather, what his choices are. I only illustrate texts I truly believe in, and never go against them. Sometimes when I'm working on a picture book, it feels like I'm making a little film—selecting key scenes, picking the 'angle,' giving the words *visual* life. Sometimes, I feel like I'm writing music—visual music, that is. The picture book form is very musical: reading the words, looking at the pictures, turning the pages all make a rhythm. I must say that I like the whole idea of creating picture books within the standard thirty-two-page format. It's not unlike the sonnet form, in which the poet has so many lines in which to express himself. I don't feel at all constricted by this. On the contrary, the 'rules' of the form seem to set me free. I'm always discovering new things I can do.

"The picture book is an art form unto itself. Arthur and I invest our work with all we have gleaned from the tradition at its height. I look back, a little amused at the distinction I once made between 'illustration' and 'fine art.' My illustration is my fine art. I have absolutely no reason to wish to liberate, or wean myself from my dependence upon text. It is through my illustrations that I express myself most deeply and fully.''

When asked about the type of research he does for particular images, Egielski replied, "Like most illustrators, I have a clipping file. And often I do consult outside sources. For *Hey, Al* I looked at lots of jungle scenes and pictures of birds. But when you get down to it, the images are essentially suggested by the story and must fit that context. If I use outside sources, it is only as a point of departure.

"I am generally pretty regular in my work habits. I'm usually at my drawing board by eleven in the morning and work straight through till about six. I find I don't work very well at night. There's something very physical about making pictures. By the end of the day, my energy is spent. I like to keep up a good momentum—the more work I do, the better I work. Arthur and I are trying to increase our output. Ideally, I would like to be wrapping up the finishes for one book just as I'm starting the storyboard for another. I like to listen to music while I'm working, and pick the music to fit the books. When I was doing *Louis the Fish*, for example, I listened to a lot of Brian Eno. During *Pinsk*, I listened to a Russian mandolin player, and for *Hey, Al*, in which Al and his dog are transported to a tropic isle, I listened to South American music. I don't know to what extent the music influences what I do, or how specifically, but it establishes an atmosphere in which I enjoy working.''

Egielski was awarded the 1986 Bratislava Prize in Illustration for *It Happened in Pinsk*. He expressed disappointment with most contemporary picture books, and in general, with most visual art produced today. "In too many picture books, the text is thin and merely an excuse for illustrations. Publishers have sent me manuscripts with request to 'liven them up.' Well, that's impossible. If I'm given a boring text, I can only do boring pictures. I refuse those jobs; I can only illustrate text in which I truly believe. Most of the illustrations I see in picture books are equally disappointing. The trend among illustrators these days seems to be to develop a particular style and to apply it across the board. I think you should change your style in accordance with the text you're working with. The visual image has become debased. This is certainly true of political images, which, largely due to television, carry little weight. The exception here may be the cartoon, which has managed to retain some vigor. But cartoons are a narrative medium requiring some work of the reader/viewer, unlike television which does it all for you. Movies are going in the same direction. The visual pyrotechnics of Spielberg and of Lucas have produced some blockbuster images, but think back to Hitchcock, where, for example, images are so exquisitely interconnected, it was like watching music unfurl before your eyes.''

—Based on an interview by Marguerite Feitlowitz

FOR MORE INFORMATION SEE: The New York Times, December 8, 1977; Lee Kingman and others, compilers, *Illustrator of Children's Books: 1967-1976*, Horn Book, 1978;

Booklist, October 1, 1979; *The Los Angeles Times,* October 14, 1979; "Story by Arthur Yorinks, Pictures by Richard Egielski'' (videotape), Farrar, 1987.

FLEISHER, Robbin   1951-1977

BRIEF ENTRY: Born January 6, 1951, in Brooklyn, N.Y.; died April 26, 1977. Artist, animator, musician, songwriter, and author. The daughter of teachers, Fleisher received a B.A. from Hunter College and attended the Teachers College of Columbia University where she majored in art therapy and education. Her only book, *Quilts in the Attic* (Macmillan, 1977), a picture book illustrated by Ati Forberg, tells of two sisters' game with quilts found in their attic. In the simple narrative, older Natasha drapes the quilts around her and declares herself a king, the wind, a star. Each time, younger Rosie chimes "Me too,'' until Natasha becomes miffed and says, "No you're not.'' After a quarrel, the girls make up. "The way the girls work out the problems is amusing and educating . . . a fetching story,'' observed *Publishers Weekly*. Fleisher, who died at the age of twenty-six after a short illness, left many notes for future children's books. Primarily an illustrator, she was beginning to develop story ideas for preschoolers in which she used her own history—the names of beloved grandparents, stories handed down from generation to generation—to relate modern yet timeless stories of children and their world.

FORD, Brian J(ohn)   1939-

PERSONAL: Born May 13, 1939, in Chippenham, Wiltshire, England; son of William John (a chartered engineer, designer and company director) and Cicely Beryl Pryn (Biddick) Ford; married Janice May Smith (a former high school governor); children: Anthony John, Stuart Pryn, Sarah Rose Pryn, Tamsin Emily May; (foster children) Leigh Roy Mills, Timothy James Havard. *Education:* Attended Cardiff University, 1959-61. *Home:* Mill Park House, 57 Westville Rd., Cardiff CF2 5DF, Wales, United Kingdom. *Office:* Department of Zoology, P.O. Box 78, Cathays Park, Cardiff CF1, Wales, United Kingdom.

CAREER: Scientist, writer and television host. Medical Research Council, Wales, staff member, 1958-59; *South Wales Echo*, Cardiff, Wales, science columnist, 1959-62; British Broadcasting Corporation (BBC), radio and television science broadcaster, 1962—; Medical Development Trust, London, England, science consultant, 1962-63; College of Art and Design, Newport, England, lecturer in science and technology studies, 1965-67; Independent Television System, Bristol, England, and Cardiff, Wales, science telecaster, 1965-67. Chairman of "Where Are You Taking Us?'' series, 1973-74; founder and chairman of series "Science Now,'' BBC, 1975-76; director and presenter of documentary film "The Fund,'' 1976; presenter of television series "Food for Thought,'' Channel Four TV (London), 1984-86, and personal documentary series "Jenseits des Kanals,'' West German TV, 1985; hosts hi-tech television game show "Computer Challenge,'' BBC Wales. Consulting editor, Northwood Publishing, and editor, *Voice of British Industry*, London, both 1967-68.

Visiting lecturer, Foreign and Commonwealth Office, British Council, 1978. University of Cardiff, Wales, member of Court of Governors, 1981—, fellow, 1986—. Executive member of Broadcasting Committee, London, 1982-83.

MEMBER: International Society of Protozoologists, European Academy for Science, Arts and Humanities (foreign member), Royal Society of Health, Royal Microscopical Society, British Interplanetary Society, Institute of Biology, Quekett Microscopical Club, Association of British Science Writers (executive board member, 1983-86), European Union of Science Journalists' Associations (president, 1984—), Scientific and Technical Authors' Committee (chairman, 1986—), Society of Authors, Society for Basic Irreproducible Research (honorary member), British Broadcasting Corporation Club, National Book League (council member), Architecture Club, Arts Club, Savage Club (chairman of entertainments, 1986—), Linnean Society of London (fellow). *Awards, honors:* Nominated by BBC for Italia Prize, 1974, for BBC program "Heart Attack"; *Microbe Power* was selected one of New York Public Library's Books for the Teen Age, 1980, 1981, 1982; holder of Kodak Bursary Award, 1981-83; grants from the Royal Society, 1982-84, the Spencer-Tolles Fund, 1982, the Appleyard Trust of the Linnean Society, 1983, Botanical Research Fund, 1985, and the Linnean Society, 1986; Leverhulme grant, 1986-87.

WRITINGS: (Editor) *Science Diary*, Letts, 1967, 13th edition, 1979; *German Secret Weapons: Blueprint for Mars*, Ballantine, 1969; *Microbiology and Food*, Northwood, 1970; *Allied Secret Weapons: The War of Science*, Ballantine, 1971; *Nonscience and the Pseudotransmogrificationalific Egocentrified Reorientational Proclivities Inherently Intracorporated in Expertistical Cerebrointellectualised Redeploymentation with Special Reference to Quasi-Notional Fashionistic Normativity, the Indoctrinationalistic Methodological Modalities and Scalar Socioeconomic Promulgationary Improvementalisationalism Predelineated Positotaxically toward Individualistified Mass-acceptance Gratificationalistic Securipermanentalisationary Professionism; or, How to Rule the World* (scientific satire), International Publishing, 1971; *The Earth Watchers*, Frewin, 1973; *The Revealing Lens: Mankind and the Microscope*, Harrap, 1973; *The Optical Microscope Manual: Past and Present Uses and Techniques*, Crane, Russak, 1973; (with others) *The Cardiff Book*, Stewart Williams, 1973.

Microbe Power: Tomorrow's Revolution, Stein & Day, 1976; *Patterns of Sex: The Mating Urge and Our Sexual Future*, St. Martin's, 1978; *Cult of the Expert*, Hamish Hamilton, 1982; (with others) *Viral Pollution of the Environment*, CRC Press, 1983; *One Hundred One Questions about Science*, Hamish Hamilton, 1983; *One Hundred One More Questions about Science*, Hamish Hamilton, 1984; *Single Lens: The Story of the Simple Microscope*, Harper, 1985; (with others) *Sex and Your Health*, Mitchell Beazley, 1985; *COMPUTE: Why? When? How? Do I Need To?*, Hamish Hamilton, 1985; *The Food Book*, Hamish Hamilton, 1986.

Contributor to Purnell's *History of the Second World War*, 1967-68, *World Book Encyclopedia*, and *International Yearbook of Science and Technology*. Contributor of columns to *Listener*, and *Mensa Journal*. Research papers published in many journals, including *Journal of Microscopy, New Scien-*

BRIAN J. FORD

tist, British Medical Journal, Transactions of the American Microscopical Society, Radiography, Journal of Biological Education, Microscope, Nature, and *La Recherche.* Contributor of articles to *Science Digest, Times* (London), *Technology Review, Vous Saurez Tous, Medical News, New Knowledge, Mind Alive, Observer, Private Eye, Guardian,* and many other international periodicals. Editor, *Science Diary,* 1967-80, *Know Britain,* 1969-70, and *Broadcasting Bulletin,* 1983; book critic, *New Scientist,* 1970-72.

WORK IN PROGRESS: Books on his scientific work; a series of the television show "Computer Challenge" and of personal documentaries for German television; a book on coastal walks in Britain, laboratory research.

SIDELIGHTS: Ford, a descendant of the inventor/scientist Sir James Watt, is a British biologist who works in London, Brussels and New York. His books used by children include *One Hundred One Questions about Science* and *One Hundred One More Questions about Science.* He was also a member of the BBC series "Dial a Scientist." His research work has frequently been cited in standard teaching books in the United States and elsewhere. His papers on biohazard laid down the modern requirements of international law; his book *Microbe Power* had a profound effect on the launch of the biotechnology era. His discovery of the world's oldest microscope specimens (which was featured in his book *Single Lens*) has altered our view of science history. More recently, he launched a new theory on plant metabolism at the 1986 Inter-Micro meeting in Chicago, Illinois, on which he is presently working. He has also been a prolific solver of mysteries, and has worked on forensic matters in the courts of law. He has several times presented his research at the Royal Society of London.

Ford's writing career began with his desire to communicate science. "I had always wanted to help the communication of science to the people. My first articles were written when I was nineteen, and they were published when I realised that I would need extra money to see my way through college. It was the editor of the newspaper *South Wales Echo* who gave me the break and there I was—a science columnist at twenty. I also played rhythm and blues in a rock band and later had a solo spot at a nightclub. I have even played rhythm and blues on radio and television—and still go to as many gigs as I can manage."

"Telling non-specialists about scientific research is a sure way to test your own comprehension. I find it easier to write a research paper for a specialist journal than to translate it into terms that the layman can grasp. But it is an important task. We imagine that we have a gap between scientists on the one hand, and the public on the other. In fact, the gap is between one specialist and another. It is true that the taxi-driver or the architect may not understand the ramifications of molecular

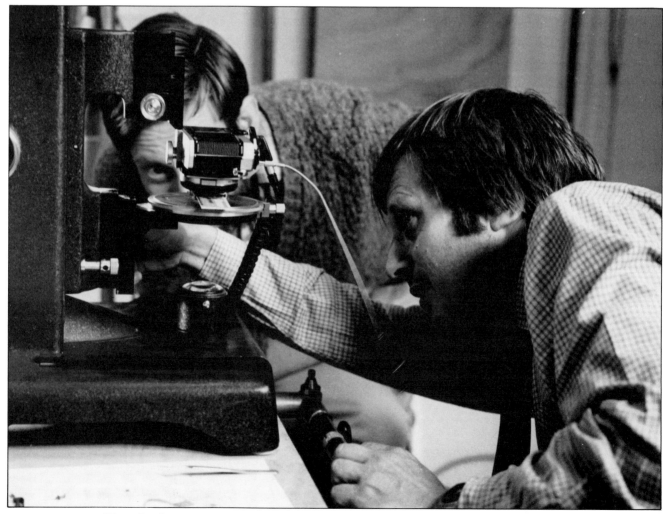

(From *Single Lens: The Story of the Simple Microscope* by Brian J. Ford. Photograph by Jaap Stolp.)

biology, but neither does the astronomer, the hematologist, or the nuclear physicist. We need to talk to each other and to embrace the culture of the public.''

Ford is a devoted family man, he and his wife are registered foster parents, and, for all his international work, he maintains close family contacts. His offspring accompany him as often as possible, and the travelling is clearly in the blood—three of the children, now grown up, live in Jeddah, Saudi Arabia, London, England, and St. Tropez, France. Jet-setting between his busy professional schedule and the various branches of the family keeps them all busy.''

Ford maintains a well-equipped private laboratory for his own study at his home in Wales. The children were all brought up to be familiar with microscopes from an early age. He commutes to work in London in the 125 m.p.h. streamlined train that runs between the two capital cities. ''It takes me an hour and forty-five minutes to travel from Cardiff to London,'' he says, ''and when I spent my formative years in North London it often took as long as that to get home. Now we live near the sea and the mountains, yet still handy for the London West End.''

Some of Ford's writings have been translated into Chinese, Japanese, Russian, French, Italian, Portugese, German and Spanish.

HOBBIES AND OTHER INTERESTS: Travel (Europe, United States, Soviet Union, India, Southeast Asia, Africa, Australasia, and the Pacific Islands), photography (some of his scientific photographs have won prizes in major competitions), rock and roll, relaxing ''with the family, on or under the ocean, celebrating the intoxicating experience of life.''

FOR MORE INFORMATION SEE: Mensa Journal, number 115, 1968; *Medical News,* October 18, 1968; *Times* (London), September 17, 1971, October 24, 1971, March 17, 1973, March 25, 1973, April 7, 1973, January 15, 1984; *Irish Press,* October 30, 1971; *Nature,* December 3, 1971, February 8, 1974, August 16, 1974, April 25, 1985, October 29, 1986, November 5, 1986; *Punch,* May 9, 1973, July 28, 1976; *Times Literary Supplement,* December 10, 1976; *Discover,* Volume II, number 10, 1981; *Scientific American,* January, 1982, July, 1985; *Science Digest,* March, 1982; *New Scientist,* January 20, 1983; *Sunday Express,* July 1, 1984; *Mensa,* January, 1985, June, 1986; *Washington Times Magazine,* April 29, 1985.

FRENCH, Michael 1944-

PERSONAL: Born December 2, 1944, in Los Angeles, Calif.; son of Richard Louis (a surgeon) and Marjorie (a nurse; maiden name, Carson) French; married Patricia Goodkind (a real estate developer), December 7, 1969; children: Timothy, Alison. *Education:* Stanford University, B.A., 1966; Northwestern University, M.S., 1967. *Home:* 463 Calle La Paz, Santa Fe, N.M. 87501. *Agent:* Lydia Galton & Associates, 351 West 19th St., New York, N.Y. 10011.

CAREER: Hill and Knowlton (international public relations firm), New York City, financial writer, 1970-72; Wilson Brothers, New York City, assistant to president, 1972-74; founder and operator of day-care center, Brooklyn Heights, N.Y., 1974-78; full-time writer, 1978—. *Military service:* U.S. Army, 1968-69. *Awards, honors: The Throwing Season* was selected one of New York Public Library's Books for the Teen

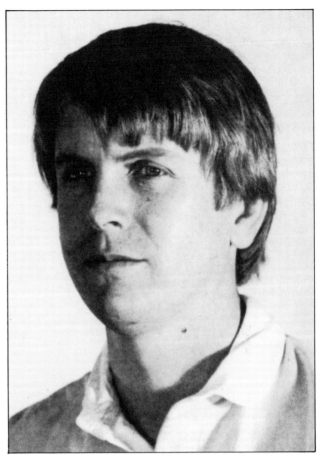

MICHAEL FRENCH

Age, 1981; finalist, Young Reader Medal from the California Reading Association, 1986, for *Pursuit.*

WRITINGS: Club Caribe (adult novel), Fawcett, 1977; *Abingdon's* (adult novel), Doubleday, 1979; *The Throwing Season* (young adult novel), Delacorte, 1980; *Rhythms* (adult novel), Doubleday, 1980; *Pursuit* (young adult novel), Delacorte, 1982; (adapter) *Flyers,* Random House, 1983; *Lifeguards Only Beyond This Point* (young adult novel), Putnam, 1984; (adapter) *Indiana Jones and the Temple of Doom: The Storybook Based on the Movie,* Random House, 1984; *Soldier Boy* (young adult novel), Putnam, 1986; *Texas Bred* (adult novel), Bantam, 1986; *Us Against Them* (young adult novel), Bantam, 1987.

WORK IN PROGRESS: An adult novel about Los Angeles society of the forties and fifties, the real estate empires there and the clash of ambitions and principles among the central characters.

SIDELIGHTS: French has been a full-time writer of novels for adults and young adults since 1978, but it wasn't always possible to devote his energies solely to his writing. ''I started at Stanford, in the creative writing program, and pretty much kept with it afterwards. I was married in 1969; my wife and I moved from Los Angeles to New York City. I worked several years for an international public relations firm, later for a Fortune 500 company, and then my wife and I started a day-care center in Brooklyn Heights [New York].

''My corporate background—the ins and outs of financing, the politics, the conflicts—has been helpful in writing my novels. But outside work is a retardant in the sense of time and energy. When you spend eight hours doing someone else's work and you come home, the last thing you want to do is write. You want to read or watch television or just talk. It takes a good deal of discipline to keep writing—particularly when it isn't selling.

"I would try to write at night *and* on weekends. And sometimes, if it was slow at the office, I would close my door and write there. It became an art—squeezing out times when you had the concentration to write intelligibly."

French admitted that he was strongly influenced by author Arthur Hailey in his first two novels. *Club Caribe* was published in 1977 as a paperback original. *Abingdon's,* his second novel, was based on the world famous Bloomingdale's department store in New York City. "I was despairing because I couldn't get any of my fiction published, and I started reading Hailey for the first time. I read *Airport, Hotel,* and *The Money-Changers.* I told myself I could do a pretty decent job in this genre. I didn't think it was beyond my capabilities, and it looked like a fair challenge, even fun. That was a definite motivation for *Club Caribe,* a book not dissimilar to *Hotel* and *Abingdon's* [1979]. Now I'm at the point where I'm not that interested in Mr. Hailey anymore, though I still enjoy reading him. *Rhythms* [1980] is a departure from the Hailey-esque genre. It's not the wildly episodic book that *Hotel* and *Abingdon's* are; it focuses on one main character, a complex and sympathetic woman who starts a disco against formidable odds. It's involved in more subtle themes and character inter-

Must be exciting, to be in the Army. You get to travel, meet people, see new things. ■ (Jacket illustration by Bob Travers from *Soldier Boy* by Michael French.)

action. Also, it's a much sexier book than I think Hailey would write."

In 1980 French sold his first young adult novel to Delacorte, a book that he had difficulty placing until his first adult novels were published. It relates the story of Henry "Indian" Chevrolet, a high school shot-putter who views his athletic ability as a means to obtaining a college scholarship. "Before *Club Caribe* I had written three novels, one, *The Throwing Season,* about corruption in high school athletics. . . . When I first sent *The Throwing Season* around, without an agent, no publisher wanted it. That's why I sat down in a mood of some discouragement and started reading Hailey, thinking if I set my sights on a particular genre, I'd have a better chance of getting published.

"My interest in writing young adult fiction is to make readers aware of their uniqueness and potentials, of the moral dilemmas that will one day confront them, and to try to broaden their worlds as good fiction sometimes can."

In his second young adult novel, *Pursuit,* French explored the relationships between four boys on a hiking trip in the Sierra mountains. The trip becomes a pursuit when one of the hikers deliberately cuts the safety rope of another, causing his death and chases the victim's brother when he refuses to cover up the death. The hunted boy faces a journey not only of survival but into himself.

"I try to research basics first. In fact, I over-research, gathering far more facts than I could ever use, because that's the only way I'll know which facts are worth using. Once the novel unfolds, inevitably there are certain gaps that I don't know how to fill, so I have to go back for more research.

"My goal is a thousand good words a day, and that usually involves two or three drafts. So I'm doing my revisions on a daily basis. Then when I finish about half the novel, I go back and do more revisions. I have a good idea what I want to do in a book before I type the first page, but as I go along I see changes have to be made. New ideas occur all the time. If they're good, they belong in the book.

"The most important time spent is in thinking out the book—planning the plot, characters, shaping the narrative, knowing the effects I want to create. The harmony, the resonance, has to feel right. The architecture has to be right. And when you've got that larger context down, you start working on the interior—first the chapters, then pages, paragraphs, sentences, working down to the smallest details, which can be the most crucial . . . the difference between a fair story and a good one.

"Writing being a solitary pursuit, one is pretty much locked to a typewriter or word processor six or seven hours a day. When I have free time, I don't like to talk or think writing. And most writers I know, if they're not talking about their work, tend to be quiet and introverted. For company I prefer a little more stimulation. The best way to enjoy writers is through their books."

HOBBIES AND OTHER INTERESTS: Tennis, cycling, mountain trekking, designing and building adobe houses.

FOR MORE INFORMATION SEE: New York Times Book Review, March 4, 1979; *Washington Post Book World,* July 29, 1979.

The sweetest roamer is a boy's young heart.
—George E. Woodberry

INA R. FRIEDMAN

FRIEDMAN, Ina R(osen) 1926-

PERSONAL: Born January 6, 1926, in Chester, Pa.; daughter of Jacob Sidney (a paper jobber) and Libby (a homemaker; maiden name, Leibowitz) Rosen; married Sol Friedman, August 11, 1946 (died November 15, 1973); married Sam D. Starobin, March 12, 1977; children: (first marriage) Ronne, Wendy, Lynn, Loren. *Education:* Pennsylvania State University, B.A., 1946. *Politics:* Democratic. *Religion:* Jewish. *Address:* c/o Houghton Mifflin, One Beacon St., Boston, Mass. 02108.

CAREER: Writer, lecturer, and storyteller. Producer of slide tape "It Wasn't Just the Nazis." *Member:* Authors Guild, Society of Children's Book Writers, Washington Independent Writers, New England Storytelling Center, National Association for the Preservation and Perpetuation of Storytelling, PEN, Hadassah. *Awards, honors:* Christopher Award, 1984, for *How My Parents Learned to Eat.*

WRITINGS: (With Ethel Dalmat) *Poetry in Prayer* (religious service), Temple Sinai, 1965; *A Collection of Temple Sinai Religious School Poetry,* Temple Sinai, 1969, new edition, 1970; *Black Cop: A Biography of Tilman O'Bryant,* Westminster Press, 1974; *Escape or Die: True Stories of Young People Who Survived the Holocaust,* Addison-Wesley, 1982; *How My Parents Learned to Eat* (ALA Notable Book; *Horn Book* honor list; illustrated by Allen Say), Houghton, 1984. Also translator of adult books from Hebrew to English.

ADAPTATIONS: "How My Parents Learned to Eat," Reading Rainbow, PBS-TV, 1987.

WORK IN PROGRESS: Picture books for kindergarten through third grades.

SIDELIGHTS: "For the past several years I have been a storyteller and lecturer in addition to being a writer. I tell stories from my book on the Holocaust, *Escape or Die: True Stories*

of Young People Who Survived the Holocaust and native American, Japanese, New England, Jewish and other types of stories. I also tell the story of Isabella Stewart Gardner, the founder of the Gardner Museum in Boston. I got into storytelling through lecturing on my book *Escape or Die.* Several people heard me tell the stories and suggested I work up a program solely of storytelling, which I did. I joined the National Association for the Preservation and Perpetuation of Storytelling and also the New England Storytelling Center. I also give workshops to students on writing, publishing and publicizing books.

"I have always been interested in writing, but as an adolescent I became afraid to show anyone my work after one aunt who had a master's degree in social work declared, 'She has no talent.' Her judgment was based on one story I had written. My advice to would-be writers: Keep writing, take writing courses to help you improve, show your work to people who can give you constructive criticism and have faith in yourself.

"My first published book, *Black Cop,* was written about a friend on the police force. My children enjoyed listening to his detective stories so I thought other students would, too. His life mirrored the civil rights movement of the 60s and 70s, and I thought this would be a good area to explore.

"To obtain material for *Escape or Die,* I travelled over 60,000 miles to five continents. I wanted to show the effect of the Nazis on individual lives, and I wanted the stories of young people to whom students could relate. *How My Parents Learned to Eat* grew out of my friendship with a Japanese woman who married an American. I thought how fortunate their children were to be brought up with two cultures. It was very exciting to receive the Christopher Award for this book."

HOBBIES AND OTHER INTERESTS: Theater, gardening, cooking, travel, swimming, tennis, collecting oral histories.

FOR MORE INFORMATION SEE: Martha E. Ward and Dorothy A. Marquardt, *Authors of Books for Young People,* supplement to the 2nd edition, Scarecrow, 1979.

FURNISS, Tim 1948-

PERSONAL: Born April 14, 1948, in Epsom, England; son of John (in business) and Marnie (Battersby) Furniss; married Susan Jacob (a trampoline instructor), January 6, 1979; children: Tom. *Education:* Attended private school in Guildford, England. *Religion:* Methodist. *Home and office:* 23 Downs Way, Epsom, Surrey KT18 5LU, England.

CAREER: Has worked as a publisher's assistant, a public relations assistant, a public relations manager, and an advertising manager. Free-lance broadcaster, writer, and public relations consultant, 1982-85; free-lance writer and broadcaster on spaceflight, 1985—. *Member:* British Interplanetary Society (fellow). *Awards, honors: Space* was chosen one of Child Study Association of America's Children's Books of the Year, 1985.

WRITINGS: A Trip to the Moon, Pitman, 1973; *A Sourcebook of Rockets, Spacecraft, and Spacemen,* Ward, Lock, 1973; *UFOs,* World, 1978; *Space Today,* Kaye & Ward, 1979; *The Story of the Space Shuttle,* Hodder & Stoughton, 1979, 3rd edition, 1986; *Space Satellites,* Hodder & Stoughton, 1980; *The Sun,* F. Watts, 1980; *Man in Space,* David & Charles, 1981; *Space Stowaway,* Kaye & Ward, 1982; *Jane's Manned*

Space is a hostile environment. ■ (Cover illustration by Andrew Farmer from *Space* by Tim Furniss.)

Spaceflight Log, Jane's Yearbooks, 1983, new edition, 1986; *Space Exploitation,* Batsford, 1983, David & Charles, 1984; *Shuttle to Mars* (juvenile novel; illustrated by Trevor Parkin), Kaye & Ward, 1983; *Our Future in Space,* F. Watts, 1985; *Space,* F. Watts, 1985; *Jane's Space Shuttle Flight Log,* Jane's Yearbooks, 1985; *Space Flight: The Records,* Guinness Superlatives England, 1985, Sterling, 1986.

Space correspondent of *Flight International,* 1984; European correspondent, *Space World,* 1984; contributor to *Space,* 1985, and *Space Flight News,* 1986.

WORK IN PROGRESS: Regular appearances on radio and television.

SIDELIGHTS: ''I have been interested in space since Gagarin's adventure in 1961. It has been my ambition to write and broadcast on space ever since I was fourteen, when in 1962 John Glenn's flight inspired me. From then on I collected news cuttings, magazine articles, pictures, and books on space. I was quite simply a 'space nut.' The sixties, culminating with Apollo on the moon, was a most exciting period for me, and then as I was beginning to write about space professionally

(two small books and some local radio), interest in the seventies dwindled to such an extent that I spent a very frustrating time waiting for the shuttle to arrive. Then pow! Everything started to happen. From 1979 onwards I wrote more books and did national radio and television, including a regular 'space spot' on national radio for kids.

''In the early seventies I went to the Cape [Kennedy] to see *Apollo XIII* and *XV* launched and met a number of the astronauts, including some that landed on the moon. I even got to wear a moon suit. I returned to cover a shuttle launch in 1985 in a more professional capacity. I would like to fly on a shuttle one day.

''I have a long way to go yet to achieve this ultimate objective, but sometimes do allow myself a smile at what perseverance, determination, enthusiasm, and luck have earned me since those days when I used to sit during school breaks trying to pick up a news station on the radio during a launch. I well remember listening in awe to Gordon Cooper's launch on my faithful blue transistor radio in 1963. I remember quite clearly thinking to myself then how good it would be to write and broadcast about space when I grew up.''

HOBBIES AND OTHER INTERESTS: Playing cricket as "cricket keeper."

GALDONE, Paul 1914-1986

OBITUARY NOTICE—See sketch in *SATA* Volume 17: Born in 1914, in Budapest, Hungary; emigrated to the United States in 1928; died of a heart attack, November 7, 1986, in Nyack, N.Y. Illustrator, author, painter, and sculptor. Galdone moved to New York City not long after arriving in the United States and worked at various jobs while attending the Art Students League and the New York School of Industrial Design at night. After four years in the art department of Doubleday & Company and a stint serving with the U.S. Army Engineer Corps during World War II, Galdone became a free-lance illustrator, including book jacket design. Throughout his career, Galdone illustrated several hundred children's books, many based on folktales and fables, including *Hans Brinker, Henny Penny, The Bremen Town Musicians,* and *The Three Bears.* He also illustrated Eve Titus's *Anatole* and *Anatole and the Cat,* which were both chosen Caldecott Honor Books. Galdone's numerous self-illustrated books include original stories and retellings such as *Paddy the Penguin, The Monkey and the Crocodile, The Town Mouse and the Country Mouse,* and *The History of Mother Twaddle and the Marvelous Achievements of Her Son Jack*—a comic adaptation of "Jack and the Beanstalk," based on an early nineteenth-century version. A nature lover, Galdone painted landscapes as well as still lifes, portraits, and nudes.

FOR MORE INFORMATION SEE: Illustrators of Children's Books: 1946-1956, Horn Book, 1958; *Books Are by People,* Citation Press, 1969; *Authors of Books for Young People,* Scarecrow, 1971; *Third Book of Junior Authors,* H. W. Wilson, 1972; *Contemporary Authors, New Revision Series,* Volume 13, Gale, 1984; *The Oxford Companion to Children's Literature,* Oxford University Press, 1984. Obituaries: *Publishers Weekly,* December 5, 1986.

GARD, (Sanford) Wayne 1899-1986

OBITUARY NOTICE: Born June 21, 1899, in Brocton, Ill.; died of pneumonia, September 24, 1986, in Dallas, Texas. Historian, educator, journalist, and author. Gard was best known as the author of *The Chisholm Trail* and several other books of interest to young adults on the history of Texas and the Southwest. Trained as a journalist, Gard initially worked part-time as a correspondent while teaching journalism at Grinnell College in Iowa. His first full-time posts as a newsman were brief stints with the *Chicago Daily News,* the *Des Moines Register,* and *Vanity Fair* magazine. In 1933 he joined the staff of the *Dallas Morning News,* where he remained as an editorial writer for thirty-one years until his retirement in 1964.

In addition to the best-selling *Chisholm Trail,* Gard wrote *Sam Bass, Frontier Justice, The Great Buffalo Hunt, Reminiscences of Range Life,* and *Rawhide Texas*—for which he received the Summerfield G. Roberts Award from the Sons of the Republic of Texas. Gard also contributed numerous articles and book reviews to magazines and periodicals, including *American Heritage, American Mercury, Reader's Digest,* and *House and Garden.*

FOR MORE INFORMATION SEE: Contemporary Authors, Volumes 1-4, revised, Gale, 1967; *Encyclopedia of American Agricultural History,* Greenwood Press, 1975; *The Reader's Encyclopedia of the American West,* Crowell, 1977. Obituaries: *Dallas Morning News,* September 27, 1986; *Dallas Times Herald,* September 27, 1986.

GARDNER, Hugh 1910-1986

OBITUARY NOTICE: Born March 28, 1910; died August 6, 1986. Civil servant and author of a children's book. Appointed Commander of the Order of the British Empire in 1953, Gardner spent nearly forty years serving Britain's Ministry of Agriculture and Fisheries. He retired in 1970 and during the ensuing ten years worked as an inspector for the Department of the Environment. In 1967 Gardner published *Tales from the Marble Mountain.*

FOR MORE INFORMATION SEE: Who's Who, 138th edition, St. Martin's, 1986. Obituaries: *Times* (London), August 18, 1986.

GASPERINI, Jim 1952-

BRIEF ENTRY: Born October 31, 1952, in New York. A graduate of Williams College, Gasperini worked in Paris, France as a technician for Stichting Video Heads and video editor for *Video* in Paris during the 1970s. Returning to New York City, he subsequently became regional manager of Ballen Booksellers International, a position he has held since 1983. Gasperini is the author of *Sail with Pirates* (1984) and *Secret of the Knights* (1984), both part of Bantam's "Time Machine" series. These "interactive" stories challenge middle-grade readers to choose their own plots, using a databank of information for help. Because its interest level extends to high school grades, *Voice of Youth Advocates (VOYA)* described the series as "excellent hi-lo material for YAs." *Mystery of Atlantis,* Gasperini's third book in the series, was published in 1985. He has also created interactive fiction software, *Star Trek: The Promethean Prophecy,* for Simon & Schuster and is now working on a computer fiction book. *Home:* 270 Riverside Dr. 12A, New York, N.Y. 10025.

GEVIRTZ, Eliezer 1950-

PERSONAL: Surname is pronounced Ge-*virtz;* born January 10, 1950, in New York, N.Y.; son of Sidney (a safety inspector) and Ellen (a homemaker; maiden name, Freymark) Gevirtz; *Education:* City College of the City University of New York, B.A. (summa cum laude), 1972; Yeshiva Hirsch Rabbinical College, rabbinical degree, 1972; Long Island University, M.S., 1974. *Religion:* Jewish. *Home:* 120 Bennett Ave., New York, N.Y. 10033.

CAREER: Yeshiva Rabbi Samson Raphael Hirsch School, New York, N.Y., part-time teacher, 1969-74, full-time teacher and guidance counselor, 1974—; Salanter-Akiva-Riverdale Academy, Riverdale, N.Y., teacher of religious and secular subjects, 1981—.

WRITINGS: Lehovin Ulehaskil: Questions and Answers on Jewish Philosophy, Jewish Education Program, 1980; *The Mystery of the Missing Pushke* (juvenile; illustrated by Chanan Mazal), Philipp Feldheim, 1982; (with Nosson Scherman) *The Story of the Chofetz Chaim* (juvenile; illustrated by Yosef Dershowitz), Mesorah, 1983. Editor of *Darkeinu* magazine and *Zeirei Forum;* contributor of *Olomeinu* magazine.

WORK IN PROGRESS: "A second mystery for Jewish youngsters."

SIDELIGHTS: "*The Mystery of the Missing Pushke* was written to provide both entertainment and some moral values (in a non-preaching format) to Jewish youth. Unfortunately, I find that many of the media's presentations to youngsters tend to exploit them through the lure of sex and violence. There is a real need for alternatives, especially for religious youth, and this book was intended as such. In it, I tried to convey the values of empathizing with those who are different and of not judging or criticizing others prematurely.

"I have long enjoyed the creative thrill in developing plots and fleshing out characters (though summoning up the patience to make them materialize on paper can be grueling). I especially liked the challenge of devising a mystery and hope to do another.

"As an Orthodox Jew, I am especially eager to try to bring the traditional Jewish values alive through contemporary plots and settings, as in *Missing Pushke.* I find it significant that the secular-based material I wrote as a teenager proved unmarketable, whereas I was able to get the more recent Jewish-based material published much more easily. Perhaps it is because I am now writing about subjects I am more familiar and comfortable with.

"For years I'd dreamed of publishing a book, but the prospects dimmed with each rejection slip. The chance finally came in an odd way—I'd volunteered to tutor a boy for his bar mitzvah; when he proved recalcitrant, his mother suggested I contact the boy's rabbi. The tutoring eventually proved fruitless, but not the contact with the rabbi, who was preparing a publication for an outreach group called the Jewish Education Program. I helped him with this and eventually wound up writing a book for him on Jewish philosophy. Likewise, the assignment for a recent book I co-authored about the Chofetz Chaim (one of the great Jewish sages of the century) came through volunteer work I'd been doing for a Jewish education group. There seems to be a message somewhere in these opportunities.

ELIEZER GEVIRTZ

He was so busy daydreaming during class, that he wasn't learning as well as he should be! ■ (From *The Mystery of the Missing Pushke* by Eliezer Gevirtz. Illustrated by Chanan Mazal.)

"Any time for writing is mainly confined to the summer. During the school year I am quite preoccupied working with some 150 students in two Jewish schools in New York. Despite the occasional 'battle fatigue,' I enjoy the work and especially the chance to see the students progress and develop. They also occasionally provide ideas for characters or plot incidents. And I'm really excited when I see them revealing literary or artistic talent.

"I look upon writing as a way of communicating with those in the present and of leaving a legacy to those in the future. My ultimate role model is the great rabbi called the Chofetz Chaim, whose works and saintly personal example can still inspire Jews of all ages everywhere."

HOBBIES AND OTHER INTERESTS: Reading biographies, listening to music.

Across the fields of yesterday
   He sometimes comes to me,
A little lad just back from play—
   The lad I used to be.

              —Thomas S. Jones, Jr.

MARY GILMORE

GILMORE, Mary (Jean Cameron) 1865-1962

PERSONAL: Born July 16, 1865 (other sources cite August 16), near Goulburn, New South Wales, Australia; died December 3, 1962, in Sydney, Australia; married William Alexander Gilmore in 1897; children: William Dysart. *Education:* Educated in New South Wales, Australia.

CAREER: Poet. Early in career worked as a school teacher; as a member of the New Australia movement, joined William Lane in founding an experimental socialist community in Paraguay, 1896-1902; after returning to Australia, 1902, contributed to labour publications in Sydney, and became women's page editor, *Sydney Worker,* 1902-30. *Member:* Fellowship of Writers, Women Writers, Lyceum Club, Women's Club. *Awards, honors:* Created Dame Commander of the Order of the British Empire, 1936, for her contribution to literature.

WRITINGS: Marri'd, and Other Verses, George Robertson, 1910; *The Tale of Tiddley Winks* (juvenile; poems), Bookfellow (Sydney), 1917; *The Passionate Heart* (poems), Angus & Robertson, 1918; *Hound of the Road* (essays), Angus & Robertson, 1922; *The Tilted Cart: A Book of Recitations* (poems), Worker Trade Union Print (Sydney), 1925; *The Wild Swan* (poems), Robertson & Mullens, 1930; *The Rue Tree* (poems), Robertson & Mullens, 1931; *Under the Wilgas* (poems), Robertson & Mullens, 1932; *Old Days, Old Ways: A Book of Recollections* (autobiography), Angus & Robertson, 1934, reprinted, 1963; *More Recollections* (autobiography), Angus & Robertson, 1935; *Battlefields* (poems), Angus & Robertson, 1939; *The Disinherited* (poems), Robertson & Mullens, 1941; *Selected Verse* (poems), Angus & Robertson, 1948, enlarged edition, edited by Robert D. Fitzgerald and T. Inglis Moore, 1969.

All Souls, Walter W. Stone, 1954; *Fourteen Men* (poems), Angus & Robertson, 1954; *Mary Gilmore* (selected poems; edited by R. D. Fitzgerald) Angus & Robertson, 1963; *Mary Gilmore: A Tribute* (selected writings; criticism and biography by Dymphna Cusack, T. I. Moore, Barrie Ovenden, and Walter Stone), Australasian Book Society, 1965; (with Lydia Pender) *Poems to Read to Young Australians* (juvenile; selected poems; illustrated by June Gulloch), Hamlyn, 1968; (with L. Pender) *Poems for Playtime* (illustrated by J. Gulloch), Hamlyn, 1969; *The Singing Tree* (juvenile; selected poems; illustrated by Astra L. Dick), Angus & Robertson, 1971; *Letters of Mary Gilmore,* selected and edited by William H. Wilde and T. I. Moore, Melbourne University Press, 1980.

Also author of *Pro Patria Australia, and Other Poems* (illustrated by Rhys Williams), 1945, and *Verse for Children,* 1955. Contributor of poetry and articles to numerous periodicals, including *Sydney Morning Herald, Sydney Daily Telegraph, Woman's Mirror,* and *New Idea.* Her work can also be found in various anthologies.

SIDELIGHTS: **July 16, 1865.** Born at her maternal grandfather's property, "Meryrale," Cottawalla, near Goulburn, New South Wales. Gilmore grew up under pioneering conditions in Australia. From her grandfather and father she learned to respect the Aborigines. "I was born near Goulburn, N.S.W. Mother N.S.W. native of N. of Ireland parentage, highly strung, nervous, bright woman, without either fads or superstitions. I was born when she was barely twenty. Father; fine looking man of splendid physique, talent for the mechanical, *very* Highland. When he was about forty he met his equal at scratch pulling; I have an idea he and the other man sat and pulled all

night without advantage on either side. My father never pulled again. He was too proud to risk a beating. He had all the Highland superstitions,—though he always *said* he didn't believe in 'em. I have them too, and I always say I don't believe in them, nor do I intellectually, but in the bedrock of my soul the belief is there.

"In my young days I was considered a prodigy of learning because I could write a fine angular hand and read a newspaper article at the age of seven. One of my earliest recollections is as a child of three sitting on my maternal grandfather's knee and spelling out of the old Family Bible 'In the Beginning was the Word.'

"My mother's people were Wesleyans of the rigid Presbyterian kind. Indeed it was simply accident that called my grandfather anything so mild as Wesleyan. No weekly newspaper was read inside his doors on Sundays, and no wicked secular music was ever heard inside his gates. . . .

"I went to school in Wagga in due time and found that I had constantly to explain myself to my fellow pupils. 'You use such long words' they used to say. I was surprised; I had no intention of using out-of-the-way language. I was a voracious reader, and spoke like a book. At this school (I was ten) I was put into a low class because I could not add up, but in six months I was in third class, and considered an exceedingly quick child. In third class we had composition and I recollect almost invariably my slate was kept to show round to the teachers. I did not think of it myself. The other girls drew my attention to the fact. When I was eight or nine I would sit for hours writing 'letters' on a slate; no one ever read them—not even myself, and as quickly as one was written it was cleaned off and another begun. At the little Brucedale (near Wagga)

Gilmore at work in her flat.

school I used to spend all my dinner hour at this, eating my lunch as I wrote.

"... I was a thin, tall, delicate child, and the hours of school took so much from my vitality that many and many a time I walked home with the calves of my legs pushing to the front in a state of nervous terror at the imaginary *something* that might be behind. In the morning there were no terrors, only in the evening. I was a child that constantly craved the affection of its nearest, or the signs of it, and because I would not sue I got, or fancied I got, least of it. It is the child that leaps on your lap and kisses you that gets the kiss, not the one that sits in the corner and longs for it, yet the first probably only kisses for love of kissing.

"After Wagga School I went to Downside School a few miles away. Here I was a bad girl. The poor old pedagogue for pedagogue he was, used to keep me in and go to his dinner. I used to climb out the window and over the fence, have my dinner and be back again before he remembered me." [Mary Cameron Gilmore, *Letters of Mary Gilmore,* edited by W. H. Wilde and T. Inglis Moore, Melbourne University Press, 1980.[1]]

1877. At the age of twelve, Gilmore left her family to work as an unofficial student teacher. Part of her day was spent teaching and part was spent learning from head teachers. "... I went to school in Cootamundra and later at Bungowannah, near Albury—a small country school among farms, where I had a bed made up in the school quite away from the house, because there was no spare room for me in the residence, where I used to lie awake in the moonlight nights trembling and cold with nervous fear, listening to the cry of the morepork in the hills, and the melancholy wail of the curlew in the flats, while my heart used to nearly burst with fright at the rustle of a mouse among the papers in the empty grate. I left here so thin and nervous I was kept at home for some time before I went to school again.

"Then I was sent to a good kind uncle—teacher at Yerong Creek, who took such pains with me that, when at sixteen I went up for examination as Pupil Teacher, I was said to have passed highest of all that year's candidates. I was given my choice of appointment in Sydney or any of half a dozen country towns. I chose Wagga as being near my own people, and because I had gone to school there. I was only a gawky country girl dressed in a home made frock when I entered the school to begin work, and when I went eagerly up to an old schoolfellow (she wore a watch and her skirt was weighted down with pennies instead of shot, and who afterwards married a clergyman and wore glasses) she coldly gave me the tips of her fingers and turned away to another girl whose dress had six pearl buttons where mine had one. But deep inside the chill that came over me was the germ of a hot feeling of hate and determination to some day make her repent of her snub. Perhaps I did, perhaps I didn't, but when for months she came to me to help her with her hardest sums, unravel the difficulties of her analysis, and give her the punctuation in the punctuation lessons, when indeed she, who previous to my coming had been the bright one, looked up to me as the bright one, then I was satisfied. My pride was soothed, I had had my revenge— and she never knew. No one who ever injured me to a deep hurting can say I ever injured them. Indeed I sometimes feel I hate so hard I *have* to be kind. ...

"Also at the time I used to often read novels till midnight and then study till daylight. I *couldn't help* reading—I read everything, Jack Harkaways, Proctor's Astronom. works, Jevons's Logic, Family Heralds, Gordon's Poems, Kendall, The Koran, fragments of newspaper stories, even if only a few inches

long—anything and everything I could get. And at this time I got my best reports as a teacher. It often seems strange to me how it should be so. ...

"I have so often been told that I have a strong personal influence over people that I begin to believe it especially as, when I look back over my life at school and as Pupil Teacher, I remember that I was either 'leader' or 'ringleader' (amongst my own particular factions or schools)—according to whether I was good or bad. I resigned my pupil teachership and took a small school in order to speedily go up for examination as a classified teacher and to avoid the training school, of which somehow I had a dread. As soon as possible I sat for examination. Feeling sure of III C. and hoping for III. B. to my surprise I came out with III. A...."[1]

1888-1889. Taught in the mining town of Silverton, where Gilmore's close association with the working-class community led to her active support of the newly-formed labour movement.

1890. Returned to Sydney, teaching first at Neutral Bay and later at Stanmore. Became actively involved with the newly-established Australian Workers Union, and acquainted with William Lane, the founder of "New Australia," a socialist utopia in Paraguay.

1896. Gilmore spent several years in Cosme, the "New Australia" colony founded by William Lane. "William Lane believed in humanity, not in the possession of things; and in the fluidity of human life, individual and sectional, rather than in the fixed. 'No one is free who has no time for thought or enjoyment. Leisure is a human necessity,' he would say and to him, indeed, leisure was as much a necessity to the individual as law to the community. So the end of his thinking and observation, based on knowledge of an older world, and

Gilmore in 1899.

fired by the freedom he had found in the U.S.A. *'Australia is half-way between England and the U.S.A.'* was the New Australia Movement, which apparently ended in Paraguay. I say apparently, because the influence of that Movement never quite died out in Australia. It educated even its opponents.

"The enrollment of members was rapid once we began seriously to work. Women paid nothing to join, men paid £60 as a paper minimum for when we thought a man worth while we took less. Needing a ship to trade when trading as a colony would begin, we bought *The Royal Tar* for £1500, and began to fit her out for the voyage. Also we began gathering in the people for the sailing. As they came to Sydney with their families and their possessions, we housed them in places we rented in Marrickville and Balmain. But the Government so hampered us in every way it could, hoping to deplete our cash resources as well as to disaffect our members, that while it did not succeed in the latter, it certainly did in regard to the former. The result was that we could not pay the baker, and the bailiffs were in for rent. But the landlord and bailiffs were so decent that it was pretended that the men in possession were members of the expedition, and the real members never knew how badly off we were. On top of this came a new exaction from the Government with the result that at a meeting of the Executive at which I was not present, it was decided to sell *The Royal Tar,* give up all idea of settlement, and repatriate everyone from what the ship would bring. When I was told of this, I said No, and that we must go on. 'But we cannot!' Mr Lane exclaimed. 'It is impossible to go on, for there is no money.' 'There will be money' I declared out of what subconscious depth I know not, adding, 'Wait, and see if I am not right.' I asked for a month's delay, then as that was refused for three weeks, then two, and in the end they agreed to a week. So I, who had no idea that I had any personal influence found myself a leader. Next day a large cheque came, and I was regarded almost as a prophetess. After that money rolled in, the ship was victualled, and the first batch of over 200 was ready for sailing.

"I have been asked, again and again, why we went to South America, and why we did not settle in Australia. The answer is easy. Neither Australia, New Zealand, nor Tasmania would give us even a foot of land. . . .

"The Spaniards, perhaps as a side inheritance from the Romans, understand colonization as no other race does. We were immediately offered, free, all the land we wanted, by the governments of the Argentine, Brazil (which of course was Portuguese), Chile, Bolivia, and Paraguay. This was not because of our excellence, but a matter of national foresight, for all these Republics in those sparse years gave free land for settlement to any immigrant nationality desiring it. So there were French, German, Welsh, Jewish, Russian, Italian and other colonies, each speaking its own language, publishing its own newspaper if it wished and had the money to do it, and each provided it kept the State laws, run self-governed. Consequently when we settled in Paraguay we spoke our own language, and had our own school. I followed John Lane as teacher when I went to the colony, which was after the break had come between the two parts. Like others we published our own Monthly journal. As far as I know, we were the only English-speaking community-settlement in South America, and though we were in a country which recognized only the Catholic religion, we had our own colony non-Catholic marriage service written by William Lane and published in the *Cosme Monthly.* This was accepted as official by the Government, whoever was our Chairman at the time being gazetted as Registrar. No Protestant clergyman ever came to the country be-

cause there were almost no Protestants to minister to, but I believe that about eight years later one did come for a time."[1]

During her years at Cosme, Gilmore taught the children, organized and administered a library for the adults, and edited the daily paper, *Cosme Evening News.*

May, 1897. Married a Cosme inhabitant, William Gilmore. Their only child, Billy, was born the following year. "I write much about Billy and little about Will. But motherhood is the thing that is of the world and for the world that says 'This have I done and this do I give,' but wifehood is the little world apart where none may come in—and so I only write of the outside things."[1]

1899. The Cosme settlement slowly disintegrated and, along with numerous others, the Gilmores made plans to return to Australia. The family was separated while her husband worked in Patagonia to raise their passage money. "And now as to why we in Cosme failed. First, we were really too few to work the land as it should have been worked, and we had no capital to buy sufficient machinery. Everything that could be made by hand and made from timber in our own forest was so made. However we built the first fireplace and chimney in Paraguay, made the first corrugated iron tank in all South America, still called the Australian tank, taught along with our recalcitrant ones the Australian method of sheep-shearing first with blades and then as they were introduced with machines, and through my recollections of how when I was a child the Australian aborigines caused wattle-seed to germinate quickly, we, for the first time since the expulsion of the Jesuits over a hundred years before, sucessfully germinated mate seed. This has meant millions of dollars in trade to South America. I may say that, in fourteen years Cosme had no death from disease, not even when bubonic plague and small pox ran through the country; and in that time no policeman had to come except as someone's guest.

"Again as to why Cosme failed.

"The law of life is movement. The circumscribed dies. Exodus is as necessary anywhere there is life, as ingress. We were the only British colony of our kind in the world. There was no other similar place with which we could have reciprocity or exchange. So, when the human cry came for change of scene, the desire for new faces, from the need of food that we could not supply, or even for another kind of girl or man to marry (for not all is affinity that is adjacent) when, I say, these things happened, and natural frictions aggravated them, there was no similar colony to go to. There was only the alien world, which was still by earlier custom the familiar world. And so the drift away began. And yet the world today, even of Australia, approaches what we advocated, and in a degree that to me is sometimes almost incredible. Even in the matter of national or community barter, which is the one thing that will release Governments from being the servants of the accumulated dollar and the all-powerful pound, even in this world begins to do what we of New Australia proposed as human. Abraham Lincoln, William Lane's hero, and for whom he called his eldest boy Charles Lincoln Lane, gave us the ideal by which we hoped to live as an abiding community, and that was 'Government of the people by the people for the people.' But we were ahead of our time. . . ."[1]

1902. Settled on the Gilmore property at Strathdownie near Casterton in Western Victoria. Became the editor of the women's page of the *Sydney Worker* newspaper, a post Gilmore held for twenty-three years.

Mary Gilmore at home.

1910. First volume of poems, *Marri'd, and Other Verses* was published. "As to whether my verses are 'me'—it depends on what one hears them say for one thing and what they find in me when they know me for another. The only thing I know is that they are the sincere cry of my heart in the better and truer ones, and of the mood in the lesser ones. They weren't written with pens, but with every cell that had sense of being in whatever is actual in what is really me. . . ."[1]

1912. Gilmore's husband joined his brother in Queensland. After his son completed his education, he joined his father and it was only during infrequent occasions that the family was reunited. At the age of forty-seven, Gilmore began her life's work as a poet, writer, and editor. Her writing for the *Worker* focused on a wide range of social and economic problems. She was concerned with the community's responsibility to youth and the aged, the sick and the helpless, the need to preserve the history of Australia, and with improving the sub-human conditions of the Aboriginals.

1925. *The Tilted Cart,* a collection of poems that dealt with Gilmore's passion to record, and to encourage others to record, the early outback life of Australia was well received. "Mechanical invention killed literary invention in Australia. The fence came too soon for us to have a literature of the frontier written in language evolved by the frontier as its own. Money came too soon as well as too easily, for invention and a world market made money as a cloud, and it only had to rain down on us. The world was filled with markets. So, land was fenced in a day, roads made, schools built, lawyers' signs put up, libraries opened, while bookshops grew in the second counter put in by silversmiths and jewellers.

"Then we brought in an imported literature where we should have been writing our own. Before we had begun to realize it, except in the far north, and the great buttes of the centre, the day of our frontier had gone, and its distinctions and its language with it. Now, a language for that period would have to be invented. That mixture of Scotch, Irish, country-and-shire-English, with its interlarding of aboriginal words, its sprinkling of Californian Spanish and its Red Indian hunting and gold-digging terms (which once was the speech of the land-ward wave inward from the sea—and the city such as the city was even then), it has all gone; and there was no one eager enough to save it. Still the field is there; and some day genius may stride forth and re-create it, and make us a literature wholly our own in expression, and as unmistakably characteristic as African is of Africa, and American of America."

[Mary Gilmore, *Old Days, Old Ways: A Book of Recollections,* Angus and Robertson, 1934.[2]]

1930. Retired from the *Worker* at the age of sixty-five, but the demands for her time and advice to aspiring writers were endless. That same year her most significant book of verse, *The Wild Swan* was published. "All my life it has been my lot to help others find themselves. My life from earliest years has been so full of observation and experience, and I realize now, too, that I had an exceptional father and mother for both were intellectual, and full of poetry and the historical sense, so that I see things in relationships unknown to most others, and can consequently show a path unseen to one seeking outlet."[1]

1936. Named a Dame of the British Empire. ". . . I have never, in writing, reached after the clothing—the jewelled or the silken words that are poetry. My house of words is a sawn timber house. It is neither a bower, a mansion, nor a battlement—all of which are poetry in its several forms. But I do rise above jingle in a sense of turning vowel sound, and, when I have time to do it, consonantal values. Usually I have not had time, and the dishes have been left to clatter on the literary shelf—or the literary dishes have been left, if that conveys it better."[1]

1945. Suffered a dual personal tragedy—son and husband died in Queensland. To assuage her grief, Gilmore gathered courage and strength from her writing, her social crusades, her active support of the Labour Party, her accumulation of Australian history, and her work with aspiring writers. "I am devoured still by other people's affairs, and I am afraid I shall have to go out into the wilderness to escape them—and I starve in the wilderness for want of people. Only as I grow old do I realize how much I have been and am a hungerer for my kind. I swore I would not read another ms. this morning; and just now is gone a working man and his novel is written in an exercise book—script. Oaths seem to be no use to me. But I do so want to get at my own work; I do not grow younger."[1]

1954. Approaching her ninetieth year and hampered by the common infirmities of old age, she published her last volume of poems, *Fourteen Men.* In her last and most beloved volume of poems, she wrote:

> "Here at this last I can come home
> And lay me down with a quiet mind;
> For the work is done that I had to do—
> A sheaf that my hand must bind."[1]

August, 1957. The Australasian Book Society commissioned William Dobell to do Gilmore's portrait. The artist found Gilmore ". . . a splendid person with a tremendous vitality and dignity which I wanted to get into paint."[1]

In Gilmore's final years she was considered a national figure—her birthdays were celebrated like holidays; streets were named after her; scholarships were awarded in her name. She was even asked to lead several local May Day processions as the May Queen.

December 3, 1962. Died at the age of ninety-seven. ". . . In regard to after death, for the most part I neither affirm nor deny. There is no argument in the mental plane that means proof to me that there is a future, yet point to the cast off feather of a sparrow, the broken leaf of a plant, and I know that what made these can also make futures. All the logic, all the argument, all the possibilities of all the ages are bound up in fragments such as these."[1]

FOR MORE INFORMATION SEE: Mary Gilmore, *Old Days, Old Ways: A Book of Recollections* (autobiography), Angus & Robertson, 1934, reprinted, 1963; M. Gilmore, *More Recollections* (autobiography), Angus & Robertson, 1935; Dymphna Cusack and others, *Mary Gilmore: A Tribute,* Australasian Book Society, 1965; Sylvia T. Lawson, *Mary Gilmore,* Oxford University Press, 1967; William H. Wilde, *Three Radicals,* Oxford University Press, 1969; Joseph Jones and Johanna Jones, *Authors and Areas of Australia,* Steck-Vaughn, 1970; M. Gilmore, *Letters of Mary Gilmore,* edited by W. H. Wilde and T. Inglis Moore, Melbourne University Press, 1980. Obituaries: *New York Times,* December 4, 1962; *Illustrated London News,* December 15, 1962.

GOODMAN, Deborah Lerme 1956-

BRIEF ENTRY: Born October 31, 1956, in New York. A writer and creator of games, Goodman has worked as an educator for several museums in Massachusetts and as education coordinator at the Smithsonian Institution in Washington, D.C. She has written several books in Bantam's "Choose Your Own Adventure" series: *The Throne of Zeus* (1985), *The Magic of the Unicorn* (1985), *The Trumpet of Terror* (1986) and *Vanished!* (1986). Goodman has also produced two books published by the Smithsonian Institution Traveling Exhibition Service: *The Magic Shuttle* (1982), in which Emily travels through time to learn about the origins of weaving; and *Bee Quilting* (1984), written with Marjorie L. Share, which provides a history of quilting and includes directions for actually making a quilt. A member of the Museum Education Roundtable and American Craft Council, Goodman contributes to periodicals, including *Threads, Cobblestone, Faces,* and *Pennywhistle Press,* and is a contributing editor to *Fiberarts. Home:* 871 Cambridge St., Cambridge, Mass. 02141.

GOULD, Chester 1900-1985

PERSONAL: Born November 20, 1900, in Pawnee, Okla.; died of congestive heart failure, May 12, 1985, in Woodstock, Ill.; son of Gilbert R. (a newspaperman) and Alice (Miller) Gould; married Edna Gauger, November 6, 1926; children: Jean (Mrs. Richard O'Connell). *Education:* Attended Oklahoma A. & M. College (now Oklahoma State University), 1919-21; Northwestern University, diploma, 1923. *Residence:* Woodstock, Ill.

CAREER: Cartoonist. *Chicago American,* Chicago, Ill., cartoonist for syndicated comic strip "Fillum Fables," 1924-29; *Chicago Daily News,* Chicago, ad illustrator, 1929-31; Chicago Tribune-New York News Syndicate, Chicago, creator of "Dick Tracy" comic strip syndicated to over five hundred newspapers, 1931-77. *Member:* National Cartoonists Society, Woodstock Country Club, Lambda Chi Alpha. *Awards, honors:* National Cartoonists Society Reuben Award for outstanding cartoonist, 1959; has also received numerous awards from law enforcement agencies and police departments, including the Police Athletic League Award, 1949, and the Associated Police Communications Officers Award, 1953.

WRITINGS: Dick Tracy and Dick Tracy, Jr. and How They Captured "Stooge" Viller, Cupples & Leon, 1933; *How Dick Tracy and Dick Tracy, Jr. Caught the Racketeers,* Cupples & Leon, 1934; *Dick Tracy, Ace Detective,* A. Whitman, 1943; *Dick Tracy Meets the Night Crawler,* A. Whitman, 1945; *The Celebrated Cases of Dick Tracy, 1931-1951,* edited by Herb

CHESTER GOULD

Galewitz, Chelsea House, 1970; *Dick Tracy, the Thirties, Tommy Guns and Hard Times*, edited by H. Galewitz, Chelsea House, 1978.

ADAPTATIONS: "Dick Tracy" (motion picture; also produced as "Dick Tracy, Detective"), starring Morgan Conway, RKO, 1945; "Dick Tracy Vs. Cueball" (motion picture), starring M. Conway, RKO, 1946; "Dick Tracy Meets Gruesome" (motion picture; also produced as "Dick Tracy Meets Karloff"), starring Ralph Byrd and Boris Karloff, RKO, 1947; "Dick Tracy's Dilemma" (motion picture), starring R. Byrd, RKO, 1947; "Dick Tracy" (television series), starring R. Byrd, ABC-TV, September 11, 1950-February 12, 1951; "Dick Tracy Show" (animated cartoon), United Productions of America, 1961.

Serials; each contains fifteen episodes; all produced by Republic Pictures: "Dick Tracy," 1936; "Dick Tracy Returns," 1938; "Dick Tracy's G-Men," 1939; "Dick Tracy Vs. Crime, Inc.," 1941, later released as "Dick Tracy Vs. the Phantom Empire," 1952.

SIDELIGHTS: **November 20, 1900.** ". . . I was born in Oklahoma and my grandfather on my mother's side was one of the men that made the trek into Oklahoma to stake out a claim.

His name was Riley Miller. He took his family there in 1892 and built a log cabin which is still standing. It's not very sturdy but it's there. On my father's side, my grandfather Gould was a minister who moved west from West Virginia. My own father was a printer and eventually the owner of a weekly newspaper. It was probably that influence which got me into the frame of mind to become a cartoonist.

"I remember very well one time when I was seven. My dad was then editing a weekly newspaper and there was to be a Pawnee County, Oklahoma political meeting. He said, 'Would you like to draw some of the men at this meeting?' Well, you can imagine how good my efforts must have been at that age. But I went over and turned out a bunch of stuff; they pasted it up in the window of the Pawnee *Courier Dispatch*, which was located right next to the post office. Everybody walked to the post office for the mail, so they had to pass my drawings. I got considerable attention and I think it's perhaps the thing that definitely turned me into this business. I have been at it since 1907." ["Interview with Chester Gould," *The Celebrated Cases of Dick Tracy 1931-1951*, edited by Herb Galewitz, Chelsea House, 1970.[1]]

"Mutt and Jeff" were early favorites. "Head and shoulders above everything else. . . . It was brand new and my father

Gould's first daily strip of "Dick Tracy," October 12, 1931. (Copyright 1931 by News Syndicate Co., Inc.)

used to buy the Oklahoma City *Daily Oklahoman* just so that I could read 'Mutt and Jeff.' 'Buster Brown' was big then too. So was 'Little Nemo,' and 'Slim Jim.'[1]

By the time Gould graduated from high school, he had already taken a correspondence course in cartooning.

1919-1921. Attended Oklahoma A. & M. College for two years until he moved to Chicago where he finished up a four-year course in commerce and marketing at Northwestern University, going to night school and working during the day drawing cartoons and doing commercial art work. "I had arrived in Chicago with $50 cash in my pocket from my hometown of Pawnee, Oklahoma on September 1, 1921, determined to be

a newspaper cartoonist. I was loaded with sample sports cartoons I had drawn for the *Daily Oklahoman* and editorial cartoons from the *Tulsa Democrat.* My aim was to crash the 'big-time' cartoon world of Sid Smith's 'The Gumps,' Frank King's 'Gasoline Alley,' and Carl Ed's 'Harold Teen,' all great comics of the time and successful for many years after. But it would be ten years (almost to the day) before I would be able to join that select group.

"To me, Chicago was a beautiful, wonderful, glamorous and peaceful place to become a millionaire, and I wouldn't dream of turning back. Becoming a millionaire, however, has proved to be one of the most elusive fantasies of my life.

(From "The First Appearance of Junior, September 8, 1932-October 12, 1932" in *Dick Tracy, the Thirties: Tommy Guns and Hard Times* by Chester Gould. Illustrated by the author.)

"My first Chicago job was far removed from the world of journalism. Newspaper jobs, as usual, were not plentiful and I wound up stacking groceries in an A & P on Devon Street. Fortunately, I was only there for a month when I heard that an artist on the Chicago *Evening Journal* was sick and I applied and got his job on a temporary basis at a surprising $30 per week. At that time, Chicago had six major daily newspapers, including the *Tribune*, the *Herald-Examiner*, the *Daily News*, the *Journal*, the *American* and the *Post*. Thereafter, I was never without a newspaper job.

"While I was not setting the world on fire, I was still doing an occasional comic strip and working with reporters on special pieces that put me close to the action. There was plenty of that in the twenties, sparked by the speakeasies which were supplied by the Beer Barons who were constantly warring with each other in a cacophony of machine guns. Though the average law-abiding citizen was more or less insulated from this unpleasant business, it was being abetted and supported by those who patronized the illegal speak.

"Without a doubt, it was this era that planted the idea of DICK TRACY in my head. The revelations of fixed juries, crooked judges, bribery of public officials and cops who looked the other way showed the crying need for a strong representative of law and order who would take an eye for an eye and a tooth for a tooth. Tracy was that man." [Chester Gould, *Dick Tracy, the Thirties, Tommy Guns and Hard Times*, Chelsea House, 1978.[2]]

1931. "Captain Joseph M. Patterson was the founder of the New York *Daily News* and also ran the syndicate that distributed its comic features. In June . . . , I sent him six strips titled 'Plainclothes Tracy.' After two months, I finally received the following wire:

"'BELIEVE PLAINCLOTHES TRACY HAS POSSIBILITIES. SEE ME IN MY *TRIBUNE* OFFICE THE 20TH.'

"Needless to say I was prompt for that appointment in the Trib Tower. Patterson changed the name of the strip to DICK TRACY and handed my submissions back to me with the advice that I would be on the payroll on the fifteenth of next month. Down in the lobby, I bought a cigar and a Coke and broke out into a cold sweat. I had achieved my goal.

"Though the work load was awesome, especially in the early years, I can say now that I doubt there is any business that can be equally as satisfying over such a long period of time.

"Most newspaper syndicates require eight to thirteen weeks lead time between receipt of material and publication. Because of this, I used to worry that some of my ideas could be stolen before they hit the presses. In order to protect myself, I would date and sign a copy of the drawing, put it into an envelope and mail it to myself. The sealed envelope would then be placed in one of my files for safekeeping.

"This was especially true of the 2-way wrist radio and TV which I originally sketched on October 17, 1945. As TV was still in its infancy, I used only the radio portion of the device at first. The Army's new walkie-talkie made the wrist radio much more plausible. A few years later, I did incorporate the TV aspect, and it has been a vital part of Tracy's gear to this very day."[2]

"Dick Tracy" started running as a Sunday page on October 4, 1931, and as a daily strip a week later. "'. . . Like all things new, it took a couple of months to catch on. Then it grew like wildfire. The salesmen would call me up and say, 'We got two new orders this morning.' There would be two or three orders a day for many, many days. However, from the very beginning I would receive letters saying what a 'horrible' strip I was doing.

"Now I am used to it and take it with a grain of salt. They don't annoy me one whit any more. The odd thing about them, however, is that they would often describe in detail the 'horrible things.' I figured that they were the types who couldn't wait until the next day to see how a particular thing turned out.

"I wanted my villains to stand out definitely so that there would be no mistake who the villain was. I once received a letter from a person asking, 'Why do you make your criminals so ugly?' I never looked at them as being ugly, but I'll tell you this. I think the ugliest thing in the world is the face of a man who has killed seven nurses—or who has kidnapped a child. His face to me is ugly. Or a man who has raped an old lady or young girl and robbed her of $3.40. I think this is an ugly man."'[1]

1941. During World War II many of the comic strip heroes went to war, but Dick Tracy was kept at home by his creator. "Somebody had to stay home and take care of these crooks. And I presume that there was so much of the Army—we were so saturated with the military—that I think leaning over backwards to be patriotic and putting on a uniform was not necessary. I think Tracy's homefront activity was just as important. An example is the Brow. He was a conniving traitor and Tracy got him."'[1]

January 21, 1946. "Dick Tracy" introduced the first two-way wrist radio.

Strip featuring Gravel Gertie in the year of her initial appearance. (Copyright 1944 by the *Chicago Tribune.*)

(From *The Celebrated Cases of Dick Tracy, 1931-1951* by Chester Gould. Illustrated by the author.)

(From the movie serial "Dick Tracy Vs. the Phantom Empire," starring Ralph Byrd. Produced by Republic Pictures Corp., 1952. Formerly released as "Dick Tracy Vs. Crime, Inc.," 1941.)

(From the movie serial "Dick Tracy's G-Men," starring Ralph Byrd. Produced by Republic Pictures Corp., 1939.)

1947. Gould introduced into the ''Tracy'' strip the first closed-circuit television (''teleguard'') to monitor criminal activities. He often utilized in his strip the possibilities of modern technology in crime prevention before anyone else, and was the first to adapt television for a burglar alarm.

1959. Given the National Cartoonists Society Reuben Award for outstanding cartoonist. About his daily work habits, Gould remarked: ''My production of Tracy is mostly a case of constant application and continuous effort. Of course any work you like is not really hard work—it's a happy operation. This is one of the most rewarding businesses in the world because all of the thinking and physical effort you put into producing a strip results in something concrete that's right there for readers to see in black and white.

''Once in a while there'll be a night when I'll wake up at 1 or 2 in the morning, and feel rested and don't want to go back to sleep, so I get up and come down to my drawing board. I'm not trying to make a hero out of myself—I just have the feeling I'd much rather be working on my strip than lying there in bed trying to figure why I can't go to sleep. So we have a lot of freedom in this business as well as being rather in a straitjacket.

''My research is going on all the time. . . . Not the kind that a college professor would do, but interesting observations such as a father would point out to his boy if they were taking a walk.

''I like to be alert to things that will make a good picture, and also fit into a good story. I have a very kind associate—a wonderful guy—who is responsible for all my technical police research. He's an ex-policeman—ex-detective—by the name of Al Valanis. He was very prominent in Chicago a few years back, at the time he perfected the method of sketching a criminal from eyewitness descriptions given to the police by a victim. He sits with me and supplies me with technical stuff. For instance, in a fingerprint room it's very important to know where the inkpad is, just what the apparatus is that holds the card, and just how you roll the fingers. Al tries to keep me on the straight and narrow on this. I slip once in a while and he gives me the old spear. He'll say, 'You'll have to do that one over—it isn't right!' Naturally, as you might suspect, I take several police magazines and bulletins, an FBI bulletin, etc., to keep myself up-to-date on routine and costuming. As an example, the State Police out here in Chicago wear a hat very much like the old Army hat, only it's a little bit modernized, whereas the Chicago Police wear a regular police cap with a checkerboard band. The checkerboard band, incidentally, is worn so people can quickly distinguish a policeman from taxi drivers and other people wearing caps, in case of a riot or other excitement. I don't make use of the checkerboard band because I try to keep my policemen universal.

''My schedule is pleasantly rigid and I'll tell you why I like it that way, after I give you a quick description of it. I do most of my writing on Friday and Monday, do a Sunday page on Tuesday, then 2 or 3 dailies on Wednesday and 3 more on

Strip showing a leaf from the "Crimestoppers Textbook." A Gould innovation, it appeared near the title of the Sunday page and was designed to draw attention to some facet of police procedure or crime prevention.

(From the daily comic strip, "Dick Tracy." Copyright 1949 by the *Chicago Tribune.*)

Thursday. Sometimes I spend some time Friday checking on the mistakes I made Thursday! I remember drawing a Sunday page one time which showed a hoodlum standing in the background, in a doorway, all through the page. Not until the strip got into print did anyone notice that this guy had on 4 different hats as he stood in that doorway! If you keep to a schedule, you can make yourself available, when needed, to your family—that's why I like it. If your wife asks, 'Will you be through with your work in time for dinner at 8?,' it's nice to be able to tell her you will, and that you'll help with some of the plans around the house.

"As far as assistants are concerned, I have a very fine, capable gent with me by the name of Richard Fletcher, who used to do a beautiful Civil War patriotic page. He does backgrounds, and helps somewhat with the technical situations as Valanis does. He can help with figures, too. I do every bit of the finished writing, I do all of my drawing, all of the penciling, including backgrounds, and I ink in my figures. My brother, Ray Gould, does the balloons after Fletcher and I are through. We've got a little team and it works out nicely.

"Quite often people ask me what the chances are of getting into this business. In my estimation, the chances have never been better! As to ideas—I think the first ingredient is *imagination!* Fortunately, God gave me what I consider a pretty good one, and I've tried to capitalize on it. I think if you can combine imagination with technical, as well as historical, facts, that out of that combination quite often can come very interesting stories and situations. The beginner should cater to the man on the street—the fellow that has to pay his bills, has to keep his children in clothes, the guy who enjoys a quiet evening at home with his shoes off. Those are the people that make America—they're the ones who are going to buy your paper. A comic strip should have no place in a paper unless it sells papers. . . ." [Chester Gould, "Dick Tracy," *Cartoonist Profile,* March, 1973.[3]]

During the 60s Gould and his wife appeared on a "This Is Your Life, Chester Gould" TV program, hosted by Ralph Edwards.

1970. "Dick Tracy" was carried in more than six hundred newspapers across the country with an estimated circulation

Gould's comic self-portrait: The creator is instructed by his own creation.

of fifty million and a readership of at least twice that. The strip had been adapted into a radio show, movie serials, feature pictures, and a television cartoon series.

Commercial product spin-offs from the "Tracy" strip included radios, watches, burglar-alarm and detective kits, masks, wallets, guns of various kinds, secret money pockets, candy, puzzles, a "Gravel Gertie" banjo, a "Sparkle Plenty" doll, and "Sparkle Plenty" Christmas-tree lights.

1972. "I have been drawing and writing Dick Tracy for 41 years. And the Lord willing, I want to go another 41 years. I'm in excellent health and I'm loaded with experience and the joy of doing my job. I consider myself a newsboy. The sole purpose of a comic strip is to sell newspapers; that makes me a newsboy. The American comic strip is responsible for and has sold more newspapers since its creation than any other feature in American journalism, and I'm proud to be part of it.

"We have a heritage of the most precious thing ever developed in the good old U.S.A.—the American newspaper and its comic strips. . . ." [Chester Gould, "The American Comic Strip Has Sold More Newspapers Than Any Other Feature in American Journalism," *Cartoonist Profile*, March, 1973.[4]]

Gould advised aspiring young cartoonists to work hard. "Speaking of young people, I have only one conviction in my mind that I can put into a couple of sentences—you can't stop a young cartoonist who wants to go to the top. But he has to be willing to use an old-fashioned system which, I'm sorry to say, not too many seem to appreciate—and that system is spelled W-O-R-K!

"It's just that simple—I don't see any mystery at all to it—it takes years—great optimism—someone with a little sunshine

in his soul—a little faith—a little belief that there is a force that will help them if they help themselves. To the quitters there's no future in this business. They might just as well hear these words because it's a tough profession. It's been very good to me—I love it—and I'm going to be around and do all I can to keep it a top business and keep it one of the happiest professions in the whole world."[4]

1977. Retired from drawing the comic strip.

May 12, 1985. Died of heart disease in Woodstock, Illinois. "I got most of my inspiration from a boyhood love of Sherlock Holmes. I was also a great follower of Edgar Allan Poe. I didn't follow many of the so-called 'popular' things that came in after 'Dick Tracy.' I followed the newspapers almost exclusively—the police news and all the information about the operation of gangsters and the war against them. And it really is a war that the police are constantly engaged in."[1]

HOBBIES AND OTHER INTERESTS: Golf, swimming, jogging, poker, driving.

FOR MORE INFORMATION SEE: Saturday Evening Post, December 17, 1949; *Holiday,* June, 1958; *Newsweek,* October 16, 1961, January 14, 1963; Herb Galewitz, editor, *The Celebrated Cases of Dick Tracy, 1931-1951,* Chelsea House, 1970; *Current Biography,* H. W. Wilson, 1971; *Washington Post,* January 15, 1971; *Cartoonist Profile,* March, 1973; Maurice Horn, *The World Encyclopedia of Comics,* Chelsea House, 1976; H. Galewitz, editor, *Dick Tracy, the Thirties, Tommy Guns and Hard Times,* Chelsea House, 1978.

Obituaries: *Los Angeles Times,* May 12, 1985; *New York Times,* May 12, 1985; *Chicago Tribune,* May 13, 1985; *Times* (London), May 14, 1985; *Time,* May 20, 1985; *Newsweek,* May 20, 1985; *Current Biography,* July, 1985.

GREGORY, Diana (Jean) 1933-

PERSONAL: Born April 27, 1933, in Pasadena, Calif.; daughter of Jessie (an interior decorator) and Marjorie (a real estate investor; maiden name, Phillips) Emerich; married John Gene Gregory, June, 1963 (divorced, 1976); children: Claudia Diane, Christopher Dean, Lisa Lynn. *Education:* Attended University of California, Los Angeles, 1951, and Pasadena City College, 1952-53 and 1966-67; Pasadena Playhouse College of Theatre Arts, B.A., 1968. *Politics:* Independent. *Religion:* Presbyterian. *Home:* 2402 71st Ave. SE, Mercer Island, Wash. 98040.

CAREER: Brangham & Brewer, Inc., Hollywood, Calif., in advertising, 1959-63; KHJ-TV, Hollywood, associate producer, 1968-71; writer, 1976—. Operated drama school for children; director for children's theater; actress. *Member:* Society of Children's Book Writers, Romance Writers of America.

WRITINGS—Young adult novels, except as indicated: *Dairy Goats* (adult; nonfiction), Arco, 1976; *Owning a Horse: A Practical Guide* (adult; nonfiction), Harper, 1977; *I'm Boo . . . That's Who!* (illustrated by Susan S. Mohn), Addison-Wesley, 1979; *There's a Caterpillar in My Lemonade* (illustrated by Channing Thieme), Addison-Wesley, 1980; *The Fog Burns Off by Eleven O'Clock,* Addison-Wesley, 1981; (with Pam Martin) *A Knight to Remember,* Simon & Schuster, 1983; *Don't Forget Me,* Bantam, 1984; *Forget Me Not,* New American Library, 1984; *Love Is in the Air* Bantam, 1985; *Two's a Crowd,*

Panel from a "Dick Tracy" comic strip, starring one of Gould's more memorable characters, "B.O. Plenty."

Diana Gregory with her "mostly" Great Dane, Bernardo.

Bantam, 1985; *Cross My Heart,* Bantam, 1986; *One Boy Too Many,* Bantam, 1987. Author of a column in *Mountain Democrat,* 1973. Contributor to juvenile and horse magazines.

WORK IN PROGRESS: Young adult novels.

SIDELIGHTS: "I am now concentrating my efforts on juvenile fiction for the age group which includes the change-over from childhood to young adulthood. I am particularly interested in problems they face and in the causes of today's youth problems. mainly the dissolution of family structure. All my fiction is based on thorough research.

"My first juvenile novel, *I'm Boo . . . That's Who!,* deals with the problems of a girl whose family is mobile, and her need for roots. That book didn't get published until I went through the motions of writing two non-fiction books in order to get a toehold inside the doorway of fiction. Who knows, someone else might have had luck without going through the nonfiction door. I didn't. Maybe I still hadn't reached the moment of being a writer.

"My second juvenile, *There's a Caterpillar in My Lemonade,* deals with a young girl whose natural father had been killed overseas in the Vietnam disaster. Until the age of thirteen she had her mother all to herself. Then her mother marries, and

she has to learn to adjust to having a father and living in a household that includes a male. *The Fog Burns Off by Eleven O'Clock* is about a girl who spends the summer visiting her divorced father and his very young mistress.

"How do I go about putting a book together? I get mad about a problem, research it as well as I can, lie down on the sofa for about four hours, then go to my typewriter and type the words 'Chapter I.' Then I forget I'm me, and the story begins. I have researched three other social problems and have tentative outlines for them. All my novels will be aimed at that particular age group who is asking questions, sometimes silently, and receiving too few answers.

"While continuing to write young adult novels, both a mix of serious and the lighter paperback type, my main focus is now on the forming of a packaging company for teen novels which are of a higher-than-average read. These are not to be dull books, but fast paced, page turning novels. More teens are reading today than ever before. I want to give them something exciting and worthwhile to read.

"At the moment we have four lines developed. One of them I am particularly excited about. It involves a dashing young man in the time of the American Revolution, written in a John Jakes style and involving plenty of espionage, secret mes-

May I suggest we join our business ventures? You know, the way other companies do. ■ (Cover photograph by Pat Hill from *Two's a Crowd* by Diana Gregory.)

sages, lots of action, and a bit of romance (but not enough to scare off any male readers). The reason I decided on doing such a line was reading about the rather frightening lack of knowledge many of today's teens have about history—anyone's history, but especially our own. I decided to do something about it. I'm not waving a flag, but I do believe there is so much richness to be learned about our own history, it's a shame not to find out about it.

"Writing and research take up about fourteen to sixteen hours of my day, which doesn't really leave time for hobbies any more. But I do like concerts—classical to rock. I try to take off a week every once in a while to do some quick traveling. Europe is my favorite. And occasionally I'll do a movie splurge—rent four or five films and pig out with popcorn."

Multiplication is vexation,
   Division is as bad;
The Rule of Three perplexes me,
   And practice drives me mad.

                          —Anonymous

GRUMMER, Arnold E(dward) 1923-

PERSONAL: Born August 19, 1923, in Spencer, Iowa; son of Edward H. (a Lutheran minister) and Anna (a housewife; maiden name, Christiansen) Grummer; married Mabel Emmel (a teacher), August 11, 1948; children: Mark, Gregory, Kimberly Grummer Schiedermayer. *Education:* Iowa State Teachers College (now University of Northern Iowa), B.A., 1949; State University of Iowa, M.A., 1952. *Politics:* Republican. *Religion:* Lutheran. *Home and office:* 1916 N. Drew St., Appleton, Wis. 54911.

CAREER: Iowa State Teachers College (now University of Northern Iowa), Cedar Falls, member of radio and television staff, 1949-51; Armstrong Cork Co., Lancaster, Pa., in advertising, 1952-53; Osage High School, Osage, Iowa, teacher of English and speech, 1954-57; Aid Association for Lutherans, Appleton, Wis., in advertising and public relations, 1957-59; Institute of Paper Chemistry, Appleton, assistant professor of general studies, 1960-70, editor of general publications, 1960-76, curator of Dard Hunter Paper Museum, 1970-76; writer, lecturer, and consultant, 1976—. *Military service:* U.S. Coast Guard, 1942-45; served in the South Pacific and Australia. *Member:* Wisconsin Alliance of Publishers and Authors.

WRITINGS: Paper by Kids, Dillon, 1980; *The Great Balloon Game Book and More Balloon Activities,* Greg Markim, 1987.

Author, editor and narrator of "Aspects of the Commercial Handmade Paper Industry of Taiwan," a film released by Institute of Paper Chemistry in 1964. Contributor to *Collier's Encyclopedia* and *Dictionary of American History.* Contributor to trade journals and newspapers in the United States and abroad, including *Paper* (London), *Sentinel* (Milwaukee), *Journal* (Milwaukee), and *One.*

WORK IN PROGRESS: Not Even Uncle Sam Wants You, a humorous novel; research on cloning trees and on paper history; hand papermaking book for adults.

SIDELIGHTS: "The material upon which these words are put is more amazing than any of the words—including the words

ARNOLD E. GRUMMER

of Aristotle, Shakespeare, Poe, or Papa Hemingway. These authors' words have penetrated the lives of relatively few people. Paper has penetrated the lives of everybody, present and future.

"It did this in one singular act. That act was the collection of radioactive debris from the atmosphere. In the form of a revolutionary filter paper, it sampled very likely the entire atmosphere of the earth, thereby tracing the travel, concentrations, ascendings and descendings geographically of residual and newly inserted radioactive debris in the atmosphere.

"On the basis of the findings, it was determined that the testing of radioactive devices in the atmosphere was a hazard to humanity. And on the basis of that conclusion, the decision was to discontinue all such testing. Since then, all over the world, no such testing in the atmosphere has taken place.

"That is paper touching the lives of everyone in the world, present and future.

"This is just one of the reasons I have found 'paper the ubiquitous' to be 'paper the incredibly fascinating.'

"So while other people might write of medicine, psychology, philosophy, spirituality, sexuality, history, poetry, or fiction, it is likely to be many reams before I exhaust the possibilities of writing on paper . . . about paper."

Grummer is the designer and manufacturer of "The Great American Paper Machine, Jr.," a hand papermaking device and kit.

HOBBIES AND OTHER INTERESTS: Hand papermaking, basic electronics, travel.

He tied nine balloons to his backyard craft, and has scheduled the blast-off for noon. ■ (From *Numbears: A Counting Book* by Kathleen Hague. Illustrated by Michael Hague.)

HAGUE, (Susan) Kathleen 1949-

PERSONAL: Born March 6, 1949, in Ventura, Calif.; daughter of John W. (an engineer and technical writer) and Sue (a landscaper; maiden name, Waggoner) Burdick; married Michael Hague (an author and illustrator of children's books), December 5, 1970; children: Meghan, Brittany, Devon. *Education:* Art Center College of Design, B.F.A. (with honors), 1971. *Home:* Colorado Springs, Colo.

CAREER: Artist. Author of children's books, 1979—. *Awards, honors:* The Man Who Kept House was chosen one of International Reading Association's Children's Choices, 1982; *The Legend of the Veery Bird* was selected one of Child Study Association of America's Children's Books of the Year, and was exhibited at Bologna International Children's Book Fair, both 1985.

WRITINGS—All illustrated by husband, Michael Hague: (Reteller with M. Hague) *East of the Sun and West of the Moon*, Harcourt, 1980; (reteller with M. Hague) *The Man Who Kept House*, Harcourt, 1981; *Alphabears: An ABC Book*, Holt, 1984; *The Legend of the Veery Bird*, Harcourt, 1985; *Numbears: A Counting Book*, Holt, 1986; *Out of the Nursery, Into the Night*, Holt, 1986.

SIDELIGHTS: "I enjoy people of all ages. Children are always fun and keep you guessing, but my best friends are few and my family is most important. I enjoy music, movies and painting. I have a deep seeded appreciation of 'good' art in most every form and admire anyone who gives all they've got—whether they succeed or not—to what they want to do."

HOBBIES AND OTHER INTERESTS: Photography.

Kathleen Hague with husband, Michael.

ARLENE HALE

HALE, Arlene   1924-1982
(Louise Christopher, Gail Everett, Will Kirkland, Mary Anne Tate, Lynn Williams)

PERSONAL: Born June 16, 1924, in New London, Iowa; died January 26, 1982; daughter of Ira Tate and Florence (Hand) Hale. *Education:* Attended Burlington College of Commerce. *Religion:* Methodist. *Residence:* New London, Iowa.

CAREER: Silas Mason Co., Burlington, Iowa, typist, 1941-43; Burlington Instrument Company, Burlington, assembly, 1943-47; Iowa-Illinois Telephone Co., New London, Iowa, accounting clerk, 1947-52; Sylvania Electric Co., Burlington, office clerk, 1952-54; free-lance writer, 1954—. *Member:* Authors Guild, Authors League of America, Mystery Writers of America.

WRITINGS—All published by Bouregy, except as indicated: *The Reluctant Heart*, 1958; *Tender Harvest*, 1959; *Blossoms in the Wind*, Winston, 1959; *Reluctant Stranger*, 1960; *School Nurse*, 1960; *Be My Love*, 1961; *Dr. Myra Comes Home*, 1962; *Listen to Your Heart*, Messner, 1962; *Ghost Town's Secret*, Abelard, 1962; *The Hungry Heart*, 1962; *Wait for Love*, 1963; *The Girl from Sherman Oaks*, 1964; *Nurse Shelley Decides*, Pyramid, 1964; *Nothing but a Stranger*, Four Winds Press, 1966; *Stay with Me, Love*, Banner Books, 1967; *The Lady Is a Nurse*, 1967; *Private Nurse*, Belmont-Tower, 1968, published as *House at Crow's Nest Island*, 1971; *Nurse in*

Residence, 1968; *The Bend of the River*, Banner Books, 1968; *Whistle Stop Nurse*, Lancer Books, 1968; *Stranger on the Beach*, 1969; *A Happy Ending*, 1969; *Nurse Rogers' Discovery*, 1969; *Share Your Heart*, 1970; (under pseudonym Will Kirkland) *Trouble on the Rimrock*, 1973; *Nurse in the Rockies*, 1980; *Lisa*, Scholastic, 1981; *The Fires of Passion*, Tiara Books, 1981; *The Impossible Love*, Scholastic, 1982.

All published by Ace: *Leave It to Nurse Cathy*, 1963; *Dude Ranch Nurse*, 1963; *Symptoms of Love*, 1964; *Nurse Marcie's Island*, 1964; *Nurse Connor Comes Home*, 1964; *Nurse on the Run*, 1965; *Disaster Area Nurse*, 1965; *Private Duty Nurse*, 1965; *Nurse on Leave*, 1965; *Chicago Nurse*, 1965; *Camp Nurse*, 1966; *Emergency for Nurse Selena*, 1966; *Mountain Nurse*, 1966; *Community Nurse*, 1967; *Nurse on the Beach*, 1967; *Lake Resort Nurse*, 1967; *Doctor's Daughter*, 1967; *University Nurse*, 1967; *Emergency Call*, 1968; *Doctor Barry's Nurse*, 1968; *Crossroads for Nurse Cathy*, 1969; *Nurse Jean's Strange Case*, 1970; *Walk Softly, Doctor*, 1972; *The Nurse from Mulberry Square*, 1972; *The Disobedient Nurse*, 1975; *Nurse from the Shadows*, 1975; *New Nurse at Crestview*, 1975; *Nurse Sue's Romance*, 1975; *Frightened Nurse*, 1975; *Nurse Julia's Tangled Loves*, 1976; *Nurse Lora's Love*, 1977; *Nurse Jan's Troubled Loves*, 1978.

All published by Dell: (Under pseudonym Louise Christopher) *Robin West: Nurse's Aide*, 1963; (under pseudonym Louise Christopher) *Robin West: Freshman Nurse*, 1964; *A Nurse for Sand Castle*, 1969; *Private Hospital*, 1970; *Orphanage Nurse*,

If it was like this on the outside, what must it be like on the inside? ■ (Jacket illustration by Ben Stahl from *The Other Side of the World* by Arlene Hale.)

1970; *Holiday to Fear,* 1970; *The New Nurses,* 1970; *Special Duty,* 1970; *Executive Nurse,* 1971; *The Secret Longing,* 1971; *Dark Flames,* 1971, large print edition, J. Curley, 1981; *The Shining Mountain,* 1972, large print edition, J. Curley, 1981; *The Reunion,* 1972; *Perilous Weekend,* 1975; *Dangerous Yesterdays,* 1975; *Midnight Nightmares,* 1975; *The Divided Heart,* 1975; *Nurse Nicole's Decision,* 1980, large print edition, Thorndike, 1981; *Love's Sweet Surrender,* 1980, large print edition, Thorndike, 1983; *In the Name of Love,* 1981.

All published by Little, Brown: *When Love Returns,* 1970; *The Season of Love,* 1971, large print edition, J. Curley, 1977; *The Runaway Heart,* 1971, large print edition, J. Curley, 1977; *A Time for Us,* 1972; *Promise of Tomorrow,* 1972; *Goodbye to Yesterday,* 1973, large print edition, G. K. Hall, 1973; *Where the Heart Is,* 1974; *Home to the Valley,* 1974; *A Glimpse of Paradise,* 1975, large print edition, G. K. Hall, 1975; *One More Bridge to Cross,* 1975; *The Other Side of the World,* 1976, large print edition, G. K. Hall, 1976; *The Winds of Summer,* 1976, large print edition, G. K. Hall, 1980; *Island of Mystery,* 1977.

All published by New American Library: *The Heart Remembers,* 1975; *In Love's Own Fashion,* 1976; *The Stormy Sea of Love,* 1976; *Love's Destiny,* 1976, large print edition, J. Curley, 1979; *Legacy of Love,* 1977, large print edition, J. Curley, 1979; *A Vote for Love,* 1977, large print edition, J. Curley, 1981; *Lovers' Reunion,* 1977, large print edition, J. Curley, 1979; *Gateway to Love,* 1977.

Under pseudonym Gail Everett; all published by Bouregy, except as indicated: *Love Is the Winner,* 1960; *Love of Laura,* 1961; *Search for Love,* 1962; *Teach Me to Love,* 1962; *Designs on Love,* 1963; *Journey for a Nurse,* Ace, 1966; *When Summer Ends,* 1968; *My Favorite Nurse,* Ace, 1968; *The Way to the Heart,* 1970.

Under pseudonym Lynn Williams; all published by Dell: *Once upon a Nightmare,* 1971; *Lake of the Wind,* 1971; *Where Is Jane?,* 1972; *Shadows over Seascape,* 1972; *Picture Her Missing,* 1973; *Rendezvous with Danger,* 1973; *Secret of Hedges Hall,* 1973; *Threads of Intrigue,* 1973; *Medley of Mystery,* 1974; *Stranger at the Gate,* 1975; *Walk a Dark Road,* 1975.

SIDELIGHTS: Although traveling was one of her main interests, Hale always lived in the rural community of New London, Iowa. "My interest in writing began with song lyrics, progressed to poetry, then to short stories, and finally to books. I have sold about 600 items, mostly short stories slanted for the juvenile field."

HOBBIES AND OTHER INTERESTS: Reading, fishing, movies, and music.

FOR MORE INFORMATION SEE: Best Sellers, October 5, 1970; Martha E. Ward and Dorothy A. Marquardt, *Authors of Books for Young People,* 2nd edition, Scarecrow, 1971.

HIND, Dolores (Ellen) 1931-

BRIEF ENTRY: Born July 17, 1931, in Welland, Ontario, Canada. A teacher and writer, Hind earned a B.A. in English and M.Ed. from the University of Toronto. She has taught music and kindergarten and was a professor at York University for two years. Since 1972, she has been a teacher and consultant in Mississauga, Ontario. All of Hind's books have been published as part of reading series for children. They include *The Animals' Walk* (Dolores Hind, Ltd., 1978), for which she

received the Federation of Women Teachers of Ontario Writer's Award in 1981, *Two by Two* (Schofield & Sims, 1984), and *So Can I* (Schofield & Sims, 1984). "Wishers," a poem in two parts, was included in Holt's "Impressions" series for third graders. "As a mother and educator I have been deeply concerned with children's creativity and curiosity, language and literature, and, most of all, appreciation of beauty," Hind observed. "Whether teaching kindergarten children or university graduate students, I have tried to instill a love of language, love of beauty, and love of life." Hind said her writing is influenced by the experiences she and her husband Donald, an account executive, have shared with their three children. Together, they restored a ninety-five-year-old farmhouse, called "Hindsite," where, according to Hind, she is "renewed and where creative thoughts begin to flow." *Home:* 60 Meadowvale Dr., Toronto, Ontario, Canada M8Z 5O1; "Hindsite," R.R. 4, Shelburne, Ontario, Canada L0N 1S0 (summers).

HOFFMAN, Edwin D.

PERSONAL: Born in New York, N.Y.; son of Joseph and Sadye (Loewenthal) Hoffman; married Jo Ann Hoff (an industrial manager), December 5, 1969; children: William Elliot. *Education:* City College (now of the City University of New York), B.S., 1940; Columbia University, M.A., 1947, Ed.D., 1952. *Office:* Department of History, West Virginia State College, Institute, W.Va. 25112.

CAREER: Allen University, Columbia, S.C., professor of history and chairman of Division of Teacher Education, 1954-58; West Virginia State College, Institute, professor of history, 1960—, provost and dean of instruction, 1966-75. *Military service:* U.S. Army, 1942-46; became first lieutenant. *Member:* American Historical Association, American Association of University Professors.

WRITINGS: Pathways to Freedom, Houghton, 1964; *Fighting Mountaineers: The Struggle for Justice in the Appalachians,* Houghton, 1979. Contributor to history journals.

SIDELIGHTS: "I have sought in my writings to inform on the role that the common people have played in the development of the American democratic tradition. I have researched and narrated dramatic episodes in which groups of ordinary Americans have struggled for justice and a better life in the face of the greed and prejudice that has too often prevailed in our nation's history. I consider myself one of the nontraditional historians who would have students and citizens focus on working people, on women, on Blacks, on Appalachians, Latinos, and Indians, rather than on those who have usually wielded power in American political and economic life."

HOOPES, Lyn L(ittlefield) 1953-

PERSONAL: Born July 14, 1953, in New York, N.Y.; daughter of Herrick Briggs (a president of a manufacturing company) and Sally (an artist; maiden name, Shore) Littlefield; married Claude Brown Hoopes (a commercial realtor), May 20, 1978; children: Nathaniel Lowrey. *Education:* Attended Smith College, 1971-72; Stanford University, B.A. (with honors), 1975. *Religion:* Christian Scientist. *Home:* 2989 Rivermeade Dr. N.W., Atlanta, Ga. 30327. *Agent:* Marilyn Marlow, Curtis Brown, 10 Astor Place, New York, N.Y. 10003.

CAREER: Harper & Row, Publishers, New York, N.Y., editorial assistant, 1975-77; Atlantic Monthly Press, Boston,

Mass., assistant editor, 1977-80; Houghton Mifflin Co., Boston, editor of children's books, 1980-82; writer, 1983—. Teacher of creative writing to children; reviewer of children's books.

WRITINGS—Juvenile: *Nana* (illustrated by Arieh Zeldich), Harper, 1981; *When I Was Little* (illustrated by Marcia Sewall), Dutton, 1983; *Daddy's Coming Home!* (illustrated by Bruce Degan), Harper, 1984; *Mommy, Daddy, Me* (illustrated by Ruth Bornstein), Harper, 1988; *Half a Button* (illustrated by Patricia Parcell Watts), Harper, 1988.

WORK IN PROGRESS: Is It Night Now?, A Name for Grandmother, Wing-a-ding, and *Max Awake,* all juveniles; a picture book about friendship.

SIDELIGHTS: "I grew up in a big family, and my mother who is an artist used to say one day we'd do a children's book together, she would paint and I would write. I remember thinking how ridiculous! Now, of course, there's nothing I would love more, and I hope one day we will. I never thought about writing, just sort of fell into it. Some of my first writing was about places I loved—a high rock overlooking a valley on my Grandmother's farm in Vermont, a hollow in one of the meadows. I remember writing about them (I was about twelve) because I loved them, but I never really thought about 'being a writer.'

"I studied English in college, read books and books and books and when I graduated I went to work in publishing. I couldn't

LYN L. HOOPES

type, but fortunately I was offered a job as a manuscript reader in a children's book department. This is where I came to love children's books and learned, slowly, how they are made and what an editor does. I moved along, and changed publishing houses a couple of times, but always stayed with children's books. Several years later, when I needed to be home with my son, writing became my focus. I write impulsively, directly out of my life and emotional self, and am always surprised to see what finds its way onto paper.

"My writing begins in emotion, a full cup of it, and in new awareness. Writing helps me to distill the feelings, find the essence. Then the books take form—or don't—out of the substance of the emotion. It is not a very calculated way of doing business, but my life seems to offer plenty of good grist, plenty to feel deeply about. My six-year-old boy—being with him, seeing and feeling through him—connects me to my own childhood directly. Not in a reminiscing way, but in a present, active way of being now, so that the child's response—the voice—comes naturally. *Daddy's Coming Home!*, for instance, there's no doubting the source of this idea. When I read this with kids in the schools I often tell them Nat wrote it when he was two—his pure joy in seeing his father, his attachment to the familiar in our lives, especially the animals, the way he loved sounds and their repetition—all of this wrote the book. Other books have come more out of my own feelings and experiences, distilled, and then cast in a frame children will respond to. So much is universal. *Half a Button* came this way, out of the joy of reunions in our family and the strange sudden sadness of saying goodbye."

I lie down and the breeze ripples all around me. ■ (From *Nana* by Lyn Littlefield Hoopes. Illustrated by Arieh Zeldich.)

HUGHES, Ted 1930-

PERSONAL: Full name, Edward J. Hughes; born August 17, 1930, in Mytholmroyd, West Yorkshire, England; son of William Henry (a joiner) and Edith (Farrar) Hughes; married Sylvia Plath (an American poet), 1956 (died 1963); married Carol Orchard, 1970; children: (first marriage) Frieda Rebecca, Nicholas Farrar. *Education:* Pembroke College, Cambridge, B.A., 1954, M.A., 1959. *Home:* Devonshire, England. *Address:* c/o Faber & Faber Ltd., 3 Queen's Square, London WC1N 3AU, England.

CAREER: Full-time writer. University of Massachusetts, Amherst, Mass., instructor, 1957-59; founding editor with Daniel Weissbrot, *Modern Poetry in Translation,* London, England, 1964-71. *Military service:* Royal Air Force, 1948-50. *Awards, honors:* First prize, Young Men's and Young Women's Hebrew Association Poetry Center contest, 1957, and first prize, Guinness Poetry Awards, 1958, both for *The Hawk in the Rain;* Guggenheim fellow, 1959-60; Somerset Maugham Award, 1960, Hawthornden Prize, 1961, and Abraham Wonsell Foundation awards, 1964-69, all for *Lupercal;* City of Florence International Poetry prize, 1969, for *Wodwo;* Premio Internazionale Taormina Prize, 1972; Queen's Medal for Poetry, 1974; *Season Songs* was a Children's Book Showcase Title, 1976; Order of the British Empire, 1977; Signal Poetry Award, 1979, for *Moon-Bells and Other Poems,* 1981, for *Under the North Star,* and 1983, for *The Rattle Bag: An Anthology of Poetry;* Royal Society of Literature Heinemann Award, 1980, for *Moortown;* honorary doctorate, Exeter College, 1982, Open University, 1983, Bradford College, 1984, and Pembroke College, 1986; Poet Laureate of England, 1984; *The Iron Man: A Story in Five Nights* (new edition) was exhibited at the Bologna International Children's Book Fair, and received the Kurt Maschler Emil Award from the National Book League (Great Britain), both 1985; Guardian Award for children's fiction, 1985, for *What Is the Truth? A Farmyard Fable for the Young.*

TED HUGHES

Crow saw the herded mountains, steaming in the morning. And he saw the sea. ■ (Jacket illustration by Leonard Baskin from *Crow: From the Life and Songs of the Crow* by Ted Hughes.)

WRITINGS—Juvenile: Meet My Folks! (verse; illustrated by George Adamson), Faber, 1961, Bobbs-Merrill, 1973; *The Earth-Owl and Other Moon-People* (verse; illustrated by R. A. Brandt), Faber, 1963, Atheneum, 1964, also published as *Moon-Whales and Other Moon Poems* (illustrated by Leonard Baskin), Viking, 1976; *How the Whale Became and Other Stories* (illustrated by G. Adamson), Faber, 1963, American edition illustrated by Rick Schreiter, Atheneum, 1964; *Nessie, the Mannerless Monster* (verse; illustrated by Gerald Rose), Chilmark, 1964, also published as *Nessie the Monster* (illustrated by Jan Pyk), Bobbs-Merrill, 1974; *The Iron Giant: A Story in Five Nights* (illustrated by Robert Nadler), Harper, 1968 (published in England as *The Iron Man: A Story in Five Nights* [illustrated by George Adamson], Faber, 1968, new edition [illustrated by Andrew Davidson], 1984; also see below); *Five Autumn Songs for Children's Voices* (verse), Gilbertson, 1968.

Season Songs (verse; illustrated by L. Baskin), Viking, 1975; *Moon-Bells and Other Poems,* Chatto & Windus, 1978; *Under the North Star* (verse; illustrated by L. Baskin), Viking, 1981; *What Is the Truth? A Farmyard Fable for the Young* (illustrated by R. J. Lloyd), Harper, 1984; *Ffangs the Vampire Bat and the Kiss of Truth* (illustrated by Chris Riddell), Faber, 1986.

Adult; verse, except as indicated: *The Hawk in the Rain,* Harper, 1957; *Pike,* Gehenna Press, 1959; *Lupercal,* Harper, 1960; (with Thom Gunn) *Selected Poems,* Faber, 1962; *The Burning of the Brothel,* Turret Books, 1966; *The Recklings,* Turret Books, 1966; *Animal Poems,* Gilbertson, 1967; *Wodwo* (miscellany), Harper, 1967; *Gravestones,* Exeter College of Art, 1967, published as *Poems,* 1968; *The Demon of Adachigahara,* music by Gordon Crosse, Oxford University Press, 1969; *I Said Goodbye to Earth,* Exeter College of Art, 1969.

The Martyrdom of Bishop Farrar, Gilbertson, 1970; *Crow: From the Life and Songs of the Crow,* Faber, 1970, revised edition, 1972, Harper, 1971; *Fighting for Jerusalem,* Mid-NAG, 1970; *Selected Poems, 1957-1967* (illustrated by L. Baskin), Faber, 1972, Harper, 1973; *Cave Birds,* Scolar Press, 1975, revised edition published as *Cave Birds: An Alchemical Cave Drama* (illustrated by L. Baskin), Faber, 1977, Viking, 1978; *The Interrogator,* Scolar Press, 1975; *Gaudete,* Harper, 1977; *Chiasmadon,* Seluzicki, 1977; *Remains of Elmet: A Pennine Sequence* (illustrated with photographs by Fay Godwin), Harper, 1979; *All around the Year* (illustrated with photographs by Michael Morpurgo), Murray, 1979; *Moortown,* Faber, 1979, Harper, 1980.

Selected Poems: 1957-1981, Faber, 1982, published in America as *New Selected Poems,* Harper, 1982; *Primer of Birds: Poems,* Phaedon Press, 1982; (with Peter Keen) *River,* Faber, 1983; *Flowers and Insects* (illustrated by L. Baskin), Knopf, in press.

Limited editions: *Scapegoats and Rabies: A Poem in Five Parts,* Poet & Printer, 1967; *Poems: Ted Hughes, Fainlight, and Sillitoe,* Rainbow Press, 1967; *A Crow Hymn,* Sceptre Press, 1970; *A Few Crows,* Rougemont Press, 1970; *Four Crow Poems,* privately printed, 1970; *Autumn Song* (verse; illustrated by Nina Carroll), privately printed, 1971; *Crow Wakes: Poems,* Poet & Printer, 1971; (with Ruth Fainlight and Alan Sillitoe) *Poems,* Rainbow Press, 1971; *In the Little Girl's Angel Gaze,* Steam Press, 1972; *Prometheus on His Crag: 21 Poems* (illustrated by L. Baskin), Rainbow Press, 1973; *Spring, Summer, Autumn, Winter* (verse), Rainbow Press, 1974; *Eclipse,* Sceptre Press, 1976; *Earth-Moon* (verse; self-illustrated), Rainbow Press, 1976; *Sunstruck,* Sceptre Press, 1977; *Orts,* Rainbow Press, 1978; *Moortown Elegies,* Rainbow Press, 1978; *A Solstice,* Sceptre Press, 1978; *Calder Valley Poems,* Rainbow Press, 1978; *The Threshold* (short story), Steam Press, 1979; *Adam and the Sacred Nine,* Rainbow Press, 1979; *Henry Williamson: A Tribute,* Rainbow Press, 1979; *Four Tales Told by an Idiot,* Sceptre Press, 1979.

Plays; juvenile: *The Coming of the Kings and Other Plays* (contains ''Beauty and the Beast'' [first broadcast in 1965; first produced in London, 1971], ''Sean, the Fool'' [first broadcast in 1968; first produced in London, 1971], ''The Devil and the Cats'' [first broadcast in 1968; first produced in

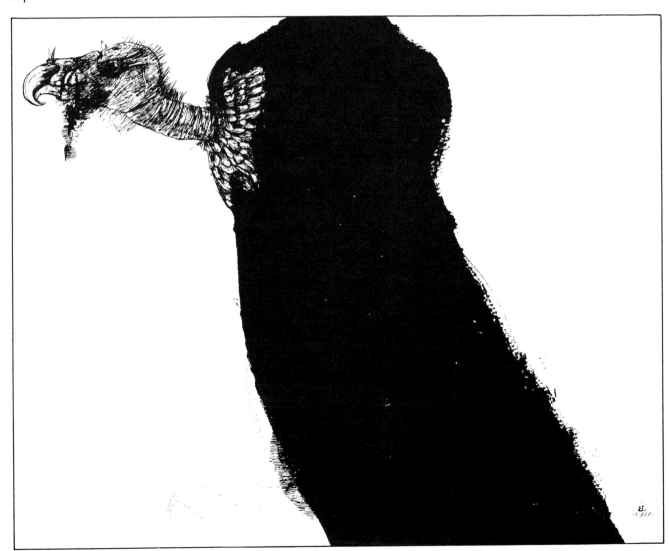

The bird is the sun's key-hole. ■ (From "The Interrogator" in *Cave Birds: An Alchemical Cave Drama* by Ted Hughes. Illustrated by Leonard Baskin.)

London, 1971], "The Coming of the Kings" [first televised in 1967; first produced in London, 1972], and "The Tiger's Bones" [first broadcast November 26, 1965]), Faber, 1970, revised edition (also contains "Orpheus" [first broadcast in 1971]), published as *The Tiger's Bones and Other Plays for Children* (illustrated by Alan E. Cober), Viking, 1974; *The Iron Man* (based on his juvenile book of the same title; first televised in 1972), Faber, 1973; "The Pig Organ; or, Pork with Perfect Pitch" (children's opera) music by Richard Blackford, first performed by the English Opera Company at the Round House, London, January, 1980.

Plays; adult: *The House of Aries*, first broadcast in 1960, published in *Audience*, spring, 1961; "The Calm," first produced in Boston, Mass., 1961; *The Wound*, first broadcast in 1962, revised version produced in London, 1972, included in *Wodwo*, Faber, 1967; "Epithalamium," first produced in London, 1963; "The House of Donkeys," first broadcast in 1965; *The Price of a Bride*, first broadcast in 1966, published in *Here, Now and Beyond*, edited by Nancy Coniston Martin, Oxford University Press, 1968; (editor) *Seneca's Oedipus* (first produced in London at National Theatre, 1968), Faber, 1969, Doubleday, 1972.

"Orghast," directed by Peter Brook, first produced in Persepolis, Iran, on the occasion of the Fifth International Arts Festival in Shiraz, 1971; *Eat Crow*, Rainbow Press, 1971; *The Story of Vasco* (adaptation of a play by Georges Schehade; first produced in London, 1974), music by G. Crosse, Oxford University Press, 1974. Also author of radio plays, "A Houseful of Women," 1961, "Difficulties of a Bridegroom," 1963, "Dogs," 1964, and "The Head of Gold," 1967.

Editor: (With Patricia Beer and Vernon Scannell) *New Poems 1962*, Hutchinson, 1962; (with T. Gunn) *Five American Poets*, Faber, 1963; *Here Today*, Hutchinson, 1963; Keith Douglas, *Selected Poems*, Chilmark, 1964; *Poetry in the Making: An Anthology of Poems and Programmes from "Listening and Writing"* (juvenile), Faber, 1967, published in America as *Poetry Is*, Doubleday, 1971; Emily Dickinson, *A Choice of Emily Dickinson's Verse*, Faber, 1968; William Shakespeare, *With Fairest Flowers While Summer Lasts: Poems from Shakespeare*, Doubleday, 1971 (published in England as *A Choice of Shakespeare's Verse*, Faber, 1971, introduction published as *Shakespeare's Poem*, Lexham Press, 1971); Sylvia Plath, *Crossing the Water: Transitional Poems*, Harper, 1971 (published in England as *Crossing the Water*, Faber, 1971); (and author of introduction) S. Plath, *Johnny Panic and the Bible of Dreams, and Other Prose Writings*, Faber, 1977, new edition, Harper, 1979; *New Poetry 6*, Hutchinson, 1980; S. Plath, *The Collected Poems of Sylvia Plath*, Harper, 1981; (with Frances McCullough) *The Journals of Sylvia Plath*, Dial, 1982; (with Seamus Heaney) *The Rattle Bag: An Anthology of Poetry* (juvenile), Faber, 1982.

Translator: (And editor) Yehuda Amichai, *Selected Poems*, Penguin, 1971; (and editor with János Csokits) János Pilinszky, *Selected Poems*, Persea Books, 1977; Charles Simic and Mark Strand, editors, *Another Republic*, Ecco Press, 1977; (and editor) Y. Amichai, *Amen*, Harper, 1977.

Contributor to anthologies, including Dannie Abse, editor, *Corgi Modern Poets in Focus 1*, Corgi Books, 1971; *Cricket's Choice*, Open Court, 1974. Contributor to numerous periodicals, including *New Yorker, The Listener, New York Review of Books, Harper's, Atlantic, Nation, Vogue, Mademoiselle,* and *Spectator.* Co-editor, *Modern Poetry in Translation* (journal), 1965—.

ADAPTATIONS—Recordings: "The Poetry and Voice of Ted Hughes," Caedmon, 1977; "Selections from Crow and Wodwo," Caedmon, 1979.

SIDELIGHTS: **August 17, 1930.** Born in Mytholmroyd, West Yorkshire, England. Hughes, whose full name is Edward J. Hughes, was the youngest of three children. His childhood was spent in West Yorkshire, where he spoke in the dialect indigenous to that region. "Whatever other speech you grow into, presumably your dialect stays alive in a sort of inner freedom, a separate little self. It makes some things more difficult . . . since it's your childhood self there inside the dialect and that is possibly your real self or the core of it. Some things it makes easier. Without it, I doubt if I would ever have written verse. And in the case of the West Yorkshire dialect, of course, it connects you directly and in your most intimate self to middle English poetry." [Egbert Faas, "Ted Hughes and Crow," *London Magazine*, January, 1971.[1]]

One of Hughes' first interests as a young boy was in animals, and this early interest later influenced his poetry themes. "My pursuit of mice at threshing time when I was a boy, snatching them from under the sheaves as the sheaves were lifted away out of the stack and popping them into my pocket till I had thirty or forty crawling around in the lining of my coat, that and my present pursuit of poems seem to me to be different stages of the same fever. In a way, I suppose, I think of poems as a sort of animal. They have their own life, like animals, by which I mean that they seem quite separate from any person, even from their author, and nothing can be added to them or

SAGE: Alas, this glorious tiger, perfect as it is in every anatomical detail, is dead. ■ (From *The Tiger's Bones and Other Plays for Children* by Ted Hughes. Illustrated by Alan E. Cober.)

taken away without maiming and perhaps even killing them. And they have a certain wisdom. They know something special . . . something perhaps which we are very curious to learn.

"Maybe my concern has been to capture not animals particularly and not poems, but simply things which have a vivid life of their own, outside mine. However all that may be, my interest in animals began when I began. My memory goes back pretty clearly to my third year, and by then I had so many of the toy lead animals you could buy in shops that they went right round our flat-topped fender, nose to tail, with some over.

"I had a gift for modelling and drawing, so when I discovered plasticine my zoo became infinite, and when an aunt bought me a thick green-backed animal book for my fourth birthday I began to draw the glossy photographs. The animals looked good in the photographs, but they looked even better in my drawings and were mine. I can remember very vividly the excitement with which I used to sit staring at my drawings, and it is a similar thing I feel nowadays with poems.

"My zoo was not entirely an indoors affair. At that time we lived in a valley in the Pennines in West Yorkshire. My brother, who probably had more to do with this passion of mine than anyone else, was a good bit older than I was, and his one interest in life was creeping about on the hillsides with a rifle.

The parkland unrolls, lush with the full ripeness of the last week in May. ■ (Jacket illustration by Leonard Baskin from *Gaudete* by Ted Hughes.)

He took me along as a retriever and I had to scramble into all kinds of places collecting magpies and owls and rabbits and weasels and rats and curlews that he shot. He could not shoot enough for me. At the same time I used to be fishing daily in the canal, with the long-handled wire-rimmed curtain mesh sort of net.

"All that was only the beginning. When I was about eight, we moved to an industrial town in south Yorkshire. Our cat went upstairs and moped in my bedroom for a week, it hated the place so much, and my brother for the same reason left home and became a gamekeeper. But in many ways that move of ours was the best thing that ever happened to me. I soon discovered a farm in the nearby country that supplied all my needs, and soon after, a private estate, with woods and lakes.

"My friends were town boys, sons of colliers and railwaymen, and with them I led one life, but all the time I was leading this other life on my own in the country. I never mixed the two lives up, except once or twice disastrously. I still have some diaries that I kept in those years: they record nothing but my catches." [Ted Hughes, *Poetry in the Making,* Faber, 1967.[2]]

1945. Began to write poetry—sagas of African tribes and poems of the American Wild West. "At about fifteen my life grew more complicated and my attitude to animals changed. I accused myself of disturbing their lives. I began to look at them, you see, from their own point of view.

"And about the same time I began to write poems. . . . At school, I was plagued by the idea that I really had much better thoughts than I could ever get into words. It was not that I could not find the words, or that the thoughts were too deep or too complicated for words. It was simply that when I tried to speak or write down the thoughts, those thoughts had vanished. All I had was a numb blank feeling, just as if somebody had asked me the name of Julius Caesar's eldest son, or said '7,283 times 6,956—quick. Think, think, think.' Now for one reason or another I became very interested in those thoughts of mine that I could never catch. Sometimes they were hardly what you could call a thought—they were a dim sort of feeling about something. They did not fit into any particular subject—history or arithmetic or anything of that sort, except perhaps English. I had the idea, which gradually grew on me, that these were the right sort of thoughts for essays, and yet probably not even essays. But for the most part they were useless to me because I could never get hold of them. Maybe when I was writing an essay I got the tail end of one, but that was not very satisfying."[2]

1954. Received degree in archaeology and anthropology from Cambridge, even though these subjects were not Hughes' first choices for a college degree. ". . . Reading English was a dead-end for me and in my last year I moved over to anthropology and archaeology, which I found absorbing.

"Cambridge is the ordeal for initiation into English society and it's a pity there's not another one. It's a most destructive experience and only tough poets like Peter Redgrove ever survive. When you think of it, hundreds of undergraduates reading English each year all want to write and 99 per cent simply disappear. In effect university is a prison from life on your last three or four most formative years. It's a most deadly institution unless you're aiming to be either a scholar or a gentleman." ["Desk Poet," *The Guardian,* March 23, 1965.[3]]

Significantly, Hughes did not write any poetry at Cambridge, although his reading of literature eventually had an important influence on his work. ". . . In the way of influences I imagine

(From "Second Glance at a Jaguar" in *Selected Poems, 1957-1967* by Ted Hughes. Illustrated by Leonard Baskin.)

everything goes into the stew. But to be specific . . . Donne . . . I once learned as many of his poems as I could and I greatly admired his satires and epistles. More than his lyrics even. As for [Dylan] Thomas, *Deaths and Entrances* was a holy book with me for quite a time when it first came out. Lawrence I read entire in my teens . . . except for all but a few of the poems. His writings coloured a whole period of my life. Blake I connect inwardly to Beethoven, and if I could dig to the bottom of my strata maybe their names and works would be the deepest traces. Yeats spellbound me for about six years. I got to him not so much through his verse as through his other interests, folklore, and magic in particular. Then that strange atmosphere laid hold of me. I fancy if there is a jury of critics sitting over what I write, and I imagine every writer has something of the sort, then Yeats is the judge.''[1]

After college, Hughes held a variety of jobs, including working as a rose gardener, a night watchman and a reader for Rank at Pinewood in England. ''Up to the age of twenty-five I read no contemporary poetry whatsoever except Eliot, Thomas and some Auden. Then I read a Penguin of American poets that came out in about 1955 and that started me writing. After writing nothing for about six years. The poems that set me off were odd pieces by Shapiro, Lowell, Merwin, Wilbur and Crowe Ransom. Crowe Ransom was the one who gave me a model I felt I could use. He helped me get my words into focus. That put me into production.

''But this whole business of influences is mysterious. Sometimes it's just a few words that open up a whole prospect. They may occur anywhere. Then again the influences that really count are most likely not literary at all. Maybe it would be best of all to have no influences.''[1]

Ted Hughes with Sylvia Plath, January, 1959.

1956. Married American poet Sylvia Plath. ''I first met Sylvia Plath in Falconer's Yard off Petty Cary in Cambridge. . . . I taught there for a bit while she finished off at Newnham and we got married the same year. We went off to America in 1957, where we both taught. We first lived in Northampton and then spent a fantastic year in Boston, where she was born. It's a strange and wonderful city. After that we did a slow tour round the States on the money we had put by. I don't know how we survived but we did. Neither of us made much from writing at that time.

''Sylvia was terribly efficient, sending all my poems out for me. . . . There was no rivalry between us as poets or in any other way. It sounds trite but you completely influence one another, if you live together. You begin to write out of one brain. Sylvia was completely original though. She may have been influenced by Stevens and Lowell in a couple of poems, but she had found her own voice. She wrote an enormous amount, eight or nine books, before Heinemann took *The Colossus* and every nine months or so the body of her manuscripts would undergo a complete change. You see, she needed to write—she could produce a characteristic poem at any time she liked.

''After we'd returned to England and were living in Chalcot Square, near Primrose Hill, we would each write poetry every day. It was all we were interested in, all we ever did. We were like two feet, each one using everything the other did. It was a working partnership and was all absorbing. We just lived it. There was an unspoken unanimity in every criticism or judgment we made. It all fitted in very well.

''Sylvia had a great desire to write stories and novels. But the poems were works of genius. She rejected a lot which seem terribly good to me. . . . If she didn't write anything for three days she'd be in a very bad way indeed. She'd written poems since she was a little girl.''[3]

1957. Publication of first major poetry collection, *The Hawk in the Rain*. ''What excites my imagination is the war between vitality and death, and my poems may be said to celebrate the exploits of the warriors of either side. Also, they are attempts to prove the realness of the world, and of myself in this world, by establishing the realness of my relation to it. Another way of saying this might be—the poems celebrate the pure solidity of my illusion of the world. Again—and probably this is the first near-truth I have put down yet—they are the only way I can unburden myself of that excess which, for their part, bulls in June bellow away.'' [Ted Hughes Writes . . . ,'' *Poetry Book Society Bulletin,* September, 1957.[4]]

1959-1960. Awarded a Guggenheim fellowship. Hughes defined his idea of a true poet as an artist who is sensitive to himself and whose work does not rely on popular issues. ''The poet's only hope is to be infinitely sensitive to what his gift is, and this in itself seems to be another gift that few poets possess. According to this sensitivity, and to his faith in it, he will go on developing as a poet, as Yeats did, pursuing those adventures, mental, spiritual and physical, whatever they may be, that his gift wants, or he will lose its guidance, lose the feel of its touch in the workings of his mind, and soon be absorbed by the impersonal dead lumber of matters in which his gift has no interest, which is a form of suicide. . . .

''His gift is an unobliging thing. He can study his art, experiment, and apply his mind and live as he pleases. But the moment of writing is too late for further improvements or adjustments. Certain memories, images, sounds, feelings, thoughts, and relationships between these, have for some rea-

The crowd was enjoying itself. Torto was weeping with shame. ■ (From *How the Whale Became and Other Stories* by Ted Hughes. Illustrated by Rick Schreiter.)

son become luminous at the core of his mind: it is in his attempt to bring them out, without impairment, into a comparatively dark world that he makes poems. At the moment of writing, the poetry is a combination, or a resultant, of all that he is, unimpeachable evidence of itself and, indirectly, of himself, and for the time of writing he can do nothing but accept it. If he doesn't approve of what is appearing, there are always plenty of ways to falsify and 'improve' it, there are always plenty of fashions as to how it should look, how it can be made more acceptable, more 'interesting,' his other faculties are only too ready to load it with their business, whereon he ceases to be a poet producing what poetry he can and becomes a cheat producing confusion." ["Ted Hughes," *London Magazine*, February, 1962.[5]]

1960. Second collection of poems, *Lupercal,* won the Hawthornden Prize the following year. "Sometimes I think my poems are merely notes. A lot of my second book, *Lupercal,* is one extended poem about one or two sensations. There are at least a dozen or fifteen poems in that book which belong organically to one another. You'll have noticed how all the animals get killed off at the end of most poems. Each one is living the redeemed life of joy. They're continually in a state of energy which men only have when they've gone mad. This strength arises from their complete unity with whatever divinity they have. They would be utterly miserable, otherwise however would they manage to live?"[3]

1961. *Meet My Folks!,* a collection of verse for children, was first published in England. "All writers agree, you cannot write about something for which you have no feeling. Unless something interests or excites you or belongs to your life in a deep way, then you just cannot think of anything to say about it. The words will not come. Now, unless you are an unusual person, you will never in this world get to know anybody quite as well as you know your relatives, and your feelings will never be tied up with anybody or with anything quite so deeply as it is with them. Accordingly, most writers find they have plenty to say about their relatives. And these feelings we have for our relatives are not unshakeably fixed to those particular people. This is one of the curious facts about feelings. If we get on well with our brother, we tend to be attracted to make friends with boys or men who remind us of our brother, and begin to feel that this new friendship is somehow using the feeling we originally had for our brother alone. In the same way, if you are a writer, and you invent a character who reminds you in some way of your brother, then all your old feelings about your brother flow into this invented character and help to bring it to life. Some very great writers have written their best books in this way, rearranging their relatives in imagination, under different names and appearances of course.

"It is not always completely easy. Our feelings about some of our relatives, particularly about our mother and father, are so complicated and so deeply rooted that they may be just too much for a writer to manage, and he finds he cannot say a thing about them. In writing these poems of mine about relatives, I found it almost impossible to write about the mother."[2]

Hughes' first children's book was followed by two more books of verse for children in 1963.

1963. Wife, Sylvia Plath, committed suicide. "Sylvia Plath was a person of many masks, both in her personal life and in her writings. Some were camouflage cliché facades, defensive mechanisms, involuntary. And some were deliberate poses, attempts to find the keys to one style or another. These were the visible faces of her lesser selves, her false or provisional selves, the minor roles of her inner drama. Though I spent

every day with her for six years, and was rarely separated from her for more than two or three hours at a time, I never saw her show her real self to anybody—except, perhaps, in the last three months of her life." [Ted Hughes, editor, *The Journals of Sylvia Plath,* Dial Press, 1982.[6]]

1964-1967. Served as a judge of the *Daily Mirror* Children's Literary Competition. ". . . By showing to a pupil's imagination many opportunities and few restraints, and instilling into him confidence and a natural motive for writing, the odds are that something—maybe not much, but something—of our common genius will begin to put a word in.

". . . As a judge of the *Daily Mirror* Children's Literary Competition . . . I have had plenty of opportunity to confirm or modify my ideas about this. Reading Milton or Keats to children is one thing. Asking them, or allowing them, to use such as models for their own writing is another. All falsities in writing—and the consequent dry-rot that spreads into the whole fabric—come from the notion that there is a stylistic ideal which exists in the abstract, like a special language, to which all men might attain. But teachers of written English should have nothing to do with that, which belongs rather to the study of manners and group jargon. Their words should be not 'How to write' but 'How to try to say what you really mean'—which is part of the search for self-knowledge and perhaps, in one form or another, grace. . . ."[2]

1968. *The Iron Man: A Story in Five Nights* was published. The story was first told to his two children, Frieda Rebecca and Nicholas Farrar. "When we tell a story to a child, to some extent we have his future in our hands insofar as we have hold of his imagination. That's the key; what affects a person's imagination affects their whole life. . . . When we tell a child a story, the child quickly finds his role; as the story proceeds the child enters a completely imaginative world, and it has to be a completely imaginative world or he jibs. If you try to introduce too much extraneous material, or connect the story too obviously to his own outside world, he resists. He doesn't want it. He wants to be enclosed completely in a totally coherent imaginative world. So to some extent he goes into a condition of trance and what he is really resisting is being jerked out of this trance. This trance is a dangerous place; a person in a trance is in a hypnotized condition and so he is completely at the mercy of any kind of suggestion. And so whatever happens to him in the story happens under conditions of hypnosis. In other words, it really happens.

"There's a blind faith that just mental, imaginative activity somehow will trigger off the right effects and put the power into the child's hands and open up the inner worlds and make the connections, that just sheer stories of any kind will do this. It's possible, maybe, to be more deliberate. . . ." [Ted Hughes, "Myth and Education," *Children's Literature in Education,* 1970.[7]]

1970. Married Carol Orchard.

Crow, the first in a series of books about Hughes' most powerful literary creation, was published. The central character—a crow—the poet defined as half-man, half-crow. ". . . Nobody knows quite how he was created, or how he appeared. He was created by God's nightmare. What exactly that is, I tried to define through the length of the poem, or the succession of poems. It's something outside God, outside the God that created Man, or the men we know, so the crow is a sort of extra-man, a shadow man. He's a man to correct man, but of course he's not a man, he's a crow: he never does quite become a man.

The Loon, the Loon
Hatched from the Moon. . . .

■ (From "The Loon" in *Under the North Star* by Ted Hughes. Illustrated by Leonard Baskin.)

"Having been created, he's put through various adventures and disasters and trials and ordeals, and the effect of these is to alter him not at all, then alter him a great deal, completely transform him, tear him to bits, put him together again, and produce him a little bit changed. And maybe his ambition is to become a man, which he never quite manages. An American artist [Leonard Baskin], who has engraved wonderful crows, suggested that we do a book—that I should simply write texts for his engravings of crows. The crow is the most intelligent of the birds. He lives in just about every piece of land on earth, and there's a great body of folklore about crows, of course. No carrion will kill a crow. The crow is the indestructible bird who suffers everything, suffers nothing—like Horatio." ["Ted Hughes's Crow," *The Listener*, July 30, 1970.[8]]

1974. Awarded the Queen's Gold Medal for Poetry. Besides being a prominent English poet of verses for adults and for children, Hughes was also highly regarded as a dramatist, having written several plays for children, radio plays, and adult drama. In 1971 he created his own language for his play "Orghast," which was first performed in Persepolis, Iran. "In writing verse, the particular combination of sounds, or the predilection for certain sequences of sounds, is unique to every poet. The signature of any painter, or any musician in music, is immediately recognizable in a very definite, final and yet finally indefinable way. So I made Orghast as we imagined the material, and I drew the language out of the material, out of my feelings about the material. I fished it out of the air, one or two roots, obviously, starting-points in certain languages, but purely peculiar to Orghast." [Ossia Trilling, "Playing with Words at Persepolis," *Theatre Quarterly*, Volume II, number 5, January-March, 1972.[9]]

Critics of Hughes' poetry often described it as "poetry of violence," to which Hughes responded: ". . . When is violence 'violence' and when is it great poetry? Can the critic distinguish? I would say that most critics cannot distinguish. The critic whose outlook is based on a rational scepticism is simply incapable of seeing Venus from any point of view but that of Adonis. He cannot distinguish between fears for his own mental security and the actions of the Universe redressing a disturbed balance. Or trying to. In other words, he is incapable of judging poetry . . . because poetry is nothing if not that, the record of just how the forces of the Universe try to redress some balance disturbed by human error. What he can do is judge works and deeds of rational scepticism within a closed society that agrees on the terms used. He can tell you why a poem is bad as a work of rational scepticism, but he cannot tell why it is good as a poem. A poem might be good as both, but it need not be. Violence that begins in an unhappy home can go one way to produce a meaningless little nightmare of murder etc. for T.V. or it can go the other way and produce those moments in Beethoven.

". . . The poem of mine usually cited for violence is the one about the Hawk Roosting, this drowsy hawk sitting in a wood and talking to itself. That bird is accused of being a fascist . . . the symbol of some horrible totalitarian genocidal dictator. Actually what I had in mind was that in this hawk Nature is thinking. Simply Nature. It's not so simple maybe because Nature is no longer so simple. I intended some Creator like the Jehovah in Job but more feminine. . . ."[1]

1979-1983. Given three Signal Poetry Awards for three verse collections: *Moon-Bells and Other Poems, Under the North Star,* and *The Rattle Bag: An Anthology of Poetry.* "You choose a subject because it serves, because you need it. We go on writing poems because one poem never gets the whole account

right. There is always something missed. At the end of the ritual up comes a goblin. Anyway within a week the whole thing has changed, one needs a fresh bulletin. And works go dead, fishing has to be abandoned, the shoal has moved on. While we struggle with a fragmentary Orestes some complete Bacchae moves past too deep down to hear. We get news of it later . . . too late. In the end, one's poems are ragged dirty undated letters from remote battles and weddings and one thing and another."[1]

FOR MORE INFORMATION SEE—Periodicals: *Poetry Book Society Bulletin,* September, 1957; *London Magazine,* February, 1962, January, 1971; "Desk Poet," *The Guardian,* March 23, 1965; *Arizona Quarterly,* spring, 1967; *Times Literary Supplement,* July 6, 1967, October 1, 1971, July 1, 1977; *Books and Bookmen,* November, 1967, February, 1971; *Book World,* December 24, 1967, February 10, 1974; *Hudson Review,* spring, 1968; *Carleton Miscellany,* summer, 1968; *Drama,* summer, 1968; *Shenandoah,* summer, 1968, winter, 1972; *Virginia Quarterly Review,* summer, 1968, spring, 1974; *New York Review,* August 1, 1968; *Comment,* September, 1968; *New York Times Book Review,* November 3, 1968, January 13, 1974, December 25, 1977; *Young Readers Review,* February, 1969.

"Ted Hughes's Crow," *Listener,* July 30, 1970; Ted Hughes, "Myth and Education," *Children's Literature in Education,* 1970; *New York Times,* March 18, 1971, July 19, 1978; *Critical Quarterly,* spring, 1971, summer, 1972; *Time,* April 5, 1971; *Newsweek,* April 12, 1971; *New York Review of Books,* July 22, 1971, March 7, 1974; *Mediterranean Review,* fall, 1971; Jean Richards, "An Interview with British Poet, Ted Hughes, Inventor of Orghast Language," *Drama and Theatre,* fall, 1971; *Commonweal,* September 17, 1971; *Saturday Review,* October 2, 1971; *Performance,* December, 1971; *Theatre Quarterly,* January-March, 1972; *Poetry,* February, 1972; *Prairie Schooner,* fall, 1972; *Contemporary Literature,* winter, 1973; *Salmagundi,* spring-summer, 1973; *Books Abroad,* winter, 1974; *New Republic,* February 16, 1974; *Nation,* March 16, 1974; *Midwest Quarterly,* summer, 1974; *Parnassus: Poetry in Review,* spring-summer, 1976; *Sewanee Review,* summer, 1976; *Encounter,* November, 1978; *The Junior Bookshelf,* August, 1980.

Books: M. L. Rosenthal, *The New Poets: American and British Poetry since World War II,* Oxford University Press, 1967; Ian Hamilton, *The Modern Poet: Essays for "The Review,"* MacDonald & Co., 1968; Monroe K. Spears, *Dionysus and the City: Modernism in Twentieth-Century Poetry,* Oxford University Press, 1970; Keith Sagar, *Ted Hughes,* Longman, 1972; *Contemporary Literary Criticism,* Gale, Volume II, 1974, Volume IV, 1975, Volume IX, 1978; K. Sagar, *The Art of Ted Hughes,* Cambridge University Press, 1975, revised edition, 1978; Lawrence R. Ries, *Wolf Masks: Violence in Contemporary Poetry,* Kennikat, 1977; *Children's Literature Review,* Volume 3, Gale, 1978; D. L. Kirkpatrick, *Twentieth-Century Children's Writers,* St. Martin's Press, 1978, new edition, 1983; Egbert Faas, *Ted Hughes: The Unaccommodated Universe,* Black Sparrow Press, 1980; Stuart Hirschberg, *Myth in the Poetry of Ted Hughes,* Wolfhound Press, 1981; *Contemporary Authors, New Revision Series,* Volume I, Gale, 1981; K. Sagar, editor, *The Achievement of Ted Hughes,* Manchester University Press, 1981; Terry Gifford and Neil Roberts, *Ted Hughes: A Critical Study,* Faber, 1981; K. Sagar and Stephen Tabor, *Ted Hughes: A Bibliography 1945-1980,* Mansell, 1983; Thomas West, *Ted Hughes,* Methuen, 1985; Leonard Scigaj, *The Poetry of Ted Hughes: Form and Imagination,* University of Iowa Press, 1986.

IPCAR, Dahlov (Zorach)   1917-

PERSONAL: Born November 12, 1917, in Windsor, Vt.; daughter of William (a sculptor) and Marguerite (a painter; maiden name, Thompson) Zorach; married Adolph Ipcar (a dairy farmer), September 29, 1936; children: Robert William, Charles. *Education:* Attended Oberlin College, 1933-34. *Home and office:* Robinhood Farm, Star Route 2, Bath, Me. 04530. *Agent:* McIntosh & Otis, Inc., 310 Madison Ave., New York, N.Y. 10017; Frost Gully Gallery, 25 Forest Ave., Portland, Me. 04101.

CAREER: Artist; author and illustrator of children's books. *Exhibitions*—One-woman: Museum of Modern Art, New York, N.Y., 1939; Bignou Gallery, New York, 1940; Passedoit Gallery, New York, 1943; Philadelphia Art Alliance, Pa., 1944; A.C.A. Gallery, New York, 1946; Farnsworth Museum, Rockland, Me., 1949, 1956, 1978-79; Wellons Gallery, New York, 1950, 1952; Children's Museum, Oakland, Calif., 1956; Portland Museum of Art, Me., 1959, 1963, 1970; Patten Free Library, Bath, Me., 1960; University of Maine, 1965, 1967, 1969, 1975; Bates College, Me., 1966, 1970, 1978; Westbrook Junior College, Me., 1966; Mary Baldwin College, Va., 1968; Fisher Gallery, Portland, Me., 1969; Shevis Gallery, Camden, Me., 1969; Maine Art Gallery, Wiscasset, Me., 1969; Dalzell-Hatfield Galleries, Los Angeles, Calif., 1970; Keystone Junior College, Pa., 1975; Delaware Art Museum Library, 1976; Frost Gully Gallery, Portland, 1977, 1985; Cape Split Place, Addison, Me., 1977; Hobe Sound Galleries, Fla., 1979; State Street Church, Portland, 1981; Curtis Library, Brunswick, Me., 1982; Maine National Bank, Portland, 1984; and others.

Two-man shows: Elmira College, N.Y., 1962; Harlow Gallery, Hallowell, Me., 1964; Priscilla Hartley Gallery, Kennebunkport, Me., 1965; Frost Gully Gallery, Portland, Me., 1974; Colby Museum of Art, Waterville, Me., 1974; Hurlbutt Gallery, Greenwich, Conn., 1978.

DAHLOV IPCAR

Group shows: Corcoran Gallery of Art Bienniel, 1939; Carnegie Institute, 1941, 1943; "14 Outstanding Women Artists," Detroit Institute, Mich., 1943; "Zorach Family," Bowdoin College, Me., 1958, "Maine '75," 1975; "76 Maine Artists," Maine State Museum, 1976; "Zorach Family," Benbow Gallery, Newport, R.I., 1977, and Frost Gully Gallery, Portland, 1980; American Academy and Institute of Arts and Letters, 1980; "Five Deborah Morton Women," Payson Gallery, Westbrook College, Me., 1982; Maine Coast Artists, Rockport, Me., 1984; Barn Gallery Invitational, Ogunquit, Me., 1984; "Maine Illustrators," Maine Coast Artists, Rockport, 1985; "Women Pioneers in Maine 1900-1945," Payson Gallery, Westbrook College, 1985; "American Institute of Architects and MCAH % for Arts," Bowdoin College, 1986; and others.

Collections: Brooklyn Museum of Art, New York; Metropolitan Museum of Art, New York, N.Y.; Whitney Museum of American Art, New York; Newark Museum, N.J.; Farleigh Dickinson University, N.J.; Portland Museum of Art, Me.; Colby College Museum of Art, Me.; Bates College, Me.; Westbrook College, Me.; University of Maine; Mary Baldwin College, Va.; Haystack Mountain School, Deer Isle, Me. Work is also included in many private collections.

Murals: U.S. Post Office, Lafollette, Tenn., 1939; U.S. Post Office, Yukon, Okla., 1941; Children's Reading Room, Patten Free Library, Bath, Me., 1978; Sun Savings and Loan Office, Auburn Mall, Me., 1979; Kingfield Elementary School, Me., 1980; Narragansett Elementary School, Gorham, Me., 1981; Poland Springs Community School, Poland, Me., 1982.

MEMBER: American Civil Liberties Union, Citizens for Safe Power (director), Bath-Brunswick Regional Arts Council (director, 1971-73). *Awards, honors: New York Herald Tribune*'s Spring Book Festival Honor Book, 1955, for *World Full of Horses;* Clara A. Haas Award of Silvermine Guild, 1957, for "Cats and Cards"; popular prize at Portland (Me.) Art Festival, 1959, for "Shore of Night"; (with husband, Adolph Ipcar) Maine State Award from the Maine Commission of Arts and Humanities, 1972, for significant contributions to Maine in the field of the arts and humanities; Junior Merit Award, Bridgeton, Me., 1973, for "Interface"; D.H.L., University of Maine, 1978; Deborah Morton Award, Westbrook College, 1978; D.F.A., Colby College, 1980; Women of Achievement Award from Westbrook College and the Junior League of Portland, Maine, 1984; Living Legacy Award from the Central Maine Area Agency on the Aging, 1986, for excellent and creative contributions of the older generation.

WRITINGS—Juvenile, all self-illustrated: *Animal Hide and Seek,* Scott, 1947; *One Horse Farm* (Junior Literary Guild selection), Doubleday, 1950; *World Full of Horses* (ALA Notable Book; Junior Literary Guild selection), Doubleday, 1955; *The Wonderful Egg,* Doubleday, 1958; *Ten Big Farms,* Knopf, 1958; *Brown Cow Farm: A Counting Book* (ALA Notable Book; Junior Literary Guild selection), Doubleday, 1959.

I Like Animals, Knopf, 1960; *Stripes and Spots* (Junior Literary Guild selection), Doubleday, 1961; *Deep Sea Farm,* Knopf, 1961; *Wild and Tame Animals* (Junior Literary Guild selection), Doubleday, 1962; *Lobsterman,* Knopf, 1962, reissued, Down East, 1977; *Black and White,* Knopf, 1963; *I Love My Anteater with an A,* Knopf, 1964; *Horses of Long Ago* (Junior Literary Guild selection), Doubleday, 1965; *The Calico Jungle,* Knopf, 1965; *Bright Barnyard,* Knopf, 1966; *The Song of the Day Birds and the Night Birds* (Junior Literary Guild selection), Doubleday, 1967; *Whisperings and Other*

(From the filmstrip "Brown Cow Farm." Produced by Weston Woods, 1966.)

Things (poetry), Knopf, 1967; *The Wild Whirlwind,* Knopf, 1968; *The Cat at Night,* Doubleday, 1969.

The Marvelous Merry-Go-Round, Doubleday, 1970; *Sir Addlepate and the Unicorn,* Doubleday, 1971; *The Cat Came Back,* Knopf, 1971; *The Biggest Fish in the Sea,* Viking, 1972; *A Flood of Creatures,* Holiday House, 1973; *The Land of Flowers,* Viking, 1974; *Bug City* (Junior Literary Guild selection), Holiday House, 1975; *Hard Scrabble Harvest,* Doubleday, 1976; *Bring in the Pumpkins,* Scholastic Book Services, 1978; *Lost and Found: A Hidden Animal Book,* Doubleday, 1981; *My Wonderful Christmas Tree,* Gannett Books, 1986.

Young adult fiction: *General Felice* (illustrated by Kenneth Longtemps), McGraw, 1967; *The Warlock of Night,* Viking, 1969; *The Queen of Spells,* Viking, 1973; *A Dark Horn Blowing* (novel), Viking, 1978.

Illustrator: Margaret Wise Brown, *The Little Fisherman,* Scott, 1945; Evelyn Beyer, *Just Like You,* Scott, 1946; John G. McCullough, *Good Work,* Scott, 1948.

Contributor of adult short stories to *Texas Quarterly, Yankee,* and *Argosy;* also contributor to *Horn Book.*

ADAPTATIONS: "Brown Cow Farm" (filmstrip), Weston Woods, 1966; "Brown Cow Farm" (recording), Weston Woods; "The Wonderful Egg" (recording), Weston Woods.

SIDELIGHTS: **November 12, 1917.** Born in Windsor, Vermont. "It never occurred to me that anyone might live a life without art. Both my parents were artists, and our home was always full of artistic activities. It was really a house of wonders. My mother was busy making batiks, embroidering bedspreads and clothes for us, hooking rugs, and, of course, painting pictures. Our walls were painted with murals of the Garden of Eden; and every piece of furniture—mostly discards from the city streets—was painted in gay colors. My father was busy carving in one room, but he could take time out to make me a costume for Hallowe'en, all covered with moons and stars and blazing suns of genuine gold leaf.

"My parents gave me no formal art training. They both felt that their own art had been hampered and misdirected by the academic training they had received—they were among the first of the modern art movement—and they wanted to see what would happen if a child's art were to develop as naturally as possible. They gave me a great deal of encouragement, and they took me to visit museums and artists' studios and showed me the best in art. Most important of all, my father taught me about integrity. He taught me that an artist must never create art to sell. If he does, it won't be Art. He must work because he has a tremendous urge to create; he must put his heart and soul into his work and do the very best he can. Then, only after the work is finished, should he try to sell it. My father also warned me against commercial art. 'Never get involved in it,' he warned. 'They'll tell you what to do; they'll pester the life out of you. You won't be able to call your soul your own!'" [Dahlov Ipcar, ''Making Pictures on the Farm,'' *The Illustrators Notebook,* edited by Lee Kingman, Horn Book, 1978.[1]]

1922. "As far back as I can remember, I have been interested in farming and animals and have wanted to live on a farm. I grew up and attended school in New York City, though I was born in Windsor, Vermont. Each summer, however, we spent in the country. I was only five years old when my parents bought our farm . . . in Robinhood, Maine. It was always run as a working farm even if we were here summers only. From the beginning my brother and I helped weed the gardens, care for the animals, cut the wood, and make hay. One summer when I was fourteen and my brother seventeen, he and I alone took in all the hay—twenty tons of it." [Dahlov Ipcar, ''We Like Being Farmers,'' *Young Wings,* March, 1951.[2]]

1924. "... At the age of seven I started a frieze that travelled around my room, full of large and fanciful animals, bright colored horses and ostriches and dinosaurs. My parents never tried to direct me. . . . The schools I attended were all 'progressive.' Perhaps through all this I have managed to keep a

little of the child's 'natural' approach to painting and fresh view point. At least, I like to think so.'' [B. M. Miller and others, compilers, *Illustrator's of Children's Books: 1946-1956,* Horn Book, 1958.[3]]

Among the several progressive schools that Ipcar attended in New York City were City and Country School, Walden School, and Lincoln School of Teacher's College. ''. . . I feel strongly that progressive education brings out the best in a creative person. . . . At the age of 16 I spent one year at Oberlin College on a full-tuition scholarship, but it was a disappointment after my more stimulating earlier education. I dropped out and have never regretted it. I feel that a person with creative talent does just as well without a formal education.'' [Lee Bennett Hopkins, ''Dahlov Ipcar,'' *Books Are by People,* Citation Press, 1969.[4]]

September 29, 1936. ''. . . When I was eighteen, I managed to marry a nice young struggling accountant, and persuaded him to try farm life. I was very lucky, because if he had been a happy accountant I would probably still be living in the city. But he didn't like city life, either, and he makes a fine dairy farmer.''[1]

During their first year of marriage, Ipcar realized a long-cherished dream when she and her husband Adolph moved to Robinhood Farm in Robinhood, Maine. ''. . . I love farm life, even though it is hard work. I think I will always feel romantic about it. There is visual beauty all around me. Color and pattern are everywhere. Haycocks and windrows form designs in the fields. Plowed fields are beautiful with the shine of light along the furrows, and the plow teams in yellow blankets with

Bring in the winter squash,
pile them high.
Bring in the pumpkins
for pumpkin pie.

(From *Hard Scrabble Harvest* by Dahlov Ipcar. Illustrated by the author.)

At the very end there comes the monarch butterfly riding a big goldbug coach pulled by six fine horseflies. The bugs on the sidelines cheer and wave as the monarch passes.

(From *Bug City* by Dahlov Ipcar. Illustrated by the author.)

red stripes. I love the browns and grays of the cows in the whitewashed barn. They seem to me as beautiful as antelopes. Even the clothes that the men wear are as bright reds and greens as you would find in any medieval miniature.... I think perhaps I first decided that I wanted to live on a farm when I was only three years old. So never underestimate how early a child's life plan is formed....''[1]

Besides assisting in the operation of their small dairy farm, Ipcar raised her two sons and continued to paint. About those early years of marriage, Ipcar once remarked: "Our sons—Bobby ... and Charlie ... join in all the farm activities. We're all busy from one year's end to the next. Each month there's a different kind of job to be done. Our farm has always been, and still is, a *one horse farm*. Somehow I doubt whether we'll ever change over to a tractor, although we talk about it. A farm would not seem a farm to me without the different animals and the work and the pleasure they give us."[2] Eventually, a tractor was acquired.

1939. Held her first one-woman show at the Museum of Modern Art's Young People's Gallery.

1944. Began illustrating children's books. Her first illustrated book was done at the request of a former teacher who asked her to illustrate Margaret Wise Brown's *The Little Fisherman*. Ipcar illustrated two more children's books by other authors before she began writing her own stories to illustrate. ". . . Fortunately, I have never had to compromise. No one has told me how to do my pictures. I have done children's books because I loved doing them. I have enjoyed all the work in-

volved. And I don't have to sell them; the publisher does that. The only thing I have to sell is the idea, or the text, for by some strange and, to my mind, backward process, it is the story that is bought, not the pictures. I write the stories too, but only as a sort of excuse for doing the pictures. I'm afraid I think as an artist, not as a writer; I think in terms of pictures. I think of something I would like to paint, and I write a story to go with it.

"But I feel a picture book, even for very young children, needs some valid idea. It must convey some message or point of view, reveal some truth about the world, or awaken some new interest in the things around us. I have a million and one ideas for pictures, but I only get about one idea a year for stories. . . .

"I have been able to do all my books and all the art work on them through the mail. I find that this gives me time to think problems through and work them out, and I am not so dependent on other people. Often I write my editor or my production manager about a problem, and by the time they reply I have solved it myself. I should think this would be rather frustrating to the editors, but they seem happy. I feel that an editor's function is not to tell us how to write or paint, but to prod us into doing our best. Sometimes a word of criticism is very helpful.''[1]

1958. "My dinosaur book, *The Wonderful Egg* . . . came from memories of my own childhood, in this case from my early love of prehistoric animals. . . . My own sons were fascinated by dinosaurs, too, and begged me to paint dinosaur pictures for them. I even made them dinosaur Easter eggs. We were a little ahead of the rest of the world, but now other children seem to have caught up with us, and they all share our interest in dinosaurs. One of the things that amused me in the reviews of this book was that some reviewers, while praising it as 'quite scientific,' took exception to the 'unscientific color.' Of course, no one knows what color dinosaurs were, and I see no reason to imagine that they were ugly putty-colored monsters, so I made them as gay in color as possible. Small reptiles are often beautifully and excitingly colored, and it seems possible that the big ones might have been also.

"Other books of mine such as *One Horse Farm* and *Ten Big Farms* are drawn directly from my farm experience, and *World Full of Horses* from my love of the old-fashioned way of life that we lived when we first came to Maine. *I Like Animals* expresses, of course, my own lifelong interest in every kind of animal life."[1]

1959. "When I first submitted my book *Brown Cow Farm*, I had planned it as a counting book from one to ten. But picture books come in standard sizes, and thirty-six pages is about the shortest. Even using double spreads for each number, ten numbers only take up twenty pages; so I padded it with a little story front and back. Peggy Lesser, of Doubleday, said, 'We like this, but it isn't either counting book or farm story. Can't you do something about it?' I wanted to keep it a counting book, but I couldn't see how to work it out. Then early one morning, about four o'clock (I always get all my best ideas at four in the morning), it came to me. Why not make this a real counting book and have it develop by tens to one hundred? All children are thrilled when they discover that once you have learned to count by tens you can count to any number, even one thousand or a million. . . ."[1]

Although Ipcar has written and illustrated many books for children, she still considers herself primarily an artist, devoting half of her time to painting. She has had numerous one-woman shows in New York City and in Maine. Her work is in several permanent museum collections throughout the country, including collections housed in the Metropolitan and Whitney Museums. "My books and my art sometimes overlap. I seem to draw ideas from each for the other. I love to paint animals more than anything else, and because I can visualize them so clearly in my mind's eye I am never dependent on models. I can show them in action as one could never capture them even with patience and a camera. My art is fairly close to nature, but not dependent on nature. I am free to do anything I choose. If I paint the things around me it is only because I find them more strange and exciting than fanciful things. But I am never earthbound; if I want to do fantastic things I can, because even the real, everyday things I paint are all done from my imagination.

"I am a firm believer in inspiration. The mind is an amazing storehouse. While mine may have a limited supply of textual material, there seems to be no end of the pictures that are stored there. I sometimes feel that I am troubled with visions; I see so many marvelous pictures when I close my eyes. They arise without any conscious effort, a multitude of completely new and beautiful designs and things I have never seen or imagined. I have seen Mexican fiestas in my mind's eye, complete with gorgeous and fantastic costumes in astounding colors. Everything is very elusive; patterns and colors change swiftly as in a kaleidoscope. I remember recently doing a painting of a snake winding down a tree, and I must have seen a hundred snakes winding down a hundred different trees, each with a different and equally beautiful change of color and design.

The little boy went down again and brought up the cat and the dog and the pot of oatmeal. Only the geese were left below, happily swimming round and round the dining room table.

"Here's your oatmeal," the little boy said, as he lugged the big pot into the bedroom. "Wouldn't you like some breakfast?"

"Oh, thank you," the old lady said. "I'm glad you rescued the oatmeal. If I have to put up with all these awful animals, I'll have to eat something to give me strength."

(From *A Flood of Creatures* by Dahlov Ipcar. Illustrated by the author.)

The cat came back,
She couldn't stay no longer.
The cat came back,
'Cause she couldn't stay away.
The cat came back,
We thought she was a goner,
But the cat came back
ON THE VERY NEXT DAY!

(From *The Cat Came Back*, adapted by Dahlov Ipcar. Illustrated by the author.)

"In general I would say that my art is happy art. A great many artists these days are afraid of cheerful pictures. They want to be taken 'seriously' and nothing insures this better than painting pictures that drip gloom and despair. This pretentious tragic posing is as ludicrous in its way as the heavy-handed Victorian attempts at pathos and melancholy.

"Perhaps I lead too happy and healthy an existence, but I much prefer to convey the beauty and excitement of simple everyday life. There is an infinite, incredible mystery in beauty. Everything living is beautifully designed. Each animal has a distinct form and personality and life of its own.''[1]

1965. Wrote and illustrated a concise historical survey of the horse—an ambitious project that ended with the publication of *Horses of Long Ago.* "Most of the books on the horse end up as a catalogue of the different breeds. I wanted to avoid this approach and give a more general picture.

"I spent a full year doing research and learned a great deal, mostly about how unreliable historians can be. I spent a lot of time trying to verify repeated references to chariot races at Stonehenge in 2500 B.C., only to find in the end that Stonehenge was not even built until 1700 B.C., and at the time there were no horses or chariots in use in Britain, not even domestic oxen to help haul the huge stones!

"I enjoyed doing this book because I have always loved both horses and the art of ancient times. I have always felt that all primitive and ancient art have something in common: a beautiful combination of simplicity and careful detail, a quality also found in the best of children's art. Children instinctively react to this quality and feel its charm. There are no more appealing or truthful pictures of ancient life than the marvelous scenes preserved in Egyptian tomb statuettes. I have tried to capture some of this quality, and tried to preserve the spirit of the original art work on which I based my research."

"The message I am trying to convey in much of my writing [is]: that the world of reality and the world of dreams and the imagination are two sides of the same experience, and neither should be rejected.

"My writing for adults and young adults is different. It is full of strange grim things. There is beauty too, for I write fantasies, and the visual part of me creates beautiful settings for my stories. But my fantasies all contain threatening elements, as most true legends and myths do. Each story I have written seems to fill a personal need to express something, something perhaps inexpressible, but very important to me emotionally. Themes reoccur: talking ravens, black bulls, war dogs. I don't think of them as symbols. To me their meaning is completely mysterious and I prefer to keep it that way.

"Perhaps Jung is right when he considers myths and legends to be part of a universal subconscious. I am continually surprised when I find parallels to my ideas in the works of other writers. Why are all these thoughts circulating 'in the air'? Or have we perhaps absorbed during childhood more legend and myth than we realize? Do the things we have read and heard sink deep within us only to surface years later in changed form? I remember a series of weird dreams of metamorphosis I had when I was ten years old—were there literary sources, or was I tapping the primeval wellspring of myth?

"I have, so far, written four novels for young adults. Each has been written under a strong compulsion. This is what we call 'inspiration.' It is a strange exciting thing, a kind of en-

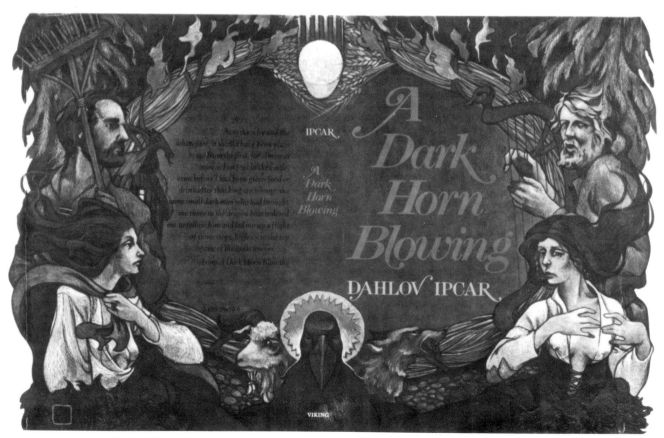

(Jacket illustration by Charles Mikolaycak from *A Dark Horn Blowing* by Dahlov Ipcar.)

(Jacket illustration by Dahlov Ipcar from *Lost and Found: A Hidden Animal Book* by Dahlov Ipcar.)

chantment. Almost all my creative ideas seem to come to me in the night or just before dawn when I awake from daydreaming. In the time between dreaming and waking there seems to be a door that opens into the creative recesses of the mind. Most of my novels begin with a single powerful visual image that grips me for no explainable reason. My . . . novel, *A Dark Horn Blowing* . . . began in this same way with one compelling scene. I wrote the first three pages laying half awake in bed. Nora hears the lowing of a cow far off, and she is drawn by the sound out across the tidal sands 'stretching silver-white far out into the bay.' There at the tide's edge the cow's lowing becomes a horn blown by a small man standing by a dark boat, and Nora can no longer turn back. She steps into the boat and all memories of her life fade away. She forgets her home, her husband, her newborn babe—she is carried across a magic sea to a strange land.

"I can identify the source of this scene. It is based on Child ballad 40 'The Queen of Elfan's Nourice.' The original is really only a ballad fragment, but even in its fragmentary form it has tremendous evocative power. I have called my magic kingdom 'Erland,' but it is, of course, the Elfland of the ballad. Norse mythology mentions a legendary King Elf, and I have often wondered if 'Elfland' was not perhaps originally his kingdom. For that reason I have given my Erland a Nordic culture and drawn on the old Norse legends for elements in my story; whereas, in the 'real' land that Nora comes from I have used elements of English-Scottish folklore, such as the power of rowanwood to protect against witchcraft.

"I thought my story would deal mainly with what became of the husband and child that Nora left behind; but, as I tried to go on with the story, I found I could not. The scenes that arose in my mind were so devastating that I kept putting it off. For three years I kept returning to the opening scene and saying to myself, 'I can't give this up.' Why that image held me so strongly, why I had to write a whole book around it, I don't know. The creative process is mysterious and endlessly fascinating to me. It seems to be similar for most writers. Some inkling of an idea surfaces from nowhere, some brief glimpse of a scene triggers an obsession until it has to grow and develop and finally become a book. I don't think any good book ever started with a cold logical decision to write on a certain topic. There is always some small germ of inspiration that starts the whole process.

"In both my painting and my writing I create worlds of the imagination. I transform ordinary reality into a reality that has special meaning to me. I hope it will also have special meaning to others. My first editor at Doubleday, Margaret [Peggy] Lesser, once said to me, 'I'm beginning to feel that the reality created by the artist's imagination is more important than actual reality.'" [Dahlov Ipcar, "Two Worlds in Balance," *Bookmark*, Moray House College (Edinburgh, Scotland), summer, 1980.⁵]

Ipcar has great respect for the state of childhood, believing that all children have a natural curiosity and love for the world around them. "I like to do art for children because I feel they love these living things as I do. They love each animal and leaf and look at it with wonder. People ask me how I manage to find my way back to the world of childhood, and I say that I am still a child at heart. Perhaps I am not really; perhaps no one can remain a child, even deep in his heart. But for me the sense of wonder is still there."¹

"Unfortunately, we live in a pragmatic society where art is not considered as important as 'practical' things. But a child raised without art is as surely deprived as a child raised without love.

(Jacket illustration by Dahlov Ipcar from *The Marvelous Merry-Go-Round* by Dahlov Ipcar.)

(Jacket illustration by Dahlov Ipcar from *Horses of Long Ago* by Dahlov Ipcar.)

"Fine art in children's book illustration is the best way to bring the creative imagination of the artist to the largest number of children. When I write and illustrate for children, I feel a strong obligation to give my best. I work with joy in the creation of beautiful books. In remembering and recapturing the intense sense of wonder that all children feel, I am continually renewed and find inspiration that carries over into all my other art forms."

A film "Dahlov Ipcar" is available abroad from the United States Information Service. Ipcar's works are included in the Kerlan Collection at the University of Minnesota and in the Archives of American Art at the Smithsonian Institute in Washington, D.C.

HOBBIES AND OTHER INTERESTS: Old folk songs, chess, gardening, nature study, promoting art legislation, and fighting against nuclear power.

FOR MORE INFORMATION SEE: Mademoiselle, February, 1949; B. M. Miller and others, compilers, *Illustrators of Children's Books: 1946-1956,* Horn Book, 1958; *Horn Book,* October, 1961, February, 1966; Diana Klemin, *The Art of Art for Children's Books,* Clarkson Potter, 1966; *Young Readers' Review,* March, 1968; Lee Kingman and others, compilers, *Illustrators of Children's Books: 1957-1966,* Horn Book, 1968; Lee Bennett Hopkins, *Books Are by People,* Citation Press, 1969; Martha E. Ward and Dorothy A. Marquardt, *Authors of Books for Young People,* 2nd edition, Scarecrow, 1971; Doris de Montreville and Donna Hill, editors, *Third Book of Junior Authors,* H. W. Wilson, 1973; Martin Dibner, *Seacoast Maine: People and Places,* Doubleday, 1973; *Down East,* April, 1974; L. Kingman, editor, *The Illustrator's Notebook,* Horn Book, 1978; L. Kingman and others, compilers, *Illustrators of Children's Books: 1967-1976,* Horn Book, 1978; Dahlov Ipcar, "Two Worlds in Balance," *Bookmark* (Edinburgh, Scotland), summer, 1980; James Plummer's Sixth Grade Class, *A Gift from Maine,* Guy Gannett, 1983; William L. Pohl, *The Voice of Maine,* Thorndike Press, 1983; *Art Gallery,* August/September, 1984; *Bittersweet,* January, 1985; Susan Ryan, "Artist and Activist," *Artists in Maine,* summer, 1986; Pat Reef, *Dahlov Ipcar: Artist* (juvenile), Kennebec River Press, 1987.

JEFFERDS, Vincent H(arris) 1916-

BRIEF ENTRY: Born August 23, 1916, in Jersey City, N.J. Company executive and author of books for children. In 1951 Jefferds began a sales and marketing career with Walt Disney Productions that spanned more than thirty years, until his retirement in 1983 as senior vice-president of marketing. During that time, he was responsible for establishing worldwide Disney book clubs, Disney ice shows, and the Disney record business. He also designed the World Showcase in Florida's Walt Disney World, introduced an exclusive line of Winnie-the-Pooh apparel and toys in conjunction with Sears & Roebuck, and designed the Orange Bird character for the Florida Citrus Commission's advertising and promotional needs. The recipient of a number of awards throughout his long career, he was named the "World's Most Outstanding Licensing Marketer" by the Nuremberg Toy Conference in 1968, and, in 1982, the "Most Creative Merchandiser" by the United States Licensed Manufacturers Association. Since his retirement, Jefferds has produced children's books featuring familiar Disney characters, including *Disney's Elegant ABC Book* (Little Simon, 1983), *Disney's Elegant Book of Manners* (Little Simon, 1985), *The Wooly Bird Meets Winnie-the-Pooh* (Golden Books, 1985), *Mickey and Donald in the Tickle Grass* (Golden Books, 1985), and *Peter Pan and the Troll* (Golden Books, 1985). In

addition to writing, Jefferds devotes his time to painting and has exhibited and sold paintings and lithographs internationally. He also continues his affiliation with Disney Productions on retainer as a senior marketing consultant. *Office:* Walt Disney Productions, 500 South Buena Vista, Burbank, Calif. 91521.

FOR MORE INFORMATION SEE: Who's Who in the West, 18th edition, Marquis, 1982; *Who's Who in America,* 43rd edition, Marquis, 1984.

KORMAN, Gordon 1963-

PERSONAL: Born October 23, 1963, in Montreal, Quebec, Canada; son of C. I. (a chartered accountant) and Bernice (a journalist; maiden name, Silverman) Korman. *Education:* New York University, B.F.A., 1985. *Home and office:* 20 Dersingham Cres., Thornhill, Ontario, Canada L3T 4E7. *Agent:* Curtis Brown Ltd., 10 Astor Place, New York, N.Y. 10003.

CAREER: Writer, 1978—. *Member:* Writers Union of Canada; Canadian Society of Children's Authors, Illustrators, and Performers (CANSCAIP); Canadian Authors' Association; ACTRA, The Society of Children's Book Writers. *Awards, honors:* Air Canada Award from Canadian Authors' Association, 1981, for Most Promising Writer under thirty-five; Ontario Youth Award from the International Year of the Youth Committee of the Ontario Government, 1985, for his contribution to children's literature.

WRITINGS: Who Is Bugs Potter?, Scholastic-TAB, 1980, Scholastic, 1984; *I Want to Go Home!,* Scholastic-TAB, 1981,

GORDON KORMAN

Paul smiled so wide it hurt his face. . . ."All systems are go." ■ (Jacket illustration by Bruce Emmett from *Don't Care High* by Gordon Korman.)

Scholastic, 1984; *Our Man Weston*, Scholastic-TAB, 1982, Scholastic, 1986; *Bugs Potter: Live at Nickaninny*, Scholastic-TAB, 1983; *No Coins, Please*, Scholastic-TAB, 1984, Scholastic, 1985; *Don't Care High*, Scholastic, 1985; *Son of Interflux* (young adult novel), Scholastic, 1986; *Raymond Jardine Lucks Out, or How to Get Rid of a Windmill* (young adult novel), Scholastic, 1987.

"Bruno and Boots" series: *This Can't Be Happening at Macdonald Hall!* (illustrated by Affie Mohammed), Scholastic-TAB (Canada), 1978, Scholastic Book Services, 1979; *Go Jump in the Pool!* (illustrated by Lea Daniel), Scholastic-TAB, 1979, Scholastic, 1982; *Beware the Fish!* (illustrated by L. Daniel), Scholastic Book Services, 1980; *The War with Mr. Wizzle*, Scholastic, 1982.

WORK IN PROGRESS: "Presently working on *The Zucchini Warriors*, the fifth in the 'Bruno and Boots' series. My fan mail asked for this one."

SIDELIGHTS: **October 23, 1963.** Born in Montreal, Canada, Korman attended local schools and enjoyed writing. "I always really enjoyed creative projects, and I always liked writing stories. I'd done a couple of speeches for speech competitions, all of which I lost, because my delivery wasn't good enough, and other things like that. If you want to win the speech contest, you sort of have to write about extinction, not how to handle your parents, or how to handle your teachers, or things designed to entertain. And I was a big writing fan. I wasn't a big reader for some reason. I was a good reader in grades one,

two, and three, but then I dropped reading in grades four, five, and six—which leads me to suspect that I may be filling in the hole that I left on the first pass. But I always tried to put in creativity where I could: if we had a sentence with all the spelling words for that week, I would try to come up with the stupidest sentences, or the funniest sentences, or the craziest sentences I could think of." [Chris Ferns, "An Interview with Gordon Korman," *Canadian Children's Literature*, number 38, 1985.]

1975. Wrote his first book, *This Can't Be Happening at Macdonald Hall!* when he was twelve years old. The book was published two years later. "When I was in 7th grade we had this English assignment which I got kind of carried away on, and I accidentally wrote the first book. You know, the characters sort of became real people to me, and they more or less wrote the book for me. The class had to read all the assignments at the end of the whole business, and a lot of people were coming to me and saying how they really liked it. I suppose anyone who writes 120 pages for class is going to attract a certain amount of attention anyway—and I just got the idea of seeing if I could get the book published. It seemed to me like a distant goal, but then again, there seemed to me no reason why it shouldn't get published, as I was pretty sure it was as good as the stuff I'd been reading. I had a lot of confidence back then—certainly in that first book, anyway. At the time, I happened to be the class monitor for the Scholastic Book Club, and it gave me this sort of corporate responsibility towards Scholastic, which of course they didn't

The next day, Simon found himself the object of much attention. ■ (Jacket illustration by Bruce Emmett from *Son of Interflux* by Gordon Korman.)

know about. So I sent the book to them when I was thinking of a publisher, and they published it.'''[1]

''I kept on writing—a book every summer—to see if I could do it again. And it turned out well. All my books have been Canadian best-sellers, and I'm proud of that. It changed my life, of course, but I've never regretted it.''

Korman's early books were directed toward the young adult market, an audience of which he was also a member. ''My books are the kind of stories I wanted to read and couldn't find when I was ten, eleven, and twelve, and young adult novels didn't exist a few years ago when I was in high school. I think that, no matter what the subject matter, kids' concerns are important, and being a kid isn't just waiting out the time between birth and the age of majority. I hope other kids see that in my work.''

1980. Departed from the exploits of his heroes Bruno and Boots, in his first book about Bugs Potter, a young rock drummer. ''Readers are really going to pick up on two things. Is it funny? And, are the people real? Those are the two most important things. Lately, I've been thinking that 'are the people real?' is even more important than 'is it funny?' It has to be a little bit funny, but with real people, and genuine character relationships. That's what the readers are going to pick up: they don't care about the structure. They won't necessarily see any structural difference between *Live at Nickaninny* and *No*

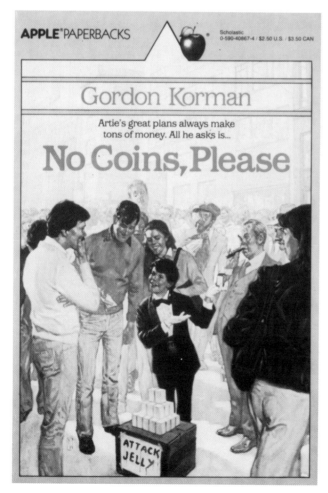

(Cover illustration from *No Coins, Please* by Gordon Korman.)

Coins, Please. If the kids say something, it's more like 'I like Bruno and Boots because they're so real.' Whereas an adult reviewer might say, 'yes, the book is good, but it does lack a little in believability.' The kids don't get that at all—they think that Bruno and Boots are real. Very rarely will there be an event where a kid will say, 'I don't buy that.' I've never seen it.'''[1]

1981. At the age of eighteen, Korman was voted the most promising writer under thirty-five by the Canadian Authors' Association. ''I've done a lot of trips across Canada and the U.S.—and the books are getting there. The kids are reading them, and they're liking them. The reactions I'm getting can be very very different, but as a rule nobody hates the books! I don't think I've excluded any kid: maybe a handful here and there. You get a number of different reactions: you get kids who just get so into the books that they take it further. You get a couple of kids who get T-shirts where one says 'Bruno' and the other says 'Boots,' and they go around self-proclaimed Bruno and Boots. Or a group of girls officially declare themselves Miss Scrimmage's Finishing School for Young Ladies. A lot of kids get very into Bugs Potter, if they're into the rock scene: they come up with their own rock groups, they do Bugs Potter things. The same with *I Want to Go Home:* a lot of people really admire Rudy Miller.

''Another reaction is that the kids who are lousy readers get into the books. Many times I've had letters from teachers saying, 'This is my fourth grade remedial reading class, and your books have sort of turned them on.' In Vancouver I was doing a tour, and I did a reading. Afterwards the teachers made all the kids do a letter home from camp, from the model of the letter in *I Want to Go Home,* and one teacher phoned me in my hotel room to tell me that her class write-off had got turned on enough to write three pages of foolscap, and that that was the first thing he'd really done. The other thing that seems to happen is that the kids get not only into the books, but into me personally—which is good, for the simple reason that it shows I have a distinctive enough style to inject my own personality into the book. So when I get to see a group of kids I'm not just this nothing coming out of a vacuum who just so happens to have his name on the books—they expect to find a certain amount of my personality in my writing. And when I talk to them I want to show them that, basically, they're right.'''[1]

Part of the appeal of Korman's heroes is the fact that they have a healthy disrespect for authority, although they draw the line between disrespect and anarchy. ''I was writing at the time of 'Animal House,' and things like that. I think one of the things which makes the books fairly strong, so that they defy being compared to things like that, is that they don't cross that line. Considering how crazy the books are, I keep a firm foot in reality. For a number of reasons: first of all, this is Scholastic—and while I could ask Scholastic to make an exception, and they probably would, Scholastic is basically a quite traditional publisher. Not so much now, perhaps, but four years ago, definitely. Also, in a book—in a movie it may be different, depending on the visual image you're portraying—in a book, if something is going to be crazy, it has to happen in the context of something fairly sane, or else you can't really appreciate how crazy it is. The reason it's great when Bruno and Boots break rules is that in the long run you know that, while they don't necessarily accept the rules themselves, they accept the basic fact that there *are* rules. They accept the fact that they are kids, and that the administration is the administration, and that that's it. And the fact that they do this makes it all the more interesting when they do decide what they can and can't do.

"Boy!" exclaimed Boots. "Were we lucky to get through this day alive!" ■ (Cover illustration by Tom Newsom from *This Can't Be Happening at Macdonald Hall!* by Gordon Korman.)

". . . With Bugs Potter, I think it's a little different. He tries to follow the rules—only there are other priorities so strong that he has to live with them first, and follow the rules whenever it fits in. He's not really actively misbehaving. . . . And Sidney Weston has a calling: so what if I break the rules, because I'm saving such and such. . . . With *No Coins, Please* it starts to become a little more ambiguous, because the sympathetic characters set up are the counsellors, almost, and the guy who's crazy is more someone to bounce off them and the other kids in the group. So Artie's motivation . . . I've been getting this real enjoyment, lately, from withholding information—I really think that if Artie had ever said why he wanted all that money it would in some way have robbed the book. . . . I think one of the most important things about *No Coins, Please* is that while Artie may violate the letter of the law, he never really violates its spirit. He doesn't really rip anybody off. He extracts a small amount of money from everybody: his fortune comes from the fact that he does it to a lot of people."[1]

In several of his books, Korman shows his young readers that young people can have power. His books appeal to young people because they show young heroes that are able to achieve in an adult world. "Whatever an adult can do, somewhere in the world there's one sixteen-year-old who can do it as well. You read about it in the paper—it just keeps coming up. And that's important, because a kid around twelve is just starting to find out that he can do certain things as well as his parents or his teachers. By the time he's fifteen he probably does some things better. You hear a lot of teachers talk about behaviour problems at the grade 7 or 8 levels—perhaps that's because in public school the teachers can do everything better than the students just by virtue of being adults, ninety-nine times out of a hundred. Whereas in high school, teachers have usually accepted that these people are almost adults and can do certain things better than them. It's not out of the ordinary to see that happen. The problem is with the age level where kids are starting to be able to do things, but it still seems unnatural. And I think that's one of the reasons why the books do well in that age bracket, which they're not really supposed to because of their presentation—because they address that situation of kids being able to triumph over the adults, and in many cases with the adults coming to terms with it."

"I think the books are very respectful of people. In some cases it may be oversimplified, but basically if someone isn't liked, it's because he deserves it. One of the things I couldn't stand about school was that it could very easily happen—it happens in the adult world, too, but in school it's most obvious—that someone could look at your face, and not like it, and want to exclude you from the group, or make your life miserable. In the Bruno and Boots books—in all the books, really—people aren't really disliked or acted against unless they've done something to deserve it. It may be a tad unrealistic—but I think it's better unrealistic. I mean, realism, yes—but who wants to read what *really* goes on? Of course, every now and then someone comes up with a super-realistic thing, and it's amazing: a movie like 'Diner,' or something like that. But for the most part, while realism is very important, something extraordinary should happen to keep your interest in the book. And that's what I like to do now."[1]

1985. Received a B.F.A. degree from New York University, and was also chosen as the recipient for the Ontario Youth Award for his contribution to children's literature.

Since his first book was published, Korman has managed to write eleven more books, complete four years of high school, and graduate after completing four years of college studies at New York University. "As a rule I've written a book every

summer. I wrote *I Want to Go Home!* in the winter—but I wouldn't do that again! It was very tough. Also, I got out of school a trimester early, so I had time to do some writing before I went away to University. The system is usually that I write a book in the summer, finish it in the first few weeks of September, and by Christmas I'm starting to think about moving on. Very casually, in conversations with my parents or my friends, I'll start throwing around a few new ideas, and even in very idle conversation something is bound to germinate in January or February. And I'll just keep thinking about it— very often I get these ideas while I'm sitting in class—and the idea begins to grow. I begin to talk about it more seriously with other people, and they give me their ideas, so that by the time I come back from school I'm usually ready to start writing."[1]

Korman's future plans include writing more books. "I see myself doing young adult fiction, but I also want to go back and do a junior fiction book again. I'm torn between doing something totally different, and going back: there's always Bruno and Boots, and I think it may be time for a new Bruno and Boots book, I'd like—I don't know whether it's a romantic notion or not—I'd like to write, not necessarily the great Novel that's going to reshape the world, but a book that makes the sort of splash that *Catch-22* made. I think that's something to aim for, eventually, anyway. But I don't see myself writing an adult book in the immediate future. What I see happening is that one day I'll set out to write about a seventeen-year-old character, and it'll just turn out that this guy isn't seventeen— he's twenty-three or so, and he's an adult. That's how I think the transition will come.

"I know that the books I enjoy most are serious books that just happen to be hilarious—so I think that's what I'm naturally going to find myself working towards. As I get older they're going to get that way. In the later books the humour hasn't been so much in the plot: quite serious things can happen, and it's in the discussion of them, or the description of them that funny things come out. I also think that *Don't Care High* is sort of a quantum leap.

". . . Another thing that's changed, for some reason, is that— there are certain ages in your life where you go through a cycle where you like to read books where everything works out, and other times when you like books where it doesn't work out—my thing now, although it's not as serious as it sounds, is a book where it usually doesn't work out. But it's O.K. because there are other things that are good."[1]

Several of Korman's books have been translated into French, Swedish, and Danish. The "Bruno and Boots" series has also been translated into Chinese.

HOBBIES AND OTHER INTERESTS: Sports, travel and music.

FOR MORE INFORMATION SEE: Ottawa Citizen, July 21, 1978; *Toronto Star,* July 29, 1978, December 14, 1982; *National Enquirer,* March 20, 1979; *Saturday Night,* November, 1979; *Canadian Statesman,* January 23, 1980; *Globe and Mail* (Toronto, Ontario), June 28, 1980, November 18, 1980; *Catholic Register,* March 14, 1981; *Jam,* spring, 1981; *Today,* June 6, 1981; *Quill and Quire,* June, 1981, May, 1982, January, 1983, February, 1983; *Journal of Commonwealth Literature,* February, 1982; *En Route,* April, 1983; *Canadian Materials,* January, 1985; *Canadian Children's Literature,* number 38, 1985; *New York Times,* July 24, 1985; *Maclean's,* October 28, 1985; *Dynamite,* number 135; *Saturday Night,* May, 1986.

KOUHI, Elizabeth   1917-

BRIEF ENTRY: Born November 24, 1917, in Ontario, Canada. Raised in a Finnish pioneering community in northwestern Ontario, Kouhi learned to speak English when she began attending classes in a one-room schoolhouse her father had helped build. With the onset of the Depression, she was forced to leave high school after only one year and spent the next four years working on the family farm. Various other jobs followed, including one as clerk for the Royal Canadian Air Force. Kouhi eventually completed her high school education and graduated from McGill University in 1949. Although interested in writing—she had written verse and prose for years—she chose the security of a teaching career, obtaining a position in a one-room schoolhouse. She later taught high school for nineteen years and retired from teaching in 1982. Kouhi, who describes her desire to write as an "incurable disease," began her first book when her own children were still young. She wrote early in the mornings and during the summers; on this schedule, fifteen years passed before *Jamie of Thunder Bay* (Borealis, 1977), a novel for children, was published.

Kouhi now devotes four to six hours a day to writing. Among her works are *North Country Spring: A Book of Verse for Children* (Penumbra, 1980); *The Story of Philip* (Queenston, 1981), which reveals to young children both the negative and positive aspects of being mentally handicapped; *Round Trip Home* (Penumbra, 1983), poetry for adults; and *Sarah Jane of Silver Islet* (Queenston, 1984), a children's novel set during the 1870s in a small, isolated community on Lake Superior. Kouhi, a member of Writers' Union of Canada and League of Canadian Poets, acts as public awareness chairperson for the Lakehead Association for the Mentally Retarded. An amateur bird-watcher, she enjoys music, art, and the theater. She and her husband have traveled to Britain, Italy, and Lapland. *Home:* 224 North Norah St., Thunder Bay, Ontario, Canada P7C 4H2.

KRAHN, Fernando   1935-

PERSONAL: Born January 4, 1935, in Santiago, Chile; son of Otto (a lawyer) and Laura (a singer; maiden name, Parada) Krahn; married María de la Luz Uribe (a writer and educator), February, 1966; children: María Fernanda, Santiago, Matías. *Education:* Attended Catholic University, Santiago, 1952-55, and University of Chile, 1954-62. *Home:* San Gaudencio 23, Sitges, Spain. *Agent:* Harriet Wasserman Literary Agency, 137 East 36th St., New York, N.Y. 10016.

CAREER: Writer and illustrator of children's books and cartoonist for magazines, 1962—; currently cartoonist for *Internacional Herald Tribune*, Paris, France, *Die Zeit*, Hamburg, West Germany, *Tages Anzeiger*, Zurich, Switzerland, *Nebelspalter*, Switzerland, and *La Vanguardia*, Barcelona, Spain. *Awards, honors: Uncle Timothy's Traviata* was included in the Children's Books Show of the American Institute of Graphic Arts, 1967/68, and *Hildegarde and Maximilian* was included, 1970; *The Life of Numbers* was chosen one of *New York Times* Outstanding Children's Books, 1970; *Lorenzo Bear and Company* was selected one of Child Study Association's Children's Books of the Year, 1971, and *Who's Seen the Scissors?*, 1975; Guggenheim fellowship for film animation experiments, 1972-73; *April Fools* was included in the Children's Book Showcase of the Children's Book Council, 1975; "Apelles Mestres" award for children's books (Spain), 1982; *Robot-Bot-Bot* and *The Mystery of the Giant Footprints* were each selected one

FERNANDO KRAHN

of the International Reading Association/Children's Book Council Children's Choices, 1985.

WRITINGS—Juvenile, except as indicated; all self-illustrated: *The Self-Made Snowman*, Lippincott, 1975; *Little Love Story*, Lippincott, 1976; *The Family Minus*, Parents Magazine Press, 1977; *A Funny Friend from Heaven*, Lippincott, 1977; *The Biggest Christmas Tree on Earth*, Atlantic-Little, Brown, 1978; *The Great Ape: Being the True Version of the Famous Saga of Adventure and Friendship Newly Discovered*, Viking, 1978; *The Family Minus's Summer House*, Parents Magazine Press, 1980; *Here Comes Alex Pumpernickel!*, Atlantic-Little, Brown, 1981; *Sleep Tight Alex Pumpernickel!*, Atlantic-Little, Brown, 1982; *The Creepy Thing* (Junior Literary Guild selection), Clarion, 1982; *The Secret in the Dungeon* (Junior Literary Guild selection), Clarion, 1983; *Mr. Top*, Morrow, 1983; *Amanda and the Mysterious Carpet*, Clarion, 1985.

Published by Delacorte: *Journeys of Sebastian*, 1968; *Hildegarde and Maximilian*, 1970; *How Santa Claus Had a Long and Difficult Journey Delivering His Presents*, 1971; *What Is a Man?*, 1972; *Sebastian and the Mushroom*, 1976.

Published by Dutton: *The Possible Worlds of Fernando Krahn* (collection of cartoons), 1965; *Gustavus and Stop*, 1968; *A Flying Saucer Full of Spaghetti*, 1970; *April Fools* (Junior Literary Guild selection), 1974; *Who's Seen the Scissors?* (Junior Literary Guild selection), 1975; *The Mystery of the Giant Footprints*, 1977; *Catch That Cat!* (Junior Literary Guild selection), 1978; *Robot-Bot-Bot* (Junior Literary Guild selection), 1979; *Arthur's Adventure in the Abandoned House*, 1981.

Illustrator and co-author: (With Carol Newman) *Strella's Children*, Atheneum, 1967; (with Alastair Reid) *Uncle Timothy's Traviata*, Delacorte, 1967; (with wife, María Luz Krahn) *The First Peko-Neko Bird*, Simon & Schuster, 1969; (with M. L. Krahn) *The Life of Numbers*, Simon & Schuster, 1970.

(From *Amanda and the Mysterious Carpet* by Fernando Krahn. Illustrated by the author.)

Other; all with wife, María de la Luz Uribe; all in Spanish: *Cuenta que te cuento*, Editorial Juventud (Barcelona, Spain), 1979; *Quien lo diría Carlota Maria*, Alfaguara (Madrid, Spain), 1981; *Doña Piñones*, Ekaré (Caracas, Venezuela), 1981; *El Cururia*, Ekaré, 1982; *La Señorita Amelia*, Destino (Barcelona), 1982; *El Vuelo de Inés*, Argos (Barcelona), 1984; *Pero Pero*, Argos, 1984.

Illustrator: Jan Wahl, *The Furious Flycycle*, Delacorte, 1968; Fred Gardner, *The Lioness Who Made Deals*, Norton, 1969; J. Wahl, *Abe Lincoln's Beard*, Delacorte, 1971; J. Wahl, *Lor-* *enzo Bear and Company*, Putnam, 1971; J. Wahl, *S.O.S. Bobomobile!; or, The Further Adventures of Melvin Spitznagle and Professor Mickimecki*, Delacorte, 1973; J. Wahl, *Mooga, Mega, Mekki*, J. Philip O'Hara, 1974; Miriam Chaikin, *Hardlucky*, Lippincott, 1975; Walt Whitman, *I Hear America Singing*, Delacorte, 1975; Yuri Suhl, *Simon Boom Gets a Letter*, Four Winds, 1976; John E. Brewton and Lorraine A. Blackburn, editors, *They've Discovered a Head in the Box for the Bread and Other Laughable Limericks*, Crowell, 1978; William Jay Smith, *Laughing Time: Nonsense Poems*, Delacorte, 1980; Jill Tomlinson, *Hilda, the Hen Who Wouldn't Give Up*,

Harcourt, 1980; Sonia Levitin, *Nobody Stole the Pie*, Harcourt, 1980.

Animated films: "The Perfect Crime," first produced in Barcelona, Spain, 1978.

Also author and illustrator of "Amanda's Fantasies" in *Cricket*, 1984—. Contributor to magazines and newspapers in the United States, France, Germany, and England, including *Esquire*, *Horizon*, *New Yorker*, *Reporter*, *Show*, *Evergreen*, *Atlantic*, *Gourmet*, *Sky*, *National Lampoon*, and *Playboy*.

ADAPTATIONS: "A Flying Saucer Full of Spaghetti" (filmstrip with teacher's guide), Weston Woods, 1977.

WORK IN PROGRESS: Animated films for television.

SIDELIGHTS: "As a little boy my 'children's books' were the last century's satirical books and news magazines that my father kept in his library.

"My father had a great talent for caricature and no doubt influenced me a lot in the comical expression of my drawings. Nevertheless, as a lawyer, he always considered drawing as a hobby. As a teenager I suggested I could pursue a career as a cartoonist, but his answer was very typical: only Picasso could earn his living just drawing.

"Maybe he was right. At that time in Chile no one lived from his drawings and I had to accept the decision to study law. But I didn't quit drawing. In my father's library I revised constantly the very old illustrated European books and magazines.

"Other things influenced me also. My father organized a circus each summer. He was a clown and each member of my family performed a number. We travelled and performed with the circus in many small towns of central Chile.

"When I was fourteen, while waiting in line to buy bread, a foreign sailor approached and offered me a second-hand book. It was *All in Lines* by Saul Steinberg. I didn't buy the bread but brought back a valuable book. It became clear to me that humour and art could be perfectly matched. It was possible, after all, to buy bread if I decided to become an artist.

"In 1962, I went to New York and started professionally as a cartoonist. It's a career I'm happy with and successful at, and I now live in Europe. Like other cartoonists I enjoy doing children's books very much.

"Since my childhood I had nurtured a special interest for cartoons and enjoyed expressing ideas graphically, avoiding the use of words."

Who's Seen the Scissors? was conceived when his daughter cut her finger using a pair of scissors. "It was a minor cut, but enough to make me feel responsible for not getting her the appropriate scissors. I left immediately with her and my two other children to buy a safer [pair].

"While we walked, I asked them to tell me what other things scissors can cut, besides paper and a finger. The list developed from the most obvious elements to the most bizarre. . . . The more absurd it was, the more they laughed. This is the way the book was born."

A wordless story *Catch That Cat!* developed from vague impressions from childhood as well as from the present. "Perhaps it was Sindicat, my children's cat that was the book's most direct motivation. Before the animal was a year old, his adventurous impulses around the neighborhood many times brought me and my family to absurd rescue missions, none in the sea, but enough to make me think that cats are a rich source of stories."

"My wife, also a Chilean, is a writer of children's books in Spain and I think it's great fun to work together."

Krahn's books for children have been translated into German, Norwegian, Swedish, Spanish, Japanese, and Danish, and are included in the Kerlan Collection at the University of Minnesota.

FOR MORE INFORMATION SEE: Martha E. Ward and Dorothy A. Marquardt, *Authors of Books for Young People*, 2nd edition, Scarecrow, 1971; *Children's Literature Review*, Volume III, Gale, 1978; Lee Kingman and others, *Illustrators of Children's Books: 1967-1976*, Horn Book, 1978; Doris de Montreville and Elizabeth D. Crawford, editors, *Fourth Book of Junior Authors and Illustrators*, H. W. Wilson, 1978; *Graphis 34*, 1978-79.

LAMBERT, David (Compton) 1932- (David Kent)

BRIEF ENTRY: Born December 27, 1932, in Southborough, Kent, England. Author of more than sixty educational books, mostly for children, Lambert graduated from the University of Cambridge in 1955 and worked for five years as an editor at Rathbone Books and, until 1967, as editorial director of textbooks at Educational Research Publications. It was at Rathbone, a now defunct British publisher of educational books for teenagers, that Lambert adopted a concise, nontechnical writing style and covered "an encyclopedic range of material," both of which led him to begin planning and writing his own texts for publishers and packagers. A full-time writer since 1967, Lambert's numerous books include *Seashore* (F. Watts, 1977), named an Outstanding Science Book for Children by the National Science Teachers Association in 1978, and *Dinosaurs* (Crown, 1978), which the *New York Times* described as "simple but literate and informed. It touches on many intriguing questions. . . ." Among his other works are *The Oceans* (Ward, Lock, 1979), *Planet Earth* (F. Watts, 1983), *The Seasons* (F. Watts, 1983), *Volcanoes* (F. Watts, 1985), and *Snakes* (F. Watts, 1986). Under the pseudonym David Kent, Lambert has written a series of children's books which explore the Bible from creation through the conversion of the Apostle Paul. All published by Warwick in 1982, the titles include *The Desert People*, *Escape from Egypt*, *Kings of Israel*, *The Last Journey*, *Miracles and Parables*, and *The Time of the Prophets*. Agent: Bruce Robertson, Diagram Visual Information Ltd., 195 Kentish Town Rd., London NW585, England.

LAMPERT, Emily 1951-

BRIEF ENTRY: Born April 26, 1951, in Boston, Mass. Co-owner of Wenham Cross Antiques in Boston, Lampert admits that she writes "nonsense and magic purely to create an escape or sometimes to exorcise a particular demon from my soul!" In her fantasy for primary-grade readers, *The Unusual Jam Adventure* (Atlantic Monthly, 1978), Pig eats breakfast jam from an unlabeled jar, sprouts wings and a horn, and, upon mailing a letter, floats through a slot marked "Unpredictable Journeys." As *Publishers Weekly* observed: "[Lampert] makes her hero's dream fantasy believable and . . . increases absurd effects with heady images and phrases." In *A Little Touch of Monster* (Atlantic Monthly, 1986), chubby, perfect Parker tires of being a "Little Angel" ignored by all and develops "a touch of monster," snarling at his family until they appease him with the attention he wants. According to *Booklist*, the story is "amusing and bound to appeal to youngsters' fantasies of always wanting to be the center of attention." *Home:* Meredith Farm, Topsfield, Mass. 01983.

LAUX, Dorothy 1920-

PERSONAL: Born August 25, 1920, in Waco, Tex.; daughter of Tommy G. and Jewel (Buice) McWilliams; married Edward E. Laux (a Baptist clergyman), May 23, 1943. *Education:* Baylor University, A.B., 1941. *Religion:* Baptist. *Home:* 6247 Annapolis, Dallas, Tex. 75214. *Agent:* c/o Broadman Press, 127 Ninth Ave. N., Nashville, Tenn. 37234.

CAREER: Writer, 1960—; Wilshire Baptist Church, Dallas, Tex., minister of childhood education, 1978-82.

WRITINGS: Did I Do That? (fiction), Broadman Press, 1970; *John, Beloved Apostle* (illustrated by William McPheeters), Broadman Press, 1977. Curriculum writer of church training material, 1960—, and of day camp materials, 1984, both for the Baptist Sunday School Board.

SIDELIGHTS: Laux and her husband, who enjoy traveling, serve as tour conductors for overseas trips. They have traveled in fifty-six countries and all fifty states. She also teaches an adult Bible study class at Wilshire Baptist Church.

DOROTHY LAUX

HOBBIES AND OTHER INTERESTS: Bird watching, china painting, ceramics, needlework, travel.

LAVIOLETTE, Emily A. 1923(?)-1975

BRIEF ENTRY: Born about 1923; died of cancer, August 31, 1975. Laviolette, who grew up in a storytelling family, made up many tales as a child to express her love for her native land, Prince Edward Island, Canada. Laviolette left school after the sixth grade, and it was not until 1974 that she wrote and illustrated the romantic tale, *A Little Island Princess* (Elaine Harrison and Associates, 1975). "The setting was pure Prince Edward Island of forty years ago, the dialogue was startlingly realistic, and the characters free of stereotype," according to Constance Mungall in *Globe and Mail*. Before she died, Laviolette wrote down the stories her grandmother had told her and more of her own, collectively published in *The Oyster and the Mermaid* (Elaine Harrison and Associates, 1975). "I think they're the best stories written," said poet and publisher Elaine Harrison. "She wrote this marvellous children's book in the last three months of her life, knowing she had only a short time to live after the doctor told her the operation was hopeless. She had hundreds of stories in her head but got only these down. Although she went only to grade six, I did not have to change a word—just punctuation a bit and paragraphing. A real storyteller unspoiled by the schools!"

It was Harrison, along with Eleanor Wheler, a retired public health nurse, who had first encouraged Laviolette to set down her stories. When faced with the author's imminent death, the pair also assumed the cost of immediate publication and distribution for both *A Little Island Princess* and *The Oyster and the Mermaid*. Letters from readers describe Laviolette's stories as charming and true-to-life. "The area is so familiar to me that I can almost see the little creatures flitting around the rocks and tidal pools of that cove," wrote one. From another, "In reading the stories I found myself enchanted and know that, for children, each of the stories is worth a night of fantastic and sweet dreams."

FOR MORE INFORMATION SEE: Constance Mungall, "Storyteller's Family Yarns Charm Island Children," *Globe and Mail*, November 12, 1975.

LE TORD, Bijou 1945-

PERSONAL: Born January 15, 1945, in St. Raphael, France; came to the United States in 1966; daughter of Jacques (an artist) and Paule (Pigoury) Le Tord. *Education:* Ecole des Beaux Arts, Lyon, France. *Politics:* Democrat. *Religion:* Protestant. *Address:* P.O. Box 2226, Sag Harbor, N.Y. 11963. *Agent:* Jane Feder, 305 East 24th St., New York, N.Y. 10010.

CAREER: Worked as a textile stylist in New York City; taught at Fashion Institute of Technology, New York City, for three years; author and illustrator of children's books, 1976—. *Member:* Society of Illustrators.

*WRITINGS—*All juvenile; all self-illustrated: *A Perfect Place to Be*, Parents Magazine Press, 1976; *The Generous Cow*, Parents Magazine Press, 1977; *Merry Xmas Hooper Dooper*, Random House, 1979; *Picking and Weaving*, Four Winds Press, 1980; *Nice and Cozy*, Four Winds Press, 1980; *An Alphabet of Sounds: Arf Boo Click*, Four Winds Press, 1981; *Rabbit Seeds*, Four Winds Press, 1984; *Good Wood Bear*, Bradbury Press, 1985; *Joseph and Nellie*, Bradbury Press, 1986.

WORK IN PROGRESS: My Grandma Leonie and *The Little Hills of Nazareth,* to be published by Bradbury.

SIDELIGHTS: ''By the time I was seven years old I had already written poems and stories for myself. I had also painted pictures to match the stories. I knew I wanted to be a writer even though I didn't quite understand what it meant to be one.

''I remember visiting Paris with my mother. I bought a supply of paper, pencils and an eraser and sat at the desk of our hotel room. I wanted to write like Colette the French writer who had lived five minutes away from where we stayed. Colette had lived at the Palais Royal and every day for a month I went to look at the windows of her apartment. I was fascinated when my mother said, 'This is where Colette used to live.' Imagine, a writer had lived there!

''I always liked words and their sounds. The way they sit on a page, their shapes delighted me. Actually, *Arf Boo Click* is an alphabet of sound words which I wrote when I began to understand the rhythm of the English language.

''When I was not writing or drawing, I would look at pictures and type in magazines and cut them out and stick them in an album. I was making my own picture books. I think this was my first awareness of what a page in a book looked like: the importance of the illustration and the perfect marriage between the picture and the type, and how sentences and phrases are perfectly linked with the illustration. I did that for a long time and for fun. I also used to draw cartoons of people and spent days drawing animals, plants, and nature. My fondness for the animal kingdom as well as my genuine interest in our planet Earth forced me to go out and look at everything around me.

''My mother was the direct influence of my appreciation of books. She made certain that I was at all times well supplied with art books, natural history books, and picture books. I still have them all. Most picture books I read and looked at were translated from American children's books. I guess when it came time for me to leave home I naturally chose to go to America.

''Poetry is really what I prefer to read. Perhaps because I find 'pictures' in a poem to look just like a painting. My father was an artist, a painter, and my early years were spent mostly in his studio watching him at work for hours. Sometimes I try to paint with words.

''I became an author and illustrator quite by chance. Although I knew that's what I wanted to be when I met M. B. Goffstein, a children's book writer, while walking my dog in Riverside Park in New York City. We became friends and she showed me her work and it made sense to me that now was the time for me to sit down and write a story. I did write a story, published it and I have never stopped since.

''Seasons like changes in the weather mean a lot to me. When fall comes around I find working a pleasure. I work many hours each day. Sometimes six days a week. Fall is the season that gets you ready for winter and what I call 'look inside' time. Winter lets you meet with yourself. I make use of these feelings and experiences, like when I see the color of leaves changing, the light in the trees, or the sky at sunset. I try to take it all in so that eventually it will come out in my books without me knowing it. In my books I try to show or explain it all in a simple way. Simplicity means honesty to me. And that is what I try to be at all times, honest. I hope that my books carry this message more than anything else. You could call me a champion of truth!

BIJOU LE TORD

''When I did books in black and white only, I carefully balanced the black line against the white paper. I made sure that both colors had enough space to move in, enough room, enough light.

''In my watercolors which so far is my favorite medium I also try to represent the light the way I sense it, and see it. Rather than saying to myself: the sky is blue, the sea is blue, therefore, I should paint it as such.

''I chose to paint *Joseph and Nellie,* the story of two fishermen at sea, mostly in blues because I felt it was the best way for me to catch the light the way I had seen it when I went out to sea. But if grey or green had been the colors I thought were right to translate what I saw, I would have painted grey or green. The color itself is not what matters to me. What is important is the mood of the book, what it implies. And if I have to change nature's colors to express it, to suit the book, I just do it. I let paint show me where the source of light is. And I go for it!

''Snow, sun, rain, wind are part of my life. What happens in the sky concerns me just as much as the world's news I hear on television or read in the newspapers. I think that's what being an artist means. To be able to take inside what happens outside. It is only part of it! Hard work is probably the most important ingredient in becoming an artist.

''I think a book should be like a relationship where you take in as much as you need at the time. Just like a friend with

"I will, I will,"said Martha...."And we will be nice and cozy." ■ (From *Nice and Cozy* by Bijou Le Tord. Illustrated by the author.)

whom you exchange ideas, feelings, experiences. I like to leave plenty of room in my books for a child to find himself or herself, get a sense of his or her own space. Room for him or her to grow in, express his or her taste. Not mine!

"I hope that my books are and have done just that."

HOBBIES AND OTHER INTERESTS: Poetry, fine arts, travel, music, people.

What we want is to see the child in pursuit of knowledge, and not knowledge in pursuit of the child.
—George Bernard Shaw

LEVINSON, Riki

BRIEF ENTRY: Born in Brooklyn, N.Y. Assistant publisher and art director at E. P. Dutton, Levinson writes children's books about family life because she finds the topic "a warm and personal experience to write about. It is reassuring, to me, that children don't change, no matter what period they live in." Her picture book *Watch the Stars Come Out* (Dutton, 1985) was named an American Library Association Notable Book and *Booklist* Children's Editor's Choice, among others. *Publishers Weekly* observed that in this tale of a young brother and sister's immigration to America and passage through Ellis Island during the late 1800s the "story and the authentic scenes on board the boat make the experience profoundly personal to the reader.'' ''Young readers can return to the book many times with satisfaction,'' added *School Library Journal*. ''There is a lot to see, to guess at and talk about.'' Also highly praised were the softly muted illustrations drawn by Diane Goode. *Horn Book* compared them to ''old photographs . . . images seen through a kind of veil, memories softened by time so the remembered joy transcends past sadness or difficulty. . . .'' Levinson's most recent book is entitled *I Go with My Family to Grandma's* (Dutton, 1986). Her upcoming works included *Touch! Touch!, DinnieAbbieSister-r-r!, Our Home Is the Sea,* and *Early in the Morning*. Included among her memberships are the Authors Guild and American Institute of Graphic Arts. *Office:* E. P. Dutton, 2 Park Ave., New York, N.Y. 10016.

LEVOY, Myron

PERSONAL: Born in New York, N.Y.; married wife, Beatrice (a junior high school teacher); children: Deborah, David. *Education:* City College of New York, B.S.; Purdue University, M.Sc. *Home:* N.J. *Agent:* Susan Cohen, Writers House, Inc., 21 West 26th St., New York, N.Y. 10010.

CAREER: Writer. Previously worked as chemical engineer. *Awards, honors: Book World*'s Children's Spring Book Festival honor book, and one of Child Study Association of America's Children's Books of the Year, both 1972, and a Children's Book Showcase selection, 1973, all for *The Witch of Fourth Street, and Other Stories;* New Jersey Institute of Technology Authors Award, 1973, for *Penny Tunes and Princesses; Boston Globe-Horn Book* Award honor book for fiction, American Book Award finalist, Woodward Park School

MYRON LEVOY

With bells like these, you will sing as you go. ■ (From *The Witch of Fourth Street and Other Stories* by Myron Levoy. Illustrated by Gabriel Lisowski.)

Annual Book Award, Jane Addams Children's Book Award honor book, and New Jersey Institute of Technology Authors Award, all 1978, Dutch Silver Pencil Award, and Austrian State Prize for Children's Literature, both 1981, and Buxtehuder Bulle Award, Buxtehuder, West Germany, and German State Prize for Children's Literature, both 1982, all for *Alan and Naomi; A Shadow Like a Leopard* was named one of American Library Association's Best Books for Young Adults, 1981, and received the Woodward Park School Annual Book Award, and was one of New York Public Library's Books for the Teen Age, both 1982.

WRITINGS—Juvenile: Penny Tunes and Princesses (illustrated by Ezra Jack Keats), Harper, 1972; *The Witch of Fourth Street, and Other Stories* (illustrated by Gabriel Lisowski), Harper, 1972; *Alan and Naomi* (*Horn Book* honor list), Harper, 1977; *A Shadow Like a Leopard,* Harper, 1981; *Three Friends,* Harper, 1984; *The Hanukkah of Great-Uncle Otto* (illustrated by Donna Ruff), Jewish Publication Society, 1984; *Pictures of Adam,* Harper, 1986.

Adult: *A Necktie in Greenwich Village* (novel), Vanguard, 1968.

Contributor of short stories and poems to periodicals, including *Antioch Review, Massachusetts Review,* and *New York Quarterly*.

ADAPTATIONS: "The Witch of Fourth Street and Other Stories," Listening Library.

WORK IN PROGRESS: A book for children, *The Magic Hat of Mortimer Wintergreen;* an adult novel.

SIDELIGHTS: "In my work for children and adults, my continuing concern has been for the 'outsider,' the loner. The Jewish boy facing anti-Semitism and the deeply troubled refugee girl he befriends (*Alan and Naomi*); the bisexual girl who believes she's losing her only friend and the sensitive chess prodigy who feels alone and strange (*Three Friends*); the ghetto boy, torn between two worlds, who carries a knife but writes poetry (*A Shadow Like a Leopard*)—all must come to terms with and face their own uniqueness. Their stories are open-ended; there are no pat solutions, but rather, growth and discovery, with more struggles ahead to be met, one hopes, with greater strength and insight."

HOBBIES AND OTHER INTERESTS: Reading, art, tennis, handball, cross-country skiing, and walking in Manhattan.

FOR MORE INFORMATION SEE: Washington Post Book World, May 7, 1972; *New York Times Book Review,* June 18, 1972; *Horn Book,* June, 1972, August, 1972, December, 1977, September/October, 1985; Martha E. Ward and Dorothy A. Marquardt, *Authors of Books for Young People,* supplement to the second edition, Scarecrow, 1979; *English Journal,* October, 1980; Sally Holmes Holtze, editor, *Fifth Book of Junior Authors and Illustrators,* H. W. Wilson, 1983; Alleen Pace Nilsen and Kenneth L. Donelson, *Literature for Today's Young Adults,* 2nd edition, Scott Foresman, 1985; Jim Trelease, *The Read-Aloud Handbook,* Penguin, 1985.

VARIAN MACE

MACE, Varian 1938-

PERSONAL: Born June 12, 1938, in American Falls, Idaho; daughter of Maurice Austin (a lumber worker) and Irene (a telephone operator; maiden name, White) Rickett; married William Phil Mace (an attorney), March, 1960; children: Douglas, Gregory, Richard. *Education:* University of California, Berkeley, B.A., 1960. *Politics:* Independent. *Home and studio:* 1342 Bennett Rd., Paradise, Calif. 95969.

CAREER: Commercial and fine artist; illustrator. Has designed fashion ads, magazine covers, posters, and greeting cards. Designed and painted, as a volunteer, two room murals for Ponderosa Elementary School, Paradise, Calif.

EXHIBITIONS—One-person shows: Home Sales Show and Reception, Paradise, Calif., 1983; Bank of Paradise, 1983; Paradise Frame Shop, 1983; Hospice House of Paradise, 1984; Feather River Hospital, Paradise, 1984; Art Works Gallery, Fair Oaks, Calif., 1984; Equinox Gallery, Grass Valley, Calif., 1984; Thistledown Gallery, Chico, Calif., 1984; Per Che' No!, Chico, 1985; Butte County Library, Paradise, 1985; Nut Tree Complex, Vacaville, Calif., 1986; Coffee Tree, Vacaville, Calif., 1986.

Group shows: Shibui Gallery, Paradise, Calif., 1977-79; Silver Dollar Fair, Chico, Calif., 1980; Fischer Gallery, Chico, 1981; Ruth Carlson Gallery, Mendocino, Calif., 1982—; Mendocino Art Center, Mendocino, 1982—; Winnie Porter Fine Art Show, Oroville, Calif., 1982, 1983; North Valley Plaza Fine Art Show, Chico, 1982, 1983; Delta Zi Art Show, Chico, 1983; Fine Arts Gallery, Marysville, Calif., 1983—; Art Works Gallery, Fair Oaks, Calif., 1983-85; Vagabond Rose Gallery, Gridley, Calif., 1983—; California Arts League, Sacramento, 1983; American Association of University Women Art Show, Chico, 1983; Omni Arts Show, Chico, 1983; Chico Professional Women in Art Show, 1078 Gallery, 1983; Art Etc. Art Show to Benefit the Special Olympics, Chico, 1983; Creative Art Center, Chico, 1984; American Association of University Women Night with Women in the Arts Show, Chico, 1984; "Summer Sensations," Mendon's Nursery, Paradise, 1984; Equinox Gallery, Grass Valley, Calif., 1984—; Ansel Ball Memorial Award Show, Paradise Art Center, 1984; Thistledown Gallery, Chico, 1984, 1985; Black Oak Gallery, Chico, 1985—; House of Color, Kachina Gallery, Paradise, 1985—; Frigulti-Black Gallery, Visalia, Calif., 1986; Bill Dodge Gallery, Carmel, Calif., 1986.

MEMBER: National League of American Pen Women, Professional Women Artists of Chico, Society of Children's Book Writers and Illustrators. *Awards, honors: Nature's Pets* was chosen one of Child Study Association of America's Children's Books of the Year, 1975; two first place awards from Silver Dollar Fair, Chico, Calif., 1980; honorable mention, 1982, and "Best of Show," 1983, from Winnie Porter Fine Art Show, Oroville, Calif.

ILLUSTRATOR: Beverly Frazier, *Small World Cook and Color Book,* Troubador, 1971; B. Frazier, *Nature Crafts and Projects,* Troubador, 1972; *Butte Remembers,* Butte County Branch, National League of American Pen Women, 1973; Malcolm Whyte, *The Meanings of Christmas,* Troubador, 1973; John Kipping, *Nature's Pets,* Troubador, 1975; Evelyn Feltman, *The Story of Santa Claus Land,* Paradise Pine, 1978; Ann Moen, *Fairy Tales Color and Story Album,* Troubador, 1979.

SIDELIGHTS: "I began my growing up in a very small Sierra Nevada community in California near Mt. Lassen, called Clear Creek. My father worked in a lumber mill near Westwood,

(From *Fairy Tales Color and Story Album* by Ann Moen. Illustrated by Varian Mace.)

where I rode the bus to school every day. Our home in Clear Creek was a little red log cabin and in the backyard ran the creek with the same name.

"As an only child, I spent many hours entertaining myself. There were not many children who lived close by, and we had no television until I was long gone to college.

"I remember during those long, snowy, winter days making many messes with various art projects. At a young age I began to experience a great delight in drawing pictures from piles of comic books that my uncles would bring as gifts when they came for visits.

"I actually began to teach myself to draw by this method. At one time I had my room 'papered' with my interpretations of Wonder Woman.

"My parents were wonderful in that they never seemed to mind all of my 'messes,' and I always had enough art supplies to 'play with.'

"In spring and summer time the 'clear creek' which flowed through our backyard was a constant source of delight for me, and I'm sure a source of concern to my parents. Icy-cold and sparkling clear, it was full of wonderful things: rocks, fish, plants, and bubbles. I spent many pleasant hours sitting on a little log bridge with cold toes dangling in the water.

"My love of drawing began in those early years and has never left me."

Mace attended the University of California at Berkeley, where she was selected a winner in the Mademoiselle College Board

Art Contest and was sent to New York City to work on a fashion magazine. "The experience was so totally different than anything I had ever done. It really introduced me to what commercial art was.

"If I ever thought I was painting just to sell, I would never paint again. There is a delicate balance between making money and being creative. I want to maintain my own standards yet still please other people." [*Butte County Arts Commission Newsletter,* December, 1983.]

Mace's goals are "to paint for the rest of my life and to continue to expand my work. I'd like to have a studio-gallery where the public could come and see my art. I want to continue to work in the fine art medium and still make someone happy by painting their favorite teddy."[1]

HOBBIES AND OTHER INTERESTS: Art and painting. "Collecting items to use in paintings seems to use up all of my time and interest."

FOR MORE INFORMATION SEE: Sacramento Bee, March 2, 1971; *Chico Enterprise-Record* (Calif.), October 5, 1973, October 22, 1973, November 9, 1986; *Paradise Post,* November 16, 1973, December 10, 1975; July 6, 1984, October 24, 1986; *Butte County Arts Commission Newsletter,* December, 1983; *Independent Messenger,* October 11, 1984.

MAYS, Lucinda L(a Bella)   1924-

PERSONAL: Born June 16, 1924, in Latrobe, Pa.; daughter of Nick (a carpenter) and Angela (Palese) La Bella; married William E. Mays (a sales manager), December 14, 1943; children: William M., Richard, Robin. *Education:* Washington University, St. Louis, Mo., B.A., 1962, M.A., 1968. *Politics:* Independent. *Religion:* Protestant. *Home and office:* 940 Beaver Lane, Glenview, Ill. 60025. *Agent:* Dorothy Markinko, McIntosh & Otis, Inc., 475 Fifth Ave., New York, N.Y. 10017.

CAREER: Parkway School District, Creve Coeur, Mo., fifth grade teacher, 1962-65; Normandy High School, Normandy, Mo., English teacher, 1965-69; Pleasant Ridge School, Glenview, Ill., sixth grade teacher, 1969-72; Providence Day School, Charlotte, N.C., head of social studies department, 1973-75; writer, 1975—. Teacher at Columbia College, Chicago, Ill., spring, 1980. Board member of National Endowment for the Humanities, Italian-American oral history project at University of Illinois at Chicago Circle. *Member:* Society of Midland Authors (treasurer, 1981-83; recording secretary and newsletter editor, 1983—), American-Italian Historical Society, League of Women Voters, Off-Campus Writers' Workshop. *Awards, honors:* Society of Midland Authors Award for best juvenile book, 1979, for *The Other Shore; The Other Shore* was selected as a Notable Book in Social Studies by *Social Education,* 1979, *The Candle and the Mirror,* 1982.

WRITINGS: The Other Shore (young adult), Atheneum, 1979; *The Candle and the Mirror* (Junior Literary Guild selection), Atheneum, 1982.

WORK IN PROGRESS: Alessandro, Son of ?, a story of a fifteen year old who discovers his father is a heretic; *Strawberries and Grizzly Bears,* the recreation of a seventeen-year-old loner who has tried to commit suicide; *Labefana and the Curse of the Three Wise Men,* an Epiphany tale for children; *When Mother Won't Answer My Questions,* for children; *Dis-*

LUCINDA L. MAYS

senters and Social Issues of the Twentieth Century; The Tenth Pain, an adult novel of the Lawrence, Massachusetts textile strike of 1912.

SIDELIGHTS: "My interest in the great migration of the turn of the century began with a research project in college. Since the Italian-Americans I knew as a child were not like those depicted on television or in films, I decided another version was in order. *The Other Shore* is neither a whitewash nor an indictment, as many books about this ethnic group have been, but an honest and sincere attempt to explain why Italians coming to this country at the turn of the century acted as they did and are what they are.

"In my book, Gabriella's father is like my own, who—though he immigrated to Pennsylvania along with my grandfather—encountered many of the hardships of Pietro DeLuca in the book. During the first part of this century, at least a dozen labor activists of Italian ancestry devoted their lives to improving the labor and living conditions among the ethnic groups. Today they are unknown to all except labor historians. Several characters in both my books were inspired by these men and their activities.

"I enjoy writing and teaching young adults because I know and understand them and enjoy their curiosity, enthusiasm, energy, and sense of justice. They are our hope for the future. However, if they cop out with drugs and/or alcohol, instead of using their pent-up indignation fighting abuses, we are all the losers (theme of *Strawberries and Grizzly Bears*).

"I am deeply concerned about the amount of the world's resources (human and natural) being utilized for war-related activities, the proliferation of toxic waste dumps, the increase in

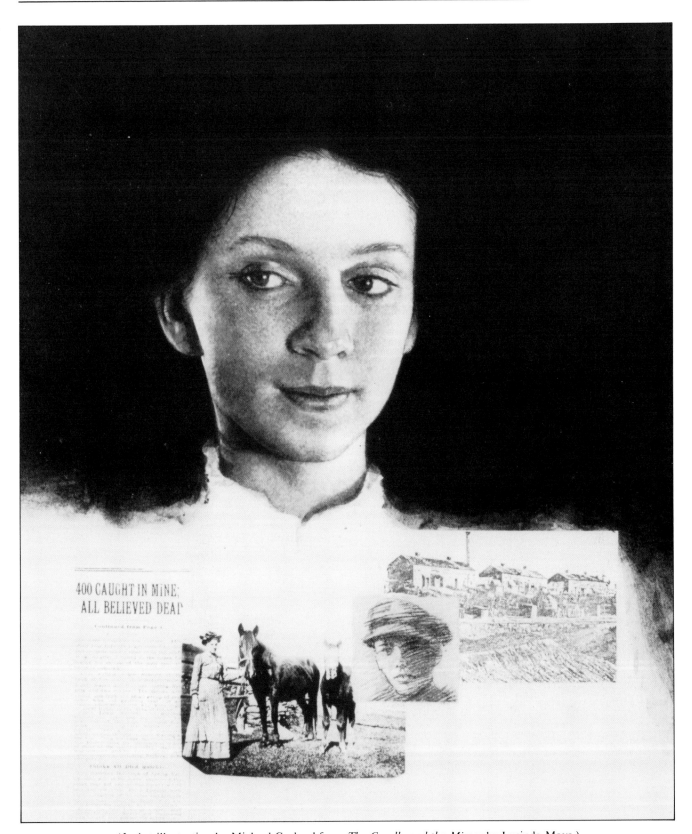

(Jacket illustration by Michael Garland from *The Candle and the Mirror* by Lucinda Mays.)

world population, the break-up of the family, commercial television's influence and the *APATHY* so prevalent today.

"The younger generation have the ability, optimism and energy to work for world betterment. It is our task to inspire and guide them in that direction."

HOBBIES AND OTHER INTERESTS: The environment, politics, nuclear freeze, conservation, population control, gardening, travel.

The Youth of a Nation are the trustees of Posterity.
—Benjamin Disraeli

JUDITH W. McINERNEY

McINERNEY, Judith W(hitelock)   1945-

PERSONAL: Surname pronounced "Mac 'n Ernie"; born June 1, 1945, in Chicago, Ill.; daughter of Leon Marshall (a pharmacist) and Mary Ann (McKenna) Whitelock; married Stephen Vincent McInerney (a businessman), June 10, 1967; children: Shamus Matthew, Kelly Elizabeth, Jennifer Kathleen, Megan Louise. *Education:* Marquette University, B.A., 1967. *Religion:* Roman Catholic. *Home:* 6019 Tonkowa Trail, Georgetown, Tex. 78628.

CAREER: Commercial Glazing Co., Inc., Nashville, Tenn., treasurer, 1970—; writer. *Member:* Decatur Arts Council, Children's Reading Roundtable. *Awards, honors:* Critic's Choice Award from the International Reading Association/Children's Book Council Joint Committee, 1984, and Young Hoosier Book Award from the Association of Indiana Media Educators, 1986, both for *Judge Benjamin: The Superdog Secret.*

WRITINGS—Juvenile; "Judge Benjamin" series; all illustrated by Leslie Morrill; all published by Holiday House: *Judge Benjamin: Superdog,* 1982; . . . *The Superdog Secret,* 1983; . . . *The Superdog Rescue,* 1984; . . . *The Superdog Surprise,* 1985; . . . *The Superdog Gift,* 1986.

Author of "Judy's Journal," a weekly column in *Metropolis News,* 1960-63. Editor of Centennial Edition of *Metropolis News,* 1966-67.

WORK IN PROGRESS: A comic mystery for another possible series.

SIDELIGHTS: "Life in a small town would be very dull without imagination. When I was just a toddler, we moved from Chicago to the southernmost tip of Illinois, a tiny town called Metropolis. I hardly knew then, but I certainly know now,

what a pump primer those early years were to my creative streak. It was a safe place, a quiet place, where I could take the long way home from school and find more flowers, pet more stray dogs, look for more lost pennies. I loved it.

"So many people who meet me and know I now have four children and through those children meet their friends, work with their teachers and librarians and learn about other children, assume that it is the love of these present day children that motivates me. But I think it goes back, rather, to the child in me, the one who wandered around that little town having a great time making up my own princes and dragons. Somehow, that child never really grew up and I think I'm all the luckier for it. Writing was one of those marvelous natural progressions and it seems almost fated that children's books should be my outlet.

"My first published work was at the wizened age of seven— a sympathetic weekly newspaper editor witnessed a determined Brownie troop scribe demanding to see her minutes in print. He succumbed. He printed them. And I floated for weeks buoyed by the idea that putting words on paper could create such euphoria. How much of my present determination I owe to that dear editor, Sam Smith of the *Metropolis News*! By the time I was a teenager, I was penning a 'Judy's Journal' column of teenage news and opinions and pestering Sam on a regular basis.

"I found my 'Prince Charming' during my Marquette years and four days after graduating from the college of journalism, we married and set on our search for the happily ever after. The years that followed came to include a son, three daughters,

Being an only dog was all I had ever known. ■ (From *Judge Benjamin: Superdog* by Judith Whitelock McInerney. Illustrated by Leslie Morrill.)

and a two hundred pound St. Bernard whose love and protection was considerably cheaper than a nanny. During those days the time and money juggle put my writing on hold, but eventually, as the kids gained independence and my husband no longer needed me as an active partner at his business, creativity fever took hold again. Judge Benjamin, our two hundred pound St. Bernard, became the focused narrator in a comedy adventure series that began with a little story and a lot of encouragement from Holiday House in New York.

"In 1980, Margery Cuyler picked my manuscript from a stack of unsoliciteds and offered me that first contract. The thrill of my first small-town by-line came back to me. Now I'm looking forward to a long and passionate affair with my typewriter. I can keep my small-town heart alive in the happy endings that children's stories allow.

"Now that I've rediscovered writing I may never stop. And now that college tuition for those four inspirations of mine looms closer and closer on the horizon, I probably *have* to keep at it!"

Judge Benjamin: Superdog has been published in France.

FOR MORE INFORMATION SEE: Russell Friedman, editor, *Holiday House: The First Fifty Years*, Holiday House, 1985.

He wears the rose
Of youth upon him.

—William Shakespeare

MEARIAN, Judy Frank   1936-

PERSONAL: Surname is pronounced *Mare*-i-an; born November 26, 1936, in Cincinnati, Ohio; daughter of Norris Clinton (an insurance adjuster) and Laura Jemima (a teacher; maiden name, Stowe) Frank; married Robert Mike Mearian (an actor), May 28, 1970. *Education:* Indiana University, A.B., 1958; Yale University, M.F.A., 1961. *Home:* 185 West End Ave., New York, N.Y. 10023. *Agent:* Connie Clausen Associates, 250 East 87th St., New York, N.Y. 10028.

CAREER: English teacher at high school in Long Island, N.Y., 1958-59; actress on stage, radio, and television in New York, N.Y., 1961-80; script writer for soap operas, 1980—. *Member:* American Federation of Television and Radio Artists (past member of national board), Actors' Fund of America, Actors Equity Association, Screen Actors Guild, Episcopal Actors' Guild.

WRITINGS: Two Ways about It (juvenile), Dial, 1979; *Someone Slightly Different* (juvenile), Dial, 1980.

SIDELIGHTS: "Although I look forward to writing for others someday, just now I'm enjoying writing for pre-teens and teens. That seems to be an age when people first become aware of serious adult problems without the advantage of knowing 'this too shall pass.' The letters from young readers have been worth any work involved.

Mom says Lou's home life is hard on her, and I guess it's true. Her parents are always yelling at each other. ■ (Jacket illustration by Diane De Groat from *Two Ways about It* by Judy Frank Mearian.)

JUDY FRANK MEARIAN

"I write on buses as I travel to and from auditions. My work as an actress has taken me to almost every state in the union, including Hawaii. The people I've met and the experiences I've had as a performer have been extremely helpful to me as a writer. I've played on Broadway, Off-Broadway, and Off-Off-Broadway, done television soap operas and commercials, radio, endless narrations and industrials, national companies, and bus and truck tours. I've sung in nightclubs and actually worked on a real, traveling showboat. I feel very fortunate to be part of the acting profession, but I also love to write. As an actress, the perfect role rarely comes along. As a writer, I can create any character I choose."

HOBBIES AND OTHER INTERESTS: Travel.

FOR MORE INFORMATION SEE: Theatre World, Volume XXII, 1965-66, Volume XXIV, 1967-68; *Washington Post,* February 10, 1980.

MELADY, John   1938-

BRIEF ENTRY: Surname is pronounced Muh-lay-dee; born September 12, 1938, in Seaforth, Ontario, Canada. A secondary school vice principal in Ontario since 1967, Melady previously taught in elementary and secondary schools. Besides writing, he travels extensively—including North and South America, Europe, and Asia—has done radio and television shows, lectures, and leads workshops in schools from the elementary to university level. Journalistic in style, two of his books deal with themes of war. *Escape from Canada! The Untold Story of German POWs in Canada, 1939-1945* (Macmillan of Canada, 1981) describes the Canadian internment camps and escape attempts of German servicemen imprisoned there during World War II, while *Korea: Canada's Forgotten War* (Macmillan of Canada, 1983) is filled with the personal recollections of Canadians who fought in that war. For young

readers, Melady has written *Cross of Valor* (Scholastic-Tab, 1985), a collection of stories about ordinary people who have performed heroic acts. "*Cross of Valor* is a thought-provoking read," according to Tim Wynne-Jones in *Globe and Mail,* "especially for the child who has unconsciously come to measure courage against the latest antics of Sylvester Stallone or a host of other comic-book he-men." A columnist for *Catholic Register* and a book reviewer for *Globe and Mail,* Melady is also the author of *Explosion* (Mika, 1980) and a contributor to *The Shaping of Ontario* (Mika, 1985). He is a member of the Ontario Secondary School Teacher's Federation, Writers' Union of Canada, and Royal Canadian Military Institute. *Home:* R.R. 3, Brighton, Ontario, Canada K0K 1H0.

MERTZ, Barbara (Gross)   1927-
(Barbara Michaels, Elizabeth Peters)

PERSONAL: Born September 29, 1927, in Canton, Ill.; daughter of Earl D. (a printer) and Grace (a teacher; maiden name, Tregellas) Gross; married Richard R. Mertz (a professor of history), June 18, 1950 (divorced, 1968); children: Elizabeth Ellen, Peter William. *Education:* University of Chicago, Ph.B., 1947, M.A., 1950, Ph.D., 1952. *Politics:* Liberal. *Agent:* Dominick Abel Literary Agency, 498 West End Ave., #12-C, New York, N.Y. 10024.

CAREER: Historian and writer. *Member:* Egypt Exploration Society, American Research Council in Egypt, Society for the Study of Egyptian Antiquities, American Association of University Women, Critics Circle, Authors Guild, Authors League of America, Mystery Writers of America, National Organization for Women. *Awards, honors: Be Buried in the Rain* was selected one of *School Library Journal*'s Best Books for Young Adults, 1985; First "Anthony" Grandmaster's Award, 1986.

WRITINGS—Published by Coward: *Temples, Tombs, and Hieroglyphs: The Story of Egyptology,* 1964; *Red Land, Black Land: The World of the Ancient Egyptians,* 1966; (with Richard R. Mertz) *Two Thousand Years in Rome,* 1968.

Under pseudonym Barbara Michaels; all novels; published by Dodd, except as indicated: *The Master of Blacktower,* Appleton, 1966; *Sons of the Wolf,* Meredith Press, 1967; *Ammie, Come Home,* Meredith Press, 1969; *Dark on the Other Side,* 1970, large print edition, G. K. Hall, 1983; *Crying Child,* 1971; *Greygallows,* 1972; *Witch,* 1973; *House of Many Shadows,* 1974; *The Sea King's Daughter,* 1975; *Patriot's Dream,* 1976; *Wings of the Falcon,* 1977, large print edition, G. K. Hall, 1982; *Wait for What Will Come,* 1978; *Walker in Shadows,* 1979; *The Wizard's Daughter,* 1980, large print edition, G. K. Hall, 1981; *Someone in the House,* 1981, large print edition, G. K. Hall, 1982; *Black Rainbow,* Congdon & Weed, 1982, large print edition, G. K. Hall, 1983; *Here I Stay,* Congdon & Weed, 1983, large print edition, G. K. Hall, 1984; (contributor) *Tales of the Uncanny: True Stories of the Unexplained,* Random, 1983; *The Grey Beginning,* Congdon & Weed, 1984, large print edition, G. K. Hall, 1985; *Be Buried in the Rain,* Atheneum, 1985; *Shattered Silk,* Atheneum, 1986.

Under pseudonym Elizabeth Peters; all novels; published by Dodd, except as indicated: *The Jackal's Head,* Meredith Press, 1968; *The Camelot Caper,* Meredith Press, 1969; *The Dead Sea Cipher,* 1970; *The Night of 400 Rabbits,* 1971; *The Seventh Sinner,* 1972; *Borrower of Night,* 1973; *The Murders of Richard III,* 1974; *Crocodile on the Sandbank,* 1975; *Legend in Green Velvet,* 1976; *Devil-May-Care,* 1977; *Street of the*

BARBARA MERTZ

Five Moons, 1978; *Summer of the Dragon*, 1979; *The Love Talker*, 1980, large print edition, G. K. Hall, 1980; *The Curse of the Pharaohs*, 1981; *The Copenhagen Connection*, Congdon & Lattes, 1982, large print edition, G. K. Hall, 1982; *Silhouette in Scarlet*, Congdon & Weed, 1983, large print edition, G. K. Hall, 1983; *Die for Love*, Congdon & Weed, 1984; *The Mummy Case*, Congdon & Weed, 1985, large print edition, G. K. Hall, 1985; *Lion in the Valley: An Amelia Peabody Mystery*, Atheneum, 1986; *Trojan Gold*, Atheneum, 1987.

ADAPTATIONS: "Ammie, Come Home" (television movie), ABC-TV, 1969.

WORK IN PROGRESS: Under pseudonym Barbara Michaels, *Sifted Shadows* (tentative title), to be published by Atheneum; another book under pseudonym Elizabeth Peters.

SIDELIGHTS: "I was born in a small town in central Illinois where I lived till I was eight. My grandmother lived on a farm nearby, and visits to her were thrilling—feeding the lambs, playing with the farm animals, berrying, and so on. When I was eight my parents moved to Oak Park, a suburb of Chicago. We lived there until I finished high school. Oak Park-River Forest High School was considered one of the best in the country and I was lucky to have superb teachers. I majored in history, but it was in a high school creative writing class that I first discovered that I loved to write. It was poetry then, of course—most adolescents write poetry, about love and spring and other original topics. I had my first writing thrill then, when my teacher called me out of a class (really a no-no in those stricter days) to ask me whether I had copied a sonnet I

had turned in for an assignment. It was called 'To a Book,' and I prefer not to remember anything else about it. I wasn't even insulted at being, however delicately, accused of plagiarism; I was so thrilled she thought it that good. She went on to explain she didn't think I had deliberately copied, but she suspected I might have been influenced unconsciously by something I had read. Not until she had sent it to *Saturday Review*, and found that none of the readers recognized it, did she really believe I had written it myself. I don't suppose any of my later triumphs ever surpassed that moment, because it was the first time anyone took my writing seriously.

"I did nothing with writing for years after that. In college I was supposed to major in education, since I come from a family of excellent teachers. But I found it very boring, and I had fallen in love with ancient Egypt—and by a strange coincidence there was the Oriental Institute right across campus. Before long I was majoring in Egyptology instead of education; I went straight through and got my Ph.D. I was unable to work in the field, however, because I had gotten married and my husband's occupation took us away from any area where I might have hoped to teach or excavate. Two children also kept me busy—but the main reason I didn't work

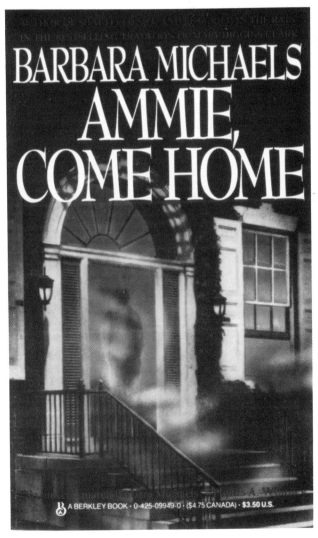

There was a sharp snap, and the door, caught by the wind, crashed back against the wall. ■ (Cover illustration from *Ammie, Come Home* by Barbara Michaels.)

was because I couldn't find employment in my specialized field.

"My husband's work took him abroad several times and I loved travelling. I have always been interested in history, the earlier the better, and in art and architecture, so Europe was a thrill from start to finish and I collected a lot of material that was later useful for backgrounds to my books. It was at this time that I started writing again. Once the children were in school I had a little time, and I needed to do something to stretch my mind. My first three books were popular nonfiction—two on ancient Egypt, one on Rome. Writing those books was a learning experience. I loved doing them, but they were a lot of work. I also loved reading romantic suspense, and at about that time the genre became more popular, so I decided to try my hand. *The Master of Blacktower* was the result—very derivative, but again very educational because I learned a lot about plotting and character development. I also learned that writing is hard work!

"My husband and I were divorced in 1968 and since then I have been writing two books a year and raising my children, plus a number of cats and two dogs—full time work, I assure you. Some years ago, when the children were grown, I decided it was time for me to indulge in the one thing I wanted and had not yet attained—that beautiful old house in the country which I had written about in so many of my ghostly stories. After looking at dozens of houses and exhausting two kindly realtors, I found my house. The oldest part of it is pre-1800; the main house was finished in 1820, by a man named John Jones (really) whose young wife Phoebe was buried in the backyard. Some of the neighbors say Phoebe haunts the house. Maybe she does. It is the friendliest, warmest house I have ever lived in, so if Phoebe is still here I guess she doesn't mind my being with her. I hope to stay here, with my animals and my plants and my fine neighbors until my arthritis gets so bad I can no longer climb my spiral staircase. In the meantime I have material for several more ghost stories. I don't believe in ghosts, but I love to read about them and write about them."

Some of Mertz's books have been recorded on cassette.

HOBBIES AND OTHER INTERESTS: Reading, needlework, cats, music, football.

FOR MORE INFORMATION SEE: Publishers Weekly, October 9, 1978; *Washington Post Book World,* January 6, 1980; *Times Literary Supplement,* July 10, 1981; Kathryn Falk, *Love's Leading Ladies,* Pinnacle Books, 1982; *Sun* (Baltimore, Md.), July 8, 1984; *School Library Journal,* October, 1986.

MICHEL, Anna 1943-

PERSONAL: Born December 12, 1943, in Mishawaka, Ind.; daughter of Raymond (a contractor) and Yolanda (a homemaker; maiden name, Ricci) Rossi; married Robert Michel (a data base analyst), August 4, 1973; children: Mia. *Education:* Indiana University, B.A., 1967; Bank Street College, M.S., 1975. *Home:* 40 Noe Place, Beacon Falls, Conn. 06403.

CAREER: Actress in summer stock and repertory and on tour, 1967-69; Commercial Analysts, New York, N.Y., marketing research interviewer, 1968-69; substitute teacher, 1970-72, remedial reading teacher, 1972-74, assistant teacher, 1974-75, all at schools in New York City; International Play Group, New York City, co-teacher, 1975-76; First Presbyterian Nursery School, New York City, head teacher, 1976-79; author,

1976—. Volunteer art teacher at a day care center, 1972; volunteer teacher of American sign language at Columbia University, 1975-77.

WRITINGS: Little Wild Chimpanzee (juvenile; illustrated by Peter Parnall and Virginia Parnall), Pantheon, 1978; *Little Wild Elephant* (juvenile; illustrated by P. Parnall and V. Parnall), Pantheon, 1979; *Little Wild Lion Cub* (juvenile; illustrated by Tony Chen), Pantheon, 1980; *The Story of Nim: The Chimp Who Learned Language* (juvenile; illustrated with photographs by Herbert S. Terrace and Susan Kuklin), Knopf, 1980.

ADAPTATIONS—Cassettes; produced by Random House: "Little Wild Chimpanzee"; "Little Wild Lion Cub"; "Little Wild Elephant."

WORK IN PROGRESS: A juvenile book on deafness.

SIDELIGHTS: "If there are books available on subjects that really interest children, teachers can stimulate reading. I have seen that most children are interested in animals, so animal life seemed like a good general area to write about. I want to present accurate and interesting information without diluting it in the fashion of some textbooks, so it was necessary for me to narrow down the subject as much as possible. I had read Jane Goodall's *In the Shadow of Man* and was fascinated by the behavior of the wild chimpanzees she had studied. I liked the idea of doing further research on chimpanzees and then sharing it.

"I believe it is important for children to realize that animals are not the property of human beings to be put at their service. If life on earth is to survive, children must grow into responsible adults who respect all life. I want to tell them that chimpanzees and other wild animals live more fulfilled and natural lives apart from humans. For this reason, I chose to write about wild chimpanzees, rather than captive ones, and to include no people in *Little Wild Chimpanzee.*

"Since the birth of my daughter five years ago, I have concentrated all my energy and time on her. Just recently I have begun to write again."

Little Wild Chimpanzee and *Little Wild Lion Cub* have been translated into Afrikaans, and *The Story of Nim* has been translated into French.

ANNA MICHEL

Though so much of Nim's behavior was childlike, he also behaved in ways that were pure chimpanzee. ■ (Photograph from *The Story of Nim: The Chimp Who Learned Language* by Anna Michel.)

HOBBIES AND OTHER INTERESTS: Skating, bicycling and reading.

MOLDON, Peter L(eonard)   1937-

PERSONAL: Born March 31, 1937, in London, England; son of Leonard George Newton and Elsie Irene (Howe) Moldon. *Education:* Attended Regent Polytechnic, 1958-59. *Politics:* Socialist. *Religion:* "Agnostic." *Home:* 11 Oxlip Rd., Witham, Essex CM8 2XY, England.

CAREER: Glaxo, Greenford, Middlesex, England, laboratory technician in anaerobic vaccine department, 1957-58; SCM Press, London, England, production assistant and book designer, 1965; Faber and Faber Ltd., London, production assistant and book designer, 1965-83; free-lance writer and de-

signer, 1983—. *Military service:* Royal Air Force, 1955-57, senior aircraftsman. *Awards, honors: Your Book of Ballet* was selected as one of the Children's Books of the Year, 1974, by the National Book League, and shown at the 1974 Frankfurt Book Fair.

WRITINGS: Your Book of Ballet (juvenile; self-illustrated), Faber, 1974, revised edition, 1980; *Nureyev* (adult), Dance Books Ltd., 1976; (contributor) *The Joy of Knowledge Encyclopaedia,* Mitchell Beazley, 1976. Contributor to *Dancing Times.*

WORK IN PROGRESS: "My magnum opus!," a stage biography of Dame Margot Fonteyn, covering the years 1958 to 1986.

SIDELIGHTS: "For as far back as I can recall I have drawn and painted. My early schooling occurred during the war and, because of frequent air-raids, I was able to spend less time on the three Rs and more on art. In one of the junior classes we had to keep a diary in an exercise book, and my short paragraph in longhand each day was really an excuse for some elaborate drawing that took up most of the page. My diary so impressed the teacher that all the other teachers got to know about it and asked to see it. So, in a way, that could be seen as my first illustrated book!

"My love of books also began then. The few books I was given as presents were read time and time again. I always remember the thrill of buying my first book—*Lone Pine Five* by Malcolm Saville—from the recently opened bookshop in the town. I still have it in its frayed dustwrapper along with thousands of other volumes, both new and secondhand. And, of course, we had a local library. After I had read just about every book in the children's section, I borrowed books from the adult's library using my parents' tickets. In addition to reading most of the works on the fiction shelves—with a predeliction for the whodunnits of Carter Dickson/John Dickson Carr—I read books on art and even made a careful study of lettering and perspective, which might have been considered boring subjects for an eleven-year-old. As it turned out, the lettering would prove its worth when I eventually became a typographer.

"In such a dull Middlesex town as Feltham there was little in the way of entertainment apart from the local 'flea pit,' The Playhouse. With my father away in the Royal Air Force, my mother took me to see every sort of film; and with two programmes a week and a different movie on Sunday, that was a lot of films. Even when I see those films of the 1940s on television, I'm convinced that they are better made and more enjoyable than nearly all those made today. And perhaps those black and white movies were a subconscious influence when I came to prefer drawing in pen or pencil to painting in colour.

"From my father I inherited not only my talent for drawing but also my love of music. He could play the violin and piano, and I can still vividly recall him playing on the upright organ in our tiny lounge while I sang in a passable treble. The classical 78s we had were played until they were almost worn out

by the old wind-up gramophone with its needles that needed changing after every record. I got to know the classical repertory through hearing the Proms on headphones as I lay in bed on summer evenings. Eventually I went to the Albert Hall myself, and bought an electric player and my first LPs (then a novelty).

"As a child I was taken to pantomimes at Richmond Theatre (Surrey) and also caught the death throes of the Music Hall at both Kingston and Chiswick Empire. When I was old enough to go up to London by myself, I went to the commercial theatre and saw all the great actors, including Gielgud, Olivier, Richardson, and Edith Evans. At the Old Vic, where I saw my first professional Shakespearean play, I was fortunate to see Richard Burton's Hamlet, Henry V, Othello, Iago, and Coriolanus, and the memory of those performances is still more vivid to me than performances seen in recent years.

"It was inevitable that my passion for all the arts would make it essential for me to go to the ballet. On one fateful night in the summer of 1955 I sat at last in the old gallery at Covent Garden to see Fonteyn and Somes in *Swan Lake*. That evening began my life-long addiction to the ballet and admiration for Dame Margot Fonteyn.

"At school I was mistakenly placed in the science stream, but after a year in a laboratory I gave up science for good. However, while working at Glaxo I studied drawing and theatre design at evening classes. Unfortunately there are only a small number of stage designers employed in Britain, and I realised that I was not really good enough to join their illustrious ranks.

"After a series of routine office jobs, my love of books eventually led me to become a book designer. While I was at Fabers, the children's editor asked me one day whom I'd recommend to write a book on ballet for the 'Your Book' series; half-jokingly I replied, 'How about me?' After the editorial board had read an article I had written for the *Dancing Times* on Nijinsky's ballet *L'Après-midi d'un faune* they gave me the go-ahead, and the book was published in 1974. As well as writing and designing the book, I also drew the illustrations, which had to be in black and white. They were done in brush and Indian ink (I've always preferred the flowing line of a brush to the scratchy line from a pen). What was left out was as important as what I put in. Reluctantly I avoided solid blacks as they might not have printed satisfactorily in letterpress. I think the resultant drawings avoided the cuteness which besets so many of the drawings for books on the ballet.

"The book was well received, and when a new edition was prepared I rewrote much of the text and was able to juggle the pages to include an extra chapter without increasing the extent. I drew three more illustrations and chose many new photographs for the plates, increasing the number in the process from twelve to sixteen pages. Of course it was impossible to put in everything I would like to have said in a mere eighty pages of text, but I consider the book a useful beginner's guide to the ballet—whether child or adult—written from the viewpoint of a non-dancer."

(From *Your Book of Ballet* by Peter L. Moldon. Illustrated by the author.)

MOORE, Patrick (Alfred) 1923-

PERSONAL: Born March 4, 1923, in Pinner, Middlesex, England; son of Charles (an army officer) and Gertrude (White) Moore. *Education:* Educated at private schools in England. *Politics:* Conservative. *Home and office:* Farthings, 39 West St., Selsey, Sussex, England. *Agent:* Hilary Rubinstein, A. P.

Watt Ltd., 26-28 Bedford Row, London WC1R 4HL, England.

CAREER: Free-lance writer, 1952—. Lecturer in Europe and United States on astronomy topics. Regular broadcaster on British Broadcasting Corporation television program, "The Sky at Night," 1957—; Armagh Planetarium, Armagh, Northern Ireland, director, 1965-68. *Military service:* Royal Air Force, Bomber Command, 1940-45; became Flight Lieutenant.

MEMBER: International Astronomical Union, Royal Astronomical Society (fellow), British Astronomical Association (director of Mercury and Venus section, 1954-63; director of lunar section, 1965—; president, 1982-84), Royal Society of Arts (fellow), Children's Writers Group of London (chairman, 1964-65). *Awards, honors:* Honorary member of the Astronomical Society of USSR, 1960; Lorimer Gold Medal, 1962, Goodacre Gold Medal, 1965, Guido Horn d'Arturo Medal, 1969, and Amateur Astronomers' Medal, New York City, 1970, all for services to astronomy; Officer Order of the British Empire, 1968; D.Sc., University of Lancaster, 1974; Jackson Gold Medal, 1979, for work on mapping the moon; Dorothea Klumpko-Roberts Medal from the Astronomical Society of the

Pacific, 1980, for literary services to astronomy; honorary fellow of the Royal Astronomical Society of New Zealand, 1984.

WRITINGS—Juvenile: *The Master of the Moon* (science fiction), Museum Press, 1952; *Planet of Fear*, Museum Press, 1953; (with A. L. Helm) *Out into Space*, Museum Press, 1954; *Island of Fear*, Museum Press, 1954; *Frozen Planet*, Museum Press, 1954; *The True Book about Worlds around Us*, Miller, 1954, published as *The Worlds around Us*, Abelard, 1956; *Destination Luna: The Thrilling Story of a Boy's Adventurous Trip to the Moon* (science fiction), Lutterworth, 1955; *Quest of the Spaceways*, Muller, 1955; *Mission to Mars*, Burke, 1955, revised edition, 1974.

World of Mists, Muller, 1956; *Domes of Mars*, Burke, 1956, revised edition, 1974; *The Boys' Book of Space*, Roy, 1956, 6th edition, Burke, 1963; *Wheel in Space*, Lutterworth, 1956; *The True Book about the Earth*, Muller, 1956; *Voices of Mars*, Burke, 1957, revised edition, 1974; *The True Book about Earthquakes and Volcanoes*, Muller, 1957; *Isaac Newton*, A. & C. Black, 1957, Putnam, 1958; *The Earth, Our Home*, Abelard, 1957, new edition, Transworld, 1977; *Peril on Mars* (science fiction), Burke, 1958, Putnam, 1965; *Your Book of*

PATRICK MOORE

Astronomy, Faber, 1958, 4th edition, 1979; *The Boys' Book of Astronomy*, Roy, 1958; *The True Book about Man*, Sportshelf, 1958; *Rockets and Earth Satellites*, Muller, 1959, 2nd edition, 1960; *Raiders of Mars*, Burke, 1959, revised edition, 1974.

Astronautics, Methuen, 1960; *Captives of the Moon*, Burke, 1960; *Stars and Space*, A. & C. Black, 1960, 4th revised edition, 1972; *Wanderer in Space* (science fiction), Burke, 1961; (with Henry Brinton) *Exploring Maps*, Odhams, 1962, (illustrated by Cyril Deakins) Hawthorn, 1967; (with Paul Murdin) *The Astronomer's Telescope*, Brockhampton, 1962; *Crater of Fear*, Harvey, 1962; *Invader from Space*, Burke, 1963; *The True Book about Roman Britain*, Muller, 1964; (with H. Brinton) *Exploring the Weather*, Odhams, 1964, published in America (illustrated by C. Deakins), Transatlantic, 1969.

Exploring the World, Oxford University Press, 1966, F. Watts, 1968; *Exploring the Planetarium*, Odhams, 1966; *Legends of the Stars*, Odhams, 1966, 2nd revised edition, Hamlyn, 1973; (with H. Brinton) *Exploring Other Planets* (illustrated by C. Deakins), Hawthorn, 1967; (with H. Brinton) *Exploring Earth History*, Odhams, 1967; *Exploring the Galaxies*, Odhams, 1968; *Exploring the Stars*, Odhams, 1968; *Planet of Fire* (science fiction), World's Work, 1969.

Seeing Stars, B.B.C., 1970, Rand McNally, 1971; (with Charles A. Cross) *Mars: The Red World*, World's Work, 1971, Crown, 1973; *Young Astronomer and His Telescope*, Lutterworth, 1976; *The Moon Raiders*, Collins, 1978; *Killer Comet*, Collins, 1978; *Fun to Know about the Mysteries of Space*, Armada Books, 1979.

The Secret of the Black Hole, Collins, 1980; *The Space Shuttle Action Book* (illustrated by Tom Stimpson), Random House, 1983; (with Heather Couper) *Halley's Comet Pop-Up Book*, Dean, 1985; *Astronomy for the Under-Tens*, George Philip, 1987. Also author of *Conquest of Air: Wright Brothers*, Lutterworth.

Other: (Translator from the French) Gerard de Vaucouleurs, *Planet Mars*, Macmillan, 1950; *A Guide to the Moon*, Norton, 1953, revised edition published as *New Guide to the Moon*, Norton, 1977; *Suns, Myths, and Men*, Muller, 1954, published as *The Story of Man and the Stars*, Norton, 1955, revised edition, 1969; *A Guide to the Planets*, Norton, 1954, revised edition, 1960, published as *The New Guide to the Planets*, 1972.

(With Hugh Percival Wilkins) *The Moon*, Macmillan, 1955, new edition, Mitchell Beazley, 1981; (with Irving Geis) *Earth Satellite: The New Satellite Projects Explained*, Eyre & Spottiswoode, 1955, published as *Earth Satellites*, Norton, 1956, revised edition, 1958; *The Planet Venus*, Faber, 1956, Macmillan, 1957, new edition (with Garry Hunt), 1983; (with H. P. Wilkins) *How to Make and Use a Telescope*, Norton, 1956 (published in England as *Making and Using a Telescope*, Eyre & Spottiswoode, 1956); *Guide to Mars*, Muller, 1956, Norton, 1978; *Science and Fiction*, Harrap, 1957, Norwood, 1980; *The Amateur Astronomer*, Norton, 1957, published as *Amateur Astronomy*, 1968, 7th revised edition, Lutterworth, 1974; *The Solar System*, Methuen, 1958, Criterion, 1961; (editor with David R. Bates) *Space Research and Exploration*, Sloane, 1958; *Space Exploration*, Cambridge University Press, 1958.

Guide to the Stars, Norton, 1960; (with H. Brinton) *Navigation*, Methuen, 1961; *Astronomy*, Oldbourne, 1961, 4th revised edition published as *The Story of Astronomy*, Macdonald

& Co., 1972, published as *The Picture History of Astronomy*, Grosset, 1961, 3rd edition, 1967; *The Stars*, Weidenfeld & Nicholson, 1962; (with Francis L. Jackson) *Life in the Universe*, Norton, 1962; *The Planets*, Norton, 1962; *The Observer's Book of Astronomy*, Warne, 1962, 6th revised edition, 1978; *Telescopes and Observatories*, John Day, 1962; (editor) H. Brinton, *Spain* (illustrated by Vernon Berry), Dufour, 1962; (editor) E. H. Jolley, *Telecommunications* (illustrated by K. M. Sibley), Dufour, 1963; *Survey of the Moon*, Norton, 1963; *Space in the Sixties*, Penguin, 1963; (editor) *Practical Amateur Astronomy*, Lutterworth, 1963, published as *A Handbook of Practical Amateur Astronomy*, Norton, 1964; *Exploring the Moon*, Odhams, 1964; *Caverns of the Moon*, Burke, 1964, large print edition, Ulverscroft, 1965, new edition, Burke, 1975; *The Sky at Night*, Volume I, Eyre & Spottiswoode, 1964, Norton, 1965, Volume II, Eyre & Spottiswoode, 1968, Volume III, B.B.C., 1970, Volume IV, B.B.C., 1972, Volume V, B.B.C., 1976, Volume VI, B.B.C., 1979, Volume VII, B.B.C., 1980; (with F. L. Jackson) *Life on Mars*, Routledge & Kegan Paul, 1965, Norton, 1966; (with A. MacVicar) *Space Adventure*, Burke, 1965.

(With Hilary Rubinstein) *The New Look of the Universe*, Norton, 1966; *Stars in Space*, Dufour, 1966; *Naked-Eye Astronomy*, Norton, 1966; *Basic Astronomy*, Oliver & Boyd, 1967; (with Peter J. Cattermole) *The Craters of the Moon*, Norton, 1967; (editor) *The Amateur Astronomer's Glossary*, Norton, 1967, revised edition, *A to Z of Astronomy*, Fontana, 1976; *Armagh Observatory: A History, 1790-1967*, Armagh Observatory, 1967; (editor) W. D. Ewart, *Building a Ship*, Dufour, 1968; *Space: The Story of Man's Greatest Feat of Exploration*, Lutterworth, 1968, Natural History Press, 1969, 3rd edition, Lutterworth, 1970; (author of revision) Mervyn A. Ellison, *The Sun and Its Influence*, 3rd edition (Moore was not associated with earlier editions), American Elsevier, 1968; *The Sun*, Norton, 1968; *Moon Flight Atlas*, Rand McNally, 1969, revised edition, Philip & Son, 1970; *Astronomy and Space Research*, National Book League (London), 1969; *The Development of Astronomical Thought*, Oliver & Boyd, 1969, State Mutual Bank, 1985.

The Atlas of the Universe, Rand McNally, 1970, new edition published as *The Rand McNally New Concise Atlas of the Universe*, 1978, 2nd revised edition published as *The New Atlas of the Universe*, Crown, 1984; *Astronomy for Ordinary Level*, Duckworth, 1970, 2nd revised edition, 1973; (author of introduction) Arthur C. Clarke, *Islands in the Sky*, Sidgwick & Jackson, 1971; *The Astronomers of Birr Castle*, Mitchell Beazley, 1971; *Stories of Science and Invention*, Oxford University Press, 1972; *Can You Speak Venusian?*, David & Charles, 1972, Norton, 1973, 2nd revised edition published as *Can You Speak Venusian? A Guide to Independent Thinkers*, I. Henry, 1977; (with David A. Hardy) *Challenge of the Stars*, Mitchell Beazley, 1972, 2nd revised edition published as *The New Challenge of the Stars* (illustrated by David Hardy), Rand McNally, 1978; (with Desmond Leslie) *How Britain Won the Space Race*, Mitchell Beazley, 1972; (with Lawrence R. Clarke) *How to Recognize the Stars*, Corgi Books, 1972; *The Southern Stars*, Rigby, 1973; *Colour Star Atlas*, Lutterworth, 1973, published in America as *Color Star Atlas*, Crown, 1973; *The Starlit Sky*, South African Broadcasting Co., 1973; *Man the Astronomer*, Priory, 1973; (editor and contributor) *Astronomical Telescopes and Observatories for Amateurs*, David & Charles, 1973; (author of revision) James S. Pickering, *1001 Questions Answered about Astronomy*, Dodd, 1973; (translator from the French) E. M. Antoniadi, *The Planet Mercury*, Keith Reid, 1974; (with Iain Nicolson) *Black Holes in Space*, Orbach & Chambers, 1974, Norton, 1976; *The Comets*, Keith Reid, 1974; *Watchers of the Stars*, Putnam, 1974.

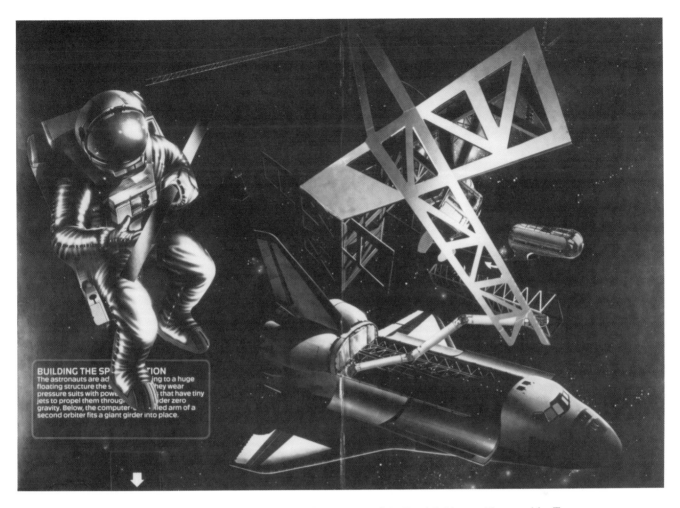

(From *The Space Shuttle Action Book* [pop-up book] by Patrick Moore. Illustrated by Tom Stimpson.)

(With Charles Cross) *Atlas of Mercury*, Mitchell Beazley, 1977; *The Stars Above*, Jarrold, 1977; *Spy in Space*, Armada, 1977; (editor) *Modern Astronomy*, Norton, 1977; *Guide to Comets*, Lutterworth, 1977; *Let's Look at the Sky: The Planets* (illustrated by L. Clarke and J. Knox), Severn House, 1978; *Let's Look at the Sky: The Stars* (illustrated by L. Clarke and J. Knox), Severn House, 1978; *The Next Fifty Years in Space*, Taplinger, 1978; (with P. Collins) *The Astronomy of Southern Africa*, Hale, 1977, Howard Timmins, 1979; *Astronomy Quiz Book*, Carousel Books, 1978; *Man's Future in Space*, Wayland, 1979; *The Terror Star*, Armada Books, 1979.

The Guinness Book of Astronomy Facts and Feats, Guinness Superlatives, 1980, 3rd edition, 1984; *Pocket Guide to Astronomy*, Simon & Schuster, 1980; (with Clyde Tomebaugh) *Out of the Darkness: The Planet Pluto*, Lutterworth, 1980, Stackpole, 1981; (with G. Hunt) *Jupiter*, Rand McNally, 1981; (editor) Bertrand M. Peek, *The Planet Jupiter: The Observer's Handbook*, Faber, 1981; *Pocket Guide to the Stars and Planets*, Mitchell Beazley, 1981; *The Unfolding Universe*, Crown, 1982; (with G. Hunt) *Saturn*, Rand McNally, 1982; (with G. Hunt) *Rand McNally Atlas of the Solar System*, Rand McNally, 1983; *Travellers in Space and Time*, Doubleday, 1983; (with John Mason) *Halley's Comet*, Patrick Stephens, 1984, published in America as *The Return of Halley's Comet*, Norton, 1984; *Patrick Moore's History of Astronomy*, revised edition, Merrimack, 1984; (with P. Cattermole) *The Story of the Earth*, Cambridge University Press, 1985; *Armchair Astronomy*, Patrick Stephens, 1985, published as *Patrick Moore's Armchair Astronomy*, Norton, 1986; *Stargazing: Astronomy without a Telescope*, Barron, 1985; (editor with I. Nicolson) *The Universe*, Macmillan, 1985; *Sky at Night 8*, Patrick Stephens, 1985; *Man and the Stars*, Mitchell Beazley, 1986; *Exploring the Night Sky with Binoculars*, Cambridge University Press, 1986.

Also author of *Man* published by Muller. Editor with Laura E. Salt of Oxford Children's Reference Library, Volumes 1-20, Oxford University Press, 1966-1973. Editor, *Yearbook of Astronomy*, Norton, 1962—.

SIDELIGHTS: ''During my boyhood I had a great deal of illness and could play no games, which is probably why, at the age of 63, I am still a regular cricketer and tennis player! My interest in astronomy began at the age of six, when I read a book about it. I joined the British Astronomical Association at the age of eleven in 1934 (the youngest-ever member), and published my first paper about the moon's surface in 1936. From 1982-84 I served as the president of the Association.

''I missed attending the University because the war broke out in 1939, and I 'manoeuvred' my age and the medical exam, becoming a flyer with the Royal Air Force Bomber Command. Subsequently, after being somewhat knocked around I was demobilized one day after the end of the war, and I intended to go to Cambridge, but wrote a book—*Guide to the Moon*—which 'caught on' and never had time to do it.

"The University of Lancaster has awarded me an honorary doctorate of science for my work in mapping the moon, in which I was heavily involved in the pre-Apollo period (I spent some time working at observatories in the United States). I feel today that my real role is in encouraging others, and I think it is fair to say that many astronomers both amateur and professional have begun their careers because of my books and broadcasts.

"The thirtieth anniversary of the British Broadcasting Corporation's program 'The Sky at Night' is in April, 1987. I have been broadcasting for this program since April, 1957 and have not missed a month since. This is now the longest running television programme in the world, excluding such things as the news.

"I speak French as well as the average schoolboy, but otherwise I believe in speaking English! I particularly like Scandinavia, notably Iceland, which I know well.

"I am a xylophone player and played in the Royal Command Performance in 1982. I have composed Viennese waltzes, some of which are regularly broadcast. A record of my music was recently produced. I have also written two comic operas, 'Theseus'' and 'Perseus.'

"Minor Planet No. 2602 has been named 'Moore' after me. It was discovered by Dr. E. Bowell of the Lowell Observatory in 1984.''

HOBBIES AND OTHER INTERESTS: Cricket, tennis, chess, music.

FOR MORE INFORMATION SEE: Martha E. Ward and Dorothy A. Marquardt, *Authors of Book for Young People,* 2nd edition, Scarecrow, 1971; Doris de Montreville and Elizabeth D. Crawford, *Fourth Book of Junior Authors and Illustrators,* H. W. Wilson, 1978.

NERLOVE, Miriam 1959-

BRIEF ENTRY: Born July 24, 1959, in Minneapolis, Minn. Although Nerlove began her career primarily as an illustrator of children's books, she later found additional and challenging awards in creating her own text. A free-lance illustrator for magazines, newspapers, and books, Nerlove illustrated Marilyn Singer's *Lizzie Silver of Sherwood Forest* (Harper, 1980) and Marya Dantzer-Rosenthal's *Some Things Are Different, Some Things Are the Same* (Albert Whitman, 1986). Her self-illustrated book for preschoolers, *I Made a Mistake* (Atheneum, 1985), is based on a jump rope rhyme. Speaking in nonsense verses, a young girl confesses her mistakes: "I went to the bathroom to brush my hair, / I made a mistake . . . and brushed a bear," and "I went to the kitchen to bake a pie, / I made a mistake . . . and baked a fly." According to *School Library Journal,* "These downright ridiculous verses provide just the type of humor that preschoolers enjoy." In addition to catchy verse, *Booklist* noted that "witty pen lines and subdued washes bring everything to life in a fresh, open way." Forthcoming books by the author-illustrator include *I Meant to Clean My Room Today* and *Zigzag People,* based on an anonymous poem. Nerlove has worked as a photo library assistant and is a member of the Children's Reading Round Table. *Residence:* Evanston, Ill.

Sunlight runs a race with rain,
All the world grows young again.

—Mathilde Blind

NESS, Evaline (Michelow) 1911-1986

OBITUARY NOTICE—See sketch in *SATA* Volume 26: Married name Evaline Bayard; born April 24, 1911, in Union City, Ohio; died of a heart attack, August 12, 1986, in Kingston, N.Y. Artist and author. Early in her career Ness worked as an artist's model and fashion illustrator, but she was best known as an award-winning author and illustrator of children's books. Among her self-illustrated works are *Josefina February, A Gift for Sula Sula,* and *Sam, Bangs, and Moonshine,* which earned her the Caldecott Medal in 1967. Ness also illustrated other writers' works, including Sorche Nic Leodhas's *All in the Morning Early* and Rebecca Caudill's *A Pocketful of Cricket,* both runners-up for the Caldecott Medal.

FOR MORE INFORMATION SEE: Books Are by People, Citation Press, 1969; *Third Book of Junior Authors,* H. W. Wilson, 1972; *Contemporary Authors, New Revision Series,* Volume 5, Gale, 1982; *Who's Who in American Art,* 16th edition, Bowker, 1984; *Something About the Author Autobiography Series,* Volume 1, Gale, 1986. Obituaries: *New York Times,* August 14, 1986; *Publishers Weekly,* August 29, 1986; *AB Bookman's Weekly,* September 8, 1986.

NESTOR, William P(rodromos) 1947-

PERSONAL: Born July 29, 1947, in Atlantic City, N.J.; son of George Peter (in federal aviation research) and Sophie (a communications specialist; maiden name, Prodromos) Nestor; married Florence Karis (a teacher), November 1, 1970; children: W. Ryan. *Education:* Glassboro State College, B.A., 1970; Antioch Graduate School (Keene, N.H.), M.S., 1975. *Religion:* Greek Orthodox. *Home:* 14 Greenleaf St., Brattleboro, Vt. 05301. *Office:* Solar Vision, Inc., Peterborough, N.H. 03458.

CAREER: Attleboro Public Schools, elementary teacher, Attleboro, Mass., 1970-72; Millburn Public Schools, Millburn, N.J., elementary teacher, 1972-74; New Hampshire Environmental Education Center, Hillsboro, director, 1974-75; New England College, Henniker, N.H., assistant professor of environmental studies, natural history, and education, 1975-80; Hitchcock Center for the Environment, Amherst, Mass., executive director, 1980-82; New England Solar Energy Association, Brattleboro, Vt., editor of *Northeast Sun,* 1982-84; Solar Vision, Inc. (publishers), Peterborough, N.H., 1984—. Consultant on education and environmental studies. *Member:* National Science Teachers Association. *Awards, honors: Into Winter: Discovering A Season* was named an outstanding science book for children by the Children's Book Council and the National Science Teachers Association Joint Committee, 1982.

WRITINGS: Into Winter: Discovering a Season (juvenile; illustrated by Susan Banta), Houghton, 1982. Contributor to newsletters.

WORK IN PROGRESS: View from Wantastiquet, about human and natural history of the three corners in New England.

SIDELIGHTS: "Growing up in an outdoors-focused family environment awakened in me a respect and love for the natural world. The nurturing of instincts, understandings, and sensory awareness was keenly developed through the hunting, fishing and other outdoor family activities which occupied an essential part and much time in my young life. Because of the orientation of my youth, [my] quest [for discoveries] now includes

WILLIAM P. NESTOR

my son, Ryan, my wife, Flo, and countless students. My travel and teaching adventures focus on investigations of cultures and natural systems. My life, as all life, is imbedded in its roots, an inextricably interwoven web of natural and human ecosystems.

"My experience with elementary-age students emphasized the wealth of opportunity for enhancing education through the natural curiosity inherent in human interaction with the natural environment. _Into Winter_ provides natural history information about the winter season while fostering exploration and discovery through a variety of activities for experiencing the natural world in winter."

HOBBIES AND OTHER INTERESTS: Bicycling, canoeing, snow-shoeing, cross-country skiing, racquetball, wilderness travel.

NOBLE, Iris   1922-1986

OBITUARY NOTICE—See sketch in _SATA_ Volume 5: Born February 22, 1922, in Calgary, Alberta, Canada; died June 30, 1986, in Patzcuaro, Mexico. Author. Noble, an American citizen born abroad, is best remembered for her young adult biographies. Among these are _Nellie Bly: First Woman Reporter, Leonardo da Vinci: The Universal Genius, Emmeline and Her Daughters: The Pankhurst Suffragettes,_ and _Nazi Hunter: Simon Wiesenthal._ Noble won a silver medal from the Commonwealth Club of California in 1962 for _First Woman Ambulance Surgeon: Emily Barringer._ She also wrote several novels, including _One Golden Summer_ and _Megan._

FOR MORE INFORMATION SEE: Contemporary Authors, New Revision Series, Volume 2, Gale, 1981. Obituaries: _New York People's Daily World,_ August 9, 1986.

O'CONNELL, Margaret F(orster)   1935-1977

PERSONAL: Born January 7, 1935, in Wilmington, Del.; died November 6, 1977, in Freeport, Bahamas; daughter of Albert E. (an executive) and Margaret (Moir) Forster; divorced. _Education:_ Pennsylvania State University, B.S., 1957; Harvard University, certificate in business administration, 1958; graduate study at New York University, 1959. _Home:_ New York, N.Y.

CAREER: Abraham & Straus (department store), in book department, 1958-59; Thomas Y. Crowell Co., New York, N.Y., assistant manager of trade, publicity, and advertising, 1959-61; Random House, Inc., New York City, director of library promotion, 1961-63; _New York Times Book Review,_ New York City, associate children's editor, 1963-74, editor, 1974-77. _Member:_ National Society of Literature and the Arts, National Book Critics Circle, Overseas Press Club, New York Historical Society, Friends of International Board on Books for Young People.

WRITINGS: The Magic Cauldron: Witchcraft for Good and Evil (juvenile), S. G. Phillips, 1975. Author of column "PTA Books for Children," 1972-74. Contributor to _Crowell-Collier Yearbook._ Contributor to magazines for adults and children, including _ETC: Journal of General Semantics._ Member of advisory board of _Brain/Mind/Bulletin._

SIDELIGHTS: "In writing _The Magic Cauldron,_ at first what I found about witches was 'bad.' My newspaperwoman's instinct told me that if something is all bad, or all good—look further. You will find shades of gray. So I did. And I was amply rewarded because a new world opened up with my research. As a matter of fact, if I had looked no further than the subject I researched, it would have been a loss—at least I feel so. Fortunately I was able to extrapolate what I found about witchcraft and myths into other areas of human en-

MARGARET F. O'CONNELL

deavor. One of them is political philosophy, another is the sociological picture, and more particularly, I have gained a perspective in the human condition, which to me is perhaps the most important gain I made.''

FOR MORE INFORMATION SEE: Mary Sam Ward, editor, *Delaware Women Remembered,* Modern Press, 1977. Obituaries: *New York Times,* November 9, 1977.

PANOWSKI, Eileen Thompson 1920-
(Eileen Thompson)

PERSONAL: Born March 17, 1920, in Lincoln, Neb.; daughter of Hugh (in the heating business) and Nelle (a housewife; maiden name, Masters) Thompson; married John B. Panowski (a chemist), September 5, 1942; children: Thomas Michael, Bruce Philip, Daryl Anne and Lynn Eileen (twins). *Education:* Miami University, Oxford, Ohio, B.A., 1941; Famous Writers School, 1953; University of New Mexico, M.A., 1971, Ph.D., 1985. *Politics:* Independent. *Religion:* Methodist. *Home and office:* 722 Solar Rd. N.W., Albuquerque, N.M. 87107. *Agent:* Ann Elmo Agency, 60 East 42nd St., New York, N.Y. 10165.

CAREER: Los Alamos Scientific Laboratory, Los Alamos, N.M., radiochemistry technician, 1956-64; writer, 1960—; Bradbury Science Hall, Los Alamos, N.M., museum guide, 1968-77. *Member:* American Association of University Women, Authors Guild, Phi Beta Kappa. *Awards, honors:* First prize, American Association of University Women Writer's Project for short stories, 1962, for ''The Kestrel''; runner-up, Edgar Allan Poe Award from the Mystery Writers of America, 1966, for *The Apache Gold Mystery.*

EILEEN THOMPSON PANOWSKI

WRITINGS—All under name Eileen Thompson: *The Blue-Stone Mystery,* Abelard, 1963; *The Spanish Deed Mystery* (illustrated by James Russell), Abelard, 1964; *The Apache Gold Mystery* (illustrated by J. Russell), Abelard, 1965; *The Dog Show Mystery* (illustrated by J. Russell), Abelard, 1966; *The Golden Coyote* (Junior Literary Guild selection; illustrated by Richard Cuffari), Simon & Schuster, 1971; *White Falcon: An Indian Boy in Early America* (illustrated by Leonard Everett Fisher), Doubleday, 1977.

SIDELIGHTS: ''I can't remember a time when I didn't write, but always poems, not stories. It was only when I was grown, and only after I discovered I'd never be a very good poet, that I realized I could turn to fiction.''

Panowski, who lives in the Southwest, is interested in history and archaeology. ''*The Golden Coyote* has been a natural outgrowth of interest and locale. More than that, though, it has been a special book for me. When I began writing it, every small bit of information, every turn of plot seemed to come to hand when needed, to slip together like pieces of a puzzle. It was an odd and exhilarating feeling. The main story line and the characters were with me from beginning to end, seeming to gain depth and rightness as I proceeded. So my feeling for the book became very deep and very personal. I have tried to make it as authentic as I could, but I was even more concerned with saying something that would have as much relevance today as it would have had 500 years ago. I don't think people have basically changed that much. I hope I have also managed to interest and amuse the reader. If so, what more could an author ask?''

Panowski received her masters and doctorate degrees in anthropology. ''For years I have enjoyed tramping around and exploring ruins of prehistoric settlements in northern New Mexico. My decision to get advanced degrees in anthropology is a result of that.''

HOBBIES AND OTHER INTERESTS: Camping, fishing.

FOR MORE INFORMATION SEE: Martha E. Ward and Dorothy A. Marquardt, *Authors of Books for Young People,* 2nd edition, Scarecrow, 1971.

PIERCE, Tamora 1954-

BRIEF ENTRY: Born December 13, 1954, in Connellsville, Pa. A writer of fantasy novels for young adults, Pierce is continually in the process of researching a wide variety of interests, such as the occult, Japanese history, martial arts, radio history and production, specific periods of European history, social work, adolescent psychology, and music. She has worked as a social worker, assistant to literary agents, and, since 1982, as creative director of ZPPR Productions Inc. in New York City. ''I grew up poor and am constantly striving to improve my economic lot,'' said Pierce. ''I enjoy writing for teenagers, because I feel—due to my own experience— that books can mean more to teenagers. Sometimes they serve as the only indication you aren't alone out there.''

Four fantasy novels, all published by Atheneum, comprise Pierce's tetralogy ''The Song of the Lioness.'' *Voice of Youth Advocates (VOYA)* described the series as a combination of ''medieval history, science fiction and sorcery.'' The titles are *Alanna: The First Adventure* (1983), for which Pierce received the New Jersey Authors Award, *In the Hand of the Goddess* (1984), *The Woman Who Rides Like a Man* (1986), and *Li-*

oness Rampant (in press). Each novel centers around the adventures of Alanna, who surreptitiously becomes a page at court and later a knight errant in her own right. "Alanna is a charming heroine who has her difficulties, but she wins out because she perseveres," observed *School Library Journal.* "This series is sprightly, filled with adventure and marvelously satsifying." Pierce's anticipated works include two more young adult novels, a historical/occult novel for adults, a stage play, and four radio plays involving the modern-day adventures of Vlad Drakul—Count Dracula. *Home and office:* c/o Kelley, 527 Fowler Ave., Pelham Manor, N.Y. 10803.

FOR MORE INFORMATION SEE: Contemporary Authors, Volume 118, Gale, 1986.

PIOWATY, Kim Kennelly 1957-

PERSONAL: Born September 7, 1957, in Spokane, Wash.; daughter of Thomas A. Kennelly (a teacher) and Mikell (a leasing agent; maiden name, O'Neil) Williams; married Timothy W. Piowaty (an insurance agent), September 6, 1975; children: Tara Marie, Katherine Deirdre. *Education:* University of Florida, B.A., 1977; also attended University of North Florida, 1977-78. *Politics:* "Moderate." *Religion:* Episcopalian. *Home:* 703 Milan Court, Altamonte Springs, Fla. 32714.

CAREER: Writer, 1976—; W. C. Cherry Elementary School, Clay County, Fla., reading specialist, 1979-80.

WRITINGS: Don't Look in Her Eyes (juvenile novel), Atheneum, 1983. Contributor to local newspapers.

SIDELIGHTS: "I began my novel as a short story in a creative writing class at the University of Florida when I was nineteen. The teacher encouraged me to try expanding it to novel form and over the next four years I worked on it whenever I had a spare moment. Finally, I sent it unsolicited to Atheneum. They sent it back, but with a very nice typed letter saying they liked the first five chapters and if I would rewrite the other sixteen chapters they might be interested in seeing it again. At that time my daughter, Tara, was ten months old and I began taking her to a babysitter three mornings a week and completely rewrote those chapters in three months. This time Atheneum accepted my novel for publication. This shows that editors do read unsolicited manuscripts and, although difficult, it is possible to sell that first time manuscript without an agent.

Kim Kennelly Piowaty with her family.

"At the time I began my novel, my younger brother and sister and I were attempting to help our father, who had had a complete psychotic breakdown. I am the oldest of five children, and all of us had lived with only my father since I was fourteen. I think my drive to see my short story through to completion as a novel was in part due to my own need to understand and deal with my father's mental illness.

"I have been very busy the last few years raising two beautiful little girls. I plan to resume my writing career soon."

QUIGG, Jane (Hulda) (?)-1986

OBITUARY NOTICE: Born in Marlborough, Conn.; died following a long illness, April 9, 1986, in Connecticut; buried in Marlborough Cemetery, Marlborough, Connecticut. Educator and author of children's books. A schoolteacher for thirty-two years, Quigg was recognized for her teaching and writing with an award from the West Hartford Connecticut Education Association in 1961. She contributed stories and articles to magazines and wrote several books for children, including *Looking for Lucky, Jenny Jones and Skid, Fun for Freddy, Jiggy Likes Nantucket, Miss Brimble's Happy Birthday,* and *Ted and Bobby Look for Something Special.*

FOR MORE INFORMATION SEE—Obituaries: *Hartford Courant,* April 11, 1986.

RANSOM, Candice F. 1952-

BRIEF ENTRY: Born July 10, 1952, in Washington, D.C. Author of books for young adults. Ransom, who has written since she was seven, relates: "The books I wrote in elementary school were feeble imitations of Nancy Drew or *Lassie Come Home,* in which I was always the main character. As a lonely child growing up in rural Fairfax County, I wrote to while away long evenings, and who else would I rather have read about having wonderful adventures than myself?" After high school, Ransom worked as a secretary for various computer and data base companies but never lost her desire to become a writer. Her first young adult novel, a mystery titled *The Silvery Past* (Scholastic) was published in 1982. She has since written numerous others, as well as contributed articles and short stories to periodicals such as *Seventeen, Jack and Jill, Country Living, Rural Living,* and *Writer's Digest.* A love for history led her to write historical romance novels, including *Amanda* (1984), *Susannah* (1984), *Kathleen* (1985), *Emily* (1985), *Nicole* (1986), and *Sabrina* (1986), all part of Scholastic's "Sunfire" series. *Emily* was a finalist for the 1985 Romance Writers of America Golden Medallion Award. Ransom is currently working on a four-book series for preteens, based on her own preteen years. "Much of my material comes from within, drawn from my own past, which I remember vividly," she said, "and a lot of my childhood interests have carried over into my profession." Ransom is a member of the Society of Children's Book Writers and Children's Book Guild of Washington, D.C. *Home:* 14400 Awbrey Patent Dr., Centreville, Va. 22020.

Our days, our deeds, all we achieve or are,
Lay folded in our infancy; the things
Of good or ill we choose while yet unborn.
—John Townsend Trowbridge

ROOP, Constance Betzer 1951-

BRIEF ENTRY: Born June 18, 1951, in Elkhorn, Wis. A science educator in Wisconsin schools, Roop and her husband Peter have collaborated on a series of joke books for children and are now completing several science books. "Peter and I are committed to children," said Roop. "I am hopeful that through our books we can help young people to discover the joy of learning." According to Roop, two of the science book topics are incorporated into her earth science curriculum. The husband-and-wife team have also collaborated on two historical fiction books, including *Keep the Lights Burning, Abbie* (Carolrhoda, 1985), based on a true incident in which a light-keeper's daughter must keep the lights burning by herself when a storm delays her father's return. "The Roops have kept all the inherent excitement in the story, though their sentences are short and their phrasing brief and to the point," observed *Booklist.* "All in all," added *School Library Journal,* "one of the best historical beginning-to-reads—a refreshing cold blast of salty real life." Roop has contributed articles to *Learning Magazine* and *Curriculum Review,* and science book reviews to *Appraisal.* An avid reader, she developed an interest in children's books while pursuing a master's degree in science education, which she received from Boston College in 1980. Besides teaching and writing, Roop is a consultant for D.C. Heath Co. and a workshop coordinator for Duquesne University. *Home and office:* 1904 North Superior St., Appleton, Wis. 54911.

ROOP, Peter 1951-

BRIEF ENTRY: Born March 8, 1951, in Winchester, Mass. An educator in Wisconsin schools and universities, Roop was named Reading Teacher of the Year in 1983 by the Mideast Wisconsin Reading Council and, in 1986, Outstanding Elementary Educator in Appleton by the Mielke Foundation, Outstanding Elementary Educator for Wisconsin and Wisconsin Teacher of the Year by the Wisconsin Department of Public Instruction. With his wife, Constance Betzer, Roop is co-author of a series of joke books and two historical fiction books for children. His solo efforts include *Little Blaze and Buffalo Jump, Siskimi, Natosi* (all Montana Council for Education, 1984), and *The Cry of the Conch* (Press Pacifica, 1984). In addition, he has contributed numerous articles and book reviews to periodicals such as *Cricket, Cobblestone, Jack and Jill,* and *School Library Journal.* Roop has served as president of the Wisconsin Regional Writers Association for several years and, among other activities, is a member of the Children's Literature Association and National Council of Teachers of English. Along with his wife, he is also a consultant for D.C. Heath Co. and a workshop coordinator for Duquesne University. *Home and office:* 1904 North Superior St., Appleton, Wis. 54911.

ROSS, David 1896-1975

PERSONAL: Born July 7, 1896, in New York, N.Y.; died November 12, 1975, in New York, N.Y.; son of Samuel and Fanny (Schmuller) Ross; married second wife, Beatrice Pons, October 14, 1937; children: (first marriage) David Andrews, Jr., Helen (Mrs. Banice Webber); (second marriage) Jonathan. *Education:* Attended Rutgers College (now University) and New York University. *Residence:* New York, N.Y.

CAREER: Radio announcer and commentator, 1926-58 (reader of poetry on "Poet's Gold," Columbia Broadcasting System-

Radio, 1934-42, "Words in the Night," National Broadcasting Co. Radio, 1953-58, and "A Rendezvous with David Ross"); writer and poet, 1958-75. Had worked as vaudeville actor, superintendent of an orphan asylum, and journalist; had appeared on television, narrated films, and made sound recordings; gave readings of his works at Library of Congress and at universities. *Member:* Poetry Society of America (past vice-president; member of board of directors, 1966-75), Academy of American Poets, Players Club. *Awards, honors:* Gold medal from American Academy of Arts and Letters, 1933; lyric poem award from Poetry Society of America, 1967; Christopher Morley Prize for light verse from Poetry Society of America, 1969, for "Elegy for an Overworked Undertaker."

WRITINGS: (Editor) *Poet's Gold: An Anthology of Poems to Be Read Aloud,* Macauley Co., 1933, 3rd edition, Devin-Adair, 1956; (editor) *The Illustrated Treasury of Poetry for Children* (illustrated by Burmah Burris and others), Grosset, 1970. Also author of a book of poems, *Wintry Errand,* as yet unpublished. Contributor of poems to literary magazines.

OBITUARIES: New York Times, November 14, 1975; *AB Bookman's Weekly,* December 8, 1975.

ROTH, Harold

BRIEF ENTRY: Born in Austria. A photographer whose photos have appeared in books, calendars, and magazines internationally, Roth creates photo essay books for middle-graders. In *First Class! The Postal System in Action* (Pantheon, 1983), Roth uses a concise text and black-and-white photographs to illustrate the workings of the United States Postal Service, including pick-up, sorting, stamping, packing, and delivering of mail. With a similar format, *A Day at the Races* (Pantheon, 1983) gives a behind-the-scenes look at a racetrack, showing trainers, exercise riders, veterinarians, and jockeys doing their jobs. *Bike Factory* (Pantheon, 1985) depicts the production line from beginning of assembly to finished bike at the Massachusetts Columbia Manufacturing Company. "A simple, satisfactory introduction where such a book is needed," observed *Booklist.* Roth has also produced a "Babies Love . . ." series of photo board books published by Putnam including, among others, *Babies Love a Goodnight Hug, Babies Love Nursery School, Babies Love Spring Days,* and *Babies Love the Playground. Residence:* New York.

ROBERT E. RUBINSTEIN

(From the movie "Who Wants to Be a Hero!" Released by Learning Corporation of America, 1981.)

RUBINSTEIN, Robert E(dward)   1943-

PERSONAL: Born November 12, 1943, in Boston, Mass.; son of Jack S. (a broker) and Augusta F. (a teacher; maiden name, Borenstein) Rubinstein; married Pearl Elizabeth Geschmay (a teacher of violin), April 30, 1972; children: Joshua, Seth, Shoshanna. *Education:* Queens College of the City University of New York, B.A., 1965; Northeastern University, M.A., 1967; University of Oregon, M.S., 1979. *Politics:* Democrat. *Religion:* Jewish. *Home:* 90 East 49th Ave., Eugene, Ore. 97405.

CAREER: Boston Public Library, Boston, Mass., children's librarian, 1965-66; professional storyteller, 1965—; Volunteers in Service to America (VISTA), Washington, D.C., volunteer worker in Eugene, Ore., 1968-69; Roosevelt Junior High School, Eugene, teacher of language arts, 1969—; writer, 1973—. Guest lecturer and performer at Cabrillo College and conventions; coordinator of community activities for the Eugene Education Association. *Member:* American Storytelling Resource Center, National Association for the Preservation and Perpetuation of Storytelling, Northwest Storytellers, National Story League, National Education Association, Authors Guild, Society of Children's Book Writers (Northwest regional advisor, 1982-86), Kappa Tau Alpha. *Awards, honors: When Sirens Scream* was chosen one of American Library Association's Notable Young Adult Novels, 1983; finalist, American Library Association and General Mills West Coast Storytelling Competition, 1985; Noel Connall Instructional and Professional Development Award from Oregon Education Association, 1986, for teaching.

WRITINGS—Young adult novels: *Who Wants to Be a Hero!*, Dodd, 1979; *When Sirens Scream*, Dodd, 1981.

Cassettes—all self-produced: "The Day the Rabbi Stopped the Sun and Other Jewish Tales," 1983; "Tales of Mystery/Tales of Terror," 1984; "Tale-Telling Techniques" (videocassette), 1985.

Contributor of more than one-hundred articles to education journals and popular magazines, including *Northwest, World Over, The Writer, Writing!, Child Life, Phi Delta Kappan, Teacher, Instructor, Oregonian, Learning,* and *California Today.*

ADAPTATIONS: "Who Wants to Be a Hero!" (film; produced for the cable television program "Showtime"), Learning Corp. of America, 1981.

WORK IN PROGRESS: Odin's Day of Doom and *The Start of Something Deadly,* both young adult novels; *Find the Missing Pieces,* poetic images of a child experiencing divorce.

SIDELIGHTS: "After serving as a VISTA volunteer in Eugene, Oregon, I began teaching and helped to develop the unique, totally elective program at Roosevelt Junior High School. During my years there, I have created and taught a wide variety of language arts and social studies classes, including storytelling, monsters, short story writing, Jewish culture, Arthur and Merlyn, sports history, playwriting, medieval history, personal communications, children's literature, and mystery stories.

"Since 1965 I have performed professionally as a storyteller, having learned the art as a children's librarian for the Boston Public Library. I have performed and given workshops for various organizations in Oregon and other states. For the past seventeen years I have directed the Roosevelt Troupe of Tellers, performing troups of seventh, eighth, and ninth-grade students who travel statewide. These troupes, which I originated, entertain elementary school students in their classrooms. They have appeared on state and local television, and were featured in three national magazine articles. According to the National Storytelling Resource Center in Tennessee, this is the only troupe of its kind in the nation. In 1983 the Troupe of Tellers was given one of the state of Oregon's 'Great Kids' public service awards.

"Each of my novels focuses on contemporary themes. *Who Wants to Be a Hero!*, which has been translated into Danish, deals with the responsibilities of being a hero. *When Sirens Scream*, also translated into Danish, concerns the benefits and questions involved with nuclear power plants.

"Stories reach the hearts and the minds of people, especially children, much faster than any other form of teaching and learning. From stories, people learn by example, and the insights endure. Storytelling is one of, if not the most, effective teaching method—and the oldest. Hopefully, more will discover the power of the tale."

Rubinstein has performed nationally in Georgia, New York, Florida, California, Tennessee, Oklahoma, Washington, Indiana, and as an invited guest presenter and performer at the Bay Arts Storytelling Festival in Berkeley, Calif., and at the Oregon Pavilion at Expo '86.

HOBBIES AND OTHER INTERESTS: Singing, bowling, softball, tennis, odd facts, people-watching.

RUSHMORE, Robert (William)   1926-1986

OBITUARY NOTICE—See sketch in *SATA* Volume 8: Born July 7 (one source says July 12), 1926, in Tuxedo Park, N.Y.; died after a long illness, September 20, 1986, in Poughkeepsie, N.Y.; cremated; ashes interred at St. Mary's Cemetery, Tuxedo Park, N.Y. Singer, journalist, and author. Trained as a baritone, Rushmore performed in Europe, but he was best known for his comprehensive history of vocal music, *The Singing Voice*. During the 1950's he worked for the U.S. Department of Information, writing for the Russian-language magazine *Amerika*. Rushmore subsequently focused his attention on writing books, including short story collections, novels, and two biographies for young adults. Among these were *The Life of George Gershwin, Who'll Burn the House Down?, The Unsubstantial Castle, A Life in the Closet*, and *If My Love Leaves Me*. A longtime trustee of Poets and Writers, Incorporated, Rushmore contributed articles and stories to such periodicals as *Mademoiselle, Opera News, Collier's*, and *Saturday Review*. He was working on a history of black opera singers at the time of his death.

FOR MORE INFORMATION SEE—Obituaries: *New York Times*, September 24, 1986; *Times Herald-Record* (Middletown, N.Y.), September 24, 1986.

Soap and education are not as sudden as a massacre, but they are more deadly in the long run.
—Mark Twain
(pseudonym of Samuel Langhorne Clemens)

SATCHWELL, John

BRIEF ENTRY: Author of informational books for children, Satchwell has taught engineering in London. His series of books about early math concepts features a friendly, green monster who introduces opposites in *Big and Little*, counting in *Counting*, sorting and grouping in *Odd One Out*, and both two- and three-dimensional shapes in *Shapes* (all Random House, 1984). *Energy at Work* (Lothrop, 1981), for middle-graders, includes two board games found on the inside covers and provides a basic study of energy—its forms, uses, conservation, and future. "With lots of 'pop' appeal (instructions on growing mung bean sprouts as 'fast food') and lots of solid information, the book succeeds," according to *School Library Journal*. A contributor of articles to scientific journals, Satchwell has also written *Future Sources* (F. Watts, 1981), discussing wind, water, solar, and atomic power as sources of energy; and *Fire* (Dial, 1983), depicting its nature, value, and danger.

SCHOLZ, Jackson (Volney)   1897-1986

OBITUARY NOTICE: Born March 15, 1897, in Buchanan, Mich.; died October 26, 1986, in Delray Beach, Fla.; cremated; ashes scattered at sea. Athlete and author. At one time considered the fastest man in the world, Scholz won a 1924 Olympic gold medal for the two-hundred-meter race. His loss in the one-hundred-meter race that same year was later recreated in "Chariots of Fire," which won the 1981 Academy Award for best motion picture. Scholz declined to see the movie because his surname was mispronounced throughout the film. He was the author of more than thirty books, including sports fiction for children. Among these writings are *Fighting Coach, Fullback for Sale, Center Field Jinx, Backfield Buckaroo*, and *The Big Mitt*. In addition, Scholz contributed more than three hundred stories to magazines.

FOR MORE INFORMATION SEE: More Junior Authors, H. W. Wilson, 1963; *Contemporary Authors*, Volumes 5-8, revised, Gale, 1969; *Authors of Books for Young People*, 2nd edition, 1971; *Who's Who in Track and Field*, Arlington House, 1973; *People Weekly*, May 10, 1982. Obituaries: *New York Times*, October 30, 1986; *Chicago Tribune*, October 31, 1986; *Washington Post*, November 1, 1986; *Facts on File*, November 7, 1986.

SCHUR, Maxine   1948-

BRIEF ENTRY: Born October 21, 1948, in San Francisco, Calif. After graduating from the University of California at Berkeley, Schur and her husband Stephen, a systems analyst, set out on a two-year tour of the world, traveling by bus, train, car, plane, donkey, truck, and tramp steamer to more than forty countries. After living briefly in Switzerland, Turkey, and Australia, they settled in Wellington, New Zealand in 1972, where Schur became a film editor and actress on the New Zealand Broadcasting Corporation television soap opera "Close to Home." "My mind, though, was haunted by exotic scenes, unforgettable people, and incredible anecdotes, 'traveller's tales,'" she said. Schur, who had begun writing down her adventures while residing in southern Turkey, sold her stories to the New Zealand Department of Education to be made into storybooks for school children.

Schur has written several other books for children, including *Schnook the Peddler* (Dillon, 1985), set in turn-of-the-century Russia, in which a young Jewish boy learns a lesson in forgiveness, charity, and love after stealing and then returning a Hanukkah dreidel to the peddler who owns it. "The lesson," observed *School Library Journal*, "is subtly woven into this brief yet poetic tale." Schur is also the author of *Hannah Szenes: A Song of Light* (Jewish Publication Society of America, 1986), a biography of the Jewish heroine who lost her life in a rescue mission to help European Jews during World War II; *Samantha's Surprise: A Christmas Story* (Pleasant, 1986); and two earlier books, *Weka Won't Learn* (Viking Sevenseas, 1977) and *The Witch at the Wellington Library* (Viking Sevenseas, 1978). Her anticipated works for children include a novel entitled *The Circlemaker*. *Home:* 736 28th Ave., San Mateo, Calif. 94403.

SHACHTMAN, Tom   1942-

PERSONAL: Born in 1942, in New York, N.Y.; married Harriet Shelare (an executive producer); children: two. *Education:* Tufts University, B.S., 1963; Carnegie-Mellon University, M.F.A., 1966. *Agent:* Mel Berger, William Morris Agency, 1350 Avenue of the Americas, New York, N.Y. 10019.

CAREER: Free-lance writer, producer, and director for television, 1966-76; National Geographic Society, Washington, D.C., assistant chief of the television division, 1969-70; New York University, New York, N.Y., adjunct lecturer in film and television, 1977—; Harvard University, Cambridge, Mass., adjunct lecturer in film and television, 1985—. *Member:* Writ-

ers Guild of America (East), Authors Guild. *Awards, honors:* Shubert fellowship, 1965-66; Gold Award from Atlanta Film Festival, Award from New York International Film Festival, and Golden Gate Award from San Francisco Film Festival, all 1972, all for "Children of Poverty"; Gold Award from Virgin Islands Film Festival, and Award from New York International Film Festival, both 1973, both for "Children of Trouble"; Gold Award from Virgin Islands Film Festival, Award from New York International Film Festival, and local Emmy awards, all 1975, all for "Children of Violence"; local Emmy award for "Winning Isn't Everything," 1977, and for other works; *Growing Up Masai* was selected as a Notable Children's Trade Book in the Field of Social Studies by the joint committee of the National Council for Social Studies and the Children's Book Council, 1982.

WRITINGS: The Day America Crashed, Putnam, 1979; *Edith and Woodrow* (nonfiction), Putnam, 1981, large print edition, Thorndike Press, 1981; *The Birdman of St. Petersburg* (juvenile), Macmillan, 1981; *Growing Up Masai* (juvenile; illustrated with photographs by D. Renn), Macmillan, 1981; *The Phony War, 1939-1940*, Harper, 1982; *Decade of Shocks, 1963-1974*, Simon & Schuster, 1983; *Parade!* (juvenile; Junior Literary Guild selection; illustrated with photographs by Chuck Saaf), Macmillan, 1985; *America's Birthday: The Fourth of July* (illustrated with photographs by Chuck Saaf), Macmillan, 1986; (with Robert Lamphere) *The FBI-KGB War*, Random House, 1986; (with Harriet Shelare) *Video Basics*, Holt, 1987. Also author of one-act plays and films.

At Herald Square at 4:30 a.m., the noise level is as high as the sky. ■ (From *Parade!* by Tom Shachtman. Photograph by Chuck Saaf.)

TOM SHACHTMAN

Television scripts: "The Twenty-First Century" (series), Columbia Broadcasting System, Inc. (CBS-TV), 1966-69; "Discovery," American Broadcasting Companies, Inc. (ABC-TV), 1970-71; "NBC Reports," National Broadcasting Company, Inc. (NBC-TV), 1971; "Children of Poverty" (trilogy; includes "Children of Poverty," "Children of Trouble," and "Children of Violence"), starring Peter Falk and Edwin Newman, NBC-TV, 1972-75; "Broken Treaty at Battle Mountain," starring Robert Redford, Public Broadcasting Service (PBS-TV), 1973; "The Masks We Wear," ABC-TV, 1973; "Rainbow Sundae," ABC-TV, 1973-75; "Sixty Minutes," CBS-TV, 1974; "Decades of Decision," PBS-TV, 1976; "Mary Kate's War," PBS-TV, 1976; "Not Worth a Continental," PBS-TV, 1976; "Look Back in Sorrow," PBS-TV, 1976; "The Last Frontier," syndicated, 1976; "We Are about Caring," syndicated; "That's the Spirit," syndicated, 1980-82; "Made in America," syndicated, 1987. Also author of dialogue of Werner Herzog's "Nosferatu" (adapted from novel *Dracula* by Bram Stoker), Twentieth-Century Fox, 1979.

WORK IN PROGRESS: The Gilded Leaf, a family biography of the R. J. Reynolds tobacco family, written with Patrick Reynolds, to be published by Little, Brown in 1988; a juvenile novel, *Beachmaster,* to be published by Holt in 1988.

SIDELIGHTS: "Writing for children is a happy obligation for an author blessed with two boys, and my editors have been kind enough to allow me to write about things which interest me greatly. I try to be reasonably definitive about my subjects, whether that be a tribe of people I've visited in Africa, my crazy pal Ralph who takes care of injured birds, the year-long effort to plan New York's annual Thanksgiving Day parade, or the art and craft of video.

"Thinking in visual terms is something I've been trained to do by years of filmmaking and working with videotape, both as a writer and as a producer. Crystalization of the image—whether in words or in pictures—is the essence of 'writing' children's books. Many writers of adult books shy away from creating works for children, possibly because they don't wish to change styles. I hope the prose in my children's books is at least as clear and lucid as it is in those I create for adult readers."

"When creating books such as *Parade!,* that are heavily illustrated, I write sparingly, with an eye toward images. And when I write history for adults—my main passion and occupation these days—what really moves me are the monumental dramas of the past which I try my best to portray in words.

"*Parade!* began with my wish to convey the energy, planning and cooperation of the many souls joined together in one undertaking that finally reaches the public and is seen and heard in a small moment of time. To me, the annual Macy's Thanksgiving Day Parade had always embodied the best in marching and display, and I was pleased when Macy's agreed to allow us to document the designing, construction, rehearsal, costuming, and myriad other aspects that go into the making of this enormous parade. I'd been to the blowing-up-of-the-balloons the night before the parade many times, but knowing the background of that magical time before the dawn only increased my appreciation of the spectacle. In all, Chuck Saaf and I spent almost two years trying to capture the wonder, the color, and intense happiness of the big parade—and, as with the parade-makers themselves at the moment they begin to march down the avenue, the work and effort have faded away and there is nothing now but the excitement.

"I am, I suppose, a curious amalgam of influences and traits. When I made a series of award-winning documentary films, I functioned more as a playwright than as a reporter; teaching writing to film and TV students at New York University, I rely more on my degree in psychology than on my master's in play writing."

FOR MORE INFORMATION SEE: New York Times, March 26, 1979; *Dallas Morning News,* May 6, 1979; *Los Angeles Times,* May 17, 1979.

SHEFTS, Joelle

BRIEF ENTRY: Born in San Antonio, Tex. An illustrator and filmmaker, Shefts graduated from Pratt Institute with a degree in fine arts. Her films have been shown nationally and on German television. According to *Publishers Weekly,* in Janet Taylor Lisle's *The Dancing Cats of Applesap* (Bradbury, 1984), Shefts "provides illustrations reflecting its hilarious surprises and tensions." With gray-washed drawings, Shefts depicts shy Melba, a ten-year-old who hides from her peers at old-fashioned Jiggs' Drug Store, with Jr. Jiggs, the owner, and Miss Toonie, his taciturn employee who has filled the premises with a hundred stray cats. When the store is threatened with closure, Melba overcomes her shyness and turns it into a showplace of cats dancing to the music of Mr. Jiggs's guitar. "Shefts' illustrations of the three misfits and the wiley cats are enchanting," noted *School Library Journal.* Shefts also illustrated Susan Sussman's *Casey the Nomad* (Albert Whitman, 1985). *Residence:* New York.

Some of my best friends are children. In fact, all of my best friends are children.

—J.D. Salinger

STASIAK, Krystyna

PERSONAL: Born in Poland; became a permanent resident of United States, 1969; daughter of Eugeniusz and Natalia Stasiak. *Education:* Academy of Fine Arts, Warsaw, Poland, M.A., 1969. *Home:* 5421 N. East River Rd., #507, Chicago, Ill. 60656.

CAREER: Free-lance artist. *Exhibitions*—One-man shows: Galerie Galaxie, Detroit, Mich., 1965; Sherman's, Chicago, Ill., 1971. Group shows: Five Artists Show, Wayne State University, Detroit, 1965; Wilder Public Library, Detroit, 1965; ''Art and Child'' Exhibit, Hall of Nations, Detroit, 1972; ''Chicago Books 1973,'' Chicago, 1973; ''Illustration Chicago,'' Chicago, 1974; ARC Gallerie, Chicago, 1975. Has also exhibited in Warsaw, Budapest, and throughout Central and Western Europe. *Awards, honors:* Third place, Award from ''Fraternita' Mondiale'' poster art competition, Milan, Italy, 1967.

WRITINGS—Self-illustrated: *Zoie the Zebra*, Scott, Foresman, 1974, large print edition, Macomb County School District (Mich.), 1974.

Illustrator: Maria Czerkawska, *Zolte chodaczki* (title means ''The Little Yellow Clogs''), Nasza Ksiegarnia (Poland), 1964; Wanda Grodzienska, *Marek Sumak i jogo koledzy* (title means ''Marc Sumak and His Friends''), Nasza Ksiegarnia, 1964; Sylwester Banas, *Przyjaciolki z VB* (title means ''Girlfriends from a Classroom VB''), Nasza Ksiegarnia, 1964; Mikolaj Kozakiewicz, *Zlota doxa* (title means ''The Golden Doxa''), Nasza Ksiegarnia, 1964; Rudyard Kipling, *Just So Stories,* Coronet, 1965; *American Folk Stories,* Coronet, 1966; *American Indian Stories,* Coronet, 1967; *Mother Goose Rhymes,* Scott, Foresman, 1967.

Maria Lastowiecka, *Mis i lalka* (title means ''A Teddybear and a Doll''), Nasza Ksiegarnia, 1973; *Illustrated Poems for Children,* Hubbard Press, 1973; *Stories from around the World,* Hubbard Press, 1974; Alma Gilleo, editor, *King Grisly-Beard,* Society for Visual Education, 1976; A. Gilleo, editor, *The Wild Swans,* Society for Visual Education, 1976; Jakob Grimm and Wilhelm Grimm, *Patterns Far and Near*, Argus Communications, 1976.

Margaret Hillert, *The Purple Pussycat,* Follett, 1980; M. Hillert, *Four Good Friends,* Follett, 1980; Betty Ren Wright, *I Like Being Alone,* Raintree, 1981; Daisy Kouzel, Yao-wen Li and Gloria Skurzynski, *Three Folktales,* Houghton, 1981; Sylvia Root Tester, *Learning about Ghosts,* Childrens Press, 1981; Laura Alden, *Learning about Fairies,* Childrens Press, 1982; M. Hillert, *The Cow That Got Her Wish,* Follett, 1982; M. Hillert, *The Witch Who Went for a Walk,* Follett, 1982; Barbara Gregorich and Joan Hoffman, editors, *Say Good Night,* School Zone, 1984; L. Alden, *Learning about Unicorns,* Childrens Press, 1985; *Magic Popcorn,* Doubleday, 1985.

ADAPTATIONS: ''King Grisly-Beard'' (cassette), Society for Visual Education, 1976; ''The Wild Swans'' (cassette), Society for Visual Education, 1976; ''Mother Goose Rhymes'' (record), Shield Productions/Jamar Records.

WORK IN PROGRESS: A collection of legends from Poland.

(From *Learning about Ghosts* by Sylvia R. Tester. Illustrated by Krystyna Stasiak.)

KRYSTYNA STASIAK

SIDELIGHTS: ''I was born in Poland. Although I have a *drop* of French blood inherited from my great-great-grandmother, and although I like the French language and am charmed by French music, literature and art—I feel I am an absolute one hundred percent *slavic soul* with an extremely romantic, passionate, sensitive and sometimes unpractical nature.

''From my earliest childhood I was subtly guided by my parents to the world of music. Somehow, equally subtly, I managed to skip my ballet or piano lessons many times and hide myself with some paper and crayons in my own magic world of colors and shapes. Although music is still the main ruler of my inner life, I try to express myself in the world of colors and forms.

''I love animals. To me an animal is not *it*. They are *he* or *she*. They have *personality*. Where could one find a better example of a friendship between two creatures than in a friendship of a sightless cow and a duck? And such friendship really, truly does exist. If you remember, 'Humphrey the Whale' took the wrong course from the Pacific Ocean to a sweetwater river. I am absolutely positive that Humphrey was truly happy in the river! After spending his life in the Pacific Ocean, where he was just one of the whales in the boundless water around him, he must have imagined that the river was still the same old blue Pacific but that he, Humphrey, grew up and became the biggest whale in the whole world. Instead of the boundless water around him before, now he could touch the shores with his fingertips.

''I like to travel. Last summer I traveled by car through the Alps from Italy through Switzerland to Tirol in Austria. The

trip was absolutely fabulous in shapes and colors—the hairpin-like serpentine road, marvelous greenery, silver of the mountains, azure of the sky. I was waiting for the red-hooded gnomes to come out from their holes, and, of course, they did.

''I like the mystery of how people touch on others lives for just one moment, or for a while or forever. I enjoy letters from people I have never met who have seen my art and liked it.''

HOBBIES AND OTHER INTERESTS: Oil painting, graphics, music, literature, languages, physical activities, skiing, tennis, traveling.

STEGEMAN, Janet Allais   1923- (Kate Britton)

BRIEF ENTRY: Born October 18, 1923, in Oak Park, Ill. A writer of books for children and young adults, Stegeman spent her early years in an Illinois farming community before moving with her family to Atlanta, Georgia. There, too ill from undiagnosed congenital defects to attend school, she began writing plays that were acted out by her sister and neighbors. Another family move took her to Cincinnati where her health improved and she was able to attend school. College life, an early marriage to medical student John Stegeman during the first year of World War II, and work as a medical researcher ''left definite marks on me and what I try to say. The irony of losing our second little boy to congenital heart disease after all that research was the clincher. I remember sitting on my bed . . . telling 'Whoever Is In Charge' I wanted to be a writer, WAS GOING TO BE A WRITER!''

Stegeman and her husband are co-authors of *Caty: A Biography of Catharine Littlefield Greene* (University of Georgia Press, 1977). Stegeman herself has written *Last Seen on Hopper's Lane,* a suspense novel for young adults, in which a girl stumbles upon a drug transaction, is kidnapped, and eventually escapes. ''What sets the book apart is the author's success in worrying the reader,'' according to *New York Times Book Review.* ''In the prolonged suspense there are real chills. . . . A good read.'' Under the pseudonym Kate Britton, Stegeman wrote *Nightmare at Lilybrook* (Bouregy, 1979), a romance for young adults. Stegeman also has contributed poems, short stories, and articles to magazines and local newspapers. Besides interests in art, music, sailing, and hiking—with reading at the top of the list—she dabbles in painting and photography. *Agent:* Curtis Brown, Ltd., Ten Astor Place, New York, N.Y. 10003.

STEVENS, Kathleen   1936-

PERSONAL: Born February 16, 1936, in Brooklyn, N.Y.; daughter of William Patrick (an insurance agent) and Mary (a homemaker; maiden name, Miner) O'Halloran; married Leonard Stevens (a high school principal), November 19, 1960; children: Mary Beth, Barbara, Larry. *Education:* Georgian Court College, A.B., 1957; Glassboro State College, M.A., 1972. *Home:* 506 Ardmore Ave., Pitman, N.J. 08071. *Office:* Glassboro State College, Glassboro, N.J. 08028.

CAREER: Pitman High School, Pitman, N.J., teacher of English and Spanish, 1957-60; Glassboro State College, Glassboro, N.J., instructor, 1972-79, assistant professor of communications, 1979—. *Member:* Society of Children's Book Writers.

I'm . . . ready to build a cottage on a bit of land and raise turnips for a living. ■ (From *Molly, McCullough, and Tom the Rogue* by Kathleen Stevens. Illustrated by Margot Zemach.)

KATHLEEN STEVENS

WRITINGS—Juvenile: *The Beast in the Bathtub* (illustrated by Ray Bowler), Childerset (Australia), 1980, Gareth Stevens, 1985; *Molly, McCullough, and Tom the Rogue* (illustrated by Margot Zemach), Crowell, 1983. Contributor of articles and stories to magazines and newspapers, including *Cricket* and *Highlights for Children.*

WORK IN PROGRESS: Children's books.

SIDELIGHTS: "My first children's book, *The Beast in the Bathtub,* came to publication by a curious route. Originally published in the children's magazine *Cricket,* the story was read by the director of an Australian company, who expressed interest in publishing it as a picture book. Later, the book was also published in England, in both hard and soft cover, and then in Japan, and finally in the United States. I've been to England, but not to Australia or Japan, so *The Beast* has seen more of the world than I have.

"My second book, *Molly, McCullough, and Tom the Rogue,* went a more conventional route. An editor at T. Y. Crowell had rejected one story I wrote, but asked to see other work. I sent her *Molly,* and it was subsequently published with full-color illustrations by Margot Zemach.

"Many of my children's stories have grown from incidents in my family life. *The Beast in the Bathtub* originated with the difficulties I had trying to pack three lively youngsters off to bed at night. For *Molly,* I took the traditional folklore theme of a rogue who has the tables turned on him, and added a new twist as Molly matches wits with the conniving Tom.

"I'm a 'late vocation' to the work of writing children's stories. As a youngster I planned to write children's stories when I grew up. That intention was somehow lost in the ensuing years, but resurfaced as my own children were growing up and I was reading books with them."

SZUDEK, Agnes S(usan) P(hilomena) (Mary McCaffrey)

BRIEF ENTRY: Born in Scotland. An educator and author of children's books, Szudek was raised in England "in the beautiful east-midlands county of Northhamptonshire. . . . Our home was on the road to Rockingham Village one mile away . . . overlooked by the magnificent Rockingham Castle." Childhood pastimes remain vivid in Szudek's mind, and serve as impetus for her stories. Of the nearly dozen children's books to her credit, Szudek admits that her favorites feature the character Victoria Plumb who appears in *Victoria Plumb* (Hutchinson, 1978) and *Victoria and the Parrots Gang* (Hutchinson, 1979). The author describes Victoria as a "modern, zany, young girl," the product of her own "tomboy youth." A reviewer for *Junior Bookshelf* agreed, calling the heroine "mad, mad as a hatter. . . . a worthy sister of my-naughty-little sister and Pippi Longstocking."

In 1980 Szudek, who is married to a Pole, received the Polish Gold Cross of Merit in recognition of her services to Polish culture abroad, for *Stories from Poland* (British Broadcasting Corp., 1972) and *The Amber Mountain* (Hutchinson, 1976). Under the pseudonym Mary McCaffrey, she is the author of *The Mighty Muddle* (Eel Pie, 1981), a collection of four unrelated stories ("The Mighty Muddle," "The King's Laundry," "Godolfus and Riftikin," and "The Seafaring Piano"), and four children's novels: *Smoke-Drift to Heaven* (Abelard, 1981), *One Way to Rome* (Abelard, 1982), *My Brother Ange* (Crowell, 1982), and *Night of the Tiger* (Abelard, 1983). Szudek attended the Montessori Training Centre in Yorkshire and Maria Assumpta Training College in London and has taught at several schools in Northhamptonshire and London. Aside from writing, she spends her time singing, dancing, painting, and playing the piano. She also thoroughly enjoys storytelling and lecturing at schools, libraries, and bookshops, due to a "bite from the acting bug [that] has never healed. Never will!"

THOMPSON, Hilary 1943-

BRIEF ENTRY: Born October 8, 1943, in Yorkshire, England. Educator, playwright, poet, and illustrator. As assistant professor of English at Acadia University and a writer, Thompson allows "one activity to feed the other," admitting that her students give her insights which become part of her thinking process as a writer. Thompson has written several plays for children, including *Anansi the Spider, Anancy and Lizard, The Quarelling Quails* (all Nova Scotia Dramatists' Co-op, 1977), and *Madame Fou-Fou and the Apricot Mousse; or, Cinderella Comes of Age: A Play for Children or Puppets* (Nova Scotia Dramatists' Co-op, 1979). She describes her only self-illustrated children's story, *Warm Is a Circle* (Lancelot Press, 1979), as "a series of images which allowed me the freedom to illustrate." Thompson's adult works include two plays, "Northern Lights" and "The Flower That Fades," and a poetry chapbook, *Only So Far* (Fiddlehead Poetry Books, 1982). Currently, she is at work on a children's novel entitled *The Giant under the Mountain,* and another book of poetry. Thompson is a member of the Children's Literature Association, Children's Theatre Association of America, and Association of Canadian University Teachers of English. *Office:* English Dept., Acadia University, Wolfville, Nova Scotia, Canada B0P 1X0.

It is better to be a young June-bug than an old bird of paradise.

—Mark Twain
(pseudonym of Samuel Langhorne Clemens)

TREADGOLD, Mary 1910-

PERSONAL: Born April 16, 1910, in London, England; daughter of John R. W. (a stockbroker) and Hilda (Edwards) Treadgold. *Education:* Bedford College, London, B.A. (with honors), 1934, M.A., 1936. *Politics:* Conservative. *Home:* England. *Agent:* Jonathan Cape, Ltd., 30 Bedford Sq., London WC1B 3EL, England.

CAREER: Raphael Tuck (publisher), London, England, 1937-38; William Heinemann Ltd., (publisher), London, editor, 1938-40; British Broadcasting Corp., World Service, producer, literary editor, 1941-60; Jonathan Cape Ltd. (publisher), London, England, literary adviser for children's books, 1963-65. *Member:* P.E.N. (English center; member of executive committee, 1956-70; chairman of program committee, 1959-63). *Awards, honors:* Carnegie Medal from the British Library Association, for the outstanding children's book of the year, 1941, for *We Couldn't Leave Dinah; The "Polly Harris"* was selected one of Child Study Association of America's Children's Books of the Year, 1970.

WRITINGS—Juvenile fiction, except as noted: *We Couldn't Leave Dinah* (illustrated by Stuart Tresilian), J. Cape, 1941, Merrimack, 1980, also published in U.S. as *Left Till Called For,* Doubleday, 1941; *No Ponies* (illustrated by Ruth Gervis), J. Cape, 1946, Merrimack, 1981; *The "Polly Harris",* J. Cape, 1949, revised edition (illustrated by Pat Marriott), T. Nelson, 1970, also published as *The Mystery of the "Polly Harris",* Doubleday, 1951; *The Running Child* (adult), J. Cape, 1951; *The Heron Ride* (illustrated by Victor Ambrus), J. Cape, 1962; *The Winter Princess* (illustrated by Pearl Falconer), Brockhampton Press, 1962, Van Nostrand, 1964; *Return to the Heron* (illustrated by V. Ambrus), J. Cape, 1963; *The Weather Boy* (illustrated by Robert Geary), Brockhampton Press, 1964, Van Nostrand, 1965; *Maid's Ribbons* (illustrated by Susannah Holden), T. Nelson (London), 1965, (New York), 1967; *Elegant Patty* (illustrated by Lynette Hemmant), Hamish Hamilton, 1967; *Poor Patty* (illustrated by L. Hemmant), Hamish Hamilton, 1968; *This Summer, Last Summer* (illustrated by Mary Russon), Hamish Hamilton, 1968; *The Humbugs* (illustrated by Faith Jaques), Hamish Hamilton, 1968; *The Rum Day of the Vanishing Pony* (illustrated by Michael Heslop), Brockhampton Press, 1970; *Journey from the Heron,* Cape, 1981, Merrimack, 1983.

SIDELIGHTS: "I started 'writing' at the age of seven—which merely meant: I carefully and ceaselessly copied out other writers' fairy tales in a green-covered exercise book and presented them to my mother on her birthday as my own. She most kindly didn't mention that the whole lot were ones she herself had read to me. I did rather better at age ten. I was at a truly wonderful dance and drama school. Its delightful heads, Ruby Ginner and Irene Mauwer, encouraged us all to be creative, so I came up with a one-act play called 'The Stolen Plans.' It was set in the reign of Queen Elizabeth the First and the only line I remember is some character coming on to an empty stage, facing the audience, putting a finger to his lips, and whispering dramatically 'Hish!' and going off. This potted melodrama was truly original at last and got itself used as a curtain-raiser at a distinguished charity matinee. And I do remember standing in the wings and saying 'Mummy, mummy, why's the whole audience *laughing?* It's a *serious* play!'

"After that episode I more or less subsided writing, except for school reports that said 'Mary is good at composition, but must try harder at her arithmetic.' Not till the early days of the War in 1940 did I really *write.* It was this way: after school I'd gone to University to study English literature which I really

MARY TREADGOLD

and truly loved all the time at school. At college, of course, I had to write many, many essays and even a thesis, so without realizing it I was being thoroughly grounded in the actual craft of writing.

"I wanted to go into publishing and I managed to get a post as children's editor at a firm of children's publishers, and it was there I came into contact with both good children's books and the quite appalling manuscripts sent in by people who wanted to be writers and were never ever going to be. And I used to mumble 'I could do better myself.' Just then Hitler took the Channel Islands which were where I'd spent so many wonderful holidays. I was so enraged I sat down and wrote—mainly in the air raid shelter as the bombs rained down on London— *We Couldn't Leave Dinah,* which to my complete surprise, won me the famous Carnegie Medal. And in the intervals of being a very busy BBC producer—my job during and after the war—I went on as a writer from there.

"Looking back, I think if I had to pick on a motto for myself as writer I'd choose 'Everything comes in handy.' Because for most writers everything does, even if they're not always pleasant things. For me: Horses and riding, dancing and drama, places and houses, and above all *people,* because a story is always about people in the end. And to all young aspiring writers I'd recommend my motto 'Everything comes in handy.' And do remember to jot experiences down in a notebook as you go along, because they may come in handy, but only if you can remember them."

Treadgold speaks some French and German; she has traveled in the Far East, the Middle East, the United States, and many of the countries in Europe.

HOBBIES AND OTHER INTERESTS: Cooking, reading, folk music, talking and a long time ago—riding and hill walking.

FOR MORE INFORMATION SEE: Margery Fisher, *Intent upon Reading,* Brockhampton Press, 1963; Roger Lancelyn Green, *Tellers of Tales,* F. Watts, 1965; Brian Doyle, *Who's Who of Children's Literature,* Schocken Books, 1968; *Author's Choice,* Crowell, 1971.

UNDERHILL, Liz 1936-

BRIEF ENTRY: Born March 13, 1936, in Worthing, England. Artist, author and illustrator of children's books. After graduating from Portsmouth College of Art in 1970 with a B.A. in art and design, Underhill held positions as part-time tutor and art teacher. She became a full-time artist in 1977; more recently, in 1982, she began a career as an author-illustrator of picturebooks. *Junior Bookshelf* described Underhill's illustrations in her *Pigs Might Fly* (Methuen, 1984) as "superb: colourful but never brash . . . brimming with life . . . strikingly original." Likewise, *Publishers Weekly* called the anthropomorphic animal portraits in *Jack of All Trades* (Godine, 1985) "witty paintings, lavishly colored and detailed." In the story, a young pup named Jack imagines himself in a variety of careers, including fisherman, musician, teacher, lawyer, and bank teller. "Underhill illuminates with a fine brush," observed *Times Literary Supplement,* "in unusual combinations of color." Among the author-illustrator's anticipated works is a pop-up book entitled *The Lucky Coin. Home:* 32 Abbey Rd., Bourne, Lincolnshire PE10 9EP, England.

FOR MORE INFORMATION SEE: Country Life, September, 1984.

UNWIN, Nora S. 1907-1982

*OBITUARY NOTICE—*See sketch in *SATA* Volume 3: Born February 22, 1907, in Surbiton, Surrey, England; died January 5, 1982. Educator, artist and author. As a professional artist Unwin exhibited works in Europe, North and South America, and the Near and Far East, winning awards from such organizations as the Society of American Graphic Artists, the National Academy of Design, and the National Association of Women Artists. Educated in Great Britain at the Kingdom School of Art and the Royal College of Art, she received her diploma in design in 1931 and later worked as an illustrator, engraver, and part-time teacher in both England and the United States. From 1957 to 1959 she served as director of art at Tenacre Country Day School in Massachusetts. Throughout her career, Unwin illustrated nearly one hundred children's books, but did not begin writing her own until 1939, when she published *Round the Year.* She followed this work with several more, including *Lucy and the Little Red Horse; Poquito, the Little Mexican Duck; The Midsummer Witch;* and *Sinbad, the Cygnet.*

FOR MORE INFORMATION SEE: Contemporary Authors, Volumes 21-24, revised, Gale, 1977; *Who's Who in Art,* 20th edition, Art Trade Press, 1982; *The Oxford Companion to Children's Literature,* Oxford University Press, 1984. Obituaries: *Who's Who,* 134th edition, St. Martin's, 1982; *Who's Who in Art,* 21st edition, Art Trade Press, 1984.

Few boys are born with talents that excel,
But all are capable of living well.
                                        —William Cowper

URIS, Leon (Marcus) 1924-

PERSONAL: Born August 3, 1924, in Baltimore, Md.; son of Wolf William and Anna (Blumberg) Uris; married Betty Katherine Beck, 1945 (divorced January, 1968); married Margery Edwards, September 8, 1968 (died February 20, 1969); married Jill Peabody (a photographer), February 15, 1970; children: (first marriage) Karen Lynn, Mark Jay, Michael Cady; (third marriage) Rachael. *Education:* Attended public schools in Baltimore, Md. *Residence:* Aspen, Colo. *Agent:* Willis Kingsley Wing, 24 East 38th St., New York, N.Y. 10016.

CAREER: Former newspaper driver, *San Francisco Call-Bulletin,* San Francisco, Calif. Full-time writer, 1950—. *Military service:* U.S. Marine Corps, 1942-45. *Member:* Writers League, Screenwriters Guild. *Awards, honors:* Daroff Memorial Award, 1959; National Institute of Arts and Letters grant, 1959; Honorary Doctorate University of Colorado, 1976, Santa Clara University, 1977, Wittenberg University, 1980, Lincoln College, 1985; John F. Kennedy Medal from Irish/American Society of New York, 1977; Gold Medal from Eire Society of Boston, 1978; Jobotinsky Medal from State of Israel, 1980; (with wife, Jill Uris) Hall Fellowship, Concord Academy, 1980; Scopus Award from the Hebrew University of Jerusalem, 1981; *Exodus* was selected one of New York Public Library's Books for the Teen Age, 1980, 1981, and 1982.

*WRITINGS—*All published by Doubleday, except as indicated: *Battle Cry,* Putnam, 1953; *The Angry Hills,* Random House, 1955; *Exodus,* 1957; (with Dimitrios Haussiadis) *Exodus Revisited* (photo-essay), 1959 (published in England as *In the Steps of Exodus,* Heinemann, 1962); *Mila 18,* 1961; *Armageddon,* 1964; *The Third Temple,* published with *Strike Zion* by William Stevenson, Bantam, 1967; *Topaz,* McGraw, 1967; *QB VII,* 1970; (with wife, Jill Uris) *Ireland, a Terrible Beauty: The Story of Ireland Today* (photo-essay), 1975; *Trinity,* 1976; (with J. Uris) *Jerusalem, Song of Songs* (photo-essay), 1981; *The Haj,* 1984.

Contributor to anthologies including *Fabulous Yesterdays,* Harper, 1961; F. Van Wyck Mason, compiler, *American Men at Arms,* Little, Brown, 1965; Samuel Sobel, editor, *A Treasury of Jewish Sea Stories,* Jonathan David, 1965; Allan Dulles, *Great Spy Stories from Fiction,* Harper, 1969. Contributor to periodicals including *Esquire, Coronet, Ladies' Home Journal,* and *TWA Ambassador.*

Screenplays: "Battle Cry," 1955; "Gunfight at the O.K. Corral," Paramount, 1957.

ADAPTATIONS: "Battle Cry" (motion picture), starring Van Heflin, James Whitmore, Tab Hunter, and Dorothy Malone, Warner Bros., 1955; "The Angry Hills" (motion picture), Metro-Goldwyn-Mayer, 1959; "Exodus" (motion picture), starring Paul Newman and Eva Marie Saint, United Artists, 1960; "Topaz" (motion picture), United Artists, 1969; (also adaptor with Walt Smith) "Ari" (musical version of *Exodus*), first produced on Broadway at Mark Hellinger Theater, January 15, 1971; "QB VII" (movie for television), starring Ben Gazarra, Leslie Carron, Anthony Hopkins, and Lee Remick, ABC-TV, April, 1974.

SIDELIGHTS: Uris was born in Baltimore, August 3, 1924. His father emigrated from Poland/Russia after World War I, spending a year as a pioneer in Palestine en route to America. The name Uris is a derivative of Yerushalami which means "Jerusalemite." His mother, Anna Blumberg, was born in Havre de Grace, Maryland. Her parents likewise were Russian/Polish immigrants.

Leon Uris. (Portrait by Leslie Emery.)

A product of a broken home, Uris spent his boyhood in Norfolk, Baltimore and finally in Philadelphia. He never graduated and was considered a poor student, flunking English three times, ''It's a good thing English and writing have nothing to do with each other.''

Uris wanted to be a writer and nothing but a writer from earliest memory. He composed an operetta inspired by the death of his dog at the age of seven which began a large collection of unproduced plays and unpublished manuscripts over two decades. Coming from a poor, big city Jewish left-wing background, he vowed never to write about how the world and his Jewishness did him wrong. ''The market is glutted with the self-pitying prose of the Jewish writers. There is so much good about being Jewish, about loving the Irish, about standing up for injustice, I can't waste my time with that other junk.'' He feels that this attitude has cost him a lot of points with the critical establishment which he feels dotes, disproportionately, on losers and their tales of woe.

A month after Pearl Harbor he ran away from home and joined the Marine Corps at the age of seventeen. His tour of duty took him to San Diego, New Zealand and Hawaii and into combat at Guadalcanal and Tarawa. He served as a radio operator and never rose over the rank of PFC. He returned to the States suffering from the effects of malaria, dengue fever, recurring asthma and unfit for further overseas duty. Faced with a medical discharge he wangled himself a limited duty post in San Francisco in order to remain in the service until the end of the war.

In San Francisco he met and later married a lady Marine sergeant, Betty Beck, of Waterloo, Iowa. After the war they settled in San Francisco, where they had their first child, Karen, in 1946.

Uris went from failure to failure in writing. Discouraged, he got a job as a newspaper home delivery district manager for the now defunct *Call-Bulletin*. He had developed the typical block against writing, but in 1950 did an article which was purchased by *Esquire* and the check for three hundred dollars proved to be the catalyst to start the long delayed novel about the Marine Corps.

Writing every night till well after midnight and on his days off for eighteen hours, the novel took form in the attic of his home in Larkspur, the Marin County suburb of San Francisco. Son Mark was born in 1950 and soon became accustomed to the lullaby of the second hand typewriter. The result, *Battle Cry* was greeted with a sense of relief by critics and readers who had had their fill of downbeat World War II novels.

(From *Ireland, a Terrible Beauty: The Story of Ireland Today* by Jill and Leon Uris. Photograph by Jill Uris.)

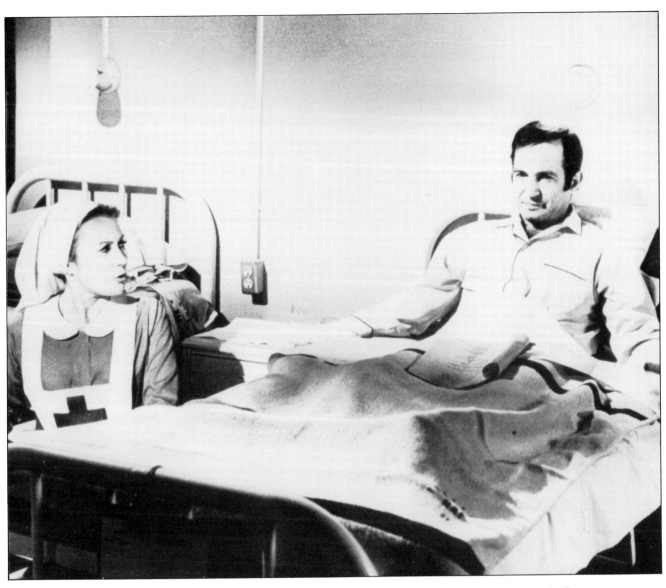

(From the television movie "QB VII," starring Ben Gazzara and Juliet Mills. The six-and-a-half hour film received thirteen Emmy Award nominations, one of which Mills won for best supporting actress.)

Battle Cry did not come without sacrifice and heartbreak. Says Uris, "If anyone wants to be a writer, I'll put him into business. I'll give him the first sheet of paper." The book was rejected by a dozen publishers, sometimes in the form of denunciations. During this period his daughter had a near fatal attack of polio. (She fully recovered.)

Their third child, Michael Cady, was born in 1953 to coincide with the publication of *Battle Cry* by G. P. Putnam's Sons. Mike's unusual middle name was after the editor, Howard Cady, who never lost faith in Uris even after his house had rejected the book.

"Like most writers and most human beings," says Uris, "I hated the war, but unlike most modern novelists, I did not hate the men who fought the war and I believed in what I was fighting for. It was a different era then. I respected my officers and revere the memory of the time I served. The Marine Corps pushed me into finding strengths I never knew I had. Perhaps I would have never known. I owe them my becoming a man and the ordeals I underwent laid a foundation of stamina I had to have later as a novelist."

Warner Brothers purchased the screen rights and Uris went to Hollywood to write the film. "Life in a studio for a novelist was as hectic and brutal as has been depicted. Sound was the last thing that came into film and by the time writers were needed, a hierarchy had been long established of star, director and producer. They pay lip service to the writer and the story, but contractually he could be and generally was fired on a whim or for making a stand for his story." Nonetheless, Uris had the backing of the Marine Corps which was necessary for the filming and he fought it through.

The family moved to Encino in Los Angeles where he wrote his second novel, *The Angry Hills*, a spy-chase based loosely on the diary of an uncle who had fought in Greece with the Palestinian Brigade, a Jewish unit of the British forces. G. P. Putnam, the publisher of *Battle Cry*, rejected and literally denounced the book. It was published in 1955 by Random House.

"Everyone has one novel in him, his own life story," says Uris. "It is that second novel that separates the men from the boys." Although it received moderate public acceptance, *The*

Angry Hills was extremely important in that it opened the way for his involvement in Palestine, later Israel, where he had a large family on his father's side.

Uris went from screenplay to screenplay and from studio to studio without success. Trouble with conspiring agents and unwilling to accept the Hollywood hierarchy led to a trail of unproduced scripts and firings. He had gained a reputation as a "one shot" writer and was on the verge of leaving Hollywood.

An interview with the producer, Hall Wallis, changed everything. Wallis had purchased an article about Tombstone, Arizona and although Uris had never written a western, he was assigned on a hunch to develop a story. The result was one of the classic westerns, "Gunfight at the O.K. Corral." "Hal and the director, John Sturges were the first two who truly respected the writer and stayed off my back . . . it was that simple."

The idea of Israel obsessed Uris now. He was hesitant about taking on so vast a project until he felt more mature as a writer, but after "Gunfight," could wait no longer, despite the fact he had now established himself as a first rank screenwriter.

Unable to finance the research, he sold the book on Israel in advance to MGM, then headed by Dory Schary. Before de-

Department of Internal Production, a division of Sûreté, functioned with much the same duties as the American FBI. ■ (Jacket illustration by Leonard Leone from *Topaz* by Leon Uris.)

parting for Israel he spent months reading hundreds of books and underwent spartan physical training to prepare for anything.

Arriving in Israel in March of 1956 he embarked on a grueling schedule of some 12,000 miles travel inside a country the size of Connecticut, conducted hundreds of interviews, took as many photographs and taped several miles of notes out of the archives. Realizing he would have to stay longer, he sent for his family. Their stay was cut short by the Sinai Campaign in the fall of '56. After evacuating his family, Uris went into the Sinai as a correspondent.

Financial resources depleted, Uris and the family dog rejoined Betty and the children in Rome where they sailed back to the States over Christmas, dead broke. His position to Bennett Cerf of Random House was that he had given everything to the project and demanded the publisher show the same faith by supporting him during the writing. Cerf declined and Uris was able to get a "contract of sorts" from Doubleday. The year of 1957 was spent writing his novel, taking time out to do some script doctoring in order to keep the family afloat.

Exodus was published in 1958 and became one of the all-time successes in American publishing history. In addition to some fifty regular translations there were a dozen or more "unauthorized" editions reaching into every corner of the communist countries. It is impossible to estimate the tens of millions who read it or the important and positive impact it had for the state of Israel at that time. "It took me all my life to become an overnight success."

While awaiting publication of *Exodus,* Uris sold the movie rights to *The Angry Hills,* and started the screenplay. He travelled to Athens on a location trip which eventually took him to Berlin for a story conference with the director, Robert Aldrich, who was shooting a film there. Although adverse to travelling in Germany because of the Holocaust, Uris took it on as a personal challenge and the seed was born for a future book. "I was eventually fired from *The Angry Hills* because Aldrich said, 'I didn't understand the characters in the novel,'" Uris recalls. "From the results of the film, neither did he."

Exodus contained an account of the Warsaw Ghetto which continued to fascinate Uris. Walter Mirisch gave him the go-ahead to develop a film on the ghetto, but a misunderstanding developed and Uris went on alone and decided to do it as a novel instead. From New York to London to Israel he tracked down survivors of the ghetto and the fighters of the historic forty-two day stand against the German Army. The last leg took him to Warsaw where a now suspicious Polish government withdrew co-operation forcing him to his information covertly. "It was hairy," he remembers, "but certain people came through despite the risk." The result, *Mila 18,* is Uris' proudest book. "I was advised by everyone not to follow up with a ghetto story after *Exodus.* It was the one thing I wrote not caring if it sold ten copies or ten thousand. I simply had to tell the story."

A by-product of the Israel phase of the research on *Mila 18* was a book of photographs, *Exodus Revisited,* in collaboration with the great Greek photographer, Dimitrios Harissiadis.

With the germ of a German novel brewing for years, Uris set out on his most difficult research task to date, taking him beyond Germany to the Soviet Union. "If it was rough in Poland, it was hell in Russia and East Germany. The whole story will have to wait till my memoirs. I'm damned lucky I didn't end up in a camp in Siberia."

(The musical production of "Ari," starring David Cryer and Constance Towers, based on the novel *Exodus,* opened at the Mark Hellinger Theater, January 24, 1971.)

His marriage of two decades was now running a rocky course. He lived and worked in Malibu after a separation and spent most of 1964 in Mexico writing an original screenplay about the Revolution. The film was never made.

One of the most important and dramatic events in Uris' life came as a result of something he had written in *Exodus*. The name of a Dr. Wladislav Dering was mentioned as among those committing atrocities against the Jews in Auschwitz.

Dering, alive in London, brought a libel suit. As a member of the Free Polish Forces Dering had escaped extradition on a warrant as a war criminal, and fled to British Somaliland where he remained for a decade as a medical officer. He returned to England after receiving an O.B.E. for distinguished service to the Crown.

Certain his research was correct on Dering, Uris gathered a few slim clues, enough to convince him Dering had performed

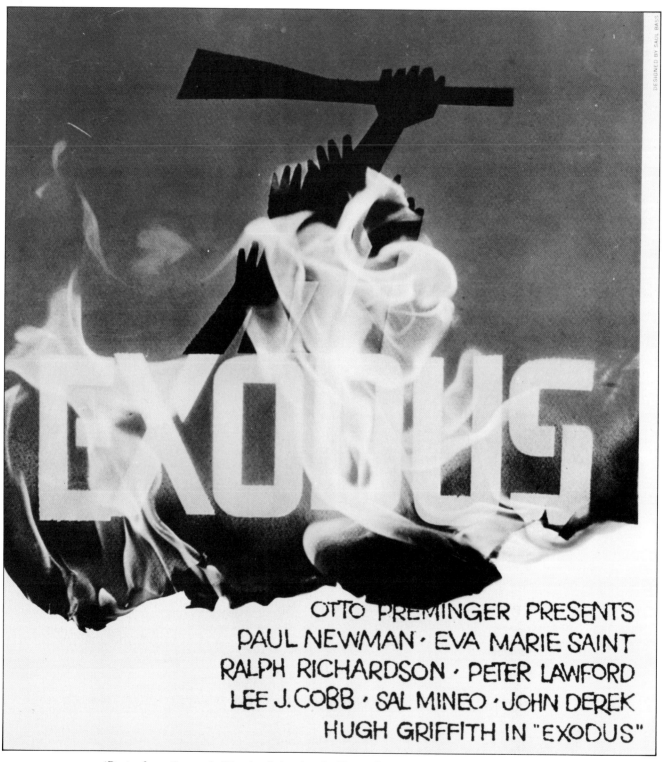

(Poster from the movie "Exodus," showing the illustrative style made famous by Saul Bass.)

castrations and ovariectomies as part of the Nazi experiments toward sterilizing the Jewish race. Because so many years had passed and so many of Dering's victims were either dead, dispersed or unable to identify him, Uris was urged to apologize in open court on risk of losing every penny he had. He decided to fight the case.

For two years, his solicitor, Soloman Kaufman, did a monumental job of gathering evidence and witnesses. The case came before the court in London in April, 1964 and went on to become "one of the most spectacular and important cases in British history." It was conducted in Greek, Polish, Hebrew, English, German, Czech, Russian and Ladino with scores of witnesses appearing from every part of the world. Leader of the defense, Lord Gerald Gardiner, later became Lord Chancellor of England.

Uris agreed that he could not support the statements made in *Exodus* of "seventeen thousand operations without anesthetic" and that he had indeed libelled Dering. His case was that Dering's character wasn't worth anything, a contention upheld by the jury which awarded the doctor a half-penny known as "contemptuous damages." "The issue at stake was how far a man can go and still claim membership in the human

(From the movie "Exodus," starring Paul Newman. Released by United Artists Corp., 1960.)

race,'' Uris said. ''As a Jew and a father and an American, I had no choice but to fight. The British court vindicated my entire position.''

Dering died of stomach cancer a year after the trial. Although Dering was obliged to pay all court costs, Uris chose not to burden the widow with the loss of her entire inheritance.

Returning to Mexico, Uris agreed to another reconciliation with his wife who had come to London to stand with him during the trial. While he wrapped up his work in Mexico, she moved with the family to Aspen, a place he had come to love as a skier.

In Acapulco during this period, he befriended Phillipe Thyraud de Vosjoli, a French diplomat who had defected his post in Washington and fled in protest against De Gaulle's anti-American position. De Vosjoli entrusted Uris with his papers concerning the decade he headed the French Intelligence Service in the Western Hemisphere. After Uris returned to Aspen, de Vosjoli sent him a startling outline of a fiction based on his life. Uris offered him half the proceeds if he could use the material for a novel and the Frenchman agreed.

Uris had fought quietly with his publishers from the onset of his career for better contractual conditions and a full share of paperback rights which he felt belonged solely to the author. He left Doubleday over this and signed with Harper & Row for the unwritten work based on de Vosjoli's story.

In 1965, after a final separation from Betty, Uris instituted divorce proceedings. It was a bitterly fought divorce lasting over two years.

During the same period, Harper & Row reneged on their contract alleging they were afraid of libel suits from de Gaulle and Fidel Castro who were depicted harshly in the manuscript. Working desperately to save the novel, Uris wrote 20,000 additional words in a three week period between sessions of the prolonged divorce hearings. McGraw-Hill finally took the book though offering a greatly reduced contract.

He was in New York working on the *Topaz* galleys when the Six Day War broke out between Israel and the Arabs. Oscar Dystel, president of Bantam Books and Uris' oldest friend in the publishing business, urged him to write a back-up piece for the Canadian writer William Stevenson who had just returned from Israel. Stevenson flew to Israel while the smoke of combat was yet unsettled and returned in less than ten days with 50,000 words. Meanwhile, Uris, locked up in his suite at the Algonquin Hotel, wrote a supporting essay. The book, *Strike Zion*, was published as a paperback and on the newsstands in less than a fortnight after it's conception.

Uris went to Israel immediately afterwards on a magazine assignment and realized a life dream of seeing the Old City of Jerusalem and standing before the Western Wall.

Topaz, the de Vosjoli revelations, was finally published in 1967 and became an international shocker causing deep repercussions inside the French government.

(From the movie "Gunfight at the O.K. Corral," starring Kirk Douglas and Burt Lancaster. Screenplay by Leon Uris. Copyright © 1957 by Paramount Pictures Corp.)

(From the movie "Battle Cry," starring Aldo Ray, Tab Hunter, and James Whitmore. Copyright 1954 by Warner Brothers Pictures, Inc.)

After his final separation from Betty, Uris took up with Margery Edwards of Philadelphia, a beautiful woman in her mid-twenties. A graduate of Skidmore she came to Aspen after modelling in New York. Unable to marry because of the lengthy divorce proceedings, they were a constant and devoted couple.

In the spring of 1968, Uris worked in Hollywood on the adaptation of *Topaz* for Alfred Hitchcock. "I learned more about film from Hitch in a few months than the rest of my film career combined. But, as with Otto Preminger on *Exodus*, I was fired . . . not, mind you, over the writing but because neither of them could stand a mere screenwriter as their peer."

After leaving *Topaz* Uris went to work on "Ari" a musical version of *Exodus*, collaborating with an Aspen buddy, Walt Smith who did the music while he wrote the lyrics and the book.

In September of 1968, Uris married Margery in Beverly Hills. After accepting an invitation to a state banquet at the White House from President Johnson, they departed for England to research for a novel based on the Dering trial. It was during this period he first became aware of the troubles in Northern Ireland by nightly BBC broadcasts of the civil rights riots.

Returning to their Aspen home early in 1969, an enormous tragedy occurred. Margery committed suicide just five months after their marriage. On the surface, there seemed no ready reason. She was an extremely cheerful woman, much in love, with no obvious problems. Speculation has only been speculation. Most of what caused her action will remain a secret forever. "No one comes out of a thing like this whole," Uris

said. "No one can describe the pain. Once you decide you are going to survive you don't know how much of you is left and you can't really know till you face a test."

Three months after Margery's death, Uris met a transplanted Bostonian, Jill Peabody who co-directed a photography institute in Aspen. Although only twenty-two years of age, she showed great maturity in helping him through the period of suffering and a relationship grew from the backwash of tragedy. Uris realized that the key to his future existence was at the typewriter. Strengthened by Jill's presence and now associated with the dean of American editors, Ken McCormick, he took on the challenge of a novel although he was in extremely poor condition.

In February of 1970 he married Jill in a ceremony at the Algonquin Hotel, the famed literary hostelry in New York and an integral part of his life for two decades. For her twenty-third birthday in April, he completed *QB VII* and dedicated the book to his new bride.

During the interim (the end of '69) two young Broadway producers, Ken Gaston and Leonard Goldberg became interested in "Ari" (the musical). Uris and wife took off for a belated honeymoon and research trip for "Ari" travelling to Israel, Cyprus and Europe. They returned to the States in June, 1970 and moved into Manhattan. Joined by Walt Smith, they began preparation of the show.

Before rehearsals were slated to begin in the autumn, Uris and wife vacationed for a few days in Montauk where disaster struck in the form of a freak accident in a beach vehicle. Jill

(From the movie "The Angry Hills," starring Robert Mitchum. Released by Metro-Goldwyn-Mayer, 1959.)

suffered a fractured skull which required emergency brain surgery. Her life was saved by Dr. Robert Sengstaken, but in the following days both her life and the extent of the damage lay in the balance.

Showing "uncommon courage" she left her hospital bed to join Uris in Philadelphia where "Ari" had it's first tryout and began the long hard road back to health. Considering the type of injury, her full recovery is still looked upon as a medical miracle. "Jill and I are unusual in that we are two people who literally owe each other our lives," he says.

After tryouts in Philadelphia and Washington, "Ari" opened in New York and folded after twenty performances, Uris' first out and out flop. "All losers have a sorry story," says Uris, "and I'm no exception. The critics landed on me with both feet; it was the coldest January in memory and we were in the middle of a severe recession. 'Ari' may not have been 'My Fair Lady,' but it was an absolutely lovely show and would have found it's audience. It deserved a life of it's own."

Jill and Uris travelled to Israel shortly after "Ari" closed to start research on a planned novel on the Russian Jews. Depressed over Jill's health, the loss of "Ari" and not fully recovered from Margery's death he was in no condition to begin a new project.

Subsequently, he travelled around the world with his son, Mike (Jill was medically unable to accompany him past Istanbul) gathering more material, but in the end he abandoned the idea. "The Jews were starting to get out of Russia and millions of

words were already being written. I don't follow headlines," he says, "I like to make them." Afghanistan, Pakistan and New Zealand were part of the itinerary. Meanwhile Jill had gone to Ireland and her letters about the place and people greatly interested Uris.

Ireland and the recent troubles in the north continued to intrigue Uris. In 1972 the Urises went over to scout out the situation. After a week in both the Republic and Ulster, he was hooked. Jill, hoping to get some magazine work, took a set of photographs of such magnitude, she was offered a book contract.

Thus began the most arduous and demanding of all his research trips. Ireland meant that a new culture, new history, new religion, new people had to be learned. "As the plane came down for a landing after crossing the country and I was committed, I wondered to myself what the hell I was doing here."

Using a flat in Dublin as their base, the couple embarked on their undertaking from the scenic splendors of the west to street warfare in Belfast and Derry. Working under every possible condition, including gunfire, Jill grew daily into a great photographer while Uris hounded down his story in every corner of the land. Returning home after the better part of a year with a ton of research books, their projects went into motion.

A joint work, a photo-essay entitled, *Ireland, a Terrible Beauty* was published in December, 1975. The collaboration produced "perhaps the most definitive book of it's kind ever done on Ireland. It has received vast public acceptance as well as critical acclaim. The publishers had little faith in the photo-essay, there were innumerable hassles, and the book came out months late.'' Even after it was published it was poorly marketed and only took off in sales when the Urises hit the road and sold it personally to the Irish community.

In March, 1976, after two and a half years of writing, Uris' novel, *Trinity* was published and it stormed to the top of the best-seller lists where it stayed for over a hundred weeks. On July 4, 1976 on America's Bicentennial it was the number one novel in the country. It had the same impact with the Irish as *Exodus* had had with the Jews two decades earlier and brought him a legion of new readers. ''To find Ireland this late in my career was something I never expected,'' Uris reflects. Asked about the tremendous upgrade of quality in his writing, he answers, ''*Trinity* is a product of my life with Jill. She gave me peace and conditions I never had as a writer. She gave me help as an editor. I had to get better.''

Uris was determined to keep the film rights to *Trinity* and produce it as an independent, ''but the road has been hard and

the sea full of sharks.'' Nine years of failure have not dimmed his enthusiasm. He still retains the motion picture rights and feels that eventually a film, honest to the novel, will be produced.

In 1976 Uris became interested in the candidacy of Senator Henry Jackson for the presidency, and for several months left Aspen to campaign actively during the primaries, sometimes giving up to ten speeches a day. Uris considers it one of the most important and uplifting experiences of his life. To be part of a national election with all the emotionalism, patriotism, tension and nearness to such a potential seat of power gave him rewards he never expected from the experience ''although it was utterly backbreaking work in which one finds instant humility.''

In 1978 the Urises set out on another joint venture to the city of Jerusalem. While Uris assisted his wife with the same kind of help as in the previous work in Ireland, he also gathered material for a novel. Jill was left more on her own to photograph on a dawn to midnight schedule, often in dangerous

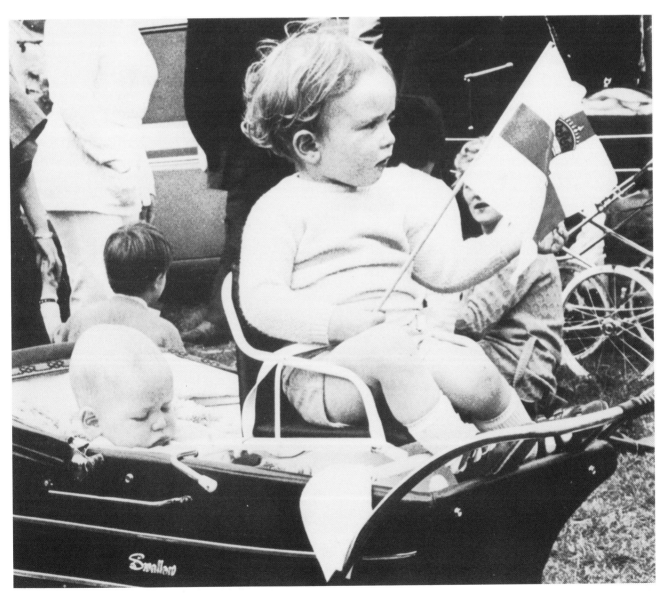

For a passing moment there was a family of man in Ulster. ■ (From *Ireland, a Terrible Beauty: The Story of Ireland Today* by Jill and Leon Uris. Photograph by Jill Uris.)

locations and situations. Their schedule ran them into exhaustion. R & R was chartering a small yacht and cruising the Greek Islands. Renewed, they finished their location work in Jerusalem by the end of the year and returned to Aspen. Uris worked on the 100,000-word text of the book for the next year and a half. The history of Jerusalem goes back over three thousand years and the author found himself involved in the most demanding task he ever undertook as a writer. The finished work, *Jerusalem, Song of Songs* contains nearly three hundred of Jill's photographs and was published by Doubleday in the autumn of 1981.

Uris' text is considered somewhat "off the wall," particularly his expose and accounts of Biblical history and the beginnings of Christianity and Islam. Despite some penetrating and unpopular conclusions, the text remains unchallenged by churchmen and scholars. The couple are devout Zionists and make a powerful statement for a united Jerusalem under Jewish rule. Success of the book was assured when the Literary Guild purchased it before publication. After publication the Urises made a seventeen city promotion tour. The tour undoubtedly helped sales, but rigors cooled them once and for all on the high profile life. "We loved the attention, the crowds and, pardon me, the glamour," Uris says, "but we could have traded it anywhere along the line for a quiet evening at home. We aren't actors or politicians or sports personalities who require constant public adulation. Writers and photographers are essentially loners who are apt to be uncomfortable at a rostrum or before TV cameras. When this tour ended, we both decided

to severely curtail future outside engagements. For us, it's a strain and the atmosphere on tour is not natural."

Meanwhile, research on the new novel was proving extremely difficult. During most of 1980 the Urises travelled to Central America, the Carribean and Israel, but he was unable to get a handle on his subject. During their travels they spent a month in the summer of 1980 in Ireland where Jill photographed enough for a new picture book, *Ireland Revisited,* which was published in 1982.

After publication of *Ireland Revisited,* they made yet another visit to Israel where Uris tried to nail down his new novel. He had always wanted to have a final say about the Middle-East. He [wrote the novel] through Arab eyes. "I tackled a heavy duty program to learn the Irish culture and history, but that was nothing beside trying to make sense out of the Arab and Moslem world." The deeper he probed, the more he realized that he was hitting both fertile and virgin ground as a novelist. He also knew that much of what he would say would be unpopular in certain liberal Jewish and Arab quarters. "The Arabs have a long, tormented history of tribal warfare, blood feuds, repression and ancient anti-semitism. I knew I would be called a racist by some but I felt even more strongly that the Western democracies were naive about the Arab world and even more naive about the danger they pose to our very existence. I decided to write it as I saw it with no apologies. It was the toughest decision I ever had to make as a writer. To know what I knew and to walk away from it would have been

Leon and Jill Uris.

a betrayal. I could never have called myself a writer again. Too damned many writers duck the hard stuff as it is.''

The writing and completion of the novel was a ''trip through hell,'' recalls Uris. ''I would get into my office at noon and by two I would be sleeping on my couch. I was in a state of depression most of the book because it's revelations tortured me. I also knew I had to tell the truth on every line and every page and I did tell the truth although the truth was ugly.''

More difficulties were in store for the Urises during the writing of *The Haj*, when they underwent a series of illnesses and personal crises. During the writing of *The Haj*, it was discovered that Uris had a large chest tumor lodged between his lung and aorta and had to go in for ''life and death'' surgery. The tumor proved benign but was the size of a baseball and required major and painful surgery to remove it.

One positive note about the experience Uris remembers, ''When you reach the age of fifty you realize that the end is closer than the beginning. I think everyone goes into a funk when he realizes he is not immortal. Yet, on the night before surgery I was out raising hell. I remember crossing a particular street when the reality occurred to me and I asked myself who in the world would I trade places with at this minute? The answer was . . . nobody. I was quite satisfied with my life and at peace and absolutely unafraid. It was a remarkable experience.''

During the same period one of his children contracted Hodgkins Disease and after a long agonizing fight, fully recovered. Jill had another miscarriage and Uris had knee surgery for the second time. ''All of this along with writing *The Haj* was like going through the seven lean years of the Bible.''

Jill became pregnant again and was in her seventh month when *The Haj* was published in the spring of 1984. The book was launched in Denver where a dozen Doubleday executives came in to join the week-long festivities. The launching did much to boost the image of Colorado as a place for writers.

Rachael Jackson Uris was born May 24, 1984 after an extremely difficult pregnancy. ''Having a baby at age sixty is the most wonderful bonus a man can have. When my first family was born I was struggling to make ends meet and the role of a father then was to wait in the hospital ante-room and drink black coffee. Being in at the birth, remaining in the hospital and being able to now spend every day with her is a gift I never expected. I don't know why the hell we waited so long. All of my fears were for nothing. Yes, we plan to have more children, God willing.''

The Haj became an instant best-seller, but as Uris suspected, there was a lot of uproar over it. ''Americans are reluctant to believe ill about other people. None the less, I had to tell this story regardless of the consequences although I'm sorry I had to write it.''

''I've received too much mail from too many people knowledgeable on the subject who have told me how right I was. Our military and state department people read *The Haj* as a text book before going to service in that part of the world. And every day that goes past in the Iran-Iraq War and in Lebanon and elsewhere serves to prove my words. Some critics and a few Arab groups harped and carped but no one . . . and I mean no one has yet to point out a single error in the book.''

With *The Haj* off Uris' chest, he made a long delayed film deal for *Mila 18* with Paramount Studios. After writing a screenplay, the project remains in development.

Uris also re-wrote his musical play, ''Ari'' making the new version suitable for regional theatre and cities outside the Broadway stage. He re-named the work ''Exodus, the Musical'' and has it on hold for a future production in Denver.

''Privacy has become a major problem. Most serious writers, and I don't mean the New York crowd, are retiring people and don't take to the spotlight. Finding new and interesting friends is difficult. Aspen provides a perfect sanctuary.'' The Urises are excellent ''sunny day'' skiers. Uris is a hacker at tennis and both enjoy long mountain walks with Rachael and their German shepherds. When the baby was coming Uris sold his motorcycles and sports cars and started ''acting his age.''

Uris is now planning his work so that he doesn't have to research out of the country and wants to write more ''from [my] desk.'' Uris identifies himself as an unabashed American and a Jew and politically a ''Roosevelt Democrat.'' Once a hard drinker with a reputation as a fast liver, Uris has become both domesticated and moderate in his life with Jill. As artists, they are apt to be on the liberal side of issues such as women's lib, gay rights, blacks, the pill, abortion, pot smoking and the like. Yet, Uris retains a great deal of the 'old Marine' posture in love of country, a stiff attitude toward the Russians and the ''old values''of family and loyalty.

His taste in music, literature and art are conventional. He distrusts a great deal of modern art and music and what he considers to be ''a phony establishment that has perpetrated mediocracy.'' John Steinbeck had the most influence on him as a youth. His closest friend and oldest associate is his lawyer and business manager of two decades, Herbert Schlosberg of Los Angeles.

To aspiring young writers, Uris says, ''If you spend the rest of your life digging sixteen tons of coal a day, it will be easier than becoming a novelist. An author requires more stamina and concentration and fanatical belief in himself than any artist. Unless you are into something like painting the Sistine Chapel, an artist's work is over in a week, a month, maybe a year. A novelist has to sustain it for five years sometimes. If an aspirant doesn't give himself twenty years to make it, he's kidding himself. In short, one must apply the seat of one's pants to the seat of the chair and write. There is no other way.''

HOBBIES AND OTHER INTERESTS: Skiing, bowling, and tennnis.

FOR MORE INFORMATION SEE: Library Journal, February 15, 1953; *Saturday Review*, April 25, 1953, September 27, 1958; *New York Herald Tribune Book Review*, September 28, 1958, August 16, 1959; *Christian Science Monitor*, December 4, 1958, November 16, 1967; *Miami Herald*, January 9, 1959; *Pittsburgh Press*, February 24, 1959; *Nation*, April 11, 1959; Leon Uris, ''The Most Heroic Story of Our Century,'' *Coronet*, November, 1960; *Los Angeles Times*, November 10, 1960; Martha Boaz, *The Quest for Truth*, Scarecrow, 1961; *Commentary*, October, 1961; *New York Review of Books*, April 16, 1964; *New York Times Book Review*, June 28, 1964, October 15, 1967, March 14, 1976, April 3, 1977; *Atlantic*, July, 1964; *Auschwitz in England*, Stein & Day, 1965; William Stevenson, *Strike Zion*, Bantam, 1967; *The Israel Honorarium*, Israeli Publishing Institute, 1968.

Barbara Thomas, ''Novelist Uris' Muse Is Peace,'' *Atlanta Journal*, August 16, 1974; Nellie Blagden, ''To Jill and Leon Uris 'Our Marriage Is Like the Welding of Two Generations,''' *People Weekly*, January 2, 1976; Stanton Peckham, ''Leon Uris,'' *Publishers Weekly*, March 29, 1976; Kathy

Hacker, "Author Uris—Always a Cause with a Capital 'C,'" *Philadelphia Bulletin*, March 31, 1976; *Chicago Tribune*, June 26, 1976; *Baltimore Sun*, October 31, 1976; *Authors in the News*, Volumes 1 and 2, Gale, 1976; *Contemporary Literary Criticism*, Volume VII, Gale, 1977; Michael Mulnix, "The Battle Cries of Leon Uris," *Writer's Digest*, November, 1977; *Author Speaks*, Bowker, 1977; *Washington Post*, May 2, 1978; *Boston Evening Globe*, May 8, 1978; *Jerusalem Post*, November, 1978; *Current Biography*, H. W. Wilson, 1979; *Denver Post*, October 24, 1982; *Electricity*, June, 1984.

WALSH, Ellen Stoll 1942-

PERSONAL: Born September 2, 1942, in Baltimore, Md.; daughter of Joseph Adolphus (a businessman) and Nell (Orum) Stoll; married David Albert Walsh (a professor), August 25, 1964; children: Benjamin Martin. *Education:* Maryland Institute of Art, B.F.A., 1964; attended University of Minnesota, 1966-69. *Home:* 29 West St., Fairport, N.Y. 14450.

CAREER: Writer and illustrator. Free-lance illustrator for Houghton Mifflin, 1984—. *Awards, honors:* Merit Award from Art Directors Club 59th Annual Exhibition, and Award of Excellence from American Institute of Graphic Arts, both 1980, both for *Brunus and the New Bear; Theodore All Grown Up* was chosen one of International Reading Association's Children's Choices, 1982; Ezra Jack Keats Fellow at the Kerlan Collection, University of Minnesota, 1986.

WRITINGS—Self-illustrated children's books: *Brunus and the New Bear*, Doubleday, 1979; *Theodore All Grown Up*, Doubleday, 1981.

ADAPTATIONS—Filmstrips: "Brunus and the New Bear," Imperial Educational Resources, 1980; "Theodore All Grown Up," narrated by Frances Sternhagen, music by Michael Barber, Spoken Arts, 1982.

SIDELIGHTS: "I was born in Baltimore and grew up in the midst of a very large family. There were ten children in all, and those of us who were older shared the responsibility of looking after the younger ones. Life was often chaotic with so many people around, but there were many wonderful moments. We were all very close then, and though we are now scattered around the country, we feel closer than ever.

"As a child I loved to read and draw and was very fond of sports. I enjoyed being by myself and would spend hours alone in the woods, often practicing to be an Indian. One of my first great disappointments was learning that no matter how hard I practiced being an Indian, I could never grow up to be one. I loved summer camp, and when I was too old to be a camper, I worked as counselor until I graduated from college.

"When I graduated I married David Walsh, and after a short year in Washington, D.C., we moved to Minneapolis. David worked for his Ph.D. at the University of Minnesota while I worked at the University of Minnesota Press and studied Latin. During our Minneapolis years we spent nine months travelling in the Mediterranean while David did research for his degree. We now live in the village of Fairport, near Rochester, New York, with our son, Ben.

"Since 1973 David, Ben and I have spent several weeks each summer participating in the archaeological excavation of the twelfth-century abbey of St. Mary's, Bordesley, in Worcestershire, England. We love England and our work at Bordesley, and we look forward to being there year after year.

ELLEN STOLL WALSH

"It never occurred to me to write children's books until my son Ben was three years old. Ben was curled up in my arms and we were reading *Alexander and the Wind-Up Mouse* by Leo Leonni. And all of a sudden I realized that I wanted to write and illustrate children's books more than anything else. I started immediately and from scratch. Since Alexander was a cut paper book, my first attempt was with cut paper. I experimented with a number of media and finally decided on colored inks. I was amazed to find out how difficult it is to write a good children's story. I quickly learned that no matter how nice the pictures are, if a story is not well thought out, an editor will not give it a second thought!

"The first step in making a picture book is finding a good idea for a story. This is probably the most difficult time for me. During this 'waiting period' I read a lot of other people's stories, talk and listen to children to find out what is important to them and probe my childhood and my son's for interesting material. I always try out lots of ideas before settling down to one that I think is not only important to write about, but will be visually exciting as well.

"Once I have a good idea for a story it grows so fast and in so many directions that I often have to remind myself to stop and remember what the original idea was all about. I find it almost impossible to confine myself to an outline, but write pages and pages trying to find the best way to tell my story.

"While I'm writing my stories I begin to imagine what the characters who move through them look like, and I want to see them on paper. Drawing my characters helps establish their personalities and makes them and my stories come alive for me. It is unwise but often difficult to resist beginning to illustrate a story before it is finished, especially since the story is still undergoing change and a favorite illustration may no longer be appropriate when the story is finished. If you have ever tried to work around a well turned sentence or paragraph in order to save it, even though it no longer fits in with what you are writing, then you can imagine how difficult it is to edit out a favorite illustration.

"It takes weeks of writing before a story will feel right to me, and after so much writing the story is invariably too long. I must always keep in mind what the real point of my story is as I cut and chop my favorite paragraphs and sentences. After weeks of work I hope to end up with a story that is no more than eight hundred words long and appears to have been written effortlessly.

"After my story is finished it will take me about nine months to complete the illustrations. The medium that I like best is colored inks which I apply with pen and brush after carefully drawing the design first in pencil. I will often use black and white photographs to establish the way a person stands or sits in my illustrations. Once the basic proportions of a figure are set down I put the photographs aside and work from nature and my imagination. I am currently working on two books in which the main characters are fully dressed bi-pedal piglets. Of course these piglets cannot be photographed or drawn from nature, so I have found it necessary (and very satisfying) to make clay models of them to work from."

Brunus and the New Bear and *Theodore All Grown Up* have been published in England and France.

HOBBIES AND OTHER INTERESTS: "Reading, especially eighteenth- and nineteenth-century English literature and English detective fiction. I love to travel, especially to places of historical interest with an emphasis on the middle ages. I enjoy archaeology, and in addition to our work at Bordesley Abbey, my husband and I have dug at an Anglo-Saxon church and at two Roman sites, one in Yugoslavia and one in England. I like classical music, especially Mozart and Beethoven, and enjoy listening to (and learning about) traditional folk music from the British Isles."

WELLS, Helen   1910-1986
(Francine Lewis)

PERSONAL: Name legally changed; born March 29, 1910, in Danville, Ill.; died February 10, 1986; daughter of Henry M. and Henrietta (a pianist; maiden name, Basch) Weinstock. *Education:* New York University, B.S. (with honors), 1934; New York University, School of Continuing Education, 1962; Programming and Systems Institute, New York, N.Y., diploma, 1969. *Politics:* Democrat. *Home:* New York, N.Y. *Agent:* McIntosh & Otis, Inc., 18 East 41st St., New York, N.Y.

CAREER: Full-time professional writer. Rockefeller Institute of InterAmerican Affairs, four-year volunteer escorting Latin-American visitors to U.S., New York, N.Y. Instructor at Institute of Children's Literature, Redding Ridge, Conn., beginning 1976. *Member:* Authors Guild, Mystery Writers of America (board of directors, 1970-77; national secretary, 1973-75), Writers Roundtable, National Arts Club, Women's National Book Association.

WRITINGS: The Girl in the White Coat, Messner, 1953; *Escape by Night: A Story of the Underground Railroad,* Winston, 1953; *A Flair for People,* Messner, 1955; *Adam Gimble, Pioneer Trader,* McKay, 1955; *Introducing Patti Lewis, Home Economist,* Messner, 1956; *A City for Jean,* Funk, 1956; *Barnum, Showman of America,* McKay, 1957; *Doctor Betty,* Messner, 1969.

HELEN WELLS

"Cherry Ames" series; all published by Grosset: *Cherry Ames, Student Nurse* (illustrated by Ralph Crosby Smith), 1943; . . . *Army Nurse,* 1944; . . . *Chief Nurse,* 1944; . . . *Senior Nurse,* 1944; . . . *Flight Nurse,* 1945; . . . *Private Duty Nurse,* 1946; . . . *Veterans' Nurse,* 1946; . . . *Visiting Nurse,* 1947; . . . *Cruise Nurse,* 1948; (with Julia Campbell Tatham) . . . *Boarding School Nurse,* 1956; . . . *Department Store Nurse,* 1956; . . . *Camp Nurse,* 1957; *Cherry Ames' Book of First Aid and Home Nursing,* 1959; *Cherry Ames at Hilton Hospital,* 1959; *Cherry Ames, Island Nurse,* 1960; . . . *Rural Nurse,* 1961; . . . *Staff Nurse,* 1962; . . . *Companion Nurse,* 1964; . . . *Jungle Nurse,* 1965; *Mystery in the Doctor's Office,* 1966; *Ski Nurse Mystery,* 1968; *Cherry Ames: The Mystery of Rogue's Cave,* 1972; . . . *The Case of the Dangerous Remedy,* 1978; . . . *The Case of the Forgetful Patient,* 1978.

"Vicki Barr" series; all published by Grosset: *Silver Wings for Vicki,* 1947; *Vicki Finds the Answer,* 1947; *The Hidden Valley Mystery,* 1948; *The Secret of Magnolia Manor,* 1949; *Peril over the Airport,* 1953; *The Search for the Missing Twin,* 1954; *The Mystery of the Vanishing Lady,* 1954; *The Ghost at the Waterfall,* 1956; *The Clue of the Gold Coin,* 1958; *The Silver Ring Mystery,* 1960; *The Clue of the Carved Ruby,* 1961; *The Mystery of Flight 908,* 1962; *The Brass Idol Mystery,* 1964.

Under pseudonym Francine Lewis; "Polly French" series, all published by A. Whitman: *Polly French of Whitford High,* 1952; . . . *Finds Out,* 1953; . . . *Takes Charge,* 1954; . . . *and the Surprising Stranger,* 1955.

Also author of radio shows and short stories for adults.

SIDELIGHTS: Born March 29, 1910, in Danville, Illinois. Her brother, Robert Wells, reflected on his life with his sister, Helen: "We were born in the very house our mother and all her siblings were born. Danville is pretty much the town that Cherry Ames lived in, and our house was her house. It was a big, comfortable, old-fashioned kind of house with lots of space surrounding it and a yard full of fruit trees. As soon as she was big enough, Helen learned to climb trees, and in the summer would bring a cushion up with her, settle into a comfortable branch, and spend the afternoon reading. She was always reading and writing; writing was as natural to her as breathing.

"One side of our house was covered with an enormous grape arbor. Helen made a whole world for herself there. She would throw elaborate tea parties for her dolls, for which Mother would prepare doll-sized sandwiches from oyster crackers—split in half, buttered, jellied. Sometimes I was invited to attend, but not always—I was just the little brother, after all! One summer, I recall, it must have been 1917, when I was about four years old, and had on a soldier suit I loved to wear, I was made to play the wounded soldier while Helen and her friend, Betty Lou Wilson, were the Red Cross nurses. It seemed I spent every afternoon lying in a doll's bed, under a tree in the front yard while the two administering angels stuffed me with malted milk tablets that tasted awful.

"Our mother was a very gifted pianist, in fact, *the pianist* of Danville. Whenever singers came to town on tour, it was always Mother who was called upon to accompany them. She was so skillful—if a singer changed key because the high notes were out of reach, Mother 'covered' flawlessly; she was so empathetic, she actually breathed with them. Both Helen and

"This," said Cherry, "is pretty wonderful!" ■ (Jacket illustration from *Cherry Ames, Department Store Nurse* by Helen Wells.)

Cherry leaned forward, stirred by the strange story. ■ (From *Cherry Ames, Visiting Nurse* by Helen Wells.)

I were taught by her from an early age. I eventually lost interest, but my sister had talent and continued.

"Our father was born and raised in Vienna, the youngest son in a large, wealthy family. His mother died when he was small, and his father remarried. He was told by his father that he would never be obliged to work, that he would become a gentleman scholar instead. In spirit, our father remained a gentleman scholar. However, as our grandfather died when our father was nine and the relatives took all the money, he did indeed have to work. He came to the States and eventually became associated with National Cash Register. When Helen was about seven, Dad was offered a New York territory. He was very keen on this, for though he liked Danville, he wanted us to have broader educational and cultural opportunities.

"My sister loved New York from the moment we arrived. She was an honor student and skipped a couple of grades, as I recall. She won the Gottheil Medal from Temple Emanu-El, where she was confirmed. My sister also took piano lessons from a wonderful English woman who had a studio at Carnegie Hall. Every year there was an ambitious recital in which my sister and mother were frequently featured playing duets. Helen was always given the more brilliant part. These recitals were big, splendid occasions—they spent months preparing, and it showed.

"Most every summer we returned to Danville to visit with our relatives. Our uncle was another important influence for us.

He had no children of his own, and lavished quite a lot of attention on us. He was a very wise man, and very scrupulous in the equality of his treatment of Helen and me, but always careful not to appear in competition with our father. Whereas our father was interested in our moral, spiritual and artistic welfare, our uncle taught us to appreciate America. Dad's influence was decidedly European and Jewish (both our parents were Jews, and we were raised with a consciousness of that tradition), whereas our uncle's ancestors fought for the States during the American Revolution. He was a direct descendant of George Washington's mother. He would take us driving on Saturday evenings when the farmers came to town, and sometimes take us to Feldkamp's for ice cream sodas.

"Helen was barely sixteen when she was graduated from high school, too young, dad thought, to go on to college. Extension courses at Columbia were permitted, however. She attended the Art Students League as well, where her creative talents did not go without notice or praise.

"Two years later, Helen enrolled in New York University, majoring in philosophy with a minor in sociology and psychology. Again she was an honor student." Wells was the first woman editor of *The Arch*, the campus literary magazine.

"She worked as a social worker after graduation in 1934. Her supervisor was stunned by a hair-raising vivid report of a slum

In the next few days, the silent flier improved more than Cherry had dared hope. ■ (From *Cherry Ames, Chief Nurse* by Helen Wells.)

Illustration from the first of the Cherry Ames series. ■ (Jacket illustration by Ralph Crosby Smith from *Cherry Ames, Student Nurse* by Helen Wells.)

family Helen had written, and recognized immediately that she was a writer. She introduced her to an editor, who helped my sister break into magazine writing. But Helen kept her job as social worker for four or five more years. Although she took her job very seriously—this was the Depression and times were hard for all of us—her primary interest was writing. She spent whatever free time she had at her desk, creating, imagining. One year, one of her short stories won a thousand-dollar prize—a fortune in those days. She and her best friend had a wonderful time with the money, with no regrets.

"A lifelong Democrat, she was also involved in politics. The Spanish Civil War was a cause that meant a lot to her, and one day at a rally she put a nice little diamond ring she was wearing into the contribution basket. Whether that ring ever made it to the Loyalists is another question, but that's the way Helen was. There's a biblical saying, 'If a stranger asks for your shirt, give him your coat.'

"During the late 1930s, she wrote a very ambitious novel about social issues and their process of resolution—a fictionalized account of the late Depression. She was exploring the ways in which young people responded to existing problems and tried to generate solutions. I don't know if she ever tried to publish that book. She threw most of it away, which I think was a great shame, because even now, parts of it come back to me, and very powerfully.

"Helen was of course best known for the 'Cherry Ames' and 'Vicki Barr' mystery/adventure series. These books are quite valuable now, and Florida State University will house the two series, as well as manuscripts and certain papers. A private collector had also come forward with a bid, but I wanted these materials to be available to the public. Her readers meant so much to her. She received fan mail literally by the pound!

"Helen was scrupulous about research, and spent a lot of time in hospitals talking with nurses. She even traveled to specialized facilities. She'd stop at nothing to get the information she needed. She worked very, very hard. She saw so much more than the rest of us. Her descriptions of a leaf, a dress, an opera, a bird, were incredibly passionate and detailed. She experienced things very deeply, and then made a gift of those experiences.

"Beginning in 1958, she began to travel extensively. Most every year a major trip was undertaken. She was especially drawn to Toledo, Spain, birthplace of our paternal grandmother. She went back to Spain several times and once had an itinerary of holy places. She spoke Spanish, having learned it in high school. She also traveled to Italy, Scandinavia, the British Isles, Israel, Egypt, Austria, Germany, Russia, Portugal, Mexico, and Brazil. She 'covered' the States, especially appreciating the Pacific Northwest. She loved Brazil, and often spoke of retiring there.

"Helen had great style, gave resplendent parties, and had lots of friends. She subscribed to the Metropolitan Opera and the Philharmonic. Sometimes she would drag me along, but I must admit, I once slept through Mahler! I preferred to hear Helen's vivid descriptions of what she had heard and seen. She also loved the theatre, not so much Broadway, but downtown off the beaten track.

"Many of her friends were writers. She was active in the Mystery Writers of America, the Writers Roundtable and the Institute of Children's Literature where she was a teacher to aspiring children's writers. The 1986 Juvenile Series Writers Conference, held in Corning, New York, was dedicated to my sister's memory."

Phyllis Whitney, a member of the Mystery Writers of America, remembered her colleague as "a very lovely and soft-spoken person. Everyone remarked her gentleness—she was terribly, terribly gentle. I suspect she had very deep emotions, but didn't often let them out. She could feel very strongly about certain causes—one of which was the creation of a writers' union—to the point almost of losing herself. Helen Wells was one of the most generous people I have ever known. Our writing community will miss her greatly."

The "Cherry Ames" and "Vicki Barr" series have also been published in numerous countries, including Canada, Britain, Norway, Sweden, Denmark, Finland, Iceland, Japan, France, Italy, Holland, and Bolivia.

—Based on an interview by Marguerite Feitlowitz

HOBBIES AND OTHER INTERESTS: "Fascinated by electronic data processing—have training in computer programming—because machine language is a new and everyday language."

FOR MORE INFORMATION SEE: Martha E. Ward and Dorothy A. Marquardt, *Authors of Books for Young People,* 2nd edition, Scarecrow, 1971. Obituaries: *New York Times,* February 13, 1986.

WHEELER, Cindy 1955-

PERSONAL: Born May 17, 1955, in Montgomery, Ala.; daughter of Kenneth Bradford (a school supervisor) and Joanne (a teacher; maiden name, Dingus) Wheeler; married Robert Patrick Lee (in publishing), July 26, 1980; children: Sally Virginia. *Education:* Auburn University, B.F.A., 1977; graduate study at School of Visual Arts, 1980. *Religion:* Episcopalian. *Home and office:* Box 157, Glynwood Farm, Cold Spring, N.Y. 10516.

CAREER: Zibart's Bookstore, Nashville, Tenn., children's book buyer and sales clerk, 1977-78; Alfred A. Knopf (publishers), New York, N.Y., editorial secretary in juvenile department, 1977-80; free-lance illustrator and author, 1980—; Lothrop, Lee & Shepard, New York, assistant to art director, 1984-85. *Awards, honors: Rose* was exhibited at the Bologna International Children's Book Fair, 1985; Alabama Author's Award from the Alabama Library Association, 1985, for *Marmalade's Christmas Present.*

WRITINGS: Rose (self-illustrated), Knopf, 1985; *Spring Is Here!* (coloring book), Happy House, 1986; *Merry Christmas, Little Mouse* (coloring book; illustrated by Jan Brett), Happy House, 1986; *A Day on the Farm* (coloring book), Happy House,

CINDY WHEELER

Marmalade sees Robin. ■ (From *A Good Day, A Good Night* by Cindy Wheeler. Illustrated by the author.)

1987; *A New House for Little Mouse* (picture book; illustrated by Stella Ormai), Happy House, 1987.

"Marmalade" series; all self-illustrated; all published by Knopf, except as indicated: *A Good Day, A Good Night* (Junior Literary Guild selection), Lippincott, 1980; *Marmalade's Snowy Day*, 1982; . . . *Yellow Leaf*, 1982; . . . *Nap*, 1983; . . . *Picnic*, 1983; . . . *Christmas Present* (Junior Literary Guild selection), 1984.

Illustrator: Charlotte Zolotow, *One Step, Two*, Lothrop, revised edition, 1981; Random House editors, *The Scaredy Cats and the Haunted House*, Random House, 1982; Susan Talanda, *Dad Told Me Not To*, Carnival Press, 1983; Carol A. Marron, *Someone Just Like Me*, Carnival Press, 1983; Alice Schertle, *That Olive!*, Lothrop, 1986.

SIDELIGHTS: "Decorative arts and crafts were a family tradition. My grandfather was a very gifted man, having the energy and know-how to take on any challenging project. He has made most of my furniture—a rocking chair, tables, lamps, a dresser—as well as dulcimers, grandfather clocks, looms, and the list goes on and on. He would derive great pleasure from taking something discarded and making it into something useful, and often unusual. Any space left in the house was filled with my father's creations. He is a whittler of anything from totem poles to African masks. A big locust log was always propped up on wooden blocks in the driveway, ready to be given a whole new life as a bear or strange sort of bird, or better yet, a little of everything! There were always many projects going on around the house, and it had a strong influence in developing my creativity.

"Equally important to this setting is the fact that many members of my family, including my parents, are teachers. When my father is not whittling, he is supervising the Hendersen County Schools' physical education programs. My mother taught English and history at a junior high and worked as an assistant director for a girls' summer camp for many years. As a result, I spent fifteen summers of my life going to camp!

"My aunt, Patty Dingus, who lived near my grandparents in Dungannon, Virginia, also taught school. She has been instrumental in supplying me with ideas and projects for children's books. *A Good Day, A Good Night* was one of the first of these projects, in which we collaborated while I was in high school. As an art student at Auburn University I was encouraged to revise *A Good Day, A Good Night* as an illustration seminar by my professor and dear friend, Mr. Guy Bost. While crediting people, I realize I must also mention Meow Meow, our fourteen-year-old cat, whose habit of sleeping in the bird feeder inspired the cover for *A Good Day, A Good Night*."

Wheeler describes Marmalade, the main character in *A Good Day, A Good Night* as "very mischievous, and sort of an old curmudgeon. He's just a cat, a typical cat who never wants to do anything he's supposed to and has his own way of handling things." [Sara Lambert, "Accent: Cindy Wheeler and Marmalade the Cat . . .," *Times News* (Hendersonville, N.C.), 1982.[1]]

In 1978 Wheeler moved to New York where she quickly sold her story of Marmalade. "When I told [my parents] I was going to move to New York, they were skeptical, like any good parents should be. But they were very supportive and encouraging, once they got used to the idea."[1]

Wheeler lives with her husband and daughter on a farm in Cold Spring, New York. Her two cats in part led to her book

Marmalade's Christmas Present. "Last fall I decided that my very spoiled, over-fed, over-loved angel of a black cat—Kitty Rat—needed a companion, since I seemed to be spending more and more time away from home. I had recently taken a studio in the town of Cold Spring to work in. A neighbor's cat had just produced a litter of beautiful white kittens. I was charmed beyond my will power and one of the little rascals came home with me. Little did I know that it would be at least six months until we could resume any semblance to normalcy in our life from the moment the little pink-eared guy seduced me. About that time, my editor was asking for a Christmas Marmalade book. Searching for an idea, I realized how completely consumed I had become in the adjustment of my new little kitten to my betrayed and broken-hearted black cat. The new book and the new cat became naturally entwined and before I knew it, *Marmalade's Christmas Present* had taken shape.

". . . Seven months [after] the arrival of Rabbit (Sassafras in the book), my husband and I . . . finally made the adjustment, and though Kitty Rat wouldn't admit it for a minute, I'm sure I catch a little wink passing between those two cats sometimes as I'm turning my back."

"Writing and illustrating books for children gives me a chance to stay in touch with some of the first emotions I experienced as a child. With each of my books I try to share, simply and clearly, those feelings the way I remember them—uncomplicated, unsuspicious, happiness in its purest and most all-encompassing form.

"I now have a one-year-old baby girl, Sally Virginia, who is busy supplying me with new ideas for more books. I'm working out a new series which will be underway soon. Meanwhile, I am cultivating the perfect 'test market!'"

HOBBIES AND OTHER INTERESTS: Gardening, knitting, swimming, and being out of doors.

FOR MORE INFORMATION SEE: Sara Lambert, "Accent: Cindy Wheeler and Marmalade the Cat . . .," *Times News* (Hendersonville, N.C.), 1982.

WILKIN, Eloise (Burns) 1904-

PERSONAL: Born March 30, 1904, in Rochester, N.Y.; married; children: four. *Education:* Attended Rochester Institute of Technology. *Home:* 504 Suburban Ct., Rochester, N.Y. 14620.

CAREER: Free-lance artist and illustrator. *Awards, honors:* New York *Herald Tribune*'s Spring Book Festival Award, younger honor, 1940, for *A Good House for Mother*, middle-honor, 1950, for *The Tune Is in the Tree;* "Lilybet" (lithograph) won the Ewald Eisenhardt Memorial Merit Award for excellence in printmaking, 1944; *The Boy with a Drum* was chosen one of Child Study Association of America's Children's Books of the Year, 1969, and *I Hear: Sounds in a Child's World*, 1971. *Exhibitions:* Hartnett Gallery, Rochester, N.Y., 1982.

WRITINGS—All for children; all self-illustrated: *Song of Praise*, American Heritage Press, 1970; *The Baby Book*, Golden Press, 1973; *Baby's Mother Goose*, Golden Press, 1975; *Baby's Christmas*, Random House, 1980; *How Big Is Baby?*, Golden Press, 1980; *Baby Listens*, Golden Press, 1981; *Baby Looks*, Golden Press, 1981; *Four Baby's First Golden Books*, Golden Press, 1981; *The Little Book*, Golden Press, 1981; *My Good-*

Eloise Wilkin (left) with sister, Esther, at an autographing session.

night Book, Golden Press, 1981; *Rock-A-Bye Baby: Nursery Songs and Cradle Games,* Random House, 1981; *My Good Morning Book,* Golden Books, 1983; *Baby's Bedtime,* Grosset, 1985; *Baby's House,* Grosset, 1985; *Baby's Playground,* Grosset, 1985; *Baby's Toys,* Grosset, 1985; *The Eloise Wilkin Treasury,* Golden Books, 1985.

Illustrator; all for children: Alice Dalgliesh, *The Choosing Book,* Macmillan, 1932; Esther Burns (pseudonym of Esther Wilkin), *Mrs. Peregrine and the Yak,* Holt, 1938; Amy W. Stone, *Going-on-Nine,* Lothrop, 1939; E. Burns, *Mrs. Peregrine at the Fair,* Messner, 1939; Irmengarde Eberle, *A Good House for a Mouse,* Messner, 1940; Myra R. Richardson, *Sheep Wagon Family,* R. M. McBride, 1941; Frances A. Bacon, *Kitty Come Down,* Oxford University Press, 1944; Elizabeth Honness, *The Great Gold Piece Mystery,* Oxford University Press, 1944, Lippincott, 1960; Lucy Sprague Mitchell, *The New House in the Forest,* Simon & Schuster, 1946; Gertrude Crampton, *Noises and Mr. Flibberty-Jib,* Simon & Schuster, 1947; L. S. Mitchell, *Fix it, Please!,* Simon & Schuster, 1947; Kathryn Jackson and Byron Jackson, *Busy Timmy,* Simon & Schuster, 1948, reissued, Grosset, 1962; Martha Gwinn Kiser, *Rainbow for Me,* Random House, 1948; Edith Osswald, *Come Play House,* Simon & Schuster, 1948, reissued, Golden Press, 1965; Ruth Shane and Harold Shane, *The New Baby,* Simon & Schuster, 1948, reissued, Golden Press, 1979; M. G. Kiser, *Sunshine for Merrily,* Random House, 1949; Milton I. Levine and Jean H. Seligmann, *A Baby Is Born: The Story of How Life Begins,* Simon & Schuster, 1949; Mary K. Reely, *Seatmates,* F. Watts, 1949; *Santa's Workshop,* Capitol, 1949; Jane Watson, *Good Morning and Good Night,* Simon & Schuster, 1949; Louise P. Woodcock, *Guess Who Lives Here,* Simon & Schuster, 1949.

The Busy ABC, Whitman Publishing, 1950; Maud Hart Lovelace, *The Tune Is in the Tree,* Crowell, 1950; Jane Werner (pseudonym of Jane Werner Watson), *The Christmas Story,*

Simon & Schuster, 1952; *Prayers for Children,* Simon & Schuster, 1952, reprinted, Golden Press, 1972; Ruth J. Buntain, *The Birthday Story,* Holiday House, 1953; Patsy Scarry, *My Kitten,* Simon & Schuster, 1953; P. Scarry, *My Teddy Bear,* Simon & Schuster, 1953; L. Woodcock, *Wiggles,* Simon & Schuster, 1953; Jakob Grimm and Wilhelm Grimm, *Hansel and Gretel,* Simon & Schuster, 1954, reissued, Golden Press, 1976; J. Werner, reteller, *First Bible Stories,* Simon & Schuster, 1954; L. Woodcock, *Hi Ho! Three in a Row,* Simon & Schuster, 1954; Clement C. Moore, *The Night before Christmas,* Simon & Schuster, 1955; P. Scarry, *My Puppy,* Simon & Schuster, 1955; R. Shane and H. Shane, *The Twins: The Story of Two Little Girls Who Look Alike,* Simon & Schuster, 1955; P. Scarry, *My Baby Brother,* Simon & Schuster, 1956; J. Watson, *My Little Golden Book about God,* Simon & Schuster, 1956; P. Scarry, *My Snuggly Bunny,* Simon & Schuster, 1956; J. Watson, *My First Book about God,* Simon & Schuster, 1957; J. Watson, *Wonders of Nature,* Simon & Schuster, 1957, published as *Wonders of Nature: A Child's First Book about Our Wonderful World,* 1958, revised edition published as *My Big Book of the Outdoors,* Golden Books, 1983; J. Watson, *A Catholic Child's Book about God,* Simon & Schuster, 1958, J. Watson, *A Giant Little Golden Book of Birds,* Simon & Schuster, 1958, reissued, Golden Press, 1977; J. Watson, *This World of Ours,* Golden Press, 1959.

P. Scarry, *My Pets* (contains *My Puppy, My Kitten,* and *My Snuggly Bunny*), Golden Press, 1960; *The Lord's Prayer,* commentary by Eloise Wilkin, Golden Press, 1961; Clara Cassidy, *We Like Kindergarten,* Golden Press, 1965, reissued, 1977; Bertha M. Parker, *The Wonders of the Season,* Golden Press, 1966, new edition, published as *My Big Book of Seasons,* Golden Books, 1983; Esther Wilkin, *Play with Me,* Golden Press, 1967; Patricia M. Zens, *The Thank You Book,* Golden Press, 1967; Esther Wilkin, *So Big,* Golden Press, 1968, reissued, 1976; Sheryl Horvath, *The Little Book,* Golden Press, 1969.

David L. Harrison, *The Boy with a Drum*, Golden Press, 1971; Lucille Ogle and Tina Thoburn, *I Hear: Sounds in a Child's World*, American Heritage Press, 1971; Esther Wilkin, selector, *The Golden Treasury of Prayers for Boys and Girls*, Golden Press, 1975; Esther Wilkin, *To You from Me*, Golden Press, 1977; Ruthanna Long, adapter, *The Once-upon-a-Time Scratch and Sniff Book*, Golden Press, 1978; *Ladybuy, Ladybug, and Other Nursery Rhymes*, Random House, 1979; *Mother Goose Nursery Rhymes*, Random House, 1979.

Esther Wilkin, *Little Prayers*, Golden Books, 1980; Joan Esley, *The Visit*, Rand McNally, 1980; Josette Frank, editor, *Poems to Read to the Very Young*, Random House, 1982; J. W. Watson, *Good Night*, Golden Press, 1983; *Prayers for a Small Child*, Random House, 1984; Jean Monrad, *How Many Kisses Good Night*, Random House, 1986. Also illustrator of J. Cushman's *We Help Mommy*, Western Publishing, and *Six Little Golden Books*, Golden Press.

SIDELIGHTS: As a child in New York City, Wilkin won the Wanamaker Award for her drawing of a Pilgrim returning home. That was the impetus needed to push her artistic talents to the forefront. Her family returned to Rochester, New York, the place of her birth, and quite naturally sent their talented daugh-

(From "Spring Rain" by Marchette Chute in *Poems to Read to the Very Young*, selected by Josette Frank. Illustrated by Eloise Wilkin.)

(From *My Goodnight Book* by Eloise Wilkin. Illustrated by the author.)

ter to Mechanics Institute, the forerunner of the Rochester Institute of Technology to study art. "After completing the illustration course at the Institute of Technology in Rochester, I commenced free-lancing." [Bertha Mahony Miller and others, compilers, *Illustrators of Children's Books: 1744-1945*, Horn Book, 1947.[1]]

"After a year [I] went to New York with a portfolio bigger than I was."[1]

"I just went to the library and got a list of all the publishers. In those days, you could meet the top art directors (just by walking into the office). It was easier than it is now." [Sue Oppenheimer, "Wilkin: Still Creating Memorable Pictures," *Brighton-Pittsford Post*, July 28, 1982.[2]]

"My first morning [in New York] I went into the Century Company, came back with a book to illustrate, and wired home to my family that I was made!"[1] She soon found herself illustrating for publishers Scribner, Little, Brown, Rand McNally, Random House, and Macmillan, as well.

In 1944, Wilkin was granted an exclusive contract with Golden Press, where she illustrated an average of one book every three months. "I have found it a most satisfying experience because

of the opportunity of working in color and because of the subject matter—a familiar one to me, the small child in the daily rounds of his activities."[1]

Wilkin married and packed away her watercolors for ten years to rear her growing family and to manage the household. The family lived in a house overlooking Canandaigua Lake. "One of my nicest memories is seeing, through a huge, high window, the moon coming up, reflecting on the lake, and throwing shadows from the trees in front of the house. . . . I'm great on moonlight scenes and scenes through windows, but I never think I do justice to them." [Selma Wakem Wilson, "Introducing . . . Eloise Wilkins" (*sic*), *Upstate New York*, January 13, 1980.[3]]

She resumed her career with the illustrations for *Mrs. Peregrine and the Yak* written by her sister, which was a prize winner in the Julia Ellsworth Ford Foundation Contest. She illustrated several of her sister's books. Both women share the same married surname, "sisters married brothers," explained the artist. [Martha Jane Hines, "Artist Often Models Tots After Her Own Grandchildren," *The Daily Herald* (Columbia, Tennessee), June 12, 1983.[4]]

Most of Wilkin's work is executed in crayon or watercolor outlined in ink. "A lithograph is rather cumbersome."[2] The

(From *Baby's Christmas* by Eloise Wilkin. Illustrated by the author.)

imported pens she used for many years to draw fine lines are no longer available. "I can't do hair the way I like it. The lines are not as fine as they were. That's one way you can tell my earlier work."[4]

Characteristic qualities of her work are Victorian interiors, plump children, and patterns of small flowers, checkers, plaids, and stripes. "I have a fascination with the period around the turn of the century; their interiors were so ugly. . . . At the same time, they have a homeyness that's appealing."[2]

Her fascination with houses and furnishings is reflected in her illustrations. She carefully researches with such sources as the 1901 *Sears and Roebuck Catalogue* and *The Victorian Home in America* to render her lifelike antique purses, candelabra, opera glasses, wallpaper design, and wicker chairs. Her illustrations carry a local flavor as well. "My things definitely are Rochester. The houses I do, the seasons—it's in my bones."[3]

The artist sees in her grandchildren a wealth of opportunity by using them as models for her book characters. She relies on a Polaroid camera to capture their action because they "wouldn't sit still long enough to be sketched."[3] She incorporates their artwork into her artwork as well. The rear view of a fat cat, crayoned by grandson John, hangs on the door of her apartment, and on the wall in a scene from one of her books.

Her grandchildren encouraged her to design a doll. Several years of sculpting a model into a life-like newborn culminated in a sale of "Baby Dear" to Vogue Doll Company in 1960. In F.A.O. Schwarz toy store "Baby Dear" caught the eye of

Nikita Khrushchev who bought thirteen dolls to take home to Russia. Several other doll creations followed.

Another of Wilkin's interests is "making doll houses for my granddaughters. I'm sending on (a picture of) the latest one for Elizabeth . . . who lives in England. It is a replica of our home in Canandaigua and so successful my son asked me where I got the picture of our living room when I showed it to him."[4] In one unique touch, she created a tiny dining room mural which she described as a "panoramic view of the farm (with) dogs, cats, pony, horse, ducks and family all in it."[4]

Wilkins reflected on her lengthy career as a book illustrator, which now includes almost a hundred books: "I don't like the deadlines, but I love my work. When I'm doing a picture, I enter into it myself and stay 'til I'm done."[3]

FOR MORE INFORMATION SEE: Bertha Mahony and others, compilers, *Illustrators of Children's Books: 1744-1945,* Horn Book, 1947; B. Mahony and others, compilers, *Illustrators of Children's Books: 1946-1956,* Horn Book, 1958; Martha E. Ward and Dorothy A. Marquardt, *Illustrators of Books for Young People,* Scarecrow, 1975; *Upstate New York,* January 13, 1980; *Brighton-Pittsford Post,* July 28, 1982; *The Daily Herald* (Columbia, Tennessee), June 12, 1983.

For God's sake give me the young man who has brains enough to make a fool of himself!

—Robert Louis Stevenson

YORINKS, Arthur   1953-
(Alan Yaffe)

PERSONAL: Born August 21, 1953, in Roslyn, N.Y.; son of Alexander (a mechanical engineer) and Shirley (Kron) Yorinks. *Education:* Attended New School for Social Research and Hofstra New College, 1971. *Home:* 181 Thompson St., New York, N.Y. 10012. *Agent:* Gloria Loomis, Watkins-Loomis Agency, 150 East 35th St., New York, N.Y. 10016.

CAREER: Writer. Cornell University, Ithaca, N.Y., instructor in theatre arts, 1972-79. Writer, teacher, and performer at American Mime Theatre, 1972-79. Founder of Moving Theatre, 1979; associate director of New Works Project in New York, N.Y. *Awards, honors: School Library Journal* named *Louis the Fish* one of the best books of 1980; Editor's Choice from *Booklist,* 1984, for *It Happened in Pinsk;* author of Caldecott Medal Book *Hey, Al,* 1987.

WRITINGS—Juveniles: Sid and Sol (illustrated by Richard Egielski), Farrar, Straus, 1977; (under pseudonym Alan Yaffe) *The Magic Meatballs* (illustrated by Karen B. Anderson), Dial, 1979; *Louis the Fish* (illustrated by R. Egielski), Farrar, Straus, 1980; *It Happened in Pinsk,* (illustrated by R. Egielski), Farrar, Straus, 1983; *Hey, Al* (illustrated by R. Egielski), Farrar, Straus. 1986.

Plays: "Six" (one-act), first produced in New York City at Hunter College Playhouse, November, 1973; "The Horse" (one-act), first produced in New York City at Cornelia Street Cafe, November, 1978; "Crackers" (one-act), first produced in New York City at Theatre of the Open Eye, June, 1979; "The King" (one-act), first produced in New York City at South Street Theatre, July, 1980; "Kissers" (one-act), first produced in New York City at South Street Theatre, July, 1980; "Piece for a Small Cafe" (one-act), first produced in New York City at Cornelia Street Cafe, February, 1981; "Piece

Richard Egielski and Arthur Yorinks.

for a Larger Cafe'' (one-act), first produced in New York City at Cornelia Street Cafe, April, 1982; ''Leipziger Kerzenspiel'' (opera), first produced in Mt. Holyoke at Mt. Holyoke College, 1984; ''The Juniper Tree'' (opera; first produced at the American Repertory Theater in Cambridge, Mass., 1985), Dunvagen Music, 1985.

ADAPTATIONS: (Author of screenplay) ''Sid and Sol,'' Four Penny Productions, 1982; ''Louis the Fish,'' Reading Rainbow, PBS-TV, 1983; ''Louis the Fish'' and ''Sid and Sol'' have both been adapted into a cassette with hardcover book by Random House.

WORK IN PROGRESS: Max Strickman, a novel for young adults; ''*Bravo Minski*'', a picture book about a scientist; opera version of *It Happened in Pinsk* for the Vineyard Theatre; another opera with Philip Glass based on an Edgar Allan Poe story.

SIDELIGHTS: ''I spent a lot of time alone as a kid, because my brother and sister were considerably older than I, and too as a writer, I spend a lot of time working by myself in a tiny room in the late hours of the night. Because of this, perhaps to offset it, in all of my artistic life I have also collaborated with visual artists, a theatre company, and musicians.

''It seems I've always been involved in some form of the arts. At six I began formal classical piano training with Robert Bedford, which lasted for seven years. A young perfectionist, Bedford was the earliest professional influence on me. I learned a great deal of what it means to be an artist from him. My mother was another influence. Trained as a fashion illustrator, she would pass time painting and drawing at the kitchen table where I watched, copied, and tried my hand. While she worked she loved to tell me her dreams. The combination was very strange—looking at her pictures, listening to her voice, taking in her dreams.

Al, a nice man, a quiet man, a janitor, lived in one room on the West Side with his faithful dog, Eddie. ■ (From *Hey, Al* by Arthur Yorinks. Illustrated by Richard Egielski.)

The world didn't know what to do. "We have to stop this trembling," they complained. ■ (From *Sid and Sol* by Arthur Yorinks. Illustrated by Richard Egielski.)

''I think it was through those early years of watching and drawing with my mother that pictures became very important to me.

''Another important collaborator early on was Michael De-Paolo, an illustrator friend whom I've known since sixth grade. Together as teenagers we traveled to Manhattan to see buildings, subways, to visit galleries, museums—a never-satisfied thirst for art began then. We'd walk around and I'd tell him stories, point things out, prodding him, saying 'Look, *that* would make a great painting!' and then tell him exactly how to go about it—the *antithesis* of a good collaboration! In junior high school, we made comic books together; I wrote the stories, and Michael did the illustrations.

''I didn't come across picture books until high school. Discovering Tomi Ungerer, William Steig, particularly Maurice Sendak, was a turning point. I was already a young adult and I saw clearly that their books weren't just kids books. They were for everyone. They had such depth and excitement and had everything I was interested in—drama, pictures, rhythm, music.

''At the age of sixteen, I summoned all the courage I had and did something that was to have an *enormous* effect on my life and work: I showed up at Maurice Sendak's door unannounced. Maurice was then living in Manhattan. It was presumptuous of me, bordering on obnoxious, but my way of learning was always to talk to people I considered among the best at what they did. I was with a friend and felt so nervous about my plan that I didn't tell him where we were headed until we reached the Village. The more he said, 'You're nuts,' the more I had to do it. I walked up to Maurice's door, and as I was about to ring the bell, I lost my nerve. Just as I turned to leave, the door opened and a man (Sendak? I wasn't even certain it was him) said, 'Can I help you?'

'''Would you like to see some of my stories?' I blurted out.

'''Well,' he said in a slightly flustered voice, 'send them to me.'

''I had them with me and I simply handed him my bundle. To have my work read and commented on by Maurice Sendak was a dream come true. We have been friends now for over fifteen years. Maurice has been a big help and a constant inspiration. I still think he is the contemporary standard for picture books and children's literature in general.

''Graduating high school a year early and not having any desire to go on to college, I explored many roads. I became involved in theater by studying ballet and acting and ended up at the American Mime Theatre. For ten years I wrote plays, performed and taught with the theatre company. Looking back, this was excellent training for picture books. In a mime play there is no dialogue. The spectacle is all images. Plot, relationships, passage of time are all communicated through action and the 'pictures' made by the performers. In a real sense, the actors *are* the pictures. The scripts I wrote were blocks of prose—this happens, then this happens, then this. I had to deal with character, situation, place and narrative without describing anything. This, as I was to learn, was pretty much the best way to write picture books.

''During that time, I was also writing and peddling my stories. I had sold a manuscript to a publisher, but as yet they hadn't found an illustrator, a situation which was to drag on for years before it fell apart altogether. I was miserable, as this was my first book, and it was sitting there, crying out for pictures. One day I was talking with Sendak, who told me that he'd had a student at Parsons who would be terrific for my work. His name was Richard (Sendak was not able to remember his last name). And then he described him in a way that only

Ah, Pinsk. Could there be a lovelier city? No. ■ (From *It Happened in Pinsk* by Arthur Yorinks. Illustrated by Richard Egielski.)

Sendak can. It must have been fate, because one day I went to Parsons to meet Maurice, and I saw the person he had described standing near the elevator. I was shy, but *desperate,* so I tapped him on the shoulder and said, 'Richard.' He turned around and looked at me as if I was about to pick his pocket! When I explained how I came to recognize him, he calmed down. It turned out that he had brought his portfolio and we went into a classroom to talk. I had never seen work like his. Maurice was absolutely right about Richard Egielski being the perfect illustrator for my stories. We have done four books together so far, and look forward to many more.

"The coincidental aspect of Richard's and my coming together doesn't end there. Richard and I worked out a project—my story, his sketches. I brought just the story to Michael di Capua at Farrar, Straus, Giroux, which had bought my ill-fated first story. Michael liked it, and said, 'You know, I think I know an illustrator who might be right for this. A while ago I saw the portfolio of an artist named Richard Egielski.' I burst out laughing, because Richard had already done the dummy. We showed it to Michael and he bought the package. *Sid and Sol,* our first joint book, came out in 1977.

"When Richard and I first started working together, I had to learn a new language. After he'd read *Sid and Sol* and said he wanted to do a storyboard for it, we talked briefly and then he went off to do his work. One day, he came over, saying 'I've got it! I've got it!' and opened a five-by-eight inch notebook. On one page, in a space maybe three-by-five inches, was his plan for the entire book. Each page was represented by a scribble about a half-inch long. I thought this was a practical joke. And yet—as I was to learn—Richard knew exactly what was going on in those little, little pictures. To anyone else, it's hieroglyphics. Richard sees in the squiggles not only a representation of the images he has in mind, but the time and space relations among the images. I have actually learned to read these little drawings. I realize that what had appeared to me to be nonsense was rhythm. Once you've learned to read them, you can see in the thumbnail sketches the pacing and the movement of the whole book. And musicality is crucial in picture books: the reader's desire to turn the page, to read, to look, to again turn the page must be determined by the rhythm, indeed the music, born of the marriage of text and pictures."

Although each book Yorinks and Egielski have done together has unfolded differently, the team has developed a basic approach. "By the time I show Richard a story, it's almost finished. It may need some fine tuning, but essentially it's all there. If he likes it, we talk—generally quite briefly—about how I came up with the story, what inspired it, what I was reading at the time I wrote it. I never have any kind of image of what the book should look like or what the pictures should feel like. The real fun for me is having to wait while Richard does his storyboard. When he shows it to me, it's like Christmas. All of a sudden I see things I never would have thought of in conjunction with the story. They were buried—apparently without my being conscious of them—in the text.

"*Louis the Fish* (1980) after a lot of hard work writing came together as a picture book fairly easily. I changed two or three words in the final draft, but that was the extent of the revision. I remember telling Richard that Kafka's *The Metamorphosis,* in which a man turns into an insect, was the inspiration for the story. Later, he told me that as he was working, he recalled that in high school when he first studied Kafka, the teacher had broken the story up into discrete, yet connected, sections. Richard's recollection of his first experience with the story that inspired *Louis* enabled him to bring something very spe-

cial to that book. And for my part, I was fascinated that Richard's first exposure to Kafka had such strong pictorial overtones—he went to an art high school and was trained to *look at* literature in a way that most literature students, like myself, are not.

"*It Happened in Pinsk*" (1983) was not quite as easy. As we looked at the storyboard, we saw problems. What we discovered was that there were some snags we hadn't noticed in the text that were showing up in the pictures. As soon as I fixed those spots in the story, Richard ceased to have problems with the illustrations. *Pinsk* grew out of my reverence for Gogol, and particularly my love for his story, 'The Nose,' in which one morning a man wakes up without his nose. As is my habit, when I have read and loved a work by a given author, I read everything he's done, as well as biographies of him. The only way I've really learned to write is to have read authors I admire. When Richard and I talked about my story, I mentioned Gogol and my infatuation with pre-revolutionary Russia. I would have loved to have opened my piece with a two- or three-page description of Nevsky Avenue—something I couldn't do in a picture book.

"Richard's double-page spread more than satisfied the craving I had to have the street described. It's very filmic, as though the camera was coming from a great distance at a very slow pace, lighting one image after another, after another. You get many tantalizing hints about what is going to happen in the book from this one illustration. You know, Gogol has a great line about learning to write: 'Stay in your room,' he said, 'and describe it in great detail.' However, within the constrictions of the picture book, I'm not permitted to explain the text in detail, but as Richard echoed the text in his visuals, nothing was lost—in fact, much was gained.

"I was so steeped in Gogol and his period that I wanted my story to feel like a translation from the Russian. There are deliberately awkward, foreign-sounding phrases.

"The title came about in a funny way. I knew I wanted a city that sounded like *insk.* But I didn't want Minsk, since that's a city in which a lot of stories have been set. I got out a map of Russia, looked it over—none too carefully, apparently— and found nothing. So I started making up names, and came up with Pinsk. I was astonished when my publisher told me there really was a Pinsk!

"I am very fond of stories in which fantastical things happen matter-of-factly. Stories that recount outlandish events almost journalistically. Gogol and Kafka, for example, describe things that are unbelievable, but make them so believable, that we take them for truth. And, of course, on a certain level it is. I strive for this quality in my own work.

"When I start writing, I don't know for what type of reader the piece is intended. Very descriptive works are not right for the picture-book form. Whether or not a story turns out to be for children has nothing to do with its level of sophistication. Kids are extremely perceptive. There is little that is truly beyond their grasp. I would hope that the stories in our picture books work on many levels, so that both children and adults will enjoy them. Often, picture books are read to children by an adult. If the grown-up is bored, that boredom will be communicated to the child. If the adult is excited, the child will be encouraged to read—not just our books, but others."

Yorinks' characters tend to be alienated people who feel ill-at-ease in their own skin. When asked if he intends to make a political statement through these characters, Yorinks replied, "No, definitely not. I feel that, for me, art and politics rarely

Al, from Al's Pet Store, found him on the bus going up Flatbush. ■ (From *Louis the Fish* by
Arthur Yorinks. Illustrated by Richard Egielski.)

make good partners. Frankly, I'm not interested in political
statements in art, which is not to say I'm not interested in
politics. But I believe firmly that for any kind of statement—
political or otherwise—to have weight, it must have validity
on the individual level. Statements intended for the masses
which do not take the individual into account are, I believe,
inherently impoverished.

"My stories begin on a psychological level. They ask questions, 'Who am I?' 'Why am I who I am?' 'What does it mean

to be human?' In that sense, perhaps, my stories are political
because to answer these questions, we must take other people
into account. The tales of Hans Christian Andersen are very
political—'The Emperor's New Clothes' is a prime political
statement. It is also a brilliant piece of literature.''

When asked about the abiding impression left by his stories—
to 'live and let live'—Yorinks allowed that, "In the largest
possible sense, I suppose that is political. But when I write, I
am thinking about writing, about literature, not about politics.

I work intuitively with a lot happening unconsciously. I tend to discover what I had in mind *after* I see a finished piece—often after I've seen Richard's illustrations.

"Sometimes it is hard to keep going, given the kind of idiosyncratic, very personal books we do. Richard and I consider picture books a venerable art form. Unfortunately, this view seems not to be widespread. In too many picture books today, the text is thin and the pictures slick and graphic. The 'Age of Spielberg and Lucas,' I call it—shallow images that don't resonate, like the videos on MTV. I see this as a sign that our culture is deteriorating.

"It's interesting to look back at the history of children's books in this country since the 1950s. The late fifties and early sixties were 'boom years' in children's book publishing. A lot of publishers were staying alive on children's books. Some very gifted people came into the field. In the sixties, in particular, a lot of money was available for schools and libraries. The Head Start program came into existence then; 'Sesame Street' was developed soon afterward. Not that everything being published then was brilliant, or even good, but a lot of attention was being paid to children, and to how they thought, to what got them excited, to what made them tick.

"Then suddenly, in the later part of the decade, children's book publishing became very political. A primary criterion of the time was 'relevance', 'social consciousness.' This led, in my opinion, to a general downward slide in the artistic quality of children's books. Picture books became teaching tools with artistry and literary quality as secondary considerations. The notion that picture books are primarily an art form was all but lost. A lot of what is passed off as fantasy in picture books is little more than escapism. The level of craft, particularly in graphics, is quite high, but there is a hollowness and an absence of the qualities that make them *art*. They have become commercial in the worst possible way. The licensing of characters for use on tee-shirts, mugs, trinkets and so on is very distressing to me. The current trend in pop-up books is also, in my opinion, a bastardization. There is a marvelous tradition of mechanical books, but these were a veritable form, not a gimmick. It's rare now to walk into a bookstore and find an original picture book unrelated to a movie, television series, or some other piece of fluff from media-land. The salt on the wound is that frequently the TV series and/or film is made first, the book is merely a spin-off. The implications of this are extremely disturbing.

"Children's first books are often picture books. From picture books, children get their first inkling about literature and visual art. The importance of picture books is therefore profound. The stories and images adults make for children may well say more about a given society than anything else. Children deserve the best we can offer—authentic and uncompromising art."

—Based on an interview by Marguerite Feitlowitz

FOR MORE INFORMATION SEE: New York Times, December 8, 1977, December 15, 1985; *New York Times Book Review*, December 10, 1978, November 23, 1980, December 18, 1983, September 21, 1986; *Booklist*, October 1, 1979; *Los Angeles Times*, October 14, 1979; Selma Lanes, *The Art of Maurice Sendak*, Abrams, 1980; *Publishers Weekly*, December 23, 1983; Michael Walsh, "The Maturing of Minimalism," *Time*, December 23, 1985; *Village Voice*, February 25, 1986; *Philadelphia Inquirer*, October 8, 1986, October 10, 1986; "Story by Arthur Yorinks, Pictures by Richard Egielski" (video; thirty-five minutes; VHS or Beta tape), Farrar, Straus, 1987.

ZALLINGER, Peter Franz 1943-

PERSONAL: Born November 29, 1943, in New Haven, Conn.; son of Rudolph Franz (an artist and educator) and Jean (an illustrator and educator; maiden name, Day) Zallinger. *Education:* Yale University, B.A., 1965. *Home:* 646 Orange St., #3D, New Haven, Conn. 06511.

CAREER: Free-lance illustrator. *Military service:* U.S. Naval Reserve, active duty, 1966-69. *Exhibitions:* Peabody Museum of Natural History, New Haven, Conn.; Los Angeles County Museum of Natural History traveling exhibition. Work is included in the permanent collections of Yale University, New Haven, and the Museum of the Academy of Natural Sciences, Philadelphia, Penn. *Member:* Society of Vertebrate Paleontology. *Awards, honors: The Total Turtle* was chosen one of Child Study Association of America's Children's Books of the Year, 1975; *Dinosaurs* was chosen one of *Saturday Review*'s Best Books of the Year, 1977.

WRITINGS—Juvenile; all self-illustrated: *Dinosaurs*, Random House, 1977; *Prehistoric Animals*, Random House, 1978; *Dinosaurs and Other Archosaurs*, Random House, 1986.

Illustrator: John Waters, *The Mysterious Eel*, Hastings, 1973; Ross E. Hutchins, *Paper Hornets*, Addisonian, 1973; Martha E. Reeves, *The Total Turtle*, Crowell, 1975.

SIDELIGHTS: "I teach drawing, illustration and linear perspective at Lyme Academy of Fine Arts in Old Lyme, Conn, and at Paier College of Art in Hamden, Conn. The names 'Tam,' 'Tammy,' 'Tam Van Benoit,' or 'Tammy Benoit' have

PETER FRANZ ZALLINGER

been hidden in my book and poster illustrations since 1977. She is the daughter of my best friend and my goddaughter.

''I sang at Carnegie Hall in 1965—I can't seem to find my medium.''

HOBBIES AND OTHER INTERESTS: Woodworking, model ship and boat building.

ZELINSKY, Paul O. 1953-

PERSONAL: Born February 14, 1953, in Evanston, Ill.; son of Daniel (a professor of mathematics) and Zelda (a medical illustrator; maiden name, Oser) Zelinsky; married Deborah Hallen (a musician), December 31, 1981; children: Anna. *Education:* Attended Yale University, B.A., 1974; Tyler School of Art, M.F.A., 1976. *Office:* 160 Columbia Hts., Brooklyn, N.Y. 11201.

CAREER: Artist, author and illustrator of books for children, 1977—. *Member:* Graphic Artists Guild, Children's Illustrators and Authors. *Awards, honors: How I Hunted the Little Fellows* was chosen one of *School Library Journal*'s Best Books, 1979, *The Maid and the Mouse and the Odd-Shaped House: A Story in Rhyme*, 1981, *Ralph S. Mouse*, 1982, and *Rumpelstiltskin*, 1986; *How I Hunted the Little Fellows* was chosen for the American Institute of Graphic Arts Book Show, 1980, *The Maid and the Mouse and the Odd-Shaped House: A Story in Rhyme*, 1982; *Three Romances* was included in the Society of Illustrators Show, 1982, and *Rumpelstiltskin*, 1986; *The Maid and the Mouse and the Odd-Shaped House: A Story in Rhyme* was chosen one of *New York Times* Best Illustrated Children's Books of the Year, 1981, and *The Story of Mrs. Lovewright and Purrless Her Cat*, 1985; *The Maid and the Mouse and the Odd-Shaped House: A Story in Rhyme* was chosen one of International Reading Association's Children's

PAUL O. ZELINSKY

Ralph was an unusual mouse. ■ (From *Ralph S. Mouse* by Beverly Cleary. Illustrated by Paul O. Zelinsky.)

Choices, 1982; illustrator of Beverly Cleary's Newbery Award book, *Dear Mr. Henshaw* which was chosen one of *New York Times* Outstanding Books of the Year, one of *School Library Journal*'s Best Books, and received the Christopher Award, all 1983, and the Garden State Children's Book Award (younger fiction) from the New Jersey Library Association, 1985; Parents' Choice Award from the Parents' Choice Foundation, 1984, for *The Lion and the Stoat*, 1985, for *The Story of Mrs. Lovewright and Her Purrless Cat*, and 1986, for *Rumpelstiltskin; The Maid and the Mouse and the Odd-Shaped House: A Story in Rhyme* was included in *Horn Book*'s ''Graphic Gallery'' of outstanding picture books, 1984; *Hansel and Gretel* was selected a Notable Children's Book by the Association for Library Service to Children, 1984; *The Story of Mrs. Lovewright and Her Purrless Cat* was selected one of Child Study Association of America's Children's Books of the Year, 1985; Caldecott Honor Book from the American Library Association, and exhibited at the Bologna International Children's Book Fair, both 1985, both for *Hansel and Gretel; Rumpelstiltskin* was chosen one of *Redbook*'s ten best children's books, 1986, and named a Caldecott Honor Book from the American Library Association, 1987.

WRITINGS—For children; self-illustrated; fiction: (Adapter) *The Maid and the Mouse and the Odd-Shaped House: A Story in Rhyme*, Dodd, 1981; *The Lion and the Stoat*, Greenwillow, 1984, large print edition, 1984; (reteller) *Rumpelstiltskin* (*Horn Book* honor list), Dutton, 1986.

Illustrator; for children; all fiction, except as noted: Avi, *Emily Upham's Revenge; or, How Deadwood Dick Saved the Banker's Niece: A Massachusetts Adventure*, Pantheon, 1978; Boris Zhitkov, *How I Hunted the Little Fellows* (ALA Notable Book), translated from the Russian by Djemma Bider, Dodd, 1979; Avi, *The History of Helpless Harry: To Which Is Added a Variety of Amusing and Entertaining Adventures*, Pantheon, 1980; Winifred Rosen, *Three Romances: Love Stories from Camelot Retold*, Knopf, 1981; Naomi Lazard, *What Amanda Saw*, Greenwillow, 1981; Beverly Cleary, *Ralph S. Mouse*, Morrow, 1982; Mirra Ginsburg, adapter, *The Sun's Asleep behind the Hill*, Greenwillow, 1982; David Kherdian, *The Song in the Walnut Grove*, Knopf, 1982; B. Cleary, *Dear Mr. Hen-*

shaw (ALA Notable Book; *Horn Book* honor list), Morrow, 1983; Jack Prelutsky, *Zoo Doings: Animal Poems*, Greenwillow, 1983; Rika Lesser, reteller, *Hansel and Gretel*, Dodd, 1984; Lore Segal, *The Story of Mrs. Lovewright and Purrless Her Cat*, Knopf, 1985.

Adult: Rika Lesser, *Etruscan Things* (poetry), Braziller, 1983.

ADAPTATIONS: "Hansel and Gretel" (cassette; filmstrip with cassette), Random House, 1986.

SIDELIGHTS: Zelinsky was born and raised in a suburb of Chicago. His early memory of picture books included, "The Little Golden Book *The Tawny, Scrawny Lion* with Tenggren's illustrations. And I liked *The Story of Ferdinand*. It wasn't long ago that I looked at it again, the first time since childhood, and saw the corks hanging from the trees. I never knew that was a joke! I liked Margaret Wise Brown's *The Color Kittens*. But beyond these impressions, I don't have a good recollection of other books from my childhood." [Sylvia and Kenneth Marantz, "Interview with Paul O. Zelinsky," *Horn Book*, May-June, 1986. Amended by Paul O. Zelinsky.[1]]

During his school years, Zelinsky did not consciously decide to become an illustrator and children's author. While an undergraduate student at Yale University, however, he decided on an art career and was greatly impressed by children's illustrator Maurice Sendak, who made him aware of children's illustrations. "I would look at them in stores, but it didn't occur to me that I could create them for a livelihood until I took a course at Yale with Maurice Sendak, a seminar initiated by a student who had convinced him to teach it. At that point I had already decided to be an art major, and was already worrying about making a living. I thought that making picture books would be something I could do."[1]

His career as an illustrator began with the help of an uncle who worked for the *New York Times*. "He suggested I show some of my drawings to their art director. Because I was an art major and did real paintings, I didn't feel as if my ego was at stake. I showed drawings to the art director. He liked them, and I went home with an assignment. The real possibility of a career in illustration fell into my lap, more or less.

"I went on painting and thought I might teach. Then I got my master's in painting and got a short-term teaching job. I found out that I was a lousy teacher and that teaching wasn't what I wanted to do. In the meantime I had been visiting publishers with a portfolio, feeling all the while that I didn't have anything personal at stake because I was really a painter. In my art education the word *illustration* had been a term of derision. I was embarrassed to tell my painting teachers for some time what I was doing. I was actually taken aback when I found that William Bailey, one of my favorite painting teachers at Yale had seen some of my books and thought they were *wonderful*—a word he used for almost nothing."[1]

Zelinsky's first book for children was Avi's *Emily Upham's Revenge*, illustrated in 1978. "I was first given *Emily Upham's Revenge* because there was something in my portfolio that looked Victorian. When I did the *Little Fellows* which is set in the 1890s, I got worried that I would be typecast as working in a nineteenth-century style. I guess I didn't really want to be pegged. I would never want to do all my books in the same style. Different writing calls for different drawing. When I look at a text, I don't usually know how it should look right away, but I often know what it shouldn't look like, and that's enough to start with.

"For Cleary's *Ralph S. Mouse* I visited a real classroom to see how big fifth-graders actually are. I bought a mouse. I named him, or her, Ralph. She posed pretty well, didn't run around too fast. The next day she ran around even slower. After a couple of days, she was barely moving. Then she died. I had to buy Ralph II, who just wouldn't stay still. I returned Ralph II to the store with instructions to tell anyone who bought him that he was soon going to be famous."[1]

Three years later, in 1981, Zelinsky expanded the scope of his career by writing and illustrating his own children's book, which was an adaptation of a folktale that was found in a Bridgeport, Connecticut school teacher's 1897 notebook. The tale, entitled *The Maid and the Mouse and the Odd-Shape House*, is actually a puzzle that takes its clues from its words and pictures. "The text came from a school notebook in the editor's grandmother's house. It was pretty crude and dated and took a lot of changing. It sounded like an 1890s idea of a funny rhyme. From the start I thought of the book as a sort

Next door is a gas station that goes ping-ping, ping-ping every time a car drives in. They turn off the pinger at 10:00 p.m. ■ (From *Dear Mr. Henshaw* by Beverly Cleary. Illustrated by Paul O. Zelinsky.)

Rumpelstiltskin
RETOLD & ILLUSTRATED BY
PAUL O. ZELINSKY

(Jacket illustration by Paul O. Zelinsky from *Rumpelstiltskin*, retold by Paul O. Zelinsky.)

of board game, very flat and ornamental. At first I thought I was inspired to know in just what period to set the book, but later I realized that I was only thinking along the lines of Mother Goose which is always eighteenth-century English. I drew lots of Wee Maids before arriving at the final exaggerated character. I had just recently looked at Sendak's *Hector Protector;* the ridiculous size of the woman's bonnet and bows suggested I could get away with a loonier Wee Maid than I might otherwise have dared. The editor later thought she looked like the 'old maid' character in the card game. I do remember that I played 'Old Maid,' but I don't recall what she looked like. She could have been my subconscious source."[1]

When asked if he had a general "Zelinsky style" that he uses in his illustrations, the artist responded, "Instead of a style I have a chain, a continuous chain, of ways that I work. I try to make the book talk, as it talks to me, and not worry about whether it is in my style or not. In my different books, I may have covered the range that I can work in: from extremely detailed, rounded images in real space, such as the almost photographic images in *How I Hunted the Little Fellows* to *The Maid and the Mouse and the Odd-Shaped House.* It seems to me that everything else I've done fits somewhere on a continuum between the two.

"I get a kick out of doing each book differently. I've been pleased that people like all the variation in what I do, because I expected to be called on the carpet for not having a style—the pictorial equivalent of a voice for an author. I figure a style will come on its own."[1]

In 1985 Zelinsky realized an old ambition to illustrate the classic tale of *Hansel and Gretel.* "From the time I started illustrating children's books I've always wanted to do *Hansel and Gretel.* I was disappointed that everyone else was doing it, too. I hadn't seen any *Hansel and Gretel* book that expressed the story for me, that seemed remotely right. The story is very serious. I don't mean that it's not happy. But it's deep; it's rich emotionally and deals with very basic fears. It's about how infants become their own people, how they come to realize that they're not an outgrowth of their parents.

"Before I did the book, I made a concentrated effort not to look at other versions because I didn't want to be responding or reacting to them. I was trying to put down the intense response I've always had to the story. When I remembered it, the image I first thought of wasn't the gingerbread house; it was the children lost in the woods: how big the woods are and how small the children are. The idea of thousands of birds in the vast forest eating up all the crumbs is a grand, dramatic image that I responded to when I first heard the story as a child.

"Rika Lesser's text was almost finished by the time I started the pictures. I was dividing it into pages while the story was still in a rough form. Then Rika actually did make some changes based on the pictures, which is a nice way to work."[1]

(From *Three Romances: Love Stories from Camelot Retold* by Winifred Rosen. Illustrated by Paul O. Zelinsky.)

Hansel carefully gathered them up and stuffed the pocket of his jacket with as many as would go in. ■ (From *Hansel and Gretel*, retold by Rika Lesser. Illustrated by Paul O. Zelinsky.)

Illustrated with Zelinsky's oil paintings, the 1985 version of *Hansel and Gretel* by Rika Lesser is based on the original transcription of Wilhelm Grimm. "I was looking at seventeenth-century Dutch genre paintings—like Steen's—that are full of characters. I went to the Metropolitan Museum of Art and sketched. When I was thinking of an approach to *Hansel and Gretel*, I got just the right feeling from those paintings. Genre paintings don't have the kind of emotional distance that some other classical paintings have. You can look at them as illustrations—really look at the people, get involved in what they're doing, be amused by them, and not have a layer of 'Great Art' come between you and the painting. I hope my finished pictures have some of the qualities of those genre paintings."[1]

Zelinsky's illustrations for the book were first done in watercolor and then overpainted transparently in oils. "I did pencil drawings which I tore out of the sketch book as I did them, so I could flip through them. The drawings were fairly detailed but small. Because of time constraints, I ended up taking slides of those pencil sketches and projecting them full-sized onto stretched paper. Then I made the underpainting in black and white. The dummy had been done before I knew the exact proportions of the book and how much space the text would take. With the slides I could project the paintings onto the paper at an angle and change their proportions—squash them sideways or elongate them. In the first forest scene everything is actually twenty per cent wider than in the sketch because there was more text than I had anticipated. I wanted to make the woods very big and the children very small. Sometimes I had to keep exerting an effort because the children got bigger and the woods smaller. I went walking in the woods of western Connecticut to get a feeling of woods. Without those walks I wouldn't have thought there would be so many large fallen trees."[1]

Besides *Hansel and Gretel* which was a 1985 Caldecott Honor Book, Zelinsky has illustrated several award-winning children's books such as *Ralph S. Mouse* by Beverly Cleary, *Emily Upham's Revenge* by Avi, and Jack Prelutsky's *Zoo Doings: Animal Poems*. "If a picture book is an art form, the art happens at the stage when you are choosing what you will illustrate. That's when the rhythm is set and when the general emotional impact, if there is any, gets set up. Choosing the scenes to illustrate is the first thing that I do. I start out knowing the number of pages, which makes an enormous difference, and with a text that seems to break in certain places. Maybe a surprise in the text really needs to be accompanied by a visual surprise at the exact moment. Sometimes an image has to take a double-page spread or a single-page. Just dealing with the text from the beginning sets alot of constraints on what is and is not going to be pictured.

"Telling the story through the pictures means: how do you get from one picture to the next in a visual and logical progression? There may or may not be changes in the scale or scheme. Selecting the pictures is making the whole book into what you want it to be."[1]

Zelinsky's work in progress includes a notebook full of ideas for stories and the possibility of a board book for younger children. "The idea of books that are like catalogues with a word and an object are not that interesting for me. I would like to do a board book if I could do more than just a catalogue. I do my books mainly for myself. It seems to work that way. If the narrative has a childlike feeling, it should come through."[1]

HOBBIES AND OTHER INTERESTS: Cooking, eating.

FOR MORE INFORMATION SEE: Sylvia Marantz and Kenneth Marantz, "Interview with Paul O. Zelinsky," *Horn Book*, May/June, 1986.

ZEMACH, Kaethe 1958-

PERSONAL: Born March 18, 1958, in Boston, Mass.; daughter of Harvey Fischtrom (a writer of children's books under pseudonym, Harve Zemach) and Margot Zemach (an illustrator of children's books); married Ray Bird (a musician). *Education:* Attended schools in England, Denmark, and the United States. *Home:* 2423 Oregon St., Berkeley, Calif. 94705.

CAREER: Artist, writer. *Awards, honors: The Princess and Froggie* was selected as a Children's Book of the Year by the Child Study Association, 1975, and was included in the Children's Book Showcase, 1976.

WRITINGS: (With Harve Zemach) *The Princess and Froggie* (juvenile; short stories; illustrated by mother, Margot Zemach), Farrar, Straus, 1975; (adapter and illustrator) *The Beautiful Rat* (Japanese folk tale), Four Winds, 1979.

Illustrator: Norman Rosten, *The Wineglass: A Passover Story*, Walker, 1978; Yuri Suhl, *The Purim Goat*, Four Winds, 1980; Eve Bunting, *The Traveling Men of Ballycoo*, Harcourt, 1983.

ADAPTATIONS: "The Princess and Froggie" (filmstrip with cassette), Doubleday Multimedia, (cassette with hardcover book), Random House.

SIDELIGHTS: "I feel that my work with children's books is still in an experimental stage, and I hope that in the future it will blossom into the stories and illustrations which will stand strong and be entertaining for children and adults alike."

Bird! You get off my daddy's head! ■ (From *The Princess and Froggie* by Harve and Kaethe Zemach. Illustrated by Margot Zemach.)

Cumulative Indexes

CUMULATIVE INDEX TO ILLUSTRATIONS AND AUTHORS

Illustrations Index

(In the following index, the number of the volume in which an illustrator's work appears is given *before* the colon, and the page on which it appears is given *after* the colon. For example, a drawing by Adams, Adrienne appears in Volume 2 on page 6, another drawing by her appears in Volume 3 on page 80, another drawing in Volume 8 on page 1, and another drawing in Volume 15 on page 107.)

YABC

Index citations including this abbreviation refer to listings appearing in *Yesterday's Authors of Books for Children,* also published by the Gale Research Company, which covers authors who died prior to 1960.

Aas, Ulf, *5:* 174
Abbé, S. van. *See* van Abbé, S.
Abel, Raymond, *6:* 122; *7:* 195; *12:* 3; *21:* 86; *25:* 119
Abrahams, Hilary, *26:* 205; *29:* 24-25
Abrams, Kathie, *36:* 170
Abrams, Lester, *49:* 26
Accorsi, William, *11:* 198
Acs, Laszlo, *14:* 156; *42:* 22
Adams, Adrienne, *2:* 6; *3:* 80; *8:* 1; *15:* 107; *16:* 180; *20:* 65; *22:* 134-135; *33:* 75; *36:* 103, 112; *39:* 74
Adams, John Wolcott, *17:* 162
Adamson, George, *30:* 23, 24
Adkins, Alta, *22:* 250
Adkins, Jan, *8:* 3
Adler, Peggy, *22:* 6; *29:* 31
Adler, Ruth, *29:* 29
Adragna, Robert, *47:* 145
Agard, Nadema, *18:* 1
Agre, Patricia, *47:* 195
Ahl, Anna Maria, *32:* 24
Aichinger, Helga, *4:* 5, 45
Aitken, Amy, *31:* 34
Akaba, Suekichi, *46:* 23
Akasaka, Miyoshi, *YABC 2:* 261
Akino, Fuku, *6:* 144
Alain, *40:* 41
Alajalov, *2:* 226
Albrecht, Jan, *37:* 176
Albright, Donn, *1:* 91
Alcorn, John, *3:* 159; *7:* 165; *31:* 22; *44:* 127; *46:* 23, 170
Alda, Arlene, *44:* 24
Alden, Albert, *11:* 103
Aldridge, Andy, *27:* 131
Alex, Ben, *45:* 25, 26
Alexander, Lloyd, *49:* 34
Alexander, Martha, *3:* 206; *11:* 103; *13:* 109; *25:* 100; *36:* 131
Alexeieff, Alexander, *14:* 6; *26:* 199
Aliki. *See* Brandenberg, Aliki
Allamand, Pascale, *12:* 9
Allan, Judith, *38:* 166
Alland, Alexander, *16:* 255
Alland, Alexandra, *16:* 255

Allen, Gertrude, *9:* 6
Allen, Graham, *31:* 145
Allen, Rowena, *47:* 75
Allison, Linda, *43:* 27
Almquist, Don, *11:* 8; *12:* 128; *17:* 46; *22:* 110
Aloise, Frank, *5:* 38; *10:* 133; *30:* 92
Althea. *See* Braithwaite, Althea
Altschuler, Franz, *11:* 185; *23:* 141; *40:* 48; *45:* 29
Ambrus, Victor G., *1:* 6-7, 194; *3:* 69; *5:* 15; *6:* 44; *7:* 36; *8:* 210; *12:* 227; *14:* 213; *15:* 213; *22:* 209; *24:* 36; *28:* 179; *30:* 178; *32:* 44, 46; *38:* 143; *41:* 25, 26, 27, 28, 29, 30, 31, 32; *42:* 87; *44:* 190
Ames, Lee J., *3:* 12; *9:* 130; *10:* 69; *17:* 214; *22:* 124
Amon, Aline, *9:* 9
Amoss, Berthe, *5:* 5
Amundsen, Dick, *7:* 77
Amundsen, Richard E., *5:* 10; *24:* 122
Ancona, George, *12:* 11
Anderson, Alasdair, *18:* 122
Anderson, Brad, *33:* 28
Anderson, C. W., *11:* 10
Anderson, Carl, *7:* 4
Anderson, Doug, *40:* 111
Anderson, Erica, *23:* 65
Anderson, Laurie, *12:* 153, 155
Anderson, Wayne, *23:* 119; *41:* 239
Andrew, John, *22:* 4
Andrews, Benny, *14:* 251; *31:* 24
Angel, Marie, *47:* 22
Angelo, Valenti, *14:* 8; *18:* 100; *20:* 232; *32:* 70
Anglund, Joan Walsh, *2:* 7, 250-251; *37:* 198, 199, 200
Anno, Mitsumasa, *5:* 7; *38:* 25, 26-27, 28, 29, 30, 31, 32
Antal, Andrew, *1:* 124; *30:* 145
Apple, Margot, *33:* 25; *35:* 206; *46:* 81
Appleyard, Dev, *2:* 192
Aragonés, Sergio, *48:* 23, 24, 25, 26, 27

Araneus, *40:* 29
Archer, Janet, *16:* 69
Ardizzone, Edward, *1:* 11, 12; *2:* 105; *3:* 258; *4:* 78; *7:* 79; *10:* 100; *15:* 232; *20:* 69, 178; *23:* 223; *24:* 125; *28:* 25, 26, 27, 28, 29, 30, 31, 33, 34, 35, 36, 37; *31:* 192, 193; *34:* 215, 217; *YABC 2:* 25
Arenella, Roy, *14:* 9
Armer, Austin, *13:* 3
Armer, Laura Adams, *13:* 3
Armer, Sidney, *13:* 3
Armitage, David, *47:* 23
Armitage, Eileen, *4:* 16
Armstrong, George, *10:* 6; *21:* 72
Arno, Enrico, *1:* 217; *2:* 22, 210; *4:* 9; *5:* 43; *6:* 52; *29:* 217, 219; *33:* 152; *35:* 99; *43:* 31, 32, 33; *45:* 212, 213, 214
Arnosky, Jim, *22:* 20
Arrowood, Clinton, *12:* 193; *19:* 11
Arting, Fred J., *41:* 63
Artzybasheff, Boris, *13:* 143; *14:* 15; *40:* 152, 155
Aruego, Ariane, *6:* 4
  See also Dewey, Ariane
Aruego, Jose, *4:* 140; *6:* 4; *7:* 64; *33:* 195; *35:* 208
Asch, Frank, *5:* 9
Ashby, Gail, *11:* 135
Ashby, Gwynneth, *44:* 26
Ashley, C. W., *19:* 197
Ashmead, Hal, *8:* 70
Assel, Steven, *44:* 153
Astrop, John, *32:* 56
Atene, Ann, *12:* 18
Atherton, Lisa, *38:* 198
Atkinson, J. Priestman, *17:* 275
Atkinson, Wayne, *40:* 46
Attebery, Charles, *38:* 170
Atwood, Ann, *7:* 9
Augarde, Steve, *25:* 22
Austerman, Miriam, *23:* 107
Austin, Margot, *11:* 16
Austin, Robert, *3:* 44
Averill, Esther, *1:* 17; *28:* 39, 40, 41

Axeman, Lois, *2:* 32; *11:* 84; *13:* 165; *22:* 8; *23:* 49
Ayer, Jacqueline, *13:* 7
Ayer, Margaret, *15:* 12

B.T.B. *See* Blackwell, Basil T.
Babbitt, Bradford, *33:* 158
Babbitt, Natalie, *6:* 6; *8:* 220
Bachem, Paul, *48:* 180
Back, George, *31:* 161
Bacon, Bruce, *4:* 74
Bacon, Paul, *7:* 155; *8:* 121; *31:* 55
Bacon, Peggy, *2:* 11, 228; *46:* 44
Baker, Alan, *22:* 22
Baker, Charlotte, *2:* 12
Baker, Jeannie, *23:* 4
Baker, Jim, *22:* 24
Baldridge, Cyrus LeRoy, *19:* 69; *44:* 50
Balet, Jan, *11:* 22
Balian, Lorna, *9:* 16
Ballantyne, R. M., *24:* 34
Ballis, George, *14:* 199
Baltzer, Hans, *40:* 30
Bang, Molly Garrett, *24:* 37, 38
Banik, Yvette Santiago, *21:* 136
Banner, Angela. *See* Maddison, Angela Mary
Bannerman, Helen, *19:* 13, 14
Bannon, Laura, *6:* 10; *23:* 8
Baptist, Michael, *37:* 208
Bare, Arnold Edwin, *16:* 31
Bare, Colleen Stanley, *32:* 33
Bargery, Geoffrey, *14:* 258
Barker, Carol, *31:* 27
Barker, Cicely Mary, *49:* 50, 51
Barkley, James, *4:* 13; *6:* 11; *13:* 112
Barks, Carl, *37:* 27, 28, 29, 30-31, 32, 33, 34
Barling, Tom, *9:* 23
Barlow, Perry, *35:* 28
Barlowe, Dot, *30:* 223
Barlowe, Wayne, *37:* 72
Barner, Bob, *29:* 37
Barnes, Hiram P., *20:* 28
Barnett, Moneta, *16:* 89; *19:* 142; *31:* 102; *33:* 30, 31, 32; *41:* 153
Barney, Maginel Wright, *39:* 32, 33, 34; *YABC 2:* 306
Barnum, Jay Hyde, *11:* 224; *20:* 5; *37:* 189, 190
Barrauds, *33:* 114
Barrer-Russell, Gertrude, *9:* 65; *27:* 31
Barrett, Angela, *40:* 136, 137
Barrett, John E., *43:* 119
Barrett, Ron, *14:* 24; *26:* 35
Barron, John N., *3:* 261; *5:* 101; *14:* 220
Barrows, Walter, *14:* 268
Barry, Ethelred B., *37:* 79; *YABC 1:* 229
Barry, James, *14:* 25
Barry, Katharina, *2:* 159; *4:* 22
Barry, Robert E., *6:* 12
Barry, Scott, *32:* 35
Bartenbach, Jean, *40:* 31
Barth, Ernest Kurt, *2:* 172; *3:* 160; *8:* 26; *10:* 31

Barton, Byron, *8:* 207; *9:* 18; *23:* 66
Barton, Harriett, *30:* 71
Bartram, Robert, *10:* 42
Bartsch, Jochen, *8:* 105; *39:* 38
Bascove, Barbara, *45:* 73
Baskin, Leonard, *30:* 42, 43, 46, 47; *49:* 125, 126, 128, 129, 133
Bass, Saul, *49:* 192
Bassett, Jeni, *40:* 99
Batchelor, Joy, *29:* 41, 47, 48
Bate, Norman, *5:* 16
Bates, Leo, *24:* 35
Batet, Carmen, *39:* 134
Batherman, Muriel, *31:* 79; *45:* 185
Batten, John D., *25:* 161, 162
Battles, Asa, *32:* 94, 95
Bauernschmidt, Marjorie, *15:* 15
Baum, Allyn, *20:* 10
Baum, Willi, *4:* 24-25; *7:* 173
Baumann, Jill, *34:* 170
Baumhauer, Hans, *11:* 218; *15:* 163, 165, 167
Bayley, Dorothy, *37:* 195
Bayley, Nicola, *40:* 104; *41:* 34, 35
Baynes, Pauline, *2:* 244; *3:* 149; *13:* 133, 135, 137-141; *19:* 18, 19, 20; *32:* 208, 213, 214; *36:* 105, 108
Beame, Rona, *12:* 40
Beard, Dan, *22:* 31, 32
Beard, J. H., *YABC 1:* 158
Bearden, Romare, *9:* 7; *22:* 35
Beardsley, Aubrey, *17:* 14; *23:* 181
Bearman, Jane, *29:* 38
Beaton, Cecil, *24:* 208
Beaucé, J. A., *18:* 103
Beck, Charles, *11:* 169
Beck, Ruth, *13:* 11
Becker, Harriet, *12:* 211
Beckett, Sheilah, *25:* 5; *33:* 37, 38
Beckhoff, Harry, *1:* 78; *5:* 163
Beckman, Kaj, *45:* 38, 39, 40, 41
Beckman, Per, *45:* 42, 43
Bedford, F. D., *20:* 118, 122; *33:* 170; *41:* 220, 221, 230, 233
Bee, Joyce, *19:* 62
Beeby, Betty, *25:* 36
Beech, Carol, *9:* 149
Beek, *25:* 51, 55, 59
Beerbohm, Max, *24:* 208
Behr, Joyce, *15:* 15; *21:* 132; *23:* 161
Behrens, Hans, *5:* 97
Beisner, Monika, *46:* 128, 131
Belden, Charles J., *12:* 182
Belina, Renate, *39:* 132
Bell, Corydon, *3:* 20
Beltran, Alberto, *43:* 37
Bemelmans, Ludwig, *15:* 19, 21
Benda, Wladyslaw T., *15:* 256; *30:* 76, 77; *44:* 182
Bendick, Jeanne, *2:* 24
Bennett, F. I., *YABC 1:* 134
Bennett, Jill, *26:* 61; *41:* 38, 39; *45:* 54
Bennett, Rainey, *15:* 26; *23:* 53
Bennett, Richard, *15:* 45; *21:* 11, 12, 13; *25:* 175
Bennett, Susan, *5:* 55
Bentley, Carolyn, *46:* 153

Bentley, Roy, *30:* 162
Benton, Thomas Hart, *2:* 99
Berelson, Howard, *5:* 20; *16:* 58; *31:* 50
Berenstain, Jan, *12:* 47
Berenstain, Stan, *12:* 47
Berg, Joan, *1:* 115; *3:* 156; *6:* 26, 58
Berg, Ron, *36:* 48, 49; *48:* 37, 38
Berger, William M., *14:* 143; *YABC 1:* 204
Bering, Claus, *13:* 14
Berkowitz, Jeanette, *3:* 249
Bernadette. *See* Watts, Bernadette
Bernath, Stefen, *32:* 76
Bernstein, Ted, *38:* 183
Bernstein, Zena, *23:* 46
Berrill, Jacquelyn, *12:* 50
Berry, Erick. *See* Best, Allena.
Berry, William A., *6:* 219
Berry, William D., *14:* 29; *19:* 48
Berson, Harold, *2:* 17-18; *4:* 28-29, 220; *9:* 10; *12:* 19; *17:* 45; *18:* 193; *22:* 85; *34:* 172; *44:* 120; *46:* 42
Bertschmann, Harry, *16:* 1
Beskow, Elsa, *20:* 13, 14, 15
Best, Allena, *2:* 26; *34:* 76
Bethers, Ray, *6:* 22
Bettina. *See* Ehrlich, Bettina
Betts, Ethel Franklin, *17:* 161, 164-165; *YABC 2:* 47
Bewick, Thomas, *16:* 40-41, 43-45, 47; *YABC 1:* 107
Bezencon, Jacqueline, *48:* 40
Biamonte, Daniel, *40:* 90
Bianco, Pamela, *15:* 31; *28:* 44, 45, 46
Bible, Charles, *13:* 15
Bice, Clare, *22:* 40
Biggers, John, *2:* 123
Bileck, Marvin, *3:* 102; *40:* 36-37
Bimen, Levent, *5:* 179
Binks, Robert, *25:* 150
Binzen, Bill, *24:* 47
Birch, Reginald, *15:* 150; *19:* 33, 34, 35, 36; *37:* 196, 197; *44:* 182; *46:* 176; *YABC 1:* 84; *YABC 2:* 34, 39
Bird, Esther Brock, *1:* 36; *25:* 66
Birmingham, Lloyd, *12:* 51
Biro, Val, *1:* 26; *41:* 42
Bischoff, Ilse, *44:* 51
Bjorklund, Lorence, *3:* 188, 252; *7:* 100; *9:* 113; *10:* 66; *19:* 178; *33:* 122, 123; *35:* 36, 37, 38, 39, 41, 42, 43; *36:* 185; *38:* 93; *47:* 106; *YABC 1:* 242
Blackwell, Basil T., *YABC 1:* 68, 69
Blades, Ann, *16:* 52; *37:* 213
Blair, Jay, *45:* 46; *46:* 155
Blaisdell, Elinore, *1:* 121; *3:* 134; *35:* 63
Blake, Quentin, *3:* 170; *9:* 21; *10:* 48; *13:* 38; *21:* 180; *26:* 60; *28:* 228; *30:* 29, 31; *40:* 108; *45:* 219; *46:* 165, 168; *48:* 196
Blake, Robert J., *37:* 90
Blake, William, *30:* 54, 56, 57, 58, 59, 60
Blass, Jacqueline, *8:* 215

Blegvad, Erik, *2:* 59; *3:* 98; *5:* 117; *7:* 131; *11:* 149; *14:* 34, 35; *18:* 237; *32:* 219; *YABC 1:* 201
Bliss, Corinne Demas, *37:* 38
Bloch, Lucienne, *10:* 12
Bloom, Lloyd, *35:* 180; *36:* 149; *47:* 99
Blossom, Dave, *34:* 29
Blumenschein, E. L., *YABC 1:* 113, 115
Blumer, Patt, *29:* 214
Blundell, Kim, *29:* 36
Boardman, Gwenn, *12:* 60
Bobri, *30:* 138; *47:* 27
Bock, Vera, *1:* 187; *21:* 41
Bock, William Sauts, *8:* 7; *14:* 37; *16:* 120; *21:* 141; *36:* 177
Bodecker, N. M., *8:* 13; *14:* 2; *17:* 55-57
Boehm, Linda, *40:* 31
Bohdal, Susi, *22:* 44
Bolian, Polly, *3:* 270; *4:* 30; *13:* 77; *29:* 197
Bolognese, Don, *2:* 147, 231; *4:* 176; *7:* 146; *17:* 43; *23:* 192; *24:* 50; *34:* 108; *36:* 133
Bond, Arnold, *18:* 116
Bond, Barbara Higgins, *21:* 102
Bond, Felicia, *38:* 197; *49:* 55, 56
Bonn, Pat, *43:* 40
Bonners, Susan, *41:* 40
Bonsall, Crosby, *23:* 6
Booth, Franklin, *YABC 2:* 76
Booth, Graham, *32:* 193; *37:* 41, 42
Bordier, Georgette, *16:* 54
Boren, Tinka, *27:* 128
Borja, Robert, *22:* 48
Born, Adolf, *49:* 63
Bornstein, Ruth, *14:* 44
Borten, Helen, *3:* 54; *5:* 24
Bossom, Naomi, *35:* 48
Boston, Peter, *19:* 42
Bosustow, Stephen, *34:* 202
Bottner, Barbara, *14:* 46
Boucher, Joelle, *41:* 138
Boulat, Pierre, *44:* 40
Bourke-White, Margaret, *15:* 286-287
Boutet de Monvel, M., *30:* 61, 62, 63, 65
Bowen, Richard, *42:* 134
Bowen, Ruth, *31:* 188
Bower, Ron, *29:* 33
Bowser, Carolyn Ewing, *22:* 253
Boyd, Patti, *45:* 31
Boyle, Eleanor Vere, *28:* 50, 51
Bozzo, Frank, *4:* 154
Bradford, Ron, *7:* 157
Bradley, Richard D., *26:* 182
Bradley, William, *5:* 164
Brady, Irene, *4:* 31; *42:* 37
Bragg, Michael, *32:* 78; *46:* 31
Braithwaite, Althea, *23:* 12-13
Bram, Elizabeth, *30:* 67
Bramley, Peter, *4:* 3
Brandenberg, Aliki, *2:* 36-37; *24:* 222; *35:* 49, 50, 51, 52, 53, 54, 56, 57
Brandenburg, Jim, *47:* 58
Brandi, Lillian, *31:* 158
Brandon, Brumsic, Jr., *9:* 25

Bransom, Paul, *17:* 121; *43:* 44
Brenner, Fred, *22:* 85; *36:* 34; *42:* 34
Brett, Bernard, *22:* 54
Brett, Harold M., *26:* 98, 99, 100
Brett, Jan, *30:* 135; *42:* 39
Brewer, Sally King, *33:* 44
Brewster, Patience, *40:* 68; *45:* 22, 183
Brick, John, *10:* 15
Bridge, David R., *45:* 28
Bridgman, L. J., *37:* 77
Bridwell, Norman, *4:* 37
Briggs, Raymond, *10:* 168; *23:* 20, 21
Brigham, Grace A., *37:* 148
Bright, Robert, *24:* 55
Brinckloe, Julie, *13:* 18; *24:* 79, 115; *29:* 35
Brion, *47:* 116
Brisley, Joyce L., *22:* 57
Brock, Charles E., *15:* 97; *19:* 247, 249; *23:* 224, 225; *36:* 88; *42:* 41, 42, 43, 44, 45; *YABC 1:* 194, 196, 203
Brock, Emma, *7:* 21
Brock, Henry Matthew, *15:* 81; *16:* 141; *19:* 71; *34:* 115; *40:* 164; *42:* 47, 48, 49; *49:* 66
Brodkin, Gwen, *34:* 135
Bromhall, Winifred, *5:* 11; *26:* 38
Brooke, L. Leslie, *16:* 181-183, 186; *17:* 15-17; *18:* 194
Brooker, Christopher, *15:* 251
Broomfield, Maurice, *40:* 141
Brotman, Adolph E., *5:* 21
Brown, Buck, *45:* 48
Brown, David, *7:* 47; *48:* 52
Brown, Denise, *11:* 213
Brown, Ford Madox, *48:* 74
Brown, Judith Gwyn, *1:* 45; *7:* 5; *8:* 167; *9:* 182, 190; *20:* 16, 17, 18; *23:* 142; *29:* 117; *33:* 97; *36:* 23, 26; *43:* 184; *48:* 201, 223; *49:* 69
Brown, Marc Tolon, *10:* 17, 197; *14:* 263
Brown, Marcia, *7:* 30; *25:* 203; *47:* 31, 32, 33, 34, 35, 36-37, 38, 39, 40, 42, 43, 44; *YABC 1:* 27
Brown, Margery W., *5:* 32-33; *10:* 3
Brown, Palmer, *36:* 40
Brown, Paul, *25:* 26; *26:* 107
Browne, Anthony, *45:* 50, 51, 52
Browne, Dik, *8:* 212
Browne, Gordon, *16:* 97
Browne, Hablot K., *15:* 65, 80; *21:* 14, 15, 16, 17, 18, 19, 20; *24:* 25
Browning, Coleen, *4:* 132
Browning, Mary Eleanor, *24:* 84
Bruce, Robert, *23:* 23
Brude, Dick, *48:* 215
Brule, Al, *3:* 135
Bruna, Dick, *43:* 48, 49, 50
Brundage, Frances, *19:* 244
Brunhoff, Jean de, *24:* 57, 58
Brunhoff, Laurent de, *24:* 60
Brunson, Bob, *43:* 135
Bryan, Ashley, *31:* 44
Brychta, Alex, *21:* 21

Bryson, Bernarda, *3:* 88, 146; *39:* 26; *44:* 185
Buba, Joy, *12:* 83; *30:* 226; *44:* 56
Buchanan, Lilian, *13:* 16
Bucholtz-Ross, Linda, *44:* 137
Buchs, Thomas, *40:* 38
Buck, Margaret Waring, *3:* 30
Buehr, Walter, *3:* 31
Buff, Conrad, *19:* 52, 53, 54
Buff, Mary, *19:* 52, 53
Bull, Charles Livingston, *18:* 207
Bullen, Anne, *3:* 166, 167
Burbank, Addison, *37:* 43
Burchard, Peter, *3:* 197; *5:* 35; *6:* 158, 218
Burger, Carl, *3:* 33; *45:* 160, 162
Burgeson, Marjorie, *19:* 31
Burgess, Gelett, *32:* 39, 42
Burkert, Nancy Ekholm, *18:* 186; *22:* 140; *24:* 62, 63, 64, 65; *26:* 53; *29:* 60, 61; *46:* 171; *YABC 1:* 46
Burn, Doris, *6:* 172
Burnett, Virgil, *44:* 42
Burningham, John, *9:* 68; *16:* 60-61
Burns, Howard M., *12:* 173
Burns, Jim, *47:* 70
Burns, M. F., *26:* 69
Burns, Raymond, *9:* 29
Burns, Robert, *24:* 106
Burr, Dane, *12:* 2
Burra, Edward, *YABC 2:* 68
Burri, René, *41:* 143
Burridge, Marge Opitz, *14:* 42
Burris, Burmah, *4:* 81
Burroughs, John Coleman, *41:* 64
Burroughs, Studley O., *41:* 65
Burton, Marilee Robin, *46:* 33
Burton, Virginia Lee, *2:* 43; *44:* 49, 51; *YABC 1:* 24
Busoni, Rafaello, *1:* 186; *3:* 224; *6:* 126; *14:* 5; *16:* 62-63
Butterfield, Ned, *1:* 153; *27:* 128
Buzonas, Gail, *29:* 88
Buzzell, Russ W., *12:* 177
Byard, Carole M., *39:* 44
Byars, Betsy, *46:* 35
Byfield, Barbara Ninde, *8:* 18
Byfield, Graham, *32:* 29
Byrd, Robert, *13:* 218; *33:* 46

Caddy, Alice, *6:* 41
Cady, Harrison, *17:* 21, 23; *19:* 57, 58
Caldecott, Randolph, *16:* 98, 103; *17:* 32-33, 36, 38-39; *26:* 90; *YABC 2:* 172
Calder, Alexander, *18:* 168
Calderon, W. Frank, *25:* 160
Caldwell, Doreen, *23:* 77
Caldwell, John, *46:* 225
Callahan, Kevin, *22:* 42
Callahan, Philip S., *25:* 77
Cameron, Julia Margaret, *19:* 203
Campbell, Ann, *11:* 43
Campbell, Walter M., *YABC 2:* 158
Camps, Luis, *28:* 120-121
Canright, David, *36:* 162
Caras, Peter, *36:* 64

Caraway, James, *3:* 200-201
Carbe, Nino, *29:* 183
Carigiet, Alois, *24:* 67
Carle, Eric, *4:* 42; *11:* 121; *12:* 29
Carlson, Nancy L., *41:* 116
Carr, Archie, *37:* 225
Carrick, Donald, *5:* 194; *39:* 97; *49:* 70
Carrick, Malcolm, *28:* 59, 60
Carrick, Valery, *21:* 47
Carroll, Lewis. *See* Dodgson, Charles L.
Carroll, Ruth, *7:* 41; *10:* 68
Carter, Barbara, *47:* 167, 169
Carter, Harry, *22:* 179
Carter, Helene, *15:* 38; *22:* 202, 203; *YABC 2:* 220-221
Cartlidge, Michelle, *49:* 65
Carty, Leo, *4:* 196; *7:* 163
Cary, *4:* 133; *9:* 32; *20:* 2; *21:* 143
Cary, Page, *12:* 41
Case, Sandra E., *16:* 2
Cassel, Lili. *See* Wronker, Lili Cassel
Cassel-Wronker, Lili.
       See also Wronker, Lili Cassel
Cassels, Jean, *8:* 50
Castellon, Federico, *48:* 45, 46, 47, 48
Castle, Jane, *4:* 80
Cather, Carolyn, *3:* 83; *15:* 203; *34:* 216
Cauley, Lorinda Bryan, *44:* 135; *46:* 49
Cayard, Bruce, *38:* 67
Cellini, Joseph, *2:* 73; *3:* 35; *16:* 116; *47:* 103
Chabrian, Debbi, *45:* 55
Chagnon, Mary, *37:* 158
Chalmers, Mary, *3:* 145; *13:* 148; *33:* 125
Chamberlain, Christopher, *45:* 57
Chamberlain, Margaret, *46:* 51
Chambers, C. E., *17:* 230
Chambers, Dave, *12:* 151
Chambers, Mary, *4:* 188
Chambliss, Maxie, *42:* 186
Chandler, David P., *28:* 62
Chapman, C. H., *13:* 83, 85, 87
Chapman, Frederick T., *6:* 27; *44:* 28
Chapman, Gaynor, *32:* 52, 53
Chappell, Warren, *3:* 172; *21:* 56; *27:* 125
Charles, Donald, *30:* 154, 155
Charlip, Remy, *4:* 48; *34:* 138
Charlot, Jean, *1:* 137, 138; *8:* 23; *14:* 31; *48:* 151
Charlton, Michael, *34:* 50; *37:* 39
Charmatz, Bill, *7:* 45
Chartier, Normand, *9:* 36
Chase, Lynwood M., *14:* 4
Chastain, Madye Lee, *4:* 50
Chauncy, Francis, *24:* 158
Chen, Tony, *6:* 45; *19:* 131; *29:* 126; *34:* 160
Cheney, T. A., *11:* 47
Cheng, Judith, *36:* 45
Chermayeff, Ivan, *47:* 53
Cherry, Lynne, *34:* 52
Chess, Victoria, *12:* 6; *33:* 42, 48, 49; *40:* 194; *41:* 145

Chessare, Michele, *41:* 50
Chesterton, G. K., *27:* 43, 44, 45, 47
Chestnutt, David, *47:* 217
Chevalier, Christa, *35:* 66
Chew, Ruth, *7:* 46
Chifflart, *47:* 113, 127
Chin, Alex, *28:* 54
Cho, Shinta, *8:* 126
Chollick, Jay, *25:* 175
Chorao, Kay, *7:* 200-201; *8:* 25; *11:* 234; *33:* 187; *35:* 239
Christelow, Eileen, *38:* 44
Christensen, Gardell Dano, *1:* 57
Christiansen, Per, *40:* 24
Christy, Howard Chandler, *17:* 163-165, 168-169; *19:* 186, 187; *21:* 22, 23, 24, 25
Chronister, Robert, *23:* 138
Church, Frederick, *YABC 1:* 155
Chute, Marchette, *1:* 59
Chwast, Jacqueline, *1:* 63; *2:* 275; *6:* 46-47; *11:* 125; *12:* 202; *14:* 235
Chwast, Seymour, *3:* 128-129; *18:* 43; *27:* 152
Cirlin, Edgard, *2:* 168
Clark, Victoria, *35:* 159
Clarke, Harry, *23:* 172, 173
Claverie, Jean, *38:* 46
Clayton, Robert, *9:* 181
Cleaver, Elizabeth, *8:* 204; *23:* 36
Cleland, T. M., *26:* 92
Clement, Charles, *20:* 38
Clevin, Jörgen, *7:* 50
Clifford, Judy, *34:* 163; *45:* 198
Coalson, Glo, *9:* 72, 85, *25:* 155; *26:* 42; *35:* 212
Cober, Alan E., *17:* 158; *32:* 77; *49:* 127
Cochran, Bobbye, *11:* 52
CoConis, Ted, *4:* 41; *46:* 41
Coerr, Eleanor, *1:* 64
Coes, Peter, *35:* 172
Coggins, Jack, *2:* 69
Cohen, Alix, *7:* 53
Cohen, Vincent O., *19:* 243
Cohen, Vivien, *11:* 112
Colbert, Anthony, *15:* 41; *20:* 193
Colby, C. B., *3:* 47
Cole, Herbert, *28:* 104
Cole, Olivia H. H., *1:* 134; *3:* 223; *9:* 111; *38:* 104
Collier, David, *13:* 127
Collier, John, *27:* 179
Colonna, Bernard, *21:* 50; *28:* 103; *34:* 140; *43:* 180
Cone, Ferne Geller, *39:* 49
Cone, J. Morton, *39:* 49
Conklin, Paul, *43:* 62
Connolly, Jerome P., *4:* 128; *28:* 52
Connolly, Peter, *47:* 60
Conover, Chris, *31:* 52; *40:* 184; *41:* 51; *44:* 79
Converse, James, *38:* 70
Cook, G. R., *29:* 165
Cookburn, W. V., *29:* 204
Cooke, Donald E., *2:* 77
Coombs, Charles, *43:* 65

Coombs, Patricia, *2:* 82; *3:* 52; *22:* 119
Cooney, Barbara, *6:* 16-17, 50; *12:* 42; *13:* 92; *15:* 145; *16:* 74, 111; *18:* 189; *23:* 38, 89, 93; *32:* 138; *38:* 105; *YABC 2:* 10
Cooper, Mario, *24:* 107
Cooper, Marjorie, *7:* 112
Copelman, Evelyn, *8:* 61; *18:* 25
Copley, Heather, *30:* 86; *45:* 57
Corbett, Grahame, *30:* 114; *43:* 67
Corbino, John, *19:* 248
Corcos, Lucille, *2:* 223; *10:* 27; *34:* 66
Corey, Robert, *9:* 34
Corlass, Heather, *10:* 7
Cornell, James, *27:* 60
Cornell, Jeff, *11:* 58
Corrigan, Barbara, *8:* 37
Corwin, Judith Hoffman, *10:* 28
Cory, Fanny Y., *20:* 113; *48:* 29
Cosgrove, Margaret, *3:* 100; *47:* 63
Costabel, Eva Deutsch, *45:* 66, 67
Costello, David F., *23:* 55
Courtney, R., *35:* 110
Couture, Christin, *41:* 209
Covarrubias, Miguel, *35:* 118, 119, 123, 124, 125
Coville, Katherine, *32:* 57; *36:* 167
Cox, *43:* 93
Cox, Charles, *8:* 20
Cox, Palmer, *24:* 76, 77
Craft, Kinuko, *22:* 182; *36:* 220
Craig, Helen, *49:* 76
Crane, Alan H., *1:* 217
Crane, H. M., *13:* 111
Crane, Jack, *43:* 183
Crane, Walter, *18:* 46-49, 53-54, 56-57, 59-61; *22:* 128; *24:* 210, 217
Crawford, Will, *43:* 77
Credle, Ellis *1:* 69
Crews, Donald, *32:* 59, 60
Crofut, Susan, *23:* 61
Crowell, Pers, *3:* 125
Cruikshank, George, *15:* 76, 83; *22:* 74, 75, 76, 77, 78, 79, 80, 81, 82, 84, 137; *24:* 22, 23
Crump, Fred H., *11:* 62
Cruz, Ray, *6:* 55
Cstari, Joe, *44:* 82
Cuffari, Richard, *4:* 75; *5:* 98; *6:* 56; *7:* 13, 84, 153; *8:* 148, 155; *9:* 89; *11:* 19; *12:* 55, 96, 114; *15:* 51, 202; *18:* 5; *20:* 139; *21:* 197; *22:* 14, 192; *23:* 15, 106; *25:* 97; *27:* 133; *28:* 196; *29:* 54; *30:* 85; *31:* 35; *36:* 101; *38:* 171; *42:* 97; *44:* 92, 192; *45:* 212, 213; *46:* 36, 198
Cugat, Xavier, *19:* 120
Cumings, Art, *35:* 160
Cummings, Chris, *29:* 167
Cummings, Pat, *42:* 61
Cummings, Richard, *24:* 119
Cunette, Lou, *20:* 93; *22:* 125
Cunningham, Aline, *25:* 180
Cunningham, David, *11:* 13
Cunningham, Imogene, *16:* 122, 127

Curry, John Steuart, *2:* 5; *19:* 84; *34:* 36
Curtis, Bruce, *23:* 96; *30:* 88; *36:* 22

Dabcovich, Lydia, *25:* 105; *40:* 114
Dain, Martin J., *35:* 75
Dalton, Anne, *40:* 62
Daly, Niki, *37:* 53
Dalziel, Brothers, *33:* 113
D'Amato, Alex, *9:* 48; *20:* 25
D'Amato, Janet, *9:* 48; *20:* 25; *26:* 118
Daniel, Alan, *23:* 59; *29:* 110
Daniel, Lewis C., *20:* 216
Daniels, Steve, *22:* 16
Dann, Bonnie, *31:* 83
Danska, Herbert, *24:* 219
Danyell, Alice, *20:* 27
Darley, F.O.C., *16:* 145; *19:* 79, 86, 88, 185; *21:* 28, 36; *35:* 76, 77, 78, 79, 80-81; *YABC 2:* 175
Darling, Lois, *3:* 59; *23:* 30, 31
Darling, Louis, *1:* 40-41; *2:* 63; *3:* 59; *23:* 30, 31; *43:* 54, 57, 59
Darrow, Whitney, Jr., *13:* 25; *38:* 220, 221
Darwin, Beatrice, *43:* 54
Darwin, Len, *24:* 82
Dastolfo, Frank, *33:* 179
Dauber, Liz, *1:* 22; *3:* 266; *30:* 49
Daugherty, James, *3:* 66; *8:* 178; *13:* 27-28, 161; *18:* 101; *19:* 72; *29:* 108; *32:* 156; *42:* 84; *YABC 1:* 256; *YABC 2:* 174
d'Aulaire, Edgar, *5:* 51
d'Aulaire, Ingri, *5:* 51
David, Jonathan, *19:* 37
Davidson, Kevin, *28:* 154
Davidson, Raymond, *32:* 61
Davis, Allen, *20:* 11; *22:* 45; *27:* 222; *29:* 157; *41:* 99; *47:* 99
Davis, Bette J., *15:* 53; *23:* 95
Davis, Dimitris, *45:* 95
Davis, Jim, *32:* 63, 64
Davis, Marguerite, *31:* 38; *34:* 69, 70; *YABC 1:* 126, 230
Davisson, Virginia H., *44:* 178
Dawson, Diane, *24:* 127; *42:* 126
Dean, Bob, *19:* 211
de Angeli, Marguerite, *1:* 77; *27:* 62, j65, 66, 67, 69, 70, 72; *YABC 1:* 166
Deas, Michael, *27:* 219, 221; *30:* 156
de Bosschère, Jean, *19:* 252; *21:* 4
De Bruyn, M(onica) G., *13:* 30-31
De Cuir, John F., *1:* 28-29
Degen, Bruce, *40:* 227, 229
De Grazia, *14:* 59; *39:* 56, 57
de Groat, Diane, *9:* 39; *18:* 7; *23:* 123; *28:* 200-201; *31:* 58, 59; *34:* 151; *41:* 152; *43:* 88; *46:* 40, 200; *49:* 163
de Groot, Lee, *6:* 21
Delacre, Lulu, *36:* 66
Delaney, A., *21:* 78
Delaney, Ned, *28:* 68
de Larrea, Victoria, *6:* 119, 204; *29:* 103

Delessert, Etienne, *7:* 140; *46:* 61, 62, 63, 65, 67, 68; *YABC 2:* 209
Delulio, John, *15:* 54
Demarest, Chris L., *45:* 68-69, 70
De Mejo, Oscar, *40:* 67
Denetsosie, Hoke, *13:* 126
Dennis, Morgan, *18:* 68-69
Dennis, Wesley, *2:* 87; *3:* 111; *11:* 132; *18:* 71-74; *22:* 9; *24:* 196, 200; *46:* 178
Denslow, W. W., *16:* 84-87; *18:* 19-20, 24; *29:* 211
de Paola, Tomie, *8:* 95; *9:* 93; *11:* 69; *25:* 103; *28:* 157; *29:* 80; *39:* 52-53; *40:* 226; *46:* 187
Detmold, Edward J., *22:* 104, 105, 106, 107; *35:* 120; *YABC 2:* 203
Detrich, Susan, *20:* 133
DeVelasco, Joseph E., *21:* 51
de Veyrac, Robert, *YABC 2:* 19
DeVille, Edward A., *4:* 235
Devito, Bert, *12:* 164
Devlin, Harry, *11:* 74
Dewey, Ariane, *7:* 64; *33:* 195; *35:* 208
See also Aruego, Ariane
Dewey, Kenneth, *39:* 62
de Zanger, Arie, *30:* 40
Diamond, Donna, *21:* 200; *23:* 63; *26:* 142; *35:* 83, 84, 85, 86-87, 88, 89; *38:* 78; *40:* 147; *44:* 152
Dick, John Henry, *8:* 181
Dickens, Frank, *34:* 131
Dickey, Robert L., *15:* 279
DiFate, Vincent, *37:* 70
DiFiori, Lawrence, *10:* 51; *12:* 190; *27:* 97; *40:* 219
Di Grazia, Thomas, *32:* 66; *35:* 241
Dillard, Annie, *10:* 32
Dillon, Corinne B., *1:* 139
Dillon, Diane, *4:* 104, 167; *6:* 23; *13:* 29; *15:* 99; *26:* 148; *27:* 136, 201
Dillon, Leo, *4:* 104, 167; *6:* 23; *13:* 29; *15:* 99; *26:* 148; *27:* 136, 201
DiMaggio, Joe, *36:* 22
Dinan, Carol, *25:* 169
Dines, Glen, *7:* 66-67
Dinesen, Thomas, *44:* 37
Dinnerstein, Harvey, *42:* 63, 64, 65, 66, 67, 68
Dinsdale, Mary, *10:* 65; *11:* 171
Disney, Walt, *28:* 71, 72, 73, 76, 77, 78, 79, 80, 81, 87, 88, 89, 90, 91, 94
Dixon, Maynard, *20:* 165
Doares, Robert G., *20:* 39
Dobias, Frank, *22:* 162
Dobrin, Arnold, *4:* 68
Docktor, Irv, *43:* 70
Dodd, Ed, *4:* 69
Dodd, Lynley, *35:* 92
Dodgson, Charles L., *20:* 148; *33:* 146; *YABC 2:* 98
Dodson, Bert, *9:* 138; *14:* 195; *42:* 55
Dohanos, Stevan, *16:* 10
Dolesch, Susanne, *34:* 49
Dolson, Hildegarde, *5:* 57

Domanska, Janina, *6:* 66-67; *YABC 1:* 166
Domjan, Joseph, *25:* 93
Donahue, Vic, *2:* 93; *3:* 190; *9:* 44
Donald, Elizabeth, *4:* 18
Donna, Natalie, *9:* 52
Doré, Gustave, *18:* 169, 172, 175; *19:* 93, 94, 95, 96, 97, 98, 99, 100, 101, 102, 103, 104, 105; *23:* 188; *25:* 197, 199
Doremus, Robert, *6:* 62; *13:* 90; *30:* 95, 96, 97; *38:* 97
Dorfman, Ronald, *11:* 128
Doty, Roy, *28:* 98; *31:* 32; *32:* 224; *46:* 157
Dougherty, Charles, *16:* 204; *18:* 74
Douglas, Aaron, *31:* 103
Douglas, Goray, *13:* 151
Dowd, Vic, *3:* 244; *10:* 97
Dowden, Anne Ophelia, *7:* 70-71; *13:* 120
Dowdy, Mrs. Regera, *29:* 100.
See also Gorey, Edward
Doyle, Richard, *21:* 31, 32, 33; *23:* 231; *24:* 177; *31:* 87
Draper, Angie, *43:* 84
Drath, Bill, *26:* 34
Drawson, Blair, *17:* 53
Drescher, Joan, *30:* 100, 101; *35:* 245
Drew, Patricia, *15:* 100
Drummond, V. H., *6:* 70
du Bois, William Pène, *4:* 70; *10:* 122; *26:* 61; *27:* 145, 211; *35:* 243; *41:* 216
Duchesne, Janet, *6:* 162
Dudash, Michael, *32:* 122
Duer, Douglas, *34:* 177
Duffy, Joseph, *38:* 203
Duffy, Pat, *28:* 153
Duke, Chris, *8:* 195
Dulac, Edmund, *19:* 108, 109, 110, 111, 112, 113, 114, 115, 117; *23:* 187; *25:* 152; *YABC 1:* 37; *YABC 2:* 147
Dulac, Jean, *13:* 64
Dunn, Harvey, *34:* 78, 79, 80, 81
Dunn, Phoebe, *5:* 175
Dunn, Iris, *5:* 175
Dunnington, Tom, *3:* 36; *18:* 281; *25:* 61; *31:* 159; *35:* 168; *48:* 195
Dutz, *6:* 59
Duvoisin, Roger, *2:* 95; *6:* 76-77; *7:* 197; *28:* 125; *30:* 101, 102, 103, 104, 105, 107; *47:* 205
Dypold, Pat, *15:* 37

E.V.B. *See* Boyle, Eleanor Vere (Gordon)
Eachus, Jennifer, *29:* 74
Eagle, Michael, *11:* 86; *20:* 9; *23:* 18; *27:* 122; *28:* 57; *34:* 201; *44:* 189
Earle, Olive L., *7:* 75
Earle, Vana, *27:* 99
Eastman, P. D., *33:* 57
Easton, Reginald, *29:* 181
Eaton, Tom, *4:* 62; *6:* 64; *22:* 99; *24:* 124
Ebel, Alex, *11:* 89

Ebert, Len, *9:* 191; *44:* 47
Echevarria, Abe, *37:* 69
Eckersley, Maureen, *48:* 62
Ede, Janina, *33:* 59
Edens, Cooper, *49:* 81, 82, 83, 84, 85
Edgar, Sarah E., *41:* 97
Edrien, *11:* 53
Edwards, Freya, *45:* 102
Edwards, George Wharton, *31:* 155
Edwards, Gunvor, *2:* 71; *25:* 47;
  32: 71
Edwards, Jeanne, *29:* 257
Edwards, Linda Strauss, *21:* 134;
  39: 123; *49:* 88-89
Eggenhofer, Nicholas, *2:* 81
Egielski, Richard, *11:* 90; *16:* 208;
  33: 236; *38:* 35; *49:* 91, 92, 93,
  95, 212, 213, 214, 216
Ehlert, Lois, *35:* 97
Ehrlich, Bettina, *1:* 83
Eichenberg, Fritz, *1:* 79; *9:* 54;
  19: 248; *23:* 170; *24:* 200;
  26: 208; *YABC 1:* 104-105;
  YABC 2: 213
Einsel, Naiad, *10:* 35; *29:* 136
Einsel, Walter, *10:* 37
Einzig, Susan, *3:* 77; *43:* 78
Eitzen, Allan, *9:* 56; *12:* 212; *14:* 226;
  21: 194; *38:* 162
Eldridge, Harold, *43:* 83
Elgaard, Greta, *19:* 241
Elgin, Kathleen, *9:* 188; *39:* 69
Ellacott, S. E., *19:* 118
Elliott, Sarah M., *14:* 58
Emberley, Ed, *8:* 53
Emberley, Michael, *34:* 83
Emery, Leslie, *49:* 187
Emmett, Bruce, *49:* 147
Engle, Mort, *38:* 64
Englebert, Victor, *8:* 54
Enos, Randall, *20:* 183
Enright, Maginel Wright, *19:* 240,
  243; *39:* 31, 35, 36
Enrique, Romeo, *34:* 135
Erhard, Walter, *1:* 152
Erickson, Phoebe, *11:* 83
Erikson, Mel, *31:* 69
Ernst, Lisa Campbell, *47:* 147
Escourido, Joseph, *4:* 81
Esté, Kirk, *33:* 111
Estoril, Jean, *32:* 27
Estrada, Ric, *5:* 52, 146; *13:* 174
Etchemendy, Teje, *38:* 68
Ets, Marie Hall, *2:* 102
Eulalie, *YABC 2:* 315
Evans, Katherine, *5:* 64
Ewing, Juliana Horatia, *16:* 92

Falconer, Pearl, *34:* 23
Falls, C. B., *1:* 19; *38:* 71, 72, 73, 74
Falter, John, *40:* 169, 170
Farmer, Andrew, *49:* 102
Farmer, Peter, *24:* 108; *38:* 75
Farquharson, Alexander, *46:* 75
Farrell, David, *40:* 135
Fatigati, Evelyn, *24:* 112
Faul-Jansen, Regina, *22:* 117
Faulkner, Jack, *6:* 169

Fava, Rita, *2:* 29
Fax, Elton C., *1:* 101; *4:* 2; *12:* 77;
  25: 107
Fay, *43:* 93
Federspiel, Marian, *33:* 51
Feelings, Tom, *5:* 22; *8:* 56; *12:* 153;
  16: 105; *30:* 196; *49:* 37
Fehr, Terrence, *21:* 87
Feiffer, Jules, *3:* 91; *8:* 58
Feigeles, Neil, *41:* 242
Feller, Gene, *33:* 130
Fellows, Muriel H., *10:* 42
Felts, Shirley, *33:* 71; *48:* 59
Fennelli, Maureen, *38:* 181
Fenton, Carroll Lane, *5:* 66; *21:* 39
Fenton, Mildred Adams, *5:* 66; *21:* 39
Ferguson, Walter W., *34:* 86
Fetz, Ingrid, *11:* 67; *12:* 52; *16:* 205;
  17: 59; *29:* 105; *30:* 108, 109;
  32: 149; *43:* 142
Fiammenghi, Gioia, *9:* 66; *11:* 44;
  12: 206; *13:* 57, 59
Field, Rachel, *15:* 113
Fine, Peter K., *43:* 210
Finger, Helen, *42:* 81
Fink, Sam, *18:* 119
Finlay, Winifred, *23:* 72
Fiorentino, Al, *3:* 240
Firmin, Charlotte, *29:* 75; *48:* 70
Fischel, Lillian, *40:* 204
Fischer, Hans, *25:* 202
Fisher, Leonard Everett, *3:* 6; *4:* 72,
  86; *6:* 197; *9:* 59; *16:* 151, 153;
  23: 44; *27:* 134; *29:* 26; *34:* 87,
  89, 90, 91, 93, 94, 95, 96;
  40: 206; *YABC 2:* 169
Fisher, Lois, *20:* 62; *21:* 7
Fisk, Nicholas, *25:* 112
Fitschen, Marilyn, *2:* 20-21; *20:* 48
Fitzgerald, F. A., *15:* 116; *25:* 86-87
Fitzhugh, Louise, *1:* 94; *9:* 163;
  45: 75, 78
Fitzhugh, Susie, *11:* 117
Fitzsimmons, Arthur, *14:* 128
Fix, Philippe, *26:* 102
Flack, Marjorie, *21:* 67; *YABC 2:* 122
Flagg, James Montgomery, *17:* 227
Flax, Zeona, *2:* 245
Fleishman, Seymour, *14:* 232; *24:* 87
Fleming, Guy, *18:* 41
Floethe, Richard, *3:* 131; *4:* 90
Floherty, John J., Jr., *5:* 68
Flora, James, *1:* 96; *30:* 111, 112
Florian, Douglas, *19:* 122
Flory, Jane, *22:* 111
Floyd, Gareth, *1:* 74; *17:* 245; *48:* 63
Fluchère, Henri A., *40:* 79
Flynn, Barbara, *7:* 31; *9:* 70
Fogarty, Thomas, *15:* 89
Folger, Joseph, *9:* 100
Folkard, Charles, *22:* 132; *29:* 128,
  257-258
Foott, Jeff, *42:* 202
Forberg, Ati, *12:* 71, 205; *14:* 1;
  22: 113; *26:* 22; *48:* 64, 65
Ford, George, *24:* 120; *31:* 70, 177
Ford, H. J., *16:* 185-186
Ford, Pamela Baldwin, *27:* 104
Foreman, Michael, *2:* 110-111

Forrester, Victoria, *40:* 83
Fortnum, Peggy, *6:* 29; *20:* 179;
  24: 211; *26:* 76, 77, 78; *39:* 78;
  YABC 1: 148
Foster, Brad W., *34:* 99
Foster, Genevieve, *2:* 112
Foster, Gerald, *7:* 78
Foster, Laura Louise, *6:* 79
Foster, Marian Curtis, *23:* 74; *40:* 42
Foucher, Adèle, *47:* 118
Fowler, Mel, *36:* 127
Fox, Charles Phillip, *12:* 84
Fox, Jim, *6:* 187
Fracé, Charles, *15:* 118
Frame, Paul, *2:* 45, 145; *9:* 153;
  10: 124; *21:* 71; *23:* 62; *24:* 123;
  27: 106; *31:* 48; *32:* 159; *34:* 195;
  38: 136; *42:* 55; *44:* 139
Francois, André, *25:* 117
Francoise. See Seignobosc, Francoise
Frank, Lola Edick, *2:* 199
Frank, Mary, *4:* 54; *34:* 100
Franké, Phil, *45:* 91
Frankel, Julie, *40:* 84, 85, 202
Frankenberg, Robert, *22:* 116; *30:* 50;
  38: 92, 94, 95
Franklin, John, *24:* 22
Frascino, Edward, *9:* 133; *29:* 229;
  33: 190; *48:* 80, 81, 82, 83, 84-
  85, 86
Frasconi, Antonio, *6:* 80; *27:* 208
Fraser, Betty, *2:* 212; *6:* 185; *8:* 103;
  31: 72, 73; *43:* 136
Fraser, Eric, *38:* 78; *41:* 149, 151
Fraser, F. A., *22:* 234
Frazetta, Frank, *41:* 72
Freas, John, *25:* 207
Freeman, Don, *2:* 15; *13:* 249;
  17: 62-63, 65, 67-68; *18:* 243;
  20: 195; *23:* 213, 217; *32:* 155
Fregosi, Claudia, *24:* 117
French, Fiona, *6:* 82-83
Friedman, Judith, *43:* 197
Friedman, Marvin, *19:* 59; *42:* 86
Frinta, Dagmar, *36:* 42
Frith, Michael K., *15:* 138; *18:* 120
Fritz, Ronald, *46:* 73
Fromm, Lilo, *29:* 85; *40:* 197
Frost, A. B., *17:* 6-7; *19:* 123, 124,
  125, 126, 127, 128, 129, 130;
  YABC 1: 156-157, 160;
  YABC 2: 107
Fry, Guy, *2:* 224
Fry, Rosalie, *3:* 72; *YABC 2:* 180-181
Fry, Rosalind, *21:* 153, 168
Fryer, Elmer, *34:* 115
Fuchs, Erich, *6:* 84
Fuchshuber, Annegert, *43:* 96
Fufuka, Mahiri, *32:* 146
Fujikawa, Gyo, *39:* 75, 76
Fulford, Deborah, *23:* 159
Fuller, Margaret, *25:* 189
Funai, Mamoru, *38:* 105
Funk, Tom, *7:* 17, 99
Furchgott, Terry, *29:* 86
Furukawa, Mel, *25:* 42

Gaberell, J., *19:* 236

Gackenbach, Dick, *19:* 168; *41:* 81; *48:* 89, 90, 91, 92, 93, 94
Gaetano, Nicholas, *23:* 209
Gag, Flavia, *17:* 49, 52
Gág, Wanda, *YABC 1:* 135, 137-138, 141, 143
Gagnon, Cécile, *11:* 77
Gal, Laszlo, *14:* 127
Galdone, Paul, *1:* 156, 181, 206; *2:* 40, 241; *3:* 42, 144; *4:* 141; *10:* 109, 158; *11:* 21; *12:* 118, 210; *14:* 12; *16:* 36-37; *17:* 70-74; *18:* 111, 230; *19:* 183; *21:* 154; *22:* 150, 245; *33:* 126; *39:* 136, 137; *42:* 57
Gallagher, Sears, *20:* 112
Galster, Robert, *1:* 66
Galsworthy, Gay John, *35:* 232
Gammell, Stephen, *7:* 48; *13:* 149; *29:* 82; *33:* 209; *41:* 88
Gannett, Ruth Chrisman, *3:* 74; *18:* 254; *33:* 77, 78
Gantschev, Ivan, *45:* 32
Garbutt, Bernard, *23:* 68
Garcia, *37:* 71
Gardner, Earle, *45:* 167
Gardner, Joan, *40:* 87
Gardner, Joel, *40:* 87, 92
Gardner, John, *40:* 87
Gardner, Lucy, *40:* 87
Gardner, Richard. *See* Cummings, Richard, *24:* 119
Garland, Michael, *36:* 29; *38:* 83; *44:* 168; *48:* 78, 221, 222; *49:* 161
Garnett, Eve, *3:* 75
Garnett, Gary, *39:* 184
Garraty, Gail, *4:* 142
Garrett, Agnes, *46:* 110; *47:* 157
Garrett, Edmund H., *20:* 29
Garrison, Barbara, *19:* 133
Gates, Frieda, *26:* 80
Gaughan, Jack, *26:* 79; *43:* 185
Gaver, Becky, *20:* 61
Gay, Zhenya, *19:* 135, 136
Geary, Clifford N., *1:* 122; *9:* 104
Gee, Frank, *33:* 26
Geer, Charles, *1:* 91; *3:* 179; *4:* 201; *6:* 168; *7:* 96; *9:* 58; *10:* 72; *12:* 127; *39:* 156, 157, 158, 159, 160; *42:* 88, 89, 90, 91
Gehm, Charlie, *36:* 65
Geisel, Theodor Seuss, *1:* 104-105, 106; *28:* 108, 109, 110, 111, 112, 113
Geldart, William, *15:* 121; *21:* 202
Genia, *4:* 84
Gentry, Cyrille R., *12:* 66
George, Jean, *2:* 113
Gérard, Jean Ignace, *45:* 80
Gérard, Rolf, *27:* 147, 150
Geritz, Franz, *17:* 135
Gerlach, Geff, *42:* 58
Gerrard, Roy, *47:* 78
Gershinowitz, George, *36:* 27
Gerstein, Mordicai, *31:* 117; *47:* 80, 81, 82, 83, 84, 85, 86
Gervase, *12:* 27
Getz, Arthur, *32:* 148

Gibbons, Gail, *23:* 78
Gibbs, Tony, *40:* 95
Gibran, Kahlil, *32:* 116
Giesen, Rosemary, *34:* 192-193
Giguère, George, *20:* 111
Gilbert, John, *19:* 184; *YABC 2:* 287
Gilbert, W. S., *36:* 83, 85, 96
Giles, Will, *41:* 218
Gill, Margery, *4:* 57; *7:* 7; *22:* 122; *25:* 166; *26:* 146, 147
Gillen, Denver, *28:* 216
Gillette, Henry J., *23:* 237
Gilliam, Stan, *39:* 64, 81
Gilman, Esther, *15:* 124
Giovanopoulos, Paul, *7:* 104
Githens, Elizabeth M., *5:* 47
Gladstone, Gary, *12:* 89; *13:* 190
Gladstone, Lise, *15:* 273
Glanzman, Louis S., *2:* 177; *3:* 182; *36:* 97, 98; *38:* 120, 122
Glaser, Milton, *3:* 5; *5:* 156; *11:* 107; *30:* 26; *36:* 112
Glass, Andrew, *36:* 38; *44:* 133; *48:* 205
Glass, Marvin, *9:* 174
Glasser, Judy, *41:* 156
Glattauer, Ned, *5:* 84; *13:* 224; *14:* 26
Glauber, Uta, *17:* 76
Gleeson, J. M., *YABC 2:* 207
Glegg, Creina, *36:* 100
Gliewe, Unada, *3:* 78-79; *21:* 73; *30:* 220
Glovach, Linda, *7:* 105
Gobbato, Imero, *3:* 180-181; *6:* 213; *7:* 58; *9:* 150; *18:* 39; *21:* 167; *39:* 82, 83; *41:* 137, 251
Goble, Paul, *25:* 121; *26:* 86; *33:* 65
Goble, Warwick, *46:* 78, 79
Godal, Eric, *36:* 93
Godfrey, Michael, *17:* 279
Goembel, Ponder, *42:* 124
Goffstein, M. B., *8:* 71
Golbin, Andrée, *15:* 125
Goldfeder, Cheryl, *11:* 191
Goldsborough, June, *5:* 154-155; *8:* 92, *14:* 226; *19:* 139
Goldstein, Leslie, *5:* 8; *6:* 60; *10:* 106
Goldstein, Nathan, *1:* 175; *2:* 79; *11:* 41, 232; *16:* 55
Goodall, John S., *4:* 92-93; *10:* 132; *YABC 1:* 198
Goode, Diane, *15:* 126
Goodelman, Aaron, *40:* 203
Goodenow, Earle, *40:* 97
Goodwin, Harold, *13:* 74
Goodwin, Philip R., *18:* 206
Goor, Nancy, *39:* 85, 86
Goor, Ron, *39:* 85, 86
Gordon, Gwen, *12:* 151
Gordon, Margaret, *4:* 147; *5:* 48-49; *9:* 79
Gorecka-Egan, Erica, *18:* 35
Gorey, Edward, *1:* 60-61; *13:* 169; *18:* 192; *20:* 201; *29:* 90, 91, 92-93, 94, 95, 96, 97, 98, 99, 100; *30:* 129; *32:* 90; *34:* 200. *See also* Dowdy, Mrs. Regera

Gorsline, Douglas, *1:* 98; *6:* 13; *11:* 113; *13:* 104; *15:* 14; *28:* 117, 118; *YABC 1:* 15
Gosner, Kenneth, *5:* 135
Gotlieb, Jules, *6:* 127
Gough, Philip, *23:* 47; *45:* 90
Gould, Chester, *49:* 112, 113, 114, 116, 117, 118
Govern, Elaine R., *26:* 94
Grabianski, *20:* 144
Grabiański, Janusz, *39:* 92, 93, 94, 95
Graboff, Abner, *35:* 103, 104
Graham, A. B., *11:* 61
Graham, L., *7:* 108
Graham, Margaret Bloy, *11:* 120; *18:* 305, 307
Grahame-Johnstone, Anne, *13:* 61
Grahame-Johnstone, Janet, *13:* 61
Grainger, Sam, *42:* 95
Gramatky, Hardie, *1:* 107; *30:* 116, 119, 120, 122, 123
Grandville, J. J., *45:* 81, 82, 83, 84, 85, 86, 87, 88; *47:* 125
Granger, Paul, *39:* 153
Grant, Gordon, *17:* 230, 234; *25:* 123, 124, 125, 126; *YABC 1:* 164
Grant, (Alice) Leigh, *10:* 52; *15:* 131; *20:* 20; *26:* 119; *48:* 202
Graves, Elizabeth, *45:* 101
Gray, Harold, *33:* 87, 88
Gray, Reginald, *6:* 69
Green, Eileen, *6:* 97
Green, Michael, *32:* 216
Greenaway, Kate, *17:* 275; *24:* 180; *26:* 107; *41:* 222, 232; *YABC 1:* 88-89; *YABC 2:* 131, 133, 136, 138-139, 141
Greenwald, Sheila, *1:* 34; *3:* 99; *8:* 72
Gregorian, Joyce Ballou, *30:* 125
Gregory, Frank M., *29:* 107
Greiffenhagen, Maurice, *16:* 137; *27:* 57; *YABC 2:* 288
Greiner, Robert, *6:* 86
Gretter, J. Clemens, *31:* 134
Gretz, Susanna, *7:* 114
Gretzer, John, *1:* 54; *3:* 26; *4:* 162; *7:* 125; *16:* 247; *18:* 117; *28:* 66; *30:* 85, 211; *33:* 235
Grey Owl, *24:* 41
Gri, *25:* 90
Grieder, Walter *9:* 84
Grifalconi, Ann, *2:* 126; *3:* 248; *11:* 18; *13:* 182; *46:* 38
Griffin, Gillett Good, *26:* 96
Griffin, James, *30:* 166
Griffiths, Dave, *29:* 76
Gringhuis, Dirk, *6:* 98; *9:* 196
Gripe, Harald, *2:* 127
Grisha, *3:* 71
Gropper, William, *27:* 93; *37:* 193
Grose, Helen Mason, *YABC 1:* 260; *YABC 2:* 150
Grossman, Nancy, *24:* 130; *29:* 101
Grossman, Robert, *11:* 124; *46:* 39
Groth, John, *15:* 79; *21:* 53, 54
Gruelle, Johnny, *35:* 107
Gschwind, William, *11:* 72
Guggenheim, Hans, *2:* 10; *3:* 37; *8:* 136

Guilbeau, Honoré, *22:* 69
Gundersheimer, Karen, *35:* 240
Gusman, Annie, *38:* 62
Gustafson, Scott, *34:* 111; *43:* 40
Guthrie, Robin, *20:* 122
Gwynne, Fred, *41:* 94, 95
Gyberg, Bo-Erik, *38:* 131

Haas, Irene, *17:* 77
Hader, Berta H., *16:* 126
Hader, Elmer S., *16:* 126
Hafner, Marylin, *22:* 196, 216; *24:* 44;
    30: 51; *35:* 95
Hague, Michael, *32:* 128; *48:* 98, 99,
    100-101, 103, 105, 106-107, 108,
    109, 110; *49:* 121
Halas, John, *29:* 41, 47, 48
Haldane, Roger, *13:* 76; *14:* 202
Hale, Irina, *26:* 97
Hale, Kathleen, *17:* 79
Haley, Gail E., *43:* 102, 103, 104, 105
Hall, Chuck, *30:* 189
Hall, Douglas, *15:* 184; *43:* 106, 107
Hall, H. Tom, *1:* 227; *30:* 210
Hall, Sydney P., *31:* 89
Hall, Vicki, *20:* 24
Hallinan, P. K., *39:* 98
Halpern, Joan, *10:* 25
Halverson, Janet, *49:* 38, 42, 44
Hamberger, John, *6:* 8; *8:* 32; *14:* 79;
    34: 136
Hamil, Tom, *14:* 80; *43:* 163
Hamilton, Bill and Associates, *26:* 215
Hamilton, Helen S., *2:* 238
Hamilton, J., *19:* 83, 85, 87
Hammond, Chris, *21:* 37
Hammond, Elizabeth, *5:* 36, 203
Hampshire, Michael, *5:* 187;
    7: 110-111; *48:* 150
Hampson, Denman, *10:* 155; *15:* 130
Hampton, Blake, *41:* 244
Handforth, Thomas, *42:* 100, 101,
    102, 103, 104, 105, 107
Handville, Robert, *1:* 89; *38:* 76;
    45: 108, 109
Hane, Roger, *17:* 239; *44:* 54
Haney, Elizabeth Mathieu, *34:* 84
Hanley, Catherine, *8:* 161
Hann, Jacquie, *19:* 144
Hannon, Mark, *38:* 37
Hanson, Joan, *8:* 76; *11:* 139
Hardy, David A., *9:* 96
Hardy, Paul, *YABC 2:* 245
Harlan, Jerry, *3:* 96
Harnischfeger, *18:* 121
Harper, Arthur, *YABC 2:* 121
Harrington, Richard, *5:* 81
Harris, Susan Yard, *42:* 121
Harrison, Florence, *20:* 150, 152
Harrison, Harry, *4:* 103
Harrison, Jack, *28:* 149
Hart, William, *13:* 72
Hartelius, Margaret, *10:* 24
Hartshorn, Ruth, *5:* 115; *11:* 129
Harvey, Bob, *48:* 219
Harvey, Gerry, *7:* 180
Hassall, Joan, *43:* 108, 109
Hassell, Hilton, *YABC 1:* 187

Hasselriis, Else, *18:* 87; *YABC 1:* 96
Hauman, Doris, *2:* 184; *29:* 58, 59;
    32: 85, 86, 87
Hauman, George, *2:* 184; *29:* 58, 59;
    32: 85, 86, 87
Hausherr, Rosmarie, *15:* 29
Hawkinson, John, *4:* 109; *7:* 83;
    21: 64
Hawkinson, Lucy, *21:* 64
Haxton, Elaine, *28:* 131
Haydock, Robert, *4:* 95
Hayes, Geoffrey, *26:* 111; *44:* 133
Haywood, Carolyn, *1:* 112; *29:* 104
Healy, Daty, *12:* 143
Hearon, Dorothy, *34:* 69
Hechtkopf, H., *11:* 110
Hedderwick, Mairi, *30:* 127; *32:* 47;
    36: 104
Hefter, Richard, *28:* 170; *31:* 81, 82;
    33: 183
Heigh, James, *22:* 98
Heighway, Richard, *25:* 160
Heinly, John, *45:* 113
Hellebrand, Nancy, *26:* 57
Heller, Linda, *46:* 86
Hellmuth, Jim, *38:* 164
Helms, Georgeann, *33:* 62
Helweg, Hans, *41:* 118
Henderson, Keith, *35:* 122
Henkes, Kevin, *43:* 111
Henneberger, Robert, *1:* 42; *2:* 237;
    25: 83
Henriksen, Harold, *35:* 26; *48:* 68
Henry, Everett, *29:* 191
Henry, Thomas, *5:* 102
Hensel, *27:* 119
Henstra, Friso, *8:* 80; *36:* 70; *40:* 222;
    41: 250
Hepple, Norman, *28:* 198
Herbert, Wally, *23:* 101
Herbster, Mary Lee, *9:* 33
Hergé. *See* Rémi, Georges
Hermanson, Dennis, *10:* 55
Herrington, Roger, *3:* 161
Heslop, Mike, *38:* 60; *40:* 130
Hess, Richard, *42:* 31
Hester, Ronnie, *37:* 85
Heustis, Louise L., *20:* 28
Heyduck-Huth, Hilde, *8:* 82
Heyer, Hermann, *20:* 114, 115
Heyman, Ken, *8:* 33; *34:* 113
Heywood, Karen, *48:* 114
Hickling, P. B., *40:* 165
Higginbottom, J. Winslow, *8:* 170;
    29: 105, 106
Hildebrandt, Greg, *8:* 191
Hildebrandt, Tim, *8:* 191
Hilder, Rowland, *19:* 207
Hill, Gregory, *35:* 190
Hill, Pat, *49:* 120
Hillier, Matthew, *45:* 205
Hillman, Priscilla, *48:* 115
Himler, Ronald, *6:* 114; *7:* 162; *8:* 17,
    84, 125; *14:* 76; *19:* 145; *26:* 160;
    31: 43; *38:* 116; *41:* 44, 79;
    43: 52; *45:* 120; *46:* 43
Himmelman, John, *47:* 109
Hinds, Bill, *37:* 127, 130
Hiroshige, *25:* 71

Hirsh, Marilyn, *7:* 126
Hitz, Demi, *11:* 135; *15:* 245
Hnizdovsky, Jacques, *32:* 96
Ho, Kwoncjan, *15:* 132
Hoban, Lillian, *1:* 114; *22:* 157;
    26: 72; *29:* 53; *40:* 105, 107, 195;
    41: 80
Hoban, Tana, *22:* 159
Hoberman, Norman, *5:* 82
Hockerman, Dennis, *39:* 22
Hodgell, P. C., *42:* 114
Hodges, C. Walter, *2:* 139; *11:* 15;
    12: 25; *23:* 34; *25:* 96; *38:* 165;
    44: 197; *45:* 95; *YABC 2:* 62-63
Hodges, David, *9:* 98
Hodgetts, Victoria, *43:* 132
Hofbauer, Imre, *2:* 162
Hoff, Syd, *9:* 107; *10:* 128; *33:* 94
Hoffman, Rosekrans, *15:* 133
Hoffman, Sanford, *38:* 208
Hoffmann, Felix, *9:* 109
Hofsinde, Robert, *21:* 70
Hogan, Inez, *2:* 141
Hogarth, Burne, *41:* 58
Hogarth, Paul, *41:* 102, 103, 104;
    YABC 1: 16
Hogarth, William, *42:* 33
Hogenbyl, Jan, *1:* 35
Hogner, Nils, *4:* 122; *25:* 144
Hogrogian, Nonny, *3:* 221; *4:* 106-107;
    5: 166; *7:* 129; *15:* 2; *16:* 176;
    20: 154; *22:* 146; *25:* 217;
    27: 206; *YABC 2:* 84, 94
Hokusai, *25:* 71
Holberg, Richard, *2:* 51
Holdcroft, Tina, *38:* 109
Holder, Heidi, *36:* 99
Holiday, Henry, *YABC 2:* 107
Holl, F., *36:* 91
Holland, Brad, *45:* 59, 159
Holland, Janice, *18:* 118
Holland, Marion, *6:* 116
Holldobler, Turid, *26:* 120
Holling, Holling C., *15:* 136-137
Hollinger, Deanne, *12:* 116
Holmes, B., *3:* 82
Holmes, Bea, *7:* 74; *24:* 156; *31:* 93
Holmgren, George Ellen, *45:* 112
Holt, Norma, *44:* 106
Holtan, Gene, *32:* 192
Holz, Loretta, *17:* 81
Homar, Lorenzo, *6:* 2
Homer, Winslow, *YABC 2:* 87
Honigman, Marian, *3:* 2
Honoré, Paul, *42:* 77, 79, 81, 82
Hood, Susan, *12:* 43
Hook, Frances, *26:* 188; *27:* 127
Hook, Jeff, *14:* 137
Hook, Richard, *26:* 188
Hoover, Carol A., *21:* 77
Hoover, Russell, *12:* 95; *17:* 2;
    34: 156
Hoppin, Augustus, *34:* 66
Horder, Margaret, *2:* 108
Horen, Michael, *45:* 121
Horvat, Laurel, *12:* 201
Horvath, Ferdinand Kusati, *24:* 176
Hotchkiss, De Wolfe, *20:* 49

Hough, Charlotte, *9:* 112; *13:* 98; *17:* 83; *24:* 195
Houlihan, Ray, *11:* 214
Housman, Laurence, *25:* 146, 147
Houston, James, *13:* 107
How, W. E., *20:* 47
Howard, Alan, *16:* 80; *34:* 58; *45:* 114
Howard, J. N., *15:* 234
Howard, John, *33:* 179
Howard, Rob, *40:* 161
Howe, Stephen, *1:* 232
Howell, Pat, *15:* 139
Howell, Troy, *23:* 24; *31:* 61; *36:* 158; *37:* 184; *41:* 76, 235; *48:* 112
Howes, Charles, *22:* 17
Hubley, Faith, *48:* 120-121, 125, 130, 131, 132, 134
Hubley, John, *48:* 125, 130, 131, 132, 134
Hudnut, Robin, *14:* 62
Huffaker, Sandy, *10:* 56
Huffman, Joan, *13:* 33
Huffman, Tom, *13:* 180; *17:* 212; *21:* 116; *24:* 132; *33:* 154; *38:* 59; *42:* 147
Hughes, Arthur, *20:* 148, 149, 150; *33:* 114, 148, 149
Hughes, David, *36:* 197
Hughes, Shirley, *1:* 20, 21; *7:* 3; *12:* 217; *16:* 163; *29:* 154
Hugo, Victor, *47:* 112
Hülsmann, Eva, *16:* 166
Hummel, Berta, *43:* 137, 138, 139
Hummel, Lisl, *29:* 109; *YABC 2:* 333-334
Humphrey, Henry, *16:* 167
Humphreys, Graham, *25:* 168
Hunt, James, *2:* 143
Hurd, Clement, *2:* 148, 149
Hurd, Peter; *24:* 30, 31, *YABC 2:* 56
Hurd, Thacher, *46:* 88-89
Hugo, Victor, *47:* 112
Hürlimann, Ruth, *32:* 99
Hustler, Tom, *6:* 105
Hutchins, Pat, *15:* 142
Hutchinson, William M., *6:* 3, 138; *46:* 70
Hutchison, Paula, *23:* 10
Hutton, Clarke, *YABC 2:* 335
Hutton, Kathryn, *35:* 155
Hutton, Warwick, *20:* 91
Huyette, Marcia, *29:* 188
Hyman, Trina Schart, *1:* 204; *2:* 194; *5:* 153; *6:* 106; *7:* 138, 145; *8:* 22; *10:* 196; *13:* 96; *14:* 114; *15:* 204; *16:* 234; *20:* 82; *22:* 133; *24:* 151; *25:* 79, 82; *26:* 82; *29:* 83; *31:* 37, 39; *34:* 104; *38:* 84, 100, 128; *41:* 49; *43:* 146; *46:* 91, 92, 93, 95, 96, 97, 98, 99, 100, 101, 102, 103, 104-105, 108, 109, 111, 197; *48:* 60, 61

Ichikawa, Satomi, *29:* 152; *41:* 52; *47:* 133, 134, 135, 136
Ide, Jacqueline, *YABC 1:* 39
Ilsley, Velma, *3:* 1; *7:* 55; *12:* 109; *37:* 62; *38:* 184

Inga, *1:* 142
Ingraham, Erick, *21:* 177
Innocenti, Roberto, *21:* 123
Inoue, Yosuke, *24:* 118
Ipcar, Dahlov, *1:* 124-125; *49:* 137, 138, 139, 140-141, 142, 143, 144, 145
Irvin, Fred, *13:* 166; *15:* 143-144; *27:* 175
Irving, Jay, *45:* 72
Irving, Laurence, *27:* 50
Isaac, Joanne, *21:* 76
Isadora, Rachel, *43:* 159, 160
Ishmael, Woodi, *24:* 111; *31:* 99
Ives, Ruth, *15:* 257

Jackson, Michael, *43:* 42
Jacobs, Barbara, *9:* 136
Jacobs, Lou, Jr., *9:* 136; *15:* 128
Jacques, Robin, *1:* 70; *2:* 1; *8:* 46; *9:* 20; *15:* 187; *19:* 253; *32:* 102, 103, 104; *43:* 184; *YABC 1:* 42
Jagr, Miloslav, *13:* 197
Jakubowski, Charles, *14:* 192
Jambor, Louis, *YABC 1:* 11
James, Derek, *35:* 187; *44:* 91
James, Gilbert, *YABC 1:* 43
James, Harold, *2:* 151; *3:* 62; *8:* 79; *29:* 113
James, Will, *19:* 150, 152, 153, 155, 163
Janosch. *See* Eckert, Horst
Jansons, Inese, *48:* 117
Jansson, Tove, *3:* 90; *41:* 106, 108, 109, 110, 111, 113, 114
Jaques, Faith, *7:* 11, 132-33; *21:* 83, 84
Jaques, Frances Lee, *29:* 224
Jauss, Anne Marie, *1:* 139; *3:* 34; *10:* 57, 119; *11:* 205; *23:* 194
Jeffers, Susan, *17:* 86-87; *25:* 164-165; *26:* 112
Jefferson, Louise E., *4:* 160
Jeruchim, Simon, *6:* 173; *15:* 250
Jeschke, Susan, *20:* 89; *39:* 161; *41:* 84; *42:* 120
Jessel, Camilla, *29:* 115
Joerns, Consuelo, *38:* 36; *44:* 94
John, Diana, *12:* 209
John, Helen, *1:* 215; *28:* 204
Johns, Jeanne, *24:* 114
Johnson, Bruce, *9:* 47
Johnson, Crockett. *See* Leisk, David
Johnson, D. William, *23:* 104
Johnson, Harper, *1:* 27; *2:* 33; *18:* 302; *19:* 61; *31:* 181; *44:* 46, 50, 95
Johnson, Ingrid, *37:* 118
Johnson, James David, *12:* 195
Johnson, James Ralph, *1:* 23, 127
Johnson, Jane, *48:* 136
Johnson, John E., *34:* 133
Johnson, Larry, *47:* 56
Johnson, Margaret S., *35:* 131
Johnson, Milton, *1:* 67; *2:* 71; *26:* 45; *31:* 107
Johnson, Pamela, *16:* 174
Johnson, William R., *38:* 91
Johnstone, Anne, *8:* 120; *36:* 89

Johnstone, Janet Grahame, *8:* 120; *36:* 89
Jones, Carol, *5:* 131
Jones, Elizabeth Orton, *18:* 124, 126, 128-129
Jones, Harold, *14:* 88
Jones, Jeff, *41:* 64
Jones, Laurian, *25:* 24, 27
Jones, Robert, *25:* 67
Jones, Wilfred, *35:* 115; *YABC 1:* 163
Joyner, Jerry, *34:* 138
Jucker, Sita, *5:* 93
Judkis, Jim, *37:* 38
Juhasz, Victor, *31:* 67
Jullian, Philippe, *24:* 206; *25:* 203
Jupo, Frank, *7:* 148-149
Justice, Martin, *34:* 72

Kahl, M. P., *37:* 83
Kahl, Virginia, *48:* 138
Kakimoo, Kozo, *11:* 148
Kalett, Jim, *48:* 159, 160, 161
Kalin, Victor, *39:* 186
Kalmenoff, Matthew, *22:* 191
Kalow, Gisela, *32:* 105
Kamen, Gloria, *1:* 41; *9:* 119; *10:* 178; *35:* 157
Kandell, Alice, *35:* 133
Kane, Henry B., *14:* 90; *18:* 219-220
Kane, Robert, *18:* 131
Kappes, Alfred, *28:* 104
Karalus, Bob, *41:* 157
Karlin, Eugene, *10:* 63; *20:* 131
Kasuya, Masahiro, *41:* 206-207
Katona, Robert, *21:* 85; *24:* 126
Kauffer, E. McKnight, *33:* 103; *35:* 127
Kaufman, Angelika, *15:* 156
Kaufman, Joe, *33:* 119
Kaufman, John, *13:* 158
Kaufmann, John, *1:* 174; *4:* 159; *8:* 43, 1; *10:* 102; *18:* 133-134; *22:* 251
Kaye, Graham, *1:* 9
Kazalovski, Nata, *40:* 205
Keane, Bil, *4:* 135
Keats, Ezra Jack, *3:* 18, 105, 257; *14:* 101, 102; *33:* 129
Keegan, Marcia, *9:* 122; *32:* 93
Keely, John, *26:* 104; *48:* 214
Keen, Eliot, *25:* 213
Keeping, Charles, *9:* 124, 185; *15:* 28, 134; *18:* 115; *44:* 194, 196; *47:* 25
Keith, Eros, *4:* 98; *5:* 138; *31:* 29; *43:* 220
Kelen, Emery, *13:* 115
Keller, Arthur I., *26:* 106
Keller, Dick, *36:* 123, 125
Keller, Holly, *45:* 79
Keller, Ronald, *45:* 208
Kelley, True, *41:* 114, 115; *42:* 137
Kellogg, Steven, *8:* 96; *11:* 207; *14:* 130; *20:* 58; *29:* 140-141; *30:* 35; *41:* 141; *YABC 1:* 65, 73
Kelly, Walt, *18:* 136-141, 144-146, 148-149
Kemble, E. W., *34:* 75; *44:* 178; *YABC 2:* 54, 59

Kemp-Welsh, Lucy, *24:* 197
Kennedy, Paul Edward, *6:* 190; *8:* 132; *33:* 120
Kennedy, Richard, *3:* 93; *12:* 179; *44:* 193; *YABC 1:* 57
Kent, Jack, *24:* 136; *37:* 37; *40:* 81
Kent, Rockwell, *5:* 166; *6:* 129; *20:* 225, 226, 227, 229
Kepes, Juliet, *13:* 119
Kerr, Judity, *24:* 137
Kessler, Leonard, *1:* 108; *7:* 139; *14:* 107, 227; *22:* 101; *44:* 96
Kesteven, Peter, *35:* 189
Ketcham, Hank, *28:* 140, 141, 142
Kettelkamp, Larry, *2:* 164
Key, Alexander, *8:* 99
Kiakshuk, *8:* 59
Kiddell-Monroe, Joan, *19:* 201
Kidder, Harvey, *9:* 105
Kidwell, Carl, *43:* 145
Kieffer, Christa, *41:* 89
Kiff, Ken, *40:* 45
Kilbride, Robert, *37:* 100
Kimball, Yeffe, *23:* 116; *37:* 88
Kincade, Orin, *34:* 116
Kindred, Wendy, *7:* 151
King, Robin, *10:* 164-165
King, Tony, *39:* 121
Kingman, Dong, *16:* 287; *44:* 100, 102, 104
Kingsley, Charles, *YABC 2:* 182
Kipling, John Lockwood, *YABC 2:* 198
Kipling, Rudyard, *YABC 2:* 196
Kipniss, Robert, *29:* 59
Kirchhoff, Art, *28:* 136
Kirk, Ruth, *5:* 96
Kirk, Tim, *32:* 209, 211
Kirmse, Marguerite, *15:* 283; *18:* 153
Kirschner, Ruth, *22:* 154
Klapholz, Mel, *13:* 35
Kleinman, Zalman, *28:* 143
Kliban, B., *35:* 137, 138
Knight, Ann, *34:* 143
Knight, Christopher, *13:* 125
Knight, Hilary, *1:* 233; *3:* 21; *15:* 92, 158-159; *16:* 258-260; *18:* 235; *19:* 169; *35:* 242; *46:* 167; *YABC 1:* 168-169, 172
Knotts, Howard, *20:* 4; *25:* 170; *36:* 163
Kobayashi, Ann, *39:* 58
Kocsis, J. C. *See* Paul, James
Koehn, Ilse, *34:* 198
Koering, Ursula, *3:* 28; *4:* 14; *44:* 53
Koerner, Henry. *See* Koerner, W.H.D.
Koerner, W.H.D., *14:* 216; *21:* 88, 89, 90, 91; *23:* 211
Koffler, Camilla, *36:* 113
Komoda, Kiyo, *9:* 128; *13:* 214
Konashevicha, V., *YABC 1:* 26
Konigsburg, E. L., *4:* 138; *48:* 141, 142, 144, 145
Kooiker, Leonie, *48:* 148
Korach, Mimi, *1:* 128-129; *2:* 52; *4:* 39; *5:* 159; *9:* 129; *10:* 21; *24:* 69
Koren, Edward, *5:* 100
Kossin, Sandy, *10:* 71; *23:* 105
Kostin, Andrej, *26:* 204

Kovacević, Zivojin, *13:* 247
Krahn, Fernando, *2:* 257; *34:* 206; *49:* 152
Kramer, Anthony, *33:* 81
Kramer, Frank, *6:* 121
Krantz, Kathy, *35:* 83
Kraus, Robert, *13:* 217
Kredel, Fritz, *6:* 35; *17:* 93-96; *22:* 147; *24:* 175; *29:* 130; *35:* 77; *YABC 2:* 166, 300
Krementz, Jill, *17:* 98; *49:* 41
Kresin, Robert, *23:* 19
Krush, Beth, *1:* 51, 85; *2:* 233; *4:* 115; *9:* 61; *10:* 191; *11:* 196; *18:* 164-165; *32:* 72; *37:* 203; *43:* 57
Krush, Joe, *2:* 233; *4:* 115; *9:* 61; *10:* 191; *11:* 196; *18:* 164-165; *32:* 72, 91; *37:* 203; *43:* 57
Kubinyi, Laszlo, *4:* 116; *6:* 113; *16:* 118; *17:* 100; *28:* 227; *30:* 172; *49:* 24, 28
Kuhn, Bob, *17:* 91; *35:* 235
Künstler, Mort, *10:* 73; *32:* 143
Kurchevsky, V., *34:* 61
Kurelek, William, *8:* 107
Kuriloff, Ron, *13:* 19
Kuskin, Karla, *2:* 170
Kutzer, Ernst, *19:* 249

LaBlanc, André, *24:* 146
Laboccetta, Mario, *27:* 120
Laceky, Adam, *32:* 121
La Croix, *YABC 2:* 4
La Farge, Margaret, *47:* 141
Laimgruber, Monika, *11:* 153
Laite, Gordon, *1:* 130-131; *8:* 209; *31:* 113; *40:* 63; *46:* 117
Lamarche, Jim, *46:* 204
Lamb, Jim, *10:* 117
Lambert, J. K., *38:* 129; *39:* 24
Lambert, Saul, *23:* 112; *33:* 107
Lambo, Don, *6:* 156; *35:* 115; *36:* 146
Landa, Peter, *11:* 95; *13:* 177
Landau, Jacob, *38:* 111
Landshoff, Ursula, *13:* 124
Lane, John, *15:* 176-177; *30:* 146
Lane, John R., *8:* 145
Lang, G. D., *48:* 56
Lang, Jerry, *18:* 295
Langner, Nola, *8:* 110; *42:* 36
Lantz, Paul, *1:* 82, 102; *27:* 88; *34:* 102; *45:* 123
Larrecq, John, *44:* 108
Larsen, Suzanne, *1:* 13
Larsson, Carl, *35:* 144, 145, 146, 147, 148-149, 150, 152, 153, 154
Larsson, Karl, *19:* 177
La Rue, Michael D., *13:* 215
Lasker, Joe, *7:* 186-187; *14:* 55; *38:* 115; *39:* 47
Latham, Barbara, *16:* 188-189; *43:* 71
Lathrop, Dorothy, *14:* 117, 118-119; *15:* 109; *16:* 78-79, 81; *32:* 201, 203; *33:* 112; *YABC 2:* 301
Lattimore, Eleanor Frances, *7:* 156
Lauden, Claire, *16:* 173
Lauden, George, Jr., *16:* 173

Laune, Paul, *2:* 235; *34:* 31
Lauré, Jason, *49:* 53
Lavis, Stephen, *43:* 143
Lawrence, John, *25:* 131; *30:* 141; *44:* 198, 200
Lawrence, Stephen, *20:* 195
Lawson, Carol, *6:* 38; *42:* 93, 131
Lawson, George, *17:* 280
Lawson, Robert, *5:* 26; *6:* 94; *13:* 39; *16:* 11; *20:* 100, 102, 103; *YABC 2:* 222, 224-225, 227-235, 237-241
Lazare, Jerry, *44:* 109
Lazarevich, Mila, *17:* 118
Lazarus, Keo Felker, *21:* 94
Lazzaro, Victor, *11:* 126
Lea, Tom, *43:* 72, 74
Leacroft, Richard, *6:* 140
Leaf, Munro, *20:* 99
Leander, Patricia, *23:* 27
Lear, Edward, *18:* 183-185
Lebenson, Richard, *6:* 209; *7:* 76; *23:* 145; *44:* 191
Le Cain, Errol, *6:* 141; *9:* 3; *22:* 142; *25:* 198; *28:* 173
Lee, Doris, *13:* 246; *32:* 183; *44:* 111
Lee, Manning de V., *2:* 200; *17:* 12; *27:* 87; *37:* 102, 103, 104; *YABC 2:* 304
Lee, Robert J., *3:* 97
Leech, John, *15:* 59
Leeman, Michael, *44:* 157
Lees, Harry, *6:* 112
Legènisel, *47:* 111
Legrand, Edy, *18:* 89, 93
Lehrman, Rosalie, *2:* 180
Leichman, Seymour, *5:* 107
Leighton, Clare, *25:* 130; *33:* 168; *37:* 105, 106, 108, 109
Leisk, David, *1:* 140-141; *11:* 54; *30:* 137, 142, 143, 144
Leloir, Maurice, *18:* 77, 80, 83, 99
Lemke, Horst, *14:* 98; *38:* 117, 118, 119
Lemke, R. W., *42:* 162
Lemon, David Gwynne, *9:* 1
Lenski, Lois, *1:* 144; *26:* 135, 137, 139, 141
Lent, Blair, *1:* 116-117; *2:* 174; *3:* 206-207; *7:* 168-169; *34:* 62
Leone, Leonard, *49:* 190
Lerner, Sharon, *11:* 157; *22:* 56
Leslie, Cecil, *19:* 244
Le Tord, Bijou, *49:* 156
Levai, Blaise, *39:* 130
Levin, Ted, *12:* 148
Levine, David, *43:* 147, 149, 150, 151, 152
Levit, Herschel, *24:* 223
Levy, Jessica Ann, *19:* 225; *39:* 191
Lewin, Betsy, *32:* 114; *48:* 177
Lewin, Ted, *4:* 77; *8:* 168; *20:* 110; *21:* 99, 100; *27:* 110; *28:* 96, 97; *31:* 49; *45:* 55; *48:* 223
Lewis, Allen, *15:* 112
Leydon, Rita Flodén, *21:* 101
Lieblich, Irene, *22:* 173; *27:* 209, 214
Liese, Charles, *4:* 222
Lightfoot, Norman R., *45:* 47

Lignell, Lois, *37:* 114
Lilly, Charles, *8:* 73; *20:* 127; *48:* 53
Lilly, Ken, *37:* 224
Lim, John, *43:* 153
Lincoln, Patricia Henderson, *27:* 27
Lindberg, Howard, *10:* 123; *16:* 190
Linden, Seymour, *18:* 200-201; *43:* 140
Linder, Richard, *27:* 119
Lindman, Maj, *43:* 154
Lindsay, Vachel, *40:* 118
Line, Les, *27:* 143
Linell. *See* Smith, Linell
Lionni, Leo, *8:* 115
Lipinsky, Lino, *2:* 156; *22:* 175
Lippman, Peter, *8:* 31; *31:* 119, 120, 160
Lisker, Sonia O., *16:* 274; *31:* 31; *44:* 113, 114
Lisowski, Gabriel, *47:* 144; *49:* 157
Lissim, Simon, *17:* 138
Little, Harold, *16:* 72
Little, Mary E., *28:* 146
Livesly, Lorna, *19:* 216
Llerena, Carlos Antonio, *19:* 181
Lloyd, Errol, *11:* 39; *22:* 178
Lo, Koon-chiu, *7:* 134
Lobel, Anita, *6:* 87; *9:* 141; *18:* 248
Lobel, Arnold, *1:* 188-189; *5:* 12; *6:* 147; *7:* 167, 209; *18:* 190-191; *25:* 39, 43; *27:* 40; *29:* 174
Loefgren, Ulf, *3:* 108
Loescher, Ann, *20:* 108
Loescher, Gil, *20:* 108
Lofting, Hugh, *15:* 182-183
Loh, George, *38:* 88
Lonette, Reisie, *11:* 211; *12:* 168; *13:* 56; *36:* 122; *43:* 155
Long, Sally, *42:* 184
Longtemps, Ken, *17:* 123; *29:* 221
Looser, Heinz, *YABC 2:* 208
Lopshire, Robert, *6:* 149; *21:* 117; *34:* 166
Lord, John Vernon, *21:* 104; *23:* 25
Lorenz, Al, *40:* 146
Loretta, Sister Mary, *33:* 73
Lorraine, Walter H., *3:* 110; *4:* 123; *16:* 192
Loss, Joan, *11:* 163
Louderback, Walt, *YABC 1:* 164
Lousada, Sandra, *40:* 138
Low, Joseph, *14:* 124, 125; *18:* 68; *19:* 194; *31:* 166
Lowenheim, Alfred, *13:* 65-66
Lowitz, Anson, *17:* 124; *18:* 215
Lowrey, Jo, *8:* 133
Lubell, Winifred, *1:* 207; *3:* 15; *6:* 151
Lubin, Leonard B., *19:* 224; *36:* 79, 80; *45:* 128, 129, 131, 132, 133, 134, 135, 136, 137, 139, 140, 141; *YABC 2:* 96
Ludwig, Helen, *33:* 144, 145
Lufkin, Raymond, *38:* 138; *44:* 48
Luhrs, Henry, *7:* 123; *11:* 120
Lupo, Dom, *4:* 204
Lustig, Loretta, *30:* 186; *46:* 134, 135, 136, 137
Lydecker, Laura, *21:* 113; *42:* 53
Lynch, Charles, *16:* 33

Lynch, Marietta, *29:* 137; *30:* 171
Lyon, Elinor, *6:* 154
Lyon, Fred, *14:* 16
Lyons, Oren, *8:* 193
Lyster, Michael, *26:* 41

Maas, Dorothy, *6:* 175
Maas, Julie, *47:* 61
Macaulay, David, *46:* 139, 140-141, 142, 143, 144-145, 147, 149, 150
Macdonald, Alister, *21:* 55
MacDonald, Norman, *13:* 99
MacDonald, Roberta, *19:* 237
Mace, Varian, *49:* 159
Macguire, Robert Reid, *18:* 67
Machetanz, Fredrick, *34:* 147, 148
MacInnes, Ian, *35:* 59
MacIntyre, Elisabeth, *17:* 127-128
Mack, Stan, *17:* 129
Mackay, Donald, *17:* 60
MacKaye, Arvia, *32:* 119
MacKenzie, Garry, *33:* 159
Mackinlay, Miguel, *27:* 22
MacKinstry, Elizabeth, *15:* 110; *42:* 139, 140, 141, 142, 143, 144, 145
Maclise, Daniel, *YABC 2:* 257
Madden, Don, *3:* 112-113; *4:* 33, 108, 155; *7:* 193; *YABC 2:* 211
Maddison, Angela Mary, *10:* 83
Maestro, Giulio, *8:* 124; *12:* 17; *13:* 108; *25:* 182
Magnuson, Diana, *28:* 102; *34:* 190; *41:* 175
Maguire, Sheila, *41:* 100
Mahony, Will, *37:* 120
Mahood, Kenneth, *24:* 141
Maik, Henri, *9:* 102
Maisto, Carol, *29:* 87
Maitland, Antony, *1:* 100, 176; *8:* 41; *17:* 246; *24:* 46; *25:* 177, 178; *32:* 74
Makie, Pam, *37:* 117
Malvern, Corinne, *2:* 13; *34:* 148, 149
Mandelbaum, Ira, *31:* 115
Manet, Edouard, *23:* 170
Mangurian, David, *14:* 133
Manham, Allan, *42:* 109
Manniche, Lise, *31:* 121
Manning, Samuel F., *5:* 75
Maraja, *15:* 86; *YABC 1:* 28; *YABC 2:* 115
Marcellino, Fred, *20:* 125; *34:* 222
Marchesi, Stephen, *34:* 140; *46:* 72
Marchiori, Carlos, *14:* 60
Margules, Gabriele, *21:* 120
Mariana. *See* Foster, Marian Curtis
Marino, Dorothy, *6:* 37; *14:* 135
Markham, R. L., *17:* 240
Marokvia, Artur, *31:* 122
Marriott, Pat, *30:* 30; *34:* 39; *35:* 164, 165, 166; *44:* 170; *48:* 186, 187, 188, 189, 191, 192, 193
Mars, W. T., *1:* 161; *3:* 115; *4:* 208, 225; *5:* 92, 105, 186; *8:* 214; *9:* 12; *13:* 121; *27:* 151; *31:* 180; *38:* 102; *48:* 66
Marsh, Christine, *3:* 164

Marsh, Reginald, *17:* 5; *19:* 89; *22:* 90, 96
Marshall, Anthony D., *18:* 216
Marshall, James, *6:* 160; *40:* 221; *42:* 24, 25, 29
Martin, David Stone, *23:* 232
Martin, Fletcher, *18:* 213; *23:* 151
Martin, René, *7:* 144; *42:* 148, 149, 150
Martin, Ron, *32:* 81
Martin, Stefan, *8:* 68; *32:* 124, 126
Martinez, John, *6:* 113
Marx, Robert F., *24:* 143
Masefield, Judith, *19:* 208, 209
Mason, George F., *14:* 139
Massie, Diane Redfield, *16:* 194
Massie, Kim, *31:* 43
Mathieu, Joseph, *14:* 33; *39:* 206; *43:* 167
Matsubara, Naoko, *12:* 121
Matsuda, Shizu, *13:* 167
Matte, L'Enc, *22:* 183
Mattelson, Marvin, *36:* 50, 51
Matthews, F. Leslie, *4:* 216
Matulay, Laszlo, *5:* 18; *43:* 168
Matus, Greta, *12:* 142
Mauldin, Bill, *27:* 23
Mawicke, Tran, *9:* 137; *15:* 191; *47:* 100
Max, Peter, *45:* 146, 147, 148-149, 150
Maxie, Betty, *40:* 135
Maxwell, John Alan, *1:* 148
Mayan, Earl, *7:* 193
Mayer, Marianna, *32:* 132
Mayer, Mercer, *11:* 192; *16:* 195-196; *20:* 55, 57; *32:* 129, 130, 132, 133, 134; *41:* 144, 248, 252
Mayhew, Richard, *3:* 106
Mayo, Gretchen, *38:* 81
Mays, Victor, *5:* 127; *8:* 45, 153; *14:* 245; *23:* 50; *34:* 155; *40:* 79; *45:* 158
Mazal, Chanan, *49:* 104
Mazza, Adriana Saviozzi, *19:* 215
Mazzetti, Alan, *45:* 210
McBride, Angus, *28:* 49
McBride, Will, *30:* 110
McCaffery, Janet, *38:* 145
McCann, Gerald, *3:* 50; *4:* 94; *7:* 54; *41:* 121
McCay, Winsor, *41:* 124, 126, 128-129, 130-131
McClary, Nelson, *1:* 111
McClintock, Theodore, *14:* 141
McCloskey, Robert, *1:* 184-185; *2:* 186-187; *17:* 209; *39:* 139, 140, 141, 142, 143, 146, 147, 148
McClung, Robert, *2:* 189
McClure, Gillian, *31:* 132
McConnel, Jerry, *31:* 75, 187
McCormick, A. D., *35:* 119
McCormick, Dell J., *19:* 216
McCrady, Lady, *16:* 198; *39:* 127
McCrea, James, *3:* 122; *33:* 216
McCrea, Ruth, *3:* 122; *27:* 102; *33:* 216
McCully, Emily, *2:* 89; *4:* 120-121, 146, 197; *5:* 2, 129; *7:* 191;

11: 122; *15:* 210; *33:* 23; *35:* 244;
    37: 122; *39:* 88; *40:* 103
McCurdy, Michael, *13:* 153; *24:* 85
McDermott, Beverly Brodsky, *11:* 180
McDermott, Gerald, *16:* 201
McDonald, Jill, *13:* 155; *26:* 128
McDonald, Ralph J., *5:* 123, 195
McDonough, Don, *10:* 163
McEntee, Dorothy, *37:* 124
McFall, Christie, *12:* 144
McGee, Barbara, *6:* 165
McGregor, Malcolm, *23:* 27
McHugh, Tom, *23:* 64
McIntosh, Jon, *42:* 56
McKay, Donald, *2:* 118; *32:* 157;
    45: 151, 152
McKeating, Eileen, *44:* 58
McKee, David, *10:* 48; *21:* 9
McKie, Roy, *7:* 44
McKillip, Kathy, *30:* 153
McKinney, Ena, *26:* 39
McLachlan, Edward, *5:* 89
McLean, Sammis, *32:* 197
McLoughlin, John C., *47:* 149
McMahon, Robert, *36:* 155
McMillan, Bruce, *22:* 184
McMullan, James, *40:* 33
McNaught, Harry, *12:* 80; *32:* 136
McNaughton, Colin, *39:* 149; *40:* 108
McNicholas, Maureen, *38:* 148
McPhail, David, *14:* 105; *23:* 135;
    37: 217, 218, 220, 221; *47:* 151,
    152, 153, 154, 155, 156, 158-159,
    160, 162-163, 164
McPhee, Richard B., *41:* 133
McQueen, Lucinda, *28:* 149; *41:* 249;
    46: 206
McVay, Tracy, *11:* 68
McVicker, Charles, *39:* 150
Mead, Ben Carlton, *43:* 75
Mecray, John, *33:* 62
Meddaugh, Susan, *20:* 42; *29:* 143;
    41: 241
Melo, John, *16:* 285
Menasco, Milton, *43:* 85
Mendelssohn, Felix, *19:* 170
Meng, Heinz, *13:* 158
Mero, Lee, *34:* 68
Merrill, Frank T., *16:* 147; *19:* 71;
    YABC 1: 226, 229, 273
Meryman, Hope, *27:* 41
Meryweather, Jack, *10:* 179
Meth, Harold, *24:* 203
Meyer, Herbert, *19:* 189
Meyer, Renate, *6:* 170
Meyers, Bob, *11:* 136
Meynell, Louis, *37:* 76
Micale, Albert, *2:* 65; *22:* 185
Middleton-Sandford, Betty, *2:* 125
Mieke, Anne, *45:* 74
Mighell, Patricia, *43:* 134
Mikolaycak, Charles, *9:* 144; *12:* 101;
    13: 212; *21:* 121; *22:* 168;
    30: 187; *34:* 103, 150; *37:* 183;
    43: 179; *44:* 90; *46:* 115, 118-119;
    49: 25
Miles, Jennifer, *17:* 278
Milhous, Katherine, *15:* 193; *17:* 51
Millais, John E., *22:* 230, 231

Millar, H. R., *YABC 1:* 194-195, 203
Millard, C. E., *28:* 186
Miller, Don, *15:* 195; *16:* 71; *20:* 106;
    31: 178
Miller, Edna, *29:* 148
Miller, Frank J., *25:* 94
Miller, Grambs, *18:* 38; *23:* 16
Miller, Jane, *15:* 196
Miller, Marcia, *13:* 233
Miller, Marilyn, *1:* 87; *31:* 69; *33:* 157
Miller, Mitchell, *28:* 183; *34:* 207
Miller, Shane, *5:* 140
Mills, Yaroslava Surmach, *35:* 169,
    170; *46:* 114
Minor, Wendell, *39:* 188
Mitsuhashi, Yoko, *45:* 153
Miyake, Yoshi, *38:* 141
Mizumura, Kazue, *10:* 143; *18:* 223;
    36: 159
Mochi, Ugo, *8:* 122; *38:* 150
Modell, Frank, *39:* 152
Mohr, Nicholasa, *8:* 139
Moldon, Peter L., *49:* 168
Momaday, N. Scott, *48:* 159
Montresor, Beni, *2:* 91; *3:* 138;
    38: 152, 153, 154, 155, 156-157,
    158, 159, 160
Moon, Carl, *25:* 183, 184, 185
Moon, Eliza, *14:* 40
Moon, Ivan, *22:* 39; *38:* 140
Moore, Agnes Kay Randall, *43:* 187
Moore, Mary, *29:* 160
Mora, Raul Mina, *20:* 41
Mordvinoff, Nicolas, *15:* 179
Morgan, Tom, *42:* 157
Morrill, Les, *42:* 127
Morrill, Leslie, *18:* 218; *29:* 177;
    33: 84; *38:* 147; *44:* 93; *48:* 164,
    165, 167, 168, 169, 170, 171;
    49: 162
Morris, *47:* 91
Morrison, Bill, *42:* 116
Morrow, Gray, *2:* 64; *5:* 200; *10:* 103,
    114; *14:* 175
Morton, Lee Jack, *32:* 140
Morton, Marian, *3:* 185
Moses, Grandma, *18:* 228
Moskof, Martin Stephen, *27:* 152
Moss, Donald, *11:* 184
Moss, Geoffrey, *32:* 198
Most, Bernard, *48:* 173
Moyers, William, *21:* 65
Moyler, Alan, *36:* 142
Mozley, Charles, *9:* 87; *20:* 176, 192,
    193; *22:* 228; *25:* 205; *33:* 150;
    43: 170, 171, 172, 173, 174;
    YABC 2: 89
Mueller, Hans Alexander, *26:* 64;
    27: 52, 53
Mugnaini, Joseph, *11:* 35; *27:* 52, 53;
    35: 62
Müller, Jörg, *35:* 215
Muller, Steven, *32:* 167
Mullins, Edward S., *10:* 101
Munari, Bruno, *15:* 200
Munowitz, Ken, *14:* 148
Muñoz, William, *42:* 160
Munsinger, Lynn, *33:* 161; *46:* 126
Munson, Russell, *13:* 9

Murphy, Bill, *5:* 138
Murphy, Jill, *37:* 142
Murr, Karl, *20:* 62
Murray, Ossie, *43:* 176
Mussino, Attilio, *29:* 131
Mutchler, Dwight, *1:* 25
Myers, Bernice, *9:* 147; *36:* 75
Myers, Lou, *11:* 2

Nachreiner, Tom, *29:* 182
Nakai, Michael, *30:* 217
Nakatani, Chiyoko, *12:* 124
Nash, Linell, *46:* 175
Naso, John, *33:* 183
Nason, Thomas W., *14:* 68
Nasser, Muriel, *48:* 74
Nast, Thomas, *21:* 29; *28:* 23
Natti, Susanna, *20:* 146; *32:* 141, 142;
    35: 178; *37:* 143
Navarra, Celeste Scala, *8:* 142
Naylor, Penelope, *10:* 104
Nebel, M., *45:* 154
Neebe, William, *7:* 93
Needler, Jerry, *12:* 93
Neel, Alice, *31:* 23
Neely, Keith R., *46:* 124
Negri, Rocco, *3:* 213; *5:* 67; *6:* 91,
    108; *12:* 159
Neill, John R., *18:* 8, 10-11, 21, 30
Ness, Evaline, *1:* 164-165; *2:* 39; *3:* 8;
    10: 147; *12:* 53; *26:* 150, 151,
    152, 153; *49:* 30, 31, 32
Neville, Vera, *2:* 182
Newberry, Clare Turlay, *1:* 170
Newfeld, Frank, *14:* 121; *26:* 154
Newman, Ann, *43:* 90
Newsom, Carol, *40:* 159; *44:* 60;
    47: 189
Newsom, Tom, *49:* 149
Ng, Michael, *29:* 171
Nicholson, William, *15:* 33-34; *16:* 48
Nicklaus, Carol, *45:* 194
Nickless, Will, *16:* 139
Nicolas, *17:* 130, 132-133;
    YABC 2: 215
Niebrugge, Jane, *6:* 118
Nielsen, Jon, *6:* 100; *24:* 202
Nielsen, Kay, *15:* 7; *16:* 211-213, 215,
    217; *22:* 143; *YABC 1:* 32-33
Niland, Deborah, *25:* 191; *27:* 156
Niland, Kilmeny, *25:* 191
Ninon, *1:* 5; *38:* 101, 103, 108
Nissen, Rie, *44:* 35
Nixon, K., *14:* 152
Noble, Trinka Hakes, *39:* 162
Noguchi, Yoshie, *30:* 99
Nolan, Dennis, *42:* 163
Noonan, Julia, *4:* 163; *7:* 207; *25:* 151
Nordenskjold, Birgitta, *2:* 208
Norman, Mary, *36:* 138, 147
Norman, Michael, *12:* 117; *27:* 168
Numeroff, Laura Joffe, *28:* 161;
    30: 177
Nussbaumer, Paul, *16:* 219; *39:* 117
Nyce, Helene, *19:* 219
Nygren, Tord, *30:* 148

Oakley, Graham, *8:* 112; *30:* 164, 165

Oakley, Thornton, *YABC 2:* 189
Obligado, Lilian, *2:* 28, 66-67; *6:* 30; *14:* 179; *15:* 103; *25:* 84
Obrant, Susan, *11:* 186
O'Brien, John, *41:* 253
Odell, Carole, *35:* 47
O'Donohue, Thomas, *40:* 89
Oechsli, Kelly, *5:* 144-145; *7:* 115; *8:* 83, 183; *13:* 117; *20:* 94
Offen, Hilda, *42:* 207
Ogden, Bill, *42:* 59; *47:* 55
Ogg, Oscar, *33:* 34
Ohlsson, Ib, *4:* 152; *7:* 57; *10:* 20; *11:* 90; *19:* 217; *41:* 246
Ohtomo, Yasuo, *37:* 146; *39:* 212, 213
O'Kelley, Mattie Lou, *36:* 150
Oliver, Jenni, *23:* 121; *35:* 112
Olschewski, Alfred, *7:* 172
Olsen, Ib Spang, *6:* 178-179
Olugebefola, Ademola, *15:* 205
O'Neil, Dan IV, *7:* 176
O'Neill, Jean, *22:* 146
O'Neill, Rose, *48:* 30, 31
O'Neill, Steve, *21:* 118
Ono, Chiyo, *7:* 97
Orbaan, Albert, *2:* 31; *5:* 65, 171; *9:* 8; *14:* 241; *20:* 109
Orbach, Ruth, *21:* 112
Orfe, Joan, *20:* 81
Ormsby, Virginia H., *11:* 187
Orozco, José Clemente, *9:* 177
Orr, Forrest W., *23:* 9
Orr, N., *19:* 70
Osborne, Billie Jean, *35:* 209
Osmond, Edward, *10:* 111
O'Sullivan, Tom, *3:* 176; *4:* 55
Otto, Svend, *22:* 130, 141
Oudry, J. B., *18:* 167
Oughton, Taylor, *5:* 23
Övereng, Johannes, *44:* 36
Overlie, George, *11:* 156
Owens, Carl, *2:* 35; *23:* 521
Owens, Gail, *10:* 170; *12:* 157; *19:* 16; *22:* 70; *25:* 81; *28:* 203, 205; *32:* 221, 222; *36:* 132; *46:* 40; *47:* 57
Oxenbury, Helen, *3:* 150-151; *24:* 81

Padgett, Jim, *12:* 165
Page, Homer, *14:* 145
Paget, Sidney, *24:* 90, 91, 93, 95, 97
Pak, *12:* 76
Palazzo, Tony, *3:* 152-153
Palladini, David, *4:* 113; *40:* 176, 177, 178-179, 181, 224-225
Pallarito, Don, *43:* 36
Palmer, Heidi, *15:* 207; *29:* 102
Palmer, Jan, *42:* 153
Palmer, Juliette, *6:* 89; *15:* 208
Palmer, Lemuel, *17:* 25, 29
Palmquist, Eric, *38:* 133
Panesis, Nicholas, *3:* 127
Papas, William, *11:* 223
Papin, Joseph, *26:* 113
Papish, Robin Lloyd, *10:* 80
Paradis, Susan, *40:* 216
Paraquin, Charles H., *18:* 166
Paris, Peter, *31:* 127

Park, Seho, *39:* 110
Park, W. B., *22:* 189
Parker, Lewis, *2:* 179
Parker, Nancy Winslow, *10:* 113; *22:* 164; *28:* 47, 144
Parker, Robert, *4:* 161; *5:* 74; *9:* 136; *29:* 39
Parker, Robert Andrew, *11:* 81; *29:* 186; *39:* 165; *40:* 25; *41:* 78; *42:* 123; *43:* 144; *48:* 182
Parks, Gordon, Jr., *33:* 228
Parnall, Peter, *5:* 137; *16:* 221; *24:* 70; *40:* 78
Parnall, Virginia, *40:* 78
Parrish, Anne, *27:* 159, 160
Parrish, Dillwyn, *27:* 159
Parrish, Maxfield, *14:* 160, 161, 164, 165; *16:* 109; *18:* 12-13; *YABC 1:* 149, 152, 267; *YABC 2:* 146, 149
Parry, David, *26:* 156
Parry, Marian, *13:* 176; *19:* 179
Partch, Virgil, *45:* 163, 165
Pascal, David, *14:* 174
Pasquier, J. A., *16:* 91
Paterson, Diane, *13:* 116; *39:* 163
Paterson, Helen, *16:* 93
Paton, Jane, *15:* 271; *35:* 176
Patterson, Robert, *25:* 118
Paul, James, *4:* 130; *23:* 161
Paull, Grace, *24:* 157
Payne, Joan Balfour, *1:* 118
Payson, Dale, *7:* 34; *9:* 151; *20:* 140; *37:* 22
Payzant, Charles, *21:* 147
Peake, Mervyn, *22:* 136, 149; *23:* 162, 163, 164; *YABC 2:* 307
Pearson, Larry, *38:* 225
Peat, Fern B., *16:* 115
Peck, Anne Merriman, *18:* 241; *24:* 155
Pederson, Sharleen, *12:* 92
Pedersen, Vilhelm, *YABC 1:* 40
Peek, Merle, *39:* 168
Peet, Bill, *2:* 203; *41:* 159, 160, 161, 162, 163
Peltier, Leslie C., *13:* 178
Pendle, Alexy, *7:* 159; *13:* 34; *29:* 161; *33:* 215
Pennington, Eunice, *27:* 162
Peppé, Mark, *28:* 142
Peppe, Rodney, *4:* 164-165
Perl, Susan, *2:* 98; *4:* 231; *5:* 44-45, 118; *6:* 199; *8:* 137; *12:* 88; *22:* 193; *34:* 54-55; *YABC 1:* 176
Perry, Patricia, *29:* 137; *30:* 171
Perry, Roger, *27:* 163
Perske, Martha, *46:* 83
Pesek, Ludek, *15:* 237
Petersham, Maud, *17:* 108, 147-153
Petersham, Miska, *17:* 108, 147-153
Peterson, R. F., *7:* 101
Peterson, Russell, *7:* 130
Petie, Haris, *2:* 3; *10:* 41, 118; *11:* 227; *12:* 70
Petrides, Heidrun, *19:* 223
Peyo, *40:* 56, 57
Peyton, K. M., *15:* 212
Pfeifer, Herman, *15:* 262

Phillips, Douglas, *1:* 19
Phillips, F. D., *6:* 202
Phillips, Thomas, *30:* 55
"Phiz." *See* Browne, Hablot K.
Piatti, Celestino, *16:* 223
Picarella, Joseph, *13:* 147
Pickard, Charles, *12:* 38; *18:* 203; *36:* 152
Picken, George A., *23:* 150
Pickens, David, *22:* 156
Pienkowski, Jan, *6:* 183; *30:* 32
Pimlott, John, *10:* 205
Pincus, Harriet, *4:* 186; *8:* 179; *22:* 148; *27:* 164, 165
Pinkney, Jerry, *8:* 218; *10:* 40; *15:* 276; *20:* 66; *24:* 121; *33:* 109; *36:* 222; *38:* 200; *41:* 165, 166, 167, 168, 169, 170, 171, 173, 174; *44:* 198; *48:* 51
Pinkwater, Daniel Manus, *46:* 180, 181, 182, 185, 188, 189, 190
Pinkwater, Manus, *8:* 156; *46:* 180
Pinto, Ralph, *10:* 131; *45:* 93
Pitz, Henry C., *4:* 168; *19:* 165; *35:* 128; *42:* 80; *YABC 2:* 95, 176
Pitzenberger, Lawrence J., *26:* 94
Plummer, William, *32:* 31
Pogány, Willy, *15:* 46, 49; *19:* 222, 256; *25:* 214; *44:* 142, 143, 144, 145, 146, 147, 148
Poirson, V. A., *26:* 89
Polgreen, John, *21:* 44
Politi, Leo, *1:* 178; *4:* 53; *21:* 48; *47:* 173, 174, 176, 178, 179, 180, 181
Polonsky, Arthur, *34:* 168
Polseno, Jo, *1:* 53; *3:* 117; *5:* 114; *17:* 154; *20:* 87; *32:* 49; *41:* 245
Ponter, James, *5:* 204
Poortvliet, Rien, *6:* 212
Portal, Colette, *6:* 186; *11:* 203
Porter, George, *7:* 181
Potter, Beatrix, *YABC 1:* 208-210, 212, 213
Potter, Miriam Clark, *3:* 162
Powers, Richard M., *1:* 230; *3:* 218; *7:* 194; *26:* 186
Powledge, Fred, *37:* 154
Pratt, Charles, *23:* 29
Price, Christine, *2:* 247; *3:* 163, 253; *8:* 166
Price, Edward, *33:* 34
Price, Garrett, *1:* 76; *2:* 42
Price, Hattie Longstreet, *17:* 13
Price, Norman, *YABC 1:* 129
Price, Willard, *48:* 184
Primavera, Elise, *26:* 95
Primrose, Jean, *36:* 109
Prince, Leonora E., *7:* 170
Prittie, Edwin J., *YABC 1:* 120
Provensen, Alice, *37:* 204, 215, 222
Provensen, Martin, *37:* 204, 215, 222
Pucci, Albert John, *44:* 154
Pudlo, *8:* 59
Purdy, Susan, *8:* 162
Puskas, James, *5:* 141
Pyk, Jan, *7:* 26; *38:* 123

Pyle, Howard, *16:* 225-228, 230-232, 235; *24:* 27; *34:* 124, 125, 127, 128

Quackenbush, Robert, *4:* 190; *6:* 166; *7:* 175, 178; *9:* 86; *11:* 65, 221; *41:* 154; *43:* 157
Quennell, Marjorie (Courtney), *29:* 163, 164
Quidor, John, *19:* 82
Quirk, Thomas, *12:* 81

Rackham, Arthur, *15:* 32, 78, 214-227; *17:* 105, 115; *18:* 233; *19:* 254; *20:* 151; *22:* 129, 131, 132, 133; *23:* 175; *24:* 161, 181; *26:* 91; *32:* 118; *YABC 1:* 25, 45, 55, 147; *YABC 2:* 103, 142, 173, 210
Rafilson, Sidney, *11:* 172
Raible, Alton, *1:* 202-203; *28:* 193; *35:* 181
Ramsey, James, *16:* 41
Rand, Paul, *6:* 188
Ransome, Arthur, *22:* 201
Rao, Anthony, *28:* 126
Raphael, Elaine, *23:* 192
Rappaport, Eva, *6:* 190
Raskin, Ellen, *2:* 208-209; *4:* 142; *13:* 183; *22:* 68; *29:* 139; *36:* 134; *38:* 173, 174, 175, 176, 177, 178, 179, 180, 181
Ratzkin, Lawrence, *40:* 143
Rau, Margaret, *9:* 157
Raverat, Gwen, *YABC 1:* 152
Ravielli, Anthony, *1:* 198; *3:* 168; *11:* 143
Ray, Deborah, *8:* 164; *29:* 238
Ray, Ralph, *2:* 239; *5:* 73
Raymond, Larry, *31:* 108
Rayner, Mary, *22:* 207; *47:* 140
Raynor, Dorka, *28:* 168
Raynor, Paul, *24:* 73
Razzi, James, *10:* 127
Read, Alexander D. ''Sandy,'' *20:* 45
Reed, Tom, *34:* 171
Reid, Stephen, *19:* 213; *22:* 89
Reinertson, Barbara, *44:* 150
Reiniger, Lotte, *40:* 185
Reiss, John J., *23:* 193
Relf, Douglas, *3:* 63
Relyea, C. M., *16:* 29; *31:* 153
Rémi, Georges, *13:* 184
Remington, Frederic, *19:* 188; *41:* 178, 179, 180, 181, 183, 184, 185, 186, 187, 188
Renlie, Frank, *11:* 200
Reschofsky, Jean, *7:* 118
Réthi, Lili, *2:* 153; *36:* 156
Reusswig, William, *3:* 267
Rey, H. A., *1:* 182; *26:* 163, 164, 166, 167, 169; *YABC 2:* 17
Reynolds, Doris, *5:* 71; *31:* 77
Rhead, Louis, *31:* 91
Rhodes, Andrew, *38:* 204
Ribbons, Ian, *3:* 10; *37:* 161; *40:* 76

Rice, Elizabeth, *2:* 53, 214
Rice, James, *22:* 210
Rice, Eve, *34:* 174, 175
Richards, George, *40:* 116, 119, 121; *44:* 179
Richards, Henry, *YABC 1:* 228, 231
Richardson, Ernest, *2:* 144
Richardson, Frederick, *18:* 27, 31
Richman, Hilda, *26:* 132
Richmond, George, *24:* 179
Rieniets, Judy King, *14:* 28
Riger, Bob, *2:* 166
Riley, Kenneth, *22:* 230
Ringi, Kjell, *12:* 171
Rios, Tere. *See* Versace, Marie
Ripper, Charles L., *3:* 175
Ritz, Karen, *41:* 117
Rivkin, Jay, *15:* 230
Rivoche, Paul, *45:* 125
Roach, Marilynne, *9:* 158
Robbin, Jodi, *44:* 156, 159
Robbins, Frank, *42:* 167
Roberts, Cliff, *4:* 126
Roberts, Doreen, *4:* 230; *28:* 105
Roberts, Jim, *22:* 166; *23:* 69; *31:* 110
Roberts, W., *22:* 2, 3
Robinson, Charles, *3:* 53; *5:* 14; *6:* 193; *7:* 150; *7:* 183; *8:* 38; *9:* 81; *13:* 188; *14:* 248-249; *23:* 149; *26:* 115; *27:* 48; *28:* 191; *32:* 28; *35:* 210; *36:* 37; *48:* 96
Robinson, Charles [1870-1937], *17:* 157, 171-173, 175-176; *24:* 207; *25:* 204; *YABC 2:* 308-310, 331
Robinson, Jerry, *3:* 262
Robinson, Joan G., *7:* 184
Robinson, T. H., *17:* 179, 181-183; *29:* 254
Robinson, W. Heath, *17:* 185, 187, 189, 191, 193, 195, 197, 199, 202; *23:* 167; *25:* 194; *29:* 150; *YABC 1:* 44; *YABC 2:* 183
Roche, Christine, *41:* 98
Rocker, Fermin, *7:* 34; *13:* 21; *31:* 40; *40:* 190, 191
Rockwell, Anne, *5:* 147; *33:* 171, 173
Rockwell, Gail, *7:* 186
Rockwell, Harlow, *33:* 171, 173, 175
Rockwell, Norman, *23:* 39, 196, 197, 199, 200, 203, 204, 207; *41:* 140, 143; *YABC 2:* 60
Rodegast, Roland, *43:* 100
Rodriguez, Joel, *16:* 65
Roever, J. M., *4:* 119; *26:* 170
Roffey, Maureen, *33:* 142, 176, 177
Rogasky, Barbara, *46:* 90
Rogers, Carol, *2:* 262; *6:* 164; *26:* 129
Rogers, Frances, *10:* 130
Rogers, Walter S., *31:* 135, 138
Rogers, William A., *15:* 151, 153-154; *33:* 35
Rojankovsky, Feodor, *6:* 134, 136; *10:* 183; *21:* 128, 129, 130; *25:* 110; *28:* 42
Rorer, Abigail, *43:* 222
Rosamilia, Patricia, *36:* 120
Rose, Carl, *5:* 62
Rose, David S., *29:* 109

Rosenblum, Richard, *11:* 202; *18:* 18
Rosier, Lydia, *16:* 236; *20:* 104; *21:* 109; *22:* 125; *30:* 151, 158; *42:* 128; *45:* 214
Ross. *See* Thomson, Ross
Ross, Clare Romano, *3:* 123; *21:* 45; *48:* 199
Ross, Dave, *32:* 152
Ross, Herbert, *37:* 78
Ross, John, *3:* 123; *21:* 45
Ross, Johnny, *32:* 190
Ross, Larry, *47:* 168
Ross, Tony, *17:* 204
Rossetti, Dante Gabriel, *20:* 151, 153
Roth, Arnold, *4:* 238; *21:* 133
Rotondo, Pat, *32:* 158
Roughsey, Dick, *35:* 186
Rouille, M., *11:* 96
Rounds, Glen, *8:* 173; *9:* 171; *12:* 56; *32:* 194; *40:* 230; *YABC 1:* 1-3
Rowe, Gavin, *27:* 144
Rowell, Kenneth, *40:* 72
Roy, Jeroo, *27:* 229; *36:* 110
Rubel, Nicole, *18:* 255; *20:* 59
Rubel, Reina, *33:* 217
Rud, Borghild, *6:* 15
Rudolph, Norman Guthrie, *17:* 13
Rue, Leonard Lee III, *37:* 164
Ruffins, Reynold, *10:* 134-135; *41:* 191, 192-193, 194-195, 196
Ruhlin, Roger, *34:* 44
Ruse, Margaret, *24:* 155
Rush, Peter, *42:* 75
Russell, E. B., *18:* 177, 182
Russo, Susan, *30:* 182; *36:* 144
Ruth, Rod, *9:* 161
Rutherford, Meg, *25:* 174; *34:* 178, 179
Rutland, Jonathan, *31:* 126
Ryden, Hope, *8:* 176
Rymer, Alta M., *34:* 181
Rystedt, Rex, *49:* 80

Saaf, Chuck, *49:* 179
Sabaka, Donna R., *21:* 172
Sabin, Robert, *45:* 35
Sacker, Amy, *16:* 100
Saffioti, Lino, *36:* 176; *48:* 60
Sagsoorian, Paul, *12:* 183; *22:* 154; *33:* 106
Saint Exupéry, Antoine de, *20:* 157
St. John, J. Allen, *41:* 62
Saldutti, Denise, *39:* 186
Sale, Morton, *YABC 2:* 31
Sambourne, Linley, *YABC 2:* 181
Sampson, Katherine, *9:* 197
Samson, Anne S., *2:* 216
Sancha, Sheila, *38:* 185
Sand, George X., *45:* 182
Sandberg, Lasse, *15:* 239, 241
Sanders, Beryl, *39:* 173
Sanderson, Ruth, *21:* 126; *24:* 53; *28:* 63; *33:* 67; *41:* 48, 198, 199, 200, 201, 202, 203; *43:* 79; *46:* 36, 44; *47:* 102; *49:* 58
Sandin, Joan, *4:* 36; *6:* 194; *7:* 177; *12:* 145, 185; *20:* 43; *21:* 74;

26: 144; *27:* 142; *28:* 224, 225; *38:* 86; *41:* 46; *42:* 35
Sandland, Reg, *39:* 215
Sandoz, Edouard, *26:* 45, 47
San Souci, Daniel, *40:* 200
Sapieha, Christine, *1:* 180
Sarg, Tony, *YABC 2:* 236
Sargent, Robert, *2:* 217
Saris, *1:* 33
Sarony, *YABC 2:* 170
Sasek, Miroslav, *16:* 239-242
Sassman, David, *9:* 79
Sätty, *29:* 203, 205
Sauber, Rob, *40:* 183
Savage, Steele, *10:* 203; *20:* 77; *35:* 28
Savitt, Sam, *8:* 66, 182; *15:* 278; *20:* 96; *24:* 192; *28:* 98
Say, Allen, *28:* 178
Scabrini, Janet, *13:* 191; *44:* 128
Scarry, Huck, *35:* 204-205
Scarry, Richard, *2:* 220-221; *18:* 20; *35:* 193, 194-195, 196, 197, 198, 199, 200-201, 202
Schaeffer, Mead, *18:* 81, 94; *21:* 137, 138, 139; *47:* 128
Scharl, Josef, *20:* 132; *22:* 128
Scheel, Lita, *11:* 230
Scheib, Ida, *29:* 28
Schermer, Judith, *30:* 184
Schick, Joel, *16:* 160; *17:* 167; *22:* 12; *27:* 176; *31:* 147, 148; *36:* 23; *38:* 64; *45:* 116, 117
Schindelman, Joseph, *1:* 74; *4:* 101; *12:* 49; *26:* 51; *40:* 146
Schindler, Edith, *7:* 22
Schindler, S. D., *38:* 107; *46:* 196
Schlesinger, Bret, *7:* 77
Schmid, Eleanore, *12:* 188
Schmiderer, Dorothy, *19:* 224
Schmidt, Elizabeth, *15:* 242
Schneider, Rex, *29:* 64; *44:* 171
Schoenherr, Ian, *32:* 83
Schoenherr, John, *1:* 146-147, 173; *3:* 39, 139; *17:* 75; *29:* 72; *32:* 83; *37:* 168, 169, 170; *43:* 164, 165; *45:* 160, 162
Schomburg, Alex, *13:* 23
Schongut, Emanuel, *4:* 102; *15:* 186; *47:* 218, 219
Schoonover, Frank, *17:* 107; *19:* 81, 190, 233; *22:* 88, 129; *24:* 189; *31:* 88; *41:* 69; *YABC 2:* 282, 316
Schottland, Miriam, *22:* 172
Schramm, Ulrik, *2:* 16; *14:* 112
Schreiber, Elizabeth Anne, *13:* 193
Schreiber, Ralph W., *13:* 193
Schreiter, Rick, *14:* 97; *23:* 171; *41:* 247; *49:* 131
Schroeder, E. Peter, *12:* 112
Schroeder, Ted, *11:* 160; *15:* 189; *30:* 91; *34:* 43
Schrotter, Gustav, *22:* 212; *30:* 225
Schucker, James, *31:* 163
Schulz, Charles M., *10:* 137-142
Schwartz, Amy, *47:* 191
Schwartz, Charles, *8:* 184
Schwartz, Daniel, *46:* 37
Schwartzberg, Joan, *3:* 208
Schweitzer, Iris, *2:* 137; *6:* 207

Schweninger, Ann, *29:* 172
Scott, Anita Walker, *7:* 38
Scott, Art, *39:* 41
Scott, Frances Gruse, *38:* 43
Scott, Julian, *34:* 126
Scott, Roszel, *33:* 238
Scott, Trudy, *27:* 172
Scribner, Joanne, *14:* 236; *29:* 78; *33:* 185; *34:* 208
Scrofani, Joseph, *31:* 65
Seaman, Mary Lott, *34:* 64
Searle, Ronald, *24:* 98; *42:* 172, 173, 174, 176, 177, 179
Searle, Townley, *36:* 85
Sebree, Charles, *18:* 65
Sedacca, Joseph M., *11:* 25; *22:* 36
Ségur, Adrienne, *27:* 121
Seignobosc, Francoise, *21:* 145, 146
Sejima, Yoshimasa, *8:* 187
Selig, Sylvie, *13:* 199
Seltzer, Isadore, *6:* 18
Seltzer, Meyer, *17:* 214
Sempé, Jean-Jacques, *47:* 92; *YABC 2:* 109
Sendak, Maurice, *1:* 135, 190; *3:* 204; *7:* 142; *15:* 199; *17:* 210; *27:* 181, 182, 183, 185, 186, 187, 189, 190-191, 192, 193, 194, 195, 197, 198, 199, 203; *28:* 181, 182; *32:* 108; *33:* 148, 149; *35:* 238; *44:* 180, 181; *45:* 97, 99; *46:* 174; *YABC 1:* 167
Sengler, Johanna, *18:* 256
Seredy, Kate, *1:* 192; *14:* 20-21; *17:* 210
Sergeant, John, *6:* 74
Servello, Joe, *10:* 144; *24:* 139; *40:* 91
Seton, Ernest Thompson, *18:* 260-269, 271
Seuss, Dr. *See* Geisel, Theodor
Severin, John Powers, *7:* 62
Sewall, Marcia, *15:* 8; *22:* 170; *37:* 171, 172, 173; *39:* 73; *45:* 209
Seward, Prudence, *16:* 243
Sewell, Helen, *3:* 186; *15:* 308; *33:* 102; *38:* 189, 190, 191, 192
Shahn, Ben, *39:* 178; *46:* 193
Shalansky, Len, *38:* 167
Shanks, Anne Zane, *10:* 149
Sharp, William, *6:* 131; *19:* 241; *20:* 112; *25:* 141
Shaw, Charles, *21:* 135; *38:* 187; *47:* 124
Shaw, Charles G., *13:* 200
Shearer, Ted, *43:* 193, 194, 195, 196
Shecter, Ben, *16:* 244; *25:* 109; *33:* 188, 191; *41:* 77
Shefcik, James, *48:* 221, 222
Shefts, Joelle, *48:* 210
Shekerjian, Haig, *16:* 245
Shekerjian, Regina, *16:* 245; *25:* 73
Shenton, Edward, *45:* 187, 188, 189; *YABC 1:* 218-219, 221
Shepard, Ernest H., *3:* 193; *4:* 74; *16:* 101; *17:* 109; *25:* 148; *33:* 152, 199, 200, 201, 202, 203, 204, 205, 206, 207; *46:* 194;

YABC 1: 148, 153, 174, 176, 180-181
Shepard, Mary, *4:* 210; *22:* 205; *30:* 132, 133
Sherman, Theresa, *27:* 167
Sherwan, Earl, *3:* 196
Shields, Charles, *10:* 150; *36:* 63
Shields, Leonard, *13:* 83, 85, 87
Shillabeer, Mary, *35:* 74
Shilston, Arthur, *49:* 61
Shimin, Symeon, *1:* 93; *2:* 128-129; *3:* 202; *7:* 85; *11:* 177; *12:* 139; *13:* 202-203; *27:* 138; *28:* 65; *35:* 129; *36:* 130; *48:* 151; *49:* 59
Shinn, Everett, *16:* 148; *18:* 229; *21:* 149, 150, 151; *24:* 218
Shore, Robert, *27:* 54; *39:* 192, 193; *YABC 2:* 200
Shortall, Leonard, *4:* 144; *8:* 196; *10:* 166; *19:* 227, 228-229, 230; *25:* 78; *28:* 66, 167; *33:* 127
Shortt, T. M., *27:* 36
Shtainments, Leon, *32:* 161
Shulevitz, Uri, *3:* 198-199; *17:* 85; *22:* 204; *27:* 212; *28:* 184
Shute, Linda, *46:* 59
Siberell, Anne, *29:* 193
Sibley, Don, *1:* 39; *12:* 196; *31:* 47
Sidjakov, Nicolas, *18:* 274
Siebel, Fritz, *3:* 120; *17:* 145
Siegl, Helen, *12:* 166; *23:* 216; *34:* 185, 186
Sills, Joyce, *5:* 199
Silverstein, Alvin, *8:* 189
Silverstein, Shel, *33:* 211
Silverstein, Virginia, *8:* 189
Simon, Eric M., *7:* 82
Simon, Hilda, *28:* 189
Simon, Howard, *2:* 175; *5:* 132; *19:* 199; *32:* 163, 164, 165
Simont, Marc, *2:* 119; *4:* 213; *9:* 168; *13:* 238, 240; *14:* 262; *16:* 179; *18:* 221; *26:* 210; *33:* 189, 194; *44:* 132
Sims, Blanche, *44:* 116
Singer, Edith G., *2:* 30
Singer, Gloria, *34:* 56; *36:* 43
Singer, Julia, *28:* 190
Sivard, Robert, *26:* 124
Skardinski, Stanley, *23:* 144; *32:* 84
Slackman, Charles B., *12:* 201
Slater, Rod, *25:* 167
Sloan, Joseph, *16:* 68
Sloane, Eric, *21:* 3
Slobodkin, Louis, *1:* 200; *3:* 232; *5:* 168; *13:* 251; *15:* 13, 88; *26:* 173, 174, 175, 176, 178, 179
Slobodkina, Esphyr, *1:* 201
Small, W., *33:* 113
Smalley, Janet, *1:* 154
Smedley, William T., *34:* 129
Smee, David, *14:* 78
Smith, A. G., Jr., *35:* 182
Smith, Alvin, *1:* 31, 229; *13:* 187; *27:* 216; *28:* 226; *48:* 149; *49:* 60
Smith, Anne Warren, *41:* 212
Smith, Carl, *36:* 41
Smith, Doris Susan, *41:* 139

Smith, E. Boyd, *19:* 70; *22:* 89; *26:* 63; *YABC 1:* 4-5, 240, 248-249
Smith, Edward J., *4:* 224
Smith, Eunice Young, *5:* 170
Smith, Howard, *19:* 196
Smith, Jacqueline Bardner, *27:* 108; *39:* 197
Smith, Jessie Willcox, *15:* 91; *16:* 95; *18:* 231; *19:* 57, 242; *21:* 29, 156, 157, 158, 159, 160, 161; *34:* 65; *YABC 1:* 6; *YABC 2:* 180, 185, 191, 311, 325
Smith, Kenneth R., *47:* 182
Smith, L. H., *35:* 174
Smith, Lee, *29:* 32
Smith, Linell Nash, *2:* 195
Smith, Maggie Kaufman, *13:* 205; *35:* 191
Smith, Moishe, *33:* 155
Smith, Philip, *44:* 134; *46:* 203
Smith, Ralph Crosby, *2:* 267; *49:* 203
Smith, Robert D., *5:* 63
Smith, Susan Carlton, *12:* 208
Smith, Terry, *12:* 106; *33:* 158
Smith, Virginia, *3:* 157; *33:* 72
Smith, William A., *1:* 36; *10:* 154; *25:* 65
Smollin, Mike, *39:* 203
Smyth, M. Jane, *12:* 15
Snyder, Andrew A., *30:* 212
Snyder, Jerome, *13:* 207; *30:* 173
Snyder, Joel, *28:* 163
Sofia, *1:* 62; *5:* 90; *32:* 166
Sokol, Bill, *37:* 178; *49:* 23
Sokolov, Kirill, *34:* 188
Solbert, Ronni, *1:* 159; *2:* 232; *5:* 121; *6:* 34; *17:* 249
Solonevich, George, *15:* 246; *17:* 47
Sommer, Robert, *12:* 211
Sorel, Edward, *4:* 61; *36:* 82
Sotomayor, Antonio, *11:* 215
Soyer, Moses, *20:* 177
Spaenkuch, August, *16:* 28
Spanfeller, James, *1:* 72, 149; *2:* 183; *19:* 230, 231, 232; *22:* 66; *36:* 160, 161; *40:* 75
Sparks, Mary Walker, *15:* 247
Spence, Geraldine, *21:* 163; *47:* 196
Spence, Jim, *38:* 89
Spiegel, Doris, *29:* 111
Spier, Jo, *10:* 30
Spier, Peter, *3:* 155; *4:* 200; *7:* 61; *11:* 78; *38:* 106
Spilka, Arnold, *5:* 120; *6:* 204; *8:* 131
Spivak, I. Howard, *8:* 10
Spollen, Christopher J., *12:* 214
Spooner, Malcolm, *40:* 142
Sprattler, Rob, *12:* 176
Spring, Bob, *5:* 60
Spring, Ira, *5:* 60
Springer, Harriet, *31:* 92
Spurrier, Steven, *28:* 198
Spy. *See* Ward, Leslie
Staffan, Alvin E., *11:* 56; *12:* 187
Stahl, Ben, *5:* 181; *12:* 91; *49:* 122
Stair, Gobin, *35:* 214
Stamaty, Mark Alan, *12:* 215
Stanley, Diane, *3:* 45; *37:* 180

Stasiak, Krystyna, *49:* 181
Steadman, Ralph, *32:* 180
Steichen, Edward, *30:* 79
Steig, William, *18:* 275-276
Stein, Harve, *1:* 109
Steinberg, Saul, *47:* 193
Steinel, William, *23:* 146
Steiner, Charlotte, *45:* 196
Stephens, Charles H., *YABC 2:* 279
Stephens, William M., *21:* 165
Steptoe, John, *8:* 197
Stern, Simon, *15:* 249-250; *17:* 58; *34:* 192-193
Stevens, Janet, *40:* 126
Stevens, Mary, *11:* 193; *13:* 129; *43:* 95
Stevenson, James, *42:* 182, 183
Stewart, Arvis, *33:* 98; *36:* 69
Stewart, Charles, *2:* 205
Stiles, Fran, *26:* 85
Stillman, Susan, *44:* 130
Stimpson, Tom, *49:* 171
Stinemetz, Morgan, *40:* 151
Stirnweis, Shannon, *10:* 164
Stobbs, William, *1:* 48-49; *3:* 68; *6:* 20; *17:* 117, 217; *24:* 150; *29:* 250
Stock, Catherine, *37:* 55
Stolp, Jaap, *49:* 98
Stone, David, *9:* 173
Stone, David K., *4:* 38; *6:* 124; *9:* 180; *43:* 182
Stone, Helen, *44:* 121, 122, 126
Stone, Helen V., *6:* 209
Stratton, Helen, *33:* 151
Stratton-Porter, Gene, *15:* 254, 259, 263-264, 268-269
Streano, Vince, *20:* 173
Strodl, Daniel, *47:* 95
Strong, Joseph D., Jr., *YABC 2:* 330
Ströyer, Poul, *13:* 221
Strugnell, Ann, *27:* 38
Stubis, Talivaldis, *5:* 182, 183; *10:* 45; *11:* 9; *18:* 304; *20:* 127
Stubley, Trevor, *14:* 43; *22:* 219; *23:* 37; *28:* 61
Stuecklen, Karl W., *8:* 34, 65; *23:* 103
Stull, Betty, *11:* 46
Suba, Susanne, *4:* 202-203; *14:* 261; *23:* 134; *29:* 222; *32:* 30
Sugarman, Tracy, *3:* 76; *8:* 199; *37:* 181, 182
Sugita, Yutaka, *36:* 180-181
Sullivan, Edmund J., *31:* 86
Sullivan, James F., *19:* 280; *20:* 192
Sumichrast, Jözef, *14:* 253; *29:* 168, 213
Sumiko, *46:* 57
Summers, Leo, *1:* 177; *2:* 273; *13:* 22
Svolinsky, Karel, *17:* 104
Swain, Su Zan Noguchi, *21:* 170
Swan, Susan, *22:* 220-221; *37:* 66
Sweat, Lynn, *25:* 206
Sweet, Darryl, *1:* 163; *4:* 136
Sweet, Ozzie, *31:* 149, 151, 152
Sweetland, Robert, *12:* 194
Swope, Martha, *43:* 160
Sylvester, Natalie G., *22:* 222
Szafran, Gene, *24:* 144

Szasz, Susanne, *13:* 55, 226; *14:* 48
Szekeres, Cyndy, *2:* 218; *5:* 185; *8:* 85; *11:* 166; *14:* 19; *16:* 57, 159; *26:* 49, 214; *34:* 205

Taback, Simms, *40:* 207
Tafuri, Nancy, *39:* 210
Tait, Douglas, *12:* 220
Takakjian, Portia, *15:* 274
Takashima, Shizuye, *13:* 228
Talarczyk, June, *4:* 173
Tallon, Robert, *2:* 228; *43:* 200, 201, 202, 203, 204, 205, 206, 207, 209
Tamas, Szecskó, *29:* 135
Tamburine, Jean, *12:* 222
Tandy, H. R., *13:* 69
Tannenbaum, Robert, *48:* 181
Tanobe, Miyuki, *23:* 221
Tarkington, Booth, *17:* 224-225
Taylor, Ann, *41:* 226
Taylor, Isaac, *41:* 228
Teale, Edwin Way, *7:* 196
Teason, James, *1:* 14
Teeple, Lyn, *33:* 147
Tee-Van, Helen Damrosch, *10:* 176; *11:* 182
Tempest, Margaret, *3:* 237, 238
Temple, Herbert, *45:* 201
Templeton, Owen, *11:* 77
Tenggren, Gustaf, *18:* 277-279; *19:* 15; *28:* 86; *YABC 2:* 145
Tenney, Gordon, *24:* 204
Tenniel, John, *YABC 2:* 99
Thacher, Mary M., *30:* 72
Thackeray, William Makepeace, *23:* 224, 228
Thamer, Katie, *42:* 187
Thelwell, Norman, *14:* 201
Theobalds, Prue, *40:* 23
Theurer, Marilyn Churchill, *39:* 195
Thistlethwaite, Miles, *12:* 224
Thollander, Earl, *11:* 47; *18:* 112; *22:* 224
Thomas, Allan, *22:* 13
Thomas, Art, *48:* 217
Thomas, Eric, *28:* 49
Thomas, Harold, *20:* 98
Thomas, Mark, *42:* 136
Thomas, Martin, *14:* 255
Thompson, Arthur, *34:* 107
Thompson, George, *22:* 18; *28:* 150; *33:* 135
Thompson, George, W., *33:* 135
Thompson, Julie, *44:* 158
Thomson, Arline K., *3:* 264
Thomson, Hugh, *26:* 88
Thomson, Ross, *36:* 179
Thorne, Diana, *25:* 212
Thorvall, Kerstin, *13:* 235
Thurber, James, *13:* 239, 242-245, 248-249
Tibbles, Paul, *45:* 23
Tichenor, Tom, *14:* 207
Tiegreen, Alan, *36:* 143; *43:* 55, 56, 58
Tilney, F. C., *22:* 231
Timbs, Gloria, *36:* 90
Timmins, Harry, *2:* 171

Tinkelman, Murray, *12:* 225; *35:* 44
Titherington, Jeanne, *39:* 90
Tolford, Joshua, *1:* 221
Tolkien, J. R. R., *2:* 243; *32:* 215
Tolmie, Ken, *15:* 292
Tomei, Lorna, *47:* 168, 171
Tomes, Jacqueline, *2:* 117; *12:* 139
Tomes, Margot, *1:* 224; *2:* 120-121;
    16: 207; *18:* 250; *20:* 7; *25:* 62;
    27: 78, 79; *29:* 81, 199; *33:* 82;
    36: 186, 187, 188, 189, 190;
    46: 129
Toner, Raymond John, *10:* 179
Toothill, Harry, *6:* 54; *7:* 49; *25:* 219;
    42: 192
Toothill, Ilse, *6:* 54
Topolski, Feliks, *44:* 48
Torbert, Floyd James, *22:* 226
Torrey, Marjorie, *34:* 105
Toschik, Larry, *6:* 102
Totten, Bob, *13:* 93
Travers, Bob, *49:* 100
Tremain, Ruthven, *17:* 238
Tresilian, Stuart, *25:* 53; *40:* 212
Trez, Alain, *17:* 236
Trier, Walter, *14:* 96
Trimby, Elisa, *47:* 199
Tripp, F. J., *24:* 167
Tripp, Wallace, *2:* 48; *7:* 28; *8:* 94;
    10: 54, 76; *11:* 92; *31:* 170, 171;
    34: 203; *42:* 57
Trnka, Jiri, *22:* 151; *43:* 212, 213,
    214, 215; *YABC 1:* 30-31
Troughton, Joanna, *37:* 186; *48:* 72
Troyer, Johannes, *3:* 16; *7:* 18
Trudeau, G. B., *35:* 220, 221, 222;
    48: 119, 123, 126, 127, 128-129,
    133
Tsinajinie, Andy, *2:* 62
Tsugami, Kyuzo, *18:* 198-199
Tuckwell, Jennifer, *17:* 205
Tudor, Bethany, *7:* 103
Tudor, Tasha, *18:* 227; *20:* 185, 186,
    187; *36:* 111; *YABC 2:* 46, 314
Tulloch, Maurice, *24:* 79
Tunis, Edwin, *1:* 218-219; *28:* 209,
    210, 211, 212
Turkle, Brinton, *1:* 211, 213; *2:* 249;
    3: 226; *11:* 3; *16:* 209; *20:* 22;
    YABC 1: 79
Turska, Krystyna, *12:* 103; *31:* 173,
    174-175
Tusan, Stan, *6:* 58; *22:* 236-237
Tworkov, Jack, *47:* 207
Tzimoulis, Paul, *12:* 104

Uchida, Yoshiko, *1:* 220
Uderzo, *47:* 88
Ulm, Robert, *17:* 238
Unada. *See* Gliewe, Unada
Underwood, Clarence, *40:* 166
Ungerer, Tomi, *5:* 188; *9:* 40; *18:* 188;
    29: 175; *33:* 221, 222-223, 225
Unwin, Nora S., *3:* 65, 234-235;
    4: 237; *44:* 173, 174; *YABC 1:* 59;
    YABC 2: 301
Uris, Jill, *49:* 188, 197
Utpatel, Frank, *18:* 114

Utz, Lois, *5:* 190

Van Abbé, S., *16:* 142; *18:* 282;
    31: 90; *YABC 2:* 157, 161
Van Allsburg, Chris, *37:* 205, 206
Vandivert, William, *21:* 175
Van Everen, Jay, *13:* 160;
    YABC 1: 121
Van Horn, William, *43:* 218
Van Loon, Hendrik Willem, *18:* 285,
    289, 291
Van Sciver, Ruth, *37:* 162
Van Stockum, Hilda, *5:* 193
Van Wely, Babs, *16:* 50
Varga, Judy, *29:* 196
Vasiliu, Mircea, *2:* 166, 253; *9:* 166;
    13: 58
Vaughn, Frank, *34:* 157
Vavra, Robert, *8:* 206
Vawter, Will, *17:* 163
Veeder, Larry, *18:* 4
Velasquez, Eric, *45:* 217
Vendrell, Carme Solé, *42:* 205
Ver Beck, Frank, *18:* 16-17
Verney, John, *14:* 225
Verrier, Suzanne, *5:* 20; *23:* 212
Versace, Marie, *2:* 255
Vestal, H. B., *9:* 134; *11:* 101; *27:* 25;
    34: 158
Vickrey, Robert, *45:* 59, 64
Victor, Joan Berg, *30:* 193
Viereck, Ellen, *3:* 242; *14:* 229
Vigna, Judith, *15:* 293
Vilato, Gaspar E., *5:* 41
Vimnèra, A., *23:* 154
Vincent, Eric, *34:* 98
Vincent, Félix, *41:* 237
Vip, *45:* 164
Vo-Dinh, Mai, *16:* 272
Vogel, Ilse-Margret, *14:* 230
Voigt, Erna, *35:* 228
Vojtech, Anna, *42:* 190
von Schmidt, Eric, *8:* 62
von Schmidt, Harold, *30:* 80
Vosburgh, Leonard, *1:* 161; *7:* 32;
    15: 295-296; *23:* 110; *30:* 214;
    43: 181
Voter, Thomas W., *19:* 3, 9
Vroman, Tom, *10:* 29

Waber, Bernard, *47:* 209, 210, 211,
    212, 213, 214
Wagner, John, *8:* 200
Wagner, Ken, *2:* 59
Waide, Jan, *29:* 225; *36:* 139
Wainwright, Jerry, *14:* 85
Wakeen, Sandra, *47:* 97
Waldman, Bruce, *15:* 297; *43:* 178
Waldman, Neil, *35:* 141
Walker, Charles, *1:* 46; *4:* 59; *5:* 177;
    11: 115; *19:* 45; *34:* 74
Walker, Dugald Stewart, *15:* 47;
    32: 202; *33:* 112
Walker, Gil, *8:* 49; *23:* 132; *34:* 42
Walker, Jim, *10:* 94

Walker, Mort, *8:* 213
Walker, Norman, *41:* 37; *45:* 58
Walker, Stephen, *12:* 229; *21:* 174
Wallace, Beverly Dobrin, *19:* 259
Waller, S. E., *24:* 36
Wallner, Alexandra, *15:* 120
Wallner, John C., *9:* 77; *10:* 188;
    11: 28; *14:* 209; *31:* 56, 118;
    37: 64
Wallower, Lucille, *11:* 226
Walters, Audrey, *18:* 294
Walther, Tom, *31:* 179
Walton, Tony, *11:* 164; *24:* 209
Waltrip, Lela, *9:* 195
Waltrip, Mildred, *3:* 209; *37:* 211
Waltrip, Rufus, *9:* 195
Wan, *12:* 76
Ward, John, *42:* 191
Ward, Keith, *2:* 107
Ward, Leslie, *34:* 126; *36:* 87
Ward, Lynd, *1:* 99, 132, 133, 150;
    2: 108, 158, 196, 259; *18:* 86;
    27: 56; *29:* 79, 187, 253, 255;
    36: 199, 200, 201, 202, 203, 204,
    205, 206, 207, 209; *43:* 34
Ward, Peter, *37:* 116
Warner, Peter, *14:* 87
Warren, Betsy, *2:* 101
Warren, Marion Cray, *14:* 215
Warshaw, Jerry, *30:* 197, 198; *42:* 165
Washington, Nevin, *20:* 123
Washington, Phyllis, *20:* 123
Waterman, Stan, *11:* 76
Watkins-Pitchford, D. J., *6:* 215, 217
Watson, Aldren A., *2:* 267; *5:* 94;
    13: 71; *19:* 253; *32:* 220; *42:* 193,
    194, 195, 196, 197, 198, 199,
    200, 201; *YABC 2:* 202
Watson, Gary, *19:* 147; *36:* 68;
    41: 122; *47:* 139
Watson, J. D., *22:* 86
Watson, Karen, *11:* 26
Watson, Wendy, *5:* 197; *13:* 101;
    33: 116; *46:* 163
Watts, Bernadette, *4:* 227
Watts, John, *37:* 149
Webber, Helen, *3:* 141
Webber, Irma E., *14:* 238
Weber, Florence, *40:* 153
Weber, William J., *14:* 239
Webster, Jean, *17:* 241
Wegner, Fritz, *14:* 250; *20:* 189;
    44: 165
Weidenear, Reynold H., *21:* 122
Weihs, Erika, *4:* 21; *15:* 299
Weil, Lisl, *7:* 203; *10:* 58; *21:* 95;
    22: 188, 217; *33:* 193
Weiner, Sandra, *14:* 240
Weisgard, Leonard, *1:* 65; *2:* 191,
    197, 204, 264-265; *5:* 108; *21:* 42;
    30: 200, 201, 203, 204; *41:* 47;
    44: 125; *YABC 2:* 13
Weiss, Ellen, *44:* 202
Weiss, Emil, *1:* 168; *7:* 60
Weiss, Harvey, *1:* 145, 223; *27:* 224,
    227
Weiss, Nicki, *33:* 229
Weissman, Bari, *49:* 72
Wells, Frances, *1:* 183

Wells, H. G., *20:* 194, 200
Wells, Rosemary, *6:* 49; *18:* 297
Wells, Susan, *22:* 43
Wendelin, Rudolph, *23:* 234
Wengenroth, Stow, *37:* 47
Werenskiold, Erik, *15:* 6
Werner, Honi, *24:* 110; *33:* 41
Werth, Kurt, *7:* 122; *14:* 157; *20:* 214; *39:* 128
Westerberg, Christine, *29:* 226
Weston, Martha, *29:* 116; *30:* 213; *33:* 85, 100
Wetherbee, Margaret, *5:* 3
Wexler, Jerome, *49:* 73
Wheatley, Arabelle, *11:* 231; *16:* 276
Wheeler, Cindy, *49:* 205
Wheeler, Dora, *44:* 179
Wheelright, Rowland, *15:* 81; *YABC 2:* 286
Whistler, Rex, *16:* 75; *30:* 207, 208
White, David Omar, *5:* 56; *18:* 6
Whitear, *32:* 26
Whithorne, H. S., *7:* 49
Whitney, George Gillett, *3:* 24
Whittam, Geoffrey, *30:* 191
Wiberg, Harald, *38:* 127
Wiese, Kurt, *3:* 255; *4:* 206; *14:* 17; *17:* 18-19; *19:* 47; *24:* 152; *25:* 212; *32:* 184; *36:* 211, 213, 214, 215, 216, 217, 218; *45:* 161
Wiesner, David, *33:* 47
Wiesner, William, *4:* 100; *5:* 200, 201; *14:* 262
Wiggins, George, *6:* 133
Wikkelsoe, Otto, *45:* 25, 26
Wikland, Ilon, *5:* 113; *8:* 150; *38:* 124, 125, 130
Wilbur, C. Keith, M.D., *27:* 228
Wilcox, J.A.J., *34:* 122
Wilcox, R. Turner, *36:* 219
Wild, Jocelyn, *46:* 220-221, 222
Wilde, George, *7:* 139
Wildsmith, Brian, *16:* 281-282; *18:* 170-171
Wilkin, Eloise, *36:* 173; *49:* 208, 209, 210
Wilkinson, Gerald, *3:* 40
Wilkoń, Józef, *31:* 183, 184
Wilks, Mike, *34:* 24; *44:* 203
Williams, Ferelith Eccles, *22:* 238
Williams, Garth, *1:* 197; *2:* 49, 270; *4:* 205; *15:* 198, 302-304, 307; *16:* 34; *18:* 283, 298-301; *29:* 177, 178, 179, 232-233, 241-245, 248; *40:* 106; *YABC 2:* 15-16, 19
Williams, J. Scott, *48:* 28
Williams, Kit, *44:* 206-207, 208, 209, 211, 212

Williams, Maureen, *12:* 238
Williams, Patrick, *14:* 218
Williams, Richard, *44:* 93
Wilson, Charles Banks, *17:* 92; *43:* 73
Wilson, Dagmar, *10:* 47
Wilson, Edward A., *6:* 24; *16:* 149; *20:* 220-221; *22:* 87; *26:* 67; *38:* 212, 214, 215, 216, 217
Wilson, Forrest, *27:* 231
Wilson, Gahan, *35:* 234; *41:* 136
Wilson, Jack, *17:* 139
Wilson, John, *22:* 240
Wilson, Maurice, *46:* 224
Wilson, Patten, *35:* 61
Wilson, Peggy, *15:* 4
Wilson, Rowland B., *30:* 170
Wilson, Tom, *33:* 232
Wilson, W. N., *22:* 26
Wilwerding, Walter J., *9:* 202
Winchester, Linda, *13:* 231
Wind, Betty, *28:* 158
Windham, Kathryn Tucker, *14:* 260
Winslow, Will, *21:* 124
Winsten, Melanie Willa, *41:* 41
Winter, Milo, *15:* 97; *19:* 221; *21:* 181, 203, 204, 205; *YABC 2:* 144
Winter, Paula, *48:* 227
Wise, Louis, *13:* 68
Wiseman, Ann, *31:* 187
Wiseman, B., *4:* 233
Wishnefsky, Phillip, *3:* 14
Wiskur, Darrell, *5:* 72; *10:* 50; *18:* 246
Wittman, Sally, *30:* 219
Woehr, Lois, *12:* 5
Wohlberg, Meg, *12:* 100; *14:* 197; *41:* 255
Woldin, Beth Weiner, *34:* 211
Wolf, J., *16:* 91
Wolf, Linda, *33:* 163
Wondriska, William, *6:* 220
Wonsetler, John C., *5:* 168
Wood, Grant, *19:* 198
Wood, Muriel, *36:* 119
Wood, Myron, *6:* 220
Wood, Owen, *18:* 187
Wood, Ruth, *8:* 11
Woodson, Jack, *10:* 201
Woodward, Alice, *26:* 89; *36:* 81
Wool, David, *26:* 27
Wooten, Vernon, *23:* 70
Worboys, Evelyn, *1:* 166-167
Worth, Jo, *34:* 143
Worth, Wendy, *4:* 133
Wosmek, Frances, *29:* 251
Wrenn, Charles L., *38:* 96; *YABC 1:* 20, 21
Wright, Dare, *21:* 206
Wright, George, *YABC 1:* 268

Wright, Joseph, *30:* 160
Wronker, Lili Cassel, *3:* 247; *10:* 204; *21:* 10
Wyatt, Stanley, *46:* 210
Wyeth, Andrew, *13:* 40; *YABC 1:* 133-134
Wyeth, Jamie, *41:* 257
Wyeth, N. C., *13:* 41; *17:* 252-259, 264-268; *18:* 181; *19:* 80, 191, 200; *21:* 57, 183; *22:* 91; *23:* 152; *24:* 28, 99; *35:* 61; *41:* 65; *YABC 1:* 133, 223; *YABC 2:* 53, 75, 171, 187, 317

Yang, Jay, *1:* 8; *12:* 239
Yap, Weda, *6:* 176
Yaroslava. *See* Mills, Yaroslava Surmach
Yashima, Taro, *14:* 84
Ylla. *See* Koffler, Camilla
Yohn, F. C., *23:* 128; *YABC 1:* 269
Young, Ed, *7:* 205; *10:* 206; *40:* 124; *YABC 2:* 242
Young, Noela, *8:* 221

Zacks, Lewis, *10:* 161
Zaffo, George, *42:* 208
Zaidenberg, Arthur, *34:* 218, 219, 220
Zalben, Jane Breskin, *7:* 211
Zallinger, Jean, *4:* 192; *8:* 8, 129; *14:* 273
Zallinger, Rudolph F., *3:* 245
Zeck, Gerry, *40:* 232
Zeiring, Bob, *42:* 130
Zeldich, Arieh, *49:* 124
Zelinsky, Paul O., *14:* 269; *43:* 56; *49:* 218, 219, 220, 221, 222-223
Zemach, Margot, *3:* 270; *8:* 201; *21:* 210-211; *27:* 204, 205, 210; *28:* 185; *49:* 22, 183, 224
Zemsky, Jessica, *10:* 62
Zepelinsky, Paul, *35:* 93
Zimmer, Dirk, *38:* 195; *49:* 71
Zimnik, Reiner, *36:* 224
Zinkeisen, Anna, *13:* 106
Zoellick, Scott, *33:* 231
Zonia, Dhimitri, *20:* 234-235
Zweifel, Francis, *14:* 274; *28:* 187
Zwinger, Herman H., *46:* 227

Author Index

The following index gives the number of the volume in which an author's biographical sketch, Brief Entry, or Obituary appears.

This index includes references to all entries in the following series, which are also published by Gale Research Company.

YABC—*Yesterday's Authors of Books for Children: Facts and Pictures about Authors and Illustrators of Books for Young People from Early Times to 1960*, Volumes 1-2

CLR—*Children's Literature Review: Excerpts from Reviews, Criticism, and Commentary on Books for Children*, Volumes 1-12

SAAS—*Something about the Author Autobiography Series*, Volumes 1-4

A

Aardema, Verna 1911- 4
Aaron, Chester 1923- 9
Aaseng, Nate
  See Aaseng, Nathan
Aaseng, Nathan 1938-
  Brief Entry 38
Abbott, Alice
  See Borland, Kathryn Kilby
Abbott, Alice
  See Speicher, Helen Ross (Smith)
Abbott, Jacob 1803-1879 22
Abbott, Manager Henry
  See Stratemeyer, Edward L.
Abbott, Sarah
  See Zolotow, Charlotte S.
Abdul, Raoul 1929- 12
Abel, Raymond 1911- 12
Abell, Kathleen 1938- 9
Abercrombie, Barbara (Mattes)
  1939- 16
Abernethy, Robert G. 1935- 5
Abisch, Roslyn Kroop 1927- 9
Abisch, Roz
  See Abisch, Roslyn Kroop
Abodaher, David J. (Naiph)
  1919- 17
Abolafia, Yossi
  Brief Entry 46
Abrahall, C. H.
  See Hoskyns-Abrahall, Clare
Abrahall, Clare Hoskyns
  See Hoskyns-Abrahall, Clare
Abrahams, Hilary (Ruth)
  1938- 29
Abrahams, Robert D(avid)
  1905- 4
Abrams, Joy 1941- 16
Abrams, Lawrence F.
  Brief Entry 47
Achebe, Chinua 1930- 40
  Brief Entry 38
Ackerman, Eugene 1888-1974 10

Acs, Laszlo (Bela) 1931- 42
  Brief Entry 32
Acuff, Selma Boyd 1924- 45
Ada, Alma Flor 1938- 43
Adair, Margaret Weeks
  (?)-1971 10
Adam, Cornel
  See Lengyel, Cornel Adam
Adams, Adrienne 1906- 8
Adams, Andy
  1859-1935 .... YABC 1
Adams, Dale
  See Quinn, Elisabeth
Adams, Harriet S(tratemeyer)
  1893(?)-1982 1
  Obituary 29
Adams, Harrison
  See Stratemeyer, Edward L.
Adams, Hazard 1926- 6
Adams, Laurie 1941- 33
Adams, Richard 1920- 7
Adams, Ruth Joyce 14
Adams, William Taylor
  1822-1897 28
Adamson, Gareth 1925-1982 46
  Obituary 30
Adamson, George Worsley
  1913- 30
Adamson, Graham
  See Groom, Arthur William
Adamson, Joy 1910-1980 11
  Obituary 22
Adamson, Wendy Wriston
  1942- 22
Addona, Angelo F. 1925- 14
Addy, Ted
  See Winterbotham, R(ussell)
  R(obert)
Adelberg, Doris
  See Orgel, Doris
Adelson, Leone 1908- 11
Adkins, Jan 1944- 8
  See also CLR 7

Adler, C(arole) S(chwerdtfeger)
  1932- 26
Adler, David A. 1947- 14
Adler, Irene
  See Penzler, Otto
  See Storr, Catherine (Cole)
Adler, Irving 1913- 29
  Earlier sketch in SATA 1
Adler, Larry 1939- 36
Adler, Peggy 22
Adler, Ruth 1915-1968 1
Adoff, Arnold 1935- 5
  See also CLR 7
Adorjan, Carol 1934- 10
Adrian, Mary
  See Jorgensen, Mary Venn
Adshead, Gladys L. 1896- 3
Aesop, Abraham
  See Newbery, John
Agapida, Fray Antonio
  See Irving, Washington
Agard, Nadema 1948- 18
Agle, Nan Hayden 1905- 3
Agnew, Edith J(osephine)
  1897- 11
Ahern, Margaret McCrohan
  1921- 10
Ahl, Anna Maria 1926- 32
Ahlberg, Allan
  Brief Entry 35
Ahlberg, Janet
  Brief Entry 32
Aichinger, Helga 1937- 4
Aiken, Clarissa (Lorenz)
  1899- 12
Aiken, Conrad (Potter)
  1889-1973 30
  Earlier sketch in SATA 3
Aiken, Joan 1924- 30
  Earlier sketch in SATA 2
  See also CLR 1
  See also SAAS 1
Ainsworth, Norma 9
Ainsworth, Ruth 1908- 7

Ainsworth, William Harrison
  1805-1882 24
Aistrop, Jack 1916- 14
Aitken, Amy 1952-
  Brief Entry 40
Aitken, Dorothy 1916- 10
Akaba, Suekichi 1910- 46
Akers, Floyd
  See Baum, L(yman) Frank
Alain
  See Brustlein, Daniel
Albert, Burton, Jr. 1936- 22
Alberts, Frances Jacobs 1907- 14
Albion, Lee Smith 29
Albrecht, Lillie (Vanderveer)
  1894- 12
Alcock, Gudrun
  Brief Entry 33
Alcock, Vivien 1924- 45
  Brief Entry 38
Alcorn, John 1935- 31
  Brief Entry 30
Alcott, Louisa May
  1832-1888 ....YABC 1
  See also CLR 1
Alda, Arlene 1933- 44
  Brief Entry 36
Alden, Isabella (Macdonald)
  1841-1930 ....YABC 2
Alderman, Clifford Lindsey
  1902- 3
Alderson, Sue Ann 1940-
  Brief Entry 48
Aldis, Dorothy (Keeley)
  1896-1966 2
Aldiss, Brian W(ilson) 1925- 34
Aldon, Adair
  See Meigs, Cornelia
Aldous, Allan (Charles) 1911- 27
Aldrich, Ann
  See Meaker, Marijane
Aldrich, Thomas Bailey
  1836-1907 17
Aldridge, Alan 1943(?)-
  Brief Entry 33
Aldridge, Josephine Haskell 14
Alegria, Ricardo E. 1921- 6
Aleksin, Anatolii (Georgievich)
  1924- 36
Alex, Ben [a pseudonym]
  1946- 45
Alex, Marlee [a pseudonym]
  1948- 45
Alexander, Anna Cooke 1913- 1
Alexander, Frances 1888- 4
Alexander, Jocelyn (Anne) Arundel
  1930- 22
Alexander, Linda 1935- 2
Alexander, Lloyd 1924- 49
  Earlier sketch in SATA 3
  See also CLR 1, 5
Alexander, Martha 1920- 11
Alexander, Rae Pace
  See Alexander, Raymond Pace
Alexander, Raymond Pace
  1898-1974 22
Alexander, Sue 1933- 12
Alexander, Vincent Arthur 1925-1980
  Obituary 23

Alexeieff, Alexandre A.
  1901- 14
Alger, Horatio, Jr. 1832-1899 16
Alger, Leclaire (Gowans)
  1898-1969 15
Aliki
  See Brandenberg, Aliki
  See also CLR 9
Alkema, Chester Jay 1932- 12
Allamand, Pascale 1942- 12
Allan, Mabel Esther 1915- 32
  Earlier sketch in SATA 5
Allard, Harry
  See Allard, Harry G(rover), Jr.
Allard, Harry G(rover), Jr.
  1928- 42
Allee, Marjorie Hill
  1890-1945 17
Allen, Adam [Joint pseudonym]
  See Epstein, Beryl and Epstein,
  Samuel
Allen, Alex B.
  See Heide, Florence Parry
Allen, Allyn
  See Eberle, Irmengarde
Allen, Betsy
  See Cavanna, Betty
Allen, Gertrude E(lizabeth)
  1888- 9
Allen, Jack 1899-
  Brief Entry 29
Allen, Jeffrey (Yale) 1948- 42
Allen, Leroy 1912- 11
Allen, Linda 1925- 33
Allen, Marjorie 1931- 22
Allen, Maury 1932- 26
Allen, Merritt Parmelee
  1892-1954 22
Allen, Nina (Strömgren)
  1935- 22
Allen, Rodney F. 1938- 27
Allen, Ruth
  See Peterson, Esther (Allen)
Allen, Samuel (Washington)
  1917- 9
Allen, T. D. [Joint pseudonym]
  See Allen, Terril Diener
Allen, Terril Diener 1908- 35
Allen, Terry D.
  See Allen, Terril Diener
Allen, Thomas B(enton)
  1929- 45
Allen, Tom
  See Allen, Thomas B(enton)
Allerton, Mary
  See Govan, Christine Noble
Alleyn, Ellen
  See Rossetti, Christina (Georgina)
Allington, Richard L(loyd)
  1947- 39
  Brief Entry 35
Allison, Bob 14
Allison, Linda 1948- 43
Allmendinger, David F(rederick), Jr.
  1938- 35
Allred, Gordon T. 1930- 10
Allsop, Kenneth 1920-1973 17
Almedingen, E. M.
  1898-1971 3

Almedingen, Martha Edith von
  See Almedingen, E. M.
Almquist, Don 1929- 11
Alsop, Mary O'Hara
  1885-1980 34
  Obituary 24
  Earlier sketch in SATA 5
Alter, Robert Edmond
  1925-1965 9
Althea
  See Braithwaite, Althea 23
Altschuler, Franz 1923- 45
Altsheler, Joseph A(lexander)
  1862-1919 ....YABC 1
Alvarez, Joseph A. 1930- 18
Ambler, C(hristopher) Gifford 1886-
  Brief Entry 29
Ambrose, Stephen E(dward)
  1936- 40
Ambrus, Gyozo (Laszlo)
  1935- 41
  Earlier sketch in SATA 1
Ambrus, Victor G.
  See Ambrus, Gyozo (Laszlo)
  See also SAAS 4
Amerman, Lockhart
  1911-1969 3
Ames, Evelyn 1908- 13
Ames, Gerald 1906- 11
Ames, Lee J. 1921- 3
Ames, Mildred 1919- 22
Amon, Aline 1928- 9
Amoss, Berthe 1925- 5
Anastasio, Dina 1941- 37
  Brief Entry 30
Anckarsvard, Karin
  1915-1969 6
Ancona, George 1929- 12
Andersdatter, Karla M(argaret)
  1938- 34
Andersen, Hans Christian
  1805-1875 ....YABC 1
  See also CLR 6
Andersen, Ted
  See Boyd, Waldo T.
Andersen, Yvonne 1932- 27
Anderson, Bernice G(oudy)
  1894- 33
Anderson, Brad(ley Jay)
  1924- 33
  Brief Entry 31
Anderson, C(larence) W(illiam)
  1891-1971 11
Anderson, Clifford [Joint pseudonym]
  See Gardner, Richard
Anderson, Ella
  See MacLeod, Ellen Jane (Anderson)
Anderson, Eloise Adell 1927- 9
Anderson, George
  See Groom, Arthur William
Anderson, Grace Fox 1932- 43
Anderson, J(ohn) R(ichard) L(ane)
  1911-1981 15
  Obituary 27
Anderson, Joy 1928- 1
Anderson, LaVere (Francis Shoenfelt)
  1907- 27
Anderson, Leone Castell 1923-
  Brief Entry 49

Anderson, (John) Lonzo
1905- 2
Anderson, Lucia (Lewis)
1922- 10
Anderson, Madelyn Klein 28
Anderson, Margaret J(ean)
1931- 27
Anderson, Mary 1939- 7
Anderson, Mona 1910- 40
Anderson, Norman D(ean)
1928- 22
Anderson, Poul (William) 1926-
Brief Entry 39
Anderson, Rachel 1943- 34
Andre, Evelyn M(arie) 1924- 27
Andree, Louise
See Coury, Louise Andree
Andrews, Benny 1930- 31
Andrews, F(rank) Emerson
1902-1978 22
Andrews, J(ames) S(ydney)
1934- 4
Andrews, Jan 1942-
Brief Entry 49
Andrews, Julie 1935- 7
Andrews, Laura
See Coury, Louise Andree
Andrews, Roy Chapman
1884-1960 19
Andrézel, Pierre
See Blixen, Karen (Christentze
Dinesen)
Andriola, Alfred J. 1912-1983
Obituary 34
Andrist, Ralph K. 1914- 45
Anfousse, Ginette 1944-
Brief Entry 48
Angel, Marie (Felicity) 1923- 47
Angeles, Peter A. 1931- 40
Angell, Judie 1937- 22
Angell, Madeline 1919- 18
Angelo, Valenti 1897- 14
Angelou, Maya 1928- 49
Angier, Bradford 12
Angle, Paul M(cClelland) 1900-1975
Obituary 20
Anglund, Joan Walsh 1926- 2
See also CLR 1
Angrist, Stanley W(olff)
1933- 4
Anita
See Daniel, Anita
Annett, Cora
See Scott, Cora Annett
Annixter, Jane
See Sturtzel, Jane Levington
Annixter, Paul
See Sturtzel, Howard A.
Anno, Mitsumasa 1926- 38
Earlier sketch in SATA 5
See also CLR 2
Anrooy, Frans van
See Van Anrooy, Francine
Antell, Will D. 1935- 31
Anthony, Barbara 1932- 29
Anthony, C. L.
See Smith, Dodie
Anthony, Edward 1895-1971 21
Anticaglia, Elizabeth 1939- 12

Antolini, Margaret Fishback
1904-1985
Obituary 45
Anton, Michael (James) 1940- ... 12
Antonacci, Robert J(oseph)
1916- 45
Brief Entry 37
Aoki, Hisako 1942- 45
Apfel, Necia H(alpern) 1930-
Brief Entry 41
Aphrodite, J.
See Livingston, Carole
Appel, Benjamin 1907-1977 39
Obituary 21
Appel, Martin E(liot) 1948- 45
Appel, Marty
See Appel, Martin E(liot)
Appiah, Peggy 1921- 15
Apple, Margot
Brief Entry 42
Applebaum, Stan 1929- 45
Appleton, Victor [Collective
pseudonym] 1
Appleton, Victor II [Collective
pseudonym] 1
See also Adams, Harriet
S(tratemeyer)
Apsler, Alfred 1907- 10
Aquillo, Don
See Prince, J(ack) H(arvey)
Aragonés, Sergio 1937- 48
Brief Entry 39
Arbuckle, Dorothy Fry 1910-1982
Obituary 33
Arbuthnot, May Hill
1884-1969 2
Archer, Frank
See O'Connor, Richard
Archer, Jules 1915- 4
Archer, Marion Fuller 1917- 11
Archibald, Joe
See Archibald, Joseph S(topford)
Archibald, Joseph S(topford)
1898-1986 3
Obituary 47
Arden, Barbie
See Stoutenburg, Adrien
Arden, William
See Lynds, Dennis
Ardizzone, Edward 1900-1979 ... 28
Obituary 21
Earlier sketch in SATA 1
See also CLR 3
Ardley, Neil (Richard) 1937- 43
Arehart-Treichel, Joan 1942- 22
Arenella, Roy 1939- 14
Arkin, Alan (Wolf) 1934-
Brief Entry 32
Armer, Alberta (Roller) 1904- 9
Armer, Laura Adams
1874-1963 13
Armitage, David 1943-
Brief Entry 38
Armitage, Ronda (Jacqueline)
1943- 47
Brief Entry 38
Armour, Richard 1906- 14
Armstrong, George D. 1927- 10

Armstrong, Gerry (Breen)
1929- 10
Armstrong, Louise 43
Brief Entry 33
Armstrong, Richard 1903- 11
Armstrong, William H. 1914- 4
See also CLR 1
Arndt, Ursula (Martha H.)
Brief Entry 39
Arneson, D(on) J(on) 1935- 37
Arnett, Carolyn
See Cole, Lois Dwight
Arno, Enrico 1913-1981 43
Obituary 28
Arnold, Caroline 1944- 36
Brief Entry 34
Arnold, Elliott 1912-1980 5
Obituary 22
Arnold, Oren 1900- 4
Arnoldy, Julie
See Bischoff, Julia Bristol
Arnosky, Jim 1946- 22
Arnott, Kathleen 1914- 20
Arnov, Boris, Jr. 1926- 12
Arnow, Harriette (Louisa Simpson)
1908-1986 42
Obituary 47
Arnstein, Helene S(olomon)
1915- 12
Arntson, Herbert E(dward)
1911- 12
Aronin, Ben 1904-1980
Obituary 25
Arora, Shirley (Lease) 1930- 2
Arquette, Lois S(teinmetz)
1934- 1
See Duncan, Lois S(teinmetz)
Arrowood, (McKendrick Lee) Clinton
1939- 19
Arthur, Robert
See Feder, Robert Arthur
Arthur, Ruth M(abel)
1905-1979 7
Obituary 26
Artis, Vicki Kimmel 1945- 12
Artzybasheff, Boris (Miklailovich)
1899-1965 14
Aruego, Ariane
See Dewey, Ariane
Aruego, Jose 1932- 6
See also CLR 5
Arundel, Honor (Morfydd)
1919-1973 4
Obituary 24
Arundel, Jocelyn
See Alexander, Jocelyn (Anne)
Arundel
Asbjörnsen, Peter Christen
1812-1885 15
Asch, Frank 1946- 5
Ash, Jutta 1942- 38
Ashabranner, Brent (Kenneth)
1921- 1
Ashby, Gwynneth 1922- 44
Ashe, Geoffrey (Thomas)
1923- 17
Asher, Sandy (Fenichel)
1942- 36
Brief Entry 34

Ashey, Bella
  See Breinburg, Petronella
Ashford, Daisy
  See Ashford, Margaret Mary
Ashford, Margaret Mary
  1881-1972 10
Ashley, Bernard 1935- 47
  Brief Entry 39
  See also CLR 4
Ashley, Elizabeth
  See Salmon, Annie Elizabeth
Ashton, Warren T.
  See Adams, William Taylor
Asimov, Issac 1920- 26
  Earlier sketch in SATA 1
  See also CLR 12
Asimov, Janet
  See Jeppson, J(anet) O(pal)
Asinof, Eliot 1919- 6
Astley, Juliet
  See Lofts, Nora (Robinson)
Aston, James
  See White, T(erence) H(anbury)
Atene, Ann
  See Atene, (Rita) Anna
Atene, (Rita) Anna 1922- 12
Atkinson, Allen
  Brief Entry 46
Atkinson, M. E.
  See Frankau, Mary Evelyn
Atkinson, Margaret Fleming 14
Atticus
  See Davies, (Edward) Hunter
  See Fleming, Ian (Lancaster)
Atwater, Florence (Hasseltine
  Carroll) 16
Atwater, Montgomery Meigs
  1904- 15
Atwater, Richard Tupper 1892-1948
  Brief Entry 27
Atwood, Ann 1913- 7
Aubry, Claude B. 1914-1984 29
  Obituary 40
Augarde, Steve 1950- 25
Augelli, John P(at) 1921- 46
Ault, Phillip H. 1914- 23
Ault, Rosalie Sain 1942- 38
Ault, Roz
  See Ault, Rosalie Sain
Aung, (Maung) Htin 1910- 21
Aung, U. Htin
  See Aung, (Maung) Htin
Auntie Deb
  See Coury, Louise Andree
Auntie Louise
  See Coury, Louise Andree
Austin, Elizabeth S. 1907- 5
Austin, Margot 11
Austin, Oliver L., Jr. 1903- 7
Austin, Tom
  See Jacobs, Linda C.
Averill, Esther 1902- 28
  Earlier sketch in SATA 1
Avery, Al
  See Montgomery, Rutherford
Avery, Gillian 1926- 7
Avery, Kay 1908- 5
Avery, Lynn
  See Cole, Lois Dwight

Avi
  See Wortis, Avi
Ayars, James S(terling) 1898- 4
Ayer, Jacqueline 1930- 13
Ayer, Margaret 15
Aylesworth, Jim 1943- 38
Aylesworth, Thomas G(ibbons)
  1927- 4
  See also CLR 6
Aymar, Brandt 1911- 22
Ayres, Carole Briggs
  See Briggs, Carole S(uzanne)
Ayres, Patricia Miller 1923-1985
  Obituary 46
Azaid
  See Zaidenberg, Arthur

B

B
  See Gilbert, W(illiam) S(chwenk)
B., Tania
  See Blixen, Karen (Christentze
  Dinesen)
BB
  See Watkins-Pitchford, D. J.
Baastad, Babbis Friis
  See Friis-Baastad, Babbis
Bab
  See Gilbert, W(illiam) S(chwenk)
Babbis, Eleanor
  See Friis-Baastad, Babbis
Babbitt, Natalie 1932- 6
  See also CLR 2
Babcock, Dennis Arthur
  1948- 22
Bach, Alice (Hendricks)
  1942- 30
  Brief Entry 27
Bach, Richard David 1936- 13
Bachman, Fred 1949- 12
Bacmeister, Rhoda W(arner)
  1893- 11
Bacon, Elizabeth 1914- 3
Bacon, Joan Chase
  See Bowden, Joan Chase
Bacon, Josephine Dodge (Daskam)
  1876-1961 48
Bacon, Margaret Hope 1921- 6
Bacon, Martha Sherman
  1917-1981 18
  Obituary 27
  See also CLR 3
Bacon, Peggy 1895- 2
Bacon, R(onald) L(eonard)
  1924- 26
Baden-Powell, Robert (Stephenson
  Smyth) 1857-1941 16
Baerg, Harry J(ohn) 1909- 12
Bagnold, Enid 1889-1981 25
  Earlier sketch in SATA 1
Bahr, Robert 1940- 38
Bahti, Tom
  Brief Entry 31
Bailey, Alice Cooper 1890- 12
Bailey, Bernadine Freeman 14
Bailey, Carolyn Sherwin
  1875-1961 14
Bailey, Jane H(orton) 1916- 12

Bailey, Maralyn Collins (Harrison)
  1941- 12
Bailey, Matilda
  See Radford, Ruby L.
Bailey, Maurice Charles
  1932- 12
Bailey, Ralph Edgar 1893- 11
Baird, Bil 1904- 30
Baird, Thomas P. 1923- 45
  Brief Entry 39
Baity, Elizabeth Chesley
  1907- 1
Bakeless, John (Edwin) 1894- 9
Bakeless, Katherine Little
  1895- 9
Baker, Alan 1951- 22
Baker, Augusta 1911- 3
Baker, Betty (Lou) 1928- 5
Baker, Charlotte 1910- 2
Baker, Elizabeth 1923- 7
Baker, Gayle C(unningham)
  1950- 39
Baker, James W. 1924- 22
Baker, Janice E(dla) 1941- 22
Baker, Jeannie 1950- 23
Baker, Jeffrey J(ohn) W(heeler)
  1931- 5
Baker, Jim
  See Baker, James W.
Baker, Laura Nelson 1911- 3
Baker, Margaret 1890- 4
Baker, Margaret J(oyce)
  1918- 12
Baker, Mary Gladys Steel
  1892-1974 12
Baker, (Robert) Michael
  1938- 4
Baker, Nina (Brown)
  1888-1957 15
Baker, Rachel 1904-1978 2
  Obituary 26
Baker, Samm Sinclair 1909- 12
Baker, Susan (Catherine)
  1942- 29
Balaam
  See Lamb, G(eoffrey) F(rederick)
Balch, Glenn 1902- 3
Baldridge, Cyrus LeRoy 1889-
  Brief Entry 29
Balducci, Carolyn Feleppa
  1946- 5
Baldwin, Anne Norris 1938- 5
Baldwin, Clara 11
Baldwin, Gordo
  See Baldwin, Gordon C.
Baldwin, Gordon C. 1908- 12
Baldwin, James 1841-1925 24
Baldwin, James (Arthur)
  1924- 9
Baldwin, Margaret
  See Weis, Margaret (Edith)
Baldwin, Stan(ley C.) 1929-
  Brief Entry 28
Bales, Carol Ann 1940-
  Brief Entry 29
Balet, Jan (Bernard) 1913- 11
Balian, Lorna 1929- 9
Ball, Zachary
  See Masters, Kelly R.

Ballantine, Lesley Frost
  See Frost, Lesley
Ballantyne, R(obert) M(ichael)
  1825-1894 .... *24*
Ballard, Lowell Clyne
  1904-1986 .... *12*
  Obituary *49*
Ballard, (Charles) Martin
  1929- *1*
Ballard, Mignon Franklin 1934-
  Brief Entry *49*
Balogh, Penelope 1916-1975 ...... *1*
  Obituary *34*
Balow, Tom 1931- *12*
Baltzer, Hans (Adolf) 1900- *40*
Bamfylde, Walter
  See Bevan, Tom
Bamman, Henry A. 1918- *12*
Bancroft, Griffing 1907- *6*
Bancroft, Laura
  See Baum, L(yman) Frank
Bandel, Betty 1912- *47*
Baner, Skulda V(anadis)
  1897-1964 .... *10*
Bang, Betsy (Garrett) 1912- *48*
  Brief Entry *37*
Bang, Garrett
  See Bang, Molly Garrett
Bang, Molly Garrett 1943- *24*
  See also CLR 8
Banks, Laura Stockton Voorhees
  1908(?)-1980
  Obituary *23*
Banks, Sara (Jeanne Gordon Harrell)
  1937- *26*
Banner, Angela
  See Maddison, Angela Mary
Bannerman, Helen (Brodie Cowan
  Watson) 1863(?)-1946 .... *19*
Banning, Evelyn I. 1903- *36*
Bannon, Laura (?)-1963 .... *6*
Barbary, James
  See Baumann, Amy (Brown)
Barbary, James
  See Beeching, Jack
Barbe, Walter Burke 1926- *45*
Barber, Antonia
  See Anthony, Barbara
Barber, Linda
  See Graham-Barber, Lynda
Barber, Richard (William)
  1941- *35*
Barbour, Ralph Henry
  1870-1944 .... *16*
Barclay, Isabel
  See Dobell, I.M.B.
Bare, Arnold Edwin 1920- *16*
Bare, Colleen Stanley *32*
Barish, Matthew 1907- *12*
Barker, Albert W. 1900- *8*
Barker, Carol (Minturn) 1938- *31*
Barker, Cicely Mary
  1895-1973 .... *49*
  Brief Entry *39*
Barker, Melvern 1907- *11*
Barker, S. Omar 1894- *10*
Barker, Will 1908- *8*
Barkhouse, Joyce 1913-
  Brief Entry *48*

Barkley, James Edward 1941- *6*
Barks, Carl 1901- *37*
Barnaby, Ralph S(tanton)
  1893- *9*
Barner, Bob 1947- *29*
Barnes, (Frank) Eric Wollencott
  1907-1962 .... *22*
Barnes, Malcolm 1909(?)-1984
  Obituary *41*
Barnett, Lincoln (Kinnear)
  1909-1979 .... *36*
Barnett, Moneta 1922-1976 ...... *33*
Barnett, Naomi 1927- *40*
Barney, Maginel Wright
  1881-1966 .... *39*
  Brief Entry *32*
Barnhart, Clarence L(ewis)
  1900- *48*
Barnouw, Adriaan Jacob 1877-1968
  Obituary *27*
Barnouw, Victor 1915- *43*
  Brief Entry *28*
Barnstone, Willis 1927- *20*
Barnum, Jay Hyde
  1888(?)-1962 .... *20*
Barnum, Richard [Collective
  pseudonym] *1*
Baron, Virginia Olsen 1931- *46*
  Brief Entry *28*
Barr, Donald 1921- *20*
Barr, George 1907- *2*
Barr, Jene 1900-1985 .... *16*
  Obituary *42*
Barrer, Gertrude
  See Barrer-Russell, Gertrude
Barrer-Russell, Gertrude
  1921- *27*
Barrett, Ethel
  Brief Entry *44*
Barrett, Judith 1941- *26*
Barrett, Ron 1937- *14*
Barrett, William E(dmund) 1900-1986
  Obituary *49*
Barrie, J(ames) M(atthew)
  1860-1937 .... *YABC 1*
Barris, George 1925- *47*
Barrol, Grady
  See Bograd, Larry
Barry, James P(otvin) 1918- *14*
Barry, Katharina (Watjen)
  1936- *4*
Barry, Robert 1931- *6*
Barry, Scott 1952- *32*
Bartenbach, Jean 1918- *40*
Barth, Edna 1914-1980 .... *7*
  Obituary *24*
Barthelme, Donald 1931- *7*
Bartholomew, Barbara 1941-
  Brief Entry *42*
Bartlett, Philip A. [Collective
  pseudonym] *1*
Bartlett, Robert Merill 1899- *12*
Barton, Byron 1930- *9*
Barton, Harriett
  Brief Entry *43*
Barton, May Hollis [Collective
  pseudonym] *1*
  See also Adams, Harriet
  S(tratemeyer)

Bartos-Hoeppner, Barbara
  1923- *5*
Bartsch, Jochen 1906- *39*
Baruch, Dorothy W(alter)
  1899-1962 .... *21*
Bas, Rutger
  See Rutgers van der Loeff, An(na)
  Basenau
Bashevis, Isaac
  See Singer, Isaac Bashevis
Baskin, Leonard 1922- *30*
  Brief Entry *27*
Bason, Lillian 1913- *20*
Bassett, Jeni 1960(?)-
  Brief Entry *43*
Bassett, John Keith
  See Keating, Lawrence A.
Batchelor, Joy 1914-
  Brief Entry *29*
Bate, Lucy 1939- *18*
Bate, Norman 1916- *5*
Bates, Barbara S(nedeker)
  1919- *12*
Bates, Betty 1921- *19*
Batey, Tom 1946-
  Brief Entry *41*
Batherman, Muriel
  See Sheldon, Muriel
Batiuk, Thomas M(artin) 1947-
  Brief Entry *40*
Batson, Larry 1930- *35*
Battaglia, Aurelius
  Brief Entry *33*
Batten, H(arry) Mortimer
  1888-1958 .... *25*
Batten, Mary 1937- *5*
Batterberry, Ariane Ruskin
  1935- *13*
Batterberry, Michael (Carver)
  1932- *32*
Battles, Edith 1921- *7*
Baudouy, Michel-Aime 1909- *7*
Bauer, Caroline Feller 1935-
  Brief Entry *46*
Bauer, Fred 1934- *36*
Bauer, Helen 1900- *2*
Bauer, Marion Dane 1938- *20*
Bauernschmidt, Marjorie
  1926- *15*
Baum, Allyn Z(elton) 1924- *20*
Baum, L(yman) Frank
  1856-1919 .... *18*
Baum, Willi 1931- *4*
Baumann, Amy (Brown)
  1922- *10*
Baumann, Elwood D.
  Brief Entry *33*
Baumann, Hans 1914- *2*
Baumann, Kurt 1935- *21*
Bawden, Nina
  See Kark, Nina Mary
  See also CLR 2
Bayer, Jane E. (?)-1985
  Obituary *44*
Bayley, Nicola 1949- *41*
Baylor, Byrd 1924- *16*
  See also CLR 3
Baynes, Pauline (Diana)
  1922- *19*

Beach, Charles
See Reid, (Thomas) Mayne
Beach, Charles Amory [Collective
pseudonym] 1
Beach, Edward L(atimer)
1918- 12
Beach, Stewart Taft 1899- 23
Beachcroft, Nina 1931- 18
Bealer, Alex W(inkler III)
1921-1980 8
Obituary 22
Beals, Carleton 1893- 12
Beals, Frank Lee 1881-1972
Obituary 26
Beame, Rona 1934- 12
Beamer, (G.) Charles, (Jr.)
1942- 43
Beaney, Jan
See Udall, Jan Beaney
Beard, Charles Austin
1874-1948 18
Beard, Dan(iel Carter)
1850-1941 22
Bearden, Romare (Howard)
1914- 22
Beardmore, Cedric
See Beardmore, George
Beardmore, George
1908-1979 20
Bearman, Jane (Ruth) 1917- 29
Beatty, Elizabeth
See Holloway, Teresa (Bragunier)
Beatty, Hetty Burlingame
1907-1971 5
Beatty, Jerome, Jr. 1918- 5
Beatty, John (Louis)
1922-1975 6
Obituary 25
Beatty, Patricia (Robbins)
1922- 30
Earlier sketch in SATA 1
See also SAAS 4
Bechtel, Louise Seaman
1894-1985 4
Obituary 43
Beck, Barbara L. 1927- 12
Becker, Beril 1901- 11
Becker, John (Leonard) 1901- 12
Becker, Joyce 1936- 39
Becker, May Lamberton
1873-1958 33
Beckett, Sheilah 1913- 33
Beckman, Gunnel 1910- 6
Beckman, Kaj
See Beckman, Karin
Beckman, Karin 1913- 45
Beckman, Per (Frithiof) 1913- 45
Bedford, A. N.
See Watson, Jane Werner
Bedford, Annie North
See Watson, Jane Werner
Beebe, B(urdetta) F(aye)
1920- 1
Beebe, (Charles) William
1877-1962 19
Beeby, Betty 1923- 25
Beech, Webb
See Butterworth, W. E.
Beeching, Jack 1922- 14

Beeler, Nelson F(rederick)
1910- 13
Beers, Dorothy Sands 1917- 9
Beers, Lorna 1897- 14
Beers, V(ictor) Gilbert 1928- 9
Begley, Kathleen A(nne)
1948- 21
Behn, Harry 1898-1973 2
Obituary 34
Behnke, Frances L. 8
Behr, Joyce 1929- 15
Behrens, June York 1925- 19
Behrman, Carol H(elen) 1925- 14
Beiser, Arthur 1931- 22
Beiser, Germaine 1931- 11
Belair, Richard L. 1934- 45
Belaney, Archibald Stansfeld
1888-1938 24
Belknap, B. H.
See Ellis, Edward S(ylvester)
Bell, Corydon 1894- 3
Bell, Emily Mary
See Cason, Mabel Earp
Bell, Gertrude (Wood) 1911- 12
Bell, Gina
See Iannone, Jeanne
Bell, Janet
See Clymer, Eleanor
Bell, Margaret E(lizabeth)
1898- 2
Bell, Norman (Edward) 1899- 11
Bell, Raymond Martin 1907- 13
Bell, Robert S(tanley) W(arren)
1871-1921
Brief Entry 27
Bell, Thelma Harrington
1896- 3
Bellairs, John 1938- 2
Belloc, (Joseph) Hilaire (Pierre)
1870-1953 ....YABC 1
Bellville, Cheryl Walsh 1944-
Brief Entry 49
Bell-Zano, Gina
See Iannone, Jeanne
Belpré, Pura 1899-1982 16
Obituary 30
Belting, Natalie Maree 1915- 6
Belton, John Raynor 1931- 22
Beltran, Alberto 1923- 43
Belvedere, Lee
See Grayland, Valerie
Bemelmans, Ludwig
1898-1962 15
See also CLR 6
Benary, Margot
See Benary-Isbert, Margot
Benary-Isbert, Margot
1889-1979 2
Obituary 21
See also CLR 12
Benasutti, Marion 1908- 6
Benchley, Nathaniel (Goddard)
1915-1981 25
Obituary 28
Earlier sketch in SATA 3
Benchley, Peter 1940- 3
Bender, Lucy Ellen 1942- 22

Bendick, Jeanne 1919- 2
See also CLR 5
See also SAAS 4
Bendick, Robert L(ouis)
1917- 11
Benedict, Dorothy Potter
1889-1979 11
Obituary 23
Benedict, Lois Trimble
1902-1967 12
Benedict, Rex 1920- 8
Benedict, Stewart H(urd)
1924- 26
Benét, Laura 1884-1979 3
Obituary 23
Benét, Stephen Vincent
1898-1943 ....YABC 1
Benet, Sula 1903(?)-1982 21
Obituary 33
Benezra, Barbara 1921- 10
Benham, Leslie 1922- 48
Benham, Lois (Dakin) 1924- 48
Benjamin, Nora
See Kubie, Nora (Gottheil) Benjamin
Bennett, Dorothea
See Young, Dorothea Bennett
Bennett, Jay 1912- 41
Brief Entry 27
See also SAAS 4
Bennett, Jill (Crawford) 1934- 41
Bennett, John 1865-1956 .....YABC 1
Bennett, Rachel
See Hill, Margaret (Ohler)
Bennett, Rainey 1907- 15
Bennett, Richard 1899- 21
Bennett, Russell H(oradley)
1896- 25
Benson, Sally 1900-1972 35
Obituary 27
Earlier sketch in SATA 1
Bentley, Judith (McBride)
1945- 40
Bentley, Nicolas Clerihew 1907-1978
Obituary 24
Bentley, Phyllis (Eleanor)
1894-1977 6
Obituary 25
Bentley, Roy 1947- 46
Berelson, Howard 1940- 5
Berends, Polly Berrien 1939-
Brief Entry 38
Berenstain, Janice 12
Berenstain, Michael 1951-
Brief Entry 45
Berenstain, Stan(ley) 1923- 12
Beresford, Elisabeth 25
Berg, Björn 1923-
Brief Entry 47
Berg, Dave
See Berg, David
Berg, David 1920- 27
Berg, Jean Horton 1913- 6
Berg, Joan
See Victor, Joan Berg
Berg, Ron 1952- 48
Bergaust, Erik 1925-1978 20
Berger, Gilda
Brief Entry 42
Berger, Josef 1903-1971 36

Berger, Melvin H. 1927- 5
  See also SAAS 2
Berger, Terry 1933- 8
Bergey, Alyce (Mae) 1934- 45
Berkebile, Fred D(onovan) 1900-1978
  Obituary 26
Berkey, Barry Robert 1935- 24
Berkowitz, Freda Pastor 1910- 12
Berliner, Don 1930- 33
Berliner, Franz 1930- 13
Berlitz, Charles L. (Frambach)
  1913- 32
Berman, Linda 1948- 38
Berna, Paul 1910- 15
Bernadette
  See Watts, Bernadette
Bernard, George I. 1949- 39
Bernard, Jacqueline (de Sieyes)
  1921-1983 8
  Obituary 45
Bernays, Anne
  See Kaplan, Anne Bernays
Bernstein, Joanne E(ckstein)
  1943- 15
Bernstein, Theodore M(enline)
  1904-1979 12
  Obituary 27
Berrien, Edith Heal
  See Heal, Edith
Berrill, Jacquelyn (Batsel)
  1905- 12
Berrington, John
  See Brownjohn, Alan
Berry, B. J.
  See Berry, Barbara J.
Berry, Barbara J. 1937- 7
Berry, Erick
  See Best, Allena Champlin
Berry, Jane Cobb 1915(?)-1979
  Obituary 22
Berry, Joy Wilt
  Brief Entry 46
Berry, William D(avid) 1926- 14
Berson, Harold 1926- 4
Berwick, Jean
  See Meyer, Jean Shepherd
Beskow, Elsa (Maartman)
  1874-1953 20
Best, (Evangel) Allena Champlin
  1892-1974 2
  Obituary 25
Best, (Oswald) Herbert 1894- 2
Bestall, Alfred (Edmeades) 1892-1986
  Obituary 48
Betancourt, Jeanne 1941-
  Brief Entry 43
Beth, Mary
  See Miller, Mary Beth
Bethancourt, T. Ernesto 1932- 11
  See also CLR 3
Bethell, Jean (Frankenberry)
  1922- 8
Bethers, Ray 1902- 6
Bethune, J. G.
  See Ellis, Edward S(ylvester)
Betteridge, Anne
  See Potter, Margaret (Newman)
Bettina
  See Ehrlich, Bettina

Bettmann, Otto Ludwig 1903- 46
Betts, James [Joint pseudonym]
  See Haynes, Betsy
Betz, Eva Kelly 1897-1968 10
Bevan, Tom
  1868-1930(?) .... YABC 2
Bewick, Thomas 1753-1828 16
Beyer, Audrey White 1916- 9
Bezencon, Jacqueline (Buxcel)
  1924- 48
Bhatia, June
  See Forrester, Helen
Bialk, Elisa 1
Bianco, Margery (Williams)
  1881-1944 15
Bianco, Pamela 1906- 28
Bibby, Violet 1908- 24
Bible, Charles 1937- 13
Bice, Clare 1909-1976 22
Bickerstaff, Isaac
  See Swift, Jonathan
Biegel, Paul 1925- 16
Biemiller, Carl L(udwig)
  1912-1979 40
  Obituary 21
Bienenfeld, Florence L(ucille)
  1929- 39
Bierhorst, John 1936- 6
Bileck, Marvin 1920- 40
Bill, Alfred Hoyt 1879-1964 44
Billings, Charlene W(interer)
  1941- 41
Billington, Elizabeth T(hain)
  Brief Entry 43
Billout, Guy René 1941- 10
Binkley, Anne
  See Rand, Ann (Binkley)
Binzen, Bill 24
Binzen, William
  See Binzen, Bill
Birch, Reginald B(athurst)
  1856-1943 19
Birmingham, Lloyd 1924- 12
Biro, Val 1921- 1
Bischoff, Julia Bristol
  1909-1970 12
Bishop, Bonnie 1943- 37
Bishop, Claire (Huchet) 14
Bishop, Curtis 1912-1967 6
Bishop, Elizabeth 1911-1979
  Obituary 24
Bisset, Donald 1910- 7
Bitter, Gary G(len) 1940- 22
Bixby, William (Courtney)
  1920-1986 6
  Obituary 47
Bjerregaard-Jensen, Vilhelm Hans
  See Hillcourt, William
Bjorklund, Lorence F.
  1913-1978 35
  Brief Entry 32
Black, Algernon David 1900- 12
Black, Irma S(imonton)
  1906-1972 2
  Obituary 25
Black, Mansell
  See Trevor, Elleston
Black, Susan Adams 1953- 40

Blackburn, Claire
  See Jacobs, Linda C.
Blackburn, John(ny) Brewton
  1952- 15
Blackburn, Joyce Knight
  1920- 29
Blackett, Veronica Heath
  1927- 12
Blackton, Peter
  See Wilson, Lionel
Blades, Ann 1947- 16
Bladow, Suzanne Wilson
  1937- 14
Blaine, John
  See Goodwin, Harold Leland
Blaine, John
  See Harkins, Philip
Blaine, Margery Kay 1937- 11
Blair, Anne Denton 1914- 46
Blair, Eric Arthur 1903-1950 29
Blair, Helen 1910-
  Brief Entry 29
Blair, Jay 1953- 45
Blair, Ruth Van Ness 1912- 12
Blair, Walter 1900- 12
Blake, Olive
  See Supraner, Robyn
Blake, Quentin 1932- 9
Blake, Robert 1949- 42
Blake, Walker E.
  See Butterworth, W. E.
Blake, William 1757-1827 30
Bland, Edith Nesbit
  See Nesbit, E(dith)
Bland, Fabian [Joint pseudonym]
  See Nesbit, E(dith)
Blane, Gertrude
  See Blumenthal, Gertrude
Blassingame, Wyatt Rainey
  1909-1985 34
  Obituary 41
  Earlier sketch in SATA 1
Blauer, Ettagale 1940- 49
Bleeker, Sonia 1909-1971 2
  Obituary 26
Blegvad, Erik 1923- 14
Blegvad, Lenore 1926- 14
Blishen, Edward 1920- 8
Bliss, Corinne D(emas) 1947- 37
Bliss, Reginald
  See Wells, H(erbert) G(eorge)
Bliss, Ronald G(ene) 1942- 12
Bliven, Bruce, Jr. 1916- 2
Blixen, Karen (Christentze Dinesen)
  1885-1962 44
Bloch, Lucienne 1909- 10
Bloch, Marie Halun 1910- 6
Bloch, Robert 1917- 12
Blochman, Lawrence G(oldtree)
  1900-1975 22
Block, Irvin 1917- 12
Blocksma, Mary
  Brief Entry 44
Blood, Charles Lewis 1929- 28
Bloom, Freddy 1914- 37
Bloom, Lloyd
  Brief Entry 43
Blos, Joan W(insor) 1928- 33
  Brief Entry 27

Blough, Glenn O(rlando)
1907- *1*
Blue, Rose 1931- *5*
Blumberg, Rhoda 1917- *35*
Blume, Judy (Sussman) 1938- *31*
Earlier sketch in SATA 2
See also CLR 2
Blumenthal, Gertrude 1907-1971
Obituary *27*
Blumenthal, Shirley 1943- *46*
Blutig, Eduard
See Gorey, Edward St. John
Bly, Janet Chester 1945- *43*
Bly, Robert W(ayne) 1957-
Brief Entry *48*
Bly, Stephen A(rthur) 1944- *43*
Blyton, Carey 1932- *9*
Blyton, Enid (Mary)
1897-1968 .... *25*
Boardman, Fon Wyman, Jr.
1911- *6*
Boardman, Gwenn R. 1924- *12*
Boase, Wendy 1944- *28*
Boatner, Mark Mayo III
1921- *29*
Bobbe, Dorothie 1905-1975 .... *1*
Obituary *25*
Bobri
See Bobritsky, Vladimir
Bobri, Vladimir
See Bobritsky, Vladimir
Bobritsky, Vladimir 1898- *47*
Brief Entry *32*
Bock, Hal
See Bock, Harold I.
Bock, Harold I. 1939- *10*
Bock, William Sauts
Netamux'we *14*
Bodecker, N. M. 1922- *8*
Boden, Hilda
See Bodenham, Hilda Esther
Bodenham, Hilda Esther
1901- *13*
Bodie, Idella F(allaw) 1925- *12*
Bodker, Cecil 1927- *14*
Bodsworth, (Charles) Fred(erick)
1918- *27*
Boeckman, Charles 1920- *12*
Boegehold, Betty (Doyle) 1913-1985
Obituary *42*
Boesch, Mark J(oseph) 1917- *12*
Boesen, Victor 1908- *16*
Boggs, Ralph Steele 1901- *7*
Bograd, Larry 1953- *33*
Bohdal, Susi 1951- *22*
Boles, Paul Darcy 1916-1984 ..... *9*
Obituary *38*
Bolian, Polly 1925- *4*
Bollen, Roger 1941(?)-
Brief Entry *29*
Bolliger, Max 1929- *7*
Bolognese, Don(ald Alan)
1934- *24*
Bolton, Carole 1926- *6*
Bolton, Elizabeth
See Johnston, Norma
Bolton, Evelyn
See Bunting, Anne Evelyn
Bond, Felicia 1954- *49*

Bond, Gladys Baker 1912- *14*
Bond, J. Harvey
See Winterbotham, R(ussell)
R(obert)
Bond, Michael 1926- *6*
See also CLR 1
See also SAAS 3
Bond, Nancy (Barbara) 1945- *22*
See also CLR 11
Bond, Ruskin 1934- *14*
Bonehill, Captain Ralph
See Stratemeyer, Edward L.
Bonestell, Chesley 1888-1986
Obituary *48*
Bonham, Barbara 1926- *7*
Bonham, Frank 1914- *49*
Earlier sketch in SATA 1
See also SAAS 3
Bonn, Pat
See Bonn, Patricia Carolyn
Bonn, Patricia Carolyn 1948- *43*
Bonner, Mary Graham
1890-1974 .... *19*
Bonners, Susan
Brief Entry *48*
Bonsall, Crosby (Barbara Newell)
1921- *23*
Bontemps, Arna 1902-1973 .... *44*
Obituary *24*
Earlier sketch in SATA 2
See also CLR 6
Bonzon, Paul-Jacques 1908- *22*
Booher, Dianna Daniels 1948- *33*
Bookman, Charlotte
See Zolotow, Charlotte S.
Boone, Pat 1934- *7*
Boorman, Linda (Kay) 1940- *46*
Booth, Ernest Sheldon
1915-1984 .... *43*
Booth, Graham (Charles)
1935- *37*
Bordier, Georgette 1924- *16*
Boring, Mel 1939- *35*
Borja, Corinne 1929- *22*
Borja, Robert 1923- *22*
Borland, Hal 1900-1978 .... *5*
Obituary *24*
Borland, Harold Glen
See Borland, Hal
Borland, Kathryn Kilby 1916- *16*
Born, Adolf 1930- *49*
Bornstein, Ruth 1927- *14*
Borski, Lucia Merecka *18*
Borten, Helen Jacobson 1930- *5*
Borton, Elizabeth
See Treviño, Elizabeth B. de
Bortstein, Larry 1942- *16*
Bosco, Jack
See Holliday, Joseph
Boshell, Gordon 1908- *15*
Boshinski, Blanche 1922- *10*
Bosse, Malcolm J(oseph)
1926- *35*
Bossom, Naomi 1933- *35*
Boston, Lucy Maria (Wood)
1892- *19*
See also CLR 3
Bosworth, J. Allan 1925- *19*
Bothwell, Jean *2*

Botkin, B(enjamin) A(lbert)
1901-1975 .... *40*
Botting, Douglas (Scott)
1934- *43*
Bottner, Barbara 1943- *14*
Boulle, Pierre (Francois Marie-Louis)
1912- *22*
Bourdon, David 1934- *46*
Bourne, Leslie
See Marshall, Evelyn
Bourne, Miriam Anne 1931- *16*
Boutet De Monvel, (Louis) M(aurice)
1850(?)-1913 .... *30*
Bova, Ben 1932- *6*
See also CLR 3
Bowden, Joan Chase 1925-
Brief Entry *38*
Bowen, Betty Morgan
See West, Betty
Bowen, Catherine Drinker
1897-1973 .... *7*
Bowen, David
See Bowen, Joshua David
Bowen, Joshua David 1930- *22*
Bowen, Robert Sidney 1900(?)-1977
Obituary *21*
Bowie, Jim
See Stratemeyer, Edward L.
Bowler, Jan Brett
See Brett, Jan
Bowman, James Cloyd
1880-1961 .... *23*
Bowman, John S(tewart)
1931- *16*
Bowman, Kathleen (Gill) 1942-
Brief Entry *40*
Boyce, George A(rthur) 1898- *19*
Boyd, Pauline
See Schock, Pauline
Boyd, Selma
See Acuff, Selma Boyd
Boyd, Waldo T. 1918- *18*
Boyer, Robert E(rnst) 1929- *22*
Boyle, Ann (Peters) 1916- *10*
Boyle, Eleanor Vere (Gordon)
1825-1916 .... *28*
Boylston, Helen (Dore)
1895-1984 .... *23*
Obituary *39*
Boynton, Sandra 1953-
Brief Entry *38*
Boz
See Dickens, Charles
Bradbury, Bianca 1908- *3*
Bradbury, Ray (Douglas)
1920- *11*
Bradford, Ann (Liddell) 1917-
Brief Entry *38*
Bradford, Karleen 1936- *48*
Bradford, Lois J(ean) 1936- *36*
Bradley, Duane
See Sanborn, Duane
Bradley, Virginia 1912- *23*
Brady, Esther Wood 1905- *31*
Brady, Irene 1943- *4*
Brady, Lillian 1902- *28*
Bragdon, Elspeth 1897- *6*
Bragdon, Lillian (Jacot) *24*

Bragg, Mabel Caroline
  1870-1945 24
Bragg, Michael 1948- 46
Braithwaite, Althea 1940- 23
Bram, Elizabeth 1948- 30
Brancato, Robin F(idler)
  1936- 23
Brandenberg, Aliki (Liacouras)
  1929- 35
  Earlier sketch in SATA 2
Brandenberg, Franz 1932- 35
  Earlier sketch in SATA 8
Brandhorst, Carl T(heodore)
  1898- 23
Brandon, Brumsic, Jr. 1927- 9
Brandon, Curt
  See Bishop, Curtis
Brandreth, Gyles 1948- 28
Brandt, Catharine 1905- 40
Brandt, Keith
  See Sabin, Louis
Branfield, John (Charles)
  1931- 11
Branley, Franklyn M(ansfield)
  1915- 4
Branscum, Robbie 1937- 23
Bransom, (John) Paul
  1885-1979 43
Bratton, Helen 1899- 4
Braude, Michael 1936- 23
Braymer, Marjorie 1911- 6
Brecht, Edith 1895-1975 6
  Obituary 25
Breck, Vivian
  See Breckenfeld, Vivian Gurney
Breckenfeld, Vivian Gurney
  1895- 1
Breda, Tjalmar
  See DeJong, David C(ornel)
Breinburg, Petronella 1927- 11
Breisky, William J(ohn) 1928- 22
Brennan, Joseph L. 1903- 6
Brennan, Tim
  See Conroy, Jack (Wesley)
Brenner, Barbara (Johnes)
  1925- 42
  Earlier sketch in SATA 4
Brenner, Fred 1920- 36
  Brief Entry 34
Brent, Hope 1935(?)-1984
  Obituary 39
Brent, Stuart 14
Brett, Bernard 1925- 22
Brett, Grace N(eff) 1900-1975 23
Brett, Hawksley
  See Bell, Robert S(tanley) W(arren)
Brett, Jan 1949- 42
Brewer, Sally King 1947- 33
Brewster, Benjamin
  See Folsom, Franklin
Brewton, John E(dmund)
  1898- 5
Brick, John 1922-1973 10
Bridgers, Sue Ellen 1942- 22
  See also SAAS 1
Bridges, Laurie
  See Bruck, Lorraine
Bridges, William (Andrew)
  1901- 5

Bridwell, Norman 1928- 4
Brier, Howard M(axwell)
  1903-1969 8
Briggs, Carole S(uzanne) 1950-
  Brief Entry 47
Briggs, Katharine Mary 1898-1980
  Obituary 25
Briggs, Peter 1921-1975 39
  Obituary 31
Briggs, Raymond (Redvers)
  1934- 23
  See also CLR 10
Bright, Robert 1902- 24
Brightwell, L(eonard) R(obert) 1889-
  Brief Entry 29
Brimberg, Stanlee 1947- 9
Brin, Ruth F(irestone) 1921- 22
Brinckloe, Julie (Lorraine)
  1950- 13
Brindel, June (Rachuy) 1919- 7
Brindze, Ruth 1903- 23
Brink, Carol Ryrie 1895-1981 31
  Obituary 27
  Earlier sketch in SATA 1
Brinsmead, H(esba) F(ay)
  1922- 18
Briquebec, John
  See Rowland-Entwistle, (Arthur)
  Theodore (Henry)
Brisco, Pat A.
  See Matthews, Patricia
Brisco, Patty
  See Matthews, Patricia
Briscoe, Jill (Pauline) 1935-
  Brief Entry 47
Brisley, Joyce Lankester
  1896- 22
Britt, Albert 1874-1969
  Obituary 28
Britt, Dell 1934- 1
Brittain, William 1930- 36
Britton, Kate
  See Stegeman, Janet Allais
Britton, Louisa
  See McGuire, Leslie (Sarah)
Bro, Margueritte (Harmon)
  1894-1977 19
  Obituary 27
Broadhead, Helen Cross
  1913- 25
Brochmann, Elizabeth (Anne)
  1938- 41
Brock, Betty 1923- 7
Brock, C(harles) E(dmund)
  1870-1938 42
  Brief Entry 32
Brock, Emma L(illian)
  1886-1974 8
Brock, H(enry) M(atthew)
  1875-1960 42
Brockett, Eleanor Hall
  1913-1967 10
Brockman, C(hristian) Frank
  1902- 26
Broderick, Dorothy M. 1929- 5
Brodie, Sally
  See Cavin, Ruth (Brodie)
Broekel, Rainer Lothar 1923- 38

Broekel, Ray
  See Broekel, Rainer Lothar
Bröger, Achim 1944- 31
Brokamp, Marilyn 1920- 10
Bromhall, Winifred 26
Brommer, Gerald F(rederick)
  1927- 28
Brondfield, Jerome 1913- 22
Brondfield, Jerry
  See Brondfield, Jerome
Bronson, Lynn
  See Lampman, Evelyn Sibley
Bronson, Wilfrid Swancourt
  1894-1985
  Obituary 43
Brooke, L(eonard) Leslie
  1862-1940 17
Brooke-Haven, P.
  See Wodehouse, P(elham)
  G(renville)
Brookins, Dana 1931- 28
Brooks, Anita 1914- 5
Brooks, Barbara
  See Simons, Barbara B(rooks)
Brooks, Charlotte K. 24
Brooks, Gwendolyn 1917- 6
Brooks, Jerome 1931- 23
Brooks, Lester 1924- 7
Brooks, Maurice (Graham)
  1900- 45
Brooks, Polly Schoyer 1912- 12
Brooks, Ron(ald George) 1948-
  Brief Entry 33
Brooks, Walter R(ollin)
  1886-1958 17
Brosnan, James Patrick 1929- 14
Brosnan, Jim
  See Brosnan, James Patrick
Broun, Emily
  See Sterne, Emma Gelders
Brower, Millicent 8
Brower, Pauline (York) 1929- 22
Browin, Frances Williams
  1898- 5
Brown, Alexis
  See Baumann, Amy (Brown)
Brown, Bill
  See Brown, William L.
Brown, Billye Walker
  See Cutchen, Billye Walker
Brown, Bob
  See Brown, Robert Joseph
Brown, Buck 1936- 45
Brown, Conrad 1922- 31
Brown, David
  See Myller, Rolf
Brown, Dee (Alexander)
  1908- 5
Brown, Eleanor Frances 1908- 3
Brown, Elizabeth M(yers)
  1915- 43
Brown, Fern G. 1918- 34
Brown, (Robert) Fletch 1923- 42
Brown, George Earl
  1883-1964 11
Brown, George Mackay 1921- 35
Brown, Irene Bennett 1932- 3
Brown, Irving
  See Adams, William Taylor

Brown, Ivor (John Carnegie)
1891-1974 5
Obituary 26
Brown, Joe David 1915-1976 44
Brown, Judith Gwyn 1933- 20
Brown, Lloyd Arnold
1907-1966 36
Brown, Marc Tolon 1946- 10
Brown, Marcia 1918- 47
Earlier sketch in SATA 7
See also CLR 12
Brown, Margaret Wise
1910-1952 ....YABC 2
See also CLR 10
Brown, Margery 5
Brown, Marion Marsh 1908- 6
Brown, Myra Berry 1918- 6
Brown, Palmer 1919- 36
Brown, Pamela 1924- 5
Brown, Robert Joseph 1907- 14
Brown, Rosalie (Gertrude) Moore
1910- 9
Brown, Roswell
See Webb, Jean Francis (III)
Brown, Roy (Frederick) 1921-1982
Obituary 39
Brown, Vinson 1912- 19
Brown, Walter R(eed) 1929- 19
Brown, Will
See Ainsworth, William Harrison
Brown, William L(ouis)
1910-1964 5
Browne, Anthony (Edward Tudor)
1946- 45
Brief Entry 44
Browne, Dik
See Browne, Richard
Browne, Hablot Knight
1815-1882 21
Browne, Matthew
See Rands, William Brighty
Browne, Richard 1917-
Brief Entry 38
Browning, Robert
1812-1889 ....YABC 1
Brownjohn, Alan 1931- 6
Bruce, Dorita Fairlie 1885-1970
Obituary 27
Bruce, Mary 1927- 1
Bruchac, Joseph III 1942- 42
Bruck, Lorraine 1921-
Brief Entry 46
Bruemmer, Fred 1929- 47
Bruna, Dick 1927- 43
Brief Entry 30
See also CLR 7
Brunhoff, Jean de 1899-1937 24
See also CLR 4
Brunhoff, Laurent de 1925- 24
See also CLR 4
Brustlein, Daniel 1904- 40
Brustlein, Janice Tworkov 40
Bryan, Ashley F. 1923- 31
Bryan, Dorothy (Marie) 1896(?)-1984
Obituary 39
Bryant, Bernice (Morgan)
1908- 11
Brychta, Alex 1956- 21
Bryson, Bernarda 1905- 9

Buba, Joy Flinsch 1904- 44
Buchan, Bryan 1945- 36
Buchan, John 1875-1940 ....YABC 2
Buchheimer, Naomi Barnett
See Barnett, Naomi
Buchwald, Art(hur) 1925- 10
Buchwald, Emilie 1935- 7
Buck, Lewis 1925- 18
Buck, Margaret Waring 1910- 3
Buck, Pearl S(ydenstricker)
1892-1973 25
Earlier sketch in SATA 1
Buckeridge, Anthony 1912- 6
Buckholtz, Eileen (Garber) 1949-
Brief Entry 47
Buckler, Ernest 1908-1984 47
Buckley, Helen E(lizabeth)
1918- 2
Buckmaster, Henrietta 6
Budd, Lillian 1897- 7
Buehr, Walter 1897-1971 3
Buff, Conrad 1886-1975 19
Buff, Mary Marsh 1890-1970 19
Bugbee, Emma 1888(?)-1981
Obituary 29
Bulfinch, Thomas 1796-1867 35
Bull, Angela (Mary) 1936- 45
Bull, Norman John 1916- 41
Bull, Peter (Cecil) 1912-1984
Obituary 39
Bulla, Clyde Robert 1914- 41
Earlier sketch in SATA 2
Bunin, Catherine 1967- 30
Bunin, Sherry 1925- 30
Bunting, A. E.
See Bunting, Anne Evelyn
Bunting, Anne Evelyn 1928- 18
Bunting, Eve
See Bunting, Anne Evelyn
Bunting, Glenn (Davison)
1957- 22
Burack, Sylvia K. 1916- 35
Burbank, Addison (Buswell)
1895-1961 37
Burch, Robert J(oseph) 1925- 1
Burchard, Peter D(uncan) 5
Burchard, Sue 1937- 22
Burchardt, Nellie 1921- 7
Burdick, Eugene (Leonard)
1918-1965 22
Burford, Eleanor
See Hibbert, Eleanor
Burger, Carl 1888-1967 9
Burgess, Anne Marie
See Gerson, Noel B(ertram)
Burgess, Em
See Burgess, Mary Wyche
Burgess, (Frank) Gelett
1866-1951 32
Brief Entry 30
Burgess, Mary Wyche 1916- 18
Burgess, Michael
See Gerson, Noel B(ertram)
Burgess, Robert F(orrest)
1927- 4
Burgess, Thornton W(aldo)
1874-1965 17
Burgess, Trevor
See Trevor, Elleston

Burgwyn, Mebane H. 1914- 7
Burke, David 1927- 46
Burke, John
See O'Connor, Richard
Burkert, Nancy Ekholm 1933- 24
Burland, Brian (Berkeley)
1931- 34
Burland, C. A.
See Burland, Cottie A.
Burland, Cottie A. 1905- 5
Burlingame, (William) Roger
1889-1967 2
Burman, Alice Caddy 1896(?)-1977
Obituary 24
Burman, Ben Lucien
1896-1984 6
Obituary 40
Burn, Doris 1923- 1
Burnett, Constance Buel
1893-1975 36
Burnett, Frances (Eliza) Hodgson
1849-1924 ....YABC 2
Burnford, S. D.
See Burnford, Sheila
Burnford, Sheila 1918-1984 3
Obituary 38
See also CLR 2
Burningham, John (Mackintosh)
1936- 16
See also CLR 9
Burns, Marilyn
Brief Entry 33
Burns, Paul C. 5
Burns, Raymond (Howard)
1924- 9
Burns, William A. 1909- 5
Burr, Lonnie 1943- 47
Burroughs, Edgar Rice
1875-1950 41
Burroughs, Jean Mitchell
1908- 28
Burroughs, Polly 1925- 2
Burroway, Janet (Gay) 1936- 23
Burstein, John 1949-
Brief Entry 40
Burt, Jesse Clifton 1921-1976 46
Obituary 20
Burt, Olive Woolley 1894- 4
Burton, Hester 1913- 7
See also CLR 1
Burton, Leslie
See McGuire, Leslie (Sarah)
Burton, Marilee Robin 1950- 46
Burton, Maurice 1898- 23
Burton, Robert (Wellesley)
1941- 22
Burton, Virginia Lee
1909-1968 2
See also CLR 11
Burton, William H(enry)
1890-1964 11
Busby, Edith (?)-1964
Obituary 29
Busch, Phyllis S. 1909- 30
Bushmiller, Ernie 1905-1982
Obituary 31
Busoni, Rafaello 1900-1962 16
Butler, Beverly 1932- 7

Butler, Suzanne
See Perreard, Suzanne Louise Butler
Butters, Dorothy Gilman
1923- 5
Butterworth, Emma Macalik
1928- 43
Butterworth, Oliver 1915- 1
Butterworth, W(illiam) E(dmund III)
1929- 5
Byars, Betsy (Cromer) 1928- 46
Earlier sketch in SATA 4
See also CLR 1
See also SAAS 1
Byfield, Barbara Ninde 1930- 8
Byrd, Elizabeth 1912- 34
Byrd, Robert (John) 1942- 33

C

C.3.3.
See Wilde, Oscar (Fingal O'Flahertie
Wills)
Cable, Mary 1920- 9
Cabral, O. M.
See Cabral, Olga
Cabral, Olga 1909- 46
Caddy, Alice
See Burman, Alice Caddy
Cadwallader, Sharon 1936- 7
Cady, (Walter) Harrison
1877-1970 19
Cagle, Malcolm W(infield)
1918- 32
Cahn, Rhoda 1922- 37
Cahn, William 1912-1976 37
Cain, Arthur H. 1913- 3
Cain, Christopher
See Fleming, Thomas J(ames)
Caines, Jeanette (Franklin)
Brief Entry 43
Cairns, Trevor 1922- 14
Caldecott, Moyra 1927- 22
Caldecott, Randolph (J.)
1846-1886 17
Caldwell, John C(ope) 1913- 7
Calhoun, Mary (Huiskamp)
1926- 2
Calkins, Franklin
See Stratemeyer, Edward L.
Call, Hughie Florence
1890-1969 1
Callahan, Dorothy M. 1934- 39
Brief Entry 35
Callahan, Philip S(erna) 1923- 25
Callaway, Bernice (Anne)
1923- 48
Callaway, Kathy 1943- 36
Callen, Larry
See Callen, Lawrence Willard, Jr.
Callen, Lawrence Willard, Jr.
1927- 19
Calmenson, Stephanie 1952-
Brief Entry 37
Calvert, John
See Leaf, (Wilbur) Munro
Calvert, Patricia 1931- 45
Cameron, Ann 1943- 27
Cameron, Edna M. 1905- 3

Cameron, Eleanor (Butler)
1912- 25
Earlier sketch in SATA 1
See also CLR 1
Cameron, Elizabeth
See Nowell, Elizabeth Cameron
Cameron, Elizabeth Jane
1910-1976 32
Obituary 30
Cameron, Ian
See Payne, Donald Gordon
Cameron, Polly 1928- 2
Camp, Charles Lewis 1893-1975
Obituary 31
Camp, Walter (Chauncey)
1859-1925 .... YABC 1
Campbell, Ann R. 1925- 11
Campbell, Bruce
See Epstein, Samuel
Campbell, Camilla 1905- 26
Campbell, Hope 20
Campbell, Jane
See Edwards, Jane Campbell
Campbell, Patricia J(ean)
1930- 45
Campbell, Patty
See Campbell, Patricia J(ean)
Campbell, R. W.
See Campbell, Rosemae Wells
Campbell, Rod 1945-
Brief Entry 44
Campbell, Rosemae Wells
1909- 1
Campion, Nardi Reeder 1917- 22
Candell, Victor 1903-1977
Obituary 24
Canfield, Dorothy
See Fisher, Dorothy Canfield
Canfield, Jane White
1897-1984 32
Obituary 38
Cannon, Cornelia (James) 1876-1969
Brief Entry 28
Cannon, Ravenna
See Mayhar, Ardath
Canusi, Jose
See Barker, S. Omar
Caplin, Alfred Gerald 1909-1979
Obituary 21
Capp, Al
See Caplin, Alfred Gerald
Cappel, Constance 1936- 22
Capps, Benjamin (Franklin)
1922- 9
Captain Kangaroo
See Keeshan, Robert J.
Carafoli, Marci
See Ridlon, Marci
Caras, Roger A(ndrew) 1928- 12
Carbonnier, Jeanne 1894-1974 3
Obituary 34
Care, Felicity
See Coury, Louise Andree
Carew, Jan (Rynveld) 1925-
Brief Entry 40
Carey, Bonnie 1941- 18
Carey, Ernestine Gilbreth
1908- 2

Carey, M. V.
See Carey, Mary (Virginia)
Carey, Mary (Virginia) 1925- 44
Brief Entry 39
Carigiet, Alois 1902-1985 24
Obituary 47
Carini, Edward 1923- 9
Carle, Eric 1929- 4
See CLR 10
Carleton, Captain L. C.
See Ellis, Edward S(ylvester)
Carley, V(an Ness) Royal 1906-1976
Obituary 20
Carlisle, Clark, Jr.
See Holding, James
Carlisle, Olga A(ndreyev)
1930- 35
Carlsen, G(eorge) Robert
1917- 30
Carlsen, Ruth C(hristoffer) 2
Carlson, Bernice Wells 1910- 8
Carlson, Dale Bick 1935- 1
Carlson, Daniel 1960- 27
Carlson, Nancy L(ee) 1953-
Brief Entry 45
Carlson, Natalie Savage 1906- 2
See also SAAS 4
Carlson, Vada F. 1897- 16
Carlstrom, Nancy White 1948-
Brief Entry 48
Carmer, Carl (Lamson)
1893-1976 37
Obituary 30
Carmer, Elizabeth Black
1904- 24
Carmichael, Carrie 40
Carmichael, Harriet
See Carmichael, Carrie
Carol, Bill J.
See Knott, William Cecil, Jr.
Caroselli, Remus F(rancis)
1916- 36
Carpelan, Bo (Gustaf Bertelsson)
1926- 8
Carpenter, Allan 1917- 3
Carpenter, Frances 1890-1972 3
Obituary 27
Carpenter, Patricia (Healy Evans)
1920- 11
Carr, Glyn
See Styles, Frank Showell
Carr, Harriett Helen 1899- 3
Carr, Mary Jane 2
Carrick, Carol 1935- 7
Carrick, Donald 1929- 7
Carrick, Malcolm 1945- 28
Carrighar, Sally 24
Carris, Joan Davenport 1938- 44
Brief Entry 42
Carroll, Curt
See Bishop, Curtis
Carroll, Latrobe 7
Carroll, Laura
See Parr, Lucy
Carroll, Lewis
See Dodgson, Charles Lutwidge
See also CLR 2
Carroll, Raymond
Brief Entry 47

Carruth, Hayden 1921- 47
Carse, Robert 1902-1971 5
Carson, Captain James
  See Stratemeyer, Edward L.
Carson, John F. 1920- 1
Carson, Rachel (Louise)
  1907-1964 23
Carson, Rosalind
  See Chittenden, Margaret
Carson, S. M.
  See Gorsline, (Sally) Marie
Carter, Bruce
  See Hough, Richard (Alexander)
Carter, Dorothy Sharp 1921- 8
Carter, Forrest 1927(?)-1979 32
Carter, Helene 1887-1960 15
Carter, (William) Hodding
  1907-1972 2
  Obituary 27
Carter, Katharine J(ones)
  1905- 2
Carter, Nick
  See Lynds, Dennis
Carter, Phyllis Ann
  See Eberle, Irmengarde
Carter, Samuel III 1904- 37
Carter, William E. 1926-1983 1
  Obituary 35
Cartlidge, Michelle 1950- 49
  Brief Entry 37
Cartner, William Carruthers
  1910- 11
Cartwright, Sally 1923- 9
Carver, John
  See Gardner, Richard
Cary
  See Cary, Louis F(avreau)
Cary, Barbara Knapp 1912(?)-1975
  Obituary 31
Cary, Louis F(avreau) 1915- 9
Caryl, Jean
  See Kaplan, Jean Caryl Korn
Case, Marshal T(aylor) 1941- 9
Case, Michael
  See Howard, Robert West
Casewit, Curtis 1922- 4
Casey, Brigid 1950- 9
Casey, Winifred Rosen
  See Rosen, Winifred
Cason, Mabel Earp 1892-1965 10
Cass, Joan E(velyn) 1
Cassedy, Sylvia 1930- 27
Cassel, Lili
  See Wronker, Lili Cassell
Cassel-Wronker, Lili
  See Wronker, Lili Cassell
Castellanos, Jane Mollie (Robinson)
  1913- 9
Castellon, Federico 1914-1971 48
Castillo, Edmund L. 1924- 1
Castle, Lee [Joint pseudonym]
  See Ogan, George F. and Ogan,
  Margaret E. (Nettles)
Castle, Paul
  See Howard, Vernon (Linwood)
Caswell, Helen (Rayburn)
  1923- 12
Cate, Dick
  See Cate, Richard (Edward Nelson)

Cate, Richard (Edward Nelson)
  1932- 28
Cather, Willa (Sibert)
  1873-1947 30
Catherall, Arthur 1906- 3
Cathon, Laura E(lizabeth)
  1908- 27
Catlin, Wynelle 1930- 13
Catton, (Charles) Bruce
  1899-1978 2
  Obituary 24
Catz, Max
  See Glaser, Milton
Caudill, Rebecca 1899-1985 1
  Obituary 44
Cauley, Lorinda Bryan 1951- 46
  Brief Entry 43
Cauman, Samuel 1910-1971 48
Causley, Charles 1917- 3
Cavallo, Diana 1931- 7
Cavanagh, Helen (Carol)
  1939- 48
  Brief Entry 37
Cavanah, Frances 1899-1982 31
  Earlier sketch in SATA 1
Cavanna, Betty 1909- 30
  Earlier sketch in SATA 1
  See also SAAS 4
Cavin, Ruth (Brodie) 1918- 38
Cawley, Winifred 1915- 13
Caxton, Pisistratus
  See Lytton, Edward G(eorge) E(arle)
  L(ytton) Bulwer-Lytton, Baron
Cazet, Denys 1938-
  Brief Entry 41
Cebulash, Mel 1937- 10
Ceder, Georgiana Dorcas 10
Celestino, Martha Laing
  1951- 39
Cerf, Bennett 1898-1971 7
Cerf, Christopher (Bennett)
  1941- 2
Cervon, Jacqueline
  See Moussard, Jacqueline
Cetin, Frank (Stanley) 1921- 2
Chadwick, Lester [Collective
  pseudonym] 1
Chaffee, Allen 3
Chaffin, Lillie D(orton) 1925- 4
Chaikin, Miriam 1928- 24
Challans, Mary 1905-1983 23
  Obituary 36
Chalmers, Mary 1927- 6
Chamberlain, Margaret 1954- 46
Chambers, Aidan 1934- 1
Chambers, Bradford 1922-1984
  Obituary 39
Chambers, Catherine E.
  See Johnston, Norma
Chambers, John W. 1933-
  Brief Entry 46
Chambers, Margaret Ada Eastwood
  1911- 2
Chambers, Peggy
  See Chambers, Margaret Ada
  Eastwood
Chandler, Caroline A(ugusta)
  1906-1979 22
  Obituary 24

Chandler, David Porter 1933- 28
Chandler, Edna Walker
  1908-1982 11
  Obituary 31
Chandler, Linda S(mith)
  1929- 39
Chandler, Robert 1953- 40
Chandler, Ruth Forbes
  1894-1978 2
  Obituary 26
Channel, A. R.
  See Catherall, Arthur
Chapian, Marie 1938- 29
Chapin, Alene Olsen Dalton
  1915(?)-1986
  Obituary 47
Chapman, Allen [Collective
  pseudonym] 1
Chapman, (Constance) Elizabeth
  (Mann) 1919- 10
Chapman, Gaynor 1935- 32
Chapman, Jean 34
Chapman, John Stanton Higham
  1891-1972
  Obituary 27
Chapman, Maristan [Joint pseudonym]
  See Chapman, John Stanton Higham
Chapman, Vera 1898- 33
Chapman, Walker
  See Silverberg, Robert
Chappell, Warren 1904- 6
Chardiet, Bernice (Kroll) 27
Charles, Donald
  See Meighan, Donald Charles
Charles, Louis
  See Stratemeyer, Edward L.
Charlip, Remy 1929- 4
  See also CLR 8
Charlot, Jean 1898-1979 8
  Obituary 31
Charlton, Michael (Alan)
  1923- 34
Charmatz, Bill 1925- 7
Charosh, Mannis 1906- 5
Chase, Alice
  See McHargue, Georgess
Chase, Mary (Coyle)
  1907-1981 17
  Obituary 29
Chase, Mary Ellen 1887-1973 10
Chastain, Madye Lee 1908- 4
Chauncy, Nan 1900-1970 6
  See also CLR 6
Chaundler, Christine
  1887-1972 1
  Obituary 25
Chen, Tony 1929- 6
Chenault, Nell
  See Smith, Linell Nash
Chenery, Janet (Dai) 1923- 25
Cheney, Cora 1916- 3
Cheney, Ted
  See Cheney, Theodore Albert
Cheney, Theodore Albert
  1928- 11
Cheng, Judith 1955- 36
Chermayeff, Ivan 1932- 47
Chernoff, Dorothy A.
  See Ernst, (Lyman) John

Chernoff, Goldie Taub 1909- *10*
Cherry, Lynne 1952- *34*
Cherryholmes, Anne
　　See Price, Olive
Chess, Victoria (Dickerson)
　　1939- *33*
Chessare, Michele
　　Brief Entry *42*
Chesterton, G(ilbert) K(eith)
　　1874-1936 .... *27*
Chetin, Helen 1922- *6*
Chevalier, Christa 1937- *35*
Chew, Ruth *7*
Chidsey, Donald Barr
　　1902-1981 .... *3*
　　Obituary *27*
Child, Philip 1898-1978 .... *47*
Childress, Alice 1920- *48*
　　Earlier sketch in SATA 7
Childs, (Halla) Fay (Cochrane)
　　1890-1971 .... *1*
　　Obituary *25*
Chimaera
　　See Farjeon, Eleanor
Chinery, Michael 1938- *26*
Chipperfield, Joseph E(ugene)
　　1912- *2*
Chittenden, Elizabeth F.
　　1903- *9*
Chittenden, Margaret 1933- *28*
Chittum, Ida 1918- *7*
Choate, Judith (Newkirk)
　　1940- *30*
Chorao, (Ann Mc)Kay (Sproat)
　　1936- *8*
Chorpenning, Charlotte (Lee Barrows)
　　1872-1955
　　Brief Entry *37*
Chrisman, Arthur Bowie
　　1889-1953 ....*YABC 1*
Christelow, Eileen 1943- *38*
　　Brief Entry *35*
Christensen, Gardell Dano
　　1907- *1*
Christesen, Barbara 1940- *40*
Christgau, Alice Erickson
　　1902- *13*
Christian, Mary Blount 1933- *9*
Christie, Agatha (Mary Clarissa)
　　1890-1976 .... *36*
Christopher, John
　　See Youd, (Christopher) Samuel
　　See also CLR 2
Christopher, Louise
　　See Hale, Arlene
Christopher, Matt(hew F.)
　　1917- *47*
　　Earlier sketch in SATA 2
Christopher, Milbourne
　　1914(?)-1984 .... *46*
Christy, Howard Chandler
　　1873-1952 .... *21*
Chu, Daniel 1933- *11*
Chukovsky, Kornei (Ivanovich)
　　1882-1969 .... *34*
　　Earlier sketch in SATA 5
Church, Richard 1893-1972 .... *3*
Churchill, E. Richard 1937- *11*
Chute, B(eatrice) J(oy) 1913- *2*

Chute, Marchette (Gaylord)
　　1909- *1*
Chwast, Jacqueline 1932- *6*
Chwast, Seymour 1931- *18*
Ciardi, John (Anthony)
　　1916-1986 .... *1*
　　Obituary *46*
Clair, Andrée *19*
Clampett, Bob
　　Obituary *38*
　　See Clampett, Robert
Clampett, Robert
　　1914(?)-1984 .... *44*
Clapp, Patricia 1912- *4*
　　See also SAAS 4
Clare, Helen
　　See Hunter, Blair Pauline
Clark, Ann Nolan 1898- *4*
Clark, Champ 1923- *47*
Clark, David
　　See Hardcastle, Michael
Clark, David Allen
　　See Ernst, (Lyman) John
Clark, Frank J(ames) 1922- *18*
Clark, Garel [Joint pseudonym]
　　See Garelick, May
Clark, Leonard 1905-1981 .... *30*
　　Obituary *29*
Clark, Margaret Goff 1913- *8*
Clark, Mary Higgins *46*
Clark, Mavis Thorpe *8*
Clark, Merle
　　See Gessner, Lynne
Clark, Patricia (Finrow) 1929- *11*
Clark, Ronald William 1916- *2*
Clark, Van D(eusen) 1909- *2*
Clark, Virginia
　　See Gray, Patricia
Clark, Walter Van Tilburg
　　1909-1971 .... *8*
Clarke, Arthur C(harles)
　　1917- *13*
Clarke, Clorinda 1917- *7*
Clarke, Joan 1921- *42*
　　Brief Entry *27*
Clarke, John
　　See Laklan, Carli
Clarke, Mary Stetson 1911- *5*
Clarke, Michael
　　See Newlon, Clarke
Clarke, Pauline
　　See Hunter Blair, Pauline
Clarkson, E(dith) Margaret
　　1915- *37*
Clarkson, Ewan 1929- *9*
Claverie, Jean 1946- *38*
Clay, Patrice 1947- *47*
Claypool, Jane
　　See Miner, Jane Claypool
Cleary, Beverly (Bunn) 1916- *43*
　　Earlier sketch in SATA 2
　　See also CLR 2, 8
Cleaver, Bill 1920-1981 .... *22*
　　Obituary *27*
　　See also CLR 6
Cleaver, Carole 1934- *6*
Cleaver, Elizabeth (Mrazik)
　　1939-1985 .... *23*
　　Obituary *43*

Cleaver, Hylton (Reginald)
　　1891-1961 .... *49*
Cleaver, Vera *22*
　　See also CLR 6
Cleishbotham, Jebediah
　　See Scott, Sir Walter
Cleland, Mabel
　　See Widdemer, Mabel Cleland
Clemens, Samuel Langhorne
　　1835-1910 ....*YABC 2*
Clemens, Virginia Phelps
　　1941- *35*
Clements, Bruce 1931- *27*
Clemons, Elizabeth
　　See Nowell, Elizabeth Cameron
Clerk, N. W.
　　See Lewis, C. S.
Cleveland, Bob
　　See Cleveland, George
Cleveland, George 1903(?)-1985
　　Obituary *43*
Cleven, Cathrine
　　See Cleven, Kathryn Seward
Cleven, Kathryn Seward *2*
Clevin, Jörgen 1920- *7*
Clewes, Dorothy (Mary)
　　1907- *1*
Clifford, Eth
　　See Rosenberg, Ethel
Clifford, Harold B. 1893- *10*
Clifford, Margaret Cort 1929- *1*
Clifford, Martin
　　See Hamilton, Charles H. St. John
Clifford, Mary Louise (Beneway)
　　1926- *23*
Clifford, Peggy
　　See Clifford, Margaret Cort
Clifton, Harry
　　See Hamilton, Charles H. St. John
Clifton, Lucille 1936- *20*
　　See also CLR 5
Clifton, Martin
　　See Hamilton, Charles H. St. John
Climo, Shirley 1928- *39*
　　Brief Entry *35*
Clinton, Jon
　　See Prince, J(ack) H(arvey)
Clish, (Lee) Marian 1946- *43*
Clive, Clifford
　　See Hamilton, Charles H. St. John
Cloudsley-Thompson, J(ohn) L(eonard)
　　1921- *19*
Clymer, Eleanor 1906- *9*
Clyne, Patricia Edwards *31*
Coalson, Glo 1946- *26*
Coates, Belle 1896- *2*
Coates, Ruth Allison 1915- *11*
Coats, Alice M(argaret) 1905- *11*
Coatsworth, Elizabeth
　　1893-1986 .... *2*
　　Obituary *49*
　　See also CLR 2
Cobb, Jane
　　See Berry, Jane Cobb
Cobb, Vicki 1938- *8*
　　See also CLR 2
Cobbett, Richard
　　See Pluckrose, Henry (Arthur)
Cober, Alan E. 1935- *7*

Cobham, Sir Alan
    See Hamilton, Charles H. St. John
Cocagnac, A(ugustin) M(aurice-Jean)
    1924- 7
Cochran, Bobbye A. 1949- 11
Cockett, Mary 3
Coe, Douglas [Joint pseudonym]
    See Epstein, Beryl and Epstein,
    Samuel
Coe, Lloyd 1899-1976
    Obituary 30
Coen, Rena Neumann 1925- 20
Coerr, Eleanor 1922- 1
Coffin, Geoffrey
    See Mason, F. van Wyck
Coffman, Ramon Peyton
    1896- 4
Coggins, Jack (Banham)
    1911- 2
Cohen, Barbara 1932- 10
Cohen, Daniel 1936- 8
    See also CLR 3
    See also SAAS 4
Cohen, Jene Barr
    See Barr, Jene
Cohen, Joan Lebold 1932- 4
Cohen, Miriam 1926- 29
Cohen, Peter Zachary 1931- 4
Cohen, Robert Carl 1930- 8
Cohn, Angelo 1914- 19
Coit, Margaret L(ouise) 2
Colbert, Anthony 1934- 15
Colby, C(arroll) B(urleigh)
    1904-1977 35
    Earlier sketch in SATA 3
Colby, Jean Poindexter 1909- 23
Cole, Annette
    See Steiner, Barbara A(nnette)
Cole, Davis
    See Elting, Mary
Cole, Jack
    See Stewart, John (William)
Cole, Jackson
    See Schisgall, Oscar
Cole, Joanna 1944- 49
    Brief Entry 37
    See also CLR 5
Cole, Lois Dwight
    1903(?)-1979 10
    Obituary 26
Cole, Sheila R(otenberg)
    1939- 24
Cole, William (Rossa) 1919- 9
Coleman, William L(eRoy)
    1938- 49
    Brief Entry 34
Coles, Robert (Martin) 1929- 23
Colin, Ann
    See Ure, Jean
Collier, Christopher 1930- 16
Collier, Ethel 1903- 22
Collier, James Lincoln 1928- 8
    See also CLR 3
Collier, Jane
    See Collier, Zena
Collier, Zena 1926- 23
Collins, David 1940- 7
Collins, Hunt
    See Hunter, Evan

Collins, Michael
    See Lynds, Dennis
Collins, Pat Lowery 1932- 31
Collins, Ruth Philpott 1890-1975
    Obituary 30
Collodi, Carlo
    See Lorenzini, Carlo
    See also CLR 5
Colloms, Brenda 1919- 40
Colman, Hila 1
Colman, Morris 1899(?)-1981
    Obituary 25
Colonius, Lillian 1911- 3
Colorado (Capella), Antonio J(ulio)
    1903- 23
Colt, Martin [Joint pseudonym]
    See Epstein, Beryl and Epstein,
    Samuel
Colum, Padraic 1881-1972 15
Columella
    See Moore, Clement Clarke
Colver, Anne 1908- 7
Colwell, Eileen (Hilda) 1904- 2
Combs, Robert
    See Murray, John
Comfort, Jane Levington
    See Sturtzel, Jane Levington
Comfort, Mildred Houghton
    1886- 3
Comins, Ethel M(ae) 11
Comins, Jeremy 1933- 28
Commager, Henry Steele
    1902- 23
Comus
    See Ballantyne, R(obert) M(ichael)
Conan Doyle, Arthur
    See Doyle, Arthur Conan
Condit, Martha Olson 1913- 28
Cone, Ferne Geller 1921- 39
Cone, Molly (Lamken) 1918- 28
    Earlier sketch in SATA 1
Conford, Ellen 1942- 6
    See also CLR 10
Conger, Lesley
    See Suttles, Shirley (Smith)
Conklin, Gladys (Plemon)
    1903- 2
Conklin, Paul S. 43
    Brief Entry 33
Conkling, Hilda 1910- 23
Conly, Robert Leslie
    1918(?)-1973 23
Connell, Kirk [Joint pseudonym]
    See Chapman, John Stanton Higham
Connelly, Marc(us Cook) 1890-1980
    Obituary 25
Connolly, Jerome P(atrick)
    1931- 8
Connolly, Peter 1935- 47
Conover, Chris 1950- 31
Conquest, Owen
    See Hamilton, Charles H. St. John
Conrad, Joseph 1857-1924 27
Conrad, Pam(ela) 1947-
    Brief Entry 49
Conroy, Jack (Wesley) 1899- 19
Conroy, John
    See Conroy, Jack (Wesley)

Constant, Alberta Wilson
    1908-1981 22
    Obituary 28
Conway, Gordon
    See Hamilton, Charles H. St. John
Cook, Bernadine 1924- 11
Cook, Fred J(ames) 1911- 2
Cook, Joseph J(ay) 1924- 8
Cook, Lyn
    See Waddell, Evelyn Margaret
Cooke, Ann
    See Cole, Joanna
Cooke, David Coxe 1917- 2
Cooke, Donald Ewin
    1916-1985 2
    Obituary 45
Cookson, Catherine (McMullen)
    1906- 9
Coolidge, Olivia E(nsor)
    1908- 26
    Earlier sketch in SATA 1
Coombs, Charles I(ra) 1914- 43
    Earlier sketch in SATA 3
Coombs, Chick
    See Coombs, Charles I(ra)
Coombs, Patricia 1926- 3
Cooney, Barbara 1917- 6
Cooney, Caroline B. 1947- 48
    Brief Entry 41
Cooney, Nancy Evans 1932- 42
Coontz, Otto 1946- 33
Cooper, Elizabeth Keyser 47
Cooper, Gordon 1932- 23
Cooper, James Fenimore
    1789-1851 19
Cooper, James R.
    See Stratemeyer, Edward L.
Cooper, John R. [Collective
    pseudonym] 1
Cooper, Kay 1941- 11
Cooper, Lee (Pelham) 5
Cooper, Lester (Irving)
    1919-1985 32
    Obituary 43
Cooper, Lettice (Ulpha) 1897- 35
Cooper, Susan 1935- 4
    See also CLR 4
Copeland, Helen 1920- 4
Copeland, Paul W. 23
Copley, (Diana) Heather Pickering
    1918- 45
Coppard, A(lfred) E(dgar)
    1878-1957 .... YABC 1
Corbett, Grahame 43
    Brief Entry 36
Corbett, Scott 1913- 42
    Earlier sketch in SATA 2
    See also CLR 1
    See also SAAS 2
Corbett, W(illiam) J(esse) 1938-
    Brief Entry 44
Corbin, Sabra Lee
    See Malvern, Gladys
Corbin, William
    See McGraw, William Corbin
Corby, Dan
    See Catherall, Arthur
Corcoran, Barbara 1911- 3
Corcos, Lucille 1908-1973 10

Cordell, Alexander
  See Graber, Alexander
Coren, Alan 1938- 32
Corey, Dorothy 23
Corfe, Thomas Howell 1928- 27
Corfe, Tom
  See Corfe, Thomas Howell
Corlett, William 1938- 46
  Brief Entry 39
Cormack, M(argaret) Grant
  1913- 11
Cormack, Maribelle B.
  1902-1984 39
Cormier, Robert (Edmund)
  1925- 45
  Earlier sketch in SATA 10
  See also CLR 12
Cornelius, Carol 1942- 40
Cornell, J.
  See Cornell, Jeffrey
Cornell, James (Clayton, Jr.)
  1938- 27
Cornell, Jean Gay 1920- 23
Cornell, Jeffrey 1945- 11
Cornish, Samuel James 1935- 23
Cornwall, Nellie
  See Sloggett, Nellie
Correy, Lee
  See Stine, G. Harry 10
Corrigan, (Helen) Adeline
  1909- 23
Corrigan, Barbara 1922- 8
Corrin, Sara 1918-
  Brief Entry 48
Corrin, Stephen
  Brief Entry 48
Cort, M. C.
  See Clifford, Margaret Cort
Corwin, Judith Hoffman
  1946- 10
Cosgrave, John O'Hara II 1908-1968
  Obituary 21
Cosgrove, Margaret (Leota)
  1926- 47
Cosgrove, Stephen E(dward) 1945-
  Brief Entry 40
Coskey, Evelyn 1932- 7
Cosner, Shaaron 1940- 43
Costabel, Eva Deutsch 1924- 45
Costello, David F(rancis)
  1904- 23
Cott, Jonathan 1942- 23
Cottam, Clarence 1899-1974 25
Cottler, Joseph 1899- 22
Cottrell, Leonard 1913-1974 24
The Countryman
  See Whitlock, Ralph
Courlander, Harold 1908- 6
Courtis, Stuart Appleton 1874-1969
  Obituary 29
Coury, Louise Andree 1895(?)-1983
  Obituary 34
Cousins, Margaret 1905- 2
Cousteau, Jacques-Yves 1910- 38
Coville, Bruce 1950- 32
Cowen, Eve
  See Werner, Herma
Cowie, Leonard W(allace)
  1919- 4

Cowles, Kathleen
  See Krull, Kathleen
Cowley, Joy 1936- 4
Cox, Donald William 1921- 23
Cox, Jack
  See Cox, John Roberts
Cox, John Roberts 1915- 9
Cox, Palmer 1840-1924 24
Cox, Victoria
  See Garretson, Victoria Diane
Cox, Wally 1924-1973 25
Cox, William R(obert) 1901- 46
  Brief Entry 31
Coy, Harold 1902- 3
Craft, Ruth
  Brief Entry 31
Craig, A. A.
  See Anderson, Poul (William)
Craig, Alisa
  See MacLeod, Charlotte (Matilda
  Hughes)
Craig, Helen 1934- 49
  Brief Entry 46
Craig, John Eland
  See Chipperfield, Joseph
Craig, John Ernest 1921- 23
Craig, M. Jean 17
Craig, Margaret Maze
  1911-1964 9
Craik, Dinah Maria (Mulock)
  1826-1887 34
Crane, Barbara J. 1934- 31
Crane, Caroline 1930- 11
Crane, M. A.
  See Wartski, Maureen (Ann Crane)
Crane, Roy
  See Crane, Royston Campbell
Crane, Royston Campbell 1901-1977
  Obituary 22
Crane, Stephen (Townley)
  1871-1900 .... *YABC* 2
Crane, Walter 1845-1915 18
Crane, William D(wight)
  1892- 1
Crary, Elizabeth (Ann) 1942-
  Brief Entry 43
Crary, Margaret (Coleman)
  1906- 9
Craven, Thomas 1889-1969 22
Crawford, Charles P. 1945- 28
Crawford, Deborah 1922- 6
Crawford, John E. 1904-1971 3
Crawford, Mel 1925- 44
  Brief Entry 33
Crawford, Phyllis 1899- 3
Craz, Albert G. 1926- 24
Crayder, Dorothy 1906- 7
Crayder, Teresa
  See Colman, Hila
Crayon, Geoffrey
  See Irving, Washington
Crecy, Jeanne
  See Williams, Jeanne
Credle, Ellis 1902- 1
Cresswell, Helen 1934- 48
  Earlier sketch in SATA 1
Cretan, Gladys (Yessayan)
  1921- 2

Crew, Helen (Cecilia) Coale
  1866-1941 .... *YABC* 2
Crews, Donald 1938- 32
  Brief Entry 30
  See also CLR 7
Crichton, (J.) Michael 1942- 9
Crofut, Bill
  See Crofut, William E. III
Crofut, William E. III 1934- 23
Croman, Dorothy Young
  See Rosenberg, Dorothy
Cromie, Alice Hamilton 1914- 24
Cromie, William J(oseph)
  1930- 4
Crompton, Anne Eliot 1930- 23
Crompton, Richmal
  See Lamburn, Richmal Crompton
Cronbach, Abraham
  1882-1965 11
Crone, Ruth 1919- 4
Cronin, A(rchibald) J(oseph)
  1896-1981 47
  Obituary 25
Crook, Beverly Courtney 38
  Brief Entry 35
Cros, Earl
  See Rose, Carl
Crosby, Alexander L.
  1906-1980 2
  Obituary 23
Crosher, G(eoffry) R(obins)
  1911- 14
Cross, Gillian (Clare) 1945- 38
Cross, Helen Reeder
  See Broadhead, Helen Cross
Cross, Wilbur Lucius III
  1918- 2
Crossley-Holland, Kevin 5
Crouch, Marcus 1913- 4
Crout, George C(lement)
  1917- 11
Crow, Donna Fletcher 1941- 40
Crowe, Bettina Lum 1911- 6
Crowe, John
  See Lynds, Dennis
Crowell, Grace Noll
  1877-1969 34
Crowell, Pers 1910- 2
Crowfield, Christopher
  See Stowe, Harriet (Elizabeth)
  Beecher
Crowley, Arthur M(cBlair)
  1945- 38
Crownfield, Gertrude
  1867-1945 .... *YABC* 1
Crowther, James Gerald 1899- 14
Cruikshank, George
  1792-1878 22
Crump, Fred H., Jr. 1931- 11
Crump, J(ames) Irving 1887-1979
  Obituary 21
Crunden, Reginald
  See Cleaver, Hylton (Reginald)
Cruz, Ray 1933- 6
Ctvrtek, Vaclav 1911-1976
  Obituary 27
Cuffari, Richard 1925-1978 6
  Obituary 25
Cullen, Countee 1903-1946 18

Culliford, Pierre 1928- 40
Culp, Louanna McNary
   1901-1965 2
Cumming, Primrose (Amy)
   1915- 24
Cummings, Betty Sue 1918- 15
Cummings, Parke 1902- 2
Cummings, Pat 1950- 42
Cummings, Richard
   See Gardner, Richard
Cummins, Maria Susanna
   1827-1866 .... YABC 1
Cunliffe, John Arthur 1933- 11
Cunliffe, Marcus (Falkner)
   1922- 37
Cunningham, Captain Frank
   See Glick, Carl (Cannon)
Cunningham, Cathy
   See Cunningham, Chet
Cunningham, Chet 1928- 23
Cunningham, Dale S(peers)
   1932- 11
Cunningham, E.V.
   See Fast, Howard
Cunningham, Julia W(oolfolk)
   1916- 26
   Earlier sketch in SATA 1
   See also SAAS 2
Cunningham, Virginia
   See Holmgren, Virginia
   C(unningham)
Curiae, Amicus
   See Fuller, Edmund (Maybank)
Curie, Eve 1904- 1
Curley, Daniel 1918- 23
Curry, Jane L(ouise) 1932- 1
Curry, Peggy Simson 1911- 8
Curtis, Bruce (Richard) 1944- 30
Curtis, Patricia 1921- 23
Curtis, Peter
   See Lofts, Norah (Robinson)
Curtis, Richard (Alan) 1937- 29
Curtis, Wade
   See Pournelle, Jerry (Eugene)
Cushman, Jerome 2
Cutchen, Billye Walker 1930- 15
Cutler, (May) Ebbitt 1923- 9
Cutler, Ivor 1923- 24
Cutler, Samuel
   See Folsom, Franklin
Cutt, W(illiam) Towrie 1898- 16
Cuyler, Margery Stuyvesant
   1948- 39
Cuyler, Stephen
   See Bates, Barbara S(nedeker)

                    D

Dabcovich, Lydia
   Brief Entry 47
Dahl, Borghild 1890-1984 7
   Obituary 37
Dahl, Roald 1916- 26
   Earlier sketch in SATA 1
   See also CLR 1; 7
Dahlstedt, Marden 1921- 8
Dain, Martin J. 1924- 35
Dale, Jack
   See Holliday, Joseph

Dale, Margaret J(essy) Miller
   1911- 39
Dale, Norman
   See Denny, Norman (George)
Dalgliesh, Alice 1893-1979 17
   Obituary 21
Dalton, Alene
   See Chapin, Alene Olsen Dalton
Dalton, Anne 1948- 40
Daly, Jim
   See Stratemeyer, Edward L.
Daly, Kathleen N(orah)
   Brief Entry 37
Daly, Maureen 2
   See also SAAS 1
Daly, Nicholas 1946- 37
Daly, Niki
   See Daly, Nicholas
D'Amato, Alex 1919- 20
D'Amato, Janet 1925- 9
Damrosch, Helen Therese
   See Tee-Van, Helen Damrosch
Dana, Barbara 1940- 22
Dana, Richard Henry, Jr.
   1815-1882 26
Danachair, Caoimhin O.
   See Danaher, Kevin
Danaher, Kevin 1913- 22
D'Andrea, Kate
   See Steiner, Barbara A(nnette)
Dangerfield, Balfour
   See McCloskey, Robert
Daniel, Anita 1893(?)-1978 23
   Obituary 24
Daniel, Anne
   See Steiner, Barbara A(nnette)
Daniel, Hawthorne 1890- 8
Daniels, Guy 1919- 11
Dank, Gloria Rand 1955-
   Brief Entry 46
Dank, Leonard D(ewey)
   1929- 44
Dank, Milton 1920- 31
Danziger, Paula 1944- 36
   Brief Entry 30
Darby, J. N.
   See Govan, Christine Noble
Darby, Patricia (Paulsen) 14
Darby, Ray K. 1912- 7
Daringer, Helen Fern 1892- 1
Darke, Marjorie 1929- 16
Darley, F(elix) O(ctavius) C(arr)
   1822-1888 35
Darling, David J.
   Brief Entry 44
Darling, Kathy
   See Darling, Mary Kathleen
Darling, Lois M. 1917- 3
Darling, Louis, Jr. 1916-1970 3
   Obituary 23
Darling, Mary Kathleen 1943- 9
Darrow, Whitney, Jr. 1909- 13
Darwin, Len
   See Darwin, Leonard
Darwin, Leonard 1916- 24
Dasent, Sir George Webbe 1817-1896
   Brief Entry 29

Daskam, Josephine Dodge
   See Bacon, Josephine Dodge
   (Daskam)
Dauer, Rosamond 1934- 23
Daugherty, Charles Michael
   1914- 16
Daugherty, James (Henry)
   1889-1974 13
Daugherty, Richard D(eo)
   1922- 35
Daugherty, Sonia Medvedeff (?)-1971
   Obituary 27
d'Aulaire, Edgar Parin
   1898-1986 5
   Obituary 47
d'Aulaire, Ingri (Maartenson Parin)
   1904-1980 5
   Obituary 24
Daveluy, Paule Cloutier 1919- 11
Davenport, Spencer
   See Stratemeyer, Edward L.
Daves, Michael 1938- 40
David, Jonathan
   See Ames, Lee J.
Davidson, Alice Joyce 1932-
   Brief Entry 45
Davidson, Basil 1914- 13
Davidson, Jessica 1915- 5
Davidson, Judith 1953- 40
Davidson, Margaret 1936- 5
Davidson, Marion
   See Garis, Howard R(oger)
Davidson, Mary R.
   1885-1973 9
Davidson, R.
   See Davidson, Raymond
Davidson, Raymond 1926- 32
Davidson, Rosalie 1921- 23
Davies, Andrew (Wynford)
   1936- 27
Davies, Bettilu D(onna) 1942- 33
Davies, (Edward) Hunter 1936-
   Brief Entry 45
Davies, Joan 1934-
   Brief Entry 47
Davies, Sumiko 1942- 46
Davis, Bette J. 1923- 15
Davis, Burke 1913- 4
Davis, Christopher 1928- 6
Davis, D(elbert) Dwight
   1908-1965 33
Davis, Daniel S(heldon) 1936- 12
Davis, Gibbs 1953- 46
   Brief Entry 41
Davis, Hubert J(ackson) 1904- 31
Davis, James Robert 1945- 32
Davis, Jim
   See Davis, James Robert
Davis, Julia 1904- 6
Davis, Louise Littleton 1921- 25
Davis, Marguerite 1889- 34
Davis, Mary L(ee) 1935- 9
Davis, Mary Octavia 1901- 6
Davis, Paxton 1925- 16
Davis, Robert
   1881-1949 .... YABC 1
Davis, Russell G. 1922- 3
Davis, Verne T. 1889-1973 6

Dawson, Elmer A. [Collective
pseudonym] *1*
Dawson, Mary 1919- *11*
Day, Beth (Feagles) 1924- *33*
Day, Maurice 1892-
Brief Entry *30*
Day, Thomas 1748-1789 ..... *YABC 1*
Dazey, Agnes J(ohnston) *2*
Dazey, Frank M. *2*
Deacon, Eileen
See Geipel, Eileen
Deacon, Richard
See McCormick, (George) Donald
(King)
Dean, Anabel 1915- *12*
Dean, Karen Strickler 1923- *49*
de Angeli, Marguerite 1889- *27*
Earlier sketch in SATA 1
See also CLR 1
DeArmand, Frances Ullmann
1904(?)-1984 .... *10*
Obituary *38*
Deary, Terry 1946-
Brief Entry *41*
deBanke, Cecile 1889-1965 ...... *11*
De Bruyn, Monica 1952- *13*
de Camp, Catherine C(rook)
1907- *12*
DeCamp, L(yon) Sprague
1907- *9*
Decker, Duane 1910-1964 .... *5*
DeClements, Barthe 1920- *35*
Deedy, John 1923- *24*
Deegan, Paul Joseph 1937- *48*
Brief Entry *38*
Defoe, Daniel 1660(?)-1731 ...... *22*
deFrance, Anthony
See Di Franco, Anthony (Mario)
Degen, Bruce
Brief Entry *47*
DeGering, Etta 1898- *7*
De Grazia
See De Grazia, Ted
De Grazia, Ted 1909-1982 .... *39*
De Grazia, Ettore
See De Grazia, Ted
De Groat, Diane 1947- *31*
de Grummond, Lena Young *6*
Deiss, Joseph J. 1915- *12*
DeJong, David C(ornel)
1905-1967 .... *10*
de Jong, Dola *7*
De Jong, Meindert 1906- *2*
See also CLR 1
de Kay, Ormonde, Jr. 1923- *7*
de Kiriline, Louise
See Lawrence, Louise de Kiriline
Dekker, Carl
See Laffin, John (Alfred Charles)
Dekker, Carl
See Lynds, Dennis
deKruif, Paul (Henry)
1890-1971 .... *5*
Delacre, Lulu 1957- *36*
De Lage, Ida 1918- *11*
de la Mare, Walter 1873-1956 .... *16*
Delaney, Harry 1932- *3*
Delaney, Ned 1951- *28*
Delano, Hugh 1933- *20*

De La Ramée, (Marie) Louise
1839-1908 .... *20*
Delaune, Lynne *7*
DeLaurentis, Louise Budde
1920- *12*
Delderfield, Eric R(aymond)
1909- *14*
Delderfield, R(onald) F(rederick)
1912-1972 .... *20*
De Leeuw, Adele Louise
1899- *30*
Earlier sketch in SATA 1
Delessert, Etienne 1941- *46*
Brief Entry *27*
Delmar, Roy
See Wexler, Jerome (LeRoy)
Deloria, Vine (Victor), Jr.
1933- *21*
Del Rey, Lester 1915- *22*
Delton, Judy 1931- *14*
Delulio, John 1938- *15*
Delving, Michael
See Williams, Jay
Demarest, Chris(topher) L(ynn)
1951- *45*
Brief Entry *44*
Demarest, Doug
See Barker, Will
Demas, Vida 1927- *9*
De Mejo, Oscar 1911- *40*
de Messières, Nicole 1930- *39*
Deming, Richard 1915- *24*
Dengler, Sandy 1939-
Brief Entry *40*
Denmark, Harrison
See Zelazny, Roger (Joseph
Christopher)
Denney, Diana 1910- *25*
Dennis, Morgan 1891(?)-1960 ..... *18*
Dennis, Wesley 1903-1966 .... *18*
Denniston, Elinore 1900-1978
Obituary *24*
Denny, Norman (George)
1901-1982 .... *43*
Denslow, W(illiam) W(allace)
1856-1915 .... *16*
Denzel, Justin F(rancis) 1917- *46*
Brief Entry *38*
Denzer, Ann Wiseman
See Wiseman, Ann (Sayre)
de Paola, Thomas Anthony
1934- *11*
de Paola, Tomie
See de Paola, Thomas Anthony
See also CLR 4
DePauw, Linda Grant 1940- *24*
deRegniers, Beatrice Schenk
(Freedman) 1914- *2*
Derleth, August (William)
1909-1971 .... *5*
Derman, Sarah Audrey 1915- *11*
de Roo, Anne Louise 1931- *25*
De Roussan, Jacques 1929-
Brief Entry *31*
Derry Down Derry
See Lear, Edward
Derwent, Lavinia *14*
Desbarats, Peter 1933- *39*

De Selincourt, Aubrey
1894-1962 .... *14*
Desmond, Alice Curtis 1897- *8*
Detine, Padre
See Olsen, Ib Spang
Deutsch, Babette 1895-1982 ...... *1*
Obituary *33*
De Valera, Sinead 1870(?)-1975
Obituary *30*
Devaney, John 1926- *12*
Devereux, Frederick L(eonard), Jr.
1914- *9*
Devlin, Harry 1918- *11*
Devlin, (Dorothy) Wende
1918- *11*
DeWaard, E. John 1935- *7*
DeWeese, Gene
See DeWeese, Thomas Eugene
DeWeese, Jean
See DeWeese, Thomas Eugene
DeWeese, Thomas Eugene
1934- *46*
Brief Entry *45*
Dewey, Ariane 1937- *7*
Dewey, Jennifer (Owings)
Brief Entry *48*
Dewey, Ken(neth Francis)
1940- *39*
DeWit, Dorothy (May Knowles)
1916-1980 .... *39*
Obituary *28*
Deyneka, Anita 1943- *24*
Deyrup, Astrith Johnson
1923- *24*
Diamond, Donna 1950- *35*
Brief Entry *30*
Dias, Earl Joseph 1916- *41*
Dick, Cappy
See Cleveland, George
Dick, Trella Lamson
1889-1974 .... *9*
Dickens, Charles 1812-1870 ...... *15*
Dickens, Frank
See Huline-Dickens, Frank William
Dickens, Monica 1915- *4*
Dickerson, Roy Ernest 1886-1965
Obituary *26*
Dickinson, Emily (Elizabeth)
1830-1886 .... *29*
Dickinson, Mary 1949- *48*
Brief Entry *41*
Dickinson, Peter 1927- *5*
Dickinson, Susan 1931- *8*
Dickinson, William Croft
1897-1973 .... *13*
Dickson, Helen
See Reynolds, Helen Mary
Greenwood Campbell
Dickson, Naida 1916- *8*
Dietz, David H(enry)
1897-1984 .... *10*
Obituary *41*
Dietz, Lew 1907- *11*
Di Franco, Anthony (Mario)
1945- *42*
Digges, Jeremiah
See Berger, Josef
D'Ignazio, Fred 1949- *39*
Brief Entry *35*

Di Grazia, Thomas (?)-1983 32
Dillard, Annie 1945- 10
Dillard, Polly (Hargis) 1916- 24
Dillon, Barbara 1927- 44
  Brief Entry 39
Dillon, Diane 1933- 15
Dillon, Eilis 1920- 2
Dillon, Leo 1933- 15
Dilson, Jesse 1914- 24
Dinan, Carolyn
  Brief Entry 47
Dines, Glen 1925- 7
Dinesen, Isak
  See Blixen, Karen (Christentze
  Dinesen)
Dinnerstein, Harvey 1928- 42
Dinsdale, Tim 1924- 11
Dirks, Rudolph 1877-1968
  Brief Entry 31
Disney, Walt(er Elias)
  1901-1966 28
  Brief Entry 27
DiValentin, Maria 1911- 7
Dixon, Dougal 1947- 45
Dixon, Franklin W. [Collective
  pseudonym] 1
  See also Adams, Harriet
  S(tratemeyer); McFarlane, Leslie;
  Stratemeyer, Edward L.; Svenson,
  Andrew E.
Dixon, Jeanne 1936- 31
Dixon, Peter L. 1931- 6
Doane, Pelagie 1906-1966 7
Dobell, I(sabel) M(arian) B(arclay)
  1909- 11
Dobie, J(ames) Frank
  1888-1964 43
Dobkin, Alexander 1908-1975
  Obituary 30
Dobler, Lavinia G. 1910- 6
Dobrin, Arnold 1928- 4
Dobson, Julia 1941- 48
Dockery, Wallene T. 1941- 27
"Dr. A"
  See Silverstein, Alvin
Dr. X
  See Nourse, Alan E(dward)
Dodd, Ed(ward) Benton 1902- 4
Dodd, Lynley (Stuart) 1941- 35
Dodge, Bertha S(anford)
  1902- 8
Dodge, Mary (Elizabeth) Mapes
  1831-1905 21
Dodgson, Charles Lutwidge
  1832-1898 ....YABC 2
Dodson, Kenneth M(acKenzie)
  1907- 11
Dodson, Susan 1941-
  Brief Entry 40
Doherty, C. H. 1913- 6
Dolan, Edward F(rancis), Jr.
  1924- 45
  Brief Entry 31
Dolson, Hildegarde 1908- 5
Domanska, Janina 6
Domino, John
  See Averill, Esther
Domjan, Joseph 1907- 25

Donalds, Gordon
  See Shirreffs, Gordon D.
Donna, Natalie 1934- 9
Donovan, Frank (Robert) 1906-1975
  Obituary 30
Donovan, John 1928-
  Brief Entry 29
  See also CLR 3
Donovan, William
  See Berkebile, Fred D(onovan)
Doob, Leonard W(illiam)
  1909- 8
Dor, Ana
  See Ceder, Georgiana Dorcas
Doré, (Louis Christophe Paul) Gustave
  1832-1883 19
Doremus, Robert 1913- 30
Dorian, Edith M(cEwen)
  1900- 5
Dorian, Harry
  See Hamilton, Charles H. St. John
Dorian, Marguerite 7
Dorman, Michael 1932- 7
Dorman, N. B. 1927- 39
Dorson, Richard M(ercer)
  1916-1981 30
Doss, Helen (Grigsby) 1918- 20
Doss, Margot Patterson 6
dos Santos, Joyce Audy
  Brief Entry 42
Dottig
  See Grider, Dorothy
Dotts, Maryann J. 1933- 35
Doty, Jean Slaughter 1929- 28
Doty, Roy 1922- 28
Doubtfire, Dianne (Abrams)
  1918- 29
Dougherty, Charles 1922- 18
Douglas, James McM.
  See Butterworth, W. E.
Douglas, Kathryn
  See Ewing, Kathryn
Douglas, Marjory Stoneman
  1890- 10
Douglass, Barbara 1930- 40
Douglass, Frederick
  1817(?)-1895 29
Douty, Esther M(orris)
  1911-1978 8
  Obituary 23
Dow, Emily R. 1904- 10
Dowdell, Dorothy (Florence) Karns
  1910- 12
Dowden, Anne Ophelia 1907- 7
Dowdey, Landon Gerald
  1923- 11
Dowdy, Mrs. Regera
  See Gorey, Edward St. John
Downer, Marion 1892(?)-1971 25
Downey, Fairfax 1893- 3
Downie, Mary Alice 1934- 13
Doyle, Arthur Conan
  1859-1930 24
Doyle, Donovan
  See Boegehold, Betty (Doyle)
Doyle, Richard 1824-1883 21
Drabble, Margaret 1939- 48
Draco, F.
  See Davis, Julia

Drager, Gary
  See Edens, Cooper
Dragonwagon, Crescent 1952- 41
  Earlier sketch in SATA 11
Drake, Frank
  See Hamilton, Charles H. St. John
Drapier, M. B.
  See Swift, Jonathan
Drawson, Blair 1943- 17
Dresang, Eliza (Carolyn Timberlake)
  1941- 19
Drescher, Joan E(lizabeth)
  1939- 30
Drew, Patricia (Mary) 1938- 15
Drewery, Mary 1918- 6
Drial, J. E.
  See Laird, Jean E(louise)
Drucker, Malka 1945- 39
  Brief Entry 29
Drummond, V(iolet) H. 1911- 6
Drummond, Walter
  See Silverberg, Robert
Drury, Roger W(olcott) 1914- 15
Dryden, Pamela
  See Johnston, Norma
Duane, Diane (Elizabeth) 1952-
  Brief Entry 46
du Blanc, Daphne
  See Groom, Arthur William
DuBois, Rochelle Holt
  See Holt, Rochelle Lynn
Du Bois, Shirley Graham
  1907-1977 24
Du Bois, W(illiam) E(dward)
  B(urghardt) 1868-1963 42
du Bois, William Pène 1916- 4
  See also CLR 1
DuBose, LaRocque (Russ)
  1926- 2
Du Chaillu, Paul (Belloni)
  1831(?)-1903 26
Duchesne, Janet 1930-
  Brief Entry 32
Ducornet, Erica 1943- 7
Dudley, Martha Ward 1909(?)-1985
  Obituary 45
Dudley, Nancy
  See Cole, Lois Dwight
Dudley, Robert
  See Baldwin, James
Dudley, Ruth H(ubbell) 1905- 11
Dueland, Joy V(ivian) 27
Duff, Annis (James) 1904(?)-1986
  Obituary 49
Duff, Maggie
  See Duff, Margaret K.
Duff, Margaret K. 37
Dugan, Michael (Gray) 1947- 15
Duggan, Alfred Leo
  1903-1964 25
Duggan, Maurice (Noel)
  1922-1974 40
  Obituary 30
du Jardin, Rosamond (Neal)
  1902-1963 2
Dulac, Edmund 1882-1953 19
Dumas, Alexandre (the elder)
  1802-1870 18
du Maurier, Daphne 1907- 27

Dunbar, Paul Laurence
  1872-1906 34
Dunbar, Robert E(verett)
  1926- 32
Duncan, Frances (Mary) 1942-
  Brief Entry 48
Duncan, Gregory
  See McClintock, Marshall
Duncan, Jane
  See Cameron, Elizabeth Jane
Duncan, Julia K. [Collective
  pseudonym] 1
Duncan, Lois S(teinmetz)
  1934- 36
  Earlier sketch in SATA 1
  See also SAAS 2
Duncan, Norman
  1871-1916 .... YABC 1
Duncombe, Frances (Riker)
  1900- 25
Dunlop, Agnes M.R. 3
Dunlop, Eileen (Rhona) 1938- ... 24
Dunn, Harvey T(homas)
  1884-1952 34
Dunn, Judy
  See Spangenberg, Judith Dunn
Dunn, Mary Lois 1930- 6
Dunnahoo, Terry 1927- 7
Dunne, Mary Collins 1914- 11
Dunnett, Margaret (Rosalind)
  1909-1977 42
Dunrea, Olivier 1953-
  Brief Entry 46
Dupuy, T(revor) N(evitt)
  1916- 4
Durant, John 1902- 27
Durrell, Gerald (Malcolm)
  1925- 8
Du Soe, Robert C.
  1892-1958 .... YABC 2
Dutz
  See Davis, Mary Octavia
Duvall, Evelyn Millis 1906- 9
Duvoisin, Roger (Antoine)
  1904-1980 30
  Obituary 23
  Earlier sketch in SATA 2
Dwiggins, Don 1913- 4
Dwight, Allan
  See Cole, Lois Dwight
Dyer, James (Frederick) 1934- ... 37
Dygard, Thomas J. 1931- 24
Dyke, John 1935- 35

E

E.V.B.
  See Boyle, Eleanor Vere (Gordon)
Eagar, Frances 1940- 11
Eager, Edward (McMaken)
  1911-1964 17
Eagle, Mike 1942- 11
Earle, Olive L. 7
Earnshaw, Brian 1929- 17
Eastman, Charles A(lexander)
  1858-1939 .... YABC 1
Eastman, P(hilip) D(ey)
  1909-1986 33
  Obituary 46

Eastwick, Ivy O. 3
Eaton, Anne T(haxter)
  1881-1971 32
Eaton, George L.
  See Verral, Charles Spain
Eaton, Jeanette 1886-1968 24
Eaton, Tom 1940- 22
Ebel, Alex 1927- 11
Eber, Dorothy (Margaret) Harley
  1930- 27
Eberle, Irmengarde 1898-1979 ... 2
  Obituary 23
Eccles
  See Williams, Ferelith Eccles
Eckblad, Edith Berven 1923- 23
Ecke, Wolfgang 1927-1983
  Obituary 37
Eckert, Allan W. 1931- 29
  Brief Entry 27
Eckert, Horst 1931- 8
Ede, Janina 1937- 33
Edell, Celeste 12
Edelman, Lily (Judith) 1915- ... 22
Edens, Cooper 1945- 49
Edens, (Bishop) David 1926- 39
Edey, Maitland A(rmstrong)
  1910- 25
Edgeworth, Maria 1767-1849 21
Edmonds, I(vy) G(ordon)
  1917- 8
Edmonds, Walter D(umaux)
  1903- 27
  Earlier sketch in SATA 1
  See also SAAS 4
Edmund, Sean
  See Pringle, Laurence
Edsall, Marian S(tickney)
  1920- 8
Edwards, Al
  See Nourse, Alan E(dward)
Edwards, Alexander
  See Fleischer, Leonore
Edwards, Anne 1927- 35
Edwards, Audrey 1947-
  Brief Entry 31
Edwards, Bertram
  See Edwards, Herbert Charles
Edwards, Bronwen Elizabeth
  See Rose, Wendy
Edwards, Cecile (Pepin)
  1916- 25
Edwards, Dorothy 1914-1982 4
  Obituary 31
Edwards, Gunvor 32
Edwards, Harvey 1929- 5
Edwards, Herbert Charles
  1912- 12
Edwards, Jane Campbell
  1932- 10
Edwards, Julie
  See Andrews, Julie
Edwards, Julie
  See Stratemeyer, Edward L.
Edwards, June
  See Forrester, Helen
Edwards, Linda Strauss 1948- ... 49
  Brief Entry 42
Edwards, Monica le Doux Newton
  1912- 12

Edwards, Olwen
  See Gater, Dilys
Edwards, Sally 1929- 7
Edwards, Samuel
  See Gerson, Noel B(ertram)
Egan, E(dward) W(elstead)
  1922- 35
Eggenberger, David 1918- 6
Eggleston, Edward 1837-1902 27
Egielski, Richard 1952- 49
  Earlier sketch in SATA 11
Egypt, Ophelia Settle
  1903-1984 16
  Obituary 38
Ehlert, Lois (Jane) 1934- 35
Ehrlich, Amy 1942- 25
Ehrlich, Bettina (Bauer) 1903- . 1
Eichberg, James Bandman
  See Garfield, James B.
Eichenberg, Fritz 1901- 9
Eichler, Margrit 1942- 35
Eichner, James A. 1927- 4
Eifert, Virginia S(nider)
  1911-1966 2
Einsel, Naiad 10
Einsel, Walter 1926- 10
Einzig, Susan 1922- 43
Eiseman, Alberta 1925- 15
Eisenberg, Azriel 1903- 12
Eisenberg, Phyllis Rose 1924- .. 41
Eisner, Vivienne
  See Margolis, Vivienne
Eisner, Will(iam Erwin) 1917- .. 31
Eitzen, Allan 1928- 9
Eitzen, Ruth (Carper) 1924- 9
Elam, Richard M(ace, Jr.)
  1920- 9
Elfman, Blossom 1925- 8
Elgin, Kathleen 1923- 39
Elia
  See Lamb, Charles
Eliot, Anne
  See Cole, Lois Dwight
Elisofon, Eliot 1911-1973
  Obituary 21
Elkin, Benjamin 1911- 3
Elkins, Dov Peretz 1937- 5
Ellacott, S(amuel) E(rnest)
  1911- 19
Elliott, Sarah M(cCarn) 1930- .. 14
Ellis, Anyon
  See Rowland-Entwistle, (Arthur)
  Theodore (Henry)
Ellis, Edward S(ylvester)
  1840-1916 .... YABC 1
Ellis, Ella Thorp 1928- 7
Ellis, Harry Bearse 1921- 9
Ellis, Herbert
  See Wilson, Lionel
Ellis, Mel 1912-1984 7
  Obituary 39
Ellison, Lucile Watkins 1907(?)-1979
  Obituary 22
Ellison, Virginia Howell
  1910- 4
Ellsberg, Edward 1891- 7
Elmore, (Carolyn) Patricia
  1933- 38
  Brief Entry 35

Elspeth
  See Bragdon, Elspeth
Elting, Mary 1906- 2
Elwart, Joan Potter 1927- 2
Emberley, Barbara A(nne) 8
  See also CLR 5
Emberley, Ed(ward Randolph)
  1931- 8
  See also CLR 5
Emberley, Michael 1960- 34
Embry, Margaret (Jacob)
  1919- 5
Emerson, Alice B. [Collective
  pseudonym] 1
Emerson, William K(eith)
  1925- 25
Emery, Anne (McGuigan)
  1907- 33
  Earlier sketch in SATA 1
Emmens, Carol Ann 1944- 39
Emmons, Della (Florence) Gould
  1890-1983
  Obituary 39
Emrich, Duncan (Black Macdonald)
  1908- 11
Emslie, M. L.
  See Simpson, Myrtle L(illias)
Ende, Michael 1930(?)-
  Brief Entry 42
Enderle, Judith (Ann) 1941- 38
Enfield, Carrie
  See Smith, Susan Vernon
Engdahl, Sylvia Louise 1933- 4
  See also CLR 2
Engle, Eloise Katherine 1923- 9
Englebert, Victor 1933- 8
English, James W(ilson)
  1915- 37
Enright, D(ennis) J(oseph)
  1920- 25
Enright, Elizabeth 1909-1968 9
  See also CLR 4
Enright, Maginel Wright
  See Barney, Maginel Wright
Enys, Sarah L.
  See Sloggett, Nellie
Epp, Margaret A(gnes) 20
Epple, Anne Orth 1927- 20
Epstein, Anne Merrick 1931- 20
Epstein, Beryl (Williams)
  1910- 31
  Earlier sketch in SATA 1
Epstein, Perle S(herry) 1938- 27
Epstein, Samuel 1909- 31
  Earlier sketch in SATA 1
Erdman, Loula Grace 1
Erdoes, Richard 1912- 33
  Brief Entry 28
Erhard, Walter 1920-
  Brief Entry 30
Erickson, Russell E(verett)
  1932- 27
Erickson, Sabra R(ollins)
  1912- 35
Ericson, Walter
  See Fast, Howard
Erikson, Mel 1937- 31
Erlanger, Baba
  See Trahey, Jane

Erlich, Lillian (Feldman)
  1910- 10
Ernest, William
  See Berkebile, Fred D(onovan)
Ernst, (Lyman) John 1940- 39
Ernst, Kathryn (Fitzgerald)
  1942- 25
Ernst, Lisa Campbell 1957-
  Brief Entry 44
Ervin, Janet Halliday 1923- 4
Erwin, Will
  See Eisner, Will(iam Erwin)
Eshmeyer, R(einhart) E(rnst)
  1898- 29
Espeland, Pamela (Lee) 1951-
  Brief Entry 38
Espy, Willard R(ichardson)
  1910- 38
Estep, Irene (Compton) 5
Estes, Eleanor 1906- 7
  See also CLR 2
Estoril, Jean
  See Allan, Mabel Esther
Etchemendy, Nancy 1952- 38
Etchison, Birdie L(ee) 1937- 38
Ets, Marie Hall 2
Eunson, Dale 1904- 5
Evans, Eva Knox 1905- 27
Evans, Hubert Reginald 1892-1986
  Obituary 48
Evans, Katherine (Floyd)
  1901-1964 5
Evans, Mari 10
Evans, Mark 19
Evans, Patricia Healy
  See Carpenter, Patricia
Evarts, Esther
  See Benson, Sally
Evarts, Hal G. (Jr.) 1915- 6
Everett, Gail
  See Hale, Arlene
Evernden, Margery 1916- 5
Evslin, Bernard 1922- 45
  Brief Entry 28
Ewen, David 1907-1985 4
  Obituary 47
Ewing, Juliana (Horatia Gatty)
  1841-1885 16
Ewing, Kathryn 1921- 20
Eyerly, Jeannette Hyde 1908- 4
Eyre, Dorothy
  See McGuire, Leslie (Sarah)
Eyre, Katherine Wigmore
  1901-1970 26
Ezzell, Marilyn 1937- 42
  Brief Entry 38

F

Fabe, Maxene 1943- 15
Faber, Doris 1924- 3
Faber, Harold 1919- 5
Fabre, Jean Henri (Casimir)
  1823-1915 22
Facklam, Margery Metz 1927- 20
Fadiman, Clifton (Paul) 1904- 11
Fair, Sylvia 1933- 13
Fairfax-Lucy, Brian (Fulke Cameron-
  Ramsay) 1898-1974 6
  Obituary 26

Fairlie, Gerard 1899-1983
  Obituary 34
Fairman, Joan A(lexandra)
  1935- 10
Faithfull, Gail 1936- 8
Falconer, James
  See Kirkup, James
Falkner, Leonard 1900- 12
Fall, Thomas
  See Snow, Donald Clifford
Falls, C(harles) B(uckles)
  1874-1960 38
  Brief Entry 27
Falstein, Louis 1909- 37
Fanning, Leonard M(ulliken)
  1888-1967 5
Faralla, Dana 1909- 9
Faralla, Dorothy W.
  See Faralla, Dana
Farb, Peter 1929-1980 12
  Obituary 22
Farber, Norma 1909-1984 25
  Obituary 38
Farge, Monique
  See Grée, Alain
Farjeon, (Eve) Annabel 1919- 11
Farjeon, Eleanor 1881-1965 2
Farley, Carol 1936- 4
Farley, Walter 1920- 43
  Earlier sketch in SATA 2
Farmer, Penelope (Jane)
  1939- 40
  Brief Entry 39
  See also CLR 8
Farmer, Peter 1950- 38
Farnham, Burt
  See Clifford, Harold B.
Farquhar, Margaret C(utting)
  1905- 13
Farquharson, Alexander 1944- 46
Farquharson, Martha
  See Finley, Martha
Farr, Finis (King) 1904- 10
Farrar, Susan Clement 1917- 33
Farrell, Ben
  See Cebulash, Mel
Farrington, Benjamin 1891-1974
  Obituary 20
Farrington, Selwyn Kip, Jr.
  1904- 20
Farthing, Alison 1936- 45
  Brief Entry 36
Fassler, Joan (Grace) 1931- 11
Fast, Howard 1914- 7
Fatchen, Max 1920- 20
Father Xavier
  See Hurwood, Bernhardt J.
Fatigati, (Frances) Evelyn de Buhr
  1948- 24
Fatio, Louise 6
Faulhaber, Martha 1926- 7
Faulkner, Anne Irvin 1906- 23
Faulkner, Nancy
  See Faulkner, Anne Irvin
Fax, Elton Clay 1909- 25
Feagles, Anita MacRae 9
Feagles, Elizabeth
  See Day, Beth (Feagles)
Feague, Mildred H. 1915- 14

Fecher, Constance 1911- 7
Feder, Paula (Kurzband)
1935- 26
Feder, Robert Arthur 1909-1969
Brief Entry 35
Feelings, Muriel (Grey) 1938- 16
See also CLR 5
Feelings, Thomas 1933- 8
Feelings, Tom
See Feelings, Thomas
See also CLR 5
Fehrenbach, T(heodore) R(eed, Jr.)
1925- 33
Feiffer, Jules 1929- 8
Feig, Barbara Krane 1937- 34
Feikema, Feike
See Manfred, Frederick F(eikema)
Feil, Hila 1942- 12
Feilen, John
See May, Julian
Feldman, Anne (Rodgers)
1939- 19
Félix
See Vincent, Félix
Fellows, Muriel H. 10
Felsen, Henry Gregor 1916- 1
See also SAAS 2
Felton, Harold William 1902- 1
Felton, Ronald Oliver 1909- 3
Felts, Shirley 1934- 33
Fenderson, Lewis H.
1907-1983 47
Obituary 37
Fenner, Carol 1929- 7
Fenner, Phyllis R(eid)
1899-1982 1
Obituary 29
Fenten, Barbara D(oris) 1935- 26
Fenten, D. X. 1932- 4
Fenton, Carroll Lane
1900-1969 5
Fenton, Edward 1917- 7
Fenton, Mildred Adams 1899- 21
Fenwick, Patti
See Grider, Dorothy
Feravolo, Rocco Vincent
1922- 10
Ferber, Edna 1887-1968 7
Ferguson, Bob
See Ferguson, Robert Bruce
Ferguson, Cecil 1931- 45
Ferguson, Robert Bruce 1927- 13
Ferguson, Walter (W.) 1930- 34
Fergusson, Erna 1888-1964 5
Fermi, Laura (Capon)
1907-1977 6
Obituary 28
Fern, Eugene A. 1919- 10
Ferrier, Lucy
See Penzler, Otto
Ferris, Helen Josephine
1890-1969 21
Ferris, James Cody [Collective
pseudonym] 1
See also McFarlane, Leslie;
Stratemeyer, Edward L.
Ferry, Charles 1927- 43
Fetz, Ingrid 1915- 30

Feydy, Anne Lindbergh
Brief Entry 32
See Sapieyevski, Anne Lindbergh
Fiammenghi, Gioia 1929- 9
Fiarotta, Noel 1944- 15
Fiarotta, Phyllis 1942- 15
Fichter, George S. 1922- 7
Fidler, Kathleen (Annie)
1899-1980 3
Obituary 45
Fiedler, Jean 4
Field, Edward 1924- 8
Field, Elinor Whitney 1889-1980
Obituary 28
Field, Eugene 1850-1895 16
Field, Gans T.
See Wellman, Manly Wade
Field, Rachel (Lyman)
1894-1942 15
Fife, Dale (Odile) 1910- 18
Fighter Pilot, A
See Johnston, H(ugh) A(nthony)
S(tephen)
Figueroa, Pablo 1938- 9
Fijan, Carol 1918- 12
Fillmore, Parker H(oysted)
1878-1944 .... YABC 1
Filstrup, Chris
See Filstrup, E(dward) Christian
Filstrup, E(dward) Christian
1942- 43
Filstrup, Jane Merrill
See Merrill, Jane
Filstrup, Janie
See Merrill, Jane
Finder, Martin
See Salzmann, Siegmund
Fine, Anne 1947- 29
Finger, Charles J(oseph)
1869(?)-1941 42
Fink, William B(ertrand)
1916- 22
Finke, Blythe F(oote) 1922- 26
Finkel, George (Irvine)
1909-1975 8
Finlay, Winifred 1910- 23
Finlayson, Ann 1925- 8
Finley, Martha 1828-1909 43
Firmin, Charlotte 1954- 29
Firmin, Peter 1928- 15
Fischbach, Julius 1894- 10
Fischler, Stan(ley I.)
Brief Entry 36
Fishback, Margaret
See Antolini, Margaret Fishback
Fisher, Aileen (Lucia) 1906- 25
Earlier sketch in SATA 1
Fisher, Barbara 1940- 44
Brief Entry 34
Fisher, Clavin C(argill) 1912- 24
Fisher, Dorothy Canfield
1879-1958 .... YABC 1
Fisher, John (Oswald Hamilton)
1909- 15
Fisher, Laura Harrison 1934- 5
Fisher, Leonard Everett 1924- 34
Earlier sketch in SATA 4
See also SAAS 1

Fisher, Lois I. 1948- 38
Brief Entry 35
Fisher, Margery (Turner)
1913- 20
Fisher, Robert (Tempest)
1943- 47
Fisk, Nicholas 1923- 25
Fitch, Clarke
See Sinclair, Upton (Beall)
Fitch, John IV
See Cormier, Robert (Edmund)
Fitschen, Dale 1937- 20
Fitzalan, Roger
See Trevor, Elleston
Fitzgerald, Captain Hugh
See Baum, L(yman) Frank
Fitzgerald, Edward Earl 1919- 20
Fitzgerald, F(rancis) A(nthony)
1940- 15
Fitzgerald, John D(ennis)
1907- 20
See also CLR 1
Fitzhardinge, Joan Margaret
1912- 2
Fitzhugh, Louise (Perkins)
1928-1974 45
Obituary 24
Earlier sketch in SATA 1
See also CLR 1
Flack, Marjorie
1899-1958 .... YABC 2
Flack, Naomi John (White) 40
Brief Entry 35
Flash Flood
See Robinson, Jan M.
Fleischer, Leonore 1934(?)-
Brief Entry 47
Fleischer, Max 1889-1972
Brief Entry 30
Fleischhauer-Hardt, Helga
1936- 30
Fleischman, Paul 1952- 39
Brief Entry 32
Fleischman, (Albert) Sid(ney)
1920- 8
See also CLR 1
Fleisher, Robbin 1951-1977
Brief Entry 49
Fleishman, Seymour 1918-
Brief Entry 32
Fleming, Alice Mulcahey
1928- 9
Fleming, Elizabeth P. 1888-1985
Obituary 48
Fleming, Ian (Lancaster)
1908-1964 9
Fleming, Susan 1932- 32
Fleming, Thomas J(ames)
1927- 8
Fletcher, Charlie May 1897- 3
Fletcher, Colin 1922- 28
Fletcher, Helen Jill 1911- 13
Fletcher, Richard E. 1917(?)-1983
Obituary 34
Fletcher, Rick
See Fletcher, Richard E.
Fleur, Anne 1901-
Brief Entry 31
Flexner, James Thomas 1908- 9

Flitner, David P. 1949- 7
Floethe, Louise Lee 1913- *4*
Floethe, Richard 1901- *4*
Floherty, John Joseph
  1882-1964 25
Flood, Flash
  See Robinson, Jan M.
Flora, James (Royer) 1914- 30
  Earlier sketch in SATA 1
Florian, Douglas 1950- *19*
Flory, Jane Trescott 1917- 22
Flowerdew, Phyllis 33
Floyd, Gareth 1940-
  Brief Entry *31*
Fluchère, Henri A(ndré) 1914- 40
Flynn, Barbara 1928- 9
Flynn, Jackson
  See Shirreffs, Gordon D.
Flynn, Mary
  See Welsh, Mary Flynn
Fodor, Ronald V(ictor) 1944- 25
Foley, (Anna) Bernice Williams
  1902- 28
Foley, June 1944- 44
Foley, (Mary) Louise Munro 1933-
  Brief Entry 40
Foley, Rae
  See Denniston, Elinore
Folkard, Charles James 1878-1963
  Brief Entry 28
Follett, Helen (Thomas) 1884(?)-1970
  Obituary 27
Folsom, Franklin (Brewster)
  1907- 5
Folsom, Michael (Brewster)
  1938- 40
Fontenot, Mary Alice 1910- 34
Fooner, Michael 22
Forberg, Ati 1925- 22
Forbes, Bryan 1926- 37
Forbes, Cabot L.
  See Hoyt, Edwin P(almer), Jr.
Forbes, Esther 1891-1967 .... *2*
Forbes, Graham B. [Collective
  pseudonym] *1*
Forbes, Kathryn
  See McLean, Kathryn (Anderson)
Ford, Albert Lee
  See Stratemeyer, Edward L.
Ford, Barbara
  Brief Entry *34*
Ford, Brian J(ohn) 1939- 49
Ford, Elbur
  See Hibbert, Eleanor
Ford, George (Jr.) *31*
Ford, Hilary
  See Youd, (Christopher) Samuel
Ford, Hildegarde
  See Morrison, Velma Ford
Ford, Marcia
  See Radford, Ruby L.
Ford, Nancy K(effer) 1906-1961
  Obituary 29
Foreman, Michael 1938- *2*
Forest, Antonia 29
Forester, C(ecil) S(cott)
  1899-1966 .... *13*
Forman, Brenda 1936- *4*
Forman, James Douglas 1932- 8

Forrest, Sybil
  See Markun, Patricia M(aloney)
Forrester, Helen 1919- 48
Forrester, Marian
  See Schachtel, Roger
Forrester, Victoria 1940- 40
  Brief Entry 35
Forsee, (Frances) Aylesa *1*
Fort, Paul
  See Stockton, Francis Richard
Fortnum, Peggy 1919- 26
Foster, Brad W. 1955- 34
Foster, Doris Van Liew 1899- 10
Foster, E(lizabeth) C(onnell)
  1902- 9
Foster, Elizabeth 1905-1963 10
Foster, Elizabeth Vincent
  1902- *12*
Foster, F. Blanche 1919- *11*
Foster, G(eorge) Allen
  1907-1969 26
Foster, Genevieve (Stump)
  1893-1979 .... *2*
  Obituary 23
  See also CLR 7
Foster, Hal
  See Foster, Harold Rudolf
Foster, Harold Rudolf 1892-1982
  Obituary 31
Foster, John T(homas) 1925- 8
Foster, Laura Louise 1918- 6
Foster, Margaret Lesser 1899-1979
  Obituary 21
Foster, Marian Curtis
  1909-1978 23
Fourth Brother, The
  See Aung, (Maung) Htin
Fowke, Edith (Margaret)
  1913- *14*
Fowles, John 1926- 22
Fox, Charles Philip 1913- *12*
Fox, Eleanor
  See St. John, Wylly Folk
Fox, Fontaine Talbot, Jr. 1884-1964
  Obituary 23
Fox, Fred 1903(?)-1981
  Obituary 27
Fox, Freeman
  See Hamilton, Charles H. St. John
Fox, Grace
  See Anderson, Grace Fox
Fox, Larry 30
Fox, Lorraine 1922-1975 .... *11*
  Obituary 27
Fox, Mary Virginia 1919- 44
  Brief Entry 39
Fox, Michael Wilson 1937- 15
Fox, Paula 1923- 17
  See also CLR 1
Fox, Petronella
  See Balogh, Penelope
Fox, Robert J. 1927- 33
Fradin, Dennis Brindel 1945- 29
Frame, Paul 1913-
  Brief Entry 33
Frances, Miss
  See Horwich, Frances R.
Franchere, Ruth *18*

Francis, Charles
  See Holme, Bryan
Francis, Dee
  See Haas, Dorothy F.
Francis, Dorothy Brenner
  1926- *10*
Francis, Pamela (Mary) 1926- *11*
Franco, Marjorie 38
Francois, André 1915- 25
Francoise
  See Seignobosc, Francoise
Frank, Anne 1929-1945(?)
  Brief Entry *42*
Frank, Josette 1893- *10*
Frank, Mary 1933- *34*
Frank, R., Jr.
  See Ross, Frank (Xavier), Jr.
Frankau, Mary Evelyn 1899- *4*
Frankel, Bernice 9
Frankel, Edward 1910- 44
Frankel, Julie 1947- 40
  Brief Entry 34
Frankenberg, Robert 1911- 22
Franklin, Harold 1920- 13
Franklin, Max
  See Deming, Richard
Franklin, Steve
  See Stevens, Franklin
Franzén, Nils-Olof 1916- 10
Frascino, Edward 1938- 48
  Brief Entry 33
Frasconi, Antonio 1919- 6
Fraser, Antonia (Pakenham) 1932-
  Brief Entry *32*
Fraser, Betty
  See Fraser, Elizabeth Marr
Fraser, Elizabeth Marr 1928- *31*
Fraser, Eric (George)
  1902-1983 38
Frazier, Neta Lohnes 7
Freed, Alvyn M. 1913- 22
Freedman, Benedict 1919- 27
Freedman, Nancy 1920- 27
Freedman, Russell (Bruce)
  1929- 16
Freeman, Barbara C(onstance)
  1906- 28
Freeman, Bill
  See Freeman, William Bradford
Freeman, Don 1908-1978 17
Freeman, Ira M(aximilian)
  1905- 21
Freeman, Lucy (Greenbaum)
  1916- 24
Freeman, Mae (Blacker)
  1907- 25
Freeman, Peter J.
  See Calvert, Patricia
Freeman, Tony
  Brief Entry 44
Freeman, William Bradford 1938-
  Brief Entry 48
Fregosi, Claudia (Anne Marie)
  1946- 24
French, Allen 1870-1946 ..... *YABC 1*
French, Dorothy Kayser 1926- 5
French, Fiona 1944- 6
French, Kathryn
  See Mosesson, Gloria R(ubin)

French, Michael 1944- *49*
  Brief Entry *38*
French, Paul
  See Asimov, Isaac
Freund, Rudolf 1915-1969
  Brief Entry *28*
Frewer, Glyn 1931- *11*
Frick, C. H.
  See Irwin, Constance Frick
Frick, Constance
  See Irwin, Constance Frick
Friedlander, Joanne K(ohn)
  1930- *9*
Friedman, Estelle 1920- *7*
Friedman, Frieda 1905- *43*
Friedman, Ina R(osen) 1926- *49*
  Brief Entry *41*
Friedman, Marvin 1930- *42*
  Brief Entry *33*
Friedrich, Otto (Alva) 1929- *33*
Friedrich, Priscilla 1927- *39*
Friendlich, Dick
  See Friendlich, Richard J.
Friendlich, Richard J. 1909- *11*
Friermood, Elisabeth Hamilton
  1903- *5*
Friis, Babbis
  See Friis-Baastad, Babbis
Friis-Baastad, Babbis
  1921-1970 .... *7*
Frimmer, Steven 1928- *31*
Friskey, Margaret Richards
  1901- *5*
Fritz, Jean (Guttery) 1915- *29*
  Earlier sketch in SATA 1
  See also CLR 2
  See also SAAS 2
Froissart, Jean
  1338(?)-1410(?) *28*
Froman, Elizabeth Hull
  1920-1975 .... *10*
Froman, Robert (Winslow)
  1917- *8*
Fromm, Lilo 1928- *29*
Frommer, Harvey 1937- *41*
Frost, A(rthur) B(urdett)
  1851-1928 .... *19*
Frost, Erica
  See Supraner, Robyn
Frost, Lesley 1899(?)-1983 .... *14*
  Obituary *34*
Frost, Robert (Lee) 1874-1963 .... *14*
Fry, Edward Bernard 1925- *35*
Fry, Rosalie 1911- *3*
Fuchs, Erich 1916- *6*
Fuchshuber, Annegert 1940- *43*
Fujikawa, Gyo 1908- *39*
  Brief Entry *30*
Fujita, Tamao 1905- *7*
Fujiwara, Michiko 1946- *15*
Fuka, Vladimir 1926-1977
  Obituary *27*
Fuller, Catherine L(euthold)
  1916- *9*
Fuller, Edmund (Maybank)
  1914- *21*
Fuller, Iola
  See McCoy, Iola Fuller
Fuller, Lois Hamilton 1915- *11*

Fuller, Margaret
  See Ossoli, Sarah Margaret (Fuller)
  marchesa d'
Fults, John Lee 1932- *33*
Funai, Mamoru (Rolland) 1932-
  Brief Entry *46*
Funk, Thompson
  See Funk, Tom
Funk, Tom 1911- *7*
Funke, Lewis 1912- *11*
Furchgott, Terry 1948- *29*
Furniss, Tim 1948- *49*
Furukawa, Toshi 1924- *24*
Fyleman, Rose 1877-1957 .... *21*
Fyson, J(enny) G(race) 1904- *42*

G

Gackenbach, Dick *48*
  Brief Entry *30*
Gaddis, Vincent H. 1913- *35*
Gadler, Steve J. 1905- *36*
Gaeddert, Lou Ann (Bigge)
  1931- *20*
Gàg, Flavia 1907-1979
  Obituary *24*
Gàg, Wanda (Hazel)
  1893-1946 .... *YABC 1*
  See also CLR 4
Gage, Wilson
  See Steele, Mary Q.
Gagliardo, Ruth Garver 1895(?)-1980
  Obituary *22*
Gal, Laszlo 1933-
  Brief Entry *32*
Galdone, Paul 1914-1986 .... *17*
  Obituary *49*
Galinsky, Ellen 1942- *23*
Gallant, Roy (Arthur) 1924- *4*
Gallico, Paul 1897-1976 .... *13*
Galt, Thomas Franklin, Jr.
  1908- *5*
Galt, Tom
  See Galt, Thomas Franklin, Jr.
Gamerman, Martha 1941- *15*
Gannett, Ruth Chrisman (Arens)
  1896-1979 .... *33*
Gannett, Ruth Stiles 1923- *3*
Gannon, Robert (Haines)
  1931- *8*
Gans, Roma 1894- *45*
Gantos, Jack
  See Gantos, John (Bryan), Jr.
Gantos, John (Bryan), Jr.
  1951- *20*
Garbutt, Bernard 1900-
  Brief Entry *31*
Gard, Joyce
  See Reeves, Joyce
Gard, Robert Edward 1910- *18*
Gard, (Sanford) Wayne 1899-1986
  Obituary *49*
Gardam, Jane 1928- *39*
  Brief Entry *28*
  See also CLR 12
Garden, Nancy 1938- *12*
Gardner, Dic
  See Gardner, Richard

Gardner, Hugh 1910-1986
  Obituary *49*
Gardner, Jeanne LeMonnier *5*
Gardner, John (Champlin, Jr.)
  1933-1982 .... *40*
  Obituary *31*
Gardner, Martin 1914- *16*
Gardner, Richard 1931- *24*
Gardner, Richard A. 1931- *13*
Gardner, Robert 1929-
  Brief Entry *43*
Gardner, Sheldon 1934- *33*
Garelick, May *19*
Garfield, James B. 1881-1984 ..... *6*
  Obituary *38*
Garfield, Leon 1921- *32*
  Earlier sketch in SATA 1
Garis, Howard R(oger)
  1873-1962 .... *13*
Garner, Alan 1934- *18*
Garnett, Eve C. R. *3*
Garraty, John A. 1920- *23*
Garret, Maxwell R. 1917- *39*
Garretson, Victoria Diane
  1945- *44*
Garrett, Helen 1895- *21*
Garrigue, Sheila 1931- *21*
Garrison, Barbara 1931- *19*
Garrison, Frederick
  See Sinclair, Upton (Beall)
Garrison, Webb B(lack) 1919- *25*
Garst, Doris Shannon 1894- *1*
Garst, Shannon
  See Garst, Doris Shannon
Garthwaite, Marion H. 1893- *7*
Garton, Malinda D(ean) (?)-1976
  Obituary *26*
Gasperini, Jim 1952-
  Brief Entry *49*
Gater, Dilys 1944- *41*
Gates, Doris 1901- *34*
  Earlier sketch in SATA 1
  See also SAAS 1
Gates, Frieda 1933- *26*
Gathorne-Hardy, Jonathan G.
  1933- *26*
Gatty, Juliana Horatia
  See Ewing, Juliana (Horatia Gatty)
Gatty, Margaret Scott 1809-1873
  Brief Entry *27*
Gauch, Patricia Lee 1934- *26*
Gault, Clare S. 1925- *36*
Gault, Frank 1926-1982 .... *36*
  Brief Entry *30*
Gault, William Campbell
  1910- *8*
Gaver, Becky
  See Gaver, Rebecca
Gaver, Rebecca 1952- *20*
Gay, Francis
  See Gee, H(erbert) L(eslie)
Gay, Kathlyn 1930- *9*
Gay, Zhenya 1906-1978 .... *19*
Gee, H(erbert) L(eslie) 1901-1977
  Obituary *26*
Gee, Maurice (Gough) 1931- *46*
Geer, Charles 1922- *42*
  Brief Entry *32*
Gehr, Mary *32*

Geipel, Eileen 1932- 30
Geis, Darlene 7
Geisel, Helen 1898-1967 26
Geisel, Theodor Seuss 1904- 28
  Earlier sketch in SATA 1
  See also CLR 1
Geldart, William 1936- 15
Gelinas, Paul J. 1911- 10
Gelman, Steve 1934- 3
Gemming, Elizabeth 1932- 11
Gendel, Evelyn W. 1916(?)-1977
  Obituary 27
Gentle, Mary 1956- 48
Gentleman, David 1930- 7
George, Jean Craighead 1919- 2
  See also CLR 1
George, John L(othar) 1916- 2
George, S(idney) C(harles)
  1898- 11
George, W(illiam) Lloyd 1900(?)-1975
  Obituary 30
Georgiou, Constantine 1927- 7
Gérard, Jean Ignace Isidore
  1803-1847 45
Geras, Adele (Daphne) 1944- 23
Gergely, Tibor 1900-1978
  Obituary 20
Geringer, Laura 1948- 29
Gerler, William R(obert)
  1917- 47
Gerrard, Roy 1935- 47
  Brief Entry 45
Gerson, Corinne 37
Gerson, Noel B(ertram) 1914- 22
Gerstein, Mordicai 1935- 47
  Brief Entry 36
Gesner, Clark 1938- 40
Gessner, Lynne 1919- 16
Gevirtz, Eliezer 1950- 49
Gewe, Raddory
  See Gorey, Edward St. John
Gibbons, Gail 1944- 23
  See also CLR 8
Gibbs, Alonzo (Lawrence)
  1915- 5
Gibbs, (Cecilia) May 1877-1969
  Obituary 27
Gibbs, Tony
  See Gibbs, Wolcott, Jr.
Gibbs, Wolcott, Jr. 1935- 40
Giblin, James Cross 1933- 33
Gibson, Josephine
  See Joslin, Sesyle
Gidal, Sonia 1922- 2
Gidal, Tim N(ahum) 1909- 2
Giegling, John A(llan) 1935- 17
Giff, Patricia Reilly 1935- 33
Gifford, Griselda 1931- 42
Gilbert, Ann
  See Taylor, Ann
Gilbert, Harriett 1948- 30
Gilbert, (Agnes) Joan (Sewell)
  1931- 10
Gilbert, John (Raphael) 1926- ... 36
Gilbert, Miriam
  See Presberg, Miriam Goldstein
Gilbert, Nan
  See Gilbertson, Mildred
Gilbert, Sara (Dulaney) 1943- 11

Gilbert, W(illiam) S(chwenk)
  1836-1911 36
Gilbertson, Mildred Geiger
  1908- 2
Gilbreath, Alice (Thompson)
  1921- 12
Gilbreth, Frank B., Jr. 1911- 2
Gilfond, Henry 2
Gilge, Jeanette 1924- 22
Gill, Derek L(ewis) T(heodore)
  1919- 9
Gill, Margery Jean 1925- 22
Gillett, Mary 7
Gillette, Henry Sampson
  1915- 14
Gillham, Bill
  See Gillham, William Edwin Charles
Gillham, William Edwin Charles
  1936- 42
Gilliam, Stan 1946- 39
  Brief Entry 35
Gilman, Dorothy
  See Butters, Dorothy Gilman
Gilman, Esther 1925- 15
Gilmore, Iris 1900- 22
Gilmore, Mary (Jean Cameron)
  1865-1962 49
Gilson, Barbara
  See Gilson, Charles James Louis
Gilson, Charles James Louis
  1878-1943 ....YABC 2
Gilson, Jamie 1933- 37
  Brief Entry 34
Ginsburg, Mirra 6
Giovanni, Nikki 1943- 24
  See also CLR 6
Giovanopoulos, Paul 1939- 7
Gipson, Frederick B.
  1908-1973 2
  Obituary 24
Girard, Linda Walvoord 1942- 41
Girion, Barbara 1937- 26
Gittings, Jo Manton 1919- 3
Gittings, Robert 1911- 6
Gladstone, Eve
  See Werner, Herma
Gladstone, Gary 1935- 12
Gladstone, M(yron) J. 1923- 37
Gladwin, William Zachary
  See Zollinger, Gulielma
Glanville, Brian (Lester)
  1931- 42
Glanzman, Louis S. 1922- 36
Glaser, Dianne E(lizabeth) 1937-
  Brief Entry 31
Glaser, Milton 1929- 11
Glaspell, Susan
  1882-1948 ....YABC 2
Glass, Andrew
  Brief Entry 46
Glauber, Uta (Heil) 1936- 17
Glazer, Tom 1914- 9
Gleasner, Diana (Cottle)
  1936- 29
Gleason, Judith 1929- 24
Glendinning, Richard 1917- 24
Glendinning, Sally
  See Glendinning, Sara W(ilson)

Glendinning, Sara W(ilson)
  1913- 24
Glenn, Mel 1943-
  Brief Entry 45
Gles, Margaret Breitmaier
  1940- 22
Glick, Carl (Cannon)
  1890-1971 14
Glick, Virginia Kirkus 1893-1980
  Obituary 23
Gliewe, Unada 1927- 3
Glines, Carroll V(ane), Jr.
  1920- 19
Globe, Leah Ain 1900- 41
Glovach, Linda 1947- 7
Glubok, Shirley 6
  See also CLR 1
Gluck, Felix 1924(?)-1981
  Obituary 25
Glynne-Jones, William 1907- 11
Gobbato, Imero 1923- 39
Goble, Dorothy 26
Goble, Paul 1933- 25
Goble, Warwick (?)-1943 46
Godden, Rumer 1907- 36
  Earlier sketch in SATA 3
Gode, Alexander
  See Gode von Aesch, Alexander
  (Gottfried Friedrich)
Gode von Aesch, Alexander (Gottfried
  Friedrich) 1906-1970 14
Godfrey, Jane
  See Bowden, Joan Chase
Godfrey, William
  See Youd, (Christopher) Samuel
Goettel, Elinor 1930- 12
Goetz, Delia 1898- 22
Goffstein, M(arilyn) B(rooke)
  1940- 8
  See also CLR 3
Golann, Cecil Paige 1921- 11
Golbin, Andrée 1923- 15
Gold, Phyllis 1941- 21
Gold, Sharlya 9
Goldberg, Herbert S. 1926- 25
Goldberg, Stan J. 1939- 26
Goldfeder, Cheryl
  See Pahz, Cheryl Suzanne
Goldfeder, Jim
  See Pahz, James Alon
Goldfrank, Helen Colodny
  1912- 6
Goldin, Augusta 1906- 13
Goldsborough, June 1923- 19
Goldsmith, Howard 1943- 24
Goldsmith, Oliver 1728-1774 26
Goldstein, Nathan 1927- 47
Goldstein, Philip 1910- 23
Goldston, Robert (Conroy)
  1927- 6
Goll, Reinhold W(eimar)
  1897- 26
Gonzalez, Gloria 1940- 23
Goodall, John S(trickland)
  1908- 4
Goodbody, Slim
  See Burstein, John
Goode, Diane 1949- 15

Goode, Stephen 1943-
 Brief Entry 40
Goodenow, Earle 1913- 40
Goodman, Deborah Lerme 1956-
 Brief Entry 49
Goodman, Elaine 1930- 9
Goodman, Walter 1927- 9
Goodrich, Samuel Griswold
 1793-1860 23
Goodwin, Hal
 See Goodwin, Harold Leland
Goodwin, Harold Leland
 1914- 13
Goor, Nancy (Ruth Miller)
 1944- 39
 Brief Entry 34
Goor, Ron(ald Stephen) 1940- 39
 Brief Entry 34
Goossen, Agnes
 See Epp, Margaret A(gnes)
Gordon, Bernard Ludwig
 1931- 27
Gordon, Colonel H. R.
 See Ellis, Edward S(ylvester)
Gordon, Donald
 See Payne, Donald Gordon
Gordon, Dorothy 1893-1970 20
Gordon, Esther S(aranga)
 1935- 10
Gordon, Frederick [Collective
 pseudonym] 1
Gordon, Hal
 See Goodwin, Harold Leland
Gordon, John 1925- 6
Gordon, John
 See Gesner, Clark
Gordon, Lew
 See Baldwin, Gordon C.
Gordon, Margaret (Anna)
 1939- 9
Gordon, Mildred 1912-1979
 Obituary 24
Gordon, Selma
 See Lanes, Selma G.
Gordon, Shirley 1921- 48
 Brief Entry 41
Gordon, Sol 1923- 11
Gordon, Stewart
 See Shirreffs, Gordon D.
Gordons, The [Joint pseudonym]
 See Gordon, Mildred
Gorelick, Molly C. 1920- 9
Gorey, Edward St. John
 1925- 29
 Brief Entry 27
Gorham, Charles Orson
 1911-1975 36
Gorham, Michael
 See Folsom, Franklin
Gormley, Beatrice 1942- 39
 Brief Entry 35
Gorog, Judith (Allen) 1938- 39
Gorsline, Douglas (Warner)
 1913-1985 11
 Obituary 43
Gorsline, (Sally) Marie 1928- 28
Gorsline, S. M.
 See Gorsline, (Sally) Marie

Goryan, Sirak
 See Saroyan, William
Goscinny, René 1926-1977 47
 Brief Entry 39
Gottlieb, Bill
 See Gottlieb, William P(aul)
Gottlieb, Gerald 1923- 7
Gottlieb, William P(aul) 24
Goudey, Alice E. 1898- 20
Goudge, Elizabeth 1900-1984 2
 Obituary 38
Gough, Catherine 1931- 24
Gough, Philip 1908- 45
Goulart, Ron 1933- 6
Gould, Chester 1900-1985 49
 Obituary 43
Gould, Jean R(osalind) 1919- 11
Gould, Lilian 1920- 6
Gould, Marilyn 1923- 15
Govan, Christine Noble 1898- 9
Govern, Elaine 1939- 26
Graaf, Peter
 See Youd, (Christopher) Samuel
Graber, Alexander 7
Graber, Richard (Fredrick)
 1927- 26
Grabiański, Janusz 1929-1976 39
 Obituary 30
Graboff, Abner 1919- 35
Grace, F(rances Jane) 45
Graeber, Charlotte Towner
 Brief Entry 44
Graff, Polly Anne
 See Colver, Anne
Graff, (S.) Stewart 1908- 9
Graham, Ada 1931- 11
Graham, Brenda Knight 1942- 32
Graham, Charlotte
 See Bowden, Joan Chase
Graham, Eleanor 1896-1984 18
 Obituary 38
Graham, Frank, Jr. 1925- 11
Graham, John 1926- 11
Graham, Kennon
 See Harrison, David Lee
Graham, Lorenz B(ell) 1902- 2
 See also CLR 10
Graham, Margaret Bloy 1920- 11
Graham, Robin Lee 1949- 7
Graham, Shirley
 See Du Bois, Shirley Graham
Graham-Barber, Lynda 1944- 42
Graham-Cameron, M(alcolm) G(ordon)
 1931-
 Brief Entry 45
Graham-Cameron, Mike
 See Graham-Cameron, M(alcolm)
 G(ordon)
Grahame, Kenneth
 1859-1932 .... YABC 1
 See also CLR 5
Gramatky, Hardie 1907-1979 30
 Obituary 23
 Earlier sketch in SATA 1
Grand, Samuel 1912- 42
Grandville, J. J.
 See Gérard, Jean Ignace Isidore
Grandville, Jean Ignace Isidore Gérard
 See Gérard, Jean Ignace Isidore

Grange, Peter
 See Nicole, Christopher Robin
Granger, Margaret Jane 1925(?)-1977
 Obituary 27
Granger, Peggy
 See Granger, Margaret Jane
Granstaff, Bill 1925- 10
Grant, Bruce 1893-1977 5
 Obituary 25
Grant, Cynthia D. 1950- 33
Grant, Eva 1907- 7
Grant, Evva H. 1913-1977
 Obituary 27
Grant, Gordon 1875-1962 25
Grant, Gwen(doline Ellen)
 1940- 47
Grant, (Alice) Leigh 1947- 10
Grant, Matthew C.
 See May, Julian
Grant, Maxwell
 See Lynds, Dennis
Grant, Myrna (Lois) 1934- 21
Grant, Neil 1938- 14
Gravel, Fern
 See Hall, James Norman
Graves, Charles Parlin
 1911-1972 4
Graves, Robert (von Ranke)
 1895-1985 45
Gray, Elizabeth Janet 1902- 6
Gray, Genevieve S. 1920- 4
Gray, Harold (Lincoln)
 1894-1968 33
 Brief Entry 32
Gray, Jenny
 See Gray, Genevieve S.
Gray, Marian
 See Pierce, Edith Gray
Gray, Nicholas Stuart
 1922-1981 4
 Obituary 27
Gray, Nigel 1941- 33
Gray, (Lucy) Noel (Clervaux)
 1898-1983 47
Gray, Patricia 7
Gray, Patsey
 See Gray, Patricia
Grayland, V. Merle
 See Grayland, Valerie
Grayland, Valerie 7
Great Comte, The
 See Hawkesworth, Eric
Greaves, Margaret 1914- 7
Grée, Alain 1936- 28
Green, Adam
 See Weisgard, Leonard
Green, D.
 See Casewit, Curtis
Green, Hannah
 See Greenberg, Joanne (Goldenberg)
Green, Jane 1937- 9
Green, Mary Moore 1906- 11
Green, Morton 1937- 8
Green, Norma B(erger) 1925- 11
Green, Phyllis 1932- 20
Green, Roger (Gilbert) Lancelyn
 1918- 2
Green, Sheila Ellen 1934- 8

Greenaway, Kate
1846-1901 ....YABC 2
See also CLR 6
Greenbank, Anthony Hunt
1933- 39
Greenberg, Harvey R. 1935- 5
Greenberg, Joanne (Goldenberg)
1932- 25
Greenberg, Polly 1932-
Brief Entry 43
Greene, Bette 1934- 8
See also CLR 2
Greene, Carla 1916- 1
Greene, Carol
Brief Entry 44
Greene, Constance C(larke)
1924- 11
Greene, Ellin 1927- 23
Greene, Graham 1904- 20
Greene, Laura 1935- 38
Greene, Wade 1933- 11
Greenfeld, Howard 19
Greenfield, Eloise 1929- 19
See also CLR 4
Greenhaus, Thelma Nurenberg
1903-1984 45
Greening, Hamilton
See Hamilton, Charles H. St. John
Greenleaf, Barbara Kaye
1942- 6
Greenleaf, Peter 1910- 33
Greenwald, Sheila
See Green, Sheila Ellen
Gregg, Walter H(arold) 1919- 20
Gregor, Arthur 1923- 36
Gregori, Leon 1919- 15
Gregorian, Joyce Ballou
1946- 30
Gregorowski, Christopher
1940- 30
Gregory, Diana (Jean) 1933- 49
Brief Entry 42
Gregory, Jean
See Ure, Jean
Gregory, Stephen
See Penzler, Otto
Greisman, Joan Ruth 1937- 31
Grendon, Stephen
See Derleth, August (William)
Grenville, Pelham
See Wodehouse, P(elham)
G(renville)
Gretz, Susanna 1937- 7
Gretzer, John 18
Grey, Jerry 1926- 11
Grey Owl
See Belaney, Archibald Stansfeld
Gri
See Denney, Diana
Grice, Frederick 1910- 6
Grider, Dorothy 1915- 31
Gridley, Marion E(leanor)
1906-1974 35
Obituary 26
Grieder, Walter 1924- 9
Griese, Arnold A(lfred) 1921- 9
Grifalconi, Ann 1929- 2
Griffin, Gillett Good 1928- 26
Griffin, Judith Berry 34

Griffith, Helen V(irginia)
1934- 39
Griffith, Jeannette
See Eyerly, Jeanette
Griffiths, G(ordon) D(ouglas)
1910-1973
Obituary 20
Griffiths, Helen 1939- 5
Grimm, Cherry Barbara Lockett 1930-
Brief Entry 43
Grimm, Jacob Ludwig Karl
1785-1863 22
Grimm, Wilhelm Karl
1786-1859 22
Grimm, William C(arey)
1907- 14
Grimshaw, Nigel (Gilroy)
1925- 23
Grimsley, Gordon
See Groom, Arthur William
Gringhuis, Dirk
See Gringhuis, Richard H.
Gringhuis, Richard H.
1918-1974 6
Obituary 25
Grinnell, George Bird
1849-1938 16
Gripe, Maria (Kristina) 1923- 2
See also CLR 5
Groch, Judith (Goldstein)
1929- 25
Grode, Redway
See Gorey, Edward St. John
Grohskopf, Bernice 7
Grol, Lini Richards 1913- 9
Grollman, Earl A. 1925- 22
Groom, Arthur William
1898-1964 10
Gross, Alan 1947-
Brief Entry 43
Gross, Ruth Belov 1929- 33
Gross, Sarah Chokla
1906-1976 9
Obituary 26
Grossman, Nancy 1940- 29
Grossman, Robert 1940- 11
Groth, John 1908- 21
Groves, Georgina
See Symons, (Dorothy) Geraldine
Gruelle, John (Barton)
1880-1938 35
Brief Entry 32
Gruelle, Johnny
See Gruelle, John
Gruenberg, Sidonie M(atsner)
1881-1974 2
Obituary 27
Grummer, Arnold E(dward)
1923- 49
Guck, Dorothy 1913- 27
Gugliotta, Bobette 1918- 7
Guillaume, Jeanette G. (Flierl)
1899- 8
Guillot, Rene 1900-1969 7
Gundersheimer, Karen
Brief Entry 44
Gundrey, Elizabeth 1924- 23
Gunn, James E(dwin) 1923- 35

Gunston, Bill
See Gunston, William Tudor
Gunston, William Tudor
1927- 9
Gunterman, Bertha Lisette
1886(?)-1975
Obituary 27
Gunther, John 1901-1970 2
Gurko, Leo 1914- 9
Gurko, Miriam 9
Gustafson, Anita 1942-
Brief Entry 45
Gustafson, Sarah R.
See Riedman, Sarah R.
Gustafson, Scott 1956- 34
Guthrie, Anne 1890-1979 28
Gutman, Bill
Brief Entry 43
Gutman, Naham 1899(?)-1981
Obituary 25
Guy, Rosa (Cuthbert) 1928- 14
Gwynne, Fred(erick Hubbard)
1926- 41
Brief Entry 27

H

Haas, Carolyn Buhai 1926- 43
Haas, Dorothy F. 46
Brief Entry 43
Haas, Irene 1929- 17
Haas, James E(dward) 1943- 40
Haas, Merle S. 1896(?)-1985
Obituary 41
Habenstreit, Barbara 1937- 5
Haber, Louis 1910- 12
Hader, Berta (Hoerner)
1891(?)-1976 16
Hader, Elmer (Stanley)
1889-1973 16
Hadley, Franklin
See Winterbotham, R(ussell)
R(obert)
Hadley, Lee 1934- 47
Brief Entry 38
Hafner, Marylin 1925- 7
Hager, Alice Rogers 1894-1969
Obituary 26
Haggard, H(enry) Rider
1856-1925 16
Haggerty, James J(oseph)
1920- 5
Hagon, Priscilla
See Allan, Mabel Esther
Hague, (Susan) Kathleen
1949- 49
Brief Entry 45
Hague, Michael (Riley) 1948- 48
Brief Entry 32
Hahn, Emily 1905- 3
Hahn, Hannelore 1926- 8
Hahn, James (Sage) 1947- 9
Hahn, (Mona) Lynn 1949- 9
Hahn, Mary Downing 1937-
Brief Entry 44
Haig-Brown, Roderick (Langmere)
1909-1976 12
Haight, Anne Lyon 1895-1977
Obituary 30

Haines, Gail Kay 1943- *11*
Haining, Peter 1940- *14*
Halacy, D(aniel) S(tephen), Jr.
  1919- *36*
Haldane, Roger John 1945- *13*
Hale, Arlene 1924-1982 .... *49*
Hale, Edward Everett
  1822-1909 .... *16*
Hale, Helen
  See Mulcahy, Lucille Burnett
Hale, Irina 1932- *26*
Hale, Kathleen 1898- *17*
Hale, Linda 1929- *6*
Hale, Lucretia Peabody
  1820-1900 .... *26*
Hale, Nancy 1908- *31*
Haley, Gail E(inhart) 1939- *43*
  Brief Entry *28*
Hall, Adam
  See Trevor, Elleston
Hall, Adele 1910- *7*
Hall, Anna Gertrude
  1882-1967 .... *8*
Hall, Borden
  See Yates, Raymond F(rancis)
Hall, Brian P(atrick) 1935- *31*
Hall, Caryl
  See Hansen, Caryl (Hall)
Hall, Donald (Andrew, Jr.)
  1928- *23*
Hall, Douglas 1931- *43*
Hall, Elvajean *6*
Hall, James Norman
  1887-1951 .... *21*
Hall, Jesse
  See Boesen, Victor
Hall, Katy
  See McMullan, Kate (Hall)
Hall, Lynn 1937- *47*
  Earlier sketch in SATA 2
  See also SAAS 4
Hall, Malcolm 1945- *7*
Hall, Marjory
  See Yeakley, Marjory Hall
Hall, Rosalys Haskell 1914- *7*
Hallard, Peter
  See Catherall, Arthur
Hallas, Richard
  See Knight, Eric (Mowbray)
Hall-Clarke, James
  See Rowland-Entwistle, (Arthur)
  Theodore (Henry)
Haller, Dorcas Woodbury
  1946- *46*
Halliburton, Warren J. 1924- *19*
Hallin, Emily Watson 1919- *6*
Hallinan, P(atrick) K(enneth)
  1944- *39*
  Brief Entry *37*
Hallman, Ruth 1929- *43*
  Brief Entry *28*
Hall-Quest, (Edna) Olga W(ilbourne)
  1899-1986 .... *11*
  Obituary *47*
Hallstead, William F(inn) III
  1924- *11*
Hallward, Michael 1889- *12*
Halsell, Grace 1923- *13*

Halsted, Anna Roosevelt 1906-1975
  Obituary *30*
Halter, Jon C(harles) 1941- *22*
Hamalian, Leo 1920- *41*
Hamberger, John 1934- *14*
Hamblin, Dora Jane 1920- *36*
Hamerstrom, Frances 1907- *24*
Hamil, Thomas Arthur 1928- *14*
Hamil, Tom
  See Hamil, Thomas Arthur
Hamill, Ethel
  See Webb, Jean Francis (III)
Hamilton, Alice
  See Cromie, Alice Hamilton
Hamilton, Charles Harold St. John
  1875-1961 .... *13*
Hamilton, Clive
  See Lewis, C. S.
Hamilton, Dorothy 1906-1983 ..... *12*
  Obituary *35*
Hamilton, Edith 1867-1963 ...... *20*
Hamilton, Elizabeth 1906- *23*
Hamilton, Morse 1943- *35*
Hamilton, Robert W.
  See Stratemeyer, Edward L.
Hamilton, Virginia 1936- *4*
  See also CLR 1, 11
Hamley, Dennis 1935- *39*
Hammer, Richard 1928- *6*
Hammerman, Gay M(orenus)
  1926- *9*
Hammond, Winifred G(raham)
  1899- *29*
Hammontree, Marie (Gertrude)
  1913- *13*
Hampson, (Richard) Denman
  1929- *15*
Hampson, Frank 1918(?)-1985
  Obituary *46*
Hamre, Leif 1914- *5*
Hamsa, Bobbie 1944-
  Brief Entry *38*
Hancock, Mary A. 1923- *31*
Hancock, Sibyl 1940- *9*
Handforth, Thomas (Schofield)
  1897-1948 .... *42*
Handville, Robert (Tompkins)
  1924- *45*
Hane, Roger 1940-1974
  Obituary *20*
Haney, Lynn 1941- *23*
Hanff, Helene *11*
Hanlon, Emily 1945- *15*
Hann, Jacquie 1951- *19*
Hanna, Paul R(obert) 1902- *9*
Hano, Arnold 1922- *12*
Hansen, Caryl (Hall) 1929- *39*
Hansen, Joyce 1942- *46*
  Brief Entry *39*
Hanser, Richard (Frederick)
  1909- *13*
Hanson, Joan 1938- *8*
Hanson, Joseph E. 1894(?)-1971
  Obituary *27*
Harald, Eric
  See Boesen, Victor
Harcourt, Ellen Knowles 1890(?)-1984
  Obituary *36*

Hardcastle, Michael 1933- *47*
  Brief Entry *38*
Harding, Lee 1937- *32*
  Brief Entry *31*
Hardwick, Richard Holmes, Jr.
  1923- *12*
Hardy, Alice Dale [Collective
  pseudonym] *1*
Hardy, David A(ndrews)
  1936- *9*
Hardy, Stuart
  See Schisgall, Oscar
Hardy, Thomas 1840-1928 .... *25*
Hare, Norma Q(uarles) 1924- *46*
  Brief Entry *41*
Harford, Henry
  See Hudson, W(illiam) H(enry)
Hark, Mildred
  See McQueen, Mildred Hark
Harkaway, Hal
  See Stratemeyer, Edward L.
Harkins, Philip 1912- *6*
Harlan, Elizabeth 1945- *41*
  Brief Entry *35*
Harlan, Glen
  See Cebulash, Mel
Harman, Fred 1902(?)-1982
  Obituary *30*
Harman, Hugh 1903-1982
  Obituary *33*
Harmelink, Barbara (Mary) *9*
Harmer, Mabel 1894- *45*
Harmon, Margaret 1906- *20*
Harnan, Terry 1920- *12*
Harnett, Cynthia (Mary)
  1893-1981 .... *5*
  Obituary *32*
Harper, Anita 1943- *41*
Harper, Mary Wood
  See Dixon, Jeanne
Harper, Wilhelmina
  1884-1973 .... *4*
  Obituary *26*
Harrah, Michael 1940- *41*
Harrell, Sara Gordon
  See Banks, Sara (Jeanne Gordon
  Harrell)
Harries, Joan 1922- *39*
Harrington, Lyn 1911- *5*
Harris, Aurand 1915- *37*
Harris, Christie 1907- *6*
Harris, Colver
  See Colver, Anne
Harris, Dorothy Joan 1931- *13*
Harris, Janet 1932-1979 .... *4*
  Obituary *23*
Harris, Joel Chandler
  1848-1908 .... *YABC 1*
Harris, Lavinia
  See Johnston, Norma
Harris, Leon A., Jr. 1926- *4*
Harris, Lorle K(empe) 1912- *22*
Harris, Marilyn
  See Springer, Marilyn Harris
Harris, Mark Jonathan 1941- *32*
Harris, Rosemary (Jeanne) *4*
Harris, Sherwood 1932- *25*
Harrison, C. William 1913- *35*
Harrison, David Lee 1937- *26*

Harrison, Deloris 1938- 9
Harrison, Harry 1925- 4
Harrison, Molly 1909- 41
Harshaw, Ruth H(etzel)
  1890-1968 27
Hart, Bruce 1938-
  Brief Entry 39
Hart, Carole 1943-
  Brief Entry 39
Harte, (Francis) Bret(t)
  1836-1902 26
Hartley, Ellen (Raphael)
  1915- 23
Hartley, Fred Allan III 1953- 41
Hartley, William B(rown)
  1913- 23
Hartman, Evert 1937- 38
  Brief Entry 35
Hartman, Jane E(vangeline)
  1928- 47
Hartman, Louis F(rancis)
  1901-1970 22
Hartshorn, Ruth M. 1928- 11
Harvey, Edith 1908(?)-1972
  Obituary 27
Harwin, Brian
  See Henderson, LeGrand
Harwood, Pearl Augusta (Bragdon)
  1903- 9
Haseley, Dennis
  Brief Entry 44
Haskell, Arnold 1903- 6
Haskins, James 1941- 9
  See also CLR 3
Haskins, Jim
  See Haskins, James
  See also SAAS 4
Hasler, Joan 1931- 28
Hassall, Joan 1906- 43
Hassler, Jon (Francis) 1933- 19
Hatch, Mary Cottam 1912-1970
  Brief Entry 28
Hatlo, Jimmy 1898-1963
  Obituary 23
Haugaard, Erik Christian
  1923- 4
  See also CLR 11
Hauman, Doris 1898- 32
Hauman, George 1890-1961 32
Hauser, Margaret L(ouise)
  1909- 10
Hausman, Gerald 1945- 13
Hausman, Gerry
  See Hausman, Gerald
Hautzig, Deborah 1956- 31
Hautzig, Esther 1930- 4
Havenhand, John
  See Cox, John Roberts
Havighurst, Walter (Edwin)
  1901- 1
Haviland, Virginia 1911- 6
Hawes, Judy 1913- 4
Hawk, Virginia Driving
  See Sneve, Virginia Driving Hawk
Hawkesworth, Eric 1921- 13
Hawkins, Arthur 1903- 19
Hawkins, Quail 1905- 6
Hawkinson, John 1912- 4

Hawkinson, Lucy (Ozone)
  1924-1971 21
Hawley, Mable C. [Collective
  pseudonym] 1
Hawthorne, Captain R. M.
  See Ellis, Edward S(ylvester)
Hawthorne, Nathaniel
  1804-1864 ....YABC 2
Hay, John 1915- 13
Hay, Timothy
  See Brown, Margaret Wise
Haycraft, Howard 1905- 6
Haycraft, Molly Costain
  1911- 6
Hayden, Gwendolen Lampshire
  1904- 35
Hayden, Robert C(arter), Jr.
  1937- 47
  Brief Entry 28
Hayden, Robert E(arl)
  1913-1980 19
  Obituary 26
Hayes, Carlton J. H.
  1882-1964 11
Hayes, Geoffrey 1947- 26
Hayes, John F. 1904- 11
Hayes, Will 7
Hayes, William D(imitt)
  1913- 8
Haynes, Betsy 1937- 48
  Brief Entry 37
Hays, H(offman) R(eynolds)
  1904-1980 26
Hays, Wilma Pitchford 1909- 28
  Earlier sketch in SATA 1
  See also SAAS 3
Hayward, Linda 1943-
  Brief Entry 39
Haywood, Carolyn 1898- 29
  Earlier sketch in SATA 1
Hazen, Barbara Shook 1930- 27
Head, Gay
  See Hauser, Margaret L(ouise)
Headley, Elizabeth
  See Cavanna, Betty
Headstrom, Richard 1902- 8
Heady, Eleanor B(utler) 1917- 8
Heal, Edith 1903- 7
Healey, Brooks
  See Albert, Burton, Jr.
Healey, Larry 1927- 44
  Brief Entry 42
Heaps, Willard (Allison)
  1909- 26
Hearne, Betsy Gould 1942- 38
Heath, Charles D(ickinson)
  1941- 46
Heath, Veronica
  See Blackett, Veronica Heath
Heaven, Constance
  See Fecher, Constance
Hecht, George J(oseph) 1895-1980
  Obituary 22
Hecht, Henri Joseph 1922- 9
Hechtkopf, Henryk 1910- 17
Heck, Bessie Holland 1911- 26
Hedderwick, Mairi 1939- 30
Hedges, Sid(ney) G(eorge)
  1897-1974 28

Hefter, Richard 1942- 31
Hegarty, Reginald Beaton
  1906-1973 10
Heide, Florence Parry 1919- 32
Heiderstadt, Dorothy 1907- 6
Hein, Lucille Eleanor 1915- 20
Heinemann, George Alfred 1918-
  Brief Entry 31
Heinlein, Robert A(nson)
  1907- 9
Heins, Paul 1909- 13
Heintze, Carl 1922- 26
Heinz, W(ilfred) C(harles)
  1915- 26
Heinzen, Mildred
  See Masters, Mildred
Helfman, Elizabeth S(eaver)
  1911- 3
Helfman, Harry 1910- 3
Hellberg, Hans-Eric 1927- 38
Heller, Linda 1944- 46
  Brief Entry 40
Hellman, Hal
  See Hellman, Harold
Hellman, Harold 1927- 4
Helps, Racey 1913-1971 2
  Obituary 25
Helweg, Hans H. 1917-
  Brief Entry 33
Hemming, Roy 1928- 11
Hemphill, Martha Locke
  1904-1973 37
Henderley, Brooks [Collective
  pseudonym] 1
Henderson, LeGrand
  1901-1965 9
Henderson, Nancy Wallace
  1916- 22
Henderson, Zenna (Chlarson)
  1917- 5
Hendrickson, Walter Brookfield, Jr.
  1936- 9
Henkes, Kevin 1960- 43
Henriod, Lorraine 1925- 26
Henry, Joanne Landers 1927- 6
Henry, Marguerite 11
  See also CLR 4
Henry, O.
  See Porter, William Sydney
Henry, Oliver
  See Porter, William Sydney
Henry, T. E.
  See Rowland-Entwistle, (Arthur)
    Theodore (Henry)
Henson, James Maury 1936- 43
Henson, Jim
  See Henson, James Maury
Henstra, Friso 1928- 8
Hentoff, Nat(han Irving)
  1925- 42
  Brief Entry 27
  See also CLR 1
Herald, Kathleen
  See Peyton, Kathleen (Wendy)
Herbert, Cecil
  See Hamilton, Charles H. St. John
Herbert, Don 1917- 2

Herbert, Frank (Patrick)
  1920-1986 37
  Obituary 47
  Earlier sketch in SATA 9
Herbert, Wally
  See Herbert, Walter William
Herbert, Walter William
  1934- 23
Hergé
  See Rémi, Georges
  See also CLR 6
Herkimer, L(awrence) R(ussell)
  1925- 42
Herman, Charlotte 1937- 20
Hermanson, Dennis (Everett)
  1947- 10
Hermes, Patricia 1936- 31
Herriot, James
  See Wight, James Alfred
Herrmanns, Ralph 1933- 11
Herron, Edward A(lbert)
  1912- 4
Hersey, John (Richard) 1914- 25
Hertz, Grete Janus 1915- 23
Hess, Lilo 1916- 4
Heuer, Kenneth John 1927- 44
Heuman, William 1912-1971 21
Hewes, Agnes Danforth
  1874-1963 35
Hewett, Anita 1918- 13
Hext, Harrington
  See Phillpotts, Eden
Hey, Nigel S(tewart) 1936- 20
Heyduck-Huth, Hilde 1929- 8
Heyerdahl, Thor 1914- 2
Heyliger, William
  1884-1955 .... YABC 1
Heyman, Ken(neth Louis)
  1930- 34
Heyward, Du Bose 1885-1940 21
Heywood, Karen 1946- 48
Hibbert, Christopher 1924- 4
Hibbert, Eleanor Burford
  1906- 2
Hickman, Janet 1940- 12
Hickman, Martha Whitmore
  1925- 26
Hickok, Lorena A.
  1892(?)-1968 20
Hickok, Will
  See Harrison, C. William
Hicks, Eleanor B.
  See Coerr, Eleanor
Hicks, Harvey
  See Stratemeyer, Edward L.
Hieatt, Constance B(artlett)
  1928- 4
Hiebert, Ray Eldon 1932- 13
Higdon, Hal 1931- 4
Higginbottom, J(effrey) Winslow
  1945- 29
Highet, Helen
  See MacInnes, Helen
Hightower, Florence Cole
  1916-1981 4
  Obituary 27
Highwater, Jamake 1942- 32
  Brief Entry 30

Hildebrandt, Greg 1939-
  Brief Entry 33
Hildebrandt, Tim 1939-
  Brief Entry 33
Hilder, Rowland 1905- 36
Hildick, E. W.
  See Hildick, Wallace
Hildick, (Edmund) Wallace
  1925- 2
Hill, Donna (Marie) 24
Hill, Douglas (Arthur) 1935- 39
Hill, Elizabeth Starr 1925- 24
Hill, Grace Brooks [Collective
  pseudonym] 1
Hill, Grace Livingston
  1865-1947 .... YABC 2
Hill, Helen M(orey) 1915- 27
Hill, Kathleen Louise 1917- 4
Hill, Kay
  See Hill, Kathleen Louise
Hill, Lorna 1902- 12
Hill, Margaret (Ohler) 1915- 36
Hill, Meg
  See Hill, Margaret (Ohler)
Hill, Monica
  See Watson, Jane Werner
Hill, Robert W(hite)
  1919-1982 12
  Obituary 31
Hill, Ruth A.
  See Viguers, Ruth Hill
Hill, Ruth Livingston
  See Munce, Ruth Hill
Hillcourt, William 1900- 27
Hillerman, Tony 1925- 6
Hillert, Margaret 1920- 8
Hillman, Martin
  See Hill, Douglas (Arthur)
Hillman, Priscilla 1940- 48
  Brief Entry 39
Hills, C(harles) A(lbert) R(eis)
  1955- 39
Hilton, Irene (P.) 1912- 7
Hilton, James 1900-1954 34
Hilton, Ralph 1907- 8
Hilton, Suzanne 1922- 4
Him, George 1900-1982
  Obituary 30
Himler, Ann 1946- 8
Himler, Ronald 1937- 6
Himmelman, John (Carl)
  1959- 47
Hinckley, Helen
  See Jones, Helen Hinckley
Hind, Dolores (Ellen) 1931-
  Brief Entry 49
Hines, Anna G(rossnickle) 1946-
  Brief Entry 45
Hinton, S(usan) E(loise)
  1950- 19
  See also CLR 3
Hinton, Sam 1917- 43
Hintz, (Loren) Martin 1945- 47
  Brief Entry 39
Hirsch, Phil 1926- 35
Hirsch, S. Carl 1913- 2
Hirschmann, Linda (Ann)
  1941- 40
Hirsh, Marilyn 1944- 7

Hirshberg, Al(bert Simon)
  1909-1973 38
Hiser, Iona Seibert 1901- 4
Hitchcock, Alfred (Joseph)
  1899-1980 27
  Obituary 24
Hitte, Kathryn 1919- 16
Hitz, Demi 1942- 11
Hnizdovsky, Jacques 1915- 32
Ho, Minfong 1951- 15
Hoare, Robert J(ohn)
  1921-1975 38
Hoban, Lillian 1925- 22
Hoban, Russell C(onwell)
  1925- 40
  Earlier sketch in SATA 1
  See also CLR 3
Hoban, Tana 22
Hobart, Lois 7
Hoberman, Mary Ann 1930- 5
Hobson, Burton (Harold)
  1933- 28
Hochschild, Arlie Russell
  1940- 11
Hockaby, Stephen
  See Mitchell, Gladys (Maude
  Winifred)
Hockenberry, Hope
  See Newell, Hope (Hockenberry)
Hodge, P(aul) W(illiam)
  1934- 12
Hodgell, P(atricia) C(hristine)
  1951- 42
Hodges, C(yril) Walter 1909- 2
Hodges, Carl G. 1902-1964 10
Hodges, Elizabeth Jamison 1
Hodges, Margaret Moore
  1911- 33
  Earlier sketch in SATA 1
Hodgetts, Blake Christopher
  1967- 43
Hoexter, Corinne K. 1927- 6
Hoff, Carol 1900- 11
Hoff, Syd(ney) 1912- 9
  See also SAAS 4
Hoffman, Edwin D. 49
Hoffman, Phyllis M. 1944- 4
Hoffman, Rosekrans 1926- 15
Hoffmann, E(rnst) T(heodor)
  A(madeus) 1776-1822 27
Hoffmann, Felix 1911-1975 9
Hoffmann, Margaret Jones
  1910- 48
Hoffmann, Peggy
  See Hoffmann, Margaret Jones
Hofsinde, Robert 1902-1973 21
Hogan, Bernice Harris 1929- 12
Hogan, Inez 1895- 2
Hogarth, Jr.
  See Kent, Rockwell
Hogarth, Paul 1917- 41
Hogg, Garry 1902- 2
Hogner, Dorothy Childs 4
Hogner, Nils 1893-1970 25
Hogrogian, Nonny 1932- 7
  See also CLR 2
  See also SAAS 1
Hoh, Diane 1937-
  Brief Entry 48

Hoke, Helen (L.) 1903- 15
Hoke, John 1925- 7
Holbeach, Henry
  See Rands, William Brighty
Holberg, Ruth Langland
  1889- 1
Holbrook, Peter
  See Glick, Carl (Cannon)
Holbrook, Sabra
  See Erickson, Sabra R(ollins)
Holbrook, Stewart Hall
  1893-1964 2
Holden, Elizabeth Rhoda
  See Lawrence, Louise
Holding, James 1907- 3
Holisher, Desider 1901-1972 6
Holl, Adelaide (Hinkle) 8
Holland, Isabelle 1920- 8
Holland, Janice 1913-1962 18
Holland, John L(ewis) 1919- 20
Holland, Lys
  See Gater, Dilys
Holland, Marion 1908- 6
Hollander, John 1929- 13
Hollander, Phyllis 1928- 39
Holldobler, Turid 1939- 26
Holliday, Joe
  See Holliday, Joseph
Holliday, Joseph 1910- 11
Holling, Holling C(lancy)
  1900-1973 15
  Obituary 26
Hollingsworth, Alvin C(arl)
  1930- 39
Holloway, Teresa (Bragunier)
  1906- 26
Holm, (Else) Anne (Lise)
  1922- 1
Holman, Felice 1919- 7
Holme, Bryan 1913- 26
Holmes, Marjorie 1910- 43
Holmes, Oliver Wendell
  1809-1894 34
Holmes, Rick
  See Hardwick, Richard Holmes, Jr.
Holmgren, George Ellen
  See Holmgren, Helen Jean
Holmgren, Helen Jean 1930- 45
Holmgren, Virginia C(unningham)
  1909- 26
Holmquist, Eve 1921- 11
Holt, Margaret 1937- 4
Holt, Margaret Van Vechten
  (Saunders) 1899-1963 32
Holt, Michael (Paul) 1929- 13
Holt, Rackham
  See Holt, Margaret Van Vechten
  (Saunders)
Holt, Rochelle Lynn 1946- 41
Holt, Stephen
  See Thompson, Harlan H.
Holt, Victoria
  See Hibbert, Eleanor
Holton, Leonard
  See Wibberley, Leonard (Patrick
  O'Connor)
Holyer, Erna Maria 1925- 22
Holyer, Ernie
  See Holyer, Erna Maria

Holz, Loretta (Marie) 1943- 17
Homze, Alma C. 1932- 17
Honig, Donald 1931- 18
Honness, Elizabeth H. 1904- 2
Hoobler, Dorothy 28
Hoobler, Thomas 28
Hood, Joseph F. 1925- 4
Hood, Robert E. 1926- 21
Hook, Frances 1912- 27
Hook, Martha 1936- 27
Hooker, Ruth 1920- 21
Hooks, William H(arris)
  1921- 16
Hooper, Byrd
  See St. Clair, Byrd Hooper
Hooper, Meredith (Jean)
  1939- 28
Hoopes, Lyn L(ittlefield)
  1953- 49
  Brief Entry 44
Hoopes, Ned E(dward) 1932- 21
Hoopes, Roy 1922- 11
Hoople, Cheryl G.
  Brief Entry 32
Hoover, H(elen) M(ary) 1935- ... 44
  Brief Entry 33
Hoover, Helen (Drusilla Blackburn)
  1910-1984 12
  Obituary 39
Hope, Laura Lee [Collective
  pseudonym] 1
  See also Adams, Harriet
  S(tratemeyer)
Hope Simpson, Jacynth 1930- 12
Hopf, Alice L(ightner) 1904- 5
Hopkins, A. T.
  See Turngren, Annette
Hopkins, Clark 1895-1976
  Obituary 34
Hopkins, Joseph G(erard) E(dward)
  1909- 11
Hopkins, Lee Bennett 1938- 3
  See also SAAS 4
Hopkins, Lyman
  See Folsom, Franklin
Hopkins, Marjorie 1911- 9
Hoppe, Joanne 1932- 42
Hopper, Nancy J. 1937- 38
  Brief Entry 35
Horgan, Paul 1903- 13
Hornblow, Arthur (Jr.)
  1893-1976 15
Hornblow, Leonora (Schinasi)
  1920- 18
Horne, Richard Henry
  1803-1884 29
Horner, Althea (Jane) 1926- 36
Horner, Dave 1934- 12
Hornos, Axel 1907- 20
Horvath, Betty 1927- 4
Horwich, Frances R(appaport)
  1908- 11
Horwitz, Elinor Lander 45
  Brief Entry 33
Hosford, Dorothy (Grant)
  1900-1952 22
Hosford, Jessie 1892- 5
Hoskyns-Abrahall, Clare 13
Houck, Carter 1924- 22

Hough, (Helen) Charlotte
  1924- 9
Hough, Richard (Alexander)
  1922- 17
Houghton, Eric 1930- 7
Houlehen, Robert J. 1918- 18
Household, Geoffrey (Edward West)
  1900- 14
Houselander, (Frances) Caryll
  1900-1954
  Brief Entry 31
Housman, Laurence
  1865-1959 25
Houston, James A(rchibald)
  1921- 13
  See also CLR 3
Houton, Kathleen
  See Kilgore, Kathleen
Howard, Alan 1922- 45
Howard, Alyssa
  See Buckholtz, Eileen (Garber)
Howard, Elizabeth
  See Mizner, Elizabeth Howard
Howard, Prosper
  See Hamilton, Charles H. St. John
Howard, Robert West 1908- 5
Howard, Vernon (Linwood)
  1918- 40
Howarth, David 1912- 6
Howe, Deborah 1946-1978 29
Howe, James 1946- 29
  See also CLR 9
Howell, Pat 1947- 15
Howell, S.
  See Styles, Frank Showell
Howell, Virginia Tier
  See Ellison, Virginia Howell
Howes, Barbara 1914- 5
Howker, Janni
  Brief Entry 46
Hoy, Nina
  See Roth, Arthur J(oseph)
Hoyle, Geoffrey 1942- 18
Hoyt, Edwin P(almer), Jr.
  1923- 28
Hoyt, Olga (Gruhzit) 1922- 16
Hubbell, Patricia 1928- 8
Hubley, Faith (Elliot) 1924- 48
Hubley, John 1914-1977 48
  Obituary 24
Hudson, Jeffrey
  See Crichton, (J.) Michael
Hudson, (Margaret) Kirsty
  1947- 32
Hudson, W(illiam) H(enry)
  1841-1922 35
Huffaker, Sandy 1943- 10
Huffman, Tom 24
Hughes, Dean 1943- 33
Hughes, (James) Langston
  1902-1967 33
  Earlier sketch in SATA 4
Hughes, Matilda
  See MacLeod, Charlotte (Matilda
  Hughes)
Hughes, Monica 1925- 15
  See also CLR 9

Hughes, Richard (Arthur Warren)
1900-1976 8
Obituary 25
Hughes, Sara
See Saunders, Susan
Hughes, Shirley 1929- *16*
Hughes, Ted 1930- *49*
Brief Entry *27*
See also CLR 3
Hughes, Thomas 1822-1896 .... *31*
Hughes, Walter (Llewellyn)
1910- 26
Hugo, Victor (Marie)
1802-1885 .... *47*
Huline-Dickens, Frank William
1931- *34*
Hull, Eleanor (Means) 1913- *21*
Hull, Eric Traviss
See Harnan, Terry
Hull, H. Braxton
See Jacobs, Helen Hull
Hull, Katharine 1921-1977 .... *23*
Hülsmann, Eva 1928- *16*
Hults, Dorothy Niebrugge
1898- 6
Hume, Lotta Carswell 7
Hume, Ruth (Fox) 1922-1980 26
Obituary 22
Hummel, Berta 1909-1946 .... *43*
Hummel, Sister Maria Innocentia
See Hummel, Berta
Humphrey, Henry (III) 1930- *16*
Humphreys, Graham 1945-
Brief Entry *32*
Hungerford, Pixie
See Brinsmead, H(esba) F(ay)
Hunt, Francis
See Stratemeyer, Edward L.
Hunt, Irene 1907- 2
See also CLR 1
Hunt, Joyce 1927- *31*
Hunt, Linda Lawrence 1940- *39*
Hunt, Mabel Leigh 1892-1971 .... *1*
Obituary 26
Hunt, Morton 1920- 22
Hunt, Nigel
See Greenbank, Anthony Hunt
Hunter, Bernice Thurman 1922-
Brief Entry 45
Hunter, Clingham, M.D.
See Adams, William Taylor
Hunter, Dawe
See Downie, Mary Alice
Hunter, Edith Fisher 1919- *31*
Hunter, Evan 1926- 25
Hunter, Hilda 1921- 7
Hunter, Kristin (Eggleston)
1931- *12*
See also CLR 3
Hunter, Leigh
See Etchison, Birdie L(ee)
Hunter, Mel 1927- *39*
Hunter, Mollie
See McIllwraith, Maureen
Hunter, Norman (George Lorimer)
1899- 26
Hunter Blair, Pauline 1921- *3*
Huntington, Harriet E(lizabeth)
1909- *1*

Huntsberry, William E(mery)
1916- 5
Hurd, Clement 1908- 2
Hurd, Edith Thacher 1910- 2
Hurd, Thacher 1949- 46
Brief Entry 45
Hürlimann, Bettina 1909-1983 ... 39
Obituary 34
Hürlimann, Ruth 1939- 32
Brief Entry 31
Hurwitz, Johanna 1937- 20
Hurwood, Bernhardt J. 1926- 12
Hutchens, Paul 1902-1977 31
Hutchins, Carleen Maley
1911- 9
Hutchins, Pat 1942- 15
Hutchins, Ross E(lliott) 1906- 4
Hutchmacher, J. Joseph 1929- 5
Hutto, Nelson (Allen) 1904- 20
Hutton, Warwick 1939- 20
Hyde, Dayton O(gden) 9
Hyde, Hawk
See Hyde, Dayton O(gden)
Hyde, Margaret Oldroyd
1917- 42
Earlier sketch in SATA 1
Hyde, Shelley
See Reed, Kit
Hyde, Wayne F. 1922- 7
Hylander, Clarence J.
1897-1964 7
Hyman, Robin P(hilip) 1931- *12*
Hyman, Trina Schart 1939- 46
Earlier sketch in SATA 7
Hymes, Lucia M. 1907- 7
Hyndman, Jane Andrews
1912-1978 46
Obituary 23
Earlier sketch in SATA 1
Hyndman, Robert Utley
1906(?)-1973 18

I

Iannone, Jeanne 7
Ibbotson, Eva 1925- 13
Ibbotson, M. C(hristine)
1930- 5
Ichikawa, Satomi 1949- 47
Brief Entry 36
Ilowite, Sheldon A. 1931- 27
Ilsley, Dent [Joint pseudonym]
See Chapman, John Stanton Higham
Ilsley, Velma (Elizabeth)
1918- 12
Immel, Mary Blair 1930- 28
Ingelow, Jean 1820-1897 33
Ingham, Colonel Frederic
See Hale, Edward Everett
Ingraham, Leonard W(illiam)
1913- 4
Ingrams, Doreen 1906- 20
Inyart, Gene 1927- 6
Ionesco, Eugene 1912- 7
Ipcar, Dahlov (Zorach) 1917- 49
Earlier sketch in SATA 1
Irvin, Fred 1914- 15
Irving, Alexander
See Hume, Ruth (Fox)

Irving, Robert
See Adler, Irving
Irving, Washington
1783-1859 .... *YABC* 2
Irwin, Ann(abelle Bowen)
1915- 44
Brief Entry 38
Irwin, Constance Frick 1913- 6
Irwin, Hadley [Joint pseudonym]
See Hadley, Lee and Irwin, Ann
Irwin, Keith Gordon
1885-1964 .... *11*
Isaac, Joanne 1934- 21
Isaacs, Jacob
See Kranzler, George G(ershon)
Isadora, Rachel 1953(?)-
Brief Entry 32
See also CLR 7
Isham, Charlotte H(ickox)
1912- *21*
Ish-Kishor, Judith 1892-1972 ... *11*
Ish-Kishor, Sulamith
1896-1977 .... *17*
Ishmael, Woodi 1914- *31*
Israel, Elaine 1945- *12*
Israel, Marion Louise 1882-1973
Obituary 26
Iwamatsu, Jun Atsushi 1908- 14

J

Jac, Lee
See Morton, Lee Jack, Jr.
Jackson, Anne 1896(?)-1984
Obituary 37
Jackson, C. Paul 1902- 6
Jackson, Caary
See Jackson, C. Paul
Jackson, Jesse 1908-1983 29
Obituary 48
Earlier sketch in SATA 2
Jackson, O. B.
See Jackson, C. Paul
Jackson, Robert B(lake) 1926- 8
Jackson, Sally
See Kellogg, Jean
Jackson, Shirley 1919-1965 2
Jacob, Helen Pierce 1927- *21*
Jacobi, Kathy
Brief Entry 42
Jacobs, Flora Gill 1918- 5
Jacobs, Francine 1935- 43
Brief Entry 42
Jacobs, Frank 1929- 30
Jacobs, Helen Hull 1908- 12
Jacobs, Joseph 1854-1916 25
Jacobs, Leland Blair 1907- 20
Jacobs, Linda C. 1943- 21
Jacobs, Lou(is), Jr. 1921- 2
Jacobs, Susan 1940- 30
Jacobs, William Jay 1933- 28
Jacobson, Daniel 1923- 12
Jacobson, Morris K(arl) 1906- 21
Jacopetti, Alexandra 1939- 14
Jacques, Robin 1920- 32
Brief Entry 30
Jaffee, Al(lan) 1921-
Brief Entry 37

Jagendorf, Moritz (Adolf)
1888-1981 2
Obituary 24
Jahn, (Joseph) Michael 1943- 28
Jahn, Mike
See Jahn, (Joseph) Michael
Jahsmann, Allan Hart 1916- 28
James, Andrew
See Kirkup, James
James, Dynely
See Mayne, William
James, Edwin
See Gunn, James E(dwin)
James, Harry Clebourne 1896- 11
James, Josephine
See Sterne, Emma Gelders
James, T. F.
See Fleming, Thomas J(ames)
James, Will(iam Roderick)
1892-1942 19
Jane, Mary Childs 1909- 6
Janes, Edward C. 1908- 25
Janeway, Elizabeth (Hall)
1913- 19
Janice
See Brustlein, Janice Tworkov
Janosch
See Eckert, Horst
Jansen, Jared
See Cebulash, Mel
Janson, Dora Jane 1916- 31
Janson, H(orst) W(oldemar)
1913- 9
Jansson, Tove (Marika) 1914- 41
Earlier sketch in SATA 3
See also CLR 2
Janus, Grete
See Hertz, Grete Janus
Jaques, Faith 1923- 21
Jaques, Francis Lee 1887-1969
Brief Entry 28
Jarman, Rosemary Hawley
1935- 7
Jarrell, Mary von Schrader
1914- 35
Jarrell, Randall 1914-1965 7
See also CLR 6
Jarrett, Roxanne
See Werner, Herma
Jauss, Anne Marie 1907- 10
Jayne, Lieutenant R. H.
See Ellis, Edward S(ylvester)
Jaynes, Clare [Joint pseudonym]
See Mayer, Jane Rothschild
Jeake, Samuel, Jr.
See Aiken, Conrad
Jefferds, Vincent H(arris) 1916-
Brief Entry 49
Jefferies, (John) Richard
1848-1887 16
Jeffers, Susan 17
Jefferson, Sarah
See Farjeon, Annabel
Jeffries, Roderic 1926- 4
Jenkins, Marie M. 1909- 7
Jenkins, William A(twell)
1922- 9
Jennings, Gary (Gayne) 1928- 9

Jennings, Robert
See Hamilton, Charles H. St. John
Jennings, S. M.
See Meyer, Jerome Sydney
Jennison, C. S.
See Starbird, Kaye
Jennison, Keith Warren 1911- 14
Jensen, Niels 1927- 25
Jensen, Virginia Allen 1927- 8
Jeppson, J(anet) O(pal) 1926-
Brief Entry 46
Jeschke, Susan 42
Brief Entry 27
Jessel, Camilla (Ruth) 1937- 29
Jewell, Nancy 1940-
Brief Entry 41
Jewett, Eleanore Myers
1890-1967 5
Jewett, Sarah Orne 1849-1909 15
Jezard, Alison 1919-
Brief Entry 34
Jiler, John 1946- 42
Brief Entry 35
Jobb, Jamie 1945- 29
Joerns, Consuelo 44
Brief Entry 33
John, Naomi
See Flack, Naomi John (White)
Johns, Avery
See Cousins, Margaret
Johnson, A. E. [Joint pseudonym]
See Johnson, Annabell and Johnson,
Edgar
Johnson, Annabell Jones
1921- 2
Johnson, Benj. F., of Boone
See Riley, James Whitcomb
Johnson, Charles R. 1925- 11
Johnson, Charlotte Buel
1918-1982 46
Johnson, Chuck
See Johnson, Charles R.
Johnson, Crockett
See Leisk, David (Johnson)
Johnson, D(ana) William
1945- 23
Johnson, Dorothy M(arie)
1905-1984 6
Obituary 40
Johnson, E(ugene) Harper 44
Johnson, Edgar Raymond
1912- 2
Johnson, Elizabeth 1911-1984 7
Obituary 39
Johnson, Eric W(arner) 1918- 8
Johnson, Evelyne 1932- 20
Johnson, Gaylord 1884- 7
Johnson, Gerald White
1890-1980 19
Obituary 28
Johnson, Harper
See Johnson, E(ugene) Harper
Johnson, James Ralph 1922- 1
Johnson, James Weldon
See Johnson, James William
Johnson, James William
1871-1938 31
Johnson, Jane 1951- 48
Johnson, John E(mil) 1929- 34

Johnson, LaVerne B(ravo)
1925- 13
Johnson, Lois S(mith) 6
Johnson, Lois W(alfrid) 1936- 22
Johnson, Margaret S(weet)
1893-1964 35
Johnson, Mary Frances K.
1929(?)-1979
Obituary 27
Johnson, Maud Battle 1918(?)-1985
Obituary 46
Johnson, Milton 1932- 31
Johnson, Natalie
See Robison, Nancy L(ouise)
Johnson, (Walter) Ryerson
1901- 10
Johnson, Shirley K(ing) 1927- 10
Johnson, Siddie Joe 1905-1977
Obituary 20
Johnson, Spencer 1938-
Brief Entry 38
Johnson, William R. 38
Johnson, William Weber
1909- 7
Johnston, Agnes Christine
See Dazey, Agnes J.
Johnston, Annie Fellows
1863-1931 37
Johnston, H(ugh) A(nthony) S(tephen)
1913-1967 14
Johnston, Johanna
1914(?)-1982 12
Obituary 33
Johnston, Norma 29
Johnston, Portia
See Takakjian, Portia
Johnston, Tony 1942- 8
Jonas, Ann 1932-
Brief Entry 42
See also CLR 12
Jones, Adrienne 1915- 7
Jones, Diana Wynne 1934- 9
Jones, Elizabeth Orton 1910- 18
Jones, Evan 1915- 3
Jones, Geraldine 1951- 43
Jones, Gillingham
See Hamilton, Charles H. St. John
Jones, Harold 1904- 14
Jones, Helen Hinckley 1903- 26
Jones, Helen L. 1904(?)-1973
Obituary 22
Jones, Hettie 1934- 42
Brief Entry 27
Jones, Hortense P. 1918- 9
Jones, Jessie Mae Orton 1887(?)-1983
Obituary 37
Jones, Margaret Boone
See Zarif, Margaret Min'imah
Jones, Mary Alice 6
Jones, McClure 34
Jones, Penelope 1938- 31
Jones, Rebecca C(astaldi)
1947- 33
Jones, Weyman 1928- 4
Jonk, Clarence 1906- 10
Jordan, Don
See Howard, Vernon (Linwood)
Jordan, E(mil) L(eopold) 1900-
Brief Entry 31

Jordan, Hope (Dahle) 1905- 15
Jordan, Jael (Michal) 1949- 30
Jordan, June 1936- 4
　See also CLR 10
Jordan, Mildred 1901- 5
Jorgensen, Mary Venn 36
Jorgenson, Ivar
　See Silverberg, Robert
Joseph, Joan 1939- 34
Joseph, Joseph M(aron)
　1903-1979 22
Joslin, Sesyle 1929- 2
Joyce, J(ames) Avery 11
Joyce, William 1959(?)-
　Brief Entry 46
Joyner, Jerry 1938- 34
Jucker, Sita 1921- 5
Judd, Denis (O'Nan) 1938- 33
Judd, Frances K. [Collective
　pseudonym] 1
Judson, Clara Ingram
　1879-1960 38
　Brief Entry 27
Jukes, Mavis
　Brief Entry 43
Jumpp, Hugo
　See MacPeek, Walter G.
Jupo, Frank J. 1904- 7
Juster, Norton 1929- 3
Justus, May 1898- 1
Juvenilia
　See Taylor, Ann

K

Kabdebo, Tamas
　See Kabdebo, Thomas
Kabdebo, Thomas 1934- 10
Kabibble, Osh
　See Jobb, Jamie
Kadesch, Robert R(udstone)
　1922- 31
Kahl, M(arvin) P(hilip) 1934- 37
Kahl, Virginia (Caroline)
　1919- 48
　Brief Entry 38
Kahn, Joan 1914- 48
Kahn, Roger 1927- 37
Kakimoto, Kozo 1915- 11
Kalashnikoff, Nicholas
　1888-1961 16
Kalb, Jonah 1926- 23
Kaler, James Otis 1848-1912 15
Kalnay, Francis 1899- 7
Kalow, Gisela 1946- 32
Kamen, Gloria 1923- 9
Kamerman, Sylvia E.
　See Burack, Sylvia K.
Kamm, Josephine (Hart)
　1905- 24
Kandell, Alice S. 1938- 35
Kane, Henry Bugbee
　1902-1971 14
Kane, Robert W. 1910- 18
Kanetzke, Howard W(illiam)
　1932- 38
Kanzawa, Toshiko
　See Furukawa, Toshi
Kaplan, Anne Bernays 1930- 32

Kaplan, Bess 1927- 22
Kaplan, Boche 1926- 24
Kaplan, Irma 1900- 10
Kaplan, Jean Caryl Korn
　1926- 10
Karageorge, Michael
　See Anderson, Poul (William)
Karasz, Ilonka 1896-1981
　Obituary 29
Karen, Ruth 1922- 9
Kark, Nina Mary 1925- 4
Karl, Jean E(dna) 1927- 34
Karlin, Eugene 1918- 10
Karp, Naomi J. 1926- 16
Kashiwagi, Isami 1925- 10
Kästner, Erich 1899-1974 14
　See also CLR 4
Katchen, Carole 1944- 9
Kathryn
　See Searle, Kathryn Adrienne
Katona, Robert 1949- 21
Katsarakis, Joan Harries
　See Harries, Joan
Katz, Bobbi 1933- 12
Katz, Fred 1938- 6
Katz, Jane 1934- 33
Katz, Marjorie P.
　See Weiser, Marjorie P(hillis) K(atz)
Katz, William Loren 1927- 13
Kaufman, Joe 1911- 33
Kaufman, Mervyn D. 1932- 4
Kaufmann, Angelika 1935- 15
Kaufmann, John 1931- 18
Kaula, Edna Mason 1906- 13
Kavaler, Lucy 1930- 23
Kay, Helen
　See Goldfrank, Helen Colodny
Kay, Mara 13
Kaye, Geraldine 1925- 10
Keane, Bil 1922- 4
Keating, Bern
　See Keating, Leo Bernard
Keating, Lawrence A.
　1903-1966 23
Keating, Leo Bernard 1915- 10
Keats, Ezra Jack 1916-1983 14
　Obituary 34
　See also CLR 1
Keegan, Marcia 1943- 9
Keel, Frank
　See Keeler, Ronald F(ranklin)
Keeler, Ronald F(ranklin)
　1913-1983 47
Keen, Martin L. 1913- 4
Keene, Carolyn [Collective
　pseudonym]
　See Adams, Harriet S.
Keeping, Charles (William James)
　1924- 9
Keeshan, Robert J. 1927- 32
Keir, Christine
　See Pullein-Thompson, Christine
Keith, Carlton
　See Robertson, Keith
Keith, Hal 1934- 36
Keith, Harold (Verne) 1903- 2
Keith, Robert
　See Applebaum, Stan

Kelen, Emery 1896-1978 13
　Obituary 26
Kelleam, Joseph E(veridge)
　1913-1975 31
Keller, B(everly) L(ou) 13
Keller, Charles 1942- 8
Keller, Dick 1923- 36
Keller, Gail Faithfull
　See Faithfull, Gail
Keller, Holly
　Brief Entry 42
Keller, Irene (Barron) 1927- 36
Kelley, Leo P(atrick) 1928- 32
　Brief Entry 31
Kelley, True Adelaide 1946- 41
　Brief Entry 39
Kellin, Sally Moffet 1932- 9
Kelling, Furn L. 1914- 37
Kellogg, Gene
　See Kellogg, Jean
Kellogg, Jean 1916- 10
Kellogg, Steven 1941- 8
　See also CLR 6
Kellow, Kathleen
　See Hibbert, Eleanor
Kelly, Eric P(hilbrook)
　1884-1960 .... *YABC 1*
Kelly, Martha Rose
　1914-1983 37
Kelly, Marty
　See Kelly, Martha Rose
Kelly, Ralph
　See Geis, Darlene
Kelly, Regina Z. 5
Kelly, Rosalie (Ruth) 43
Kelly, Walt(er Crawford)
　1913-1973 18
Kelsey, Alice Geer 1896- 1
Kemp, Gene 1926- 25
Kempner, Mary Jean
　1913-1969 10
Kempton, Jean Welch 1914- 10
Kendall, Carol (Seeger) 1917- 11
Kendall, Lace
　See Stoutenburg, Adrien
Kenealy, James P. 1927-
　Brief Entry 29
Kenealy, Jim
　See Kenealy, James P.
Kennedy, John Fitzgerald
　1917-1963 11
Kennedy, Joseph 1929- 14
Kennedy, Paul E(dward)
　1929- 33
Kennedy, (Jerome) Richard
　1932- 22
Kennedy, T(eresa) A. 1953- 42
　Brief Entry 35
Kennedy, X. J.
　See Kennedy, Joseph
Kennell, Ruth E(pperson)
　1893-1977 6
　Obituary 25
Kenny, Ellsworth Newcomb
　1909-1971
　Obituary 26
Kenny, Herbert A(ndrew)
　1912- 13

Kenny, Kathryn
  See Bowden, Joan Chase
  See Krull, Kathleen
Kenny, Kevin
  See Krull, Kathleen
Kent, Alexander
  See Reeman, Douglas Edward
Kent, David
  See Lambert, David (Compton)
Kent, Deborah Ann 1948- 47
  Brief Entry 41
Kent, Jack
  See Kent, John Wellington
Kent, John Wellington
  1920-1985 24
  Obituary 45
Kent, Margaret 1894- 2
Kent, Rockwell 1882-1971 6
Kent, Sherman 1903-1986 20
  Obituary 47
Kenward, Jean 1920- 42
Kenworthy, Leonard S. 1912- 6
Kenyon, Ley 1913- 6
Kepes, Juliet A(ppleby) 1919- 13
Kerigan, Florence 1896- 12
Kerman, Gertrude Lerner
  1909- 21
Kerr, Jessica 1901- 13
Kerr, (Anne) Judith 1923- 24
Kerr, M. E.
  See Meaker, Marijane
  See also SAAS 1
Kerry, Frances
  See Kerigan, Florence
Kerry, Lois
  See Duncan, Lois S(teinmetz)
Ker Wilson, Barbara 1929- 20
Kessel, Joyce Karen 1937- 41
Kessler, Ethel 1922- 44
  Brief Entry 37
Kessler, Leonard P. 1921- 14
Kesteven, G. R.
  See Crosher, G(eoffry) R(obins)
Ketcham, Hank
  See Ketcham, Henry King
Ketcham, Henry King 1920- 28
  Brief Entry 27
Kettelkamp, Larry 1933- 2
  See also SAAS 3
Kevles, Bettyann 1938- 23
Key, Alexander (Hill)
  1904-1979 8
  Obituary 23
Keyes, Daniel 1927- 37
Keyes, Fenton 1915- 34
Keyser, Marcia 1933- 42
Keyser, Sarah
  See McGuire, Leslie (Sarah)
Khanshendel, Chiron
  See Rose, Wendy
Kherdian, David 1931- 16
Kidd, Ronald 1948- 42
Kiddell, John 1922- 3
Kidwell, Carl 1910- 43
Kiefer, Irene 1926- 21
Kiesel, Stanley 1925- 35
Kikukawa, Cecily H. 1919- 44
  Brief Entry 35
Kilgore, Kathleen 1946- 42

Kilian, Crawford 1941- 35
Killilea, Marie (Lyons) 1913- 2
Kilreon, Beth
  See Walker, Barbara K.
Kimball, Yeffe 1914-1978 37
Kimbrough, Emily 1899- 2
Kimmel, Eric A. 1946- 13
Kimmel, Margaret Mary
  1938- 43
  Brief Entry 33
Kindred, Wendy 1937- 7
Kines, Pat Decker 1937- 12
King, Adam
  See Hoare, Robert J(ohn)
King, Arthur
  See Cain, Arthur H.
King, Billie Jean 1943- 12
King, (David) Clive 1924- 28
King, Cynthia 1925- 7
King, Frank O. 1883-1969
  Obituary 22
King, Marian 1900(?)-1986 23
  Obituary 47
King, Martin
  See Marks, Stan(ley)
King, Martin Luther, Jr.
  1929-1968 14
King, Reefe
  See Barker, Albert W.
King, Stephen 1947- 9
King, Tony 1947- 39
Kingman, Dong (Moy Shu)
  1911- 44
Kingman, (Mary) Lee 1919- 1
  See also SAAS 3
Kingsland, Leslie William
  1912- 13
Kingsley, Charles
  1819-1875 .... YABC 2
Kingsley, Emily Perl 1940- 33
King-Smith, Dick 1922- 47
  Brief Entry 38
Kinney, C. Cle 1915- 6
Kinney, Harrison 1921- 13
Kinney, Jean Stout 1912- 12
Kinsey, Elizabeth
  See Clymer, Eleanor
Kipling, (Joseph) Rudyard
  1865-1936 .... YABC 2
Kirk, Ruth (Kratz) 1925- 5
Kirkland, Will
  See Hale, Arlene
Kirkup, James 1927- 12
Kirkus, Virginia
  See Glick, Virginia Kirkus
Kirtland, G. B.
  See Joslin, Sesyle
Kishida, Eriko 1929- 12
Kisinger, Grace Gelvin
  1913-1965 10
Kissin, Eva H. 1923- 10
Kjelgaard, James Arthur
  1910-1959 17
Kjelgaard, Jim
  See Kjelgaard, James Arthur
Klagsbrun, Francine (Lifton) 36
Klaperman, Gilbert 1921- 33

Klaperman, Libby Mindlin
  1921-1982 33
  Obituary 31
Klass, Morton 1927- 11
Klass, Sheila Solomon 1927- 45
Kleberger, Ilse 1921- 5
Klein, Aaron E. 1930- 45
  Brief Entry 28
Klein, Gerda Weissmann
  1924- 44
Klein, H. Arthur 8
Klein, Leonore 1916- 6
Klein, Mina C(ooper) 8
Klein, Norma 1938- 7
  See also CLR 2
  See also SAAS 1
Klein, Robin 1936-
  Brief Entry 45
Klemm, Edward G., Jr. 1910- 30
Klemm, Roberta K(ohnhorst)
  1884- 30
Klevin, Jill Ross 1935- 39
  Brief Entry 38
Kliban, B. 1935- 35
Klimowicz, Barbara 1927- 10
Kline, Suzy 1943-
  Brief Entry 48
Klug, Ron(ald) 1939- 31
Knapp, Ron 1952- 34
Knebel, Fletcher 1911- 36
Knickerbocker, Diedrich
  See Irving, Washington
Knifesmith
  See Cutler, Ivor
Knight, Anne (Katherine)
  1946- 34
Knight, Damon 1922- 9
Knight, David C(arpenter) 14
Knight, Eric (Mowbray)
  1897-1943 18
Knight, Francis Edgar 14
Knight, Frank
  See Knight, Francis Edgar
Knight, Hilary 1926- 15
Knight, Mallory T.
  See Hurwood, Bernhardt J.
Knight, Ruth Adams 1898-1974
  Obituary 20
Knott, Bill
  See Knott, William Cecil, Jr.
Knott, William Cecil, Jr.
  1927- 3
Knotts, Howard (Clayton, Jr.)
  1922- 25
Knowles, Anne 1933- 37
Knowles, John 1926- 8
Knox, Calvin
  See Silverberg, Robert
Knox, (Mary) Eleanor Jessie
  1909- 30
Knox, James
  See Brittain, William
Knudsen, James 1950- 42
Knudson, Richard L(ewis)
  1930- 34
Knudson, R. R.
  See Knudson, Rozanne
Knudson, Rozanne 1932- 7
Koch, Dorothy Clarke 1924- 6

Kocsis, J. C.
   See Paul, James
Koehn, Ilse
   See Van Zwienen, Ilse (Charlotte
      Koehn)
Koerner, W(illiam) H(enry) D(avid)
   1878-1938 21
Kohl, Herbert 1937- 47
Kohler, Julilly H(ouse) 1908-1976
   Obituary 20
Kohn, Bernice (Herstein)
   1920- 4
Kohner, Frederick 1905-1986 10
   Obituary 48
Kolba, Tamara 22
Komisar, Lucy 1942- 9
Komoda, Beverly 1939- 25
Komoda, Kiyo 1937- 9
Komroff, Manuel 1890-1974 2
   Obituary 20
Konigsburg, E(laine) L(obl) 48
   Earlier sketch in SATA 4
   See also CLR 1
Koning, Hans
   See Koningsberger, Hans
Koningsberger, Hans 1921- 5
Konkle, Janet Everest 1917- 12
Koob, Theodora (Johanna Foth)
   1918- 23
Kooiker, Leonie
   See Kooyker-Romijn, Johanna Maria
Kooyker-Romijn, Johanna Maria
   1927- 48
Korach, Mimi 1922- 9
Koren, Edward 1935- 5
Korinetz, Yuri (Iosifovich)
   1923- 9
   See also CLR 4
Korman, Gordon 1963- 49
   Brief Entry 41
Korty, Carol 1937- 15
Kossin, Sandy (Sanford)
   1926- 10
Kotzwinkle, William 1938- 24
   See also CLR 6
Kouhi, Elizabeth 1917-
   Brief Entry 49
Koutoukas, H. M.
   See Rivoli, Mario
Kouts, Anne 1945- 8
Krahn, Fernando 1935- 49
   Brief Entry 31
   See also CLR 3
Kramer, Anthony
   Brief Entry 42
Kramer, George
   See Heuman, William
Kramer, Nora 1896(?)-1984 26
   Obituary 39
Krantz, Hazel (Newman)
   1920- 12
Kranzler, George G(ershon)
   1916- 28
Kranzler, Gershon
   See Kranzler, George G(ershon)
Krasilovsky, Phyllis 1926- 38
   Earlier sketch in SATA 1
Kraske, Robert
   Brief Entry 36

Kraus, Robert 1925- 4
Krauss, Ruth (Ida) 1911- 30
   Earlier sketch in SATA 1
Krautter, Elisa
   See Bialk, Elisa
Krauze, Andrzej 1947-
   Brief Entry 46
Kredel, Fritz 1900-1973 17
Krementz, Jill 1940- 17
   See also CLR 5
Krensky, Stephen (Alan)
   1953- 47
   Brief Entry 41
Kripke, Dorothy Karp 30
Kristof, Jane 1932- 8
Kroeber, Theodora (Kracaw)
   1897- 1
Kroll, Francis Lynde
   1904-1973 10
Kroll, Steven 1941- 19
Kropp, Paul (Stephen) 1948- 38
   Brief Entry 34
Krull, Kathleen 1952-
   Brief Entry 39
Krumgold, Joseph 1908-1980 48
   Obituary 23
   Earlier sketch in SATA 1
Krush, Beth 1918- 18
Krush, Joe 1918- 18
Krüss, James 1926- 8
   See also CLR 9
Kubie, Nora (Gottheil) Benjamin
   1899- 39
Kubinyi, Laszlo 1937- 17
Kuh, Charlotte 1892(?)-1985
   Obituary 43
Kujoth, Jean Spealman 1935-1975
   Obituary 30
Kullman, Harry 1919-1982 35
Kumin, Maxine (Winokur)
   1925- 12
Kunhardt, Dorothy Meserve
   1901(?)-1979
   Obituary 22
Künstler, Morton 1927- 10
Kupferberg, Herbert 1918- 19
Kuratomi, Chizuko 1939- 12
Kurelek, William 1927-1977 8
   Obituary 27
   See also CLR 2
Kurland, Gerald 1942- 13
Kurland, Michael (Joseph)
   1938- 48
Kuskin, Karla (Seidman)
   1932- 2
   See also CLR 4
   See also SAAS 3
Kuttner, Paul 1931- 18
Kuzma, Kay 1941- 39
Kvale, Velma R(uth) 1898- 8
Kyle, Elisabeth
   See Dunlop, Agnes M. R.
Kyte, Kathy S. 1946-
   Brief Entry 44

L

Lacy, Leslie Alexander 1937- 6

Ladd, Veronica
   See Miner, Jane Claypool
Lader, Lawrence 1919- 6
Lady, A
   See Taylor, Ann
Lady Mears
   See Tempest, Margaret Mary
Lady of Quality, A
   See Bagnold, Enid
La Farge, Oliver (Hazard Perry)
   1901-1963 19
La Farge, Phyllis 14
Laffin, John (Alfred Charles)
   1922- 31
La Fontaine, Jean de
   1621-1695 18
Lagercrantz, Rose (Elsa)
   1947- 39
Lagerlöf, Selma (Ottiliana Lovisa)
   1858-1940 15
   See also CLR 7
Laiken, Deirdre S(usan) 1948- 48
   Brief Entry 40
Laimgruber, Monika 1946- 11
Laing, Martha
   See Celestino, Martha Laing
Laird, Jean E(louise) 1930- 38
Laite, Gordon 1925- 31
Lake, Harriet
   See Taylor, Paula (Wright)
Laklan, Carli 1907- 5
la Mare, Walter de
   See de la Mare, Walter
Lamb, Beatrice Pitney 1904- 21
Lamb, Charles 1775-1834 17
Lamb, Elizabeth Searle 1917- 31
Lamb, G(eoffrey) F(rederick) 10
Lamb, Lynton 1907- 10
Lamb, Mary Ann 1764-1847 17
Lamb, Robert (Boyden) 1941- 13
Lambert, David (Compton) 1932-
   Brief Entry 49
Lambert, Janet (Snyder)
   1894-1973 25
Lambert, Saul 1928- 23
Lamburn, Richmal Crompton
   1890-1969 5
Lamorisse, Albert (Emmanuel)
   1922-1970 23
Lampert, Emily 1951-
   Brief Entry 49
Lamplugh, Lois 1921- 17
Lampman, Evelyn Sibley
   1907-1980 4
   Obituary 23
Lamprey, Louise
   1869-1951 .... YABC 2
Lampton, Chris
   See Lampton, Christopher
Lampton, Christopher
   Brief Entry 47
Lancaster, Bruce 1896-1963 9
Lancaster, Matthew 1973(?)-1983
   Obituary 45
Land, Barbara (Neblett) 1923- 16
Land, Jane [Joint pseudonym]
   See Borland, Kathryn Kilby and
      Speicher, Helen Ross (Smith)
Land, Myrick (Ebben) 1922- 15

Land, Ross [Joint pseudonym]
    See Borland, Kathryn Kilby and
    Speicher, Helen Ross (Smith)
Landau, Elaine 1948- 10
Landau, Jacob 1917- 38
Landeck, Beatrice 1904- 15
Landin, Les(lie) 1923- 2
Landshoff, Ursula 1908- 13
Lane, Carolyn 1926- 10
Lane, Jerry
    See Martin, Patricia Miles
Lane, John 1932- 15
Lane, Margaret 1907-
    Brief Entry 38
Lane, Rose Wilder 1886-1968 29
    Brief Entry 28
Lanes, Selma G. 1929- 3
Lang, Andrew 1844-1912 16
Lange, John
    See Crichton, (J.) Michael
Lange, Suzanne 1945- 5
Langley, Noel 1911-1980
    Obituary 25
Langner, Nola 1930- 8
Langone, John (Michael)
    1929- 46
    Brief Entry 38
Langstaff, John 1920- 6
    See also CLR 3
Langstaff, Launcelot
    See Irving, Washington
Langton, Jane 1922- 3
Lanier, Sidney 1842-1881 18
Lansing, Alfred 1921-1975 35
Lantz, Paul 1908- 45
Lantz, Walter 1900- 37
Lappin, Peter 1911- 32
Larom, Henry V. 1903(?)-1975
    Obituary 30
Larrecq, John M(aurice)
    1926-1980 44
    Obituary 25
Larrick, Nancy G. 1910- 4
Larsen, Egon 1904- 14
Larson, Eve
    See St. John, Wylly Folk
Larson, Norita D. 1944- 29
Larson, William H. 1938- 10
Larsson, Carl (Olof)
    1853-1919 35
Lasell, Elinor H. 1929- 19
Lasell, Fen H.
    See Lasell, Elinor H.
Lash, Joseph P. 1909- 43
Lasher, Faith B. 1921- 12
Lasker, David 1950- 38
Lasker, Joe 1919- 9
Lasky, Kathryn 1944- 13
    See also CLR 11
Lassalle, C. E.
    See Ellis, Edward S(ylvester)
Latham, Barbara 1896- 16
Latham, Frank B. 1910- 6
Latham, Jean Lee 1902- 2
Latham, Mavis
    See Clark, Mavis Thorpe
Latham, Philip
    See Richardson, Robert S(hirley)

Lathrop, Dorothy P(ulis)
    1891-1980 14
    Obituary 24
Lathrop, Francis
    See Leiber, Fritz
Lattimore, Eleanor Frances
    1904-1986 7
    Obituary 48
Lauber, Patricia (Grace) 1924- 33
    Earlier sketch in SATA 1
Laugesen, Mary E(akin)
    1906- 5
Laughbaum, Steve 1945- 12
Laughlin, Florence 1910- 3
Lauré, Ettagale
    See Blauer, Ettagale
Lauré, Jason 1940-
    Brief Entry 44
Laurence, Ester Hauser 1935- 7
Laurin, Anne
    See McLaurin, Anne
Lauritzen, Jonreed 1902- 13
Laux, Dorothy 1920- 49
Lavine, David 1928- 31
Lavine, Sigmund A. 1908- 3
Laviolette, Emily A. 1923(?)-1975
    Brief Entry 49
Lawrence, Ann (Margaret)
    1942- 41
Lawrence, Isabelle (Wentworth)
    Brief Entry 29
Lawrence, J. T.
    See Rowland-Entwistle, (Arthur)
    Theodore (Henry)
Lawrence, John 1933- 30
Lawrence, Josephine 1890(?)-1978
    Obituary 24
Lawrence, Linda
    See Hunt, Linda Lawrence
Lawrence, Louise 1943- 38
Lawrence, Louise de Kiriline
    1894- 13
Lawrence, Mildred 1907- 3
Lawson, Carol (Antell) 1946- 42
Lawson, Don(ald Elmer)
    1917- 9
Lawson, Marion Tubbs 1896- 22
Lawson, Robert
    1892-1957 .... YABC 2
    See also CLR 2
Laycock, George (Edwin)
    1921- 5
Lazare, Gerald John 1927- 44
Lazare, Jerry
    See Lazare, Gerald John
Lazarevich, Mila 1942- 17
Lazarus, Keo Felker 1913- 21
Lea, Alec 1907- 19
Lea, Richard
    See Lea, Alec
Leach, Maria 1892-1977 39
    Brief Entry 28
Leacroft, Helen 1919- 6
Leacroft, Richard 1914- 6
Leaf, (Wilbur) Munro
    1905-1976 20
Leaf, VaDonna Jean 1929- 26
Leakey, Richard E(rskine Frere)
    1944- 42

Leander, Ed
    See Richelson, Geraldine
Lear, Edward 1812-1888 18
    See also CLR 1
Leavitt, Jerome E(dward)
    1916- 23
LeBar, Mary E(velyn)
    1910-1982 35
LeCain, Errol 1941- 6
Lederer, Muriel 1929- 48
Lee, Amanda [Joint pseudonym]
    See Buckholtz, Eileen (Garber)
Lee, Benjamin 1921- 27
Lee, Betsy 1949- 37
Lee, Carol
    See Fletcher, Helen Jill
Lee, Dennis (Beynon) 1939- 14
    See also CLR 3
Lee, Doris (Emrick)
    1905-1983 44
    Obituary 35
Lee, (Nelle) Harper 1926- 11
Lee, John R(obert) 1923-1976 27
Lee, Manning de V(illeneuve)
    1894-1980 37
    Obituary 22
Lee, Marian
    See Clish, (Lee) Marian
Lee, Mary Price 1934- 8
Lee, Mildred 1908- 6
Lee, Robert C. 1931- 20
Lee, Robert J. 1921- 10
Lee, Roy
    See Hopkins, Clark
Lee, Tanith 1947- 8
Leekley, Thomas B(riggs)
    1910- 23
Leeming, Jo Ann
    See Leeming, Joseph
Leeming, Joseph 1897-1968 26
Leeson, R. A.
    See Leeson, Robert (Arthur)
Leeson, Robert (Arthur) 1928- 42
Lefler, Irene (Whitney) 1917- 12
Le Gallienne, Eva 1899- 9
Legg, Sarah Martha Ross Bruggeman
    (?)-1982
    Obituary 40
LeGrand
    See Henderson, LeGrand
Le Guin, Ursula K(roeber)
    1929- 4
    See also CLR 3
Legum, Colin 1919- 10
Lehn, Cornelia 1920- 46
Lehr, Delores 1920- 10
Leiber, Fritz 1910- 45
Leichman, Seymour 1933- 5
Leigh, Tom 1947- 46
Leigh-Pemberton, John 1911- 35
Leighton, Clare (Veronica Hope)
    1900(?)- 37
Leighton, Margaret 1896- 1
Leipold, L. Edmond 1902- 16
Leisk, David (Johnson)
    1906-1975 30
    Obituary 26
    Earlier sketch in SATA 1
Leister, Mary 1917- 29

Leitch, Patricia 1933- *11*
LeMair, H(enriette) Willebeek
  1889-1966
  Brief Entry *29*
Lemke, Horst 1922- *38*
Lenanton, C.
  See Oman, Carola (Mary Anima)
Lenard, Alexander 1910-1972
  Obituary *21*
L'Engle, Madeleine 1918- *27*
  Earlier sketch in SATA 1
  See also CLR 1
Lengyel, Cornel Adam 1915- *27*
Lengyel, Emil 1895-1985 .... *3*
  Obituary *42*
Lens, Sidney 1912-1986 .... *13*
  Obituary *48*
Lenski, Lois 1893-1974 .... *26*
  Earlier sketch in SATA 1
Lent, Blair 1930- *2*
Lent, Henry Bolles 1901-1973 .... *17*
Leodhas, Sorche Nic
  See Alger, Leclaire (Gowans)
Leokum, Arkady 1916(?)- *45*
Leonard, Constance (Brink)
  1923- *42*
  Brief Entry *40*
Leonard, Jonathan N(orton)
  1903-1975 .... *36*
Leong Gor Yun
  See Ellison, Virginia Howell
Lerner, Aaron B(unsen) 1920- *35*
Lerner, Carol 1927- *33*
Lerner, Marguerite Rush
  1924- *11*
Lerner, Sharon (Ruth)
  1938-1982 .... *11*
  Obituary *29*
LeRoy, Gen
  Brief Entry *36*
Lerrigo, Marion Olive 1898-1968
  Obituary *29*
LeShan, Eda J(oan) 1922- *21*
  See also CLR 6
LeSieg, Theo
  See Geisel, Theodor Seuss
Leslie, Robert Franklin 1911- *7*
Leslie, Sarah
  See McGuire, Leslie (Sarah)
Lesser, Margaret 1899(?)-1979
  Obituary *22*
Lester, Helen 1936- *46*
Lester, Julius B. 1939- *12*
  See also CLR 2
Le Sueur, Meridel 1900- *6*
Le Tord, Bijou 1945- *49*
Leutscher, Alfred (George)
  1913- *23*
Levai, Blaise 1919- *39*
Levin, Betty 1927- *19*
Levin, Marcia Obrasky 1918- *13*
Levin, Meyer 1905-1981 .... *21*
  Obituary *27*
Levine, David 1926- *43*
  Brief Entry *35*
Levine, Edna S(imon) *35*
Levine, I(srael) E. 1923- *12*
Levine, Joan Goldman *11*
Levine, Joseph 1910- *33*

Levine, Rhoda *14*
Levinson, Nancy Smiler
  1938- *33*
Levinson, Riki
  Brief Entry *49*
Levitin, Sonia 1934- *4*
  See also SAAS 2
Levoy, Myron *49*
  Brief Entry *37*
Levy, Elizabeth 1942- *31*
Lewees, John
  See Stockton, Francis Richard
Lewin, Betsy 1937- *32*
Lewin, Hugh (Francis) 1939-
  Brief Entry *40*
  See also CLR 9
Lewin, Ted 1935- *21*
Lewis, Alfred E. 1912-1968
  Brief Entry *32*
Lewis, Alice C. 1936- *46*
Lewis, Alice Hudson 1895(?)-1971
  Obituary *29*
Lewis, (Joseph) Anthony
  1927- *27*
Lewis, C(live) S(taples)
  1898-1963 .... *13*
  See also CLR 3
Lewis, Claudia (Louise) 1907- *5*
Lewis, E. M. *20*
Lewis, Elizabeth Foreman
  1892-1958 .... *YABC 2*
Lewis, Francine
  See Wells, Helen
Lewis, Hilda (Winifred) 1896-1974
  Obituary *20*
Lewis, Lucia Z.
  See Anderson, Lucia (Lewis)
Lewis, Marjorie 1929- *40*
  Brief Entry *35*
Lewis, Paul
  See Gerson, Noel B(ertram)
Lewis, Richard 1935- *3*
Lewis, Roger
  See Zarchy, Harry
Lewis, Shari 1934- *35*
  Brief Entry *30*
Lewis, Thomas P(arker) 1936- *27*
Lewiton, Mina 1904-1970 .... *2*
Lexau, Joan M. *36*
  Earlier sketch in SATA 1
Ley, Willy 1906-1969 .... *2*
Leydon, Rita (Flodén) 1949- *21*
Leyland, Eric (Arthur) 1911- *37*
L'Hommedieu, Dorothy K(easley)
  1885-1961
  Obituary *29*
Libby, Bill
  See Libby, William M.
Libby, William M. 1927-1984 .... *5*
  Obituary *39*
Liberty, Gene 1924- *3*
Liebers, Arthur 1913- *12*
Lieblich, Irene 1923- *22*
Liers, Emil E(rnest)
  1890-1975 .... *37*
Lietz, Gerald S. 1918- *11*
Lifton, Betty Jean *6*
Lightner, A. M.
  See Hopf, Alice L.

Lignell, Lois 1911- *37*
Lillington, Kenneth (James)
  1916- *39*
Lilly, Charles
  Brief Entry *33*
Lilly, Ray
  See Curtis, Richard (Alan)
Lim, John 1932- *43*
Liman, Ellen (Fogelson)
  1936- *22*
Limburg, Peter R(ichard)
  1929- *13*
Lincoln, C(harles) Eric 1924- *5*
Lindbergh, Anne
  See Sapieyevski, Anne Lindbergh
Lindbergh, Anne Morrow (Spencer)
  1906- *33*
Lindbergh, Charles A(ugustus, Jr.)
  1902-1974 .... *33*
Lindblom, Steven (Winther)
  1946- *42*
  Brief Entry *39*
Linde, Gunnel 1924- *5*
Lindgren, Astrid 1907- *38*
  Earlier sketch in SATA 2
  See also CLR 1
Lindgren, Barbro 1937-
  Brief Entry *46*
Lindman, Maj (Jan)
  1886-1972 .... *43*
Lindop, Edmund 1925- *5*
Lindquist, Jennie Dorothea
  1899-1977 .... *13*
Lindquist, Willis 1908- *20*
Lindsay, Norman (Alfred William)
  1879-1969
  See CLR 8
Lindsay, (Nicholas) Vachel
  1879-1931 .... *40*
Line, Les 1935- *27*
Linfield, Esther *40*
Lingard, Joan *8*
Link, Martin 1934- *28*
Lionni, Leo 1910- *8*
  See also CLR 7
Lipinsky de Orlov, Lino S.
  1908- *22*
Lipkind, William 1904-1974 ...... *15*
Lipman, David 1931- *21*
Lipman, Matthew 1923- *14*
Lippincott, Bertram 1898(?)-1985
  Obituary *42*
Lippincott, Joseph Wharton
  1887-1976 .... *17*
Lippincott, Sarah Lee 1920- *22*
Lippman, Peter J. 1936- *31*
Lipsyte, Robert 1938- *5*
Lisker, Sonia O. 1933- *44*
Lisle, Janet Taylor
  Brief Entry *47*
Lisle, Seward D.
  See Ellis, Edward S(ylvester)
Lisowski, Gabriel 1946- *47*
  Brief Entry *31*
Liss, Howard 1922- *4*
Lissim, Simon 1900-1981
  Brief Entry *28*
List, Ilka Katherine 1935- *6*
Liston, Robert A. 1927- *5*

Litchfield, Ada B(assett)
  1916- 5
Litowinsky, Olga (Jean) 1936- 26
Little, A. Edward
  See Klein, Aaron E.
Little, (Flora) Jean 1932- 2
  See also CLR 4
Little, Mary E. 1912- 28
Littledale, Freya (Lota) 2
Lively, Penelope 1933- 7
  See also CLR 7
Liversidge, (Henry) Douglas
  1913- 8
Livingston, Carole 1941- 42
Livingston, Myra Cohn 1926- 5
  See also CLR 7
  See also SAAS 1
Livingston, Richard R(oland)
  1922- 8
Llerena-Aguirre, Carlos Antonio
  1952- 19
Llewellyn, Richard
  See Llewellyn Lloyd, Richard
  Dafydd Vyvyan
Llewellyn, T. Harcourt
  See Hamilton, Charles H. St. John
Llewellyn Lloyd, Richard Dafydd
  Vyvyan 1906-1983 11
  Obituary 37
Lloyd, Errol 1943- 22
Lloyd, Norman 1909-1980
  Obituary 23
Lloyd, (Mary) Norris 1908- 10
Lobel, Anita 1934- 6
Lobel, Arnold 1933- 6
  See also CLR 5
Lobsenz, Amelia 12
Lobsenz, Norman M. 1919- 6
Lochak, Michèle 1936- 39
Lochlons, Colin
  See Jackson, C. Paul
Locke, Clinton W. [Collective
  pseudonym] 1
Locke, Lucie 1904- 10
Lockwood, Mary
  See Spelman, Mary
Lodge, Bernard 1933- 33
Lodge, Maureen Roffey
  See Roffey, Maureen
Loeb, Robert H., Jr. 1917- 21
Loeper, John J(oseph) 1929- 10
Loescher, Ann Dull 1942- 20
Loescher, Gil(burt Damian)
  1945- 20
Loewenstein, Bernice
  Brief Entry 40
Löfgren, Ulf 1931- 3
Lofting, Hugh 1886-1947 15
Lofts, Norah (Robinson)
  1904-1983 8
  Obituary 36
Logue, Christopher 1926- 23
Loken, Newton (Clayton)
  1919- 26
Lomas, Steve
  See Brennan, Joseph L.
Lomask, Milton 1909- 20
London, Jack 1876-1916 18

London, Jane
  See Geis, Darlene
London, John Griffith
  See London, Jack
Lonergan, (Pauline) Joy (Maclean)
  1909- 10
Lonette, Reisie (Dominee)
  1924- 43
Long, Helen Beecher [Collective
  pseudonym] 1
Long, Judith Elaine 1953- 20
Long, Judy
  See Long, Judith Elaine
Long, Laura Mooney 1892-1967
  Obituary 29
Longfellow, Henry Wadsworth
  1807-1882 19
Longman, Harold S. 1919- 5
Longsworth, Polly 1933- 28
Longtemps, Kenneth 1933- 17
Longway, A. Hugh
  See Lang, Andrew
Loomis, Robert D. 5
Lopshire, Robert 1927- 6
Lord, Athena V. 1932- 39
Lord, Beman 1924- 5
Lord, (Doreen Mildred) Douglas
  1904- 12
Lord, John Vernon 1939- 21
Lord, Nancy
  See Titus, Eve
Lord, Walter 1917- 3
Lorenz, Lee (Sharp) 1932(?)-
  Brief Entry 39
Lorenzini, Carlo 1826-1890 29
Lorraine, Walter (Henry)
  1929- 16
Loss, Joan 1933- 11
Lot, Parson
  See Kingsley, Charles
Lothrop, Harriet Mulford Stone
  1844-1924 20
Louie, Ai-Ling 1949- 40
  Brief Entry 34
Louisburgh, Sheila Burnford
  See Burnford, Sheila
Lourie, Helen
  See Storr, Catherine (Cole)
Love, Katherine 1907- 3
Love, Sandra (Weller) 1940- 26
Lovelace, Delos Wheeler
  1894-1967 7
Lovelace, Maud Hart
  1892-1980 2
  Obituary 23
Lovell, Ingraham
  See Bacon, Josephine Dodge
  (Daskam)
Lovett, Margaret (Rose) 1915- 22
Low, Alice 1926- 11
Low, Elizabeth Hammond
  1898- 5
Low, Joseph 1911- 14
Lowe, Jay, Jr.
  See Loper, John J(oseph)
Lowenstein, Dyno 1914- 6
Lowitz, Anson C.
  1901(?)-1978 18

Lowitz, Sadyebeth (Heath)
  1901-1969 17
Lowrey, Janette Sebring
  1892- 43
Lowry, Lois 1937- 23
  See also CLR 6
  See also SAAS 3
Lowry, Peter 1953- 7
Lowther, George F. 1913-1975
  Obituary 30
Lozier, Herbert 1915- 26
Lubell, Cecil 1912- 6
Lubell, Winifred 1914- 6
Lubin, Leonard B. 1943- 45
  Brief Entry 37
Lucas, E(dward) V(errall)
  1868-1938 20
Lucas, Jerry 1940- 33
Luce, Celia (Geneva Larsen)
  1914- 38
Luce, Willard (Ray) 1914- 38
Luckhardt, Mildred Corell
  1898- 5
Ludden, Allen (Ellsworth)
  1918(?)-1981
  Obituary 27
Ludlam, Mabel Cleland
  See Widdemer, Mabel Cleland
Ludwig, Helen 33
Lueders, Edward (George)
  1923- 14
Lufkin, Raymond H. 1897- 38
Lugard, Flora Louisa Shaw
  1852-1929 21
Luger, Harriett M(andelay)
  1914- 23
Luhrmann, Winifred B(ruce)
  1934- 11
Luis, Earlene W. 1929- 11
Lum, Peter
  See Crowe, Bettina Lum
Lund, Doris (Herold) 1919- 12
Lunn, Janet 1928- 4
Lurie, Alison 1926- 46
Lustig, Loretta 1944- 46
Luther, Frank 1905-1980
  Obituary 25
Luttrell, Guy L. 1938- 22
Luttrell, Ida (Alleene) 1934- 40
  Brief Entry 35
Lutzker, Edythe 1904- 5
Luzzati, Emanuele 1912- 7
Luzzatto, Paola (Caboara)
  1938- 38
Lydon, Michael 1942- 11
Lyfick, Warren
  See Reeves, Lawrence F.
Lyle, Katie Letcher 1938- 8
Lynch, Lorenzo 1932- 7
Lynch, Marietta 1947- 29
Lynch, Patricia (Nora)
  1898-1972 9
Lynds, Dennis 1924- 47
  Brief Entry 37
Lyngseth, Joan
  See Davies, Joan
Lynn, Mary
  See Brokamp, Marilyn

Lynn, Patricia
    See Watts, Mabel Pizzey
Lyon, Elinor 1921- 6
Lyon, Lyman R.
    See De Camp, L(yon) Sprague
Lyons, Dorothy 1907- 3
Lyons, Grant 1941- 30
Lystad, Mary (Hanemann)
    1928- 11
Lyttle, Richard B(ard) 1927- 23
Lytton, Edward G(eorge) E(arle)
    L(ytton) Bulwer-Lytton, Baron
    1803-1873 23

M

Maar, Leonard (F., Jr.) 1927- 30
Maas, Selve 14
Mac
    See MacManus, Seumas
Mac Aodhagáin, Eamon
    See Egan, E(dward) W(elstead)
MacArthur-Onslow, Annette
    (Rosemary) 1933- 26
Macaulay, David (Alexander)
    1946- 46
    Brief Entry 27
    See also CLR 3
MacBeth, George 1932- 4
MacClintock, Dorcas 1932- 8
MacDonald, Anson
    See Heinlein, Robert A(nson)
MacDonald, Betty (Campbell Bard)
    1908-1958 ....YABC 1
Macdonald, Blackie
    See Emrich, Duncan
Macdonald, Dwight
    1906-1982 29
    Obituary 33
MacDonald, George
    1824-1905 33
Mac Donald, Golden
    See Brown, Margaret Wise
Macdonald, Marcia
    See Hill, Grace Livingston
Macdonald, Mary
    See Gifford, Griselda
Macdonald, Shelagh 1937- 25
Macdonald, Zillah K(atherine)
    1885- 11
Mace, Elisabeth 1933- 27
Mace, Varian 1938- 49
MacFarlan, Allan A.
    1892-1982 35
MacFarlane, Iris 1922- 11
MacGregor, Ellen 1906-1954 39
    Brief Entry 27
MacGregor-Hastie, Roy 1929- 3
Machetanz, Frederick 1908- 34
Machin Goodall, Daphne
    (Edith) 37
MacInnes, Helen 1907-1985 22
    Obituary 44
MacIntyre, Elisabeth 1916- 17
Mack, Stan(ley) 17
Mackay, Claire 1930- 40
MacKaye, Percy (Wallace)
    1875-1956 32
MacKellar, William 1914- 4

Macken, Walter 1915-1967 36
Mackenzie, Dr. Willard
    See Stratemeyer, Edward L.
MacKenzie, Garry 1921-
    Brief Entry 31
MacKinstry, Elizabeth
    1879-1956 42
MacLachlan, Patricia
    Brief Entry 42
MacLean, Alistair (Stuart)
    1923- 23
MacLeod, Beatrice (Beach)
    1910- 10
MacLeod, Charlotte (Matilda Hughes)
    1922- 28
MacLeod, Ellen Jane (Anderson)
    1916- 14
MacManus, James
    See MacManus, Seumas
MacManus, Seumas
    1869-1960 25
MacMaster, Eve (Ruth) B(owers)
    1942- 46
MacMillan, Annabelle
    See Quick, Annabelle
MacPeek, Walter G.
    1902-1973 4
    Obituary 25
MacPherson, Margaret 1908- 9
    See also SAAS 4
MacPherson, Thomas George
    1915-1976
    Obituary 30
Macrae, Hawk
    See Barker, Albert W.
MacRae, Travi
    See Feagles, Anita (MacRae)
Macumber, Mari
    See Sandoz, Mari
Madden, Don 1927- 3
Maddison, Angela Mary
    1923- 10
Maddock, Reginald 1912- 15
Madian, Jon 1941- 9
Madison, Arnold 1937- 6
Madison, Winifred 5
Maestro, Betsy 1944-
    Brief Entry 30
Maestro, Giulio 1942- 8
Magorian, James 1942- 32
Maguire, Anne
    See Nearing, Penny
Maguire, Gregory 1954- 28
Maher, Ramona 1934- 13
Mäh|qvist, (Karl) Stefan
    1943- 30
Mahon, Julia C(unha) 1916- 11
Mahony, Elizabeth Winthrop
    1948- 8
Mahood, Kenneth 1930- 24
Mahy, Margaret 1936- 14
    See also CLR 7
Maidoff, Ilka List
    See List, Ilka Katherine
Maik, Henri
    See Hecht, Henri Joseph
Maiorano, Robert 1946- 43
Maitland, Antony (Jasper)
    1935- 25

Major, Kevin 1949- 32
    See also CLR 11
Makie, Pam 1943- 37
Malcolmson, Anne
    See Storch, Anne B. von
Malcolmson, David 1899- 6
Mali, Jane Lawrence 1937-
    Brief Entry 44
Mallowan, Agatha Christie
    See Christie, Agatha (Mary Clarissa)
Malmberg, Carl 1904- 9
Malo, John 1911- 4
Malory, (Sir) Thomas 1410(?)-1471(?)
    Brief Entry 33
Maltese, Michael 1908(?)-1981
    Obituary 24
Malvern, Corinne 1905-1956 34
Malvern, Gladys (?)-1962 23
Manchel, Frank 1935- 10
Manes, Stephen 1949- 42
    Brief Entry 40
Manfred, Frederick F(eikema)
    1912- 30
Mangione, Jerre 1909- 6
Mangurian, David 1938- 14
Maniscalco, Joseph 1926- 10
Manley, Deborah 1932- 28
Manley, Seon 15
    See also CLR 3
    See also SAAS 2
Mann, Peggy 6
Mannheim, Grete (Salomon)
    1909- 10
Manniche, Lise 1943- 31
Manning, Rosemary 1911- 10
Manning-Sanders, Ruth 1895- 15
Manson, Beverlie 1945-
    Brief Entry 44
Manton, Jo
    See Gittings, Jo Manton
Manushkin, Fran 1942- 7
Mapes, Mary A.
    See Ellison, Virginia Howell
Mara, Barney
    See Roth, Arthur J(oseph)
Mara, Jeanette
    See Cebulash, Mel
Marais, Josef 1905-1978
    Obituary 24
Marasmus, Seymour
    See Rivoli, Mario
Marcellino
    See Agnew, Edith J.
Marchant, Bessie
    1862-1941 ....YABC 2
Marchant, Catherine
    See Cookson, Catherine (McMulen)
Marcher, Marion Walden
    1890- 10
Marcus, Rebecca B(rian)
    1907- 9
Margaret, Karla
    See Andersdatter, Karla M(argaret)
Margolis, Richard J(ules)
    1929- 4
Margolis, Vivienne 1922- 46
Mariana
    See Foster, Marian Curtis

Marino, Dorothy Bronson
1912- 14
Maris, Ron
Brief Entry 45
Mark, Jan 1943- 22
See also CLR 11
Mark, Pauline (Dahlin) 1913- 14
Mark, Polly
See Mark, Pauline (Dahlin)
Markins, W. S.
See Jenkins, Marie M.
Markle, Sandra L(ee) 1946-
Brief Entry 41
Marko, Katherine D(olores) 28
Marks, Burton 1930- 47
Brief Entry 43
Marks, Hannah K.
See Trivelpiece, Laurel
Marks, J
See Highwater, Jamake
Marks, J(ames) M(acdonald)
1921- 13
Marks, Margaret L. 1911(?)-1980
Obituary 23
Marks, Mickey Klar 12
Marks, Peter
See Smith, Robert Kimmel
Marks, Rita 1938- 47
Marks, Stan(ley) 1929- 14
Marks-Highwater, J
See Highwater, Jamake
Markun, Patricia M(aloney)
1924- 15
Marlowe, Amy Bell [Collective
pseudonym] 1
Marokvia, Artur 1909- 31
Marokvia, Mireille (Journet)
1918- 5
Marr, John S(tuart) 1940- 48
Marrin, Albert 1936-
Brief Entry 43
Marriott, Alice Lee 1910- 31
Marriott, Pat(ricia) 1920- 35
Mars, W. T.
See Mars, Witold Tadeusz J.
Mars, Witold Tadeusz J.
1912- 3
Marsh, J. E.
See Marshall, Evelyn
Marsh, Jean
See Marshall, Evelyn
Marshall, Anthony D(ryden)
1924- 18
Marshall, (Sarah) Catherine
1914-1983 2
Obituary 34
Marshall, Douglas
See McClintock, Marshall
Marshall, Evelyn 1897- 11
Marshall, James 1942- 6
Marshall, James Vance
See Payne, Donald Gordon
Marshall, Kim
See Marshall, Michael (Kimbrough)
Marshall, Michael (Kimbrough)
1948- 37
Marshall, Percy
See Young, Percy M(arshall)

Marshall, S(amuel) L(yman) A(twood)
1900-1977 21
Marsten, Richard
See Hunter, Evan
Marston, Hope Irvin 1935- 31
Martignoni, Margaret E. 1908(?)-1974
Obituary 27
Martin, Ann M(atthews)
1955- 44
Brief Entry 41
Martin, Bill, Jr.
See Martin, William Ivan
Martin, David Stone 1913- 39
Martin, Dorothy 1921- 47
Martin, Eugene [Collective
pseudonym] 1
Martin, Frances M(cEntee)
1906- 36
Martin, Fredric
See Christopher, Matt(hew F.)
Martin, J(ohn) P(ercival)
1880(?)-1966 15
Martin, Jeremy
See Levin, Marcia Obransky
Martin, Lynne 1923- 21
Martin, Marcia
See Levin, Marcia Obransky
Martin, Nancy
See Salmon, Annie Elizabeth
Martin, Patricia Miles
1899-1986 43
Obituary 48
Earlier sketch in SATA 1
Martin, Peter
See Chaundler, Christine
Martin, René 1891-1977 42
Obituary 20
Martin, Rupert (Claude) 1905- 31
Martin, Stefan 1936- 32
Martin, Vicky
See Storey, Victoria Carolyn
Martin, William Ivan 1916-
Brief Entry 40
Martineau, Harriet
1802-1876 .... YABC 2
Martini, Teri 1930- 3
Marx, Robert F(rank) 1936- 24
Marzani, Carl (Aldo) 1912- 12
Marzollo, Jean 1942- 29
Masefield, John 1878-1967 19
Mason, Edwin A. 1905-1979
Obituary 32
Mason, F. van Wyck
1901-1978 3
Obituary 26
Mason, Frank W.
See Mason, F. van Wyck
Mason, George Frederick
1904- 14
Mason, Miriam (Evangeline)
1900-1973 2
Obituary 26
Mason, Tally
See Derleth, August (William)
Mason, Van Wyck
See Mason, F. van Wyck
Masselman, George
1897-1971 19
Massie, Diane Redfield 16

Masters, Kelly R. 1897- 3
Masters, Mildred 1932- 42
Masters, William
See Cousins, Margaret
Matchette, Katharine E. 1941- ... 38
Math, Irwin 1940- 42
Mathews, Janet 1914- 41
Mathews, Louise
See Tooke, Louise Mathews
Mathiesen, Egon 1907-1976
Obituary 28
Mathieu, Joe
See Mathieu, Joseph P.
Mathieu, Joseph P. 1949- 43
Brief Entry 36
Mathis, Sharon Bell 1937- 7
See also CLR 3
See also SAAS 3
Matson, Emerson N(els)
1926- 12
Matsui, Tadashi 1926- 8
Matsuno, Masako 1935- 6
Matte, (Encarnacion) L'Enc
1936- 22
Matthews, Ann
See Martin, Ann M(atthews)
Matthews, Ellen 1950- 28
Matthews, Jacklyn Meek
See Meek, Jacklyn O'Hanlon
Matthews, Patricia 1927- 28
Matthews, William Henry III
1919- 45
Brief Entry 28
Matthias, Catherine 1945-
Brief Entry 41
Matthiessen, Peter 1927- 27
Mattingley, Christobel (Rosemary)
1931- 37
Matulay, Laszlo 1912- 43
Matulka, Jan 1890-1972
Brief Entry 28
Matus, Greta 1938- 12
Mauser, Patricia Rhoads
1943- 37
Maves, Mary Carolyn 1916- 10
Maves, Paul B(enjamin)
1913- 10
Mawicke, Tran 1911- 15
Max, Peter 1939- 45
Maxon, Anne
See Best, Allena Champlin
Maxwell, Arthur S.
1896-1970 11
Maxwell, Edith 1923- 7
May, Charles Paul 1920- 4
May, Julian 1931- 11
May, Robert Lewis 1905-1976
Obituary 27
May, Robert Stephen 1929- 46
May, Robin
See May, Robert Stephen
Mayberry, Florence V(irginia
Wilson) 10
Mayer, Albert Ignatius, Jr. 1906-1960
Obituary 29
Mayer, Ann M(argaret) 1938- 14
Mayer, Jane Rothschild 1903- 38
Mayer, Marianna 1945- 32

Mayer, Mercer 1943- *32*
  Earlier sketch in SATA 16
  See also CLR 11
Mayerson, Charlotte Leon *36*
Mayhar, Ardath 1930- *38*
Maynard, Chris
  See Maynard, Christopher
Maynard, Christopher 1949-
  Brief Entry *43*
Maynard, Olga 1920- *40*
Mayne, William 1928- *6*
Maynes, Dr. J. O. Rocky
  See Maynes, J. Oscar, Jr.
Maynes, J. O. Rocky, Jr.
  See Maynes, J. Oscar, Jr.
Maynes, J. Oscar, Jr. 1929- *38*
Mayo, Margaret (Mary) 1935- *38*
Mays, Lucinda L(a Bella)
  1924- *49*
Mays, (Lewis) Victor, (Jr.)
  1927- *5*
Mazer, Harry 1925- *31*
Mazer, Norma Fox 1931- *24*
  See also SAAS 1
Mazza, Adriana 1928- *19*
McBain, Ed
  See Hunter, Evan
McCaffery, Janet 1936- *38*
McCaffrey, Anne 1926- *8*
McCaffrey, Mary
  See Szudek, Agnes S(usan)
  P(hilomena)
McCain, Murray (David, Jr.)
  1926-1981 .... *7*
  Obituary *29*
McCall, Edith S. 1911- *6*
McCall, Virginia Nielsen
  1909- *13*
McCallum, Phyllis 1911- *10*
McCann, Gerald 1916- *41*
McCannon, Dindga Fatima
  1947- *41*
McCarter, Neely Dixon 1929- *47*
McCarthy, Agnes 1933- *4*
McCarty, Rega Kramer 1904- *10*
McCaslin, Nellie 1914- *12*
McCaughrean, Geraldine
  See Jones, Geraldine
McCay, Winsor 1869-1934 ...... *41*
McClintock, Marshall
  1906-1967 .... *3*
McClintock, Mike
  See McClintock, Marshall
McClintock, Theodore
  1902-1971 .... *14*
McClinton, Leon 1933- *11*
McCloskey, (John) Robert
  1914- *39*
  Earlier sketch in SATA 2
  See also CLR 7
McClung, Robert M. 1916- *2*
  See also CLR 11
McClure, Gillian Mary 1948- *31*
McConnell, James Douglas
  (Rutherford) 1915- *40*
McCord, Anne 1942- *41*
McCord, David (Thompson Watson)
  1897- *18*
  See also CLR 9

McCord, Jean 1924- *34*
McCormick, Brooks
  See Adams, William Taylor
McCormick, Dell J.
  1892-1949 .... *19*
McCormick, (George) Donald (King)
  1911- *14*
McCormick, Edith (Joan)
  1934- *30*
McCourt, Edward (Alexander)
  1907-1972
  Obituary *28*
McCoy, Iola Fuller *3*
McCoy, J(oseph) J(erome)
  1917- *8*
McCoy, Lois (Rich) 1941- *38*
McCrady, Lady 1951- *16*
McCrea, James 1920- *3*
McCrea, Ruth 1921- *3*
McCullers, (Lula) Carson
  1917-1967 .... *27*
McCulloch, Derek (Ivor Breashur)
  1897-1967
  Obituary *29*
McCulloch, Sarah
  See Ure, Jean
McCullough, Frances Monson
  1938- *8*
McCully, Emily Arnold 1939- *5*
McCurdy, Michael 1942- *13*
McDearmon, Kay *20*
McDermott, Beverly Brodsky
  1941- *11*
McDermott, Gerald 1941- *16*
  See also CLR 9
McDole, Carol
  See Farley, Carol
McDonald, Gerald D.
  1905-1970 .... *3*
McDonald, Jamie
  See Heide, Florence Parry
McDonald, Jill (Masefield)
  1927-1982 .... *13*
  Obituary *29*
McDonald, Lucile Saunders
  1898- *10*
McDonnell, Christine 1949- *34*
McDonnell, Lois Eddy 1914- *10*
McEntee, Dorothy (Layng)
  1902- *37*
McEwen, Robert (Lindley) 1926-1980
  Obituary *23*
McFall, Christie 1918- *12*
McFarland, Kenton D(ean)
  1920- *11*
McFarlane, Leslie 1902-1977 ..... *31*
McGaw, Jessie Brewer 1913- *10*
McGee, Barbara 1943- *6*
McGiffin, (Lewis) Lee (Shaffer)
  1908- *1*
McGill, Marci
  See Ridlon, Marci
McGinley, Phyllis 1905-1978 ..... *44*
  Obituary *24*
  Earlier sketch in SATA 2
McGinnis, Lila S(prague)
  1924- *44*
McGough, Elizabeth (Hemmes)
  1934- *33*

McGovern, Ann *8*
McGowen, Thomas E. 1927- *2*
McGowen, Tom
  See McGowen, Thomas
McGrady, Mike 1933- *6*
McGrath, Thomas 1916- *41*
McGraw, Eloise Jarvis 1915- *1*
McGraw, William Corbin
  1916- *3*
McGregor, Craig 1933- *8*
McGregor, Iona 1929- *25*
McGuire, Edna 1899- *13*
McGuire, Leslie (Sarah) 1945-
  Brief Entry *45*
McGurk, Slater
  See Roth, Arthur J(oseph)
McHargue, Georgess *4*
  See also CLR 2
McHugh, (Berit) Elisabet 1941-
  Brief Entry *44*
McIlwraith, Maureen 1922- *2*
McInerney, Judith Whitelock
  1945- *49*
  Brief Entry *46*
McKay, Donald 1895- *45*
McKay, Robert W. 1921- *15*
McKeever, Marcia
  See Laird, Jean E(louise)
McKenzie, Dorothy Clayton
  1910-1981
  Obituary *28*
McKillip, Patricia A(nne)
  1948- *30*
McKim, Audrey Margaret
  1909- *47*
McKinley, (Jennifer Carolyn) Robin
  Brief Entry *32*
  See also CLR 10
McKown, Robin *6*
McLaurin, Anne 1953- *27*
McLean, Kathryn (Anderson)
  1909-1966 .... *9*
McLeish, Kenneth 1940- *35*
McLenighan, Valjean 1947- *46*
  Brief Entry *40*
McLeod, Emilie Warren
  1926-1982 .... *23*
  Obituary *31*
McLeod, Kirsty
  See Hudson, (Margaret) Kirsty
McLeod, Margaret Vail
  See Holloway, Teresa (Bragunier)
McLoughlin, John C. 1949- *47*
McMahan, Ian
  Brief Entry *45*
McManus, Patrick (Francis)
  1933- *46*
McMeekin, Clark
  See McMeekin, Isabel McLennan
McMeekin, Isabel McLennan
  1895- *3*
McMillan, Bruce 1947- *22*
McMullan, Kate (Hall) 1947-
  Brief Entry *48*
McMullen, Catherine
  See Cookson, Catherine (McMullen)
McMurtrey, Martin A(loysius)
  1921- *21*
McNair, Kate *3*

McNamara, Margaret C(raig)
1915-1981
Obituary 24
McNaught, Harry 32
McNaughton, Colin 1951- 39
McNeely, Jeannette 1918- 25
McNeer, May 1
McNeill, Janet 1907- 1
McNickle, (William) D'Arcy
1904-1977
Obituary 22
McNulty, Faith 1918- 12
McPhail, David M(ichael)
1940- 47
Brief Entry 32
McPharlin, Paul 1903-1948
Brief Entry 31
McPhee, Richard B(yron)
1934- 41
McPherson, James M. 1936- 16
McQueen, Lucinda
Brief Entry 48
McQueen, Mildred Hark
1908- 12
McShean, Gordon 1936- 41
McSwigan, Marie 1907-1962 24
McVicker, Charles (Taggart)
1930- 39
McVicker, Chuck
See McVicker, Charles (Taggart)
McWhirter, Norris (Dewar)
1925- 37
McWhirter, (Alan) Ross
1925-1975 37
Obituary 31
Mead, Margaret 1901-1978
Obituary 20
Mead, Russell (M., Jr.) 1935- 10
Mead, Stella (?)-1981
Obituary 27
Meade, Ellen (Roddick) 1936- 5
Meade, Marion 1934- 23
Meader, Stephen W(arren)
1892- 1
Meadow, Charles T(roub)
1929- 23
Meadowcroft, Enid LaMonte
See Wright, Enid Meadowcroft
Meaker, M. J.
See Meaker, Marijane
Meaker, Marijane 1927- 20
Means, Florence Crannell
1891-1980 1
Obituary 25
Mearian, Judy Frank 1936- 49
Medary, Marjorie 1890- 14
Meddaugh, Susan 1944- 29
Medearis, Mary 1915- 5
Mee, Charles L., Jr. 1938- 8
Meek, Jacklyn O'Hanlon 1933-
Brief Entry 34
Meek, S(terner St.) P(aul) 1894-1972
Obituary 28
Meeker, Oden 1918(?)-1976 14
Meeks, Esther MacBain 1
Meggendorfer, Lothar 1847-1925
Brief Entry 36
Mehdevi, Alexander 1947- 7

Mehdevi, Anne (Marie)
Sinclair 8
Meighan, Donald Charles
1929- 30
Meigs, Cornelia Lynde
1884-1973 6
Meilach, Dona Z(weigoron)
1926- 34
Melady, John 1938-
Brief Entry 49
Melcher, Daniel 1912-1985
Obituary 43
Melcher, Frederic Gershom 1879-1963
Obituary 22
Melcher, Marguerite Fellows
1879-1969 10
Melin, Grace Hathaway
1892-1973 10
Mellersh, H(arold) E(dward) L(eslie)
1897- 10
Meltzer, Milton 1915- 1
See also SAAS 1
Melville, Anne
See Potter, Margaret (Newman)
Melwood, Mary
See Lewis, E. M.
Melzack, Ronald 1929- 5
Memling, Carl 1918-1969 6
Mendel, Jo [House pseudonym]
See Bond, Gladys Baker
Mendonca, Susan
Brief Entry 49
See also Smith, Susan Vernon
Mendoza, George 1934- 41
Brief Entry 39
Meng, Heinz (Karl) 1924- 13
Menotti, Gian Carlo 1911- 29
Menuhin, Yehudi 1916- 40
Mercer, Charles (Edward)
1917- 16
Meredith, David William
See Miers, Earl Schenck
Meriwether, Louise 1923-
Brief Entry 31
Merriam, Eve 1916- 40
Earlier sketch in SATA 3
Merrill, Jane 1946- 42
Merrill, Jean (Fairbanks)
1923- 1
Merrill, Phil
See Merrill, Jane
Mertz, Barbara (Gross) 1927- 49
Merwin, Decie 1894-1961
Brief Entry 32
Messick, Dale 1906-
Brief Entry 48
Messmer, Otto 1892(?)-1983 37
Metcalf, Suzanne
See Baum, L(yman) Frank
Metos, Thomas H(arry) 1932- 37
Meyer, Carolyn 1935- 9
Meyer, Edith Patterson 1895- 5
Meyer, F(ranklyn) E(dward)
1932- 9
Meyer, Jean Shepherd 1929- 11
Meyer, Jerome Sydney
1895-1975 3
Obituary 25

Meyer, June
See Jordan, June
Meyer, Kathleen Allan 1918-
Brief Entry 46
Meyer, Louis A(lbert) 1942- 12
Meyer, Renate 1930- 6
Meyers, Susan 1942- 19
Meynier, Yvonne (Pollet)
1908- 14
Mezey, Robert 1935- 33
Mian, Mary (Lawrence Shipman)
1902-
Brief Entry 47
Micale, Albert 1913- 22
Michaels, Barbara
See Mertz, Barbara (Gross)
Michaels, Ski
See Pellowski, Michael J(oseph)
Michel, Anna 1943- 49
Brief Entry 40
Micklish, Rita 1931- 12
Miers, Earl Schenck
1910-1972 1
Obituary 26
Miklowitz, Gloria D. 1927- 4
Mikolaycak, Charles 1937- 9
See also SAAS 4
Mild, Warren (Paul) 1922- 41
Miles, Betty 1928- 8
Miles, Miska
See Martin, Patricia Miles
Miles, (Mary) Patricia 1930- 29
Miles, Patricia A.
See Martin, Patricia Miles
Milgrom, Harry 1912- 25
Milhous, Katherine 1894-1977 15
Militant
See Sandburg, Carl (August)
Millar, Barbara F. 1924- 12
Miller, Albert G(riffith)
1905-1982 12
Obituary 31
Miller, Alice P(atricia
McCarthy) 22
Miller, Don 1923- 15
Miller, Doris R.
See Mosesson, Gloria R(ubin)
Miller, Eddie
See Miller, Edward
Miller, Edna (Anita) 1920- 29
Miller, Edward 1905-1974 8
Miller, Elizabeth 1933- 41
Miller, Eugene 1925- 33
Miller, Frances A. 1937-
Brief Entry 46
Miller, Helen M(arkley) 5
Miller, Helen Topping 1884-1960
Obituary 29
Miller, Jane (Judith) 1925- 15
Miller, John
See Samachson, Joseph
Miller, Margaret J.
See Dale, Margaret J(essy) Miller
Miller, Marilyn (Jean) 1925- 33
Miller, Mary Beth 1942- 9
Miller, Natalie 1917-1976 35
Miller, Ruth White
See White, Ruth C.

Miller, Sandy (Peden) 1948- *41*
  Brief Entry *35*
Milligan, Spike
  See Milligan, Terence Alan
Milligan, Terence Alan 1918- *29*
Mills, Claudia 1954- *44*
  Brief Entry *41*
Mills, Yaroslava Surmach
  1925- *35*
Millstead, Thomas Edward *30*
Milne, A(lan) A(lexander)
  1882-1956 ....*YABC 1*
  See also CLR 1
Milne, Lorus J. *5*
Milne, Margery *5*
Milonas, Rolf
  See Myller, Rolf
Milotte, Alfred G(eorge)
  1904- *11*
Milton, Hilary (Herbert)
  1920- *23*
Milton, John R(onald) 1924- *24*
Milton, Joyce 1946-
  Brief Entry *41*
Milverton, Charles A.
  See Penzler, Otto
Minarik, Else Holmelund
  1920- *15*
Miner, Jane Claypool 1933- *38*
  Brief Entry *37*
Miner, Lewis S. 1909- *11*
Minier, Nelson
  See Stoutenburg, Adrien
Mintonye, Grace *4*
Mirsky, Jeannette 1903- *8*
Mirsky, Reba Paeff
  1902-1966 .... *1*
Miskovits, Christine 1939- *10*
Miss Francis
  See Horwich, Francis R.
Miss Read
  See Saint, Dora Jessie
Mister Rogers
  See Rogers, Fred (McFeely)
Mitchell, Cynthia 1922- *29*
Mitchell, (Sibyl) Elyne (Keith)
  1913- *10*
Mitchell, Gladys (Maude Winifred)
  1901-1983 .... *46*
  Obituary *35*
Mitchell, Joyce Slayton 1933- *46*
  Brief Entry *43*
Mitchell, Yvonne 1925-1979
  Obituary *24*
Mitchison, Naomi Margaret (Haldane)
  1897- *24*
Mitchnik, Helen 1901- *41*
  Brief Entry *35*
Mitsuhashi, Yoko *45*
  Brief Entry *33*
Mizner, Elizabeth Howard
  1907- *27*
Mizumura, Kazue *18*
Moché, Dinah (Rachel) L(evine)
  1936- *44*
  Brief Entry *40*
Mochi, Ugo (A.) 1889-1977 ..... *38*
Modell, Frank B. 1917- *39*
  Brief Entry *36*

Moe, Barbara 1937- *20*
Moeri, Louise 1924- *24*
Moffett, Martha (Leatherwood)
  1934- *8*
Mofsie, Louis B. 1936-
  Brief Entry *33*
Mohn, Peter B(urnet) 1934- *28*
Mohn, Viola Kohl 1914- *8*
Mohr, Nicholasa 1935- *8*
Molarsky, Osmond 1909- *16*
Moldon, Peter L(eonard)
  1937- *49*
Mole, John 1941- *36*
Molloy, Anne Baker 1907- *32*
Molloy, Paul 1920- *5*
Momaday, N(avarre) Scott
  1934- *48*
  Brief Entry *30*
Moncure, Jane Belk *23*
Monjo, F(erdinand) N.
  1924-1978 .... *16*
  See also CLR 2
Monroe, Lyle
  See Heinlein, Robert A(nson)
Monroe, Marion 1898-1983
  Obituary *34*
Monsell, Helen (Albee)
  1895-1971 .... *24*
Montana, Bob 1920-1975
  Obituary *21*
Montgomerie, Norah Mary
  1913- *26*
Montgomery, Constance
  See Cappell, Constance
Montgomery, Elizabeth Rider
  1902-1985 .... *34*
  Obituary *41*
  Earlier sketch in SATA 3
Montgomery, L(ucy) M(aud)
  1874-1942 ....*YABC 1*
  See also CLR 8
Montgomery, R(aymond) A., (Jr.)
  1936- *39*
Montgomery, Rutherford George
  1894- *3*
Montresor, Beni 1926- *38*
  Earlier sketch in SATA 3
  See also SAAS 4
Moody, Ralph Owen 1898- *1*
Moon, Carl 1879-1948 .... *25*
Moon, Grace 1877(?)-1947 .... *25*
Moon, Sheila (Elizabeth)
  1910- *5*
Mooney, Elizabeth C(omstock)
  1918-1986
  Obituary *48*
Moor, Emily
  See Deming, Richard
Moore, Anne Carroll
  1871-1961 .... *13*
Moore, Clement Clarke
  1779-1863 .... *18*
Moore, Don W. 1905(?)-1986
  Obituary *48*
Moore, Eva 1942- *20*
Moore, Fenworth
  See Stratemeyer, Edward L.

Moore, Jack (William) 1941- *46*
  Brief Entry *32*
Moore, Janet Gaylord 1905- *18*
Moore, Jim 1946- *42*
Moore, John Travers 1908- *12*
Moore, Lamont 1909-
  Brief Entry *29*
Moore, Margaret Rumberger
  1903- *12*
Moore, Marianne (Craig)
  1887-1972 .... *20*
Moore, Patrick (Alfred) 1923- *49*
  Brief Entry *39*
Moore, Ray (S.) 1905(?)-1984
  Obituary *37*
Moore, Regina
  See Dunne, Mary Collins
Moore, Rosalie
  See Brown, Rosalie (Gertrude)
  Moore
Moore, Ruth *23*
Moore, Ruth Nulton 1923- *38*
Moore, S. E. *23*
Moores, Dick
  See Moores, Richard (Arnold)
Moores, Richard (Arnold) 1909-1986
  Obituary *48*
Mooser, Stephen 1941- *28*
Mordvinoff, Nicolas
  1911-1973 .... *17*
More, Caroline [Joint pseudonym]
  See Cone, Molly Lamken and
  Strachan, Margaret Pitcairn
Morey, Charles
  See Fletcher, Helen Jill
Morey, Walt 1907- *3*
Morgan, Alfred P(owell)
  1889-1972 .... *33*
Morgan, Alison Mary 1930- *30*
Morgan, Geoffrey 1916- *46*
Morgan, Helen (Gertrude Louise)
  1921- *29*
Morgan, Helen Tudor
  See Morgan, Helen (Gertrude
  Louise)
Morgan, Jane
  See Cooper, James Fenimore
Morgan, Lenore 1908- *8*
Morgan, Louise
  See Morgan, Helen (Gertrude
  Louise)
Morgan, Shirley 1933- *10*
Morgan, Tom 1942- *42*
Morgenroth, Barbara
  Brief Entry *36*
Morrah, Dave
  See Morrah, David Wardlaw, Jr.
Morrah, David Wardlaw, Jr.
  1914- *10*
Morressy, John 1930- *23*
Morrill, Leslie H(olt) 1934- *48*
  Brief Entry *33*
Morris, Desmond (John)
  1928- *14*
Morris, Robert A. 1933- *7*
Morris, William 1913- *29*
Morrison, Bill 1935-
  Brief Entry *37*
Morrison, Dorothy Nafus *29*

Morrison, Gert W.
See Stratemeyer, Edward L.
Morrison, Lillian 1917- 3
Morrison, Lucile Phillips
1896- 17
Morrison, Roberta
See Webb, Jean Francis (III)
Morrison, Velma Ford 1909- 21
Morrison, William
See Samachson, Joseph
Morriss, James E(dward)
1932- 8
Morrow, Betty
See Bacon, Elizabeth
Morse, Carol
See Yeakley, Marjory Hall
Morse, Dorothy B(ayley) 1906-1979
Obituary 24
Morse, Flo 1921- 30
Mort, Vivian
See Cromie, Alice Hamilton
Mortimer, Mary H.
See Coury, Louise Andree
Morton, Lee Jack, Jr. 1928- 32
Morton, Miriam 1918(?)-1985 9
Obituary 46
Moscow, Alvin 1925- 3
Mosel, Arlene 1921- 7
Moser, Don
See Moser, Donald Bruce
Moser, Donald Bruce 1932- 31
Mosesson, Gloria R(ubin) 24
Moskin, Marietta D(unston)
1928- 23
Moskof, Martin Stephen
1930- 27
Moss, Don(ald) 1920- 11
Moss, Elaine Dora 1924-
Brief Entry 31
Most, Bernard 1937- 48
Brief Entry 40
Motz, Lloyd 20
Mountain, Robert
See Montgomery, R(aymond) A.,
(Jr.)
Mountfield, David
See Grant, Neil
Moussard, Jacqueline 1924- 24
Mowat, Farley 1921- 3
Moyler, Alan (Frank Powell)
1926- 36
Mozley, Charles 1915- 43
Brief Entry 32
Mrs. Fairstar
See Horne, Richard Henry
Mueller, Virginia 1924- 28
Muir, Frank 1920- 30
Mukerji, Dhan Gopal
1890-1936 40
See also CLR 10
Mulcahy, Lucille Burnett 12
Mulford, Philippa Greene
1948- 43
Mulgan, Catherine
See Gough, Catherine
Muller, Billex
See Ellis, Edward S(ylvester)
Mullins, Edward S(wift)
1922- 10

Mulock, Dinah Maria
See Craik, Dinah Maria (Mulock)
Mulvihill, William Patrick
1923- 8
Mun
See Leaf, (Wilbur) Munro
Munari, Bruno 1907- 15
See also CLR 9
Munce, Ruth Hill 1898- 12
Munowitz, Ken 1935-1977 14
Muñoz, William 1949- 42
Munro, Alice 1931- 29
Munro, Eleanor 1928- 37
Munsch, Robert N. 1945-
Brief Entry 48
Munsinger, Lynn 1951- 33
Munson(-Benson), Tunie
1946- 15
Munves, James (Albert) 1922- 30
Munzer, Martha E. 1899- 4
Murch, Mel and Starr, Ward [Joint
double pseudonym]
See Manes, Stephen
Murphy, Barbara Beasley
1933- 5
Murphy, E(mmett) Jefferson
1926- 4
Murphy, Jill 1949- 37
Murphy, Jim 1947- 37
Brief Entry 32
Murphy, Pat
See Murphy, E(mmett) Jefferson
Murphy, Robert (William)
1902-1971 10
Murphy, Shirley Rousseau
1928- 36
Murray, John 1923- 39
Murray, Marian 5
Murray, Michele 1933-1974 7
Murray, Ossie 1938- 43
Musgrave, Florence 1902- 3
Musgrove, Margaret W(ynkoop)
1943- 26
Mussey, Virginia T. H.
See Ellison, Virginia Howell
Mutz
See Kunstler, Morton
Myers, Arthur 1917- 35
Myers, Bernice 9
Myers, Caroline Elizabeth (Clark)
1887-1980 28
Myers, Elisabeth P(erkins)
1918- 36
Myers, Hortense (Powner)
1913- 10
Myers, Walter Dean 1937- 41
Brief Entry 27
See also CLR 4
See also SAAS 2
Myller, Rolf 1926- 27
Myra, Harold L(awrence)
1939- 46
Brief Entry 42
Myrus, Donald (Richard)
1927- 23

N

Nakatani, Chiyoko 1930-
Brief Entry 40

Namioka, Lensey 1929- 27
Napier, Mark
See Laffin, John (Alfred Charles)
Nash, Bruce M(itchell) 1947- 34
Nash, Linell
See Smith, Linell Nash
Nash, Mary (Hughes) 1925- 41
Nash, (Frederic) Ogden
1902-1971 46
Earlier sketch in SATA 2
Nast, Elsa Ruth
See Watson, Jane Werner
Nast, Thomas 1840-1902
Brief Entry 33
Nastick, Sharon 1954- 41
Nathan, Adele (Gutman) 1900(?)-1986
Obituary 48
Nathan, Dorothy (Goldeen)
(?)-1966 15
Nathan, Robert (Gruntal)
1894-1985 6
Obituary 43
Natti, Susanna 1948- 32
Navarra, John Gabriel 1927- 8
Naylor, Penelope 1941- 10
Naylor, Phyllis Reynolds
1933- 12
Nazaroff, Alexander I. 1898- 4
Neal, Harry Edward 1906- 5
Nearing, Penny 1916- 47
Brief Entry 42
Nebel, Gustave E. 45
Brief Entry 33
Nebel, Mimouca
See Nebel, Gustave E.
Nee, Kay Bonner 10
Needle, Jan 1943- 30
Needleman, Jacob 1934- 6
Negri, Rocco 1932- 12
Neigoff, Anne 13
Neigoff, Mike 1920- 13
Neilson, Frances Fullerton (Jones)
1910- 14
Neimark, Anne E. 1935- 4
Neimark, Paul G. 1934-
Brief Entry 37
Nelson, Cordner (Bruce) 1918-
Brief Entry 29
Nelson, Esther L. 1928- 13
Nelson, Lawrence E(rnest) 1928-1977
Obituary 28
Nelson, Mary Carroll 1929- 23
Nerlove, Miriam 1959-
Brief Entry 49
Nesbit, E(dith)
1858-1924 .... YABC 1
See also CLR 3
Nesbit, Troy
See Folsom, Franklin
Nespojohn, Katherine V.
1912- 7
Ness, Evaline (Michelow)
1911-1986 26
Obituary 49
Earlier sketch in SATA 1
See also CLR 6
See also SAAS 1
Nestor, William P(rodromos)
1947- 49

Neufeld, John 1938- 6
  See also SAAS 3
Neumeyer, Peter F(lorian)
  1929- 13
Neurath, Marie (Reidemeister)
  1898- 1
Neusner, Jacob 1932- 38
Neville, Emily Cheney 1919- 1
  See also SAAS 2
Neville, Mary
  See Woodrich, Mary Neville
Nevins, Albert J. 1915- 20
Newberry, Clare Turlay
  1903-1970 1
  Obituary 26
Newbery, John 1713-1767 20
Newcomb, Ellsworth
  See Kenny, Ellsworth Newcomb
Newcombe, Jack 45
  Brief Entry 33
Newell, Crosby
  See Bonsall, Crosby (Barbara
  Newell)
Newell, Edythe W. 1910- 11
Newell, Hope (Hockenberry)
  1896-1965 24
Newfeld, Frank 1928- 26
Newlon, (Frank) Clarke
  1905(?)-1982 6
  Obituary 33
Newman, Daisy 1904- 27
Newman, Gerald 1939- 46
  Brief Entry 42
Newman, Robert (Howard)
  1909- 4
Newman, Shirlee Petkin
  1924- 10
Newsom, Carol 1948- 40
Newton, James R(obert)
  1935- 23
Newton, Suzanne 1936- 5
Ney, John 1923- 43
  Brief Entry 33
Nic Leodhas, Sorche
  See Alger, Leclaire (Gowans)
Nichols, Cecilia Fawn 1906- 12
Nichols, Peter
  See Youd, (Christopher) Samuel
Nichols, (Joanna) Ruth 1948- 15
Nicholson, Joyce Thorpe
  1919- 35
Nickelsburg, Janet 1893- 11
Nickerson, Betty
  See Nickerson, Elizabeth
Nickerson, Elizabeth 1922- 14
Nicklaus, Carol
  Brief Entry 33
Nicol, Ann
  See Turnbull, Ann (Christine)
Nicolas
  See Mordvinoff, Nicolas
Nicolay, Helen
  1866-1954 ....YABC 1
Nicole, Christopher Robin
  1930- 5
Nielsen, Kay (Rasmus)
  1886-1957 16
Nielsen, Virginia
  See McCall, Virginia Nielsen

Niland, Deborah 1951- 27
Nixon, Hershell Howard
  1923- 42
Nixon, Joan Lowery 1927- 44
  Earlier sketch in SATA 8
Nixon, K.
  See Nixon, Kathleen Irene (Blundell)
Nixon, Kathleen Irene
  (Blundell) 14
Noble, Iris 1922-1986 5
  Obituary 49
Noble, Trinka Hakes
  Brief Entry 37
Nodset, Joan L.
  See Lexau, Joan M.
Noguere, Suzanne 1947- 34
Nolan, Dennis 1945- 42
  Brief Entry 34
Nolan, Jeannette Covert
  1897-1974 2
  Obituary 27
Nolan, Paul T(homas) 1919- 48
Nolan, William F(rancis) 1928-
  Brief Entry 28
Noonan, Julia 1946- 4
Norcross, John
  See Conroy, Jack (Wesley)
Nordhoff, Charles (Bernard)
  1887-1947 23
Nordlicht, Lillian 29
Nordstrom, Ursula 3
Norman, Charles 1904- 38
Norman, James
  See Schmidt, James Norman
Norman, Mary 1931- 36
Norman, Steve
  See Pashko, Stanley
Norris, Gunilla B(rodde)
  1939- 20
North, Andrew
  See Norton, Alice Mary
North, Captain George
  See Stevenson, Robert Louis
North, Joan 1920- 16
North, Robert
  See Withers, Carl A.
North, Sterling 1906-1974 45
  Obituary 26
  Earlier sketch in SATA 1
Norton, Alice Mary 1912- 43
  Earlier sketch in SATA 1
Norton, André
  See Norton, Alice Mary
Norton, Browning
  See Norton, Frank R(owland)
  B(rowning)
Norton, Frank R(owland) B(rowning)
  1909- 10
Norton, Mary 1903- 18
  See also CLR 6
Nöstlinger, Christine 1936-
  Brief Entry 37
  See also CLR 12
Nourse, Alan E(dward) 1928- 48
Nowell, Elizabeth Cameron 12
Numeroff, Laura Joffe 1953- 28
Nurenberg, Thelma
  See Greenhaus, Thelma Nurenberg

Nurnberg, Maxwell
  1897-1984 27
  Obituary 41
Nussbaumer, Paul (Edmond)
  1934- 16
Nyce, (Nellie) Helene von Strecker
  1885-1969 19
Nyce, Vera 1862-1925 19
Nye, Harold G.
  See Harding, Lee
Nye, Robert 1939- 6

O

Oakes, Vanya 1909-1983 6
  Obituary 37
Oakley, Don(ald G.) 1927- 8
Oakley, Graham 1929- 30
  See also CLR 7
Oakley, Helen 1906- 10
Oana, Katherine D. 1929-
  Brief Entry 37
Oana, Kay D.
  See Oana, Katherine D.
Obligado, Lilian (Isabel) 1931-
  Brief Entry 45
Obrant, Susan 1946- 11
O'Brien, Anne Sibley 1952-
  Brief Entry 48
O'Brien, Esse Forrester 1895(?)-1975
  Obituary 30
O'Brien, Robert C.
  See Conly, Robert Leslie
  See also CLR 2
O'Brien, Thomas C(lement)
  1938- 29
O'Carroll, Ryan
  See Markun, Patricia M(aloney)
O'Connell, Margaret F(orster)
  1935-1977 49
  Obituary 30
O'Connell, Peg
  See Ahern, Margaret McCrohan
O'Connor, Jane 1947-
  Brief Entry 47
O'Connor, Karen 1938- 34
O'Connor, Patrick
  See Wibberley, Leonard (Patrick
  O'Connor)
O'Connor, Richard 1915-1975
  Obituary 21
O'Daniel, Janet 1921- 24
O'Dell, Scott 1903- 12
  See also CLR 1
Odenwald, Robert P(aul)
  1899-1965 11
Odor, Ruth Shannon 1926-
  Brief Entry 44
Oechsli, Kelly 1918- 5
Ofek, Uriel 1926- 36
Offit, Sidney 1928- 10
Ofosu-Appiah, L(awrence) H(enry)
  1920- 13
Ogan, George F. 1912- 13
Ogan, M. G. [Joint pseudonym]
  See Ogan, George F. and Ogan,
  Margaret E. (Nettles)
Ogan, Margaret E. (Nettles)
  1923- 13

Ogburn, Charlton, Jr. 1911- 3
Ogilvie, Elisabeth May 1917- 40
   Brief Entry 29
O'Hagan, Caroline 1946- 38
O'Hanlon, Jacklyn
   See Meek, Jacklyn O'Hanlon
O'Hara, Mary
   See Alsop, Mary O'Hara
Ohlsson, Ib 1935- 7
Ohtomo, Yasuo 1946- 37
O'Kelley, Mattie Lou 1908- 36
Okimoto, Jean Davies 1942- 34
Olcott, Frances Jenkins
   1872(?)-1963 19
Old Boy
   See Hughes, Thomas
Old Fag
   See Bell, Robert S(tanley) W(arren)
Oldenburg, E(gbert) William
   1936-1974 35
Olds, Elizabeth 1896- 3
Olds, Helen Diehl 1895-1981 9
   Obituary 25
Oldstyle, Jonathan
   See Irving, Washington
O'Leary, Brian 1940- 6
Oleksy, Walter 1930- 33
Olesky, Walter
   See Oleksy, Walter
Oliver, John Edward 1933- 21
Olmstead, Lorena Ann 1890- 13
Olney, Ross R. 1929- 13
Olschewski, Alfred 1920- 7
Olsen, Ib Spang 1921- 6
Olson, Gene 1922- 32
Olson, Helen Kronberg 48
Olugebefola, Ademole 1941- 15
Oman, Carola (Mary Anima)
   1897-1978 35
Ommanney, F(rancis) D(ownes)
   1903-1980 23
O Mude
   See Gorey, Edward St. John
Oneal, Elizabeth 1934- 30
Oneal, Zibby
   See Oneal, Elizabeth
O'Neill, Judith (Beatrice)
   1930- 34
O'Neill, Mary L(e Duc) 1908- 2
Onslow, John 1906-1985
   Obituary 47
Opie, Iona 1923- 3
Opie, Peter (Mason)
   1918-1982 3
   Obituary 28
Oppenheim, Joanne 1934- 5
Oppenheimer, Joan L(etson)
   1925- 28
Optic, Oliver
   See Adams, William Taylor
Orbach, Ruth Gary 1941- 21
Orczy, Emmuska, Baroness
   1865-1947 40
O'Reilly, Sean
   See Deegan, Paul Joseph
Orgel, Doris 1929- 7
Oriolo, Joe
   See Oriolo, Joseph

Oriolo, Joseph 1913-1985
   Obituary 46
Orleans, Ilo 1897-1962 10
Ormai, Stella
   Brief Entry 48
Ormerod, Jan(ette Louise) 1946-
   Brief Entry 44
Ormes, Jackie
   See Ormes, Zelda J.
Ormes, Zelda J. 1914-1986
   Obituary 47
Ormondroyd, Edward 1925- 14
Ormsby, Virginia H(aire) 11
Orris
   See Ingelow, Jean
Orth, Richard
   See Gardner, Richard
Orwell, George
   See Blair, Eric Arthur
Osborne, Chester G. 1915- 11
Osborne, David
   See Silverberg, Robert
Osborne, Leone Neal 1914- 2
Osborne, Mary Pope 1949-
   Brief Entry 41
Osceola
   See Blixen, Karen (Christentze
   Dinesen)
Osgood, William E(dward)
   1926- 37
Osmond, Edward 1900- 10
Ossoli, Sarah Margaret (Fuller)
   marchesa d' 1810-1850 25
Otis, James
   See Kaler, James Otis
O'Trigger, Sir Lucius
   See Horne, Richard Henry
Ottley, Reginald (Leslie) 26
Otto, Margaret Glover 1909-1976
   Obituary 30
Ouida
   See De La Ramée, (Marie) Louise
Ousley, Odille 1896- 10
Overton, Jenny (Margaret Mary) 1942-
   Brief Entry 36
Owen, Caroline Dale
   See Snedecker, Caroline Dale
   (Parke)
Owen, Clifford
   See Hamilton, Charles H. St. John
Owen, Dilys
   See Gater, Dilys
Owen, (Benjamin) Evan
   1918-1984 38
Oxenbury, Helen 1938- 3

P

Pace, Mildred Mastin 1907- 46
   Brief Entry 29
Packard, Edward 1931- 47
Packer, Vin
   See Meaker, Marijane
Page, Eileen
   See Heal, Edith
Page, Eleanor
   See Coerr, Eleanor
Page, Lou Williams 1912- 38

Paget-Fredericks, Joseph E. P. Rous-
   Marten 1903-1963
   Brief Entry 30
Pahz, (Anne) Cheryl Suzanne
   1949- 11
Pahz, James Alon 1943- 11
Paice, Margaret 1920- 10
Paige, Harry W. 1922- 41
   Brief Entry 35
Paine, Roberta M. 1925- 13
Paisley, Tom
   See Bethancourt, T. Ernesto
Palazzo, Anthony D.
   1905-1970 3
Palazzo, Tony
   See Palazzo, Anthony D.
Palder, Edward L. 1922- 5
Palladini, David (Mario)
   1946- 40
   Brief Entry 32
Pallas, Norvin 1918- 23
Pallister, John C(lare) 1891-1980
   Obituary 26
Palmer, Bernard 1914- 26
Palmer, C(yril) Everard 1930- 14
Palmer, (Ruth) Candida 1926- 11
Palmer, Heidi 1948- 15
Palmer, Helen Marion
   See Geisel, Helen
Palmer, Juliette 1930- 15
Palmer, Robin 1911- 43
Panetta, George 1915-1969 15
Panowski, Eileen Thompson
   1920- 49
Pansy
   See Alden, Isabella (Macdonald)
Pantell, Dora (Fuchs) 1915- 39
Panter, Carol 1936- 9
Papashvily, George
   1898-1978 17
Papashvily, Helen (Waite)
   1906- 17
Pape, D(onna) L(ugg) 1930- 2
Paperny, Myra (Green) 1932-
   Brief Entry 33
Paradis, Adrian A(lexis)
   1912- 1
Paradis, Marjorie (Bartholomew)
   1886(?)-1970 17
Parenteau, Shirley (Laurolyn)
   1935- 47
   Brief Entry 40
Parish, Peggy 1927- 17
Park, Barbara 1947- 40
   Brief Entry 35
Park, Bill
   See Park, W(illiam) B(ryan)
Park, Ruth 25
Park, W(illiam) B(ryan) 1936- 22
Parker, Elinor 1906- 3
Parker, Lois M(ay) 1912- 30
Parker, Nancy Winslow 1930- 10
Parker, Richard 1915- 14
Parker, Robert
   See Boyd, Waldo T.
Parkinson, Ethelyn M(inerva)
   1906- 11
Parks, Edd Winfield
   1906-1968 10

Parks, Gordon (Alexander Buchanan)
   1912- *8*
Parley, Peter
   See Goodrich, Samuel Griswold
Parlin, John
   See Graves, Charles Parlin
Parnall, Peter 1936- *16*
Parr, Letitia (Evelyn) 1906- *37*
Parr, Lucy 1924- *10*
Parrish, Anne 1888-1957 .... *27*
Parrish, Mary
   See Cousins, Margaret
Parrish, (Frederick) Maxfield
   1870-1966 .... *14*
Parry, Marian 1924- *13*
Parsons, Tom
   See MacPherson, Thomas George
Partch, Virgil Franklin II
   1916-1984 .... *45*
   Obituary *39*
Partridge, Benjamin W(aring), Jr.
   1915- *28*
Partridge, Jenny (Lilian) 1947-
   Brief Entry *37*
Pascal, David 1918- *14*
Pascal, Francine 1938-
   Brief Entry *37*
Paschal, Nancy
   See Trotter, Grace V(iolet)
Pashko, Stanley 1913- *29*
Patent, Dorothy Hinshaw
   1940- *22*
Paterson, Diane (R. Cole) 1946-
   Brief Entry *33*
Paterson, Katherine (Womeldorf)
   1932- *13*
   See also CLR 7
Paton, Alan (Stewart) 1903- *11*
Paton, Jane (Elizabeth) 1934- *35*
Paton Walsh, Gillian 1939- *4*
   See also SAAS 3
Patten, Brian 1946- *29*
Patterson, Geoffrey 1943-
   Brief Entry *44*
Patterson, Lillie G. *14*
Paul, Aileen 1917- *12*
Paul, Elizabeth
   See Crow, Donna Fletcher
Paul, James 1936- *23*
Paul, Robert
   See Roberts, John G(aither)
Pauli, Hertha (Ernestine)
   1909-1973 .... *3*
   Obituary *26*
Paull, Grace A. 1898- *24*
Paulsen, Gary 1939- *22*
Paulson, Jack
   See Jackson, C. Paul
Pavel, Frances 1907- *10*
Payne, Donald Gordon 1924- *37*
Payne, Emmy
   See West, Emily G(ovan)
Payson, Dale 1943- *9*
Payzant, Charles *18*
Payzant, Jessie Mercer Knechtel
   See Shannon, Terry
Paz, A.
   See Pahz, James Alon

Paz, Zan
   See Pahz, Cheryl Suzanne
Peake, Mervyn 1911-1968 .... *23*
Peale, Norman Vincent 1898- *20*
Pearce, (Ann) Philippa 1920- *1*
   See also CLR 9
Peare, Catherine Owens 1911- *9*
Pears, Charles 1873-1958
   Brief Entry *30*
Pearson, Susan 1946- *39*
   Brief Entry *27*
Pease, Howard 1894-1974 .... *2*
   Obituary *25*
Peck, Anne Merriman 1884- *18*
Peck, Richard 1934- *18*
   See also SAAS 2
Peck, Robert Newton III
   1928- *21*
   See also SAAS 1
Peek, Merle 1938- *39*
Peel, Norman Lemon
   See Hirsch, Phil
Peeples, Edwin A. 1915- *6*
Peet, Bill
   See Peet, William Bartlett
   See also CLR 12
Peet, Creighton B. 1899-1977 ..... *30*
Peet, William Bartlett 1915- *41*
   Earlier sketch in SATA 2
Peirce, Waldo 1884-1970
   Brief Entry *28*
Pelaez, Jill 1924- *12*
Pellowski, Anne 1933- *20*
Pellowski, Michael J(oseph) 1949-
   Brief Entry *48*
Pelta, Kathy 1928- *18*
Peltier, Leslie C(opus) 1900- *13*
Pembury, Bill
   See Gronon, Arthur William
Pemsteen, Hans
   See Manes, Stephen
Pendennis, Arthur, Esquire
   See Thackeray, William Makepeace
Pender, Lydia 1907- *3*
Pendery, Rosemary *7*
Pendle, Alexy 1943- *29*
Pendle, George 1906-1977
   Obituary *28*
Penn, Ruth Bonn
   See Rosenberg, Ethel
Pennage, E. M.
   See Finkel, George (Irvine)
Penney, Grace Jackson 1904- *35*
Pennington, Eunice 1923- *27*
Pennington, Lillian Boyer
   1904- *45*
Penrose, Margaret
   See Stratemeyer, Edward L.
Penzler, Otto 1942- *38*
Pepe, Phil(ip) 1935- *20*
Peppe, Rodney 1934- *4*
Percy, Charles Henry
   See Smith, Dodie
Perera, Thomas Biddle 1938- *13*
Perkins, Al(bert Rogers)
   1904-1975 .... *30*
Perkins, Marlin 1905-1986 .... *21*
   Obituary *48*
Perl, Lila *6*

Perl, Susan 1922-1983 .... *22*
   Obituary *34*
Perlmutter, O(scar) William
   1920-1975 .... *8*
Perrault, Charles 1628-1703 .... *25*
Perreard, Suzanne Louise Butler 1919-
   Brief Entry *29*
Perrine, Mary 1913- *2*
Perry, Barbara Fisher
   See Fisher, Barbara
Perry, Patricia 1949- *30*
Perry, Roger 1933- *27*
Pershing, Marie
   See Schultz, Pearle Henriksen
Peters, Caroline
   See Betz, Eva Kelly
Peters, Elizabeth
   See Mertz, Barbara (Gross)
Peters, S. H.
   See Porter, William Sydney
Petersen, P(eter) J(ames)
   1941- *48*
   Brief Entry *43*
Petersham, Maud (Fuller)
   1890-1971 .... *17*
Petersham, Miska 1888-1960 ...... *17*
Peterson, Esther (Allen) 1934- ... *35*
Peterson, Hans 1922- *8*
Peterson, Harold L(eslie)
   1922- *8*
Peterson, Helen Stone 1910- *8*
Peterson, Jeanne Whitehouse
   See Whitehouse, Jeanne
Peterson, Lorraine 1940-
   Brief Entry *44*
Petie, Haris 1915- *10*
Petrides, Heidrun 1944- *19*
Petrie, Catherine 1947-
   Brief Entry *41*
Petroski, Catherine (Ann Groom)
   1939- *48*
Petrovich, Michael B(oro)
   1922- *40*
Petrovskaya, Kyra
   See Wayne, Kyra Petrovskaya
Petry, Ann (Lane) 1908- *5*
   See also CLR 12
Pevsner, Stella *8*
Peyo
   See Culliford, Pierre
Peyton, K. M.
   See Peyton, Kathleen (Wendy)
   See also CLR 3
Peyton, Kathleen (Wendy)
   1929- *15*
Pfeffer, Susan Beth 1948- *4*
   See also CLR 11
Phelan, Josephine 1905-
   Brief Entry *30*
Phelan, Mary Kay 1914- *3*
Phelps, Ethel Johnston 1914- *35*
Philbrook, Clem(ent E.) 1917- *24*
Phillips, Betty Lou
   See Phillips, Elizabeth Louise
Phillips, Elizabeth Louise
   Brief Entry *48*
Phillips, Irv
   See Phillips, Irving W.
Phillips, Irving W. 1908- *11*

Phillips, Jack
  See Sandburg, Carl (August)
Phillips, Leon
  See Gerson, Noel B(ertram)
Phillips, Loretta (Hosey)
  1893- *10*
Phillips, Louis 1942- *8*
Phillips, Mary Geisler
  1881-1964 .... *10*
Phillips, Prentice 1894- *10*
Phillpotts, Eden 1862-1960 ...... *24*
Phipson, Joan
  See Fitzhardinge, Joan M.
  See also CLR 5
  See also SAAS 3
Phiz
  See Browne, Hablot Knight
Phleger, Fred B. 1909- *34*
Phleger, Marjorie Temple
  1908(?)-1986 .... *1*
  Obituary *47*
Phypps, Hyacinthe
  See Gorey, Edward St. John
Piaget, Jean 1896-1980
  Obituary *23*
Piatti, Celestino 1922- *16*
Picard, Barbara Leonie 1917- *2*
Pickard, Charles 1932- *36*
Pickering, James Sayre
  1897-1969 .... *36*
  Obituary *28*
Pienkowski, Jan 1936- *6*
  See also CLR 6
Pierce, Edith Gray 1893-1977 ..... *45*
Pierce, Katherine
  See St. John, Wylly Folk
Pierce, Meredith Ann 1958-
  Brief Entry *48*
Pierce, Ruth (Ireland) 1936- *5*
Pierce, Tamora 1954-
  Brief Entry *49*
Pierik, Robert 1921- *13*
Pig, Edward
  See Gorey, Edward St. John
Pike, E(dgar) Royston 1896- *22*
Pilarski, Laura 1926- *13*
Pilgrim, Anne
  See Allan, Mabel Esther
Pilkington, Francis Meredyth
  1907- *4*
Pilkington, Roger (Windle)
  1915- *10*
Pinchot, David 1914(?)-1983
  Obituary *34*
Pincus, Harriet 1938- *27*
Pine, Tillie S(chloss) 1897- *13*
Pinkerton, Kathrene Sutherland
  (Gedney) 1887-1967
  Obituary *26*
Pinkney, Jerry 1939- *41*
  Brief Entry *32*
Pinkwater, Daniel Manus
  1941- *46*
  Earlier sketch in SATA 8
  See also CLR 4
  See also SAAS 3
Pinner, Joma
  See Werner, Herma

Pioneer
  See Yates, Raymond F(rancis)
Piowaty, Kim Kennelly 1957- *49*
Piper, Roger
  See Fisher, John (Oswald Hamilton)
Piper, Watty
  See Bragg, Mabel Caroline
Piro, Richard 1934- *7*
Pirsig, Robert M(aynard)
  1928- *39*
Pitman, (Isaac) James 1901-1985
  Obituary *46*
Pitrone, Jean Maddern 1920- *4*
Pitz, Henry C(larence)
  1895-1976 .... *4*
  Obituary *24*
Pizer, Vernon 1918- *21*
Place, Marian T. 1910- *3*
Plaidy, Jean
  See Hibbert, Eleanor
Plaine, Alfred R. 1898(?)-1981
  Obituary *29*
Platt, Kin 1911- *21*
Plimpton, George (Ames)
  1927- *10*
Plomer, William (Charles Franklin)
  1903-1973 .... *24*
Plotz, Helen (Ratnoff) 1913- *38*
Plowhead, Ruth Gipson
  1877-1967 .... *43*
Plowman, Stephanie 1922- *6*
Pluckrose, Henry (Arthur)
  1931- *13*
Plum, J.
  See Wodehouse, P(elham)
  G(renville)
Plum, Jennifer
  See Kurland, Michael (Joseph)
Plumb, Charles P. 1900(?)-1982
  Obituary *29*
Plume, Ilse
  Brief Entry *43*
Plummer, Margaret 1911- *2*
Podendorf, Illa E.
  1903(?)-1983 .... *18*
  Obituary *35*
Poe, Edgar Allan 1809-1849 ...... *23*
Pogány, William Andrew
  1882-1955 .... *44*
Pogány, Willy
  Brief Entry *30*
  See Pogány, William Andrew
Pohl, Frederik 1919- *24*
Pohlmann, Lillian (Grenfell)
  1902- *11*
Pointon, Robert
  See Rooke, Daphne (Marie)
Pola
  See Watson, Pauline
Polatnick, Florence T. 1923- *5*
Polder, Markus
  See Krüss, James
Polette, Nancy (Jane) 1930- *42*
Polhamus, Jean Burt 1928- *21*
Politi, Leo 1908- *47*
  Earlier sketch in SATA 1
Polking, Kirk 1925- *5*
Polland, Barbara K(ay) 1939- *44*
Polland, Madeleine A. 1918- *6*

Pollock, Bruce 1945- *46*
Pollock, Mary
  See Blyton, Enid (Mary)
Pollock, Penny 1935- *44*
  Brief Entry *42*
Pollowitz, Melinda (Kilborn)
  1944- *26*
Polonsky, Arthur 1925- *34*
Polseno, Jo *17*
Pomerantz, Charlotte *20*
Pomeroy, Pete
  See Roth, Arthur J(oseph)
Pond, Alonzo W(illiam) 1894- *5*
Pontiflet, Ted 1932- *32*
Poole, Gray Johnson 1906- *1*
Poole, Josephine 1933- *5*
  See also SAAS 2
Poole, Lynn 1910-1969 .... *1*
Poole, Peggy 1925- *39*
Poortvliet, Marien
  See Poortvliet, Rien
Poortvliet, Rien 1933(?)-
  Brief Entry *37*
Pope, Elizabeth Marie 1917- *38*
  Brief Entry *36*
Portal, Colette 1936- *6*
Porte, Barbara Ann
  Brief Entry *45*
Porter, Katherine Anne
  1890-1980 .... *39*
  Obituary *23*
Porter, Sheena 1935- *24*
Porter, William Sydney
  1862-1910 ....YABC *2*
Portteus, Eleanora Marie Manthei
  (?)-1983
  Obituary *36*
Posell, Elsa Z. *3*
Posten, Margaret L(ois) 1915- *10*
Potok, Chaim 1929- *33*
Potter, (Helen) Beatrix
  1866-1943 ....YABC *1*
  See also CLR 1
Potter, Margaret (Newman)
  1926- *21*
Potter, Marian 1915- *9*
Potter, Miriam Clark
  1886-1965 .... *3*
Pournelle, Jerry (Eugene)
  1933- *26*
Powell, A. M.
  See Morgan, Alfred P(owell)
Powell, Richard Stillman
  See Barbour, Ralph Henry
Powers, Anne
  See Schwartz, Anne Powers
Powers, Bill 1931-
  Brief Entry *31*
Powers, Margaret
  See Heal, Edith
Powledge, Fred 1935- *37*
Poynter, Margaret 1927- *27*
Prager, Arthur *44*
Preiss, Byron (Cary) *47*
  Brief Entry *42*
Prelutsky, Jack *22*
Presberg, Miriam Goldstein 1919-1978
  Brief Entry *38*
Preston, Edna Mitchell *40*

Preston, Lillian Elvira 1918- *47*
Preussler, Otfried 1923- *24*
Prevert, Jacques (Henri Marie)
  1900-1977
  Obituary *30*
Price, Christine 1928-1980 .... *3*
  Obituary *23*
Price, Garrett 1896-1979
  Obituary *22*
Price, Jennifer
  See Hoover, Helen (Drusilla
    Blackburn)
Price, Jonathan (Reeve) 1941- *46*
Price, Lucie Locke
  See Locke, Lucie
Price, Margaret (Evans) 1888-1973
  Brief Entry *28*
Price, Olive 1903- *8*
Price, Susan 1955- *25*
Price, Willard 1887-1983 .... *48*
  Brief Entry *38*
Prideaux, Tom 1908- *37*
Priestley, Lee (Shore) 1904- *27*
Prieto, Mariana B(eeching)
  1912- *8*
Primavera, Elise 1954-
  Brief Entry *48*
Prime, Derek (James) 1931- *34*
Prince, Alison 1931- *28*
Prince, J(ack) H(arvey) 1908- *17*
Pringle, Laurence 1935- *4*
  See also CLR 4
Pritchett, Elaine H(illyer)
  1920- *36*
Proctor, Everitt
  See Montgomery, Rutherford
Professor Zingara
  See Leeming, Joseph
Provensen, Alice 1918- *9*
  See also CLR 11
Provensen, Martin 1916- *9*
  See also CLR 11
Pryor, Helen Brenton
  1897-1972 .... *4*
Pucci, Albert John 1920- *44*
Pudney, John (Sleigh)
  1909-1977 .... *24*
Pugh, Ellen T. 1920- *7*
Pullein-Thompson, Christine
  1930- *3*
Pullein-Thompson, Diana *3*
Pullein-Thompson, Josephine *3*
Puner, Helen W(alker) 1915- *37*
Purdy, Susan Gold 1939- *8*
Purscell, Phyllis 1934- *7*
Putnam, Arthur Lee
  See Alger, Horatio, Jr.
Putnam, Peter B(rock) 1920- *30*
Pyle, Howard 1853-1911 .... *16*
Pyne, Mable Mandeville
  1903-1969 .... *9*

Q

Quackenbush, Robert M.
  1929- *7*
Quammen, David 1948- *7*
Quarles, Benjamin 1904- *12*

Queen, Ellery, Jr.
  See Holding, James
Quennell, Marjorie (Courtney)
  1884-1972 .... *29*
Quick, Annabelle 1922- *2*
Quigg, Jane (Hulda) (?)-1986
  Obituary *49*
Quin-Harkin, Janet 1941- *18*
Quinn, Elisabeth 1881-1962 .... *22*
Quinn, Susan
  See Jacobs, Susan
Quinn, Vernon
  See Quinn, Elisabeth

R

Rabe, Berniece 1928- *7*
Rabe, Olive H(anson)
  1887-1968 .... *13*
Rabinowich, Ellen 1946- *29*
Rabinowitz, Sandy 1954-
  Brief Entry *39*
Raboff, Ernest Lloyd
  Brief Entry *37*
Rachlin, Harvey (Brant) 1951- ... *47*
Rackham, Arthur 1867-1939 ...... *15*
Radford, Ruby L(orraine)
  1891-1971 .... *6*
Radlauer, David 1952- *28*
Radlauer, Edward 1921- *15*
Radlauer, Ruth (Shaw) 1926- *15*
Radley, Gail 1951- *25*
Rae, Gwynedd 1892-1977 .... *37*
Raebeck, Lois 1921- *5*
Raftery, Gerald (Bransfield)
  1905- *11*
Rahn, Joan Elma 1929- *27*
Raible, Alton (Robert) 1918- *35*
Raiff, Stan 1930- *11*
Rainey, W. B.
  See Blassingame, Wyatt Rainey
Ralston, Jan
  See Dunlop, Agnes M. R.
Ramal, Walter
  See de la Mare, Walter
Rana, J.
  See Forrester, Helen
Ranadive, Gail 1944- *10*
Rand, Ann (Binkley) *30*
Rand, Paul 1914- *6*
Randall, Florence Engel 1917- *5*
Randall, Janet [Joint pseudonym]
  See Young, Janet Randall and
    Young, Robert W.
Randall, Robert
  See Silverberg, Robert
Randall, Ruth Painter
  1892-1971 .... *3*
Randolph, Lieutenant J. H.
  See Ellis, Edward S(ylvester)
Rands, William Brighty
  1823-1882 .... *17*
Ranney, Agnes V. 1916- *6*
Ransom, Candice F. 1952-
  Brief Entry *49*
Ransome, Arthur (Michell)
  1884-1967 .... *22*
  See also CLR 8
Rapaport, Stella F(read) *10*

Raphael, Elaine (Chionchio)
  1933- *23*
Rappaport, Eva 1924- *6*
Rarick, Carrie 1911- *41*
Raskin, Edith (Lefkowitz)
  1908- *9*
Raskin, Ellen 1928-1984 .... *38*
  Earlier sketch in SATA 2
  See also CLR 1, 12
Raskin, Joseph 1897-1982 .... *12*
  Obituary *29*
Rasmussen, Knud Johan Victor
  1879-1933
  Brief Entry *34*
Rathjen, Carl H(enry) 1909- *11*
Rattray, Simon
  See Trevor, Elleston
Rau, Margaret 1913- *9*
  See also CLR 8
Rauch, Mabel Thompson 1888-1972
  Obituary *26*
Raucher, Herman 1928- *8*
Ravielli, Anthony 1916- *3*
Rawlings, Marjorie Kinnan
  1896-1953 ....*YABC 1*
Rawls, (Woodrow) Wilson
  1913- *22*
Ray, Deborah 1940- *8*
Ray, Irene
  See Sutton, Margaret Beebe
Ray, JoAnne 1935- *9*
Ray, Mary (Eva Pedder)
  1932- *2*
Raymond, James Crossley 1917-1981
  Obituary *29*
Raymond, Robert
  See Alter, Robert Edmond
Rayner, Mary 1933- *22*
Rayner, William 1929-
  Brief Entry *36*
Raynor, Dorka *28*
Rayson, Steven 1932- *30*
Razzell, Arthur (George)
  1925- *11*
Razzi, James 1931- *10*
Read, Elfreida 1920- *2*
Read, Piers Paul 1941- *21*
Ready, Kirk L. 1943- *39*
Reaney, James 1926- *43*
Reck, Franklin Mering 1896-1965
  Brief Entry *30*
Redding, Robert Hull 1919- *2*
Redway, Ralph
  See Hamilton, Charles H. St. John
Redway, Ridley
  See Hamilton, Charles H. St. John
Reed, Betty Jane 1921- *4*
Reed, Gwendolyn E(lizabeth)
  1932- *21*
Reed, Kit 1932- *34*
Reed, Philip G. 1908-
  Brief Entry *29*
Reed, Thomas (James) 1947- *34*
Reed, William Maxwell
  1871-1962 .... *15*
Reeder, Colonel Red
  See Reeder, Russell P., Jr.
Reeder, Russell P., Jr. 1902- *4*

Reeman, Douglas Edward 1924-
    Brief Entry 28
Rees, David Bartlett 1936- 36
Rees, Ennis 1925- 3
Reeve, Joel
    See Cox, William R(obert)
Reeves, James 1909- 15
Reeves, Joyce 1911- 17
Reeves, Lawrence F. 1926- 29
Reeves, Ruth Ellen
    See Ranney, Agnes V.
Regehr, Lydia 1903- 37
Reggiani, Renée 18
Reid, Alastair 1926- 46
Reid, Barbara 1922- 21
Reid, Dorothy M(arion) (?)-1974
    Brief Entry 29
Reid, Eugenie Chazal 1924- 12
Reid, John Calvin 21
Reid, (Thomas) Mayne
    1818-1883 24
Reid, Meta Mayne 1905-
    Brief Entry 36
Reid Banks, Lynne 1929- 22
Reiff, Stephanie Ann 1948- 47
    Brief Entry 28
Reig, June 1933- 30
Reigot, Betty Polisar 1924-
    Brief Entry 41
Reinach, Jacquelyn (Krasne)
    1930- 28
Reiner, William B(uck)
    1910-1976 46
    Obituary 30
Reinfeld, Fred 1910-1964 3
Reiniger, Lotte 1899-1981 40
    Obituary 33
Reiss, Johanna de Leeuw
    1932- 18
Reiss, John J. 23
Reit, Seymour 21
Reit, Sy
    See Reit, Seymour
Rémi, Georges 1907-1983 13
    Obituary 32
Remington, Frederic (Sackrider)
    1861-1909 41
Renault, Mary
    See Challans, Mary
Rendell, Joan 28
Rendina, Laura Cooper 1902- 10
Renick, Marion (Lewis) 1905- 1
Renken, Aleda 1907- 27
Renlie, Frank H. 1936- 11
Rensie, Willis
    See Eisner, Will(iam Erwin)
Renvoize, Jean 1930- 5
Resnick, Michael D(iamond)
    1942- 38
Resnick, Mike
    See Resnick, Michael D(iamond)
Resnick, Seymour 1920- 23
Retla, Robert
    See Alter, Robert Edmond
Reuter, Carol (Joan) 1931- 2
Revena
    See Wright, Betty Ren

Rey, H(ans) A(ugusto)
    1898-1977 26
    Earlier sketch in SATA 1
    See also CLR 5
Rey, Margret (Elizabeth)
    1906- 26
    See also CLR 5
Reyher, Becky
    See Reyher, Rebecca Hourwich
Reyher, Rebecca Hourwich
    1897- 18
Reynolds, Dickson
    See Reynolds, Helen Mary
       Greenwood Campbell
Reynolds, Helen Mary Greenwood
    Campbell 1884-1969
    Obituary 26
Reynolds, John
    See Whitlock, Ralph
Reynolds, Madge
    See Whitlock, Ralph
Reynolds, Malvina 1900-1978 44
    Obituary 24
Reynolds, Pamela 1923- 34
Rhodes, Bennie (Loran) 1927- 35
Rhodes, Frank H(arold Trevor)
    1926- 37
Rhue, Morton
    See Strasser, Todd
Rhys, Megan
    See Williams, Jeanne
Ribbons, Ian 1924- 37
    Brief Entry 30
    See also SAAS 3
Ricciuti, Edward R(aphael)
    1938- 10
Rice, Charles D(uane) 1910-1971
    Obituary 27
Rice, Dale R(ichard) 1948- 42
Rice, Edward 1918- 47
    Brief Entry 42
Rice, Elizabeth 1913- 2
Rice, Eve (Hart) 1951- 34
Rice, Inez 1907- 13
Rice, James 1934- 22
Rich, Elaine Sommers 1926- 6
Rich, Josephine 1912- 10
Richard, Adrienne 1921- 5
Richards, Curtis
    See Curtis, Richard (Alan)
Richards, Frank
    See Hamilton, Charles H. St. John
Richards, Hilda
    See Hamilton, Charles H. St. John
Richards, Kay
    See Baker, Susan (Catherine)
Richards, Laura E(lizabeth Howe)
    1850-1943 .... YABC 1
Richards, Norman 1932- 48
Richards, R(onald) C(harles) W(illiam)
    1923-
    Brief Entry 43
Richardson, Frank Howard 1882-1970
    Obituary 27
Richardson, Grace Lee
    See Dickson, Naida
Richardson, Robert S(hirley)
    1902- 8
Richelson, Geraldine 1922- 29

Richler, Mordecai 1931- 44
    Brief Entry 27
Richoux, Pat 1927- 7
Richter, Alice 1941- 30
Richter, Conrad 1890-1968 3
Richter, Hans Peter 1925- 6
Rico, Don(ato) 1917-1985
    Obituary 43
Ridge, Antonia (Florence)
    (?)-1981 7
    Obituary 27
Ridge, Martin 1923- 43
Ridley, Nat, Jr.
    See Stratemeyer, Edward L.
Ridlon, Marci 1942- 22
Riedman, Sarah R(egal) 1902- 1
Riesenberg, Felix, Jr.
    1913-1962 23
Rieu, E(mile) V(ictor)
    1887-1972 46
    Obituary 26
Riggs, Sidney Noyes 1892-1975
    Obituary 28
Rikhoff, Jean 1928- 9
Riley, James Whitcomb
    1849-1916 17
Rinard, Judith E(llen) 1947- 44
Ringi, Kjell Arne Sörensen
    1939- 12
Rinkoff, Barbara (Jean)
    1923-1975 4
    Obituary 27
Riordan, James 1936- 28
Rios, Tere
    See Versace, Marie Teresa
Ripley, Elizabeth Blake
    1906-1969 5
Ripper, Charles L. 1929- 3
Rissman, Art
    See Sussman, Susan
Rissman, Susan
    See Sussman, Susan
Ritchie, Barbara (Gibbons) 14
Ritts, Paul 1920(?)-1980
    Obituary 25
Rivera, Geraldo 1943-
    Brief Entry 28
Riverside, John
    See Heinlein, Robert A(nson)
Rivkin, Ann 1920- 41
Rivoli, Mario 1943- 10
Roach, Marilynne K(athleen)
    1946- 9
Roach, Portia
    See Takakjian, Portia
Robbins, Frank 1917- 42
    Brief Entry 32
Robbins, Raleigh
    See Hamilton, Charles H. St. John
Robbins, Ruth 1917(?)- 14
Robbins, Tony
    See Pashko, Stanley
Roberts, Bruce (Stuart) 1930- ... 47
    Brief Entry 39
Roberts, Charles G(eorge) D(ouglas)
    1860-1943
    Brief Entry 29
Roberts, David
    See Cox, John Roberts

Roberts, Elizabeth Madox
　1886-1941 33
　Brief Entry 27
Roberts, Jim
　See Bates, Barbara S(nedeker)
Roberts, John G(aither) 1913- 27
Roberts, Nancy Correll 1924-
　Brief Entry 28
Roberts, Terence
　See Sanderson, Ivan T.
Roberts, Willo Davis 1928- 21
Robertson, Barbara (Anne)
　1931- 12
Robertson, Don 1929- 8
Robertson, Dorothy Lewis
　1912- 12
Robertson, Jennifer (Sinclair)
　1942- 12
Robertson, Keith 1914- 1
Robinet, Harriette Gillem
　1931- 27
Robins, Seelin
　See Ellis, Edward S(ylvester)
Robinson, Adjai 1932- 8
Robinson, Barbara (Webb)
　1927- 8
Robinson, C(harles) A(lexander), Jr.
　1900-1965 36
Robinson, Charles 1870-1937 17
Robinson, Charles 1931- 6
Robinson, Jan M. 1933- 6
Robinson, Jean O. 1934- 7
Robinson, Jerry 1922-
　Brief Entry 34
Robinson, Joan (Mary) G(ale Thomas)
　1910- 7
Robinson, Marileta 1942- 32
Robinson, Maudie (Millian Oller)
　1914- 11
Robinson, Maurice R. 1895-1982
　Obituary 29
Robinson, Nancy K(onheim)
　1942- 32
　Brief Entry 31
Robinson, Ray(mond Kenneth)
　1920- 23
Robinson, Shari
　See McGuire, Leslie (Sarah)
Robinson, T(homas) H(eath)
　1869-1950 17
Robinson, (Wanda) Veronica
　1926- 30
Robinson, W(illiam) Heath
　1872-1944 17
Robison, Bonnie 1924- 12
Robison, Nancy L(ouise)
　1934- 32
Robottom, John 1934- 7
Roche, A. K. [Joint pseudonym]
　See Abisch, Roslyn Kroop and
　Kaplan, Boche
Roche, P(atricia) K.
　Brief Entry 34
Roche, Terry
　See Poole, Peggy
Rock, Gail
　Brief Entry 32
Rocker, Fermin 1907- 40
Rockwell, Anne F. 1934- 33

Rockwell, Gail
　Brief Entry 36
Rockwell, Harlow 33
Rockwell, Norman (Percevel)
　1894-1978 23
Rockwell, Thomas 1933- 7
　See also CLR 6
Rockwood, Joyce 1947- 39
Rockwood, Roy [Collective
　pseudonym] 1
　See also McFarlane, Leslie;
　Stratemeyer, Edward L.
Roddenberry, Eugene Wesley
　1921- 45
Roddenberry, Gene
　See Roddenberry, Eugene Wesley
Rodgers, Mary 1931- 8
Rodman, Emerson
　See Ellis, Edward S(ylvester)
Rodman, Maia
　See Wojciechowska, Maia
Rodman, Selden 1909- 9
Rodowsky, Colby 1932- 21
Roe, Harry Mason
　See Stratemeyer, Edward L.
Roever, J(oan) M(arilyn)
　1935- 26
Roffey, Maureen 1936- 33
Rogers, (Thomas) Alan (Stinchcombe)
　1937- 2
Rogers, Frances 1888-1974 10
Rogers, Fred (McFeely) 1928- 33
Rogers, Jean 1919-
　Brief Entry 47
Rogers, Matilda 1894-1976 5
　Obituary 34
Rogers, Pamela 1927- 9
Rogers, Robert
　See Hamilton, Charles H. St. John
Rogers, W(illiam) G(arland)
　1896-1978 23
Rojan
　See Rojankovsky, Feodor
　(Stepanovich)
Rojankovsky, Feodor (Stepanovich)
　1891-1970 21
Rokeby-Thomas, Anna E(lma)
　1911- 15
Roland, Albert 1925- 11
Rolerson, Darrell A(llen)
　1946- 8
Roll, Winifred 1909- 6
Rollins, Charlemae Hill
　1897-1979 3
　Obituary 26
Romano, Clare
　See Ross, Clare (Romano)
Romano, Louis 1921- 35
Rongen, Björn 1906- 10
Rood, Ronald (N.) 1920- 12
Rooke, Daphne (Marie) 1914- 12
Roop, Constance Betzer 1951-
　Brief Entry 49
Roop, Peter 1951-
　Brief Entry 49
Roos, Stephen (Kelley) 1945- 47
　Brief Entry 41
Root, Phyllis
　Brief Entry 48

Roote, Mike
　See Fleischer, Leonore
Roper, Laura Wood 1911- 34
Roscoe, D(onald) T(homas)
　1934- 42
Rose, Anna Perrot
　See Wright, Anna (Maria Louisa
　Perrot) Rose
Rose, Anne 8
Rose, Carl 1903-1971
　Brief Entry 31
Rose, Elizabeth Jane (Pretty) 1933-
　Brief Entry 28
Rose, Florella
　See Carlson, Vada F.
Rose, Gerald (Hembdon Seymour)
　1935-
　Brief Entry 30
Rose, Nancy A.
　See Sweetland, Nancy A(nn)
Rose, Wendy 1948- 12
Rosen, Michael (Wayne)
　1946- 48
　Brief Entry 40
Rosen, Sidney 1916- 1
Rosen, Winifred 1943- 8
Rosenbaum, Maurice 1907- 6
Rosenberg, Dorothy 1906- 40
Rosenberg, Ethel 3
Rosenberg, Maxine B(erta) 1939-
　Brief Entry 47
Rosenberg, Nancy Sherman
　1931- 4
Rosenberg, Sharon 1942- 8
Rosenblatt, Arthur S. 1938-
　Brief Entry 45
Rosenbloom, Joseph 1928- 21
Rosenblum, Richard 1928- 11
Rosenburg, John M. 1918- 6
Rosenthal, Harold 1914- 35
Ross, Alan
　See Warwick, Alan R(oss)
Ross, Alex(ander) 1909-
　Brief Entry 29
Ross, Clare (Romano) 1922- 48
Ross, Dave 1949- 32
Ross, David 1896-1975 49
　Obituary 20
Ross, Diana
　See Denney, Diana
Ross, Frank (Xavier), Jr.
　1914- 28
Ross, John 1921- 45
Ross, Pat 1943-
　Brief Entry 48
Ross, Tony 1938- 17
Ross, Wilda (S.) 1915-
　Brief Entry 39
Rossel, Seymour 1945- 28
Rössel-Waugh, C. C. [Joint
　pseudonym]
　See Waugh, Carol-Lynn Rössel
Rossetti, Christiana (Georgina)
　1830-1894 20
Roth, Arnold 1929- 21
Roth, Arthur J(oseph) 1925- 43
　Brief Entry 28
Roth, David 1940- 36

Roth, Harold
  Brief Entry 49
Rothkopf, Carol Z. 1929- 4
Rothman, Joel 1938- 7
Roueché, Berton 1911- 28
Roughsey, Dick 1921(?)- 35
Rounds, Glen (Harold) 1906- 8
Rourke, Constance (Mayfield)
  1885-1941 ....YABC 1
Rowe, Viola Carson 1903-1969
  Obituary 26
Rowland, Florence Wightman
  1900- 8
Rowland-Entwistle, (Arthur) Theodore
  (Henry) 1925- 31
Rowsome, Frank (Howard), Jr.
  1914-1983 36
Roy, Liam
  See Scarry, Patricia
Roy, Ron(ald) 1940- 40
  Brief Entry 35
Rubel, Nicole 1953- 18
Rubin, Eva Johanna 1925- 38
Rubinstein, Robert E(dward)
  1943- 49
Ruby, Lois 1942- 35
  Brief Entry 34
Ruchlis, Hy 1913- 3
Ruckman, Ivy 1931- 37
Ruck-Pauquèt, Gina 1931- 40
  Brief Entry 37
Rudeen, Kenneth
  Brief Entry 36
Rudley, Stephen 1946- 30
Rudolph, Marguerita 1908- 21
Rudomin, Esther
  See Hautzig, Esther
Rue, Leonard Lee III 1926- 37
Ruedi, Norma Paul
  See Ainsworth, Norma
Ruffell, Ann 1941- 30
Ruffins, Reynold 1930- 41
Rugoff, Milton 1913- 30
Ruhen, Olaf 1911- 17
Rukeyser, Muriel 1913-1980
  Obituary 22
Rumsey, Marian (Barritt)
  1928- 16
Runyan, John
  See Palmer, Bernard
Rush, Alison 1951- 41
Rush, Peter 1937- 32
Rushmore, Helen 1898- 3
Rushmore, Robert (William)
  1926-1986 8
  Obituary 49
Ruskin, Ariane
  See Batterberry, Ariane Ruskin
Ruskin, John 1819-1900 24
Russell, Charlotte
  See Rathjen, Carl H(enry)
Russell, Don(ald Bert) 1899-1986
  Obituary 47
Russell, Franklin 1926- 11
Russell, Helen Ross 1915- 8
Russell, Patrick
  See Sammis, John
Russell, Solveig Paulson
  1904- 3

Russo, Susan 1947- 30
Rutgers van der Loeff, An(na) Basenau
  1910- 22
Ruth, Rod 1912- 9
Rutherford, Douglas
  See McConnell, James Douglas
  (Rutherford)
Rutherford, Meg 1932- 34
Ruthin, Margaret 4
Rutz, Viola Larkin 1932- 12
Ruzicka, Rudolph 1883-1978
  Obituary 24
Ryan, Betsy
  See Ryan, Elizabeth (Anne)
Ryan, Cheli Durán 20
Ryan, Elizabeth (Anne) 1943- 30
Ryan, John (Gerald Christopher)
  1921- 22
Ryan, Peter (Charles) 1939- 15
Rydberg, Ernest E(mil) 1901- 21
Rydberg, Lou(isa Hampton)
  1908- 27
Rydell, Wendell
  See Rydell, Wendy
Rydell, Wendy 4
Ryden, Hope 8
Ryder, Joanne
  Brief Entry 34
Rye, Anthony
  See Youd, (Christopher) Samuel
Rylant, Cynthia 1954-
  Brief Entry 44
Rymer, Alta May 1925- 34

S

Saberhagen, Fred (Thomas)
  1930- 37
Sabin, Edwin Legrand
  1870-1952 ....YABC 2
Sabin, Francene 27
Sabin, Louis 1930- 27
Sabre, Dirk
  See Laffin, John (Alfred Charles)
Sabuso
  See Phillips, Irving W.
Sachs, Elizabeth-Ann 1946- 48
Sachs, Marilyn 1927- 3
  See also CLR 2
  See also SAAS 2
Sackett, S(amuel) J(ohn)
  1928- 12
Sackson, Sid 1920- 16
Saddler, Allen
  See Richards, R(onald) C(harles)
  W(illiam)
Saddler, K. Allen
  See Richards, R(onald) C(harles)
  W(illiam)
Sadie, Stanley (John) 1930- 14
Sadler, Catherine Edwards
  Brief Entry 45
Sadler, Mark
  See Lynds, Dennis
Sage, Juniper [Joint pseudonym]
  See Brown, Margaret Wise and
  Hurd, Edith
Sagsoorian, Paul 1923- 12

Saida
  See LeMair, H(enriette) Willebeek
Saint, Dora Jessie 1913- 10
St. Briavels, James
  See Wood, James Playsted
St. Clair, Byrd Hooper 1905-1976
  Obituary 28
Saint Exupéry, Antoine de
  1900-1944 20
  See also CLR 10
St. George, Judith 1931- 13
St. John, Nicole
  See Johnston, Norma
St. John, Philip
  See Del Rey, Lester
St. John, Wylly Folk
  1908-1985 10
  Obituary 45
St. Meyer, Ned
  See Stratemeyer, Edward L.
St. Tamara
  See Kolba, Tamara
Saito, Michiko
  See Fujiwara, Michiko
Salassi, Otto R(ussell) 1939- 38
Saldutti, Denise 1953- 39
Salkey, (Felix) Andrew (Alexander)
  1928- 35
Salmon, Annie Elizabeth
  1899- 13
Salten, Felix
  See Salzmann, Siegmund
Salter, Cedric
  See Knight, Francis Edgar
Salvadori, Mario (George)
  1907- 40
Salzer, L. E.
  See Wilson, Lionel
Salzman, Yuri
  Brief Entry 42
Salzmann, Siegmund
  1869-1945 25
Samachson, Dorothy 1914- 3
Samachson, Joseph 1906- 3
Sammis, John 1942- 4
Sampson, Fay (Elizabeth)
  1935- 42
  Brief Entry 40
Samson, Anne S(tringer)
  1933- 2
Samson, Joan 1937-1976 13
Samuels, Charles 1902- 12
Samuels, Gertrude 17
Sanborn, Duane 1914- 38
Sancha, Sheila 1924- 38
Sanchez, Sonia 1934- 22
Sánchez-Silva, José María
  1911- 16
  See also CLR 12
Sand, George X. 45
Sandak, Cass R(obert) 1950-
  Brief Entry 37
Sandberg, (Karin) Inger 1930- ... 15
Sandberg, Karl C. 1931- 35
Sandberg, Lasse (E. M.)
  1924- 15
Sandburg, Carl (August)
  1878-1967 8

Sandburg, Charles A.
  See Sandburg, Carl (August)
Sandburg, Helga 1918- *3*
Sanderlin, George 1915- *4*
Sanderlin, Owenita (Harrah)
  1916- *11*
Sanders, Winston P.
  See Anderson, Poul (William)
Sanderson, Ivan T. 1911-1973 .... *6*
Sanderson, Ruth (L.) 1951- *41*
Sandin, Joan 1942- *12*
Sandison, Janet
  See Cameron, Elizabeth Jane
Sandoz, Mari (Susette)
  1901-1966 .... *5*
Sanger, Marjory Bartlett
  1920- *8*
Sankey, Alice (Ann-Susan)
  1910- *27*
San Souci, Robert D. 1946- ... *40*
Santesson, Hans Stefan 1914(?)-1975
  Obituary *30*
Sapieyevski, Anne Lindbergh
  1940- *35*
Sarac, Roger
  See Caras, Roger A(ndrew)
Sarg, Anthony Fredrick
  See Sarg, Tony
Sarg, Tony 1880-1942 .... *YABC 1*
Sargent, Pamela *29*
Sargent, Robert 1933- *2*
Sargent, Sarah 1937- *44*
  Brief Entry *41*
Sargent, Shirley 1927- *11*
Sari
  See Fleur, Anne
Sarnoff, Jane 1937- *10*
Saroyan, William 1908-1981 ..... *23*
  Obituary *24*
Sarton, Eleanore Marie
  See Sarton, (Eleanor) May
Sarton, (Eleanor) May 1912- *36*
Sasek, Miroslav 1916-1980 .... *16*
  Obituary *23*
  See also CLR 4
Satchwell, John
  Brief Entry *49*
Sattler, Helen Roney 1921- *4*
Sauer, Julia (Lina) 1891-1983 ..... *32*
  Obituary *36*
Saul, (E.) Wendy 1946- *42*
Saunders, Caleb
  See Heinlein, Robert A(nson)
Saunders, Keith 1910- *12*
Saunders, Rubie (Agnes)
  1929- *21*
Saunders, Susan 1945- *46*
  Brief Entry *41*
Savage, Blake
  See Goodwin, Harold Leland
Savery, Constance (Winifred)
  1897- *1*
Saville, (Leonard) Malcolm
  1901-1982 .... *23*
  Obituary *31*
Saviozzi, Adriana
  See Mazza, Adriana
Savitt, Sam *8*
Savitz, Harriet May 1933- *5*

Sawyer, Ruth 1880-1970 .... *17*
Say, Allen 1937- *28*
Sayers, Frances Clarke 1897- *3*
Sazer, Nina 1949- *13*
Scabrini, Janet 1953- *13*
Scagnetti, Jack 1924- *7*
Scanlon, Marion Stephany *11*
Scarf, Maggi
  See Scarf, Maggie
Scarf, Maggie 1932- *5*
Scarlett, Susan
  See Streatfeild, (Mary) Noel
Scarry, Huck
  See Scarry, Richard, Jr.
Scarry, Patricia (Murphy)
  1924- *2*
Scarry, Patsy
  See Scarry, Patricia
Scarry, Richard (McClure)
  1919- *35*
  Earlier sketch in SATA 2
  See also CLR 3
Scarry, Richard, Jr. 1953- *35*
Schachtel, Roger (Bernard)
  1949- *38*
Schaefer, Jack 1907- *3*
Schaeffer, Mead 1898- *21*
Schaller, George B(eals)
  1933- *30*
Schatell, Brian
  Brief Entry *47*
Schatzki, Walter 1899-
  Brief Entry *31*
Schechter, Betty (Goodstein)
  1921- *5*
Scheer, Julian (Weisel) 1926- *8*
Scheffer, Victor B. 1906- *6*
Scheier, Michael 1943- *40*
  Brief Entry *36*
Schell, Mildred 1922- *41*
Schell, Orville H. 1940- *10*
Schellie, Don 1932- *29*
Schemm, Mildred Walker
  1905- *21*
Scher, Paula 1948- *47*
Scherf, Margaret 1908- *10*
Schermer, Judith (Denise)
  1941- *30*
Schertle, Alice 1941- *36*
Schick, Alice 1946- *27*
Schick, Eleanor 1942- *9*
Schick, Joel 1945- *31*
  Brief Entry *30*
Schiff, Ken 1942- *7*
Schiller, Andrew 1919- *21*
Schiller, Barbara (Heyman)
  1928- *21*
Schiller, Justin G. 1943-
  Brief Entry *31*
Schindelman, Joseph 1923-
  Brief Entry *32*
Schisgall, Oscar 1901-1984 ...... *12*
  Obituary *38*
Schlee, Ann 1934- *44*
  Brief Entry *36*
Schlein, Miriam 1926- *2*
Schloat, G. Warren, Jr. 1914- *4*
Schmid, Eleonore 1939- *12*
Schmiderer, Dorothy 1940- *19*

Schmidt, Elizabeth 1915- *15*
Schmidt, James Norman
  1912- *21*
Schneider, Herman 1905- *7*
Schneider, Laurie
  See Adams, Laurie
Schneider, Nina 1913- *2*
Schneider, Rex 1937- *44*
Schnirel, James R(einhold)
  1931- *14*
Schock, Pauline 1928- *45*
Schoen, Barbara 1924- *13*
Schoenherr, John (Carl) 1935- *37*
Scholastica, Sister Mary
  See Jenkins, Marie M.
Scholefield, Edmund O.
  See Butterworth, W. E.
Scholey, Arthur 1932- *28*
Scholz, Jackson (Volney) 1897-1986
  Obituary *49*
Schone, Virginia *22*
Schongut, Emanuel
  Brief Entry *36*
Schoonover, Frank (Earle)
  1877-1972 .... *24*
Schoor, Gene 1921- *3*
Schraff, Anne E(laine) 1939- *27*
Schrank, Joseph 1900-1984
  Obituary *38*
Schreiber, Elizabeth Anne (Ferguson)
  1947- *13*
Schreiber, Georges 1904-1977
  Brief Entry *29*
Schreiber, Ralph W(alter)
  1942- *13*
Schroeder, Ted 1931(?)-1973
  Obituary *20*
Schulman, Janet 1933- *22*
Schulman, L(ester) M(artin)
  1934- *13*
Schulte, Elaine L(ouise) 1934- *36*
Schultz, Gwendolyn *21*
Schultz, James Willard
  1859-1947 .... *YABC 1*
Schultz, Pearle Henriksen
  1918- *21*
Schulz, Charles M(onroe)
  1922- *10*
Schur, Maxine 1948-
  Brief Entry *49*
Schurfranz, Vivian 1925- *13*
Schutzer, A. I. 1922- *13*
Schuyler, Pamela R(icka)
  1948- *30*
Schwartz, Alvin 1927- *4*
  See also CLR 3
Schwartz, Amy 1954- *47*
  Brief Entry *41*
Schwartz, Ann Powers 1913- *10*
Schwartz, Charles W(alsh)
  1914- *8*
Schwartz, Daniel (Bennet) 1929-
  Brief Entry *29*
Schwartz, Elizabeth Reeder
  1912- *8*
Schwartz, Julius 1907- *45*
Schwartz, Sheila (Ruth) 1929- *27*
Schwartz, Stephen (Lawrence)
  1948- *19*

Schweitzer, Iris
  Brief Entry 36
Schweninger, Ann 1951- 29
Scoggin, Margaret C.
  1905-1968 47
  Brief Entry 28
Scoppettone, Sandra 1936- 9
Scott, Ann Herbert 1926-
  Brief Entry 29
Scott, Bill 1902(?)-1985
  Obituary 46
Scott, Cora Annett (Pipitone)
  1931- 11
Scott, Dan [House pseudonym]
  See Barker, S. Omar; Stratemeyer,
  Edward L.
Scott, Elaine 1940- 36
Scott, Jack Denton 1915- 31
Scott, John 1912-1976 14
Scott, John Anthony 1916- 23
Scott, John M(artin) 1913- 12
Scott, Sally (Elisabeth) 1948- 44
Scott, Sally Fisher 1909-1978 43
Scott, Tony
  See Scott, John Anthony
Scott, Sir Walter
  1771-1832 .... YABC 2
Scott, Warwick
  See Trevor, Elleston
Scribner, Charles, Jr. 1921- 13
Scribner, Joanne L. 1949- 33
Scrimsher, Lila Gravatt 1897-1974
  Obituary 28
Scuro, Vincent 1951- 21
Seabrooke, Brenda 1941- 30
Seaman, Augusta Huiell
  1879-1950 31
Seamands, Ruth (Childers)
  1916- 9
Searcy, Margaret Zehmer 1926-
  Brief Entry 39
Searight, Mary W(illiams)
  1918- 17
Searle, Kathryn Adrienne
  1942- 10
Searle, Ronald (William Fordham)
  1920- 42
Sears, Stephen W. 1932- 4
Sebastian, Lee
  See Silverberg, Robert
Sebestyen, Igen
  See Sebestyen, Ouida
Sebestyen, Ouida 1924- 39
Sechrist, Elizabeth Hough
  1903- 2
Sedges, John
  See Buck, Pearl S.
Seed, Jenny 1930- 8
Seed, Sheila Turner 1937(?)-1979
  Obituary 23
Seeger, Elizabeth 1889-1973
  Obituary 20
Seeger, Pete(r) 1919- 13
Seever, R.
  See Reeves, Lawrence F.
Sefton, Catherine
  See Waddell, Martin
Segal, Joyce 1940- 35
Segal, Lore 1928- 4

Seidelman, James Edward
  1926- 6
Seiden, Art(hur)
  Brief Entry 42
Seidler, Tor 1952-
  Brief Entry 46
Seidman, Laurence (Ivan)
  1925- 15
Seigel, Kalman 1917- 12
Seignobosc, Francoise
  1897-1961 21
Seixas, Judith S. 1922- 17
Sejima, Yoshimasa 1913- 8
Selden, George
  See Thompson, George Selden
  See also CLR 8
Self, Margaret Cabell 1902- 24
Selig, Sylvie 1942- 13
Selkirk, Jane [Joint pseudonym]
  See Chapman, John Stanton
  Higham
Sellers, Naomi John
  See Flack, Naomi John (White)
Selsam, Millicent E(llis)
  1912- 29
  Earlier sketch in SATA 1
  See also CLR 1
Seltzer, Meyer 1932- 17
Seltzer, Richard (Warren, Jr.)
  1946- 41
Sendak, Jack 28
Sendak, Maurice (Bernard)
  1928- 27
  Earlier sketch in SATA 1
  See also CLR 1
Sengler, Johanna 1924- 18
Senn, Steve 1950-
  Brief Entry 48
Serage, Nancy 1924- 10
Seredy, Kate 1899-1975 1
  Obituary 24
  See also CLR 10
Seroff, Victor I(lyitch)
  1902-1979 12
  Obituary 26
Serraillier, Ian (Lucien) 1912- 1
  See also CLR 2
  See also SAAS 3
Servello, Joe 1932- 10
Service, Robert W(illiam)
  1874(?)-1958 20
Serwadda, William Moses
  1931- 27
Serwer, Blanche L. 1910- 10
Seth, Marie
  See Lexau, Joan M.
Seton, Anya 3
Seton, Ernest Thompson
  1860-1946 18
Seuling, Barbara 1937- 10
Seuss, Dr.
  See Geisel, Theodor Seuss
  See also CLR 9
Severn, Bill
  See Severn, William Irving
Severn, David
  See Unwin, David S(torr)
Severn, William Irving 1914- 1
Sewall, Marcia 1935- 37

Seward, Prudence 1926- 16
Sewell, Anna 1820-1878 24
Sewell, Helen (Moore)
  1896-1957 38
Sexton, Anne (Harvey)
  1928-1974 10
Seymour, Alta Halverson 10
Shachtman, Tom 1942- 49
Shackleton, C. C.
  See Aldiss, Brian W(ilson)
Shafer, Robert E(ugene)
  1925- 9
Shahn, Ben(jamin) 1898-1969
  Obituary 21
Shahn, Bernarda Bryson
  See Bryson, Bernarda
Shane, Harold Gray 1914- 36
Shanks, Ann Zane (Kushner) 10
Shannon, George (William Bones)
  1952- 35
Shannon, Monica (?)-1965 28
Shannon, Terry 21
Shapiro, Irwin 1911-1981 32
Shapiro, Milton J. 1926- 32
Shapp, Martha 1910- 3
Sharfman, Amalie 14
Sharma, Partap 1939- 15
Sharmat, Marjorie Weinman
  1928- 33
  Earlier sketch in SATA 4
Sharmat, Mitchell 1927- 33
Sharp, Margery 1905- 29
  Earlier sketch in SATA 1
Sharp, Zerna A. 1889-1981
  Obituary 27
Sharpe, Mitchell R(aymond)
  1924- 12
Shaw, Arnold 1909- 4
Shaw, Charles (Green)
  1892-1974 13
Shaw, Evelyn 1927- 28
Shaw, Flora Louisa
  See Lugard, Flora Louisa Shaw
Shaw, Ray 7
Shaw, Richard 1923- 12
Shay, Arthur 1922- 4
Shay, Lacey
  See Shebar, Sharon Sigmond
Shea, George 1940-
  Brief Entry 42
Shearer, John 1947- 43
  Brief Entry 27
Shearer, Ted 1919- 43
Shebar, Sharon Sigmond
  1945- 36
Shecter, Ben 1935- 16
Sheedy, Alexandra (Elizabeth)
  1962- 39
  Earlier sketch in SATA 19
Sheedy, Ally
  See Sheedy, Alexandra (Elizabeth)
Sheehan, Ethna 1908- 9
Sheffield, Janet N. 1926- 26
Shefts, Joelle
  Brief Entry 49
Shekerjian, Regina Tor 16
Sheldon, Ann [Collective
  pseudonym] 1
Sheldon, Aure 1917-1976 12

Sheldon, Muriel 1926- 45
  Brief Entry 39
Shelley, Mary Wollstonecraft
  (Godwin) 1797-1851 29
Shelton, William Roy 1919- 5
Shemin, Margaretha 1928- 4
Shenton, Edward 1895-1977 45
Shepard, Ernest Howard
  1879-1976 33
  Obituary 24
  Earlier sketch in SATA 3
Shepard, Mary
  See Knox, (Mary) Eleanor Jessie
Shephard, Esther 1891-1975 5
  Obituary 26
Shepherd, Elizabeth 4
Sherburne, Zoa 1912- 3
Sherman, D(enis) R(onald)
  1934- 48
  Brief Entry 29
Sherman, Diane (Finn) 1928- 12
Sherman, Elizabeth
  See Friskey, Margaret Richards
Sherman, Harold (Morrow)
  1898- 37
Sherman, Nancy
  See Rosenberg, Nancy Sherman
Sherrod, Jane
  See Singer, Jane Sherrod
Sherry, (Dulcie) Sylvia 1932- 8
Sherwan, Earl 1917- 3
Shiefman, Vicky 22
Shields, Brenda Desmond (Armstrong)
  1914- 37
Shields, Charles 1944- 10
Shimin, Symeon 1902- 13
Shinn, Everett 1876-1953 21
Shippen, Katherine B(inney)
  1892-1980 1
  Obituary 23
Shipton, Eric 1907- 10
Shirer, William L(awrence)
  1904- 45
Shirreffs, Gordon D(onald)
  1914- 11
Sholokhov, Mikhail A. 1905-1984
  Obituary 36
Shore, June Lewis 30
Shore, Robert 1924- 39
Shortall, Leonard W. 19
Shotwell, Louisa R. 1902- 3
Showalter, Jean B(reckinridge) 12
Showell, Ellen Harvey 1934- 33
Showers, Paul C. 1910- 21
  See also CLR 6
Shreve, Susan Richards 1939- 46
  Brief Entry 41
Shtainmets, Leon 32
Shub, Elizabeth 5
Shulevitz, Uri 1935- 3
  See also CLR 5
Shulman, Alix Kates 1932- 7
Shulman, Irving 1913- 13
Shumsky, Zena
  See Collier, Zena
Shura, Mary Francis
  See Craig, Mary Francis
Shuttlesworth, Dorothy 3
Shyer, Marlene Fanta 13

Siberell, Anne 29
Sibley, Don 1922- 12
Siculan, Daniel 1922- 12
Sidjakov, Nicolas 1924- 18
Sidney, Frank [Joint pseudonym]
  See Warwick, Alan R(oss)
Sidney, Margaret
  See Lothrop, Harriet Mulford Stone
Siebel, Fritz (Frederick) 1913-
  Brief Entry 44
Siegal, Aranka 1930-
  Brief Entry 37
Siegel, Beatrice 36
Siegel, Helen
  See Siegl, Helen
Siegel, Robert (Harold) 1939- 39
Siegl, Helen 1924- 34
Silas
  See McCay, Winsor
Silcock, Sara Lesley 1947- 12
Silver, Ruth
  See Chew, Ruth
Silverberg, Robert 13
Silverman, Mel(vin Frank)
  1931-1966 9
Silverstein, Alvin 1933- 8
Silverstein, Shel(by) 1932- 33
  Brief Entry 27
  See also CLR 5
Silverstein, Virginia B(arbara
  Opshelor) 1937- 8
Silverthorne, Elizabeth 1930- 35
Simon, Charlie May
  See Fletcher, Charlie May
Simon, Hilda (Rita) 1921- 28
Simon, Howard 1903-1979 32
  Obituary 21
Simon, Joe
  See Simon, Joseph H.
Simon, Joseph H. 1913- 7
Simon, Martin P(aul William)
  1903-1969 12
Simon, Mina Lewiton
  See Lewiton, Mina
Simon, Norma 1927- 3
Simon, Seymour 1931- 4
  See also CLR 9
Simon, Shirley (Schwartz)
  1921- 11
Simon, Solomon 1895-1970 40
Simonetta, Linda 1948- 14
Simonetta, Sam 1936- 14
Simons, Barbara B(rooks)
  1934- 41
Simont, Marc 1915- 9
Simpson, Colin 1908- 14
Simpson, Harriette
  See Arnow, Harriette (Louisa)
  Simpson
Simpson, Myrtle L(illias)
  1931- 14
Sinclair, Clover
  See Gater, Dilys
Sinclair, Upton (Beall)
  1878-1968 9
Singer, Isaac Bashevis 1904- 27
  Earlier sketch in SATA 3
  See also CLR 1

Singer, Jane Sherrod
  1917-1985 4
  Obituary 42
Singer, Julia 1917- 28
Singer, Kurt D(eutsch) 1911- 38
Singer, Marilyn 1948- 48
  Brief Entry 38
Singer, Susan (Mahler) 1941- 9
Sirof, Harriet 1930- 37
Sisson, Rosemary Anne 1923- 11
Sitomer, Harry 1903- 31
Sitomer, Mindel 1903- 31
Sive, Helen R. 1951- 30
Sivulich, Sandra (Jeanne) Stroner
  1941- 9
Skelly, James R(ichard) 1927- 17
Skinner, Constance Lindsay
  1882-1939 .... YABC 1
Skinner, Cornelia Otis 1901- 2
Skipper, G. C. 1939- 46
  Brief Entry 38
Skofield, James
  Brief Entry 44
Skold, Betty Westrom 1923- 41
Skorpen, Liesel Moak 1935- 3
Skurzynski, Gloria (Joan)
  1930- 8
Slackman, Charles B. 1934- 12
Slade, Richard 1910-1971 9
Slate, Joseph (Frank) 1928- 38
Slater, Jim 1929-
  Brief Entry 34
Slaughter, Jean
  See Doty, Jean Slaughter
Sleator, William 1945- 3
Sleigh, Barbara 1906-1982 3
  Obituary 30
Slepian, Jan(ice B.) 1921-
  Brief Entry 45
Slicer, Margaret O. 1920- 4
Sloane, Eric 1910(?)-1985
  Obituary 42
Slobodkin, Florence (Gersh)
  1905- 5
Slobodkin, Louis 1903-1975 26
  Earlier sketch in SATA 1
Slobodkina, Esphyr 1909- 1
Sloggett, Nellie 1851-1923 44
Slote, Alfred 1926- 8
  See also CLR 4
Small, David 1945-
  Brief Entry 46
Small, Ernest
  See Lent, Blair
Smallwood, Norah (Evelyn)
  1910(?)-1984
  Obituary 41
Smaridge, Norah 1903- 6
Smiley, Virginia Kester 1923- 2
Smith, Anne Warren 1938- 41
  Brief Entry 34
Smith, Beatrice S(chillinger) 12
Smith, Betsy Covington 1937-
  Brief Entry 43
Smith, Betty 1896-1972 6
Smith, Bradford 1909-1964 5
Smith, Caesar
  See Trevor, Elleston

Smith, Datus C(lifford), Jr.
1907- 13
Smith, Dodie 4
Smith, Doris Buchanan 1934- 28
Smith, Dorothy Stafford
1905- 6
Smith, E(lmer) Boyd
1860-1943 .... YABC 1
Smith, E(dric) Brooks 1917- 40
Smith, Elva S(ophronia) 1871-1965
Brief Entry 31
Smith, Emma 1923-
Brief Entry 36
Smith, Eunice Young 1902- 5
Smith, Frances C. 1904- 3
Smith, Fredrika Shumway 1877-1968
Brief Entry 30
Smith, Gary R(ichard) 1932- 14
Smith, George Harmon 1920- 5
Smith, H(arry) Allen 1907-1976
Obituary 20
Smith, Howard Everett, Jr.
1927- 12
Smith, Hugh L(etcher)
1921-1968 5
Smith, Imogene Henderson
1922- 12
Smith, Jacqueline B. 1937- 39
Smith, Jean
See Smith, Frances C.
Smith, Jean Pajot 1945- 10
Smith, Jessie Willcox
1863-1935 21
Smith, Jim 1920-
Brief Entry 36
Smith, Joan 1933-
Brief Entry 46
Smith, Johnston
See Crane, Stephen (Townley)
Smith, Lafayette
See Higdon, Hal
Smith, Lee
See Albion, Lee Smith
Smith, Lillian H(elena) 1887-1983
Obituary 32
Smith, Linell Nash 1932- 2
Smith, Lucia B. 1943- 30
Smith, Marion Hagens 1913- 12
Smith, Marion Jaques 1899- 13
Smith, Mary Ellen 10
Smith, Mike
See Smith, Mary Ellen
Smith, Nancy Covert 1935- 12
Smith, Norman F. 1920- 5
Smith, Pauline C(oggeshall)
1908- 27
Smith, Philip Warren 1936- 46
Smith, Robert Kimmel 1930- 12
Smith, Robert Paul 1915-1977
Obituary 30
Smith, Ruth Leslie 1902- 2
Smith, Samantha 1972-1985
Obituary 45
Smith, Sarah Stafford
See Smith, Dorothy Stafford
Smith, Susan Carlton 1923- 12
Smith, Susan Mathias 1950- 43
Brief Entry 35
Smith, Susan Vernon 1950- 48

Smith, Vian (Crocker)
1919-1969 11
Smith, Ward
See Goldsmith, Howard
Smith, William A. 10
Smith, William Jay 1918- 2
Smith, Winsome 1935- 45
Smith, Z. Z.
See Westheimer, David
Smits, Teo
See Smits, Theodore R(ichard)
Smits, Theodore R(ichard)
1905- 45
Brief Entry 28
Smucker, Barbara (Claassen)
1915- 29
See also CLR 10
Snedeker, Caroline Dale (Parke)
1871-1956 .... YABC 2
Snell, Nigel (Edward Creagh) 1936-
Brief Entry 40
Sneve, Virginia Driving Hawk
1933- 8
See also CLR 2
Sniff, Mr.
See Abisch, Roslyn Kroop
Snodgrass, Thomas Jefferson
See Clemens, Samuel Langhorne
Snook, Barbara (Lillian)
1913-1976 34
Snow, Donald Clifford 1917- 16
Snow, Dorothea J(ohnston)
1909- 9
Snow, Richard F(olger) 1947-
Brief Entry 37
Snyder, Anne 1922- 4
Snyder, Carol 1941- 35
Snyder, Gerald S(eymour)
1933- 48
Brief Entry 34
Snyder, Jerome 1916-1976
Obituary 20
Snyder, Zilpha Keatley 1927- 28
Earlier sketch in SATA 1
See also SAAS 2
Snyderman, Reuven K. 1922- 5
Soble, Jennie
See Cavin, Ruth (Brodie)
Sobol, Donald J. 1924- 31
Earlier sketch in SATA 1
See also CLR 4
Sobol, Harriet Langsam 1936- 47
Brief Entry 34
Soderlind, Arthur E(dwin)
1920- 14
Softly, Barbara (Frewin)
1924- 12
Soglow, Otto 1900-1975
Obituary 30
Sohl, Frederic J(ohn) 1916- 10
Sokol, Bill
See Sokol, William
Sokol, William 1923- 37
Sokolov, Kirill 1930- 34
Solbert, Romaine G. 1925- 2
Solbert, Ronni
See Solbert, Romaine G.
Solomon, Joan 1930(?)-
Brief Entry 40

Solomons, Ikey, Esquire, Jr.
See Thackeray, William Makepeace
Solonevich, George 1915- 15
Solot, Mary Lynn 1939- 12
Sommer, Elyse 1929- 7
Sommer, Robert 1929- 12
Sommerfelt, Aimee 1892- 5
Sonneborn, Ruth (Cantor) A.
1899-1974 4
Obituary 27
Sorche, Nic Leodhas
See Alger, Leclaire (Gowans)
Sorel, Edward 1929-
Brief Entry 37
Sorensen, Virginia 1912- 2
Sorley Walker, Kathrine 41
Sorrentino, Joseph N. 6
Sortor, June Elizabeth 1939- 12
Sortor, Toni
See Sortor, June Elizabeth
Soskin, V. H.
See Ellison, Virginia Howell
Sotomayor, Antonio 1902- 11
Soudley, Henry
See Wood, James Playsted
Soule, Gardner (Bosworth)
1913- 14
Soule, Jean Conder 1919- 10
Southall, Ivan 1921- 3
See also CLR 2
See also SAAS 3
Spanfeller, James J(ohn)
1930- 19
Spangenberg, Judith Dunn
1942- 5
Spar, Jerome 1918- 10
Sparks, Beatrice Mathews
1918- 44
Brief Entry 28
Sparks, Mary W. 1920- 15
Spaulding, Leonard
See Bradbury, Ray
Speare, Elizabeth George
1908- 5
See also CLR 8
Spearing, Judith (Mary Harlow)
1922- 9
Specking, Inez 1890-196(?) 11
Speicher, Helen Ross (Smith)
1915- 8
Spellman, John W(illard)
1934- 14
Spelman, Mary 1934- 28
Spence, Eleanor (Rachel)
1927- 21
Spence, Geraldine 1931- 47
Spencer, Ann 1918- 10
Spencer, Cornelia
See Yaukey, Grace S.
Spencer, Donald D(ean) 1931- 41
Spencer, Elizabeth 1921- 14
Spencer, William 1922- 9
Spencer, Zane A(nn) 1935- 35
Sperry, Armstrong W.
1897-1976 1
Obituary 27
Sperry, Raymond, Jr. [Collective
pseudonym] 1

Spicer, Dorothy (Gladys)
  (?)-1975 .... *32*
Spiegelman, Judith M. *5*
Spielberg, Steven 1947- *32*
Spier, Peter (Edward) 1927- *4*
  See also CLR 5
Spilhaus, Athelstan 1911- *13*
Spilka, Arnold 1917- *6*
Spinelli, Eileen 1942- *38*
Spinelli, Jerry 1941- *39*
Spink, Reginald (William)
  1905- *11*
Spinner, Stephanie 1943- *38*
Spinossimus
  See White, William
Splaver, Sarah 1921-
  Brief Entry *28*
Spollen, Christopher 1952- *12*
Sprague, Gretchen (Burnham)
  1926- *27*
Sprigge, Elizabeth 1900-1974 ..... *10*
Spring, (Robert) Howard
  1889-1965 .... *28*
Springer, Marilyn Harris
  1931- *47*
Springstubb, Tricia 1950- *46*
  Brief Entry *40*
Spykman, E(lizabeth) C.
  19(?)-1965 .... *10*
Spyri, Johanna (Heusser)
  1827-1901 .... *19*
Squire, Miriam
  See Sprigge, Elizabeth
Squires, Phil
  See Barker, S. Omar
S-Ringi, Kjell
  See Ringi, Kjell
Srivastava, Jane Jonas
  Brief Entry *37*
Stadtler, Bea 1921- *17*
Stafford, Jean 1915-1979
  Obituary *22*
Stahl, Ben(jamin) 1910- *5*
Stahl, Hilda 1938- *48*
Stair, Gobin (John) 1912- *35*
Stalder, Valerie *27*
Stamaty, Mark Alan 1947- *12*
Stambler, Irwin 1924- *5*
Stanek, Muriel (Novella) 1915-
  Brief Entry *34*
Stang, Judit 1921-1977 .... *29*
Stang, Judy
  See Stang, Judit
Stanhope, Eric
  See Hamilton, Charles H. St. John
Stankevich, Boris 1928- *2*
Stanley, Diana 1909-
  Brief Entry *30*
Stanley, Diane 1943- *37*
  Brief Entry *32*
Stanley, Robert
  See Hamilton, Charles H. St. John
Stanli, Sue
  See Meilach, Dona Z(weigoron)
Stanstead, John
  See Groom, Arthur William
Stapleton, Marjorie (Winifred)
  1932- *28*

Stapp, Arthur D(onald)
  1906-1972 .... *4*
Starbird, Kaye 1916- *6*
Stark, James
  See Goldston, Robert
Starkey, Marion L. 1901- *13*
Starr, Ward and Murch, Mel [Joint
  double pseudonym]
  See Manes, Stephen
Starret, William
  See McClintock, Marshall
Stasiak, Krystyna *49*
Stauffer, Don
  See Berkebile, Fred D(onovan)
Staunton, Schuyler
  See Baum, L(yman) Frank
Steadman, Ralph (Idris) 1936- *32*
Stearns, Monroe (Mather)
  1913- *5*
Steele, Chester K.
  See Stratemeyer, Edward L.
Steele, Mary Q. *3*
Steele, (Henry) Max(well)
  1922- *10*
Steele, William O(wen)
  1917-1979 .... *1*
  Obituary *27*
Stegeman, Janet Allais 1923-
  Brief Entry *49*
Steig, William 1907- *18*
  See also CLR 2
Stein, Harvé 1904-
  Brief Entry *30*
Stein, M(eyer) L(ewis) *6*
Stein, Mini *2*
Stein, R(ichard) Conrad 1937- *31*
Stein, Sara Bonnett
  Brief Entry *34*
Steinbeck, John (Ernst)
  1902-1968 .... *9*
Steinberg, Alfred 1917- *9*
Steinberg, Fannie 1899- *43*
Steinberg, Fred J. 1933- *4*
Steinberg, Phillip Orso 1921- *34*
Steinberg, Rafael (Mark)
  1927- *45*
Steiner, Barbara A(nnette)
  1934- *13*
Steiner, Charlotte 1900-1981 ..... *45*
Steiner, Jörg 1930- *35*
Steiner, Stan(ley) 1925- *14*
Steiner-Prag, Hugo 1880-1945
  Brief Entry *32*
Stephens, Mary Jo 1935- *8*
Stephens, William M(cLain)
  1925- *21*
Stephensen, A. M.
  See Manes, Stephen
Stepp, Ann 1935- *29*
Steptoe, John (Lewis) 1950- *8*
  See also CLR 2, 12
Sterling, Dorothy 1913- *1*
  See also CLR 1
  See also SAAS 2
Sterling, Helen
  See Hoke, Helen (L.)
Sterling, Philip 1907- *8*
Stern, Ellen N(orman) 1927- *26*

Stern, Madeleine B(ettina)
  1912- *14*
Stern, Philip Van Doren
  1900-1984 .... *13*
  Obituary *39*
Stern, Simon 1943- *15*
Sterne, Emma Gelders
  1894-1971 .... *6*
Steurt, Marjorie Rankin 1888- *10*
Stevens, Carla M(cBride)
  1928- *13*
Stevens, Franklin 1933- *6*
Stevens, Gwendolyn 1944- *33*
Stevens, Kathleen 1936- *49*
Stevens, Patricia Bunning
  1931- *27*
Stevens, Peter
  See Geis, Darlene
Stevenson, Anna (M.) 1905- *12*
Stevenson, Augusta
  1869(?)-1976 .... *2*
  Obituary *26*
Stevenson, Burton E(gbert)
  1872-1962 .... *25*
Stevenson, James 1929- *42*
  Brief Entry *34*
Stevenson, Janet 1913- *8*
Stevenson, Robert Louis
  1850-1894 .... *YABC 2*
  See also CLR 10, 11
Stewart, A(gnes) C(harlotte) *15*
Stewart, Charles
  See Zurhorst, Charles (Stewart, Jr.)
Stewart, Elizabeth Laing
  1907- *6*
Stewart, George Rippey
  1895-1980 .... *3*
  Obituary *23*
Stewart, John (William) 1920- *14*
Stewart, Mary (Florence Elinor)
  1916- *12*
Stewart, Robert Neil
  1891-1972 .... *7*
Stewart, Scott
  See Zaffo, George J.
Stewig, John Warren 1937- *26*
Stiles, Martha Bennett *6*
Stiles, Norman B. 1942-
  Brief Entry *36*
Still, James 1906- *29*
Stillerman, Robbie 1947- *12*
Stilley, Frank 1918- *29*
Stine, G(eorge) Harry 1928- *10*
Stine, Jovial Bob
  See Stine, Robert Lawrence
Stine, Robert Lawrence 1943- *31*
Stinetorf, Louise 1900- *10*
Stirling, Arthur
  See Sinclair, Upton (Beall)
Stirling, Nora B. *3*
Stirnweis, Shannon 1931- *10*
Stobbs, William 1914- *17*
Stockton, Francis Richard
  1834-1902 .... *44*
Stockton, Frank R(ichard)
  Brief Entry *32*
  See Stockton, Francis Richard
Stoddard, Edward G. 1923- *10*
Stoddard, Hope 1900- *6*

Stoddard, Sandol
See Warburg, Sandol Stoddard
Stoiko, Michael 1919- *14*
Stoker, Abraham 1847-1912 ...... *29*
Stoker, Bram
See Stoker, Abraham
Stokes, Cedric
See Beardmore, George
Stokes, Jack (Tilden) 1923- *13*
Stokes, Olivia Pearl 1916- *32*
Stolz, Mary (Slattery) 1920- *10*
See also SAAS 3
Stone, Alan [Collective
pseudonym] *1*
See also Svenson, Andrew E.
Stone, D(avid) K(arl) 1922- *9*
Stone, Eugenia 1879-1971 .... *7*
Stone, Gene
See Stone, Eugenia
Stone, Helen V. *6*
Stone, Irving 1903- *3*
Stone, Jon 1931- *39*
Stone, Josephine Rector
See Dixon, Jeanne
Stone, Raymond [Collective
pseudonym] *1*
Stone, Richard A.
See Stratemeyer, Edward L.
Stonehouse, Bernard 1926- *13*
Stong, Phil(ip Duffield)
1899-1957 .... *32*
Storch, Anne B. von
See von Storch, Anne B.
Storey, (Elizabeth) Margaret (Carlton)
1926- *9*
Storey, Victoria Carolyn
1945- *16*
Storme, Peter
See Stern, Philip Van Doren
Storr, Catherine (Cole) 1913- *9*
Stoutenburg, Adrien 1916- *3*
Stover, Allan C(arl) 1938- *14*
Stover, Marjorie Filley 1914- *9*
Stowe, Harriet (Elizabeth) Beecher
1811-1896 .... *YABC 1*
Strachan, Margaret Pitcairn
1908- *14*
Strait, Treva Adams 1909- *35*
Strand, Mark 1934- *41*
Strange, Philippa
See Coury, Louise Andree
Stranger, Joyce
See Wilson, Joyce M(uriel Judson)
Strasser, Todd 1950- *45*
Brief Entry *41*
See also CLR 11
Stratemeyer, Edward L.
1862-1930 .... *1*
Stratford, Philip 1927- *47*
Stratton, Thomas [Joint pseudonym]
See DeWeese, Thomas Eugene
Stratton-Porter, Gene
1863-1924 .... *15*
Strayer, E. Ward
See Stratemeyer, Edward L.
Streano, Vince(nt Catello)
1945- *20*
Streatfeild, Noel 1897-1985 .... *20*
Obituary *48*

Street, Julia Montgomery
1898- *11*
Stren, Patti 1949-
Brief Entry *41*
See also CLR 5
Strete, Craig Kee 1950- *44*
Stretton, Barbara (Humphrey)
1936- *43*
Brief Entry *35*
Strong, Charles [Joint pseudonym]
See Epstein, Beryl and Epstein,
Samuel
Strong, David
See McGuire, Leslie (Sarah)
Strong, J. J.
See Strong, Jeremy
Strong, Jeremy 1949- *36*
Ströyer, Poul 1923- *13*
Stuart, David
See Hoyt, Edwin P(almer), Jr.
Stuart, Forbes 1924- *13*
Stuart, Ian
See MacLean, Alistair (Stuart)
Stuart, (Hilton) Jesse
1907-1984 .... *2*
Obituary *36*
Stuart, Sheila
See Baker, Mary Gladys Steel
Stuart-Clark, Christopher
1940- *32*
Stubis, Talivaldis 1926- *5*
Stubley, Trevor (Hugh) 1932- *22*
Stultifer, Morton
See Curtis, Richard (Alan)
Sture-Vasa, Mary
See Alsop, Mary O'Hara
Sturton, Hugh
See Johnston, H(ugh) A(nthony)
S(tephen)
Sturtzel, Howard A(llison)
1894- *1*
Sturtzel, Jane Levington
1903- *1*
Styles, Frank Showell 1908- *10*
Suba, Susanne *4*
Subond, Valerie
See Grayland, Valerie
Sudbery, Rodie 1943- *42*
Sugarman, Tracy 1921- *37*
Sugita, Yutaka 1930- *36*
Suhl, Yuri 1908- *8*
See also CLR 2
See also SAAS 1
Suid, Murray 1942- *27*
Sullivan, George E(dward)
1927- *4*
Sullivan, Mary W(ilson)
1907- *13*
Sullivan, Thomas Joseph, Jr.
1947- *16*
Sullivan, Tom
See Sullivan, Thomas Joseph, Jr.
Sumichrast, Jözef 1948- *29*
Sumiko
See Davies, Sumiko
Summers, James L(evingston) 1910-
Brief Entry *28*
Sunderlin, Sylvia 1911- *28*
Sung, Betty Lee *26*

Supraner, Robyn 1930- *20*
Surge, Frank 1931- *13*
Susac, Andrew 1929- *5*
Sussman, Susan 1942- *48*
Sutcliff, Rosemary 1920- *44*
Earlier sketch in SATA 6
See also CLR 1
Sutherland, Efua (Theodora Morgue)
1924- *25*
Sutherland, Margaret 1941- *15*
Sutherland, Zena B(ailey)
1915- *37*
Suttles, Shirley (Smith) 1922- *21*
Sutton, Ann (Livesay) 1923- *31*
Sutton, Eve(lyn Mary) 1906- *26*
Sutton, Felix 1910(?)- *31*
Sutton, Jane 1950-
Brief Entry *43*
Sutton, Larry M(atthew)
1931- *29*
Sutton, Margaret (Beebe)
1903- *1*
Sutton, Myron Daniel 1925- *31*
Svenson, Andrew E.
1910-1975 .... *2*
Obituary *26*
Swain, Su Zan (Noguchi)
1916- *21*
Swan, Susan 1944- *22*
Swarthout, Glendon (Fred)
1918- *26*
Swarthout, Kathryn 1919- *7*
Sweeney, James B(artholomew)
1910- *21*
Sweeney, Karen O'Connor
See O'Connor, Karen
Sweetland, Nancy A(nn)
1934- *48*
Swenson, Allan A(rmstrong)
1933- *21*
Swenson, May 1919- *15*
Swift, David
See Kaufmann, John
Swift, Hildegarde Hoyt 1890(?)-1977
Obituary *20*
Swift, Jonathan 1667-1745 .... *19*
Swift, Merlin
See Leeming, Joseph
Swiger, Elinor Porter 1927- *8*
Swinburne, Laurence 1924- *9*
Swindells, Robert E(dward) 1939-
Brief Entry *34*
Switzer, Ellen 1923- *48*
Sydney, Frank [Joint pseudonym]
See Warwick, Alan R(oss)
Sylvester, Natalie G(abry)
1922- *22*
Syme, (Neville) Ronald 1913- *2*
Symons, (Dorothy) Geraldine
1909- *33*
Synge, (Phyllis) Ursula 1930- *9*
Sypher, Lucy Johnston 1907- *7*
Szasz, Suzanne Shorr 1919- *13*
Szekeres, Cyndy 1933- *5*
Szudek, Agnes S(usan) P(hilomena)
Brief Entry *49*
Szulc, Tad 1926- *26*

T

Taback, Simms 1932- *40*
   Brief Entry *36*
Taber, Gladys (Bagg) 1899-1980
   Obituary *22*
Tabrah, Ruth Milander 1921- *14*
Tafuri, Nancy 1946- *39*
Tait, Douglas 1944- *12*
Takakjian, Portia 1930- *15*
Takashima, Shizuye 1928- *13*
Talbot, Charlene Joy 1928- *10*
Talbot, Toby 1928- *14*
Talker, T.
   See Rands, William Brighty
Tallcott, Emogene *10*
Tallon, Robert 1939- *43*
   Brief Entry *28*
Talmadge, Marian *14*
Tamarin, Alfred *13*
Tamburine, Jean 1930- *12*
Tannen, Mary 1943- *37*
Tannenbaum, Beulah 1916- *3*
Tannenbaum, D(onald) Leb
   1948- *42*
Tanner, Louise S(tickney)
   1922- *9*
Tanobe, Miyuki 1937- *23*
Tapio, Pat Decker
   See Kines, Pat Decker
Tarkington, (Newton) Booth
   1869-1946 .... *17*
Tarry, Ellen 1906- *16*
Tarshis, Jerome 1936- *9*
Tarsky, Sue 1946- *41*
Tashjian, Virginia A. 1921- *3*
Tasker, James *9*
Tate, Eleanora E(laine) 1948- *38*
Tate, Ellalice
   See Hibbert, Eleanor
Tate, Joan 1922- *9*
Tate, Mary Anne
   See Hale, Arlene
Tatham, Campbell
   See Elting, Mary
Taves, Isabella 1915- *27*
Taylor, Ann 1782-1866 .... *41*
   Brief Entry *35*
Taylor, Barbara J. 1927- *10*
Taylor, Carl 1937- *14*
Taylor, David 1900-1965 .... *10*
Taylor, Elizabeth 1912-1975 ...... *13*
Taylor, Florence Walton *9*
Taylor, Florence M(arion Tompkins)
   1892- *9*
Taylor, Herb(ert Norman, Jr.)
   1942- *22*
Taylor, Jane 1783-1824 .... *41*
   Brief Entry *35*
Taylor, Jerry Duncan 1938- *47*
Taylor, Kenneth N(athaniel)
   1917- *26*
Taylor, L(ester) B(arbour), Jr.
   1932- *27*
Taylor, Louise Todd 1939- *47*
Taylor, Mark 1927- *32*
   Brief Entry *28*
Taylor, Mildred D. *15*
   See also CLR 9

Taylor, Paula (Wright) 1942- *48*
   Brief Entry *33*
Taylor, Robert Lewis 1912- *10*
Taylor, Sydney (Brenner)
   1904(?)-1978 .... *28*
   Obituary *26*
   Earlier sketch in SATA 1
Taylor, Theodore 1924- *5*
   See also SAAS 4
Teague, Bob
   See Teague, Robert
Teague, Robert 1929- *32*
   Brief Entry *31*
Teal, Val 1903- *10*
Teale, Edwin Way 1899-1980 ..... *7*
   Obituary *25*
Teasdale, Sara 1884-1933 .... *32*
Tebbel, John (William) 1912- *26*
Tee-Van, Helen Damrosch
   1893-1976 .... *10*
   Obituary *27*
Teleki, Geza 1943- *45*
Telemaque, Eleanor Wong
   1934- *43*
Telescope, Tom
   See Newbery, John
Temkin, Sara Anne (Schlossberg)
   1913- *26*
Temko, Florence *13*
Tempest, Margaret Mary 1892-1982
   Obituary *33*
Templar, Maurice
   See Groom, Arthur William
Temple, Herbert 1919- *45*
Temple, Paul [Joint pseudonym]
   See McConnell, James Douglas
   (Rutherford)
Tenggren, Gustaf 1896-1970 ...... *18*
   Obituary *26*
Tennant, Kylie 1912- *6*
Tennant, Veronica 1946- *36*
Tenniel, Sir John 1820-1914
   Brief Entry *27*
Terban, Marvin
   Brief Entry *45*
ter Haar, Jaap 1922- *6*
Terhune, Albert Payson
   1872-1942 .... *15*
Terlouw, Jan (Cornelis) 1931- *30*
Terris, Susan 1937- *3*
Terry, Luther L(eonidas)
   1911-1985 .... *11*
   Obituary *42*
Terry, Walter 1913- *14*
Terzian, James P. 1915- *14*
Tester, Sylvia Root 1939-
   Brief Entry *37*
Tether, (Cynthia) Graham
   1950- *46*
   Brief Entry *36*
Thacher, Mary McGrath
   1933- *9*
Thackeray, William Makepeace
   1811-1863 .... *23*
Thaler, Michael C. 1936-
   Brief Entry *47*
Thaler, Mike
   See Thaler, Michael C.
Thamer, Katie 1955- *42*

Thane, Elswyth 1900- *32*
Tharp, Louise Hall 1898- *3*
Thayer, Jane
   See Woolley, Catherine
Thayer, Marjorie
   Brief Entry *37*
Thayer, Peter
   See Wyler, Rose
Thelwell, Norman 1923- *14*
Theroux, Paul 1941- *44*
Thieda, Shirley Ann 1943- *13*
Thiele, Colin (Milton) 1920- *14*
   See also SAAS 2
Thiry, Joan (Marie) 1926- *45*
Thistlethwaite, Miles 1945- *12*
Thollander, Earl 1922- *22*
Thomas, Allison
   See Fleischer, Leonore
Thomas, Andrea
   See Hill, Margaret (Ohler)
Thomas, Art(hur Lawrence)
   1952- *48*
   Brief Entry *38*
Thomas, Estelle Webb 1899- *26*
Thomas, H. C.
   See Keating, Lawrence A.
Thomas, Ianthe 1951-
   Brief Entry *42*
   See also CLR 8
Thomas, J. F.
   See Fleming, Thomas J(ames)
Thomas, Jane Resh 1936- *38*
Thomas, Joan Gale
   See Robinson, Joan G.
Thomas, Joyce Carol 1938- *40*
Thomas, Lowell (Jackson), Jr.
   1923- *15*
Thomas, Victoria [Joint pseudonym]
   See DeWeese, Thomas Eugene
Thompson, Brenda 1935- *34*
Thompson, Christine Pullein
   See Pullein-Thompson, Christine
Thompson, David H(ugh)
   1941- *17*
Thompson, Diana Pullein
   See Pullein-Thompson, Diana
Thompson, Eileen
   See Panowski, Eileen Thompson
Thompson, George Selden
   1929- *4*
Thompson, Harlan H. 1894- *10*
Thompson, Hilary 1943-
   Brief Entry *49*
Thompson, Josephine
   See Pullein-Thompson, Josephine
Thompson, Julian F(rancis) 1927-
   Brief Entry *40*
Thompson, Kay 1912- *16*
Thompson, Stith 1885-1976
   Obituary *20*
Thompson, Vivian L. 1911- *3*
Thomson, David (Robert Alexander)
   1914- *40*
Thomson, Peggy 1922- *31*
Thorndyke, Helen Louise
   [Collective pseudonym] *1*
Thorne, Ian
   See May, Julian

Author Index

Thornton, W. B.
  See Burgess, Thornton Waldo
Thorpe, E(ustace) G(eorge)
  1916- *21*
Thorvall, Kerstin 1925- *13*
Thrasher, Crystal (Faye)
  1921- *27*
Thum, Gladys 1920- *26*
Thum, Marcella *28*
  Earlier sketch in SATA 3
Thundercloud, Katherine
  See Witt, Shirley Hill
Thurber, James (Grover)
  1894-1961 .... *13*
Thurman, Judith 1946- *33*
Thwaite, Ann (Barbara Harrop)
  1932- *14*
Ticheburn, Cheviot
  See Ainsworth, William Harrison
Tichenor, Tom 1923- *14*
Tichy, William 1924- *31*
Tiegreen, Alan F. 1935-
  Brief Entry *36*
Tilton, Madonna Elaine 1929- *41*
Tilton, Rafael
  See Tilton, Madonna Elaine
Timmins, William F. *10*
Tiner, John Hudson 1944- *32*
Tinkelman, Murray 1933- *12*
Tinkle, (Julien) Lon
  1906-1980 .... *36*
Titler, Dale M(ilton) 1926- *35*
  Brief Entry *28*
Titmarsh, Michael Angelo
  See Thackeray, William Makepeace
Titus, Eve 1922- *2*
Tobias, Tobi 1938- *5*
  See also CLR 4
Todd, Anne Ophelia
  See Dowden, Anne Ophelia
Todd, Barbara K. 1917- *10*
Todd, H(erbert) E(atton)
  1908- *11*
Todd, Loreto 1942- *30*
Tolan, Stephanie S. 1942- *38*
Toland, John (Willard) 1912- *38*
Tolkien, J(ohn) R(onald) R(euel)
  1892-1973 .... *32*
  Obituary *24*
  Earlier sketch in SATA 2
Tolles, Martha 1921- *8*
Tolliver, Ruby C(hangos) 1922-
  Brief Entry *41*
Tolmie, Ken(neth Donald)
  1941- *15*
Tolstoi, Leo (Nikolaevich)
  1828-1910 .... *26*
Tomalin, Ruth *29*
Tomes, Margot (Ladd) 1917- *36*
  Brief Entry *27*
Tomfool
  See Farjeon, Eleanor
Tomkins, Jasper
  See Batey, Tom
Tomline, F. Latour
  See Gilbert, W(illiam) S(chwenk)
Tomlinson, Jill 1931-1976 .... *3*
  Obituary *24*

Tomlinson, Reginald R(obert)
  1885-1979(?)
  Obituary *27*
Tompert, Ann 1918- *14*
Toner, Raymond John 1908- *10*
Took, Belladonna
  See Chapman, Vera
Tooke, Louise Mathews 1950- *38*
Toonder, Martin
  See Groom, Arthur William
Toothaker, Roy Eugene 1928- *18*
Tooze, Ruth 1892-1972 .... *4*
Topping, Audrey R(onning)
  1928- *14*
Tor, Regina
  See Shekerjian, Regina Tor
Torbert, Floyd James 1922- *22*
Torgersen, Don Arthur 1934-
  Brief Entry *41*
Torrie, Malcolm
  See Mitchell, Gladys (Maude
  Winifred)
Totham, Mary
  See Breinburg, Petronella
Tournier, Michel 1924- *23*
Towne, Mary
  See Spelman, Mary
Townsend, John Rowe 1922- *4*
  See also CLR 2
  See also SAAS 2
Townsend, Sue 1946-
  Brief Entry *48*
Toye, Clive 1933(?)-
  Brief Entry *30*
Toye, William E(ldred) 1926- *8*
Traherne, Michael
  See Watkins-Pitchford, D. J.
Trahey, Jane 1923- *36*
Trapp, Maria (Augusta) von
  1905- *16*
Travers, P(amela) L(yndon)
  1906- *4*
  See also CLR 2
  See also SAAS 2
Treadgold, Mary 1910- *49*
Trease, (Robert) Geoffrey
  1909- *2*
Tredez, Alain 1926- *17*
Treece, Henry 1911-1966 .... *2*
  See also CLR 2
Tregarthen, Enys
  See Sloggett, Nellie
Tregaskis, Richard 1916-1973 ..... *3*
  Obituary *26*
Trell, Max 1900- *14*
Tremain, Ruthven 1922- *17*
Trent, Robbie 1894- *26*
Trent, Timothy
  See Malmberg, Carl
Tresilian, (Cecil) Stuart
  1891-19(?) *40*
Tresselt, Alvin 1916- *7*
Treviño, Elizabeth B(orton) de
  1904- *29*
  Earlier sketch in SATA 1
Trevor, Elleston 1920- *28*
Trevor, Glen
  See Hilton, James
Trevor, (Lucy) Meriol 1919- *10*

Trez, Alain
  See Tredez, Alain
Trimby, Elisa 1948- *47*
  Brief Entry *40*
Tripp, Eleanor B. 1936- *4*
Tripp, Paul *8*
Tripp, Wallace (Whitney)
  1940- *31*
Trivelpiece, Laurel 1926-
  Brief Entry *46*
Trivett, Daphne (Harwood)
  1940- *22*
Trnka, Jiri 1912-1969 .... *43*
  Brief Entry *32*
Trollope, Anthony 1815-1882 ..... *22*
Trost, Lucille Wood 1938- *12*
Trotter, Grace V(iolet) 1900- *10*
Troughton, Joanna (Margaret)
  1947- *37*
Troyer, Johannes 1902-1969
  Brief Entry *40*
Trudeau, G(arretson) B(eekman)
  1948- *35*
Trudeau, Garry B.
  See Trudeau, G(arretson) B(eekman)
Truesdell, Sue
  See Truesdell, Susan G.
Truesdell, Susan G.
  Brief Entry *45*
Truss, Jan 1925- *35*
Tucker, Caroline
  See Nolan, Jeannette
Tudor, Tasha *20*
Tully, John (Kimberley)
  1923- *14*
Tunis, Edwin (Burdett)
  1897-1973 .... *28*
  Obituary *24*
  Earlier sketch in SATA 1
  See also CLR 2
Tunis, John R(oberts)
  1889-1975 .... *37*
  Brief Entry *30*
Turkle, Brinton 1915- *2*
Turlington, Bayly 1919- *5*
Turnbull, Agnes Sligh *14*
Turnbull, Ann (Christine)
  1943- *18*
Turner, Alice K. 1940- *10*
Turner, Ann W(arren) 1945- *14*
Turner, Elizabeth
  1774-1846 .... YABC 2
Turner, Josie
  See Crawford, Phyllis
Turner, Philip 1925- *11*
Turner, Sheila R.
  See Seed, Sheila Turner
Turngren, Annette 1902(?)-1980
  Obituary *23*
Turngren, Ellen (?)-1964 .... *3*
Turska, Krystyna Zofia 1933- *31*
  Brief Entry *27*
Tusan, Stan 1936- *22*
Tusiani, Joseph 1924- *45*
Twain, Mark
  See Clemens, Samuel Langhorne
Tweedsmuir, Baron
  See Buchan, John
Tweton, D. Jerome 1933- *48*

Tworkov, Jack 1900-1982 47
    Obituary 31
Tyler, Anne 1941- 7

U

Ubell, Earl 1926- 4
Uchida, Yoshiko 1921- 1
    See also CLR 6
    See also SAAS 1
Udall, Jan Beaney 1938- 10
Uden, (Bernard Gilbert) Grant
    1910- 26
Udry, Janice May 1928- 4
Ullman, James Ramsey
    1907-1971 7
Ulm, Robert 1934-1977 17
Ulyatt, Kenneth 1920- 14
Unada
    See Gliewe, Unada
Uncle Gus
    See Rey, H. A.
Uncle Mac
    See McCulloch, Derek (Ivor
    Breashur)
Uncle Ray
    See Coffman, Ramon Peyton
Uncle Shelby
    See Silverstein, Shel(by)
Underhill, Alice Mertie 1900-1971
Underhill, Liz 1936-
    Brief Entry 49
Ungerer, (Jean) Thomas 1931- 33
    Earlier sketch in SATA 5
Ungerer, Tomi
    See Ungerer, (Jean) Thomas
    See also CLR 3
Unkelbach, Kurt 1913- 4
Unnerstad, Edith 1900- 3
Unrau, Ruth 1922- 9
Unstead, R(obert) J(ohn)
    1915- 12
Unsworth, Walt 1928- 4
Untermeyer, Louis 1885-1977 37
    Obituary 26
    Earlier sketch in SATA 2
Unwin, David S(torr) 1918- 14
Unwin, Nora S. 1907-1982 3
    Obituary 49
Ure, Jean 48
Uris, Leon (Marcus) 1924- 49
Usher, Margo Scegge
    See McHargue, Georgess
Uttley, Alice Jane (Taylor)
    1884-1976 3
    Obituary 26
Uttley, Alison
    See Uttley, Alice Jane (Taylor)
Utz, Lois 1932- 5
Uzair, Salem ben
    See Horne, Richard Henry

V

Vaeth, J(oseph) Gordon 1921- 17
Valen, Nanine 1950- 21
Valencak, Hannelore 1929- 42

Valens, Evans G., Jr. 1920- 1
Van Abbé, Salaman
    1883-1955 18
Van Allsburg, Chris 1949- 37
    See also CLR 5
Van Anrooy, Francine 1924- 2
Van Anrooy, Frans
    See Van Anrooy, Francine
Vance, Eleanor Graham 1908- 11
Vance, Marguerite 1889-1965 29
Vandenburg, Mary Lou 1943- 17
Vander Boom, Mae M. 14
Van der Veer, Judy
    1912-1982 4
    Obituary 33
Vandivert, Rita (Andre) 1905- 21
Van Duyn, Janet 1910- 18
Van Dyne, Edith
    See Baum, L(yman) Frank
Van Horn, William 1939- 43
Van Iterson, S(iny) R(ose) 26
Van Leeuwen, Jean 1937- 6
Van Lhin, Erik
    See Del Rey, Lester
Van Loon, Hendrik Willem
    1882-1944 18
Van Orden, M(erton) D(ick)
    1921- 4
Van Rensselaer, Alexander (Taylor
    Mason) 1892-1962 14
Van Riper, Guernsey, Jr.
    1909- 3
Van Steenwyk, Elizabeth Ann
    1928- 34
Van Stockum, Hilda 1908- 5
Van Tuyl, Barbara 1940- 11
Van Vogt, A(lfred) E(lton)
    1912- 14
Van Woerkom, Dorothy (O'Brien)
    1924- 21
Van Wormer, Joe
    See Van Wormer, Joseph Edward
Van Wormer, Joseph Edward
    1913- 35
Van-Wyck Mason, F.
    See Mason, F. van Wyck
Van Zwienen, Ilse (Charlotte Koehn)
    1929- 34
    Brief Entry 28
Varga, Judy
    See Stang, Judit
Varley, Dimitry V. 1906- 10
Vasiliu, Mircea 1920- 2
Vass, George 1927-
    Brief Entry 31
Vaughan, Carter A.
    See Gerson, Noel B(ertram)
Vaughan, Harold Cecil 1923- 14
Vaughan, Sam(uel) S. 1928- 14
Vaughn, Ruth 1935- 14
Vavra, Robert James 1944- 8
Vecsey, George 1939- 9
Veglahn, Nancy (Crary) 1937- 5
Venable, Alan (Hudson)
    1944- 8
Venn, Mary Eleanor
    See Jorgensen, Mary Venn
Ventura, Piero (Luigi) 1937-
    Brief Entry 43

Vequin, Capini
    See Quinn, Elisabeth
Verne, Jules 1828-1905 21
Verner, Gerald 1897(?)-1980
    Obituary 25
Verney, John 1913- 14
Vernon, (Elda) Louise A(nderson)
    1914- 14
Vernon, Rosemary
    See Smith, Susan Vernon
Vernor, D.
    See Casewit, Curtis
Verral, Charles Spain 1904- 11
Verrone, Robert J. 1935(?)-1984
    Obituary 39
Versace, Marie Teresa Rios
    1917- 2
Vesey, Paul
    See Allen, Samuel (Washington)
Vestly, Anne-Cath(arina)
    1920- 14
Vevers, (Henry) Gwynne
    1916- 45
Viator, Vacuus
    See Hughes, Thomas
Vicarion, Count Palmiro
    See Logue, Christopher
Vicker, Angus
    See Felsen, Henry Gregor
Vickery, Kate
    See Kennedy, T(eresa) A.
Victor, Edward 1914- 3
Victor, Joan Berg 1937- 30
Viereck, Ellen K. 1928- 14
Viereck, Phillip 1925- 3
Viertel, Janet 1915- 10
Vigna, Judith 1936- 15
Viguers, Ruth Hill 1903-1971 6
Villiard, Paul 1910-1974
    Obituary 20
Villiers, Alan (John) 1903- 10
Vincent, Eric Douglas 1953- 40
Vincent, Félix 1946- 41
Vincent, Mary Keith
    See St. John, Wylly Folk
Vinge, Joan D(ennison) 1948- 36
Vining, Elizabeth Gray
    See Gray, Elizabeth Janet
Vinson, Kathryn 1911- 21
Vinton, Iris 24
Viorst, Judith 7
    See also CLR 3
Vip
    See Partch, Virgil Franklin II
Visser, W(illiam) F(rederick)
    H(endrik) 1900-1968 10
Vlahos, Olivia 1924- 31
Vlasic, Bob
    See Hirsch, Phil
Vo-Dinh, Mai 1933- 16
Vogel, Ilse-Margret 1914- 14
Vogel, John H(ollister), Jr.
    1950- 18
Vogt, Esther Loewen 1915- 14
Vogt, Gregory
    Brief Entry 45
Vogt, Marie Bollinger 1921- 45
Voight, Virginia Frances
    1909- 8

Voigt, Cynthia 1942- *48*
  Brief Entry *33*
Voigt, Erna 1925- *35*
Voigt-Rother, Erna
  See Voigt, Erna
Vojtech, Anna 1946- *42*
von Almedingen, Martha Edith
  See Almedingen, E. M.
Von Hagen, Victor Wolfgang
  1908- *29*
von Klopp, Vahrah
  See Malvern, Gladys
Von Schmidt, Eric 1931-
  Brief Entry *36*
von Storch, Anne B. 1910- *1*
Vosburgh, Leonard (W.)
  1912- *15*
Voyle, Mary
  See Manning, Rosemary

W

Waber, Bernard 1924- *47*
  Brief Entry *40*
Waddell, Evelyn Margaret
  1918- *10*
Waddell, Martin 1941- *43*
Wade, Theodore E., Jr. 1936- ... *37*
Wagenheim, Kal 1935- *21*
Wagner, Jane *33*
Wagner, Sharon B. 1936- *4*
Wagoner, David (Russell)
  1926- *14*
Wahl, Jan 1933- *34*
  Earlier sketch in SATA 2
  See also SAAS 3
Waide, Jan 1952- *29*
Waitley, Douglas 1927- *30*
Wakefield, Jean L.
  See Laird, Jean E(louise)
Wakin, Edward 1927- *37*
Walck, Henry Z(eigler) 1908-1984
  Obituary *40*
Walden, Amelia Elizabeth *3*
Waldman, Bruce 1949- *15*
Waldron, Ann Wood 1924- *16*
Walker, Alice 1944- *31*
Walker, Barbara K. 1921- *4*
Walker, (James) Braz(elton)
  1934-1983 .... *45*
Walker, David Harry 1911- *8*
Walker, Diana 1925- *9*
Walker, Frank 1930- *36*
Walker, Holly Beth
  See Bond, Gladys Baker
Walker, Louise Jean 1891-1976
  Obituary *35*
Walker, Mildred
  See Schemm, Mildred Walker
Walker, (Addison) Mort
  1923- *8*
Walker, Pamela 1948- *24*
Walker, Stephen J. 1951- *12*
Wallace, Barbara Brooks *4*
Wallace, Beverly Dobrin
  1921- *19*
Wallace, Bill 1947-
  Brief Entry *47*

Wallace, Daisy
  See Cuyler, Margery Stuyvesant
Wallace, John A. 1915- *3*
Wallace, Nigel
  See Hamilton, Charles H. St. John
Wallace, Robert 1932- *47*
  Brief Entry *37*
Wallace-Brodeur, Ruth 1941-
  Brief Entry *41*
Waller, Leslie 1923- *20*
Wallis, G. McDonald
  See Campbell, Hope
Wallner, Alexandra 1946-
  Brief Entry *41*
Wallner, John C. 1945- *10*
Wallower, Lucille *11*
Walsh, Ellen Stoll 1942- *49*
Walsh, Jill Paton
  See Paton Walsh, Gillian
  See also CLR 2
Walter, Mildred Pitts
  Brief Entry *45*
Walter, Villiam Christian
  See Andersen, Hans Christian
Walters, Audrey 1929- *18*
Walters, Hugh
  See Hughes, Walter (Llewellyn)
Walther, Thomas A. 1950- *31*
Walther, Tom
  See Walther, Thomas A.
Waltner, Elma 1912- *40*
Waltner, Willard H. 1909- *40*
Walton, Richard J. 1928- *4*
Waltrip, Lela (Kingston)
  1904- *9*
Waltrip, Mildred 1911- *37*
Waltrip, Rufus (Charles)
  1898- *9*
Walworth, Nancy Zinsser
  1917- *14*
Wangerin, Walter, Jr. 1944- *45*
  Brief Entry *37*
Wannamaker, Bruce
  See Moncure, Jane Belk
Warbler, J. M.
  See Cocagnac, A. M.
Warburg, Sandol Stoddard
  1927- *14*
Ward, John (Stanton) 1917- *42*
Ward, Lynd (Kendall)
  1905-1985 .... *36*
  Obituary *42*
  Earlier sketch in SATA 2
Ward, Martha (Eads) 1921- *5*
Ward, Melanie
  See Curtis, Richard (Alan)
Wardell, Dean
  See Prince, J(ack) H(arvey)
Ware, Leon (Vernon) 1909- *4*
Warner, Frank A. [Collective
  pseudonym] *1*
Warner, Gertrude Chandler
  1890- *9*
Warner, Lucille Schulberg *30*
Warner, Oliver 1903-1976 .... *29*
Warren, Betsy
  See Warren, Elizabeth Avery
Warren, Billy
  See Warren, William Stephen

Warren, Cathy
  Brief Entry *46*
Warren, Elizabeth
  See Supraner, Robyn
Warren, Elizabeth Avery
  1916- *46*
  Brief Entry *38*
Warren, Joyce W(illiams)
  1935- *18*
Warren, Mary Phraner 1929- *10*
Warren, Robert Penn 1905- *46*
Warren, William Stephen
  1882-1968 .... *9*
Warrick, Patricia Scott 1925- *35*
Warsh
  See Warshaw, Jerry
Warshaw, Jerry 1929- *30*
Warshofsky, Fred 1931- *24*
Warshofsky, Isaac
  See Singer, Isaac Bashevis
Wartski, Maureen (Ann Crane) 1940-
  Brief Entry *37*
Warwick, Alan R(oss)
  1900-1973 .... *42*
Wa-sha-quon-asin
  See Belaney, Archibald Stansfeld
Washburn, (Henry) Bradford (Jr.)
  1910- *38*
Washburne, Heluiz Chandler
  1892-1970 .... *10*
  Obituary *26*
Washington, Booker T(aliaferro)
  1858(?)-1915 .... *28*
Watanabe, Shigeo 1928- *39*
  Brief Entry *32*
  See also CLR 8
Waters, John F(rederick)
  1930- *4*
Waterton, Betty (Marie) 1923- *37*
  Brief Entry *34*
Watkins-Pitchford, D. J.
  1905- *6*
  See also SAAS 4
Watson, Aldren A(uld) 1917- *42*
  Brief Entry *36*
Watson, Clyde 1947- *5*
  See also CLR 3
Watson, Helen Orr 1892-1978
  Obituary *24*
Watson, James 1936- *10*
Watson, Jane Werner 1915- *3*
Watson, Nancy Dingman *32*
Watson, Pauline 1925- *14*
Watson, Sally 1924- *3*
Watson, Wendy (McLeod)
  1942- *5*
Watson Taylor, Elizabeth
  1915- *41*
Watt, Thomas 1935- *4*
Watts, Bernadette 1942- *4*
Watts, Ephraim
  See Horne, Richard Henry
Watts, Franklin (Mowry)
  1904-1978 .... *46*
  Obituary *21*
Watts, Mabel Pizzey 1906- *11*
Waugh, Carol-Lynn Rössel
  1947- *41*
Waugh, Dorothy *11*

Wayland, Patrick
 See O'Connor, Richard
Wayne, (Anne) Jenifer
 1917-1982 32
Wayne, Kyra Petrovskaya
 1918- 8
Wayne, Richard
 See Decker, Duane
Waystaff, Simon
 See Swift, Jonathan
Weales, Gerald (Clifford)
 1925- 11
Weary, Ogdred
 See Gorey, Edward St. John
Weaver, John L. 1949- 42
Weaver, Ward
 See Mason, F. van Wyck
Webb, Christopher
 See Wibberley, Leonard (Patrick
 O'Connor)
Webb, Jean Francis (III)
 1910- 35
Webb, Sharon 1936- 41
Webber, Irma E(leanor Schmidt)
 1904- 14
Weber, Alfons 1921- 8
Weber, Lenora Mattingly
 1895-1971 2
 Obituary 26
Weber, William John 1927- 14
Webster, Alice (Jane Chandler)
 1876-1916 17
Webster, David 1930- 11
Webster, Frank V. [Collective
 pseudonym] 1
Webster, Gary
 See Garrison, Webb B(lack)
Webster, James 1925-1981 17
 Obituary 27
Webster, Jean
 See Webster, Alice (Jane Chandler)
Wechsler, Herman 1904-1976
 Obituary 20
Weddle, Ethel H(arshbarger)
 1897- 11
Wegen, Ron(ald)
 Brief Entry 44
Wegner, Fritz 1924- 20
Weihs, Erika 1917- 15
Weik, Mary Hays
 1898(?)-1979 3
 Obituary 23
Weil, Ann Yezner 1908-1969 9
Weil, Lisl 7
Weilerstein, Sadie Rose 1894- 3
Weinberg, Larry
 See Weinberg, Lawrence (E.)
Weinberg, Lawrence (E.)
 Brief Entry 48
Weiner, Sandra 1922- 14
Weingarten, Violet (Brown)
 1915-1976 3
 Obituary 27
Weingartner, Charles 1922- 5
Weir, LaVada 2
Weir, Rosemary (Green)
 1905- 21
Weis, Margaret (Edith) 1948- 38

Weisberger, Bernard A(llen)
 1922- 21
Weiser, Marjorie P(hillis) K(atz)
 1934- 33
Weisgard, Leonard (Joseph)
 1916- 30
 Earlier sketch in SATA 2
Weiss, Adelle 1920- 18
Weiss, Ann E(dwards) 1943- 30
Weiss, Ellen 1953- 44
Weiss, Harvey 1922- 27
 Earlier sketch in SATA 1
 See also CLR 4
Weiss, Malcolm E. 1928- 3
Weiss, Miriam
 See Schlein, Miriam
Weiss, Nicki 1954- 33
Weiss, Renee Karol 1923- 5
Weissenborn, Hellmuth 1898-1982
 Obituary 31
Welber, Robert 26
Welch, D'Alte Aldridge 1907-1970
 Obituary 27
Welch, Jean-Louise
 See Kempton, Jean Welch
Welch, Martha McKeen 1914-
 Brief Entry 45
Welch, Pauline
 See Bodenham, Hilda Esther
Welch, Ronald
 See Felton, Ronald Oliver
Weller, George (Anthony)
 1907- 31
Welles, Winifred 1893-1939
 Brief Entry 27
Wellman, Alice 1900-
 Brief Entry 36
Wellman, Manly Wade
 1903-1986 6
 Obituary 47
Wellman, Paul I. 1898-1966 3
Wells, H(erbert) G(eorge)
 1866-1946 20
Wells, Helen 1910-1986 49
 Earlier sketch in SATA 2
Wells, J. Wellington
 See DeCamp, L(yon) Sprague
Wells, Rosemary 18
 See also SAAS 1
Wels, Byron G(erald) 1924- 9
Welsh, Mary Flynn 1910(?)-1984
 Obituary 38
Weltner, Linda R(iverly)
 1938- 38
Welty, S. F.
 See Welty, Susan F.
Welty, Susan F. 1905- 9
Wendelin, Rudolph 1910- 23
Werner, Herma 1926- 47
 Brief Entry 41
Werner, Jane
 See Watson, Jane Werner
Werner, K.
 See Casewit, Curtis
Wersba, Barbara 1932- 1
 See also CLR 3
 See also SAAS 2
Werstein, Irving 1914-1971 14
Werth, Kurt 1896- 20

West, Anna 1938- 40
West, Barbara
 See Price, Olive
West, Betty 1921- 11
West, C. P.
 See Wodehouse, P(elham)
 G(renville)
West, Emily G(ovan) 1919- 38
West, Emmy
 See West, Emily G(ovan)
West, James
 See Withers, Carl A.
West, Jerry
 See Stratemeyer, Edward L.
West, Jerry
 See Svenson, Andrew E.
West, (Mary) Jessamyn 1902(?)-1984
 Obituary 37
West, Ward
 See Borland, Hal
Westall, Robert (Atkinson)
 1929- 23
 See also SAAS 2
Westerberg, Christine 1950- 29
Westervelt, Virginia (Veeder)
 1914- 10
Westheimer, David 1917- 14
Westmacott, Mary
 See Christie, Agatha (Mary Clarissa)
Westman, Paul (Wendell)
 1956- 39
Weston, Allen [Joint pseudonym]
 See Norton, Alice Mary
Weston, John (Harrison)
 1932- 21
Westwood, Jennifer 1940- 10
Wexler, Jerome (LeRoy)
 1923- 14
Wharf, Michael
 See Weller, George (Anthony)
Wheatley, Arabelle 1921- 16
Wheeler, Captain
 See Ellis, Edward S(ylvester)
Wheeler, Cindy 1955- 49
 Brief Entry 40
Wheeler, Janet D. [Collective
 pseudonym] 1
Wheeler, Opal 1898- 23
Whelan, Elizabeth M(urphy)
 1943- 14
Whistler, Reginald John
 1905-1944 30
Whistler, Rex
 See Whistler, Reginald John
Whitcomb, Jon 1906- 10
White, Anne Hitchcock 1902-1970
 Brief Entry 33
White, Anne Terry 1896- 2
White, Dale
 See Place, Marian T.
White, Dori 1919- 10
White, E(lwyn) B(rooks)
 1899-1985 29
 Obituary 44
 Earlier sketch in SATA 2
 See also CLR 1
White, Eliza Orne
 1856-1947 .... YABC 2

White, Florence M(eiman)
  1910- *14*
White, Laurence B., Jr. 1935- *10*
White, Ramy Allison [Collective
  pseudonym] *1*
White, Robb 1909- *1*
  See also CLR 3
  See also SAAS 1
White, Ruth C. 1942- *39*
White, T(erence) H(anbury)
  1906-1964 .... *12*
White, William, Jr. 1934- *16*
Whitehead, Don(ald) F. 1908- *4*
Whitehouse, Arch
  See Whitehouse, Arthur George
Whitehouse, Arthur George
  1895-1979 .... *14*
  Obituary *23*
Whitehouse, Elizabeth S(cott)
  1893-1968 .... *35*
Whitehouse, Jeanne 1939- *29*
Whitinger, R. D.
  See Place, Marian T.
Whitlock, Pamela 1921(?)-1982
  Obituary *31*
Whitlock, Ralph 1914- *35*
Whitman, Walt(er) 1819-1892 ..... *20*
Whitney, Alex(andra) 1922- *14*
Whitney, David C(harles)
  1921- *48*
  Brief Entry *29*
Whitney, Phyllis A(yame)
  1903- *30*
  Earlier sketch in SATA 1
Whitney, Thomas P(orter)
  1917- *25*
Wibberley, Leonard (Patrick
  O'Connor) 1915-1983 .... *45*
  Obituary *36*
  Earlier sketch in SATA 2
  See also CLR 3
Wiberg, Harald (Albin) 1908-
  Brief Entry *40*
Widdemer, Mabel Cleland
  1902-1964 .... *5*
Widenberg, Siv 1931- *10*
Wier, Ester 1910- *3*
Wiese, Kurt 1887-1974 .... *36*
  Obituary *24*
  Earlier sketch in SATA 3
Wiesner, Portia
  See Takakjian, Portia
Wiesner, William 1899- *5*
Wiggin, Kate Douglas (Smith)
  1856-1923 .... *YABC 1*
Wight, James Alfred 1916-
  Brief Entry *44*
Wikland, Ilon 1930-
  Brief Entry *32*
Wilber, Donald N(ewton)
  1907- *35*
Wilbur, C. Keith 1923- *27*
Wilbur, Richard (Purdy)
  1921- *9*
Wilcox, R(uth) Turner
  1888-1970 .... *36*
Wild, Jocelyn 1941- *46*
Wild, Robin (Evans) 1936- *46*

Wilde, Gunther
  See Hurwood, Bernhardt J.
Wilde, Oscar (Fingal O'Flahertie
  Wills) 1854-1900 .... *24*
Wilder, Cherry
  See Grimm, Cherry Barbara Lockett
Wilder, Laura Ingalls
  1867-1957 .... *29*
  See also CLR 2
Wildsmith, Brian 1930- *16*
  See also CLR 2
Wilkie, Katharine E(lliott)
  1904-1980 .... *31*
Wilkin, Eloise (Burns) 1904- *49*
Wilkins, Frances 1923- *14*
Wilkins, Marilyn (Ruth)
  1926- *30*
Wilkins, Marne
  See Wilkins, Marilyn (Ruth)
Wilkinson, (Thomas) Barry 1923-
  Brief Entry *32*
Wilkinson, Brenda 1946- *14*
Wilkinson, Burke 1913- *4*
Wilkinson, Sylvia (J.) 1940-
  Brief Entry *39*
Wilkoń, Józef 1930- *31*
Wilks, Michael Thomas 1947- *44*
Wilks, Mike
  See Wilks, Michael Thomas
Will
  See Lipkind, William
Willard, Barbara (Mary)
  1909- *17*
  See also CLR 2
Willard, Mildred Wilds 1911- *14*
Willard, Nancy 1936- *37*
  Brief Entry *30*
  See also CLR 5
Willcox, Isobel 1907- *42*
Willey, Robert
  See Ley, Willy
Williams, Barbara 1925- *11*
Williams, Beryl
  See Epstein, Beryl
Williams, Charles
  See Collier, James Lincoln
Williams, Clyde C.
  1881-1974 .... *8*
  Obituary *27*
Williams, Coe
  See Harrison, C. William
Williams, Eric (Ernest)
  1911-1983 .... *14*
  Obituary *38*
Williams, Ferelith Eccles
  1920- *22*
Williams, Frances B.
  See Browin, Frances Williams
Williams, Garth (Montgomery)
  1912- *18*
Williams, Guy R. 1920- *11*
Williams, Hawley
  See Heyliger, William
Williams, J. R.
  See Williams, Jeanne
Williams, J. Walker
  See Wodehouse, P(elham)
  G(renville)

Williams, Jay 1914-1978 .... *41*
  Obituary *24*
  Earlier sketch in SATA 3
  See also CLR 8
Williams, Jeanne 1930- *5*
Williams, Kit 1946(?)- *44*
  See also CLR 4
Williams, Leslie 1941- *42*
Williams, Louise Bonino 1904(?)-1984
  Obituary *39*
Williams, Lynn
  See Hale, Arlene
Williams, Maureen 1951- *12*
Williams, Michael
  See St. John, Wylly Folk
Williams, Patrick J.
  See Butterworth, W. E.
Williams, Selma R(uth) 1925- *14*
Williams, Slim
  See Williams, Clyde C.
Williams, Ursula Moray
  1911- *3*
Williams, Vera B. 1927-
  Brief Entry *33*
  See also CLR 9
Williams-Ellis, (Mary) Amabel
  (Nassau) 1894-1984 .... *29*
  Obituary *41*
Williamson, Henry 1895-1977 .... *37*
  Obituary *30*
Williamson, Joanne Small
  1926- *3*
Willson, Robina Beckles (Ballard)
  1930- *27*
Wilma, Dana
  See Faralla, Dana
Wilson, Beth P(ierre) *8*
Wilson, Carter 1941- *6*
Wilson, Charles Morrow
  1905-1977 .... *30*
Wilson, Christopher B. 1910(?)-1985
  Obituary *46*
Wilson, Dagmar 1916-
  Brief Entry *31*
Wilson, Dorothy Clarke 1904- *16*
Wilson, Edward A(rthur)
  1886-1970 .... *38*
Wilson, Ellen (Janet Cameron)
  (?)-1976 .... *9*
  Obituary *26*
Wilson, Eric H. 1940- *34*
  Brief Entry *32*
Wilson, Forrest 1918- *27*
Wilson, Gahan 1930- *35*
  Brief Entry *27*
Wilson, Gina 1943- *36*
  Brief Entry *34*
Wilson, (Leslie) Granville
  1912- *14*
Wilson, Hazel 1898- *3*
Wilson, John 1922- *22*
Wilson, Joyce M(uriel Judson) *21*
Wilson, Lionel 1924- *33*
  Brief Entry *31*
Wilson, Maurice (Charles John)
  1914- *46*
Wilson, Ron(ald William) *38*
Wilson, Tom 1931- *33*
  Brief Entry *30*

Wilson, Walt(er N.) 1939- *14*

Wilton, Elizabeth 1937- *14*

Wilwerding, Walter Joseph
1891-1966 .... *9*

Winchester, James H(ugh)
1917-1985 .... *30*
Obituary *45*

Winders, Gertrude Hecker *3*

Windham, Basil
See Wodehouse, P(elham)
G(renville)

Windham, Kathryn T(ucker)
1918- *14*

Windsor, Claire
See Hamerstrom, Frances

Windsor, Patricia 1938- *30*

Winfield, Arthur M.
See Stratemeyer, Edward L.

Winfield, Edna
See Stratemeyer, Edward L.

Winn, Chris 1952- *42*

Winn, Janet Bruce 1928- *43*

Winn, Marie 1936- *38*

Winston, Clara 1921-1983
Obituary *39*

Winter, Milo (Kendall)
1888-1956 .... *21*

Winter, Paula Cecelia 1929- *48*

Winter, R. R.
See Winterbotham, R(ussell)
R(obert)

Winterbotham, R(ussell) R(obert)
1904-1971 .... *10*

Winterton, Gayle
See Adams, William Taylor

Winthrop, Elizabeth
See Mahony, Elizabeth Winthrop

Wirtenberg, Patricia Z. 1932- *10*

Wise, William 1923- *4*

Wise, Winifred E. *2*

Wiseman, Ann (Sayre) 1926- *31*

Wiseman, B(ernard) 1922- *4*

Wiseman, David 1916- *43*
Brief Entry *40*

Wisler, G(ary) Clifton 1950-
Brief Entry *46*

Wisner, Bill
See Wisner, William L.

Wisner, William L.
1914(?)-1983 .... *42*

Witham, (Phillip) Ross 1917- *37*

Withers, Carl A. 1900-1970 .... *14*

Witt, Shirley Hill 1934- *17*

Wittels, Harriet Joan 1938- *31*

Wittman, Sally (Anne Christensen)
1941- *30*

Witty, Paul A(ndrew) 1898-1976
Obituary *30*

Wizard, Mr.
See Herbert, Don

Wodehouse, P(elham) G(renville)
1881-1975 .... *22*

Wodge, Dreary
See Gorey, Edward St. John

Wohlberg, Meg 1905- *41*

Wohlrabe, Raymond A. 1900- *4*

Wojciechowska, Maia 1927- *28*
Earlier sketch in SATA 1
See also CLR 1
See also SAAS 1

Wolcott, Patty 1929- *14*

Wold, Jo Anne 1938- *30*

Woldin, Beth Weiner 1955- *34*

Wolf, Bernard 1930-
Brief Entry *37*

Wolfe, Burton H. 1932- *5*

Wolfe, Louis 1905- *8*

Wolfe, Rinna (Evelyn) 1925- *38*

Wolfenden, George
See Beardmore, George

Wolff, Diane 1945- *27*

Wolff, Robert Jay 1905- *10*

Wolitzer, Hilma 1930- *31*

Wolkoff, Judie (Edwards)
Brief Entry *37*

Wolkstein, Diane 1942- *7*

Wolters, Richard A. 1920- *35*

Wondriska, William 1931- *6*

Wood, Audrey
Brief Entry *44*

Wood, Catherine
See Etchison, Birdie L(ee)

Wood, Don 1945-
Brief Entry *44*

Wood, Edgar A(llardyce)
1907- *14*

Wood, Esther
See Brady, Esther Wood

Wood, Frances Elizabeth *34*

Wood, James Playsted 1905- *1*

Wood, Kerry
See Wood, Edgar A(llardyce)

Wood, Laura N.
See Roper, Laura Wood

Wood, Nancy 1936- *6*

Wood, Phyllis Anderson
1923- *33*
Brief Entry *30*

Wood, Wallace 1927-1981
Obituary *33*

Woodard, Carol 1929- *14*

Woodburn, John Henry 1914- *11*

Woodford, Peggy 1937- *25*

Woodrich, Mary Neville
1915- *2*

Woods, George A(llan) 1926- *30*

Woods, Geraldine 1948-
Brief Entry *42*

Woods, Harold 1945-
Brief Entry *42*

Woods, Margaret 1921- *2*

Woods, Nat
See Stratemeyer, Edward L.

Woodson, Jack
See Woodson, John Waddie, Jr.

Woodson, John Waddie, Jr. *10*

Woodward, Cleveland
1900-1986 .... *10*
Obituary *48*

Woody, Regina Jones 1894- *3*

Wooldridge, Rhoda 1906- *22*

Woolley, Catherine 1904- *3*

Woolsey, Janette 1904- *3*

Worcester, Donald Emmet
1915- *18*

Work, Virginia 1946-
Brief Entry *45*

Worline, Bonnie Bess 1914- *14*

Wormser, Sophie 1896- *22*

Worth, Richard
Brief Entry *46*

Worth, Valerie 1933- *8*

Wortis, Avi 1937- *14*

Wosmek, Frances 1917- *29*

Wriggins, Sally Hovey 1922 ...... *17*

Wright, Anna (Maria Louisa Perrot)
Rose 1890-1968
Brief Entry *35*

Wright, Betty Ren
Brief Entry *48*

Wright, Dare 1926(?)- *21*

Wright, Enid Meadowcroft
1898-1966 .... *3*

Wright, Esmond 1915- *10*

Wright, Frances Fitzpatrick
1897- *10*

Wright, Judith 1915- *14*

Wright, Katrina
See Gater, Dilys

Wright, Kenneth
See Del Rey, Lester

Wright, Nancy Means *38*

Wright, R(obert) H. 1906- *6*

Wrightson, Patricia 1921- *8*
See also CLR 4
See also SAAS 4

Wronker, Lili Cassel 1924- *10*

Wulffson, Don L. 1943- *32*

Wuorio, Eva-Lis 1918- *34*
Brief Entry *28*

Wyeth, Betsy James 1921- *41*

Wyeth, N(ewell) C(onvers)
1882-1945 .... *17*

Wyler, Rose 1909- *18*

Wylie, Betty Jane *48*

Wylie, Laura
See Matthews, Patricia

Wymer, Norman George
1911- *25*

Wynants, Miche 1934-
Brief Entry *31*

Wyndham, Lee
See Hyndman, Jane Andrews

Wyndham, Robert
See Hyndman, Robert Utley

Wynter, Edward (John) 1914- *14*

Wynyard, Talbot
See Hamilton, Charles H. St. John

Wyss, Johann David Von
1743-1818 .... *29*
Brief Entry *27*

Wyss, Thelma Hatch 1934- *10*

Y

Yaffe, Alan
See Yorinks, Arthur

Yamaguchi, Marianne 1936- *7*

Yang, Jay 1941- *12*

Yarbrough, Ira 1910(?)-1983
Obituary *35*

Yaroslava
  See Mills, Yaroslava Surmach
Yashima, Taro
  See Iwamatsu, Jun Atsushi
  See also CLR 4
Yates, Elizabeth 1905- 4
Yates, Raymond F(rancis)
  1895-1966 31
Yaukey, Grace S(ydenstricker)
  1899- 5
Yeakley, Marjory Hall 1908- 21
Yeatman, Linda 1938- 42
Yensid, Retlaw
  See Disney, Walt(er Elias)
Yeo, Wilma (Lethem) 1918- 24
Yeoman, John (Brian) 1934- 28
Yep, Laurence M. 1948- 7
  See also CLR 3
Yerian, Cameron John 21
Yerian, Margaret A. 21
Yolen, Jane H. 1939- 40
  Earlier sketch in SATA 4
  See also CLR 4
  See also SAAS 1
Yonge, Charlotte Mary
  1823-1901 17
Yorinks, Arthur 1953- 49
  Earlier sketch in SATA 33
York, Andrew
  See Nicole, Christopher Robin
York, Carol Beach 1928- 6
York, Rebecca [Joint pseudonym]
  See Buckholtz, Eileen (Garber)
Yost, Edna 1889-1971
  Obituary 26
Youd, (Christopher) Samuel
  1922- 47
  Brief Entry 30
Young, Bob
  See Young, Robert W.
Young, Clarence [Collective
  pseudonym] 1
Young, Dorothea Bennett
  1924- 31
Young, Ed 1931- 10

Young, Edward
  See Reinfeld, Fred
Young, Elaine L.
  See Schulte, Elaine L(ouise)
Young, Jan
  See Young, Janet Randall
Young, Janet Randall 1919- 3
Young, Lois Horton
  1911-1981 26
Young, Margaret B(uckner)
  1922- 2
Young, Miriam 1913-1934 7
Young, (Rodney Lee) Patrick (Jr.)
  1937- 22
Young, Percy M(arshall)
  1912- 31
Young, Robert W. 1916-1969 3
Young, Scott A(lexander)
  1918- 5
Young, Vivien
  See Gater, Dilys
Youngs, Betty 1934-1985
  Obituary 42

Z

Zaffo, George J. (?)-1984 42
Zaidenberg, Arthur 1908(?)- 34
Zalben, Jane Breskin 1950- 7
Zallinger, Jean (Day) 1918- 14
Zallinger, Peter Franz 1943- 49
Zappler, Lisbeth 1930- 10
Zarchy, Harry 1912- 34
Zarif, Margaret Min'imah
  (?)-1983 33
Zaring, Jane (Thomas) 1936-
  Brief Entry 40
Zaslavsky, Claudia 1917- 36
Zeck, Gerald Anthony 1939- 40
Zeck, Gerry
  See Zeck, Gerald Anthony
Zei, Alki 24
  See also CLR 6

Zelazny, Roger (Joseph Christopher)
  1937-
  Brief Entry 39
Zelinsky, Paul O. 1953- 49
  Brief Entry 33
Zellan, Audrey Penn 1950- 22
Zemach, Harve 1933- 3
Zemach, Kaethe 1958- 49
  Brief Entry 39
Zemach, Margot 1931- 21
Zerman, Melvyn Bernard
  1930- 46
Ziemienski, Dennis 1947- 10
Zillah
  See Macdonald, Zillah K.
Zim, Herbert S(pencer) 1909- 30
  Earlier sketch in SATA 1
  See also CLR 2
  See also SAAS 2
Zim, Sonia Bleeker
  See Bleeker, Sonia
Zimelman, Nathan
  Brief Entry 37
Zimmerman, Naoma 1914- 10
Zimnik, Reiner 1930- 36
  See also CLR 3
Zindel, Bonnie 1943- 34
Zindel, Paul 1936- 16
  See also CLR 3
Ziner, (Florence) Feenie
  1921- 5
Zion, (Eu)Gene 1913-1975 18
Zollinger, Gulielma 1856-1917
  Brief Entry 27
Zolotow, Charlotte S. 1915- 35
  Earlier sketch in SATA 1
  See also CLR 2
Zonia, Dhimitri 1921- 20
Zubrowski, Bernard 1939- 35
Zupa, G. Anthony
  See Zeck, Gerald Anthony
Zurhorst, Charles (Stewart, Jr.)
  1913- 12
Zuromskis, Diane
  See Stanley, Diane
Zweifel, Frances 1931- 14
Zwinger, Ann 1925- 46